A Bibliography of Stylistics and Related Criticism, 1967–83

James R. Bennett

The Modern Language Association of America
New York 1986

Copyright © 1986 by The Modern Language Association of America

Library of Congress Cataloging in Publication Data

Bennett, James R., 1932–
  A bibliography of stylistics and related criticism, 1967–83.

  Includes indexes.
  1. Style, Literary—Bibliography. I. Title.
Z6514.S8B46   1986   [PN203]   016.809   85–25867
ISBN 0–87352–142–0
ISBN 0–87352–143–9 (pbk.)

Published by The Modern Language Association of America
10 Astor Place, New York, NY 10003

To my parents,
Volney and Mildred Bennett,
for a lifetime of support.

For what is happening at last on the frontiers of English studies is that, as in other humane disciplines that have bothered to look outwards (notably linguistics or anthropology), we are now asking questions about what we are doing and the way we are doing it with some rudimentary understanding that, as Coleridge pointed out long before Wittgenstein, the world is half composed of what we observe and half of what we create by the manner *in which* we perceive. . . . [T]he transformation that is overtaking us inside the field of English is, and must be, one of methodological awareness if progress is to be made.

Hilda Schiff, *Contemporary Approaches to English Studies.*

It was late in the 1960s when the symptoms, heretofore fugitive and for the most part manageable, could no longer be ignored. The Anglo-American literary community, which had been erected on the rock of Johnsonian empiricism and Arnoldian sensibility, found itself suddenly possessed by an alien spirit of speculation, infected by an unspeakable cant of theoretical abstractions. The signs were everywhere (as, indeed, everything seemed destined to become yet another sign): Professional meetings that might once have spent their sessions in admiring the visionary system of a Blake or a Yeats turned instead to the great system building critics and the deconstructive subverters of those systems; graduate programs in "poetics" began to displace the more familiar period specializations. . . . All at once the books that were most honored, most frequently cited or condemned, were no longer scholarly monographs on the roots of Restoration comedy or readings of the later Eliot but were instead the collected papers of the latest international symposium.

Elizabeth Bruss, *Beautiful Theories*

Acknowledgments

My wife, Jo, made it all much easier. In 1966 Richard W. Bailey initiated the annual bibliography of stylistics published in *Style*, which led eventually to this book. Jim Cowan suggested the project and remained supportive. The reference staff of the Mullins Library at the University of Arkansas — Elizabeth McKee, Larry Perry, Janet Parsch, Stephen Dew, Donna Webb, and Don Batson — answered innumerable questions cheerfully and accurately. Regina French and the Inter-Library Loan staff acquired several hundred books for me; Shirley Brindel of Acquisitions purchased dozens; Pat Crabb's Circulation staff located books quickly. My research helpers, Jack Fine and Bev Maddox, were both diligent and intelligent. Leighton Rudolph gave me his carrel, an essential workplace provided by the library. Marjorie Rudolph helped with the Russian names. John Guilds, dean of the College of Arts and Sciences at the University of Arkansas, provided a semester of research leave, which significantly reduced the duration of the project. John Stokes of the University of Arkansas Research Programs, and the typists there, Sara Holmes and Georgiana Mellot, kept the pages coming. Karen Hodges, John Childs, and Harold Mosher, Jr., offered advice and encouragement. Walter Achtert, MLA director of book publications and research programs, guided the book firmly — it seemed almost effortlessly — from conception to publication. Roslyn Schloss, the MLA's editor for the book, performed an extraordinarily careful and thorough labor; I wish I could have expressed my appreciation in person. To all of you, thank you.

Contents

Introduction

Linguistics, Literature, and Society

The unqualified acknowledgement of the autonomy of the literary text
and its corollary, the claim of the superior truth of the poet and the
emphatic assimilation of that truth by the interpreter, will hardly be found
in recent publications. The old, indeed traditional conviction that literature
has a cognitive and communicative function has come to the fore again
and has freed the literary text from its artificial isolation. As a particular
form of organizing the semantic universe, literature has been attributed
a more relative, but at the same time a more significant place. Literature
has been accepted again as part of a more comprehensive cognitive process. As such, it also justifies the attempts to increase our knowledge about
literature through scientific investigation. But this position entails an
extension of the field of interest of literary studies. The student of literature
must have access to all those disciplines that are engaged in the systematic
organization of the semantic universe: linguistics, history, sociology, philosophy, and anthropology.

Fokkema and Kunne-Ibsch, "Prospects for Further Research," *Theories
of Literature in the Twentieth Century*

Semiotics—the study of signs in all their manifestations—is like zoology, the
study of animal life in a wide variety of forms, or anthropology, the study of
human life in the great variety of the groups of humankind. The attempt to
study human language scientifically is called linguistics—the study of languages
in order to understand their structures and processes, to know the ways by which
linguistic units achieve their communicative function. Recently a resurgence of
interest in developing a scientific study of literature as a subset of language (for
such an aim is not new) has gained adherents under the labels of stylistics, poetics,
structuralism, and literary semiotics.[1] Fredric Jameson, for example, has
described structuralism as "the primacy of the linguistic model," or metaphor
(vii). The idea that, since literature is composed of language, critics of literature
should seek first and primarily to understand the structures and processes of the
language of literature and that linguistics could provide a reliable metalanguage
and system for investigation has attracted at least a minority of literary students.

Probably highly diverse experiences and motives moved individuals to this
conclusion. For some academic linguists (many of whom also taught traditional
literary courses) it was the desire to apply their knowledge of the language system
to the literature they taught. The advent of new—and, it was hoped, more
precise—techniques and the widening range of knowledge about language and

culture provided by linguistics made the conjunction of linguistics and literary criticism seem both desirable and feasible. For some literary critics it was the desire to bring some order into their study and teaching of literature. For them, the daily classroom was too fragmentary and random, lacking a disciplined progression of investigation, unproductively cumulative of disconnected data, leading nowhere.

To many linguists and traditional academic teachers and critics the personal experience of the chaos of the ascendant literary history, particularly of the historical treatment of genres, authors, and texts, was the decisive factor. The revolt was against the "petty antiquarianism" of accumulating unrelated facts: "'research' into the minutest details of the lives and quarrels of authors, parallel hunting, and source digging . . . on the vague belief that all these bricks will sometime be used in a great pyramid of learning" (Wellek 256). The often multitudinously detailed, atomistic, and uncorrelated course and comprehensive examinations of traditional literary studies sent many graduates eagerly in search of greater coherence. An equal number, reacting against a literary history that was everything but the study of literature, began to seek ways to create an aesthetic history of literature.

Others reacted to the unsupported generalizations, the complacent dogmatisms, and the nebulosities of impressionistic critical terminology— "elaborate style," "ornate form," "bright, swift melody," "muted notes," "sultry monotone," "plangent passion," "trumpet-call," "elaborate harmonies," "full orchestration," and so on. Others felt exasperated by inadequate theories and evidence and inevitably hasty conclusions. Too many studies about a text's or a writer's style were written without even asking "What is style?" Too many were written ad hoc without building on the best theories (or on any theories) and procedures of preceding studies. Too many literary critics lacked even a rudimentary understanding of basic methods of research—of the need to consider historical and linguistic contexts, for example, or to establish controls (comparisons with other texts examined in the same way) before generalizing. Too many studies, enfeebled by shoddy methods, would have to be scrapped.

Just as Bloomfield back in the 1920s welcomed Saussure and Sapir for advocating the synchronic (structural) study of language as prior to diachronic (historical) study, and just as the New Critics beginning in the 1920s had concentrated on the internal relations—the subtlety, the layeredness, the paradoxicalness—of a text, some linguists and literary critics in the 1950s insisted that the nature of literature should be understood before its history (or its interpretation) is attempted. Too often, they argued, literature had been reduced to a means to the knowledge of something else (the author, society). What was needed first was an understanding of literature, of "literariness"—not only of metaphor or point of view but of such things as ordinary versus artistic uses of language, textuality, convention, defamiliarization. To effect that kind of study, to bring about a coherent body of concepts and methods for understanding the structures and processes of literature, a new emphasis on theory was needed. Before interpreting, critics must describe a text accurately in precise terms, and before describing, critics must possess an organized body of abstract concepts: at least they must be aware of the important connection between theory and practice, since the theory one follows determines one's assumptions about the subject, the kind of questions one asks, the kind of evidence one seeks, and the use one makes of the evidence collected. "The history of thought is the history of its models. Classical mechanics, the organism, natural selection" were "systems which, first used to organize our understanding of the natural world, have then been called upon to illuminate human reality" because reality is susceptible to analysis by these models (Jameson vii). Out of these thoughts and arguments arose a confidence among critics worldwide (A. A. Hill, Anne Cluysenaar, Juryj Lotman — critics in rapidly growing numbers during the 1970s and 1980s) in the indispensableness of linguistics to the study of literature.[2] "Where what we have to describe are linguistic features, there can be no rival to contemporary linguistics as a source of such descriptions," contends Cluysenaar (20). Among a few critics this belief has become an exuberant faith in the ability of the linguistic study of literature to produce "a revolutionary . . . insight into the nature of literature, language, and man himself" (Ching 4).

But if a dislike of the disconnected empiricism and undisciplined methods of traditional literary research and an admiration for the theoretical order and terminological precision of science were immediate sources of attraction to linguistics, in the background was the growing twentieth-century preoccupation with meaning and communication, the problem of doubt and verification. Many of those devoted to the rationality of technique, who would unite linguistics and literary criticism by stressing procedure and method (and, of course, many who were not always technically based in linguistics but who were deeply interested in language — the phenomenologists and hermeneuticists, for example), were expressing their anxiety about the relation between language and phenomena.

Reaction to the scientific study of literature has been intense. In the first place, there are some who believe that because of disagreements among linguists (except in the areas of phonology and dialectology) linguistics is not enough of a discipline yet to make its standards those of all thought about language.[3] There are others who do not find linguistics as precise and adequate a method as some of its adherents claim: "Even where linguistics provides definite and well-established procedures for classing and describing elements of a text it does not solve the problem of what constitutes a pattern and hence does not provide a method for the discovery of patterns. *A fortiori*, it does not provide a procedure for the discovery of poetic patterns" (Culler 65). Others perceive a destructive obsession with methodology and theory that ignores applied criticism and in which literature "sometimes seems almost irrelevant" (Krieger xii). And there are many more who reject the idea that science (pejoratively, "scientism") or positivism can ever apply to human creativity. Opponents of the cooperation of linguistics and literary criticism have charged linguists with obtuseness and insensitivity in their approach to literature, and linguistics with offering only a superficial utility for literary criticism. Tempers have flared: "Among the barbed-wire in-words of the 1970's" is "text," "meaning something dead on the page, *Hamlet* as pickled dogfish. These are pieces from a game they play in France," where "language itself is a more fascinating problem than anything that gets done with it" (Kenner 189). And Jameson refers ominously to the "profound consonance between linguistics as a method and that systematized and disembodied nightmare which is our culture today" (ix).

Umberto Eco has translated the debate into the conflict between William and Adso in his novel *The Name of the Rose*. William believes that books are not made to be believed but to be subjected to inquiry (as in Barthes's early essays, in which literature and life are no more than languages to be studied as pure relational systems). Adso writes to be believed.

Certainly, too many of the "scientific" studies of literature squeak as pettily as the antiquarian scholarship the linguistic-literary critics seek to replace. How embarrassingly limited the actual practice of linguistic stylistics has often seemed when measured by criticism that apprehends full contexts. Too many linguistic studies of literature have exemplified what Denis Donoghue in *Ferocious Alphabets* denounces as "graphireading"—the antihumanist approach to literature that regards writing as devoid of a person's voice in a place and time, partly out of a fervor for scientific and linguistic terms (Donoghue's "graphireaders" are not linguists, however, but the deconstructionists). And too many linguists forget the precarious state of humankind, which has partly resulted from the apotheosis of science and technical reason undirected by humane and socially useful values and ends (this is not to deny the presence of social and political unawareness among some literary critics).

Trivial or antihuman linguistic studies may be the expression of an individual practitioner's inadequacies, however, since investigative programs advocated by critics trained in both linguistics and literary criticism insist on full social and authorial contextualization.[4] Critics like Roger Fowler see an invigorated future for stylistics, the confrontation of linguistics and criticism constantly enlarging "the range of techniques and concepts" of linguistics in "the service of literary and textual studies" ("Inclusive" 202).[5] The same critic encourages a close cooperation between linguists, sociolinguists, and literary critics. He even at times uses the terms "linguistics" and "sociolinguistics" interchangeably, whether to correlate linguistic forms and social structures or to suggest that "all linguistic form is socially motivated" (*Literature* 200). Already in Europe *Literatursoziologie*, the definition of literature as a social product with a social function, is deeply established. And a growing number of critics worldwide feel the future holds great promise for a significant stylistics that combines, for example, the linguistic skills of a Roman Jakobson with the social preoccupations of a David Craig (see his *Real Foundations*). The editor of *Poetics* stressed in 1980 how indispensable was contextual knowledge to meaningful literary analysis:

The aim is to produce, with the same standard of rational argumentation as in other fields of scientific research, analyses which are based on an explicit theory, logically consistent and capable of empirical interpretation. . . . [I]t is my hope that *Poetics* will in future give an appropriate amount of space to the theoretical and methodological problems of an *empirical* theory of literature. Accordingly, there should be more co-operation with related disciplines such as psychology, sociology, ethnology, anthropology and political science, so as to enable us to discuss the basic assumptions and methods of an empirical theory of literature more competently and from a broader base. . . . [C]o-operation of the type described must never lose sight of our primary aim, which is to improve the scientific study of *literary* texts in their respective contexts. (Schmidt, n.p.)

All these critics suggest that only by a careful attention to theory and method, combined with knowledge of contexts and with intuition, can the isolation of literature and literary criticism from human life be avoided and the vitality of literature and literary criticism as vehicles for moral guidance and historical revelation be affirmed.

This bibliography therefore includes a wide range of studies of the language of literature, only part of which derives from some specific formalist school. But the emphasis is on the linguistic study of literature, and this is accomplished in various ways:

1. ample representation of theoretical and practical linguistically based bibliographies and books published from 1967 through 1983 that at least partly deal with literature;
2. emphasis on reviews from journals sympathetic to the scientific study of literature;
3. survey of bibliographies in linguistically oriented books as a guide to selection (listed in the "Description of the Bibliography");
4. the appendixes.

Notes

[1] See Fries, ch. 2; Wellek; and Todorov.

[2] Juryj Lotman in *Analysis of the Poetic Text* and his other books argues for the scientific study of literature through attention to method, process, terminology, technique, and the formulation of useful questions, to free investigators from the perpetual reinvention of the wheel so characteristic of past literary studies.

[3] Owen Thomas has gone so far as to describe "the current state of linguistics" as "one of confusion. There seem to be almost as many theories as there are linguists, at least well-known linguists" (203).

[4] For examples of significant contexts long available see Ohmann or Spencer and Gregory. Or see the contexts established by the sociolinguistic critics (Aers, Bernstein, Ferguson, Fowler, Gumperz, Halliday, Hodge, Hymes, Kress, Labov, Sammons, Schmidt, Trew) or by the Marxist critics (Bennett, Bisztray, Eagleton, Jameson, Krieger, Weimann, Williams).

[5] Fowler cites research into semantic macrostructures and text modality.

Works Cited

Ching, Marvin K. L., et al., eds. *Linguistic Perspectives on Literature*. London: Routledge, 1980.

Cluysenaar, Anne. *Aspects of Literary Stylistics*. New York: St. Martin's, 1975.

Craig, David. *The Real Foundations: Literature and Social Change*. New York: Oxford UP, 1974.

Culler, Jonathan. *Structuralist Poetics*. Ithaca: Cornell UP, 1975.

Donoghue, Denis. *Ferocious Alphabets*. Boston: Little, 1981.

Eco, Umberto. *The Name of the Rose*. Trans. William Weaver. San Diego: Harcourt, 1983.

Fowler, Roger. "Inclusive (Sociolinguistic) versus Exclusive (Formalist) Stylistics: A Review of William O. Hendricks' *Grammars of Style and Styles of Grammar*." *Style* 11 (1977): 199–204.

————. *Literature as Social Discourse: The Practice of Linguistic Criticism*. Bloomington: Indiana UP, 1981.

Fries, Charles C. *Linguistics and Reading*. New York: Holt, 1962.

Jameson, Fredric. *The Prison-House of Language: A Critical Account of Structuralism and Russian Formalism*. Princeton: Princeton UP, 1972.

Kenner, Hugh. Review. *Style* 10 (1976): 189.

Krieger, Murray. *Theory of Criticism: A Tradition and Its System*. Baltimore: Johns Hopkins UP, 1976.

Lotman, Juryj. *Analysis of the Poetic Text*. Ann Arbor: Ardis, 1976.

Ohmann, Richard. *Shaw: The Style and the Man*. Middletown: Wesleyan UP, 1962.

Schmidt, Siegfried J. "Editorial." *Poetics* 9 (1980): n.p.

Spencer, John, and Michael Gregory. "An Approach to the Study of Style." *Linguistics and Style*. Ed. John Spencer. London: Oxford UP, 1964. 59–105.

Thomas, Owen. Review. *Style* 10 (1976): 203.

Todorov, Tzvetan. "Structuralism and Literature." *Approaches to Poetics*. Ed. Seymour Chatman. New York: Columbia UP, 1973. 153–68.

Wellek, René. "The Revolt against Positivism in Recent European Literary Scholarship." *Concepts of Criticism*. New Haven: Yale UP, 1963. 256–81.

Description of the Bibliography

Scope and Occasion

This bibliography of studies of the language of literature owes a great debt to several persons who made contributions in the 1950s and 1960s. In 1953 Helmut Hatzfeld published his first United States edition of *A Critical Bibliography of the New Stylistics Applied to the Romance Literatures 1900–1952*. This edition he expanded in Spanish (1955) and French (1961) editions. In 1966 he prepared a new United States edition omitting items prior to 1953, including items from 1955 to 1960, and adding about 800 items from 1960 to 1965. By this time two new bibliographies were in typescript: Louis Milic's *Style and Stylistics*, mainly on criticism in the English language, appeared in 1967, and a few months later, in 1968, *English Stylistics* by Richard W. Bailey and Dolores Burton appeared. The present bibliography carries forward the work of Hatzfeld, Milic, and Bailey and Burton through 1983.

Process of Selection

I began by making a list of books derived from the annual bibliography in *Style* (1968–81), the annual *MLA International Bibliography* (1968–81),[1] *Subject Guide to Books in Print*, and *Forthcoming Books*. As a guide to selection from the thousands of potential items, I asked the authors of books reviewed in *Style* to recommend the most outstanding studies published on stylistics between 1967 and 1983, and I surveyed the reviews and articles in *Style*; reviews in the journals *Linguistics*, *Modern Language Review*, *Yale Review*, *Australasian Universities MLA*, *Journal of Literary Semantics*, *Centrum*, and *Diacritics*; and the bibliographies in diverse books (see the beginning of section 1.0). The books cited in this bibliography represent both the amplitude and the variety of stylistic criticism, defined broadly as the theoretical or practical study of the language of literary works.

Certain arbitrary exclusions and limits should be noted. All dissertations and most purely theoretical linguistic works (lacking application to literature) are omitted.[2] Translation criticism has been omitted except for bibliographic references (1.0). Poetry textbooks and concordances have been severely limited, as have been film-literature and psychoanalytic studies (see 1.0 for bibliographies).

Although narratology (fiction poetics) is well represented, only a separate bibliography could exhibit fully such a large field of study. And only a country-by-country inspection of the *Bibliographie linguistique* can provide a relatively complete listing of books from Eastern Europe.

An Analytical Bibliography

The bibliography does not merely list titles but contains the following features to facilitate the study of stylistics:
a.   a six-part system of classification with subdivisions
b.   chronological order of entries within each part
c.   annotations
d.   book reviews
e.   a linguistics and literature chronology
f.   a classification of critics by theory and method
g.   an introductory reading list on stylistics
h.   a terminological index
i.   an author index: authors as subjects (styles studied)
j.   critic index 1: critics as subjects
k.   critic index 2: critics as contributors

The Classification

In his famous essay "Concluding Statement: Linguistics and Poetics," Roman Jakobson represents the relations of author, text, and reader in this way:

	Context Referential	
Addresser (Factor) Emotive (Function)	Message Poetic	Addressee Conative
	Contact Phatic	
	Code Metalingual	

By this system stylisticians are reminded simultaneously of the complex reality that is literature, of the complex operations necessary to release that reality, and of their role as rhetoricians in performing these operations. The top word of each pair describes the factors involved in verbal communication. "The *addresser* sends a *message* to the *addressee.* To be operative the message requires a *context* referred" and "seizable by the addressee, and either verbal or capable of being verbalized; a *code* fully, or at least partially, common to the addresser and addressee"; and, "finally, a *contact*, a physical channel" between "the addresser and the addressee, enabling both of them to enter and stay in communication." The bottom word of each pair describes the function of each factor, and the set of paired constituents dramatizes what is involved in the elusive experience of the network of language and response that is literary art. Jakobson sees truly how much communication, and especially literary communication, depends on the interrelation of diverse factors and functions. But no single bibliography can hope to represent all aspects adequately. This bibliography concentrates on the message factor and poetic function. But it encompasses also important works that connect these with the other factors and functions. Examinations of textual complexity that include inquiries into sociopolitical and ideological contexts, for example, are included.

If understanding of the language of literary texts requires a knowledge of the structures and systems of factors and functions that determine form and meaning in a text, then stylistics needs not a methodology but methodologies. Thus stylistics today multifariously seeks to gather maximal information about techniques and to develop coherent theories and precise methods for deriving that information. In addition to asking: What is style? modern linguistic critics ask: What are the properties of a text? and What is the best analytical instrument for accurately examining each property? The goal may vary—to describe meter more precisely, to classify narratives more systematically—but the contemporary linguistic critic is primarily concerned with developing the best tools for the description of each feature.

This empirical attitude seems bedrock to any reliable effort to discover what and how an author meant. Science, however, is not directionless observation, nor is stylistics random inventories. Critics probably always work on the basis of some conceptual framework, and a concept conditions the critical model and therefore what is perceived: style is ornament, idiosyncrasy, conscious choice, deviation from norms, selection from preexisting language varieties, or text features that in combination create messages. But stylistics has the great advantage of concentrating on quantitative fact and systematic methodology. Skeptical of the metaphysics of abstract definitions of style, it is better prepared to cope with abstractions. And the accumulation of empirical data through systematic analysis of the numerous style features admits any concept or practical model safely, not merely because sufficient evidence suppresses bias but because sufficient categories of text features ensure sufficient (if not perfect) analytical models.

The system of classification employed here reflects an effort to recognize the many ways readers approach texts in theory and practice and to be inclusive. The system facilitates research both within and across categories. Studies of the language of historical periods, for example, are found in 3.0. Studies of the syntax of periods, authors, and texts may be found in 3.2.2, 4.2.2, and 5.2.2 (supplemented by the terminological index).

Each entry is cited in only one category. I have tried to choose the most emphasized categories for items that could be included in more than one category. For example, I placed Karl Kroeber's *Styles in Fictional Structure: The Art of Jane Austen, Charlotte Brontë, George Eliot* in the genre section (3.2.4) instead of in the author section because his chief concern seems to be not the three novelists but the creation of a schema for the analysis of fiction.

1.0 Bibliographical Resources (entries 1–153)
    A. Annual Bibliographies and Selected Journals (1–42)
    B. Single Bibliographies, Dictionaries, Checklists, Handbooks (43–153)

2.0 General Theory and Concepts of Style (154–637)
    A. Collections by Diverse Authors (154–313)
    B. Individual, Dual, or Group Authorship (314–637)

3.0 Culture, History, and Style: The Period, the Nation, the Genre (638–1012)
    3.1 Theory (638–758)
    3.2 Practice (759–1012)
        3.2.1 Diction, Imagery, Tropes
        3.2.2 Syntax, Schemes
        3.2.3 Prosody, Sound Patterns in Prose
        3.2.4 Studies on Several Linguistic Levels

4.0 Habitual Usage: The Author (1013–276)
    4.1 Theory (1013–16)
    4.2 Practice (1017–276)
        4.2.1 Diction, Imagery, Tropes
        4.2.2 Syntax, Schemes
        4.2.3 Prosody, Sound Patterns in Prose
        4.2.4 Studies on Several Linguistic Levels

5.0 Individual Choice: The Text (1277–434)
    5.1 Theory (1277–89)
    5.2 Practice (1290–434)
        5.2.1 Diction, Imagery, Tropes
        5.2.2 Syntax, Schemes
        5.2.3 Prosody, Sound Patterns in Prose
        5.2.4 Studies on Several Linguistic Levels

6.0 Individual Response: The Reader (1435–84)
    6.1 Theory (1435–71)
    6.2 Practice (1472–84)

1.0 Bibliographical Resources

This section includes handbooks, checklists, dictionaries, encyclopedias, glossaries, and selected journals.

2.0 General Theory and Concepts of Style

In this section appear discussions of concepts of language and style, of methodologies, and of devices for the description and analysis of the language of literature. This section and the subsections on theory within each of the major divisions of the classification cover what Jonathan Culler in *The Pursuit of Signs* calls literary semiotics: the systematic description of "the modes of signification of literary discourse and the interpretive operations embodied in the institution of literature," the attempt "to discover the conventions which make meaning possible" (12, 37). Literary semiotics thus resembles the work of modern rhetoricians like the authors of *Rhétorique générale*, whose purpose is to ground the study of *elocutio* in linguistics, to explain "how and why a text is a text—that is, *what the linguistic procedures characterizing literature are*" (6). It resembles also the "structuralism" of French critics like Greimas, Bremond, Genette, and Todorov (who has employed the term "poetics" to describe his work), to whom rigorous self-consciousness about theory, methods, and devices is primary. (Structuralists ultimately include in their plans for a scientific literary criticism not only phonology but also the evolution of literature and the relations between literature and society [Todorov].)

In defense of theory, Fokkema and Kunne-Ibsch (1977), reason in this way:

> Theorizing which reduces literature to abstract, a-historical form and on that basis attempts to phrase universal laws, has so far remained in the programmatic stage. On the other hand, the hermeneutic position that deals only with the interpretation of individual works and shirks all generalization cannot further our understanding of the literary process either. The only way open for future development of our discipline is the construction of general concepts and models, which allow for individual deviations and take account of the historical basis of all literature. . . . Without conceptualization and generalization, and without the terminology of a metalanguage, no scientific discussion of the components of literature and literary history seems possible. (9)

Students of style share this concern for theory and disciplined method in the study of the elements of literature—a fully coherent and comprehensive guide to the study of irony, for example. The systematic description of principles, methods (models), and devices is fundamental. But stylistic critics usually make the application of that knowledge to the interpretation of literary texts their ultimate goal. The field of stylistics is the application of the principles and methods of linguistics to the description and interpretation of literary texts. Thus it is a part of the pursuit of meaning and value shared by rhetoric, the humanities, and the social sciences.

Anthologies also appear in this section.

3.0 Culture, History, and Style: The Period, the Nation, the Genre

Whether it is possible to speak meaningfully of a historical or national or generic "style" or "styles" is questionable. The description of the languages of literary periods, national literatures, and literary genres is in its infancy. But concern for these areas of study is increasing. The concept of genre, for example, has, in Peter Brooks's words, "assumed new importance in contemporary poetics . . . as a set of norms and expectations that structure our reading of texts" (Todorov, *Introduction to Poetics* xv). Improved methods of quantification are enabling scholars to gather the large amount of precise data necessary for certain limited generalizations (see Cluett, *Prose Style and Critical Reading*), and new methods of description and analysis of large quantities of writing are developing (see Robert Adolph, "On the Possibility of a History of Prose," in the Fall 1981 issue of *Style*, and John Smith, "Toward a Marxist Poetics," in the Winter 1982 issue).

4.0 Habitual Usage: The Author

This category closely relates to 3.0 because both deal with how milieu conditions styles. The items are assigned according to emphasis. For example, Bien's book on Kazantzakis is placed under 4.2.4 because it focuses on a single author in his milieu. The program of stylistics includes the effort to develop reliable ways to describe an author's characteristic features and to interpret their roles in the expression of the author's meanings. Obviously, quantifiable data and statistical procedures are essential to the study of an author's propensities, and as with the study of the styles of periods, nations, and genres or with any descriptive study requiring large quantities of data, the study of author styles has been tremendously facilitated by the computer. In practice, these studies have seldom been feature studies merely but have been what Richard Ohmann calls "epistemic" (*Shaw: The Style and the Man*). By linking the creating, valuing, shaping mind with text (and often with audience) they carry on humanistic investigation.

5.0 Individual Choice: The Text

In *The Pursuit of Signs* Culler contrasts literary semiotics (poetics) to practical criticism—the systematic study of modes contrasted to the production of new readings of texts. Stylistics continues the New Critical commitment to the description and interpretation of individual texts—the systematic description of the constituents of an artistic whole leading to how these elements cohere and function and communicate meaning. This activity is variously labeled "practical criticism," "literary stylistics," "discourse analysis," "text linguistics," "text criticism," "holistic criticism," and "semiotics" (Riffaterre, *Semiotics of Poetry*). Reuben Brower in *The Fields of Light* represents the intuitive and commonsense critics who have shown the way to a meaningful holistic stylistics. Brower conceives of a work of art as "imaginately organized," possessing "extraordinary relationships" (grammatical, logical, chronological, imaginal, dramatic, metaphorical, rhythmic, etc.). He seeks the full and exact definition of words by context, compares similar expressions in the text, "tracing the continuities," and then relates the constituent patterns in search of the "wonderful" experience of perceiving the sets of relations. Jakobson's minutely, almost exhaustively analytical study of Blake's "Infant Sorrow" similarly evokes the "total attitude" Brower considers fundamental to literary art, by tracing the multiple levels of paradigmatic symmetries in the poem within the syntagmatic "dramatic development." Extreme expressions of commitment to the study of the internal relations of a text are Claude Lévi-Strauss's belief in a work of art as "an object endowed with precise properties, that must be analytically isolated" and that "can be entirely defined on the grounds of such properties" (qtd. in Eco, *The Role of the Reader* 3), and Riffaterre's claim that "style is the text itself," the only analyzable corpus being the unique text (*Text Production* 207). Riffaterre adds the reader as an integral part of the "production" of a text, and critics who define discourse as "the total verbal process in its context of situation" (Coulthard) include conversational and speech-act theories and methods in the development of a "linguistics beyond the sentence."

6.0 Individual Response: The Reader

M. H. Abrams in *The Mirror and the Lamp* distinguishes four critical traditional purposes of literature since Aristotle: mimetic (represent reality), pragmatic (teach and please), expressive (project author's inner feelings), and objective (admire beauty of artifact). The rhetorical tradition of literary studies, by concentrating squarely on the pragmatic and mimetic functions, provides a significant communicational framework for stylistics leading to the reader. Affective stylistics, deconstruction, hermeneutics, phenomenology, reader response, reception aesthetics, semics, subjective criticism — these are some of the labels for the new acceptance of each reader as participant in the creation of the meaning of a text. Although in *The Pursuit of Signs* Culler contrasts the study of modes of signification (for him the purpose of literary semiotics) and the interpretation of individual texts, he includes the study of interpretive *operations* within the domain of literary semiotics.

In this section appear works that stress the phenomenology of readers, the ways they are implicated in creating the meaning of a text, the ways language and literature as systems of expression inevitably involve extralinguistic responses.

The traditional preoccupation with the text in stylistics is gradually expanding to include how readers actually perceive that text. Even the historical study of styles has begun to include that dimension. Perhaps this area of literary study will eventually be labled "pragmatics," a designation given by C. S. Peirce to the relation between language and its users and classified by him as one of the three branches of semiotics: syntactics (relation among signs), semantics (relation between signs and the outside world), and pragmatics.

Selection again depends on emphasis. Theoretical psycholinguistic and cognitive studies that offer no application to literature have been excluded (see bibliographies in 1.0). Works that fall under what Trevor Eaton calls "empirical semics"—studies that focus entirely on the responses of readers—clearly belong in this section. A distinct example of this approach is Eugene Kintgen's effort in *The Perception of Poetry* to "catch sight" of the process—the "actual experience"—of reading. (His opening chapter distinguishes his approach from various other methods.) Some of Norman Holland's criticism, however, combines text and response analysis. And Wolfgang Iser's *The Implied Reader* is classified elsewhere (5.2.4) because it deals primarily with the way a reader is implied in a particular author's compositional strategies in a specific work and their intended effects.

Entry Format

A typical entry consists of eight pieces of information. Example:

801.   Malof, Joseph. 1970. *A Manual of English Meters*. Bloomington: Indiana UP. 236 pp. Rpt. Greenwood, 1978.
Introd. on basic terms; chs. on "Foot Verse (Syllable-Stress Verse)," "Simple-Stress Verse," "Stress-Verse: The Native Meters," "Syllabic Verse," "Free Verse," and "Using the Scansion" (application to lines from *King Lear*). 6 apps., 4 of them glossaries, 1 a bib., 1 a key to quotations.
Style 7, 189–90: "a good book about prosody"; *Choice* 8, 48: outstanding "clarity," "supersedes all the partial treatments available (Hillyer, Shapiro, Deutsch, Hamilton, et al.)," "indispensable."

Analysis of Entry Format

a.   Item number. Within the subdivisions of the six parts of the bibliography, entry numbers represent a chronological listing. Because stylistics is a rapidly developing field, it is useful to see at a glance the earliest and the latest work and the evolution in each area from the 1960s to the 1980s. Easy location of individual authors is provided by the alphabetical author index.

b.   Name of the author(s), or title if the proceedings of a conference or a special number of a journal. Within a given year, listing is alphabetical by author.

c.   Year of original publication, unless otherwise indicated (as, for example, by the abbreviation "Rev. ed."), or year of translation.

d. Title.
e. Facts of publication: place, publisher, pages.
f. Subsequent appearances, indicated by the abbreviations "Rpt.," or, for translated works, original publication data.
g. Annotation. Thesis and contents generally.
h. Book reviews. Reviews are listed usually by journal volume and pages, often followed by brief excerpts. In addition to the journals surveyed during the compilation of the bibliography (listed above) I also checked each selection in *Book Review Index*.

Indexes

Indexes refer to item numbers, not to page numbers.

Index 1: Terms

Key terms employed by the authors cited in the bibliography are listed in alphabetical order. Definitions of terms would have required at least as much space as the bibliography. I have not tried to reduce the terms to an order of headings and subheadings. Rather, the index of terms reflects actual usage; the haphazardness mirrors the current proliferation. One purpose of this bibliography is to clarify the confusing quantity and diversity of overlapping terms by a classification system that connects broad areas of research and practice and by a cross-referenced terminological index that connects related terms.

Index 2: Authors and Works Studied

In this index are listed alphabetically those literary artists and those anonymous works that are studied substantially by the critics cited. These authors and works are the subject matter for the writers in indexes 3 and 4.

Index 3: Critics Studied

In this index are listed alphabetically the major critics of style and stylistics discussed substantially in the works cited in the bibliography. The list includes theoreticians, particularly linguists, who, although not directly engaged in the study of literature, have significantly influenced theoretical and practical literary criticism — for example, Chomsky, Kuhn, Saussure.

Index 4: Contributors

These are the names of the authors whose works are annotated in the bibliography. The two critic indexes provide a finding list of writers about style.

Notes

[1] Beginning in 1981, the *MLA International Bibliography*, vol. 1, includes a subject index, with headings on "Style," "Stylistic Analysis," "Stylistic Approach," "Structural Approach," "Structuralism," and related topics; and vol. 4 contains ample sections on "Criticism" (linguistic, deconstructionist, formalist, hermeneutic, Marxist, semiotic, etc.), "Literary Theory" (same areas), "Genres" (biography, drama, etc.), "Literary Forms" (epitaph, allegory, etc.), and "Professional Topics" (includes computer-assisted research). Vol. 3 retains the "Stylistics" and "Prosody" sections. The year 1981, that is, represents a breakthrough for the MLA from its traditional period/author orientation to a full recognition of the importance of discourse in contemporary criticism.

[2] See the *DAI* indexes, the "Stylistics" section of the annual *MLA International Bibliography*, vol. 3, and the annual bibliography of *Style* (annotated).

Master List of Periodicals in Alphabetical Order by Acronym

This list of acronyms follows the *MLA International Bibliography* mainly, supplemented by acronyms in the *Linguistic Bibliography/Bibliographie linguistique* and book review indexes.

Acronym	*Title*
AA	American Anthropologist (U of California, Davis)
AAm	Art in America (New York)
AHR	American History Review (Washington, DC)
AJP	American Journal of Philology (Johns Hopkins U)
AJPs	American Journal of Psychology (U of Illinois)
AJS	American Journal of Sociology (U of Chicago)
AJSem	American Journal of Semiotics (Cambridge, MA)
AL	American Literature (Duke U)
ALASH	Acta linguistica academiae scientiarum hungaricae (Budapest)
ALLCB	Bulletin of the Association for Literary and Linguistic Computing (Oxford)
ALLCJ	Association for Literary and Linguistic Computing Journal (Oxford)
Alph	Alphabet (London, Can.)
Anglia	Anglia: Zeitschrift für englische Philologie (U of Munich)
ANQ	American Notes & Queries (Lexington, KY)
AntC	L'antiquité classique (Grivegnée, Belg.)
AQ	Arizona Quarterly (U of Arizona)
AR	Antioch Review (Antioch, OH)
ARBA	American Reference Books Annual
Archiv	Archiv für das Studium der neueren Sprachen und Literaturen (Heidelberg, W. Ger.)
ArL	Archivum linguisticum: A Review of Comparative Philology and General Linguistics (U of Leeds, Eng.)
ArsS	Ars semeiotica: International Journal of American Semiotic (Amsterdam)

AS	American Speech: A Quarterly of Linguistic Usage (Duke U)
ASNP	Annali della Scuola normale superiore de Pisa (Florence)
AUMLA	Australasian Universities MLA (James Cook U, Queensland)
AWR	Anglo-Welsh Review (Cardiff, Wales)
B	Booklist (Chicago)
BA	Books Abroad (now WLT)
B&B	Books & Bookmen (London)
BBN	British Book News (London)
BC	Book Collector (London)
BCILA	Bulletin CILA (Neuchâtel)
BIQ	Blake: An Illustrated Quarterly (U of New Mexico)
Bio	Biography (U of Hawaii)
BJA	British Journal of Aesthetics (U of Sussex)
BL	Bibliographie linguistique (The Hague)
BlakeS	Blake Studies (Memphis State U)
BLS	Bulletin of Literary Semiotics (see SemS)
BMMLA	Bulletin of the Midwest Modern Language Association (U of Iowa)
BNYPL	Bulletin of the New York Public Library (now BRH)
Boundary	Boundary (U of Delaware)
BRD	Book Review Digest (New York)
BRH	Bulletin of Research in the Humanities (State U of New York, Stony Brook) (formerly BNYPL)
BRMMLA	Bulletin of the Rocky Mountain Modern Language Association (Arizona State U) (later RMR)
BSLP	Bulletin de la Société de linguistique de Paris (Paris)
BSUF	Ball State University Forum (Ball State U)
BuR	Bucknell Review (Bucknell U)
BW	Book World (Washington, DC)
ByronJ	Byron Journal (London)
C&L	Christianity and Literature (Calvin C)
CanL	Canadian Literature (U of British Columbia)
CASS	Canadian-American Slavic Studies (Arizona State U)
CAT	Cahiers d'analyse textuelle (Embourg, Belg.)
CC	Christian Century (Chicago)
CCC	College Composition and Communication (Ohio State U)
CCr	Comparative Criticism: A Yearbook (Cambridge, Eng.)
CD	Comparative Drama (Kalamazoo, MI)
CdIL	Cahiers de l'Institut de linguistique de Louvain (Belg.)
CdL	Cahiers de lexicologie (Besançon, Fr.)
CE	College English (Indiana U)

CEA	CEA Critic: An Official Journal of the College English Association (Texas A&M U)
CEAF	CEA Forum (Texas A&M U)
CentR	Centennial Review (Michigan State U)
Centrum	Centrum (U of Minnesota, Minneapolis; ceased publication)
CFS	Cahiers Ferdinand de Saussure: Revue de linguistique général (Geneva)
CG	Colloquia Germanica (U of Kentucky)
Chasqui	Chasqui: Revista de literatura latinoamericana (C of William and Mary)
ChauR	Chaucer Review: A Journal of Medieval Studies and Literary Criticism (Pennsylvania State U)
CHum	Computers and the Humanities (Osprey, FL)
Cithara	Cithara: Essays in the Judaeo-Christian Tradition (St. Bonaventure U)
CJL	Canadian Journal of Linguistics/La revue canadienne de linguistique (U of Toronto)
CJVS	Cizí jazyky ve škole (Prague)
CL	Comparative Literature (U of Oregon)
CLAJ	College Language Association Journal (Morehouse C)
ClassR	Classical Review (Brasenose C, Oxford U)
CLing	Cercetări de Lingvistică (Napoca, Rom.)
CLIO	CLIO (Indianapolis)
CLit	College Literature (West Chester State C)
CLS	Comparative Literature Studies (U of Illinois, Urbana)
CM	Carleton Miscellany (Carleton C)
ComM	Communication Monographs (Purdue U)
ComQ	Communication Quarterly (Temple U)
Comt	Commentary (New York)
Comw	Commonweal (New York)
ConL	Contemporary Literature (U of Wisconsin, Madison)
ConP	Contemporary Poetry (Bryn Mawr C)
CP	Contemporary Psychology (Washington, DC)
CPh	Classical Philology (U of Chicago)
CRCL	Canadian Review of Comparative literature/Revue canadienne de littérature comparée (U of Alberta)
Crit	Critique: Studies in Modern Fiction (Georgia Inst. of Tech.)
CritI	Critical Inquiry (U of Chicago)
Critm	Criticism: A Quarterly for Literature and the Arts (Wayne State U)
CritQ	Critical Quarterly (U of Manchester, Eng.)
CritT	Critical Texts (Columbia U)
CRL	College and Research Libraries (Chicago)

CS	Contemporary Sociology (Washington, DC)
CW	Classical World (Duquesne U)
DaF	Deutsch als Fremdsprache (Leipzig)
DAI	Dissertation Abstracts International (Ann Arbor, MI)
Daphnis	Daphnis (Berlin, W. Ger.)
Degrés	Degrés: Revue de synthese à orientation sémiologique (Brussels)
DHLR	D. H. Lawrence Review (U of Arkansas, Fayetteville, 1968–83; U of Delaware, 1984–)
Diacritics	Diacritics: A Review of Contemporary Criticism (Cornell U)
Dickensian	Dickensian (Birkbeck C, Eng.)
DicS	Dickinson Studies: Emily Dickinson (Brentwood, MD)
Dieciocho	Dieciocho: Hispanic Enlightenment, Aesthetics, and Literary Theory (Rutgers U, New Brunswick)
DQR	Dutch Quarterly Review of Anglo-American Letters (Amsterdam)
DR	Dalhousie Review (Dalhousie U)
DrR	Drama Review (School of the Arts, New York U; MIT P)
DuJ	Durham University Journal (Durham, Eng.)
DVLG	Deutsche Vierteljahresschrift für Literaturwissenschaft und Geistesgeschichte (Stuttgart)
EA	Études anglaises (Paris)
E&S	Essays and Studies (London)
Econ	Economist (London)
ECr	L'esprit créateur (Lawrence, KS)
ECS	Eighteenth-Century Studies (Ohio State U)
EG	Études germaniques (Paris)
EIC	Essays in Criticism (Keble C, Oxford U)
EJ	English Journal (Arizona State U)
ELA	Études de linguistique appliquée (Paris)
ELH	Journal of English Literary History (Johns Hopkins U)
ELN	English Language Notes (U of Colorado, Boulder)
ELT	English Literature in Transition (1880–1920) (Arizona State U)
Em	Emérita: Boletin de lingüística y filología clásica (Madrid)
Enc	Encounter (London)
EP	Essays in Poetics (U of Keele, Eng.)
ES	English Studies: A Journal of English Language and Literature (Nijmegen, Neth.)
ESA	Empirical Studies of the Arts (U of Maine)
ETC	Etcetera (San Francisco)
Euphorion	Euphorion: Zeitschrift für Literaturgeschichte (Heidelberg, W. Ger.)

Fabula	Fabula: Zeitschrift für Erzählforschung/Journal of Folklore Studies/Revue d'études sur le conte populaire (Göttingen, W. Ger.)
FdL	Forum der Letteren (Muiderberg, Neth.)
FF	French Forum (Lexington, KY)
FI	Forum Italicum: A Quarterly of Italian Studies (Tonawanda, NY)
FL	Foundations of Language (see Slang)
FM	Le français moderne (Paris)
FMLS	Forum for Modern Language Studies (U of St. Andrews, Scot.)
ForumH	Forum (U of Houston)
FQ	Film Quarterly (U of California, Berkeley)
FR	French Review: Journal of the American Association of Teachers of French (Chapel Hill, NC)
FS	French Studies: A Quarterly Review (Queen Mary C, England)
GaR	Georgia Review (U of Georgia)
Genre	Genre (U of Oklahoma)
Germanistik	Germanistik: Internationales Referatenofgan mit bibliographischen Hinweisen (Tübingen, W. Ger.)
GL	General Linguistics (Pennsylvania State U)
GL&L	German Life and Letters (Inst. of Germanic Studies, London)
Glyph	Glyph: Johns Hopkins Textual Studies
Gnomon	Gnomon: Kritische Zeitschrift für die Gesamte klassische Altertumswissenschaft (U of Munich)
GQ	German Quarterly (Princeton U)
GRM	Germanisch-Romanische Monatsschrift (Heidelberg, W. Ger.)
Gymnasium	Gymnasium: Zeitschrift für Kultur der Antike und humanistische Bildung (Norderstedt, W. Ger.)
HAB	Humanities Association Bulletin (Queen's U, Can.)
Hasifrut	Ha-Sifrut/Literature: Theory-Poetics-Hebrew and Comparative Literature (Tel Aviv)
Hephaistos	Hephaistos: A Quarterly Devoted to Computer Research in the Humanities (St. Joseph's C, Philadelphia)
Hermathena	Hermathena: A Dublin University Review (Trinity C, Dublin)
Hisp	Hispania (C of the Holy Cross)
HisR	Hispanic Review (U of Pennsylvania)
HLR	Harvard Law Review
HM	Harper's Magazine (New York)
HQ	Hopkins Quarterly (Wilfrid Laurier U, Can.)

HR	Hudson Review (New York)
HSL	Hartford Studies in Literature (U of Hartford)
HSN	Hawthorne Society Newsletter (North Texas State U)
IAN	Izvestija akademii nauk S.S.S.R., Serija literatury i jazyka (Moscow)
I&L	Ideologies and Literature (U of Minnesota, Minneapolis)
IFR	International Fiction Review (U of New Brunswick, Can.)
IJAL	International Journal of American Linguistics (U of Colorado, Boulder)
IJPs	International Journal of Psycholinguistics (The Hague)
Ind Ling	Indian Linguistics: Journal of the Linguistic Society of India (Deccan C)
IPQ	International Philosophical Quarterly (Fordham U)
IRLI	Italianistica: Rivista di letteratura italiana (Milan)
Italica	Italica (Columbia U)
ITL	ITL: Tijdschrift van het Instituut voor toegepaste linguistiek/Review of the Institute of Applied Linguistics (Louvain, Belg.)
ITT	In These Times (Chicago)
JAAC	Journal of Aesthetics and Art Criticism (Temple U)
Jabberwocky	Jabberwocky: The Journal of the Lewis Carroll Society (Staffs, Eng.)
JAE	Journal of Aesthetic Education (U of Illinois, Urbana)
JAF	Journal of American Folklore (U of Texas, Austin)
JAS	Journal of American Studies (Cambridge U)
JazA	Jazykovědńé aktuality: Zpravodaj jazykovědného sdruženi při československé akademii věd (Prague)
JbAm	Jahrbuch für Amerikastudien (Heidelberg, W. Ger.)
JC	Journal of Communication (U of Pennsylvania)
JCLTA	Journal of the Chinese Language Teachers Association (Ohio State U)
JEGP	Journal of English and Germanic Philology (U of Illinois, Urbana)
JEL	Journal of English Linguistics (Western Washington U)
JES	Journal of European Studies (U of Exeter, Eng.)
JFI	Journal of the Folklore Institute (Indiana U)
JGE	Journal of General Education (Pennsylvania State U)
JJQ	James Joyce Quarterly (U of Tulsa)
JL	Journal of Linguistics (London)
JLS	Journal of Literary Semantics (U of Kent, Eng.)
JLT	Journal of Literary Theory (formerly JPS)
JML	Journal of Modern Literature (Temple U)
JMRS	Journal of Medieval and Renaissance Studies (Duke U)
JNT	Journal of Narrative Technique (Eastern Michigan U)

JoHS	Journal of Hellenic Studies (Corpus Christi C, Oxford U)
JOP	Journal of Pragmatics (Amsterdam)
JPC	Journal of Popular Culture (Bowling Green U)
JPS	Journal of Practical Structuralism (Kingston, ON) (now JLT)
JQ	Journalism Quarterly (Ohio U)
JRS	Journal of Russian Studies (U of Nottingham, Eng.)
JSSTC	Journal of Spanish Studies, 20th Century (U of Nebraska, Lincoln)
KLit	Kritikon Litterarum: Internationale Rezensionzletschrift für Romanistik, Slavistik, Anglistik/Amerikanistik und für Linguistik (Darmstadt, W. Ger.)
KN	Kwartalnik neofilologiczny (Warsaw)
KR	Kenyon Review (Kenyon C)
KRQ	Kentucky Romance Quarterly (U of Kentucky)
Kratylos	Kratylos: Kritisches Berichts- und Rezensionsorgan für indogermanische und allgemeine Sprachwissenschaft (Wiesbaden, W. Ger.)
KSJ	Keats-Shelley Journal: Keats, Shelley, Byron, Hunt, and Their Circles (U of Pennsylvania)
L&H	Literature and History (Thames Polytech, Eng.)
Lang	Language: Journal of the Linguistic Society of America (U of California, Los Angeles)
Langages	Langages: Sémiotiques textuelles (Paris)
L&P	Literature and Psychology (Fairleigh Dickinson U)
Lang&S	Language and Style (Queens C, City U of New York)
LangS	Language Sciences (Mitaka, Jap.)
LaS	Language in Society (Cambridge U)
LB	Leuvense bijdragen: Tijdschrift voor germaanse filologie (Leuven, Belg.)
LBib	Linguistica biblica: Interdisziplinäre Zeitschrift für Theologie und Linguistik (Bonn, W. Ger.)
LeedsSE	Leeds Studies in English (U of Leeds, Eng.)
LeL	Linguistica e letteratura (Pisa)
LeS	Lingua e stile: Trimestrale di linguistica e critica letteraria (Bologna)
LFQ	Literature/Film Quarterly (Salisbury State C)
LFr	Langue française (Paris)
LiLi	LiLi: Zeitschrift für Literaturwissenschaft und Linguistik (Göttingen, W. Ger.)
Ling	Linguistics: An Interdisciplinary Journal of the Language Sciences (U Coll., London)
LingA	Linguistic Analysis (U of Washington)
LingB	Linguistische Berichte (Heidelberg, W. Ger.)

LingI	Linguistic Inquiry (MIT)
LingR	Linguistic Reporter (Washington, DC)
Lingua	Lingua (Amsterdam)
Linguistique	La linguistique (Paris)
LIP	Literature in Performance (Speech Communication Association, Annandale, VA)
Lis	Listener (London)
Lit	Littérature (Palaiseau, Fr.)
LJ	Library Journal
LL	Language Learning: A Journal of Applied Linguistics (Brattleboro, VT)
LLBA	Language & Language Behavior Abstracts
LLSEE	Linguistic & Literary Studies in Eastern Europe (Amsterdam and Philadelphia)
LNL	Linguistics in Literature (Trinity U)
LOP	Language of Poems (U of South Carolina, 1972–80)
Lore&L	Lore and Language (U of Sheffield, Eng.)
LOS	Literary Onomastics Studies (State U of New York C, Brockport)
LP	Litterair Paspoort (Amsterdam)
LRB	London Review of Books
LRN	Literary Research Newsletter (State U of New York C, Brockport)
LS	La lingue straniere (Rome)
LSE	Lund Studies in English (Lund, Swed.)
LSoc	Language in Society (U of Pennsylvania)
LT	Levende talen (Groningen, Neth.)
LuD	Linguistik und Didaktik (Munich)
MAE	Medium ævum (Balliol C, Oxford U)
Maledicta	Maledicta: The International Journal of Verbal Aggression (Waukesha, WI)
MD	Modern Drama (U of Toronto)
MFS	Modern Fiction Studies (Purdue U)
MiltonQ	Milton Quarterly (Ohio U, Athens)
MiltonS	Milton Studies (U of Pittsburgh)
Mind	Mind: A Quarterly Review of Philosophy (Birkbeck C, Oxford U)
MLJ	Modern Language Journal (Ohio State U)
MLN	Modern Language Notes (Johns Hopkins U)
MLQ	Modern Language Quarterly (U of Washington)
MLR	Modern Language Review (U of St. Andrews, Scot.)
Monatshefte	Monatshefte (U of Wisconsin, Madison)
MP	Modern Philology (U of Chicago)

MPhon	Le maître phonétique: Organe de l'Association phoné-tique internationale (London)
MQR	Michigan Quarterly Review (U of Michigan, Ann Arbor)
MS	Medieval Studies (Toronto)
MSE	Massachusetts Studies in English (U of Massachusetts, Amherst)
MSpr	Moderna sprak (Göteborg, Swed.)
Mu	Muttersprache: Zeitschrift zur Pflege und Erforschung der deutschen Sprach (Wiesbaden, W. Ger.)
N&Q	Notes & Queries (Pembroke C, Oxford U)
Nat	Nation (New York)
NCF	Nineteenth-Century Fiction (U of California, Los Angeles)
NCFS	Nineteenth-Century French Studies (State U of New York C, Fredonia)
NEQ	New England Quarterly (Northeastern U)
NGC	New German Critique (U of Wisconsin, Milwaukee)
NJL	Nordic Journal of Linguistics (U of Helsinki)
NK	Nyelvtudományi közlemények: A magyar tudományos akadémia nyelvtadományi Bizoltságá nak megbizásából (Budapest)
NL	New Letters: A Magazine of Fine Writing (formerly University Review) (U of Missouri, Kansas City)
NLH	New Literary History: A Journal of Theory and Interpre-tation (U of Virginia)
NM	Neuphilologische mitteilungen: Bulletin de la Société ne-ophilologique/Bulletin of the Modern Language So-ciety (U of Helsinki)
Novel	Novel: A Forum on Fiction (Brown U)
NR	New Republic (Washington, DC)
NS	New Statesman (London)
NsM	Neusprachliche Mitteilungen aus Wissenschaft und Praxis (Berlin, W. Ger.)
NUQ	New Universities Quarterly (Oxford) (formerly Universi-ties Quarterly)
NYRB	New York Review of Books
NYTBR	New York Times Book Review
Obs	Observer (London)
OL	Orbis Litterarum: International Review of Literary Studies (Odense, Den.)
OLR	Oxford Literary Review: A Post-Structuralist Journal (Ox-ford U)
Paideia	Paideia (Brescia)
P&L	Philosophy and Literature (U of Michigan, Dearborn)

P&R	Philosophy and Rhetoric (Pennsylvania State U)
Pensée	Pensée (Paris)
Phoenix	Phoenix: The Journal of the Classical Association of Canada (Trinity C, Toronto)
Phonetica	Phonetica: Journal of the International Society of Phonetic Sciences/Zeitschrift der Internationalen Gesellschaft für phonetische Wissenschaft (U of Kiel, W. Ger.)
PhS	Philosophical Studies: An International Journal for Philosophy in the Analytic Tradition (U of Ireland, Dublin)
PLL	Papers on Language and Literature (Southern Illinois U, Edwardsville)
PMLA	PMLA: Publications of the Modern Language Association of America (New York)
PN Review	PN Review (Manchester, Eng.)
Poetica	Poetica: Zeitschrift für Sprach und Literaturwissenschaft (U of Bochum, W. Ger.)
Poetics	Poetics: International Review for the Theory of Literature (Amsterdam)
Poétique	Poétique: Revue de théorie et d'analyse littéraires (Paris)
PoT	Poetics Today: Theory and Analysis of Literature and Communication (formerly PTL) (Tel Aviv)
PP	Philologica pragensia (Prague)
PPNCFL	Proceedings of the Pacific Northwest Conference on Foreign Languages
PQ	Philological Quarterly (U of Iowa)
PR	Partisan Review (New York)
PS	Prairie Schooner (U of Nebraska, Lincoln)
PTL	PTL: A Journal for Descriptive Poetics and Theory (ceased pub. 1979, became PoT)
QJS	Quarterly Journal of Speech (U of Massachusetts, Amherst)
QQ	Queen's Quarterly (Queen's U, Can.)
QRFS	Quarterly Review of Film Studies (South Salem, NY)
RE	La revue d'esthétique (Paris 1973–80, Toulouse 1981–)
REG	Revue des études grecques (Paris)
Ren&R	Renaissance and Reformation/Renaissance et reforme (U of Toronto)
RenD	Renaissance Drama (Evanston, IL)
RenQ	Renaissance Quarterly (New York)
RES	Review of English Studies (Oxford U)
RF	Romanische Forschungen (Frankfurt am Main, W. Ger.)
RJ	Romanistisches Jahrbuch (U of Hamburg, W. Ger.)

RLJ	Russian Language Journal (Michigan State U)
RLR	Revue des langues romanes (Montpellier, Fr.)
RLV	Revue des langues vivantes/Tijdschrift voor levende talen (1932–79)
RM	Review of Metaphysics (Washington, DC)
RMR	Rocky Mountain Review (Arizona State U)
RMS	Renaissance and Modern Studies (U of Nottingham, Eng.)
RPh	Romance Philology (U of California, Berkeley)
RR	Romanic Review (Columbia U)
RRL	Revue roumaine de linguistique (Bucharest)
RSH	Revue des sciences humaines (U of Lille)
RSQ	Rhetoric Society Quarterly (St. Cloud State U)
RSR	Religious Studies Review (Waterloo, Can.)
RTE	Research in the Teaching of English (National Council of Teachers of English, Urbana, IL)
RusL	Russian Literature (U of Amsterdam)
SAB	South Atlantic Bulletin (University, AL)
Sal	Salamagundi (Skidmore C)
SAmL	Studies in American Literature (The Hague)
Samlaren	Samlaren: Tidskrift for svensk literaturvetenskaplig forskning (Uppsala, Swed.)
S&S	Science & Society (John Jay C, City U of New York)
SAP	Studia anglica posnaniensia (Adam Mickiewica U, Pol.)
SAQ	South Atlantic Quarterly (Duke UP)
SAS	Slovo a slovesnost (Prague)
SB	Studies in Bibliography (Charlottesville, VA)
Sat Rev	Saturday Review (ceased pub.)
SBHC	Studies in Browning and His Circle (Baylor U)
SCN	Seventeenth-Century News (Pennsylvania State U)
SCR	South Carolina Review (Clemson U)
SCr	Strumenti critici: Rivista quadrimestrale di cultura e critica letteraria (Torino, It.)
SdG	Sprache der Gegenwart: Schriften des Instituts für deutsche Sprache in Mannheim
SDSN	Semiotic and Discourse Studies Newsletter (U of North Carolina, Charlotte)
SEA	Studies in English and American (Budapest)
SECOLB	SECOL Bulletin: Southeastern Conference on Linguistics (Murfreesboro, TN)
SEER	Slavonic and East European Review (U of London)
SEEJ	Slavic and East European Journal (Murray State U)
SEL	Studies in English Literature, 1500–1900 (Rice U)
Sem	Semiotext(e) (Columbia U)

Semiosis	Semiosis: Internationale Zeitschrift für Semiotik und Ästhetik (U of Stuttgart)
Semiotica	Semiotica: Journal of the International Association for Semiotic Studies/Revue de l'Association internationale de sémiotique (Indiana U)
SemS	Semiotic Scene: Bulletin of the Semiotic Society of America (ceased pub., see Semiotica)
Ser Rev	Serials Review (Ann Arbor, MI)
SFFBU	Sborník prací filosofické fakulty Brněnské univerzita (Brno)
SHR	Southern Humanities Review (Auburn U)
ShS	Shakespeare Survey (Oxford)
SIL	Studies in Linguistics (Taos, NM)
SILTA	Studi italiani di linguistica teorica ed applicata (U of Bologna)
SIR	Studies in Romanticism (Boston)
SJS	San Jose Studies (San Jose State U)
SL	Studia linguistica: Revue de linguistique générale et comparée (Lund U, Swed.)
Slang	Studies in Language (Gonzaga U) (supersedes Foundations of Language)
Slavia	Slavia (Prague)
SlavR	Slavic Review (U of Illinois, Urbana)
SlRec	Slovenská rec (Bratislava, Czech.)
SMIL	SMIL: Journal of Linguistic Calculus (Stockholm)
SN	Studia neophilogica: A Journal of Germanic and Romance Languages and Literature (Uppsala U, Swed.)
SNNTS	Studies in the Novel (North Texas State U)
Soc	Sociology (Dorridge, Eng.)
SocR	Sociological Review/Revija za socijologiju (Zagreb)
SoQ	Southern Quarterly: A Journal of the Arts in the South (Hattiesburg, MS)
SoRA	Southern Review: Literary and Interdisciplinary Essays (U of Adelaide, S. Austral.)
SP	Studies in Philology (U of North Carolina, Chapel Hill)
Spec	Speculum: A Journal of Medieval Studies (Medieval Academy of America, Cambridge, MA)
Spektator	Spektator: Tjidschrift voor Neerlandistick (U of Amsterdam)
Sprache	Die Sprache: Zeitschrift für Sprachwissenschaft (U of Vienna)
SR	Sewanee Review (U of the South)
SRNB	Sociology: Reviews of New Books (Washington, DC)
SSCJ	Southern Speech Communication Journal (U of Richmond)

SSF	Studies in Short Fiction (Newberry C)
StCL	Studii si cercetări lingvistice (Bucharest)
StCS	Studies in Contemporary Satire (Clarion State C)
StR	Structuralist Review (Queens C, City U of New York)
SfTCL	Studies in Twentieth-Century Literature (U of Nebraska, Lincoln)
Style	Style (U of Arkansas, Fayetteville, 1967–82; Northern Illinois U, 1983–)
Sub-Stance	Sub-Stance: A Review of Theory and Literary Criticism (U of Wisconsin, Madison)
TCL	Twentieth-Century Literature (Hofstra U)
TCS	Twentieth-Century Studies (U of Kent, Eng.)
Telos	Telos (St. Louis, MO)
TES	Times Educational Supplement (London)
Texte	Texte: Revue de critique et de théorie littéraire (Trinity C, Toronto)
THES	Times Higher Educational Supplement (London)
TJ	Theatre Journal (Washington, DC)
TLL	Travaux de linguistique et de littérature publiés par la Centre de philologie et de littératures romanes de l'Université de Strasbourg (U of Strasbourg, Fr.)
TLS	Times Literary Supplement (London)
TLTL	Teaching Language through Literature (Bronx, NY)
TQ	Tel Quel (Paris)
TS	Theological Studies (Georgetown U)
TSLL	Texas Studies in Literature and Language (Austin)
TT	Theology Today (Princeton Theological Seminary)
TvF	Tijdschrift voor filosofie (Leuven, Belg.)
TWC	Wordsworth Circle (Temple U)
UTQ	University of Toronto Quarterly
Verb	Verbatim (Essex, CT)
Versus	Versus: Quaderni di studi semiotici (U of Bologna)
Vir	Viriltaja: Kotikielen seuran aikakeuslehti (Helsinki)
VJa	Voprosy jazykoznanija (Moscow)
VLit	Voprosy literatury (Moscow)
VLS	Village Voice Literary Supplement (New York)
VLU	Vestnik Leningradskogo Universiteta. Serija istorii, jazyka i literatury
VP	Victorian Poetry (U of West Virginia)
VQR	Virginia Quarterly Review (Charlottesville, VA)
VS	Victorian Studies (Indiana U)
VWQ	Virginia Woolf Quarterly (Cherry Hill, NJ)
WCR	West Coast Review (Simon Fraser U)
WCRB	West Coast Review of Books (Hollywood, CA)

WHR	Western Humanities Review (U of Utah)
WLT	World Literature Today (Norman, OK) (formerly Books Abroad)
WMQ	William and Mary Quarterly (Williamsburg, VA)
Word	Word: Journal of the International Linguistic Association (Queens C, City U of New York)
WPCS	Working Papers in Cultural Studies (U of Birmingham, Eng.)
WS	Die Welt der Slaven (Munich)
WT	Western Teacher (Perth, Austral.)
YCC	Yearbook of Comparative Criticism (Pennsylvania State U)
YCGL	Yearbook of Comparative and General Literature (Indiana U)
YES	Yearbook of English Studies (U of Warwick, Eng.)
YFS	Yale French Studies (Yale U)
YR	Yale Review (Yale U)
ZAA	Zeitschrift für Anglistik und Amerikanistik (Leipzig, E. Ger.)
ZDA	Zeitschrift für deutsches Altertum und deutsche Literatur (Wiesbaden, W. Ger.)
ZDPh	Zeitschrift für deutsche Philologie (Berlin, W. Ger.)
ZFSL	Zeitschrift für französische Sprache und Literatur (Munich)
ZPSK	Zeitschrift für Phonetik, Sprachwissenschaft, und Kommunikationsforschung (Berlin, E. Ger.)
ZRP	Zeitschrift für Romanische Philologie (Tübingen, W. Ger.)
ZS	Zeitschrift für Slawistik (Berlin, E. Ger.)

THE BIBLIOGRAPHY

1.0 Bibliographical Resources (entries 1–153)

Includes bibliographies, handbooks, checklists, dictionaries, encyclopedias, glossaries, and selected journals. In addition to these resources, see the substantial bibliographies in the following books (asterisks indicate annotated): Attridge, *The Rhythms of English Poetry* (1982); Beaugrande, *Text, Discourse, and Process* (1980); Beaugrande and Dressler, *Introduction to Text Linguistics* (1981); *Bennett, *Prose Style* (1971); Brock and Scott, *Methods of Rhetorical Criticism* (1980); Carter, *Language and Literature* (1982); Chapman, *The Language of English Literature* (1982); Corti, *An Introduction to Literary Semiotics* (1978); Culler, *Structuralist Poetics* (1975) and *On Deconstruction* (1982); Dressler, *Current Trends in Textlinguistics* (following each essay) (1978); Eco, *A Theory of Semiotics* (1976); Enkvist, *Linguistic Stylistics* (1973); Elam, *The Semiotics of Theatre & Drama* (1980); *Fiske, *Introduction to Communication Studies* (1982); Fowler, *Literature as Social Discourse* (1981); Freeman, *Essays in Modern Stylistics* (1981); *Harari, *Textual Strategies* (1979); *Hawkes, *Structuralism and Semiotics* (1977); Leech, *Semantics* (1974); Leech and Short, *Style in Fiction* (1981); Riffaterre, *Semiotics of Poetry* (1978); *Norris, *Deconstruction* (1982); Rimmon-Kenan, *Narrative Fiction: Contemporary Poetics* (1983); Sammons, *Literary Sociology and Practical Criticism* (1977); Scaglione, *The Classical Theory of Composition . . .* (1972); *Scholes, *Structuralism in Literature* (1974), *Semiotics and Interpretation* (1982); Segers, *The Evaluation of Literary Texts* (1978); Shukman, *Literature and Semiotics* (1977); Suleiman and Crosman, *The Reader in the Text* (1980); Tompkins, *Reader-Response Criticism* (1980); Traugott and Pratt, *Linguistics for Students of Literature* (1980); and Wetherill, *The Literary Text* (1974).

A. Annual Bibliographies and Selected Journals (1–42)

(See Harari's annotated list of journals in *Textual Strategies*.)
1.   *American Journal of Semiotics*, 1982–.
A quarterly journal of the Semiotic Society of America, interdisciplinary, concerned with sign processes, especially human sign systems and the messages they generate. Vol. 1 contains an essay on "Greimas's Model for the Generative Trajectory of Meaning in Discourse." Vol. 2, nos. 1–2 (Spring 1983), is a special issue on Peirce's semiotic. No. 3 (Summer 1983) is devoted to Jakobson's contribution to semiotics.

2.   *American Literary Scholarship: An Annual.*
Bibliographic essays organized by major U.S. writers, periods, and genres. Index lists only names. Section on "Themes, Topics, and Criticism" usually includes something related to stylistics.

3. *Annual Bibliography of English Language and Literature* (Modern Humanities Research Assn.), 1920–.
    Stylistics section 1973–. Also see *"Festschriften* and Other Collections," "Subject, Genre, and Period Bibliographies, Checklists and Indexes," "Scholarly Method," "Language, Literature, and the Computer," "Social and Occupational" (sociolinguistics; slang, cant, jargon; technical and professional language), "Phonetics and Phonology," "Vocabulary," "Semantics," "Folklore," and various categories under "English Literature."

4. *Centrum: Working Papers of the Minnesota Center for Advanced Studies in Language, Style, and Literary Theory*, 1973–.
    Publishes papers bearing on the theory of language, style, and literature, especially with an interdisciplinary approach, including computer-aided analysis. In 1 issue: articles on "The Ideology of Speech-Act Theory," the poet as prophet, Riffaterre's *Semiotics of Poetry* applied to a poem by Emily Dickinson, oxymora, computational linguistics and discourse analysis. Also revs. of Iser's *The Act of Reading* and Bleich's *Subjective Criticism*. Reviews books. Eng.

5. *Choice.*
    A monthly book selection journal pub. by the Assn. of College and Research Libraries. 1-paragraph descriptions and assessments of books on "language and literature" appear under that heading in every number.

6. *Communications*, 1961–.
    Pub. by the École pratique des hautes études, Paris. "Has produced some of the most influential work in the field of structuralism" (Hawkes, *Structuralism and Semiotics* 182).

7. *Computers and the Humanities*, "Annual Bibliography," 1966–.
    Includes articles on literature — e.g., "Robertson Davies: The Tory Mode," "Variable Rules and Literary Style." Reviews books. Eng., Fr., Ger.

8. "Current Bibliography of Books on Rhetoric," in *RSQ.*
    The section on "Basic Rhetorical Research" includes a section on "Style"; see other sections.

9. *Diacritics: A Review of Contemporary Criticism*, 1970–.
    "A review of contemporary criticism in literature, cinema, and the arts, as well as a preview of important work in progress. . . . Diacritical discussion entails distinguishing the methodological and ideological issues which critics encounter. . . . Review articles, which are the principal component of each issue, should both provide a serious account of the work(s) under considera-

tion and allow the reviewer to respond by developing his own ideas or position." Eng.

10.   *Dissertation Abstracts International.*
Each issue has a principal section, a subject index, and an author index. See language and literature sections. And see the *Comprehensive Dissertation Index.*
     The 1981 Supp., vol. 4, includes the topics "style," "styles," "stylistic," "stylistics," "stylistique," and several related subjects ("structure," etc.).

10a.   *Essays in Poetics: Journal of British Neo-Formalist Circle,* 1976–.
"This journal studies Formalism, Structuralism and other recent progressive theories of literature and culture. It publishes both theoretical discussions and textual analysis of specific works drawn from English, American, Western and Eastern European literatures and other art forms" (from the journal's advertisement).

11.   *French Forum,* 1976–.
A journal of literary criticism that "welcomes multiplicity of approaches" — paradox in a poem, the poetics of a poet, the discourse of a play, etc. Revs. Fr. and Eng. *FF* is the publisher of French Forum Monographs on various aspects of literature — *Paradoxicality in Chrétien's "Conte del Graal," Studies in the Imagery of Montaigne's* Essais, etc.—15 vols. by 1979.

12.   *French XX Bibliography, Critical and Biographical References for the Study of French Literature since 1885.*
Vol. 7, no. 4, issue no. 34 (1982): contains a section entitled "Literary Genres, Esthetics, Stylistics, Themes: General, Novel, Poetry."

12a.   *Glyph,* 1977–.
Johns Hopkins's *Glyph* "was evidently established to accommodate if not further deconstructive efforts" (Atkins, *Reading Deconstruction/Deconstructive Reading* 1).

13.   *Journal of Literary Semantics,* 1972–.
Invites studies by theoretical linguists of traditional literary texts; publishes articles on all aspects of literary semantics, especially those of a philosophical and interdisciplinary nature. Reviews books. Eng.

14.   *Journal of Practical Structuralism,* 1979– (now *Journal of Literary Theory*).
The purpose of *JPS* is to provide a forum in which techniques of literary analysis, especially those related to structuralism, can be discussed and employed. 1 number a year. The first number contains 4 articles on Barthes's *The Pleasure of the Text*; the second is devoted to Genette's "Discours du récit" and Chatman's *Story and Discourse.* Reviews books. Eng.

15.   *Langages,* 1966–.
Notable for its exploration of linguistic-oriented criticism, with special numbers on "Linguistique et littérature," "L'analyse du discours," "L'enonciation," etc. Fr.

16.   *Language and Language Behavior Abstracts*, 1967–.
Sections on poetics, stylistics, literary criticism, discourse analysis/text linguistics, and semiotics. Each vol. selects certain journals for coverage over several years; not an annual bib. like that in *Style* or like the *MLA International Bibliography*.

17.   *Language and Style*, 1968–.
Publishes articles on style in all the arts and contexts. All theoretical approaches welcome. Reviews books. Eng., Fr., Ger.
    Ser Rev 6.3, 20: "a journal in which the major issues in stylistics are aired," an "excellent" journal, "provocative," "wide-ranging."

18.   *Language of Poems*, 1972–80.
Focused on grammar as the central cog in the meaning of a poem.

19.   *LiLi: Zeitschrift für Literaturwissenschaft und Linguistik*, 1971–.
Style 12, 63–67: *LiLi*, which derives its name from the main initials of its full title, is a "journal for the science of literature and linguistics," particularly for the development of auxiliary sciences (especially mathematically based) for the study of literature. Each issue is devoted to 1 or 2 connected themes, with "much stress laid upon method." "Anyone who is interested in linguistic (and other) approaches to literature and who has a reasonable knowledge of German should try to get a look at this journal." "The journal is . . . a highly important European contribution in linguistics, literature, and adherent areas."

20.   *Lingua e stile: Trimestrale di linguistica e critica litteraria*, 1966–.
Mainly in Ital., but also Ger., Eng., and Russ. No. 2 of vol. 18 (1982) is entirely in Ital. except for 1 article in Ger., but Eng. and Russ. summaries are provided. This number's articles deal with "Allegory and Structure in the Tale of the *Vita nuova*," the notion of verisimilitude, literary genres in the late Middle Ages, etc. Reviews books.
    Style 3, 91–93 (rev. of vol. 1, 1966): "The editors and readers of *Style* will want to warmly embrace this handsome sister-publication from Italy"; "this noteworthy effort brings Italian scholarship at once in the forefront of an . . . international effort to develop the various branches of semiotics and to provide this vast field with a sound theoretical underpinning."

21.   *Linguistic and Literary Studies in Eastern Europe*, 1979–.
A series of books on recent developments in linguistics and literary research in Eastern Europe. Eng., Ger.

22.   *Linguistic Bibliography/Bibliographie linguistique*, 1939–.
Stylistics section from its inception. See also sections on semantics, semiotics,

pragmatics and speech acts, phonology, grammar, text linguistics, prosody, sociolinguistics, and psycholinguistics. An annual bib. that contains titles in European publications mainly. [Excellent.]

23.   *Linguistics*, 1963–.
Occasional literary articles and revs. of books on literature. No. 55 (1969) contains essays on parody, feeling in literature, and "langue" and "parole." Eng., Fr., Ger.

24.   *MLA International Bibliography of Books and Articles on the Modern Languages and Literatures*, 1925–.
Vol. 3, "Linguistics," since 1968 has included a section on stylistics under "General Linguistics." Also see sections on phonology, prosody, lexis, grammar, semantics, psycholinguistics, and festschriften.

25.   *New Literary History: A Journal of Theory and Interpretation*, 1969–.
Welcomes 2 types of contributions: (1) theoretical articles (the nature of literary theory, the evolution of styles) and (2) articles from other disciplines that help define and interpret the problems of literary study. Eng.
    Katz, *Magazines for Libraries*: "a superior publication"; *Ser Rev* 6.3, 23: "Over the past ten years *NLH* has established itself as the most interesting and best-known of the new American journals that deal with issues of literary theory. . . . Most of the best literary theorists of the 1970's have appeared in its pages."

26.   *Poetics: International Review for the Theory of Literature*, 1971–.
Publishes theoretical articles with a linguistic emphasis, e.g., the theory of metrics, syntax, narrative, semantics, discourse. A double issue dealt with "Theory of Metaphor." Other numbers on "Literary Stylistics," "Structural Poetics," Formal Semantics and Literary Theory."
    Ser Rev 6.3, 27: "In a relatively new area of study . . . *Poetics* stands among the finest journals" at "a highly specialized level"; Katz, *Magazines for Libraries*: "the most abstruse literary journal in existence."

27.   *Poetics Today: Theory and Analysis of Literature and Communication*, 1979–. (formerly *PTL*)
Articles on contemporary literary theory; descriptive poetics of specific texts, writers, or genres; language in context; and communication in culture.
    The Winter 1980 number contained 2 essays on metaphor, 3 on modern theoretical trends, 2 on recent research in Germany, 2 on deconstruction, etc.
    Ser Rev 6.3, 27–28: a highly laudatory rev. based, however, on only the inaugural issue and the eds.' stated intentions. Articles in this first issue by J. Lotman, B. H. Smith, T. A. van Dijk, et al.

28.　　*Poétique: Revue de théorie et d'analyse littéraires*, 1970–.
Literary theory and its categories (genres, periods, methods of investigation, levels of analysis) in relation with concrete works of literature. Founded for the study of "literariness." Fr. See Todorov's index to "Studies on Style in *Poétique*."
"Probably the most influential review of literary criticism in France today" (Harari, *Textual Strategies* 462).

29.　　*Pre/Text, an Inter-Disciplinary Journal of Rhetoric*, 1980–.
Objectives: (1) to encourage "the rediscovery of rhetoric as historically an inter-disciplinary art," (2) to review all publications contributing to this rediscovery. Eng.

30.　　"Prosody," *MLA International Bibliography*, vol. 3.

30a.　　*Reader: Essays in Reader-Oriented Theory, Criticism, and Pedagogy* (formerly *A Newsletter of Reader-Oriented Criticism and Teaching*), 1983–.
The Spring 1983 issue treats the theme "The Ideologies of Reader-Oriented Literary Theory." The topic for the Fall issue is "Relationships between Reader-Response and Psycholinguistic Reading Theories."

30b.　　*Real: The Yearbook of Research in English and American Literature*, de Gruyter, 1982–.
An outlet for longer articles (up to 50 typescript pp.) on poetics, rhetoric, stylistics, metrics, textual criticism, and current research. Also rev. articles, reports on developments in creative literature. In vol. 1, only 2 of the 9 contributions deal with stylistics—1 on story openings, the other on genre (the fantastic).

31.　　*Rhetorica*, 1983–.
The journal of the International Society for the History of Rhetoric. Articles, book revs., bibs. Eng., Fr., Ger., Ital.

32.　　*The Rhetoric Society Quarterly*, 1968–.
The society's purpose is "to gather from all relevant fields of study . . . current knowledge of rhetoric, broadly construed." Publishes articles, revs., special bibs., and a current bib. Eng.

33.　　*Semiotica: Journal of the International Association for Semiotic Studies*, 1969–.
"Conceptions of Folklore in the Development of Literary Semiotics," "A Visual and Temporal Decoding of the Pragmatic Structure of *Jacques le fataliste*," etc. Reviews books. Eng., Fr., Ger., Russ.

34.   *Style*, 1967–.
Publishes critical analyses of literature, numerous revs., special bibs., an annual bib., surveys of national criticism, reports of teaching about stylistics or using stylistics in the classroom.
   Ser Rev 6.3, 33: "probably the best of the serials treating stylistic issues," "a treasure of some of the best criticism being written today."

35.   Stylistics "Annual Bibliography," *Style* (usually the Spring no.).
Additional bibs. and checklists may be found at the beginning of the annual bib. The 1980 bib. surveys 180 journals and *DAI*, providing 883 entries.

36.   *Tel Quel*, 1960–.
Literature, philosophy, science, and politics. "The most radical of the journals associated with structuralism and semiotics" (Hawkes, *Structuralism and Semiotics* 183). *Théorie d'ensemble* (1968) is a collection of essays by writers associated with the journal (Barthes, Derrida, Sollers, et al.). Fr.

37.   *Texas Studies in Language and Literature: A Journal of the Humanities*, 1911–.
All areas of literature, linguistics, philosophy, social studies, and nontechnical science. Eng.

38.   *Text: An Interdisciplinary Journal for the Study of Discourse*, 1981–.
Forum for interdisciplinary discourse studies (*Textwissenschaft*): texts, conversations, messages, etc. Emphasizes theory formation and development of methods of analysis. Examples for literature: "Sentence Aspect and the Movement of Narrating Time," "Words, Sentences, Texts, and All That." Eng.

39.   *Voprosy literatury*, 1957–.
Articles on theory and history of Russian and foreign literatures. Reviews books. Russ.

40.   *Yale French Studies*, 1948–.
Fr. literature and culture, related topics. Considerable attention to structuralism (e.g., nos. 44 and 45 contain essays by Todorov) and problems of contemporary criticism.

41.   *Year's Work in English Studies*, 1919–.
Vol. 60, index 2, "Authors & Subjects Treated," cites work on "Style & Stylistics."

42.   *Year's Work in Modern Language Studies*, 1930–.
Surveys fields of Romance, Celtic, Germanic, and Slavonic language and literatures. Index of vol. 42 contains the subject heading "Stylistics."

B. Single Bibliographies, Dictionaries, Checklists, Handbooks (43–153)

43.　Alston, R. C., and J. L. Rosier. 1967. "Rhetoric and Style: A Bibliographical Guide." *LeedsSE*, ns 1, 137–59.

44.　Milic, Louis T. 1967. *Style and Stylistics: An Analytical Bibliography.* New York: Free. 199 pp.
A topical arrangement, mainly in Eng. about Eng. literature and language (some Fr., a few Ger. and Ital.). 5 categories: "Theoretical," the theory of rhetoric and style from Plato to the 1960s; "Methodological," how the study of style is to be pursued; "Applied," the largest (and most selective) section, studies of particular authors, styles, periods, devices, translation, etc.; "Bibliographies"; "Omnibus." C 800 entries. 3 indexes: authors as contributors, authors as subjects, subjects and topics. Annotations by key word.
　　Style 2, 233–38: Milic stresses prose writers, especially those of the 18th cent., and several important studies are missing; but he does present a considerable amount of valuable and accurate information; *FL* 6, 590–93; *CRL* 29, 69; *QJS* 54, 164.

45.　Bailey, Richard W., and Dolores M. Burton. 1968. *English Stylistics: A Bibliography.* Cambridge: MIT P. 198 pp.
A chronological and topical arrangement of the criticism of the literature of England and America from 1500 to the 1960s. Introd. on stylistics in mid-20th cent. 1. "Bibliographical Sources." 2. "Language and Style before 1900." 3. "English Stylistics in the Twentieth Century: Defining Creativity and 'Style,'" "Modes of Stylistic Investigation," "Statistical Approaches to Style," "Problems in Translation," "Prose Stylistics," "Style in Poetry." C. 2,000 entries, about half annotated descriptively. 2 indexes: "Styles under Scrutiny" and "Critics of Style" (authors whose works appear in the bib.). No terminological index.
　　Style 2, 239–42: lacks a topical index, but a "good" and "useful" bibliography, the rhetorical section (part 2) "probably the best to be found anywhere," "relatively free of typographical error," "the page well laid-out for visibility"; *RPh* 24, 639–40; *ZAA* 17, 312–14; *GL* 9, 132–34; *FL* 6, 590–93; *MLJ* 54, 41; *VQR* 41, 115.

46.　Bailey, Richard, and Lubomír Doležel, eds. 1968. *An Annotated Bibliography of Statistical Stylistics.* Ann Arbor: Dept. of Slavic Langs. and Lits., U of Michigan. 97 pp.
More than 650 items, most annotated; organized into 7 categories; international, interdisciplinary; the first bib. exclusively devoted to statistical stylistics; author index.
　　Style 6, 67–70: topical index needed, too many relevant PhD dissertations overlooked, and other "strange omissions," but a "useful" reference work.

47.   Bennett, James R. 1968. "English Prose from Alfred to More: A Bibliography." *MS* 30, 248–59.
Annotated list of 75 items.

48.   Bennett, James R. 1968. "Style in Twentieth-Century British and American Fiction: A Bibliography." *WCR* 2, 43–51.
175 items (most of them annotated), 25 general, 150 on individual authors.

49.   Turco, Lewis. 1968. *The Book of Forms: A Handbook of Poetics.* New York: Dutton. 160 pp.
On poetry; ch. 4 explains over 175 traditional Anglo-American verse forms. The glossarial index contains over 650 entries.

50.   Deutsch, Babette. 1969. *Poetry Handbook: A Dictionary of Terms.* 3rd ed., rev., enl. New York: Funk. 201 pp.
"I tried to steer a middle course" for the general and professional reader. Terms relating to literary history generally omitted.

51.   Lanham, Richard. 1969. *A Handlist of Rhetorical Terms: A Guide for Students of English Literature.* Berkeley: U of California P. 148 pp.
An alphabetical list of classical, plus Puttenham's englished, terms. In addition the terms are classified according to divisions of rhetoric (invention, arrangement, style), by type (addition, substraction, substitution, balance, etc.), and as ornaments. Separate sections give especially useful terms, important dates, and works cited.
       SR 53, 38; *AN&Q* 7, 156–57; *QJS* 55, 85–86; *CritQ* 13, 189; *EIC* 19, 320; *ClassR* 23, 99; *RPh* 26, 743.

52.   Bausch, K.-R., J. Klegraf, and W. Wilss. 1970. *The Science of Translation: An Analytical Bibliography.* 2 vols. and a supp. Tübingen: Spangenberg. 181 pp.
Covers the years 1962–71. A third vol. is being prepared. The same authors are preparing *Materials for a History of Translation*, intended to be a truly comprehensive encyclopedic bib. covering all writings in all languages.

53.   Martin, W. 1970. *Analyse van een vocabularium met behulp van een computer.* Brussels: Aimav. 219 pp.
Contains a list of computer-assisted lexical studies and quantitative stylistics.

54.   Rossum-Guyon, Françoise van. 1970. "Point de vue ou perspective narrative." *Poétique* 4, 476–97.

55.   Todorov, Tzvetan. 1970. "Les études du style: Bibliographie sélective." *Poétique* 2, 224–32.
Current work.

56.   Tyl, Zdenek, ed. 1970. *A Tentative Bibliography of Studies in Functional Sentence Perspective*. Prague: Československa Akad. Ved. 66 pp.

57.   Harari, Josué. 1971. *Structuralists and Structuralisms: A Selected Bibliography of French Contemporary Thought (1960–1970)*. Ithaca: *Diacritics*. 82 pp.
See Miller's extension, no. 136.

58.   Murphy, James J. 1971. *Medieval Rhetoric: A Select Bibliography*. Toronto: U of Toronto P. 100 pp.
Original texts and criticism, many annotated, divided by "Background Works," "The Transitional Period (AD 400 to 1050)," "Transmission of Classical Rhetorical Traditions," "Grammar," "The Art of Letter-Writing," "The Art of Preaching," and "The University Disputation." Name index.

59.   Shibles, Warren. 1971. *Metaphor: An Annotated Bibliography and History*. Whitewater: Language. 414 pp.
An international collection (2,400 entries) with a name and term index and a metaphor index. Continued in *RSQ* 4, 5–13.
     ARBA 3, 463: "highly recommended"; *ZAA* 23, 170–71: "meritorious," "a mine of information"; *Mu* 83, 364–67; *FL* 10, 610–11.

60.   Bronzwaer, W. 1972. "A Survey of Recent Studies in Stylistics." *DQR* 2, 162–68.

61.   Kluewer, Jeffery. 1972. "An Annotated Checklist of Writings on Linguistics and Literature in the Sixties." *BNYPL* 76, 36–91.
Works written in Eng. and dealing with Eng. and Amer. literature.

62.   Malinskaja, B. A., et al., comps. 1972. *Obščeje i prikladnoje jazykoznanie: Ukazatel' literatury, izdannoi y SSSR s 1963 po 1967 god* [General and Applied Linguistics: Bibliographical Guide to Soviet Publications in Linguistics from 1963 to 1967]. Moscow: USSR Acad. of Sciences, Inst. of Scientific Information in Social Sciences.
Stylistics titles are scattered throughout: nos. 400–06, 1117–23, 3919–31, "general stylistics" 3932–90, etc. Subject and name indexes.

63.   Ozzello, Yvonne, 1972. "The Syntax of Poetry: A Selected Bibliography, 1960–1970." *Sub-Stance* 4, 79–103.
54 entries focusing on linguistic theory and models of analysis.

64.   Andrew, J. Dudley, and Gerald Bruns. 1973. "Structuralism, Narrative Analysis, and the Theory of Texts: A Checklist." *BMMLA* 6, 121–27.

65.   Bennett, James R., and Linda Stafstrom. 1973. "English and American
       Prose Style: A Bibliography of Criticism for 1968–1969." *Style* 7,
       295–348.
Organized by historical periods and individual authors; fiction and nonfiction. 554 items.

66.   Bense, Max, and Elisabeth Walther, eds. 1973. *Wörterbuch der Semio-
       tik*. Cologne: Kiepenheuer. 137 pp.
The first dictionary of semiotics.
Semiotica 13, 396–414.

67.   *Computers and the Humanities*, Mar. 1973 issue.
Lists 360 books and articles concerned with the computer study of literature
and language in its bib. for 1972.

68.   Dressler, Wolfgang, and Siegfried Schmidt. 1973. *Textlinguistik: Kom-
       mentierte Bibliographie*. Munich: Fink. 120 pp.
386 annotated titles; 69 more without comment.
Ling 141, 76–78 (Ger.).

69.   Fowler, Roger, ed. 1973. *A Dictionary of Modern Critical Terms*. Lon-
       don: Routledge. 208 pp.
"This is not an encyclopaedia. . . . Nor is this a 'dictionary' in the usual
sense, in that its primary concern is not to provide brief working definitions
of critical terms." The purpose is to encourage "a new [heuristic] perspective
on literary terminology" and "to stimulate curiosity about how literary terms
work actively for us," those terms, that is, that are "not tied down by any
immutable linguistic rule" (e.g., tension, irony, baroque, fabulation). [No
principle of selection is offered.]
    Lang&S 8, 239: "a collection of individual essays, well-written, well-
researched, with valuable bibliogaphies," but "there are lapses . . . ."; *Enc*
42, 69–72; *JES* 4, 71; *BRD* 74, 387; *LJ* 99, 744; *N&Q* 22, 522–24; *RLV* 41, 210.

70.   Hornsby, Samuel. 1973. "Style in the Bible: A Bibliography." *Style* 7,
       349–75.
Deals with the King James (1611) version; classified, annotated.

71.   Bergal, Irene, and James R. Bennett. 1974. "Tzvetan Todorov: An An-
       notated List of His Published Writings in French and English." *Style*
       8, 143–52.

72.   Doak, Robert. 1974. "Color and Light Imagery: An Annotated Bibliog-
       raphy." *Style* 8, 208–59.
Both literary and nonliterary; period and author indexes.

73. Eaton, Marcia. 1974. "Speech Acts: A Bibliography." *Centrum* 2, 57–72.
Covers 1956–; author index.

74. "French Stylistics." 1974. *Style* 8.1, 155–286.
Hatzfeld on 20th-cent. Fr. stylisticians, Antoine on "La Nouvelle critique,"
Hamon on narrative, Kress-Rosen on the "speech event," Harari on Barthes.
7 revs.; indexes of *Le français moderne*, *Poétique*, and *Change*; bibs. of Genette
and Todorov.

75. Hatzfeld, Helmut. 1974. "The Leading French Stylisticians of the Twentieth Century." *Style* 8, 3–17.
From Bally to Todorov.

76. Helgorsky, Françoise. 1974. "Studies on Style in *Le français moderne*:
An Index." *Style* 8, 109–19.
Through 1972 in 7 categories.

77. Paris, Jean, and Joseph Maier. 1974. "Studies on Style in *Change*, 1–13
(1968–1972): An Index, with Afterword." *Style* 8, 124–38.

78. Seaman, John. 1974. "The Style of Political Discourse: An Annotated
Bibliography." *Style* 8, 477–528.
Bib. of 502 items; index of authors studied.

79. See, Klaus von, ed. 1974–. *Neues Handbuch der Literaturwissenschaft.*
Wiesbaden: Akad. Verl. Athenaion.
25 vols. are planned, with emphasis on genres and styles of particular periods.
[See Escarpit, no. 133.]
    MLR 75, 937–39 (rev. of vol. 3): the complete encyclopedia is an enterprise
of "monumental proportions."

80. Todorov, Tzvetan. 1974. "Studies on Style in *Poétique*, 1970–1973: An
Index." *Style* 8, 12–23.
The first 14 issues classified into 7 categories.

81. Bennett, James R. 1975. "Stylistic Innovation and Tradition: A Bibliography." *Style* 9, 401–42.
Organized by chronological periods and alphabetically by authors.

82. DeMarco, Norman. 1975. "Bibliography of Books on Literature and
Film." *Style* 9, 593–606.
See Welch, no. 141.

83. Di Cristo, Albert. 1975. *Soixante-et-dix ans de recherches en prosodie:
Bibliographie alphabétique, thématique et chronologique* [Seventy Years

of Research in Prosody: Alphabetical, Thematic, and Chronological Bibliography]. Aix-en-Provence: Inst. de phonétique. 351 pp.
BL (1978), 2580.

84.   Morier, Henri. 1975. *Dictionnaire de poétique et de rhétorique.* 2nd ed., augmented. Paris: PUF. 1,210 pp.
"A dictionary of terms in modern poetry and rhetoric. Runs heavily to long, detailed articles, with numerous examples of use, and charts, diagrams, etc. . . . Particular attention is given to phonetics" (*Guide to Reference Books*, 1976).

85.   Murray, Roger, and Sally McNall. 1975. "Period Style: A Bibliography of Recent Theory." *Style* 9, 155–80.
Mainly from 1950–72, most items annotated.

86.   Rewa, Michael. 1975. "Style in Biography: A Bibliographical Study." *Style* 9, 181–209.
A section on general works, then special attention to Johnson, Boswell, Strachey, More, Harpsfield, Walton, North, Goldsmith, Carlyle.

87.   Ross, Harris. 1975. "A Selected Bibliography of the Relationship of Literature and Film." *Style* 9, 564–92.
Articles, many annotated. [See Welch, no. 141.]

88.   Selz, Dorothy. 1975. "Structuralism for the Non-Specialist: A Glossary and a Bibliography." *CE* 37, 160–66.

89.   Bennett, James R. 1976. "Beginning and Ending: A Bibliography." *Style* 10, 184–88.
Bib. of 36 items.

90.   Bennett, James R. 1976. "A Stylistics Checklist I." *Style* 10, 350–401.
Bib. of 237 topical entries (terms, methods, theories, critics, schools); over 400 critical references. Extensive cross-references.

91.   Cable, Thomas. 1976. "Recent Developments in Metrics." *Style* 10, 313–28.
A survey mainly of "generative metrics," beginning with "Chaucer and the Study of Prosody," the seminal article by Halle and Keyser in the Dec. 1966 issue of *College English* (187–219). Studies of traditional and structural metrics are "mentioned only in passing."

92.   Freeman, Donald C. 1976. "Literature." Ch. 11 in R. Wardlaugh and H. D. Brown, eds., *A Survey of Applied Linguistics*, Ann Arbor: U of Michigan P, 229–49.

A "sketch" of "the intellectual backgrounds and assumptions of the most promising lines of research over the last fifteen years. . . . Work in English published in North America and Great Britain since the publication of Sebeok's *Style in Language* (1960) will be the focal point." Freeman divides this work into 2 "major directions" — "endogenous" ("the search for formal structures" in literary language, works, and the work of authors) and "exogenous" ("the search for adequate" contrastive descriptions of literary language versus ordinary language, language of particular authors versus works by other authors, etc.).

93.   Gershator, Phillis. 1976. *A Bibliographic Guide to the Literature of Contemporary American Poetry, 1970–1975*. Metuchen: Scarecrow. 124 pp.
Covers reference works, anthologies, textbooks, and "works dealing with more than three poets each." Name and topic indexes.

94.   Hassel, Jon, and Valerie Staines. 1976. "An Annotated Bibliography of *Sub-Stance*." *Style* 10, 176–83.
Surveys 1971–74.

95.   Tate, Gary, ed. 1976. *Teaching Composition: 10 Bibliographical Essays*. Ft. Worth: Texas Christian UP. 304 pp.
1 of the essays is "Approaches to the Study of Style," by Edward P. J. Corbett (73–110). Others on "Structure and Form in Non-Fiction Prose," "Modes of Discourse," etc. Corbett concentrates "on those books and articles . . . most useful . . . to teachers of composition . . . on a fairly elementary level." His essay headings cover collections, bibliography, history, theory, and methodology and application.

96.   Bennett, James R. 1977. "A Stylistics Checklist II." *Style* 11, 425–45.
Continues the glossary and sources of stylistic terms; cross-referenced.

97.   Bennett, James R., et al. 1977. "The Historical Study of Style: An Annotated Bibliography." *Style* 11, 338–52.
Bib. of 102 items.

98.   Bennett, James R., et al. 1977. "The Paragraph: An Annotated Bibliography." *Style* 11, 107–18.
Bib. of 110 items.

99.   Bennett, James R., et al. 1977. "Punctuation and Style: An Annotated Bibliography." *Style* 11, 119–35.
Bib. of 176 items.

100.   Bennett, James R., et al. 1977. "Typography and Style: An Annotated Bibliography." *Style* 11, 446–51.
Bib. of 55 items.

101.   Cuddon, J. A. 1977. *A Dictionary of Literary Terms*. Garden City: Doubleday; London: Deutsch. 745 pp. Rpt. Penguin, 1982.
Definitions and discussion of about 2,000 literary terms "in regular use," including several lesser-known technical and foreign examples. [Does not reflect current critical developments.]

102.   Meyers, Robert, and Karen Hopkins. 1977. "A Speech-Act Theory Bibliography," *Centrum* 5, 73–108.
An expansion of the Eaton bib. to include the spread of the theory "beyond philosophy, linguistics and literary theory to fields as diverse as political science, legal studies, education, sociology and theology." References include only work that "explicitly employs Austin's theory and its major concepts."

103.   Nager, Rae Ann. 1977. "A Selective Annotated Bibliography of Recent Work on English Prosody." *Style* 11, 136–70.
A continuation of a bib. that appeared in *Versification*, ed. W. K. Wimsatt, this one covering 1969–75. 285 items.

104.   Bennett, James R., et al. 1978. "Author Style." *Style* 12, 83–108.
214 items cover 140 authors.

105.   Bleich, David, et al. 1978. "The Psychological Study of Language and Literature: A Selected and Annotated Bibliography." *Style* 12, 113–211.
Bib. of 819 items of works in Eng. Divided into 2 main sections with subsections. "Part I lists works on the perception and cognition of language. Part II lists works on the affective and philosophical considerations of language in relation to literature and aesthetics."

106.   Gazdar, Gerald, Ewan Klein, and Geoffrey K. Pullum. 1978. *A Bibliography of Contemporary Linguistic Research*. New York: Garland. 450 pp.
Focuses primarily on post-1970 linguistics; over 4,000 entries; organized alphabetically by author. Topic, language, and linguist indexes.

107.   McHale, Brian. 1978. "Free Indirect Discourse: A Survey of Recent Accounts." *PTL* 3, 249–88.

108.   No entry.

109.   Rajec, Elizabeth. 1978. *The Study of Names in Literature: A Bibliography*. New York: Sauer. 166 pp.
Bib. of 1,346 items, annotated, international; covers through 1977; subject index.
Style 14, 56–57.

110.   Rickert, William. 1978. "Rhyme Terms." *Style* 12, 35–46.
Defines 229 terms used to describe rhyme.

111.   Terry, Garth. 1978. *East European Languages and Literatures: A Subject and Name Index to Articles in English-Language Journals, 1900–1977.* Santa Barbara: Clio. 275 pp.
Almost 10,000 articles written in Eng. and Fr. from over 800 non-Eastern English-language journals covering over 77 years. Arranged by subject; name index.
    AUMLA 54, 296–98: "a major contribution in both depth and range" and "coherent and cohesive . . . treatment."

112.   Verschueren, Jef. 1978. *Pragmatics: An Annotated Bibliography.* Amsterdam: John Benjamins. 270 pp.
Ongoing in *JOP*: "Pragmatics: An Annotated Bibliography. First Annual Supplement (Part 1)." *JOP* 2, 373–400.

113.   Allen, Robert F., and Robert Foster. 1979. "Bibliography of Grammatical Aspects of Style." *Style* 13, 141–61.
Bib. of 95 items from 165 Fr. and Eng. language journals during 1974.

114.   Bennett, James R., and Sam Hornsby. 1979. "The Sonnet: An Annotated Bibliography from 1940 to the Present." *Style* 13, 162–77.
Criticism in the Eng. language; 107 items.

115.   Bennett, James R., et al. 1979. "History as Art: An Annotated Checklist of Criticism." *Style* 13, 5–36.
Bib. of 315 items, mainly in Eng., during the last 25 years.

116.   Childs, John, et al. 1979. "A Bibliography of the Pun." *Style* 14, 127–37.
Bib. of 84 items derived from 64 journals published between 1945 and 1970. Annotated.

117.   Congrat-Butlar, Stefan, ed. 1979. *Translation and Translators: An International Directory and Guide.* New York: Bowker. 241 pp.
Ch. 6, "Journals/Books" (79–87), lists "an international selection of American, British, Canadian, Western European, and Soviet [and Chinese] material intended for the student preparing to enter the profession, and include[s] all contemporary studies containing important bibliographies or bibliographic footnotes."

118.   Ducrot, Oswald, and Tzvetan Todorov. 1979. *Encyclopedic Dictionary of the Sciences of Language.* Baltimore: Johns Hopkins UP. 380 pp. Trans. Catherine Porter from 2nd Fr. ed. of *Dictionnaire encyclopédique des sciences du langage* (Paris: Seuil, 1973).

By "language" the authors mean natural language, not all sign systems; by "sciences" in the plural they designate their inclusion of linguistics, poetics, rhetoric, stylistics, etc. Focus is on semantics, the problem of meaning on all levels. The book is organized conceptually in 4 sections, "some fifty articles" on well-defined topics that include the definition of "about eight hundred terms." The first section, "Schools," "traces the . . . history of modern linguistics"; the second, "Fields," describes the "disciplines for which language is the object" (linguistics, stylistics, etc.); the other 2 sections describe "the principal concepts we have used." Name and term indexes 10 pp.

Style 15, 506–07: inadequate "lexicographical scope" and indexes, but contains a "fair amount of useful . . . bibliographical material" and "wide-ranging and scholarly discussion of many important current issues in linguistics"; *MLN* 95, 1054–55: "a very fine introduction," all articles "well-informed and useful" and many "models of lucidity and acumen," "excellent translation."

119.   Jackson, Dennis, et al. 1979. "The Language of Literature about War: A Selective Annotated Bibliography." *Style* 13, 162–77.
Bib. of 200 items on Eng. language criticism about writers who have written in Eng.

120.   Perri, Carmela, et al. 1979. "Allusion Studies: An International Annotated Bibliography, 1921–1977." *Style* 13, 178–225.
Studies in Eng., Fr., Ger., Ital., Scand., Span., and Russ. that treat allusion as a literary device.

121.   Woodson, Linda. 1979. *A Handbook of Modern Rhetorical Terms*. Urbana: NCTE. 78 pp.
"[A]n attempt [to begin] to bring together in one place the myriad of words that have been added to rhetoric and composition in this century," compiled "from textbooks, from theoretical studies, from pedagogical and curricular explorations, and from plain practical studies." Some classical terms "still widely used" are included. Alphabetical order. Each term is defined, "often in the words of its originator," followed by a reference. A categorical app. facilitates cross-reference. Index of names of authors cited.

Style 15, 465–66: "That this book does not [fulfill the promise of its title] is hardly surprising, but the extent of the book's lapses should sober us." It is "more useful as a bibliographical guide than as a handbook of important terms"; *Choice* 17, 206: "No principles governing choice are stated, and one therefore remains puzzled"; *CCC* 31, 235; *ARBA* 11, 521.

122.   Bullock, Chris, and David Peck, comps. 1980. *Guide to Marxist Literary Criticism*. Bloomington: Indiana UP. 176 pp.
15 chs.: "Bibliographical Tools," "General Collections," "Journals," "Marx-

ist Criticism: General," "Literary Genres: Drama," "Literary Genres: Fiction," "Literary Genres: Poetry," "National Literatures: British," "National Literatures: United States," "National Literatures: English-Canadian," "Individual Authors," "Teaching English," "Language, Linguistics, and Literacy," "Literature and Society," "Appendix: A Reading List on Mass Culture." Name and term index. ["Style" and "stylistics" do not appear in the index; see "aesthetics," "literary form," "New Criticism," "structuralism."]

Choice 18, 1068: "indispensable research tool"; *LJ* 105, 1720; *AR* 40, 241; *ARBA* 13, 616; *CC* 98, 395; *SJS* 45, 382.

123.   Childs, John, et al. 1980. "A Bibliography of the Colloquial as a Stylistic Term: An Introduction." *Style* 14, 103–26.
Bib. of 143 items published between 1945 and 1978, annotated.

124.   Crystal, David. 1980. *A First Dictionary of Linguistics and Phonetics.* London: Deutsch; Boulder: Westview. 390 pp.
"Theoretical terminology which has developed since the mid-1970s will not be found," but pragmatics is included. See "stylistics" (Crystal 337).

Style 15, 508: "a worthy counterpart" to recent dictionaries of philosophy.

125.   Gordon, W. Terrence. 1980. *Semantics: A Bibliography 1965–1978.* Metuchen: Scarecrow. 307 pp.
In addition to the work in 6 languages on semantics that belongs properly to philosophy, psychology, and anthropology, this bib. surveys the scholarship in 2 chief linguistic frameworks—transformational-generative grammar and European traditions rooted in philology. The bib. begins in 1965 with Chomsky's *Aspects of the Theory of Syntax*, which advanced the notion of a tripartite grammar (syntactic, morphophonemic, and semantic). It lists works on 20 major topics, *not* including works on general semantics (Korzybski et al.), history of semantics, teaching, translating, discourse analysis, lexicology, logical semantics, or *meaning and style*. Lexical and author indexes.

ARBA 12, 514; *Choice* 18, 504.

126.   Horner, Winifred B., ed. 1980. *Historical Rhetoric: An Annotated Bibliography of Selected Sources in English.* Boston: Hall. 294 pp.
"[A]n attempt to trace the tradition of rhetoric through its long history from ancient Greece to its evolution within the English-speaking world." The book is divided into 5 sections: classical, medieval, renaissance, 18th cent., and 19th cent. Each section contains a list of primary works arranged in chronological order and a list of secondary studies arranged alphabetically by author. Each section was prepared by a different specialist, who has written an introduction. Name and term index.

BRD 78, 120–21; *Choice* 18, 1236; *ARBA* 13, 619; *B* 78, 1118; *CRL* 43, 70; *RenQ* 21, 199; *RSQ* 11, 97–98.

127.   de Joia, Alex, and Adrian Stenton. 1980. *Terms in Systemic Linguistics: A Guide to Halliday*. New York: St. Martin's. 160 pp.
Citations from the writings of Michael Halliday designed also to provide an overview of the development of systemic thought.
Lang 57, 769.

128.   Klinkenberg, Jean-Marie. 1980. "Studies on Style in *Le Français moderne*: An Index." *Style* 14, 163–64.

129.   Miller, George. 1980. "Stylistic Rhetoric and the Analysis of Style: An Annotated Bibliography." *Style* 14, 75–102.
Analyses of classical rhetorical figures.

130.   Rose, Marilyn, ed. 1980. *Translation Spectrum: Essays in Theory and Practice*. Albany: State U of New York P. 172 pp.
See "Translation Sources in the Humanities and the Social Sciences." Name and term index. [See Bausch, no. 52; Congrat-Butlar, no 117.]
Style 17, 64–65.

131.   Bennett, James R. 1981. "A Stylistics Checklist III." *Style* 15, 326–62.
146 entries; the 3 checklists contain 625 entries and over 1,000 references.

132.   Brogan, T. V. F. 1981. *English Versification, 1570–1980: A Reference Guide with a Global Appendix*. Baltimore: Johns Hopkins UP. 824 pp.
An annotated list (6,000 entries) classified by subject, cross-referenced, and indexed by poet and author of all known printed studies of Eng. versification from the Renaissance to the present, with global aspects of versification provided by a listing of major studies in other languages.

133.   Escarpit, Robert, ed. 1981. *Dictionnaire international des terms littéraires. Fascicule I: Académie-autobiographie. Fascicule 2: Autobiographie-bourgeois*. Bern: Francke. 96 pp.
The beginning of a massive dictionary by international scholars. Entries in either Fr. or Eng. Format: etymology, definition, linguistic equivalents in other languages, bib. [See See, no. 79.]
Style 15, 501–02: "will undoubtedly displace all other literary dictionaries and glossaries when it is completed."

134.   Gould, Christopher, and Karen Hodges. 1981. "The Art of Revision." *Style* 15, 171–211.
Bib. of 356 items, mainly from 1967 through 1978, annotated.

135.   Lintvelt, Jarep. 1981. *Essai de typologie narrative: Le point de vue: Théorie et analyse*. Paris: Corti. 315 pp.
Includes Dutch and Ger. work not readily found elsewhere.

136.   Miller, Joan, comp. 1981. *French Structuralism: A Multidisciplinary Bibliography: With a Checklist of Sources for Louis Althusser, Roland Barthes, Jacques Derrida, Michel Foucault, Lucien Goldmann, Jacques Lacan, and an Update of Works on Claude Lévi-Strauss.* New York: Garland. 553 pp.

The "more than 5650 items" cover "the period from 1968 to 1978 and thus extend J. V. Harari's earlier bibliographical survey, *Structuralists and Structuralisms.*" Part 1 "lists general and introductory works for those who wish to familiarize themselves with structuralism as a whole"; part 2 "contains primary and secondary source bibliographies" for 7 important structuralists; part 3 "furnishes bibliographies on structuralism as applied or related to thirteen different disciplines." "Many items are annotated," and cross-referencing is used. Name and term indexes.

Choice 19, 746: favorable; *ARBA* 13, 572; *RSR* 9, 168.

137.   Orr, Sarah. 1981. "A Guide to *Style*: Essays and Bibliographies, Volumes XI–XIV." *Style* 15, 102–10.

138.   Orr, Sarah. 1981. "A Guide to *Style*: Reviews, Volumes XI–XIV." *Style* 15, 111–84.

139.   Rygiel, Dennis. 1981. "Style in Twentieth-Century English Literary Nonfiction: An Annotated Bibliography of Criticism, 1960–1979." *Style* 15, 127–71.

Bib. of 293 items; author index.

140.   Weimar, Klaus. 1981. *Enzyklopädie der Literaturwissenschaft.* Bern: Francke. 231 pp.

Each of the 5 major subject divisions (the encyclopedia itself, literary theory, poetics, hermeneutics, and literary history) is divided into numbered topics.

Style 15, 501–02: "There are numerous problems with this book as an 'encyclopedia,'" e.g., "chapter headings are too vague and overlapping to really describe the contents."

141.   Welch, Jeffrey. 1981. *Literature and Film: An Annotated Bibliography, 1900–1977.* New York: Garland. 350 pp.

"Lists and annotates all important books and articles published in North America and Great Britain having to do with the special relationship between films and works of literature." 3 categories define this relationship: (1) adapting process, (2) similarities and differences between film and literary genres, influences, interviews with directors, etc., and (3) teaching. Dissertations, listed separately, are not annotated. App. lists all authors of works on which films have been based and all films mentioned in the bib. An index lists all authors, works, and films cited. [See DeMarco, no. 82.]

ARBA 13, 542; *CRL* 43, 71.

142.   Borkland, Elmer. 1982. *Contemporary Literary Critics*. 2nd ed. Detroit:
        Gale. 550 pp.
Discusses 124 modern British and Amer. critics and lists their works.
LJ 107, 2248: "its reference value would be increased if there were more
information about critical movements and approaches. . . . [O]ne must protest the continued exclusion of Continental critics and the remarkable scar-
city of women critics. Nevertheless, this is valuable."

142a.   Davies, Alistair. 1982. *An Annotated Critical Bibliography of Modern-
        ism*. Brighton: Harvester; Totowa: Barnes. 261 pp.
A general section of 69 pp. followed by sections on Yeats, Wyndham Lewis,
D. H. Lawrence, and T. S. Eliot. Subject and contributor indexes.

143.   Donow, Herbert, comp. 1982. *The Sonnet in England and America:
        A Bibliography of Criticism*. Westport: Greenwood. 477 pp.
Covers sonnets written from 1530 to the end of the 19th cent., arranged by
period and author; many items annotated. Contributor, poet, and subject
indexes (subject index contains terms — "imagery," etc.).

143a.   *Garland Bibliographies of Modern Critics and Critical Schools*. New
        York: Garland. 1982–.
Each vol. includes an introd. that surveys the critic's life or the central figures
of the critical school. Each vol. is annotated and contains listings for both
primary and secondary materials. R. S. Crane, Michel Foucault, Elder Olson,
Eliseo Vivas, et al.

144.   Greimas, A. J., and J. Courtés. 1982. *Semiotics and Language: An Ana-
        lytical Dictionary*. Trans. Larry Crist et al. Bloomington: Indiana UP.
        409 pp. (*Sémiotique: Dictionnaire raisonné de la théorie du langue*.
        Paris: Hachette, 1979.)
An attempt to review, evaluate, and synthesize "the various attempts that have
been made to establish" semiotics "as a coherent theory" by establishing "a
common ground" on which semiotics and linguistics "could be brought together, compared and evaluated." The results are arranged in alphabetical
order with cross-references that constitute "the semantic context of the term"
defined. Bib. 26 pp.

145.   Hancher, Michael, and Ralph Chapman. 1982 (typescript). "Speech Acts
        and Literature: An Annotated Bibliography." Minneapolis: English
        Dept., U of Minnesota. 56 pp.
Work in progress. "The following list reports essays in literary criticism that
make use of the speech-act theories developed by J. L. Austin, John R. Searle,
and H. P. Grice."

146. Jackson, Dennis, et al. 1982. "The Style of Political Discourse: Annotated Bibliography II." *Style* 16, 101–58.
A continuation of Seaman's bib.

146a. Rice, Thomas. 1982. *James Joyce: A Guide to Research*. New York: Garland. 412 pp.
Lists more than 1,400 books and essays, including all the book-length studies of Joyce.
Choice 20, 812; *LJ* 108, 197.

147. Soufas, C. Christopher, Jr. 1982. "On the Discrimination of Contemporary Criticisms: An Annotated Introductory Bibliography." *CLit* 9, 231–66.
"My bibliography traces the history of contemporary literary criticism, beginning with structuralism but focusing primarily upon the diverse tendencies of the post-structuralist development of the last ten years."

148. Crosby, Everett, et al., comps. 1983. *Medieval Studies: A Bibliographical Guide*. New York: Garland. 700 pp.
C. 8,000 annotated entries, topically arranged. Name and collection indexes.

148a. Francis, W. Nelson, and Henry Kučera. 1983. *Frequency Analysis of English Usage: Lexicon and Grammar*. Boston: Houghton. 561 pp.
A new ed. of the analytical source of all information pertaining to the Brown Standard Corpus of American English, including word frequency research on every term included in the corpus.

149. Freedman, Sanford, and Carole Taylor. 1983. *Roland Barthes: A Bibliographical Reader's Guide*. New York: Garland. 409 pp.
Divided by primary and secondary sources. Name and term indexes.

150. Horner, Winifred, ed. 1983. *The Present State of Scholarship in Historical and Contemporary Rhetoric*. Columbia: U of Missouri P. 240 pp.
Written for the Eng. literary scholar and rhetorician who lacks a reading knowledge of Gr. and Lat. Divided into 6 sections—classical, medieval, Renaissance, 18th cent., 19th cent., and 20th cent.—each written by a specialist in the period.

150a. Lazarus, Arnold and Wendell Smith. 1983. *A Glossary of Literature and Composition*. Urbana: NCTE. 326 pp.
Concentrates on 3 major branches of Eng. studies: literature and criticism, rhetorical theory, and composition. Nearly 800 terms illustrated by literary examples, cross-referenced, and accompanied by scholarly references. Author index.

151.   Urdang, Laurence, and Frank Abate. 1983. *Literary, Rhetorical, and Linguistics Terms Index*. Detroit: Gale. 305 pp.
   Bib. of 17,000 citations to 10,000 terms.

152.   Bennett, James R. 1983. "A Stylistics Checklist IV." *Style* 17, 429–53.
   On 113 topics; the 4 checklists contain a total of 738 topics.

153.   Crosland, Andrew. Forthcoming. *Concordances: A Bibliography*. Write or call the author at the U of South Carolina, Spartanburg.

2.0 General Theory and Concepts of Style (154–637)

A. Collections by Diverse Authors (sometimes combining theory and praxis) (154–313)

154.   Fokkema, D. W., et al., eds. n.d. *Comparative Poetics — Poétique Comparative — Vergleichende Poetik in Honour of Jan Kamerbeek, Jr.* Amsterdam: Rodopi. 312 pp.
   16 essays in Eng., Fr., and Ger. on such topics as interplay of semantics, syntax, and rhythm in a poem; intersubjectivity; foregrounding of graphic elements.
   Style 14, 196–98: essays not all comparative, several excellent but the whole confusingly arranged; *JLS* 7, 57–59: "I can find little justification for either of the first two words of its title," the papers "very mixed" in quality.

155.   Handy, William, ed. 1965. *A Symposium on Formalist Criticism*. Austin: Humanities Research Center, U of Texas. 92 pp.
   Essays by Ransom, Olson, Vivas, and Burke.

156.   Lemon, Lee T., and Marion J. Reis, eds. 1965. *Russian Formalist Criticism: Four Essays*. Lincoln: Bison–U of Nebraska P. 143 pp.
   Essays by Šklovskij, Tomaševskij, and Eixenbaum. Name and term index. [See Matejka and Pomorska, no. 179, for a much fuller collection, and Erlich, no. 212, for history and doctrine.]

157.   Gorrell, Robert, ed. 1967. *Rhetoric: Theories for Application*. Champaign: NCTE. 121 pp.
   14 essays on the paragraph, field theory, styles typology, rhetorical analysis of poetry, etc.
   QJS 54, 164: compared to Steinmann's *Rhetoric*, Gorrell's "may well offer the general reader more intellectual stimulation and leave him with a better sense of balance between 'old' and 'new'"; *EJ* 57, 748.

158.   LeSage, Laurent, ed. 1967. *The French New Criticism: An Introduction and a Sampler.* University Park: Pennsylvania State UP. 229 pp.
Discusses 18 critics from Bachelard and Barthes to Starobinski and Weber, with brief passages from their writings translated into Eng.
Choice 4, 842: "not claiming" definitiveness, "clear and straightforward"; *Sat Rev* 50, 71; *TLS* 31 Aug. 1967, 782.

159.   Demetz, Peter, et al. 1968. *The Disciplines of Criticism: Essays in Literary Theory, Interpretation, and History.* New Haven: Yale UP. 613 pp.
26 essays divided into 3 groups: literary theory, literary interpretation, and literary history.
Choice 6, 206: "the narrowness of the method is paralleled by a limitation to modern Western works," but "some of the articles [Levin's, Guillén's] are well worth studying."

160.   Foucault, Michel, et al. 1968. *Théorie d'ensemble* [Theory of the Whole]. Paris: Seuil. 415 pp.

161.   *Poetik und Hermeneutik: Arbeitsergebnisse einer Forschungsgruppe. III: Die nicht mehr schönon Künste* [Poetics and Hermeneutics: Study Results of a Research Team. III: The No Longer Fine Arts]. 1968. Munich: Fink. 735 pp.
20 papers on antiaesthetic elements in art and literature—the ugly, the grotesque, etc.
MLR 65, 689–90: "long and heavy."

162.   Bennett, James R., ed. "International Stylistics." 1969. *Style* 3.1. 100 pp.
Articles on Span.-speaking America and on Italy, Sweden and Finland, Great Britain, and the Soviet Union.

163.   Burke, Virginia, ed. 1969. *The Paragraph in Context.* Indianapolis: Bobbs. 64 pp.
9 essays. Bib. 1 p.

164.   Corbett, Edward P. J., ed. 1969. *Rhetorical Analyses of Literary Works.* New York: Oxford UP. 272 pp.
14 essays divided into 4 sections: "Argument," "Arrangement," "Audience," and "Style." Bib. 39 pp.
QJS 55, 437–39: This study of "*structural* rhetorical criticism" (analysis of the "rhetorical structures *within* the work") is "interesting, but incomplete" because it only teaches us to "name our tools" but not "how well the tools work," i.e., how a work "rhetorically affected receivers," or "*functional*" rhetorical criticism. *Style* 6, 311–13: a valuable reminder that "rhetoric lives."

165.   Doležel, Lubomír, and Richard W. Bailey, eds. 1969. *Statistics and Style.* New York: Elsevier. 245 pp.
17 articles in 6 categories: theory; word-level measures; sentence-level meas-ures; poetics; studies of individual styles; history. International, interdisciplinary. Bib. 3 pp. Name and term index.
Style 5, 184–92: "vitality and increasing sophistication of statistical stylistics"; *GL* 12, 42–52; *MLR* 66, 164–65; *Mu* 81, 276–82; *Lang* 46, 227–29; *SIL* 21, 129–32; *CHum* 4, 263–72.

166.   Gerbner, George, et al. 1969. *The Analysis of Communication Content: Developments in Scientific Theories and Computer Techniques.* New York: Wiley. 597 pp.
Includes "Studying 'Style' as Deviation from Encoding Norms," "Content Analysis and the Study of Poetry," and "Categories and Procedures for Content Analysis in the Humanities."
LJ 95, 78: "requires no knowledge of advanced mathematics, and for the most part is clearly written."

167.   Love, Glen, and Michael Payne, eds. 1969. *Contemporary Essays on Style: Rhetoric, Linguistics, and Criticism.* Glenview: Scott. 307 pp.
25 essays on prose style from 1951 to 1968 arranged into 3 parts: "Style and Rhetoric," "Style and Linguistics," and "Style and Criticism." 11 deal with theories of style and the study of style, 3 with diction primarily, 6 with syntax mainly, 3 with the paragraph, and 2 on whole works. [Introductory notes to each essay helpful.] Bib. App. 6 pp.
Style 6, 222–25: "generally of high quality"; *EIC* 20, 264–68: "too miscellaneous" and "virtually an All-American team," but essays laudably often illustrate theory; *LT* (1971), 287–92: "highly recommended," "ideal textbook," "important landmark in modern English stylistics" (rev. article).

167a.   Akhmanova, Olga, ed. 1970. *The Principles and Methods of Linguostylistics.* Moscow: MGU. 93 pp.
Akhmanova's lectures for undergraduates recorded by her students since 1963 with several articles written by 2 postgraduate students. The main idea is that language not only is a system of signs to convey information but also has a symbolic function, and this is the subject of linguostylistics.
Ling 152, 73–74: "many important" themes in the field "are touched upon."

168.   Freeman, Donald, ed. 1970. *Linguistics and Literary Style.* New York: Holt. 491 pp.
23 essays spanning 3 1/2 decades but mainly pub. during the 1960s, arranged under 4 headings: "Theory," "Method," "Prose," "Metrics." "[L]inguistics

gives literary criticism a theoretical underpinning as necessary to that under-taking as mathematics is to physics. A good critic is perforce a good linguist" (Freeman 3). Headnotes to each article give background and biographical in-formation. No index.

Style 9, 121–25: "useful, practical"; *GL* 13, 118–23; *JC* 20, 296; *CLing* 16, 177–83; *JES* 1, 268.

169.   Guiraud, Pierre, and Pierre Kuentz, eds. 1970. *La stylistique: Lectures* [Stylistics: Readings]. Paris: Klincksieck. 327 pp.
Diverse short excerpts from published criticism on style, ranging from Buffon to statistical methods. Ch. 1 on theoretical problems: stylistics between lin-guistics and literature, the notion of "poetic languages" genre, the unity of a text; ch. 2, language and style: expressiveness, choice, psychology of styles; ch. 3, immanence of style; ch. 4, techniques of analysis; ch. 5, practical ana-lyses. [Excellent introd. to the stylistics of the 1950s and 1960s.] Bib. 6 pp.; name and term indexes.

170.   Lane, Michael, ed. 1970. *Structuralism: A Reader.* London: Cape. 456 pp. (*Introduction to Structuralism.* New York: Basic, 1970.)
19 selections (not all on literature) with the ed.'s introd.: Saussure, Barthes, Jakobson, Lévi-Strauss, et al. Bib. 17 pp.

NS 79, 448–49: "has an extremely useful introduction by the editor," but the selections are "a very mixed bag"; *TLS* 23 Apr. 1970, 451; *Obs* 22 Mar 1970, 33; *SocR* 18, 283.

171.   Lyons, John, ed. 1970. *New Horizons in Linguistics.* Harmondsworth: Penguin. 367 pp.
Includes J. P. Thorne, "Generative Grammar and Stylistic Analysis." Bib. 29 pp.

172.   Macksey, Richard, and Eugenio Donato, eds. 1970. *The Languages of Criticism and the Sciences of Man: The Structuralist Controversy.* Bal-timore: Johns Hopkins UP. 367 pp.
Papers from an interdisciplinary symposium at Johns Hopkins in 1966 where different approaches were argued and Europeans such as Todorov and Der-rida were introduced to the U.S. Name index. [Paperback ed. of 1972, enti-tled *The Structuralist Controversy: The Languages of Criticism and the Sciences of Man,* contains a pref. on structuralism between 1966 and 1971 and a bib. updated to 1971.]

Style 8, 78–80: the essays provide "very little" help to literary criticism; *MLR* 70, 128–30.

173. Chatman, Seymour, ed. 1971. *Literary Style: A Symposium*. New York: Oxford UP. 427 pp.
21 papers given at the 1969 Symposium on Literary Style at Villa Serbelloni, Bellagio, which reflected "a growing sense of a coherent field," especially of style as a formal property of a text, but also of the manner of an individual or group, of expressiveness, and of register. The essays are grouped by "Theory of Style," "Stylistics and Related Disciplines," "Style Features," "Period Style," "Genre Style," and "Styles of Individual Authors and Texts." Name and title indexes.
Lingua 33, 397: "both stimulating and disappointing. . . . The specialist does not get the careful theoretical discussion he wants, nor does the non-specialist receive the explanations he needs"; *KLit* 2, 71: "immensely important . . . undoubtedly marks the main trends which will determine future research"; *Ling* 194, 65–89: "this collection should be a desk-book for every student of style"; *ECr* 12, 324: "excellent"; *FL* 11, 115–39 (rev. article); *QJS* 58, 242.

174. Hauff, Jürgen, et al. 1971. *Methodendiskussion: Arbeitsbuch zur Literaturwissenschaft* [Discussion of Methods: Workbook on Literary Criticism]. Frankfurt am Main: Athenäum. 2 vols., 183 and 235 pp.
4 main sections—positivism, formalism and structuralism, interpretation, and Marxism.
MLR 69, 474–75: "a corrective to complacency."

175. Heath, Stephen, et al., eds. 1971. *Signs of the Times: Introductory Readings in Textual Semiotics*. Cambridge: Granta. 89 pp.
The 6 essays offer a "certain introduction" to "the structuration of literary works and the elaboration of the notion of text."

176. Johannesen, Richard, ed. 1971. *Contemporary Theories of Rhetoric: Selected Readings*. New York: Harper. 403 pp.
Organized into 8 parts, the first and last dealing with multiple theories, parts 2–7 with the work of 1 rhetorician (Burke, Richards, Weaver, Perelman, Toulmin, and McLuhan).
RSQ 3, 6–7: "excellent."

177. Kristeva, Julia, et al., eds. 1971. *Essays in Semiotics: Essais de sémiotique*. The Hague: Mouton. 639 pp.
Articles by Chatman, "The Semantics of Style," Genette, "Langage poétique . . . ," Uspensky on semiotics and style, and Todorov on narrative.
AA 75, 1916–18.

178. Léon, Pierre, et al., eds. 1971. *Problèmes de l'analyse textuelle/ Problems of Textual Analysis*. Montreal: Didier. 199 pp.

3 of the 17 essays are in Eng.: "Some Uses of the Grammar in Poetic Analysis" by Levin, "The Stylistic Analysis of the Literary Image" by Nesselroth, and "Discontinuity and Communication in Literature" by McLuhan.

MLR 69, 829–30: "Its value lies in four" of the papers—"by Henri Mitterand, Michael Riffaterre, Marshall McLuhan, and Gérard Genette"; *Ling* 141, 67–72: "on the whole a remarkable exception" to the rule that papers read at congresses are "frequently uneven in quality" and "confusing if not depressing when read."

179.   Matejka, Ladislav, and Krystyna Pomorska, eds. 1971. *Readings in Russian Poetics: Formalist and Structuralist Views.* Cambridge: MIT P. 306 pp.
19 essays intended "to acquaint English readers with the methodological struggles in which the leading Russian theorists of literature engaged during the 1920s and early 1930s." Name and term index 10 pp.
PS 46, 187: "valuable," "a necessary book for students of linguistics and literary theory"; *LJ* 96, 2320; *Choice* 9, 1298.

180.   Strelka, Joseph, ed. 1971. *Patterns of Literary Style.* Yearbook of Comparative Criticism 3. University Park: Pennsylvania State UP. 276 pp.
13 essays by diverse authors on such topics as narrative, mathematical analysis, free indirect style, and period style. Name index.
JLS 2, 110–14: "the volume as a whole, in spite of some outstanding contributions, is rather disappointing"; *MLR* 68, 464.

181.   Wisbey, R. A., ed. 1971. *The Computer in Literary and Linguistic Research: Papers from a Cambridge Symposium.* London: Cambridge UP. 309 pp.
Papers divided into groups, including sections on "programming the computer for literary and linguistic research" and "stylistic analysis and poetry generation."
MLR 67, 858–60: "recommended without reservation"; *Ling* 141, 97–102: "provides a general survey as well as a specialist insight," "demonstrates convincingly that neglect of computer assistance is to the detriment of the literary scientist."

182.   Babb, Howard, ed. 1972. *Essays in Stylistic Analysis.* New York: Harcourt. 392 pp.
21 essays highly various in assumptions, methods, and texts and features analyzed, the earliest pub. 1733, the latest 1966. Headnotes to each essay give context and main idea. No index.
Style 9, 126–27: "several of the essays do not in fact do much with the language of the texts."

183.   Bloomfield, Morton, ed. 1972. *In Search of Literary Theory*. Ithaca: Cornell UP. 274 pp.
        6 metatheoretical studies about theoretical scope and constraints, all affirming the rationality of literary criticism, by Abrams, Hirsch, Bloomfield, Frye, Hartman, and de Man. Name index.
        Centrum 1, 77–81: "the enterprise at hand is welcome," the essay by Abrams "the most fully thought through."

184.   Blumensath, Heinz, ed. 1972. *Strukturalismus in der Literaturwissenschaft* [Structuralism in Literary Criticism]. Cologne: Kiepenheuer. 420 pp.

185.   Dijk, Teun van, ed. 1972. "Text Grammar and Narrative Structures." *Poetics* 3. 130 pp.
        5 essays.

186.   Ihwe, Jens, ed. 1972. *Literaturwissenschaft und Linguistik: Eine Auswahl. Texte zur Theorie der Literaturwissenschaft* [Literary Criticism and Linguistics: A Selection. Essays on the Theory of Literary Criticism]. Frankfurt am Main: Fischer Taschenbuch. 2 vols., 322 and 267 pp.
        A collection of 18 essays, a shorter and revised version of *Literaturwissenschaft und Linguistik: Ergebnisse und Perspektiven* (1971), plus 2 original contributions.
        Style 11, 76–79: "irritating" method of presentation, but the "ambitious book should serve as a stimulus to further study."

187.   Kachru, Braj, and Herbert Stahlke, eds. 1972. *Current Trends in Stylistics*. Edmonton and Champaign: Linguistic Research. 286 pp.
        19 papers on a variety of theoretical and practical topics divided into 5 sections: "Traditions in Stylistics," "Current Trends in Stylistics," "Linguistic Models & Stylistics," "Applied Stylistics," "Computers & Stylistics." Bib. references follow each article. No index.
        Style 9, 112–16: "more a guide to the unsolved problems of the field," which "is not at the moment outstanding for the logic and intelligence of its theoretical debate."

188.   Koch, Walter, ed. 1972. *Strukturelle Textanalyse. Analyse du récit. Discourse Analysis*. Hildesheim: Olms. 486 pp.
        Contributions chiefly in Eng., Fr., and Ger.

189.   Rousseau, G. S., ed. 1972. *Organic Form: The Life of an Idea*. London: Routledge. 108 pp.

Essays on organic form in Plato, in the life sciences, and as a metaphor, with an introd. and a 14-pp. bib.

MLR 71, 110–12: "a lively internal debate."

190.   Shibles, Warren, ed. 1972. *Essays on Metaphor.* Whitewater: Language. 180 pp.

Claims to be "the first collection of essays on metaphor." Includes articles in rhetoric, linguistics, and the humanities by Nietzsche, S. Pepper, J. M. Murry, et al. Philosophical orientation mainly.

RSQ 4, 3–5: "selection quite good," "a much needed book."

191.   Simon, John, ed. 1972. *Modern French Criticism: From Proust and Valéry to Structuralism.* Chicago: U of Chicago P. 405 pp.

Essays on Valéry, Proust and Gourmont, Du Bos, Thibaudet, Paulhan, Breton, Bataille, Bachelard, Sartre, Merleau-Ponty, Blanchot, the Geneva School, and Barthes. In addition to an annotated bib. following each article, there is a "general" bib.; name index.

LJ 97, 1719: "well-written, informative"; *JAAC* 31, 138; *Enc* 39, 80; *Choice* 9, 822.

192.   Aitken, A. J., R. W. Bailey, and N. Hamilton-Smith, eds. 1973. *The Computer and Literary Studies.* Edinburgh: Edinburgh UP. 369 pp.

Papers given at the second Symposium on the Uses of Computers in Literary Research in 1972, divided into 7 sections: "Lexicography," "Stylistics and Vocabulary Studies," "Word Association and Thematic Analysis," "Textual and Metrical Studies," "Problems of Input and Output," "Programming for Literary Research," and "A Literary Computing Center." [Sections 2–4 of most relevance to stylistics; unity of book through statistics more than through computer.] Bib. (following some of the essays); name and term index 21 pp.

Style 10, 291–95: "this volume fairly represents the state of computer-assisted literary research, showing both its strengths and weaknesses; *MLR* 69, 597–99: "a tribute to the varied and imaginative exploitation of the computer for literary purposes."

193.   Bann, Stephen, and John Bowlt, eds. 1973. *Russian Formalism.* Edinburgh: Edinburgh UP. 178 pp.

A collection of articles in translation from Šklovskij to Todorov.

MLR 69, 713–15; *TLS* 5 Oct 1973, 1164; *LJ* 99, 1036.

194.   *Between Language and Literature.* 1973. Papers by Members of the English Inst. Cracow: Jagellonian U. 156 pp.

The title indicates the range of these 11 essays (presented in 1971): some have nothing to do with imaginative literature, some deal with imaginative literature but are extralinguistic in method, but most offer technical linguistic ana-

lyses of the language of literature. Examples of the latter: the Polish translation of *Ulysses*, a new grammar of metaphor, antimetabole in Lyly and Sidney, verbal repetition in *Piers Plowman*. (All of the literary subjects are British
and American.) References follow each essay.
   Style 9, 219–21: a "useful contribution" to the worldwide effort to develop
a linguistics-based discipline of literary criticism.

195.   Bouazis, Charles, ed. 1973. *Essais de la théorie du texte* [Essays on the
       Theory of the Text]. Paris: Galilée. 222 pp.
   A diverse collection of essays on text grammars, speech acts, semiotics, metalanguage, and connotation.
   JLS 2, 114–16: "collection as a whole demonstrates no agreement about
methods, problems, or even—which is more serious—goals."

196.   Brower, Reuben, Helen Vendler, John Hollander, eds. 1973. *I. A.
       Richards: Essays in His Honor*. New York: Oxford UP. 368 pp.
   19 essays plus an interview and poems. Bib. of Richards's books, articles, and
revs.
   Centrum 2, 90–94.

197.   Chatman, Seymour, ed. 1973. *Approaches to Poetics*. New York: Colum-
       bia UP. 168 pp.
   6 essays presented at the 1972 English Inst.: Erlich on Roman Jakobson, David-
son and Kermode on Roland Barthes, Ohmann on John Austin's speech-act
theory, Fish on stylistics and reader response, and Todorov on literary theory.
No bib. or index.
   Style 10, 254–57: "excellent book"; *YR* 63, 439–44; *KLit* 3, 320–23; *CL*
29, 76–79; *PS* 48, 91; *BRD* 74, 202; *QJS* 60, 254.

198.   Eng, Jan van der, and Mojmír Grygar, eds. 1973. *Structure of Texts and
       Semiotics of Culture*. The Hague: Mouton. 371 pp.
   Czech, Polish, Russ., and Dutch contributions to the seventh International
Congress of Slavists in Warsaw. 4 of the 12 essays are in Eng.—e.g., "Literature as Information. Some Notes on Lotman's Book *Struktura xudozestven-
nogo teksta*." No bib. or index.

199.   Polletta, Gregory, ed. 1973. *Issues in Contemporary Literary Criticism*.
       Boston: Little. 833 pp.
   46 readings divided under 5 headings: "The Place and Performance of Criticism," "The Writer's Intention," "The Literary Performance," "The Reader's
Response," and "Literature's Relation to the World." Introds. to each section
sketch "the general questions posed by the topic" and describe "the specific
questions on which the individual selections turn as well as the particular views
each critic brings to the inquiry." [No bib. or index, but an outstanding eclectic
collection.]

200. Robey, David, ed. 1973. *Structuralism: An Introduction*. Oxford: Clarendon. 153 pp.
7 lectures, only 1 of which is specifically about literature (Todorov on the tales of Henry James).
JLS 5, 98–101: "a less satisfactory book than the collections by Lane and Ehrmann"; *AUMLA* 46, 356–58.

201. Bennett, James R., ed. 1974. "French Stylistics." *Style* 8.1. 154 pp.
5 essays, 7 reviews, indexes of *Le français moderne*, *Poétique*, and *Change*, and bibs. of the work of Genette and Todorov.

202. Cohen, Ralph, ed. 1974. *New Directions in Literary History*. Baltimore: Johns Hopkins UP. 263 pp.
13 essays from *NLH* "engaged in reconsidering the systematic study of literature" and the "theoretical basis for practical inquiries." They fall into 4 groups: the "continuity . . . of relations between readers," the "processes involved in reading," the "distinction between literary and non-literary works," and genre.
AUMLA 46, 311–13: "Much of what they write is dogmatic assertion, unexamined assumption, or emphasis on the trivial or self-evident"; *MLR* 71, 112: this "fair and representative selection" from *NLH* contributes to bringing "some order into a variety of theoretical problems."

203. Enkvist, Nils E., ed. 1974. *Reports on Text Linguistics: Four Papers on Text, Style and Syntax*. Publications of the Research Inst. of the Åbo Akad. Foundation 1. Åbo, Finland. 117 pp.
2 of the papers are strictly linguistic. The 2 on literature are: "Style and Types of Context" by Enkvist and "On the Problem of Sample Length in the Study of Major Word Order Patterns in Old English and Early Middle English" by Viljo Kohonen. Bib. follows each essay.

204. Kallmeyer, Werner, et al. 1974. *Lektürekolleg zur Textlinguistik* [Textlinguistics: A Colloquium]. Frankfurt am Main: Athenäum. 280 pp. (2nd ed. 1977).
Essays by the Faculty of Linguistics and Literature at the U of Bielefeld.

205. Mitchell, J. L., ed. 1974. *Computers in the Humanities*. Edinburgh: Edinburgh UP. 318 pp.
29 papers divided into several groups, including "Literary Stylistics."
MLR 71, 106–08: "the book points to an increasing sophistication of programs and techniques for measuring style."

206. O'Toole, L. M., ed. 1974. *Four Essays in Poetics*. Colchester: U of Essex Language Centre. 89 pp.

Essays on structure and style in Russ. literature—e.g., the short story, the dialogic text and the *texte pluriel*, the function of quotation in Dostoevskij.

207.   Projektgruppe Textlinguistik Konstanz. 1974. *Probleme und Perspektivan der neueren textgrammatischen Forschung I* [Problems and Perspectives of Modern Research in Textual Grammar I]. Hamburg: Buske.

208.   Sebeok, Thomas, ed. 1974. *Linguistics and Adjacent Arts and Sciences.* Vol. 12 of *Current Trends in Linguistics.* The Hague: Mouton. 4 books, 3,037 pp.
The 4 books of the vol. contain 13 parts and 71 papers. Book 3, "Linguistics and the Verbal Arts," contains essays on "Poetics and Linguistics," "Rhetoric and Stylistics," "Literary Genres," and "Metrics" and 4 essays on folklore. Sebeok's "Semiotics: A Survey of the State of the Art" may be found in the "Semiotics" section, book 2. Bib. 20 pp.; name, term, language indexes.
    Ling 207, 53–93: the vol. is "an invaluable document for the history of science"; *Choice* 13, 362: "essential."

209.   Barbotin, Edmond, ed. 1975. *Qu'est-ce qu'un texte? Eléments pour une herméneutique* [What Is a Text? Elements for a Hermeneutics]. Paris: Corti. 205 pp.
7 essays from different text-based disciplines, from Monique Parent's survey of stylistics to Barbotin's location of meaning in the author.
    MLR 72, 643–44: "in good measure succeeds in showing" that the "intellectual and moral price" of modern hermeneutics "is very high."

210.   Brütting, Richard, and Bernhard Zimmermann, eds. 1975. *Theorie-Literatur-Praxis: Arbeitsbuch zur Literatur-theorie seit 1970* [Theory-Literature-Practice: A Workbook of Literary Theory after 1970]. Frankfurt am Main: Athenaion. 254 pp.
Rpts., except for 2 new essays by the editors.

211.   Dijk, Teun van, and J. S. Petöfi, eds. 1975. "Theory of Metaphor." *Poetics* 4.2–3. 232 pp.
9 essays, 6 in Eng.

212.   Erlich, Victor, ed. 1975. *Twentieth-Century Russian Literary Criticism.* New Haven: Yale UP. 317 pp.
Interpretive essays of well-known Russ. authors chosen as representative of certain schools or types of criticism.
    MLR 72, 255–56: the self-imposed limitations prevent the vol. from being "illustrative of the range and depth of twentieth-century Russian thinking about literature," but it is "useful and welcome."

213. Fowler, Roger, ed. 1975. *Style and Structure in Literature: Essays in the New Stylistics.* Ithaca: Cornell UP. 262 pp.
7 essays by British and U.S. scholars given at a conference at East Anglia in 1972 aimed at expressing "the great diversification of research into linguistic aspects of literature in the past few years." The 7 essays fall into 2 groups: the first 3 — by contributors D. Freeman, Epstein, and Fowler — describe exponents of style; the other 4 — by Culler, O'Toole, Rutherford, and Chatman — analyze narrative structure. Name index.
Style 10, 197–202: "a valuable addition to the fast growing literature on linguistic stylistics," but its emphasis on *new* is not justified, and the field is defined too narrowly; B. H. Smith, *On the Margins of Discourse*: "a volume in which so much that is new is old, and so much of what is both new and old is dismaying" (201); *PTL* 2, 151–82 (rev. article); *Critm* 18, 394–97; *JAAC* 36, 107–09; *Lang&S* 11, 259; *AUMLA* 47, 116; *Centrum* 4, 171–81.

214. "Frontières de la rhétorique." 1975. *Littérature* 18. 126 pp.
8 essays on such subjects as ideology, philosophical dialogue, and repetition.

215. Graff, Piotr, and Sław Krzemień-Ojak, eds. 1975. *Roman Ingarden and Contemporary Polish Aesthetics: Essays.* Trans. Piotr Graff et al. Warsaw: PWN. 268 pp.
14 essays by diverse writers on such topics as concretization, aesthetic values, and indeterminacy.
JAAC 35, 234: "oscillates between platitudinous accounts and impressive analyses of Ingarden's theories about art," not a comprehensive view of Ingarden's work; a generally favorable rev.

216. Hatzfeld, Helmut, ed. 1975. *Romanistische Stilforschung* [Essays on Romance Stylistics]. Darmstadt: Wissenschaftliche. 411 pp.
Style 10, 194–95: "This is a collection of fourteen essays assembled by the undisputed authority on Romance stylistics. . . . The contributions range in time from the very beginning of the century to the threshold of the present decade" — from Vossler (1903) to Genette (1970); *BL* (1977), 3383; (1979), 2756.

217. "Rhétorique et herméneutique." 1975. *Poétique* 23. 127 pp.
8 articles, introd. by Tzvetan Todorov.

218. Ringbom, Håkan, ed. 1975. *Style and Text: Studies Presented to Nils Erik Enkvist.* Stockholm: Språkförlaget. 441 pp.
33 papers mainly on stylistics and text linguistics (discourse analysis) in 4 sections: "Theory of Style" (7 papers), "Style and Literary Criticism" (5), "Style and Linguistic Analysis" (11), and "Text Linguistics" (10). The studies are linked by the search for "a rational *Literaturwissenschaft* which seriously tries to build

up empirically testable theories of literary communication." Chronological bib. of Enkvist's published writings from 1951 to 1973.

Style 12, 47–51: wonders at the inclusion of some of the essays "since they depart rather far from the two central themes of the book," which "suffers from . . . diffuseness of point of view and inconsistency of quality" and from poor proofreading; but in general the book is "not unworthy of its recipient"; *SMIL* 4, 41–45; *Anglia* 38, 467; *ES* 179, 575; *N&Q* 21, 397.

218a.   Shukman, Ann, ed. 1975–. *Russian Poetics in Translation*. Oxford: RPT and Holdan.
A series in Eng. of classic studies by the Russ. formalists and recent outstanding works of semiotic theory and analysis from the Soviet Union. Vol. 1: *Generating the Literary Text* (1975), 77 pp. Vol. 2: *Poetry and Prose* (1976), 84 pp. Vol. 3: *General Semiotics* (1976), 81 pp. Vol. 4: *Formalist Theory* (1977), 108 pp. Vol. 5: *Formalism: History, Comparison, Genre* (1978), 93 pp. Vol. 6: *Dramatic Structure, Poetic and Cognitive Semantics* (1979), 96 pp. Vol. 7: *Metre, Rhythm, Stanza, Rhyme* (1980), 105 pp. Vol. 8: *Film Theory and General Semiotics* (1981), 107 pp. Vol. 9: *The Poetics of Cinema* (1982), 126 pp. Vol. 10: *Baxtin School Papers* (1983), 156 pp.
MLR 75, 152 (vols. 4 and 5).

219.   Winterowd, Ross, ed. 1975. *Contemporary Rhetoric: A Conceptual Background with Readings*. New York: Harcourt. 380 pp.
In his introd. the ed. defines rhetoric as the domain of invention, arrangement, and style, and he divides his 23 selections accordingly, with introductory comments to each.
QJS 62, 321–23: the book "serves less well the values" of those in speech communication than those in Eng.; *RSQ* 5, 13–16; *Choice* 18, 627.

220.   Akhmanova, Olga, ed. 1976. *Linguostylistics: Theory and Method*. The Hague: Mouton. 125 pp. (Moscow: Moscow State U, 1972.)
Essays pub. by members of the Eng. dept. of Moscow State U as a manual for philologists and experienced teachers who join the dept. for brief periods of advanced study. The book is intended to "give an idea of recent research." Part 1, "Style as 'Language'"; part 2, "Style as 'Speech'"; part 3, "'Style' in Terms of Major Syntax"; part 4, "The Linguostylistics of Cross-Cultural Communication." Apps. on "Norm and Deviation" and "Variation and Acceptability." Bib. 2 pp.
Style 9, 222–24: "not worth very much"; *PP* 18, 111–12: "may prove useful as a guide to recent Soviet work"; *JLS* 8, 59–61.

221.   Beck, Mary A., et al., eds. 1976. *The Analysis of Hispanic Texts: Current Trends in Methodology*. Jamaica: Bilingual, York C. 355 pp.

Includes essays on such topics as the syntactic patterning in a poem, a stylistic analysis of bilingual texts, and a model of narrative analysis. The 22 essays (9 in Eng.) divide into archetypal, formalist, linguistic, Marxist, psychoanalytic, rhetorical, sociological, and structuralist sections.

222.   Bennett, James R., ed. 1976. "Recent Approaches to Style Study." *Style* 10.3. 172 pp.
5 articles, 14 reviews, and a stylistics checklist-glossary.

223.   Brady, Patrick, ed. 1976. *Phenomenology, Structuralism, Semiology.* Lewisburg: Bucknell UP. 250 pp.
The ed. provides a "review-essay" of basic concepts and major trends and divides the 13 essays into 2 parts, on phenomenology and on structuralism and semiology. Brady perceives the collection as "an appropriate moment at which to review the achievements of phenomenology and structuralism and their role in preparing the emergence of the new science, which is destined to inherit many of the aspirations of the parent movements." The phenomenology section includes 3 essays of practical literary criticism and 1 on the movement from empiricism to structuralism. The structuralism-semiology section includes essays on myth (3), French fiction theories, Todorov, semiology and literary theory, and Lévi-Strauss. No bib. or index.
Style 15, 61–64: "a very useful tool for advanced courses in semiology, and for interdisciplinary courses which deal with . . . structural epistemology"; *MLR* 69, 830–31: equally favorable rev.

224.   Butler, C. S., and R. R. K. Hartmann, eds. 1976. *A Reader on Language Variety.* Exeter: U of Exeter. 331 pp.
Includes W. Nash's paper on "the middle ground of stylistics."
JLS 6, 115–16: a favorable rev.

225.   Dijk, Teun van, ed. 1976. *Pragmatics of Language and Literature.* North-Holland Studies in Theoretical Poetics 2. Amsterdam: North-Holland; New York: Elsevier. 236 pp.
A collection of essays that provide a sample of what some advocates of "pragmatics" study. The ed. says in his pref. that many properties of sentences and discourses, and verbal communication in general, "cannot be accounted for in terms of grammatical theories of the usual kind. What is needed is a pragmatic component in which rules, conditions and constraints can be formulated based on systematic properties of (speech) acts and communicative contexts." The subjects of the essays range from macrostructures to literary discourse, speech acts, and fictivity.
Style 15, 90–94: "Pragmatics is by definition concerned with the use of language," but this collection is abstract, theoretical, logical, formal, with "no place for those who have studied the use of language in the field"; also,

the book needs "a subject index and a more thorough editorial summary giving the gist of the discussion, one subject at a time"; *JAAC* 37, 96.

226.   Enkvist, Nils E., and Viljo Kohonen, eds. 1976. *Reports on Text Linguistics: Approaches to Word Order.* Publications of the Research Inst. of the Åbo Akad. Foundation 8. Åbo, Finland. 257 pp.
14 essays, mainly theoretical and abstract, but several use literary examples, and Kohonen's essay deals with a work by Ælfric. Bib. follows each essay.

227.   Foulkes, A. P., ed. 1976. *The Uses of Criticism.* Bern: Lang. 287 pp.
A mixture of linguistic and general literary essays — 3 essays on medieval topics, the others either theoretical or pedagogical-practical.
JLS 6, 113–15: "the theoretical essays make a contribution of major importance. . . . The central direction of the book is clearly to emphasize the connexion between literature and the 'reality' outside it," which is "the most fundamental issue which confronts literary studies at present"; *MLR* 73, 585.

228.   Kindt, Walther, and Siegfried Schmidt, eds. 1976. *Interpretationanalysen: Argumentationsstrukturen in literaturwissenschaftlichen Interpretationen* [Methods of Interpretation: Structures of Argumentation in Literary Interpretation]. Munich: Fink. 194 pp.

229.   Matejka, Ladislav, and Irwin Titunik, eds. 1976. *Semiotics of Art: Prague School Contributions.* Cambridge: MIT P. 298 pp.
21 essays by Mukařovský, Bogatyrev, Brušák, Honzl, Veltruský, Jakobson, et al., concluded by an essay by the ed. on "Prague School Semiotics." Name and term index.
JAAC 35, 363: "useful anthology," "impressive"; *DrR* 20, 126; *PS* 51, 211; *CL* 30, 274; *Choice* 13, 1308.

230.   Newton-De Molina, David, ed. 1976. *On Literary Intention.* Edinburgh: U of Edinburgh P. 273 pp.
15 essays sift the issue of the intentional fallacy.
JAAC 36, 499–500: "unbalanced" and some poor essays, but "still contains much that is useful."

231.   Rump, Gerhard, ed. 1976. *Sprachnetze: Studien zur literarischen Sprachverwendung* [Linguistic Webs: Studies of Literary Use of Language]. Hildesheim: Olms. 235 pp.
Contains 4 essays dealing with language and literary use of language in the theater of Rainer Fassbinder, Agatha Christie's detective novels, André Breton and surrealism, and *Finnegans Wake.*

232.   Simpson, Lewis, ed. 1976. *The Possibilities of Order: Cleanth Brooks and His Work*. Baton Rouge: Louisiana State UP. 254 pp.
4 critical essays, a long "conversation" between Brooks and R. P. Warren, and 2 reminiscences. No bib.
   MLR 75, 150–52: "the four interpretative essays . . . are among the best so far available."

233.   Thoma, Werner, ed. 1976. "Stilistik." *LiLi* 6.22. 143 pp.
7 essays on meter, connotation, context, idiosyncrasy, etc.
   BL (1979), 2762.

234.   Bennett, James R., ed. 1977. "The Historical Study of Style." *Style* 11.3. 119 pp.
6 essays, 12 revs., bib.

235.   Lucid, Daniel, ed. and trans. 1977. *Soviet Semiotics: An Anthology*. Baltimore: Johns Hopkins UP. 259 pp.
In his introd. Lucid treats semiotics, "the science of signs," as a "structuralist discipline" [not defined] and linguistics, "the science of language," as a part of semiotics, conceptualizing this hierarchy for the study of literature: communications, cybernetics, structuralism, semiotics, linguistics, poetics. [Excellent introd. to an important collection.] The 24 essays, dating from 1962 to 1974, are grouped into 6 parts: "General Concepts," "Modeling Systems," "Communication Studies," "Text Analysis," "Art and Literature," and "Typology of Culture." Bib. 7 pp.; no index.
   Style 15, 52–55: "a good source of information on the variety of paths embarked upon by Russian semiotics in the sixties and seventies" and "shows the way in which wider and wider fields of investigation opened up to Russian semiotic theory." *Critm* 20, 421–24; *SR* 87, 628–38; *SEEJ* 22, 545–46; *SlavR* 39, 533–34; *MLN* 95, 1063–64; *SEER* 58, 121–22.

236.   Péter, M., ed. 1977. *The Structure and Semantics of the Literary Text: Struktura i semantika literaturnoso teksta*. Budapest: Akad. Kiadó. 144 pp.
Mainly 13 lectures read at the 1974 Conference at Tihany of the Subcommittee for Slavonic Poetics and Stylistics of the International Committee of Slavists. 2 papers in Eng.
   BL (1979), 2763.

237.   Plett, Heinrich von, ed. 1977. *Rhetorik: Kritische Positionen zum Stand der Forschung* [Rhetoric: Critical Opinions on the State of the Research]. Munich: Fink. 312 pp.
BL (1979), 2754.

238.   Ponsio, Augusto, ed. 1977. *Michail Bachtin: Semiotica, theoria della letteratura e marxismo* [Mixail Baxtin: Semiotics, Theory of Literature, and Marxism]. Bari: Dedalo. 265 pp.
BL (1978), 2503.

239.   Routh, Jane, and Janet Wolff, eds. 1977. *The Sociology of Literature: Theoretical Approaches.* Keele: U of Keele. 180 pp.
12 essays and the eds.' introd.: a general essay on "The Sociology of Literary Response," 1 on "The Hermeneutic Approach," 1 on "A Theory of Literature and Society," 3 essays on structuralism (includes 1 on Barthes), 5 on Marxist criticism, and 1 on Sartre. Bib. (follows each essay).
SRNB 6, 151.

240.   Schiff, Hilda, ed. 1977. *Contemporary Approaches to English Studies.* London: Heinemann Educational; New York: Barnes. 105 pp.
6 essays on such topics as literature in society, structuralism and literature, and Marxist literary criticism. The ed.'s introd. offers an explanation of the purposes of methodological analysis and proposes "questions we need to ask" in Eng. studies. Brief "further reading" follows each essay.

240a.   Andersson, Erik, ed. 1978. *Working Papers on Computer Processing of Syntactic Data.* Publications of the Research Inst. of the Åbo Akad. Foundation 37. Åbo, Finland. 108 pp.
1 ch., on topicalization, employs novels by Wyndham Lewis and Angus Wilson; another, on Swedish materials, uses a fairy tale and a young people's novel; the third essay is in Swedish.

241.   Bailey, R. W., L. Matejka, and P. Steiner, eds. 1978. *The Sign: Semiotics around the World.* Ann Arbor: Michigan Slavic Publications. 363 pp.

20 studies of the history and theory of semiotics and of individuals and national "schools" of semiotics—Todorov on Augustine, Bruss on Peirce and Jakobson, Steiner on American semiotics, etc. Bib. (following each essay).
JAAC 38, 337; *MLJ* 64, 165.

242.   Berrendonner, A., ed. 1978. *Stratégies discursives* [Discursive Strategies]. Actes du Colloque du Centre de recherches linguistiques et sémiologiques de Lyon, 1977 [Proc. of the Colloquium of the Center for Linguistic and Semiological Research at Lyon, 1977]. Lyon: PU de Lyon. 287 pp.

243.   Burks, Don, ed. 1978. *Rhetoric, Philosophy, and Literature: An Exploration.* West Lafayette: Purdue UP. 115 pp.

6 essays originally presented as lectures in 1974 by Wayne Booth, Kenneth Burke, Maurice Natanson, Lloyd Bitzer, Henry Johnstone, Jr., and Donald Bryant. The topics range from "The Pleasures and Pitfalls of Irony" by Booth to "Literature and Politics" by Bryant. [Selected for the James A. Winans–Herbert A. Wichelns Award for Distinguished Scholarship in Rhetoric, 1979.]

    Style 13, 377–78: "splendid"; *JAAC* 37, 507–08; *QJS* 65, 449–50; *P&R* 13, 198–206; *RM* 34, 783–84; *SSCJ* 45, 206–09.

244.   Dressler, Wolfgang, ed. 1978. *Current Trends in Textlinguistics.* Berlin: de Gruyter. 308 pp.
17 essays explore "recent developments within various trends," including "Stylistics and Text Linguistics" by N. E. Enkvist. Bib. (following each essay); name and term index.

    JLS 9, 110–13: "gives the information on trends in text-linguistics promised by the editor."

245.   Eaton, Trevor, ed. 1978. *Essays in Literary Semantics.* Heidelberg: Groos. 120 pp.
Previously pub. essays from *JLS.*

    MLR 75, 825–26: "if literary study is to retain intellectual respect rather than shelter in esotericism, the way forward could well be through the creative rigour that the best of these essays represent."

246.   Folejevskij, Zbigniev, et al., eds. 1978. *Canadian Contributions to the VIII International Congress of Slavists (Zagreb-Ljubljana, 1978): Tradition and Innovation in Slavic Literatures, Linguistics, and Stylistics.* Ottawa: Canadian Assn. of Slavists. 194 pp.
Part 3, "Linguistics and Stylistics," has 2 essays on stylistics. A similar collection of Amer. contributions is mainly composed of miscellaneous traditional literary essays.

247.   Hernadi, Paul, ed. 1978. *What Is Literature?* Bloomington: Indiana UP. 257 pp.
18 essays that emphasize pedagogy over aesthetics, theory, and form. Part 1, "Definitions: Theory & History"; 2, "Canon-Formation"; 3, "Acts, Effects, Artifacts." Name index. [See his related collection, *What Is Criticism?*, no. 287.]

    MLR 75, 148–49: "general usefulness."

248.   *L'Ironie.* 1978. Lyon: PUF. 115 pp.
    Style 14, 177–78: 5 essays "dealing with definitional and procedural aspects of the concept of irony"; "some narrower aspects of the . . . notion of irony" than presented by Booth and others.

249.   "Ironie." 1978. *Poétique* 36. 123 pp.
7 essays and 1 historical document.

250.   Laurenson, Diana, ed. 1978. *The Sociology of Literature: Applied Studies*. Keele: U of Keele. 284 pp.
13 essays and the ed.'s introd. on current research. Examples: "Structure and Ideology in the Novels of Doris Lessing," "Styles of Marxism; Styles of Criticism. *Wuthering Heights*: A Case Study."
Choice 16, 1576: follows companion vol., *The Sociology of Literature: Theoretical Approaches*, "essential for graduate libraries"; *SRNB* 6, 151.

251.   Plottel, Jeanine, and Hanna Charney, eds. 1978. "Intertextuality: New Perspectives in Criticism." *New York Literature Forum* 2. 308 pp.
23 mainly brief papers, only some of which focus on intertextuality, while others compare texts (mainly Fr.) in familiar fashion. Bib. 5 pp.; name and term index (for vols. 1 and 2).
Style 14, 193–95: offers no "sustained and careful" exploration of the key questions regarding intertextuality.

252.   Bloom, Harold, et al. 1979. *Deconstruction and Criticism*. New York: Seabury. 256 pp.
Essays on individual literary works by H. Bloom, de Man, Derrida, Hartman, and J. H. Miller. [A witty pref. by Hartman distinguishes vaguely between the "boa-deconstructors" Derrida, de Man, and Miller and the "barely" deconstructors Bloom and Hartman.] No index.
MLR 78, 386–88: several of the essays are "intricate on the surface" but "vacancy itself below"; *CE* 42, 25–34; *NUQ* 34, 505–12.

253.   Brown, Robert, Jr., and Martin Steinmann, eds. 1979. *Rhetoric 78: Proceedings of Theory of Rhetoric: An Interdisciplinary Conference*. Minneapolis: U of Minnesota. 419 pp.
32 highly diverse papers ranging from the nature of the paragraph to invention and speech acts, to science and rhetoric from Bacon to Hobbes, to paradox and reflexive form. Bib. (following each paper).
QJS 67, 344: "insightful" and in general "a worthwhile addition to the literature" but "uneven in quality."

254.   Burghardt, Wolfgang, and Klaus Hölker, ed. 1979. *Text Processing: Papers in Text Analysis and Text Description*. Berlin: de Gruyter. 465 pp.
15 essays written for a conference on "The Role of Grammar in Automatic and Non-Automatic Text Processing" held in 1974. 7 of the papers are in Eng., on discourse analysis and psycholinguistics. Bib. (references follow each essay).

JLS 10, 52–54: several reservations about the book—e.g., "the reader has first to cope with 15 almost completely unrelated metalingual systems."

255. Chatman, Seymour, et al., eds. 1979. *A Semiotic Landscape: Proceedings of the First Congress of the International Association for Semiotic Studies, Milan, June 1974.* The Hague: Mouton. 1,238 pp.
A highly diverse collection. Part 6, "Literature," contains 32 essays on such subjects as allusion as a linking device, structuralism, euphony, and epiphany and code in Joyce, 13 in Eng. Bib. (all titles quoted by the authors in their papers); name index.
Style 17, 56–59: "an exciting point of departure," even though semiotics is not defined and the goal of discussing "a unified objective" is not realized.

256. Dijk, Teun van, ed. 1979. "The Future of Structural Poetics." *Poetics* 8.6. 113 pp.

257. Giersing, Morten, and Ralf Pittelkow, eds. 1979. *Litteraturkritik: Aspekter af det 20. århundredes Litteraturkritik* [Literary Criticism: Aspects of Literary Criticism in the Twentieth Century]. Copenhagen: Borgen. 380 pp.
Edda 172, 361.

258. Harari, Josué, ed. 1979. *Textual Strategies: Perspectives in Post-Structuralist Criticism.* Ithaca: Cornell UP. 475 pp.
15 essays and an introd. by the ed. Bib. 22 pp.; name and term indexes.
JLS 11, 36: "excellently edited," "important essays"; *Diacritics* 12.1, 2–24; *PoT* 2, 213–55.

259. Heindrichs, Wilfried, and Gerhard Rump, eds. 1979. *Dialoge: Beiträge zur Interaktions und Diskursanalyse* [Dialogues: Contributions to the Analysis of Interaction and Discourse]. Hildesheim: Gurstenberg. 284 pp.

260. Jazayery, Mohammad Ali, et al., eds. 1979. *Linguistic and Literary Studies in Honor of Archibald A. Hill.* Linguistics and Literature/Sociolinguistics and Applied Linguistics 4. The Hague: Mouton. 392 pp.
The fourth and final installment of a multivolume festschrift (the first 3 devoted to general and theoretical linguistics). The first half of the book contains 18 essays on linguistics and literature written before 1972, most of them brief descriptive studies of a particular work or author. The second half of the book covers sociolinguistics and applied linguistics.
Style 14, 192: "suffers from the usual defects of *Festschriften*"; *SCr* 13, 502–08; *Lang* 54, 755.

261.   Koch, Walter, ed. 1979. *Semiotische Versuche zu literarischen Struktu-*
        ren [Semiotic Studies of Literary Structures]. Hildesheim: Olms. 440 pp.

262.   Lang, Berel, ed. 1979. *The Concept of Style.* Philadelphia: U of Penn-
        sylvania P. 246 pp.
        10 essays originally presented as lectures in 1977. The unifying intention is
        to encourage the study of style across the arts—literary criticism, art history,
        musicology—but most of the essays deal with verbal style. Bib. 6 pp.
        Style 15, 34–35: "plenty of stimulating ideas," "achieves its wholeness be-
        cause the persons . . . shared certain assumptions."

263.   McQuade, Donald, ed. 1979. *Linguistics, Stylistics, and the Teaching*
        of Composition. N.p. 220 pp.
        A "broad sampling" of the "recent work of composition theorists who use
        linguistics and stylistics." 14 essays and 5 revs.
        Style 15, 94–98: the writers are "more in agreement about composition"
        than about stylistics, but the views of style either as product or as process by
        paralleling composition studies "lend support to books" like this one.

264.   Nyírö, Lajos, ed. 1979. *Literature and Its Interpretation.* Trans. S. Si-
        mon. The Hague: Mouton. 302 pp.
        The ed. has an essay on "The Russian Formalist School."

265a.   Odmark, John, ed. 1979. *Language, Literature & Meaning I: Problems*
        of Literary Theory. LLSEE 1. Amsterdam: Benjamins. 467 pp.
        The 13 essays in this anthology "provide the reader with an overview of cur-
        rent Czech, Polish and Hungarian research" and "new perspectives" on "Ro-
        man Ingarden, Georg Lukács & Jan Mukařovský." All but 2 of the essays are
        in Eng.
        Style 17, 59–61: "terrible" editing and some arguments lost in abstractions
        and "impenetrable conceptualizing," but there are "several exceptions," and
        the book is significant because of the way it juxtaposes "(Prague) structural-
        ism and the phenomenology of Roman Ingarden"; *Choice* 17, 667: the es-
        says "convincingly demonstrate the vigor and independence of literary theory
        in East Europe."

265b.   Odmark, John, ed. 1980. *Language, Literature & Meaning II: Current*
        Trends in Literary Research. LLSEE 2. Amsterdam: Benjamins. 569 pp.
        12 essays and 2 bibs. have the same purpose as *Language, Literature & Mean-*
        ing I. The 2 bibs.—1 on Czech and Slovakian criticism, the other on Polish—
        and 1 essay are in Ger.

266.   Ortony, Andrew, ed. 1979. *Metaphor and Thought.* Cambridge: Cam-
        bridge UP. 501 pp.

In "Metaphor: A Multidimensional Problem," Ortony gives primacy to the modern "constructivist" view of metaphor as a way of thinking in and of itself, the world constructed from human knowledge and language. Essays divided into 6 groups: "Metaphor and Linguistic Theory," "Metaphor and Pragmatics," "Metaphor and Psychology," "Metaphor and Society," "Metaphor and Science," "Metaphor and Education." Bib. 13 pp.; name index.

Style, 17, 77–79; *Language* 56, 916–17; *Mind* 90, 448–52; *MLR* 76, 426–28: *SR* 89, 95–110; *JLS* 9, 113–15.

267.   Östman, Jan-Ola, ed. 1979. *Reports on Text Linguistics: Semantics and Cohesion*. Publications of the Research Inst. of the Åbo Akad. Foundation 41. Åbo, Finland. 192 pp.

The last in a series of papers produced by the Text Linguistics Research Group at Åbo Akad. during 1974–77 under the leadership of Nils Enkvist. The papers in section 1, on "Meaning and Semantics," stress the "many-foldedness of semantic theory." The articles on textual cohesion are more closely connected.

268.   Petit, Jean-Pierre, ed. 1979. *Discourse and Style, I.* Lyon: L'Hermès. 100 pp.

12 "working papers" sponsored by the English Dept. of the Université Jean-Moulin, Lyon III.

269.   Sacks, Sheldon, ed. 1979. *On Metaphor.* Chicago: U of Chicago P. 196 pp. (Most of this vol. appeared previously in *CritI* 5.)

Interdisciplinary essays on metaphor and its relation to cognition and perception, metaphor occupying "a central position in the understanding of understanding itself." Name and term index.

Style 17, 77: This and other recent books on metaphor reflect the impact of quantum mechanics, Kuhn's *The Structure of Scientific Revolutions*, and other sources that stress the significance of metaphor in the construal of reality.

270.   *Sémantique de la poésie* [Semantics of Poetry]. 1979. Paris: Seuil. 177 pp.

This little book contains 5 previously pub. essays or chs. by Todorov, Empson, J. Cohen, Hartman, and Rigolot on rhetorical, semantic, and linguistic approaches to signification in poetry.

271.   Sturrock, John, ed. 1979. *Structuralism and Since: From Lévi-Strauss to Derrida.* New York: Oxford UP. 190 pp.

Brief discussions of 5 critics representing a broad spectrum of disciplines—Barthes, Foucault, Lacan, Lévi-Strauss, and Derrida. Each essay gives the major works, briefly explains the major ideas, and assesses the ideas. The ed.'s introd. attempts to establish some common traits—e.g., the genealogy of the critics' ideas (e.g., Saussure) and their antirationalism. Name and term index. [Cf. Belsey, no. 561, and Kurzweill, no. 571.]

Style 17, 49–52: title misleading, for the book emphasizes *Since*, most of these critics being poststructuralists, i.e., hostile to the stability of discourse; *MLR* 76, 714; *NYQ* 34, 505–12.

272.   "Théories du texte." 1979. *Poétique* 38. 256 pp.
5 articles, 3 on Arabic and Indian theory.

273.   Ching, Marvin K. L., Michael Haley, and Ronald Lunsford, eds. 1980.
Linguistic Perspectives on Literature. London: Routledge. 332 pp.
Essays composed since 1969 selected on the basis of the eds.' faith that linguistic study of literature will produce "a revolutionary . . . insight into the nature of literature, language, and man himself." Part 1: a 35-p. introd. summarizing recent trends in linguistics and outlining the tasks of the linguistic study of literature. Part 2: 9 papers on figurative language, with opposing points of view. Part 3: 9 papers, arranged according to their concept of style, explicating literary texts. Name and term index. [An important book for the linguistic study of literature, though little is said about phonology or narrative.]
Style 17, 46–49: "Although the book does not fulfill its promise, there are some excellent papers that demonstrate what linguistic analysis can achieve. They range enormously in difficulty, however, and hardly make a coherent collection." *AUMLA* 58, 219–20: "contains a wealth" of material, "excellent example" of "research in progress," especially the 9 essays on metaphor; *MLR* 76, 906–09; *EIC* 31, 169–76; *JAAC* 39, 334.

274.   *Issues in Stylistics.* 1980. Hyderabad: Central Inst. of English and Foreign Languages. 243 pp.
17 papers originally presented at the Seminar on Stylistics at Hyderabad in 1974. "Stylistics" is conceived by all participants as the symbiosis of linguistics and criticism in search of literary interpretation and evaluation.
Style 15, 483–85: "the importance of this collection" is that it shows "the international enterprise to make literary criticism more theoretically coherent and practically precise."

275.   Mitchell, W. J. T., ed. 1980. *The Language of Images.* Chicago: U of Chicago P. 307 pp.
Studies of the "symbiotic relationship between verbal and pictorial modes in modern art and literature." Several literary essays: Quarles's *Emblemes,* spatial form in literature, etc. Name and term index.
JAE 289, 115.

276.   Petit, Jean-Pierre, ed. 1980. *Discourse and Style, II.* Lyon: L'Hermès.
110 pp.
"Covers the same areas as its predecessor (discourse analysis, linguistic and literary stylistics), as well as a few others: general and historical linguistics (from a textual angle), and lexicography."

277. Prideaux, Gary, et al., eds. 1980. *Experimental Linguistics: Integration of Theories and Applications.* Ghent: Story-Scientia. 321 pp.
Contains, e.g., Mary Marckworth and William Baker's "A Discriminant Function Analysis of Co-Variation of a Number of Syntactic Devices in Five Prose Genres."

278. "Roman Jakobson—Language and Literature." 1980. *PoT* 2.1a. 236 pp.
11 essays by or about Jakobson, on such topics as "the poetic function" and "the poetry of grammar & grammar of poetry."

279. Scott, Robert, and Bernard Brock, eds. 1980. *Methods of Rhetorical Criticism: A Twentieth-Century Perspective.* 2nd ed., rev. Detroit: Wayne State UP. 503 pp.
In their introd. the eds. employ Kuhn's *The Structure of Scientific Revolutions* to explain how traditional critical perspectives have been challenged by language-action and other new approaches. Sections on "Traditional," "Experiential," and "New Rhetorics" perspectives and on "meta-critical" approaches. Bib. 20 pp.; name and term index.

280. White, Eugene, ed. 1980. *Rhetoric in Transition: Studies in the Nature and Uses of Rhetoric.* University Park: Pennsylvania State UP. 181 pp.
10 essays on rhetoric in an effort "to come to grips with the swift changes" in our understanding of it in recent years. Name and term index.
JLS 11, 36: Valesio's *Novantiqua* is "much more ambitious and of greater interest to literary theorists."

281. Bloomfield, Morton, ed. 1981. *Allegory, Myth, and Symbol.* Cambridge: Harvard UP. 388 pp.
19 essays on "terms used to describe the polysemous meaning" of literature. Most of the articles concentrate on allegory, on particular texts or authors, and on English literature.

282. Brackert, Helmut, and Jörn Stückrath, eds. 1981. *Literaturwissenschaft: Grundkurs 1* [Literary Criticism: Introduction 1]. Reinbeck bei Hamburg: Rowohlt. 434 pp.
Essay on linguistics and text analysis, etc.

283. Brackert, Helmut, and Jörn Stückrath, eds. 1981. *Literaturwissenschaft: Grundkurs 2* [Literary Criticism: Introduction 2]. Reinbeck bei Hamburg: Rowohlt. 481 pp.
Includes an essay by Hans Gunther on Russ. and Prague formalisms, Marxist criticism, and structuralist criticism, etc.

284.   DeGeorge, Richard, ed. 1981. *Semiotic Themes*. Lawrence: U of Kansas
        P. 277 pp.
12 essays as a "contribution" to the development of "a new and somewhat
unproven theory and discipline." Includes essays on Saussure, Peirce, the semiotics of poetry, Baxtin, Derrida, and irony.

285.   Dorfmüller-Karpusa, Käthi, and János Petöfi, eds. 1981. *Text, Kontext,
        Interpretation: Einige Aspekte der texttheoretischen Forschung* [Text,
        Context, Interpretation: Aspects of Research in Text Theory]. Hamburg:
        Buske. 354 pp.
Includes 3 contributions in Eng.: an essay on text grammar and 2 bibs. on
discourse studies.

286.   Freeman, Donald C., ed. 1981. *Essays in Modern Stylistics*. London:
        Methuen. 416 pp.
Stylistics, the application of linguistics to the study of literature, is represented
here by previously pub. essays. No attempt is made to encompass the diversity of the field; most of the essays center on "modern transformational-
generative grammar and its ramifications." 16 chs. are grouped into 4 parts:
general theory and approaches to poetics, metrics, and prose style. Bib. 3 1/2
pp.; no index. [The subject needs more introductory and connecting material; for advanced students only.]
    MLR 78, 643: "I respect the concentrated analytic focus of the descriptive
chapters" (the first 3 sections), but "I would prefer more diversity"; *BBN* May
1982, 316; *TES* 11 Dec. 1981, 25.

287.   Hernadi, Paul, ed. 1981. *What Is Criticism?* Bloomington: Indiana UP.
        329 pp.
23 essays plus an introd. by the ed. Bib. 2 pp.; name index.
    GQ 55, 568: "admirable"; *AR* 40, 245; *SCR* 15, 118; *WLT* 57, 180; *TLS*
5 Feb 1982, 144.

288.   Konigsberg, Ira, ed. 1981. *American Criticism in the Poststructuralist
        Age*. Ann Arbor: U of Michigan. 186 pp.
9 symposium papers by Culler, J. H. Miller, Spivak, Fish, Morris, Girard, G.
Graff, B. H. Smith, Krieger.
    Choice 19, 1552: "little that is new" and "a mediocre standard of
production."

289.   *Poétiques de la métamorphose* [Poetics of Transformation]. 1981. St-
        Etienne: U de St-Etienne. 221 pp.
A collection of essays on the various processes of metamorphosis in literature —
e.g., from analogy or metaphor to metamorphosis.
    MLR 77, 949–50: "a rich vein of poetic expression has been opened up."

290.   Shopen, Timothy, and Joseph Williams, eds. 1981. *Style and Variables in English*. Cambridge, MA: Winthrop. 272 pp.
Essays on "The English Language as Rule-Governed Behavior: Grammatical Structure," "The English Language as Use-Governed Behavior," "Styles," "The Organization of Discourse," "Literary Style: The Personal Voice" (macrostructure, microstructure, verbal nouns, expansion and architecture, final ordering, etc.), "Sociolinguistic Variables." "Suggestions for Further Reading" following each ch.; no index.

291.   Steiner, Wendy, ed. 1981. *The Sign in Music and Literature*. Austin: U of Texas P. 237 pp.
14 papers presented at a conference in 1978, the first 8 on literature, e.g., "Inside Greimas's Square," "The Literary Artifact," "Typography, Rhymes, and Linguistic Structures in Poetry." Bib. 8 pp.
    MLR 78, 644: "most of these authors write in an impenetrable jargon" and "all seem intent on celebrating the difficulty of the text and our inability to understand it"; *JAAC* 40, 340; *GaR* 36, 449; *FQ* 35, 61.

292.   Varga, A. Kibédi, ed. 1981. *Théorie de la littérature* [Theory of Literature]. Paris: Picard. 304 pp.
Contains, e.g., "Rhétorique et stylistique" by Heinrich Plett.

293.   Young, Robert, ed. 1981. *Untying the Text: A Post Structuralist Reader*. Boston: Routledge. 326 pp.
"Whereas Todorov, Greimas or the early Barthes sought to elevate their work to the condition of a science, post-structuralist thinkers, such as Derrida, Foucault and Lacan, have questioned the status of science itself, and the possibility of the objectivity of any language of description or analysis, as well as the assumptions implicit in the Saussurian model of linguistics on which structuralism may be said to be broadly based." Contributors include Barthes, Foucault, Balibar and Macherey, Riffaterre, J. H. Miller, and de Man. 28-p. introd. by ed.; headnotes, guides to further reading following each selection. Author and term index 10 pp. [The introd., the headnotes, and, for many of the selections, the footnotes provided by the ed. and the choice of essays containing specific textual analyses make this difficult collection accessible.]
    GQ 55, 569: "an excellent introduction to recent French developments, in spite of the shortcomings of deconstruction"; *MLR* 78, 383–85: "gives a lively account of deconstructionist theory and practice" that avoids duplicating any of the material in Harari's *Textual Strategies*; *HM* 263, 68; *Choice* 19, 1062; *BRD* 78.9, 123–24.

294.   Zima, Peter, ed. 1981. *Semiotics and Dialectics: Ideology and the Text*. Amsterdam: Benjamins. 573 pp.

Has essays on Vološinov's "Marriage of Formalism and Marxism," "Kristeva's Poetics," etc.
JLS 11, 42: "important."

295.   Carter, Ronald, ed. 1982. *Language and Literature: An Introductory Reader in Stylistics*. Aspects of English. London: Allen. 256 pp.
The 12 essays were selected to show "some ways in which language and literature study can be integrated." 1 essay shows how the handling of pronouns and syntax produces the particular state of mind in a poem. Another focuses on the function of deixis in a novel. The emphasis is on practical stylistics. Glossary of main stylistic terms; bib. 8 pp.; brief subject and name index. [In keeping with the introductory character of the book, the ed. has provided introds. to each essay.]
Lang&S 16, 505: "two main reservations," "the excellent ambition of this collection is limited because the analysis starts at the wrong end"; *Lang* 60, 198–99: "a good introductory text."

296.   Carter, Ronald, and Deirdre Burton, eds. 1982. *Literary Text and Language Study*. London: Arnold. 115 pp.
Since literature is made from language, a knowledge of language is a necessary element in the interpretation of literary texts. Ch. 1, the importance and problems of adopting this interdisciplinary approach; ch. 2, lexical patterning in poetry; ch. 3, the semantic organization of fictional narrative; ch. 4, the relationship between naturally occurring conversation and language in drama. References follow each ch.; no index.

297.   Dijk, Teun van, ed. 1982. "New Developments in Cognitive Models of Discourse Processing." *Text* 2.1–3. 294 pp.
From the fields of psychology and artificial intelligence. "These developments run parallel to and now also frequently interact with similar developments in other areas of discourse analysis. . . . [L]inguistic discourse analysis has become more than a secondary paradigm, and even affects the core of linguistic theory, viz. grammar. . . . These few major areas [linguistics, psychology, sociology, anthropology] of discourse analysis are . . . paralleled with textual studies in poetics, stylistics, rhetorics, history, law, theology, semiotics, and so on."

298.   Hernadi, Paul, ed. 1982. *The Horizon of Literature*. Lincoln: U of Nebraska P. 373 pp.
24 essays revised from *BMMLA*. Part 2, "Critical Perspectives," contains essays by Andrew, Said, Jameson, Eco, Kenner.
Choice 20, 824: second section "the best," essays by Andrew and Said "superb."

299.   Herzfeld, Michael, and Margot Lenhart, eds. 1982. *Semiotics 1980*. Proc.
        of the Fifth Annual Meeting of the Semiotic Soc. of Amer., Lubbock.
        New York: Plenum. 606 pp.
        First in a series devoted to semiotics. Only a few papers on literature — e.g.,
        "The Semiosis of the Sequence of Signs in a Narrative." [See Deely and Len-
        hart, no. 308.]

300.   Jefferson, Ann, and David Robey, eds. 1982. *Modern Literary Theory:
        A Comparative Introduction*. Totowa: Barnes. 186 pp.
        Focuses on the theories of the Prague School and Roman Jakobson, Anglo-
        American New Criticism, structuralism and poststructuralism, Lacan's psy-
        choanalytic criticism and Marxist-influenced theories like those of Lukács and
        Macherey. Bib. follows each essay (annotated) and at end (9 pp.); name and
        term index. [Cf. Fokkema and Kunne-Ibsch, no. 492.]
            PN Review 30, 79–80: "most useful to the reader who already has some
        familiarity with literary theory," written in "too formal and impersonal" a
        style; *Choice* 20, 577: "unavoidable selectivity takes a . . . noticeable toll"
        but "a unique, perhaps indispensable, tool for students of literary theory";
        JLS 12, 90: recommends the book in spite of crucial gaps (Greimas, van Dijk,
        Ital. and Russ. semiotics, post-Lacanian feminism).

301.   Murphy, James J., ed. 1982. *The Rhetorical Tradition and Modern Writ-
        ing*. New York: MLA. 149 pp.
        Part 1, the need for rhetoric in U.S. education; part 2, historical perspectives —
        e.g., "Ciceronian Rhetoric and the Rise of Science; The Plain Style Reconsi-
        dered." Name and term index 7 pp.
            WLT 57, 521: will help reunify the studies of writing and literature; *Choice*
        20, 700.

302.   "The Newest Criticisms." 1982. *College Literature* 9.3. 102 pp.
        Essays on Greimas's narrative semiotics applied to a story by Faulkner, on how
        readers make meaning, etc.

302a.   Spanos, William, et al., eds. 1982. *The Question of Textuality: Strate-
        gies of Reading in Contemporary American Criticism*. Bloomington:
        Indiana UP. 372 pp.
        13 papers, with responses, presented at a 1978 symposium: "for the most part
        the Symposium speakers assumed that both American New Critical and Hu-
        manistic rhetorics are no longer viable alternatives for the critical intellectual
        in America." All previously pub. in *Boundary 2*.
            Choice 19, 1234: "best essays" by Said, H. Brown, and Poster.

303.   Strelka, Joseph, ed. 1982. *Literary Criticism and Philosophy*. University
        Park: Pennsylvania State UP. 288 pp.

11 essays divided into 3 divisions: "Basic Philosophical Foundations of Literary Criticism," "Philosophical Concepts and Implications in Literary Criticism," and "Philosophical Concepts and Implications within the Literary Work of Art." Special attention to Roman Ingarden. Name index 6 pp.

304.   Sudol, Ronald, ed. 1982. *Revising: New Essays for Teachers of Writing.* Urbana: NCTE. 187 pp.
The first 6 essays are theoretical and historical, including "H. G. Wells' *The Outline of History*: A Study in Revision."

305.   Tanner, William, and J. Dean Bishop, eds. 1982. *Rhetoric and Change.* Mesquite: Ide; Urbana: NCTE. 217 pp.
14 essays.

306.   Widdowson, Peter, ed. 1982. *Re-Reading English.* London: Methuen. 246 pp.
"This book is an attempt to take stock of the current state of that area in higher education traditionally referred to as 'English' or 'Literary Studies,' and to redirect it in response to pressing social and political needs." Bib. following chs. and at end (5 pp.); name and term index.
Enc 58, 64; *TLS* 10 Dec. 1982, 1371.

307.   Arac, Jonathan, et al., eds. 1983. *The Yale Critics: Deconstruction in America.* Minneapolis: U of Minnesota P. 222 pp.
10 essays and an introd. Mainly on the work of Bloom, de Man, Hartman, and Miller but also on Derrida, Blanchot, Nietzsche, and others. Bib. 10 pp.; name and term index.
AL 55, 678: "disciplined, surprisingly clear, and integrated"; *NR* 188, 28; *Choice* 21, 567.

308.   Deely, John, and Margot Lenhart, eds. 1983. *Semiotics 1981.* Proc. of the Sixth Annual Meeting of the Semiotic Soc. of Amer., Nashville. New York: Plenum. 555 pp.
1 section, on "Literary and Artistic Semiotics," includes papers such as "Function of the Index in Narrative" and "Representation and Subjectivity in Modern Literature." [See Herzfeld and Lenhart, no. 299.]

308a.   Horner, Winifred B., ed. 1983. *Composition and Literature.* Chicago: U of Chicago P. 184 pp.
12 essays on how to cope with "the widening gulf between research and teaching in literature and research and teaching in composition."
EJ 73, 23.

309. "The Ironic Discourse." 1983. *PoT* 4.3. 223 pp.
Contains 4 essays on irony in literature (essays also on irony in philosophy, sociology, and psycholinguistics).

310. Kappeler, Susanne, and Norman Bryson, eds. 1983. *Teaching the Text.* London: Routledge. 200 pp.
Members of the Cambridge U English faculty (including Frank Kermode and Raymond Williams) explain their approaches to topics and texts.

310a. Krupnick, Mark, ed. 1983. *Displacement: Derrida and After.* Blooming- ton: Indiana UP. 198 pp.
This collection of 7 essays and the ed.'s introd. traces "a trajectory that runs from Sigmund Freud's *The Interpretation of Dreams* to Jacques Derrida's most recent writings. The separate essays are unified . . . by the pervasive pres- ence of Derrida, the philosopher who has done most to displace the metaphysics of the presence." "Displacement provides the organizing princi- ple of this collection," for "Derridean deconstruction proceeds by way of dis- placement."
LJ 108, 1797.

311. "Metaphor." 1983. *PoT* 4.2. 167 pp.
4 essays, including 1 by Umberto Eco, a critique of an article with the author's response, 2 rev. articles, 8 revs., and a "New Books" section (8 pp.).

312. Steiner, Peter, ed. 1983. *The Prague School: Selected Writings, 1929–1946.* Austin: U of Texas P. 219 pp.
Bogatyrëv, Jakobson, Karcevskij, Mukařovský, Rieger, Vodička, and Honzl are translated into Eng. for the first time in a collection of essays revealing the diversity of the Prague School's interests: literary criticism, theory of theater, folklore, and philosophy. An introductory note accompanies each essay, and the whole concludes with a postscript tracing the roots of structuralist aes- thetics.
Lang 60, 181: "much care went into the preparation of this collection," notes "especially helpful," "a welcome addition."

313. White, Hayden, and Margaret Brose, eds. 1983. *Representing Kenneth Burke.* Baltimore: Johns Hopkins UP. 175 pp.
7 essays (3 written in 1977) by Rueckert, Jameson, Lentricchia, et al.
LJ 108, 586: "substantial help and pleasure . . . to beginners as well as specialists."

B. Individual, Dual, or Group Authorship (314–637)

314.   Saussure, Ferdinand de. 1959. *Course in General Linguistics.* Ed. Charles
        Bally, Albert Sechehaye, and Albert Riedlinger. Trans. Wade Baskin.
        New York: Philosophical Library. McGraw-Hill paperback ed., 1966.
        (*Cours de linguistique générale,* 1915.)
    The chief work by the person Jonathan Culler has called the "father of mod-
    ern linguistics."
        AJP 64, 175; *TLS* 11 Mar. 1960, 166; *CW* 53, 267; *JAF* 73, 274; *CE* 22,
    210; *MLJ* 45, 145; *AUMLA* 15, 114; *Ling* 55, 82–89 (rev. of the 1967 first vol.
    of Engler's critical ed.): "any discussion of the *Cours* which wants to be taken
    seriously will from now on have to be based on Engler's edition."

315.   Vachek, Josef. 1966. *The Linguistic School of Prague: An Introduction
        to Its Theory and Practice.* Bloomington: Indiana UP. 184 pp.
    Chs. on "Historical Aspects," "General Pattern," "Phonology," "Morphol-
    ogy," "Syntax," "Standard Language and Aesthetic Function," etc. 3 apps.
    on the Circle and the times. Bib. 13 pp.; name and term indexes.
        Anglia 87, 412–14; *SR* 33, 60–61; *MPhon* 123, 7–9; *SFFBU* 15, 180–81; *IJAL*
    33, 341–44.

316.   Bayerdörfer, Hans-Peter. 1967. *Poetik als sprachtheoretisches Problem*
        [Poetics and the Theoretical Language Problem]. Tübingen: Niemeyer.
        303 pp.
    Part 1 treats theory: langue, parole, synchrony, diachrony (Saussure), etc.; part
    2, issues of individual speech, convention, condensation, expansion, etc.
        MLR 64, 449–50: "difficult reading."

317.   Guiraud, Pierre. 1967. *La estilística.* Buenos Aires: Nova. 124 pp. (Trans.
        of *La stylistique,* 5th ed., 1967.)

318.   Hester, Marcus. 1967. *The Meaning of the Poetic Metaphor: An Analy-
        sis in the Light of Wittgenstein's Claim That Meaning Is Use.* The Hague:
        Mouton. 229 pp.
    Introd. on definitions of metaphor and method; part 1, "Wittgenstein's Theory
    of Meaning"; part 2, "Poetic Language"; part 3, "Metaphor"; part 4, "Lan-
    guage of Literary Discussion." An investigation of the relevance of imagery
    to meaning. The author argues that poetic language functions iconically,
    achieving a fusion of sense, sound, and imagery, and that poetic metaphors
    fuse meaning and form (which includes imagery). Bib. 5 pp.; name and term
    indexes.
        JAAC 28, 400–01: "thoughtful both on language and on the problems of
    metaphor and imagery"; *Style* 10, 311–12; *Ling* 58, 92–98.

319. Hirsch, E. D. 1967. *Validity in Interpretation*. New Haven: Yale UP. 287 pp.
An attack on hermeneutical skepticism in general and historicism, psychologism, and autonomism in particular and an attempt to define the grounds on which textual interpretation can claim to establish objective knowledge and to demonstrate the uniformity and universality of the principles of valid interpretation for verbal texts. Name and term index.
PR 34, 627; *N&Q* 15, 355; *Alph* 15, 70; *EIC* 18, 337; *VQR* 43, cxvi.

320. Kloepfer, Rolf. 1967. *Die Theorie der literarischen Übersetzung* [The Theory of Literary Translation]. Munich: Fink. 140 pp.
RF 79, 657–62; *LB* 56, 136–39; *GL&L* 22,415–16; *REL* 45, 502–03; *ZRP* 85, 236–39.

321. Lausberg, Heinrich. 1967. *Elemente der literarischen Rhetorik: Eine Einführung für Studierende der klassichen, romanischen, englischen und deutschen Philologie* [Elements of Literary Rhetoric: An Introduction to the Study of Classical, Romance, English, and German Philology]. 3rd ed. Munich: Hueber. 169 pp. (1st ed. 1949, 2nd ed. 1963.)
Studies of tropes based on modern linguistic theories.
ZRP 83, 89–90 (on 2nd ed.).

322. Artemenko, E. P., and N. K. Sokolova. 1968. *O nekotoryx priemax izučenija jazyka xudožestvennyx proizvedenij* [The Study of the Language of Belles Lettres]. Voronež: Izd. Voronezskogo U.

323. Fucks, Wilhelm. 1968. *Nach allen Regeln der Kunst* [According to the Rules of Art]. Stuttgart: Deutsche Verl.-Anstalt. 143 pp.
Style 5, 92–94: "Fucks reveals the elegantly formulable mathematical distributions underlying such phenomena as the length of sentences in a text and the pitches of note-pairs in a concerto. . . . This is a most seductive book in a field which many think of as rather arid. . . . a work of propaganda . . . intended to convince the uninitiated first that there are regularities . . . and then that a literary science of exact numerical description is a good thing"; *Germanistik* 10, 740; *ITL* 12, 59–72.

323a. Granger, Gilles G. 1968. *Essai d'une philosophie du style*. Paris: Colin. 313 pp.
A semiotic approach.
LFr 7, 109–12.

324. Jones, Robert. 1968. *Panorama de la nouvelle critique en France*. Paris: Soc. d'édition d'enseignement supérieur. 366 pp.
An attack on "mystical" and "*a priori* system" criticism.
MLR 65, 416–17: an unfavorable rev.

325.   Lawall, Sarah. 1968. *Critics of Consciousness: The Existential Structures of Literature.* Cambridge: Harvard UP. 281 pp.

A survey of Fr. phenomenological criticism: Béguin, Raymond, Poulet, J.-P. Richard, Starobinski, Rousset, Blanchot. Name and term index.
     MLR 65, 415–16: an unfavorable rev.

326.   Salm, Peter. 1968. *Three Modes of Criticism. The Literary Theories of Scherer, Walzel, and Staiger.* Cleveland: Case Western Reserve UP. 127 pp.
The positivist Scherer and the formalists Walzel and Staiger are compared.
     MLR 66, 231–32: "Comparative studies on different kinds of criticism such as the present work deserve every possible encouragement."

327.   Valesio, Paolo. 1968. *Strutture dell'allitterazione: Grammatica, retorica e folklore verbale* [The Structure of Alliteration: Grammar, Rhetoric, and Verbal Folklore]. Bologna: Zanichelli. 436 pp.
Style 5, 95–97: "highly important."

328.   Dupriez, Bernard. 1969. *L'étude des styles ou la commutation en littérature* [The Study of Style, or Substitution in Literature]. Paris: Didier. 333 pp. (*Edition augmentée d'une étude sur le style de Paul Claudel.* Montreal: Didier, 1970. 368 pp.)
Style 6, 314–15: first half of book surveys approaches to style, second half develops theory of "commutation," a "useful idea" but lodged in an inadequate theory; *FM* 41, 198–200; *FS* 26, 489–90; *Lingua* 26, 325–28; *ZRP* 87, 402–09; *MLR* 66, 652–53; *Sprache* 17, 66–67; *BSLP* 66, 37–39; *RLR* 79, 277–78.

329.   Gray, Bennison. 1969. *Style: The Problem and Its Solution.* The Hague: Mouton. 117 pp.
"Style" is an unnecessary entity because it is coextensive with the work itself; therefore, "there will be no new science of style." The author especially criticizes the first international conference on style in language held at Indiana U in 1958 (most of the work discussed is of the 1950s), the application of statistics to literary problems, psychological approaches to style, and the idea of style as an expression of the author. Bib. 4 pp.; name index. [A challenge to all who use the term "style." See Ellis, no. 420.]
Style 5, 177–83: generally negative; *MLR* 66, 162; *Ling* 101, 89–93.

330.   Hermand, Jost. 1969. *Synthetisches Interpretieren: Zur Methodik der Literaturwissenschaft* [Synthetic Interpretation: On the Methodology of Literary Criticism]. Munich: Nymphenburger. 269 pp.
Part 1 presents a survey of critical approaches since 1900 (psychoanalytic, Marxist, etc.); part 2 offers his synthesis.

331. Hough, Graham. 1969. *Style and Stylistics*. London: Routledge; New York: Humanities. 114 pp.

2 chs. describe the historical development of style study from Germanic philology through New Criticism and Saussure, Bally, and Cressot. Ch. 3 explores the concept of style and individual and period styles. Ch. 4 praises the contributions of 8 "practitioners." [Throughout, Hough stresses the use of careful linguistic observation for understanding the meaning of works as wholes.] Bib. 4 pp.

ES 54, 85–88: too uncritical of the "practitioners" and too unsympathetic toward statistics, but a "highly useful introduction"; *EIC* 20, 264; *LT* (1971), 287–92 (rev. article): "a disappointing little book . . . chiefly because of its Luddite tone and its traditionalism."

332. Imbert, Enrique. 1969. *Métodos de crítica literaria* [Methods of Literary Criticism]. Madrid: Revista de Occidente. 186 pp.

A general survey that includes sections on formalist and stylistic criticism. Bib. 9 pp.; name index.

333. Koch, Walter. 1969. *Von Morphem zum Textem — From Morpheme to Texteme*. Hildesheim: Olms. 258 pp.

Essays in structural linguistics and literary criticism rpt. from *Orbis* and other periodicals, 1962–67.

RPh 24, 545–46; *Anglia* 89, 476–80.

333a. Kristeva, Julia. 1969. *Sēēmēiotikē: Recherches pour une sémanalyse* [Semiotics: Research for an Analysis of Semantics]. Paris: Seuil. 379 pp.

LFr 7, 115–16; *LeS* 5, 532–34.

334. McCall, Marsh, Jr. 1969. *Ancient Rhetorical Theories of Simile and Comparison*. Cambridge: Harvard UP. 272 pp.

8 chs. on pre-Aristotle, Aristotle, *Rhetorica ad Herennium*, Cicero, Greeks of the first century BC and AD, the Senecas, Quintilian, and after Quintilian; ch. 9 a summary.

Ling 137, 95–99: "the author has fulfilled his task in an exemplary way"; "all the relevant material," "exact and careful"; *QJS* 57, 125; *AJP* 92, 360; *CW* 64, 138; *TLS* 18 Dec. 1970, 1488; *BL* (1976), 3014.

335. Mackin, John. 1969. *Classical Rhetoric for Modern Discourse*. New York: Free. 274 pp.

"A textbook for English composition and speech courses and an essay to start discussion about the art." Stresses Socratic over Aristotelian foundations. Many examples from Shakespeare. Name and term index.

QJS 56, 101: "intriguing and certainly worth consideration," but "as a textbook it may prove disappointing unless used with very advanced students"; *Choice* 7, 101.

336.   Muecke, D. C. 1969. *The Compass of Irony.* London: Methuen. 276 pp.
Has 2 purposes: "a general account of the formal qualities of irony and a classification . . . of the more familiar kinds" and a rev. of the more recent open
forms of irony. Bib. 9 pp.; name and term index. [In his pref. to the 1980
rpt. the author declares he would have made a "thorough revision of the classifications in chapters III and IV" and, "among the bookful of things that
might be added, perhaps the most essential would be a chapter on the different
ironigenic properties of theatre, narrative fiction and lyric poetry."]
    RES 21, 526: "wealth of erudition and examples" yet "methodological weak-
ness"; *TLS* 4 Sept. 1969, 970.

337.   Muschg, Walter. 1969. *Die dichterische Phantasie: Einführung in eine
Poetik* [The Poetic Imagination: Introduction to a Poetics]. Bern: Francke.
180 pp.
Relates 3 types of imagery to 3 linguistic modes (first person, second person,
third person) and 3 genres (lyric, drama, epic).
    MLR 68, 223–24: "richness" in "the teeming wealth of comment," "remark-
ably informed."

338.   Perelman, Chaim, and L. Olbrechts-Tyteca. 1969. *The New Rhetoric:
A Treatise on Argumentation.* Trans. John Wilkinson and Purcell
Weaver. Notre Dame: U of Notre Dame P. 566 pp. (*La nouvelle rhétorique: Traité de l'argumentation.* Paris: PUF, 1958.)
Builds a theory of demonstration by analyzing the "methods of proof used
in the human sciences, law, and philosophy" and the "arguments put forward by advertisers in newspapers, politicians in speeches, lawyers in plead-
ings, judges in decisions, and philosophers in treatises." Bib. 25 pp.; name
and term indexes.
    JAAC 29, 569: "highest value as a clear and masterful exposition of
Aristotelian rhetoric"; *QJS* 56, 92; *HLR* 83, 1971; *RM* 25, 363; *Choice* 7, 101.

339.   Pongs, Hermann. 1969. *Das Bild in der Dichtung. Vol. III: Der sym-
bolische Kosmos der Dichtung* [The Image in Poetry. Vol. III. The Sym-
bolical Cosmos of Poetry]. Marburg: Elwert. 822 pp.
The conclusion to his trilogy about the poetic image and the symbolic language of literature, this vol. focuses on ballad, epic, and drama.
    MLR 66, 454–56: "penetrating."

340.   Schiller, Jerome. 1969. *I. A. Richards' Theory of Literature.* New Haven: Yale UP. 189 pp.
An analysis of Richards's account of the function of literature and of poetic
language as "language which occasions multiple interpretation," the value

of which "lies in the way in which it forces the reader to become absorbed in the purposes underlying" interpretation.

MLR 67, 152–53: "a valuable elucidation."

341. Uitti, Karl. 1969. *Linguistics and Literary Theory*. Englewood Cliffs: Prentice-Hall. 272 pp.

Concentrates on contemporary research in the U.S., addressed to readers working mainly in fields other than linguistics and literary theory. Ch. 1, "basic features of the Western concept of language"; ch. 2, "linguistics and literary study as practiced in this country (and abroad) in recent years"; ch. 3, "suggestions concerning increased collaboration between the two fields." Name index.

MLR 66, 161–62: "What one needs is not the large adjectival gesture but rigorous exploration of particular possibilities."

342. Wellek, René. 1969. *The Literary Theory and Aesthetics of the Prague School*. Ann Arbor: U of Michigan Dept. of Slavic Languages and Literature. 37 pp.

On Mukařovský.

343. Butler, Christopher. 1970. *Number Symbolism*. London: Routledge. 186 pp.

Claims to be "only the briefest of introductions to a very complex subject," in chronological order—Gk. origins, early medieval Biblical exegesis, etc. Bib. 4 pp.; name and term index.

TLS 23 July 1970, 809: "covers all the fundamental theory and history of the subject"; *MLR* 67, 390–91.

344. Cambours Ocampo, Arturo. 1970. *Lenguaje y creación: Notas para una fenomenología del estilo literario* [Language and Creation: Notes toward a Phenomenology of Literary Style]. Buenos Aires: La Reja. 124 pp.

345. Caplan, Harry. 1970. *Of Eloquence: Studies in Ancient and Mediaeval Rhetoric*. Ithaca: Cornell UP. 289 pp.

10 mostly previously pub. essays ranging from the Roman period to the Middle Ages. Name and term indexes.

TLS 21 July 1972, 849: valuable "for anyone interested in the history of classical rhetoric"; *QJS* 57, 249; *Spec* 46, 413; *CW* 64, 313.

346. Cassirer, Peter. 1970. *Deskriptiv stilistik: En begrepps- och metoddiskussion* [Descriptive Stylistics: A Discussion of Concepts and Methods]. Gothenburg: Universitetet. 140 pp.

Eng. summary.

347.   Darbyshire, A. E. 1970. *A Grammar of Style*. London: Deutsch. 236 pp.
A study of how deviation from the accepted "norm" creates style. The author
employs transformational generative grammar to relate style to the 5 basic
sentence types. Term index.
Style 11, 423–24: too schematic, "too narrow and parochial," a "naive and
old-fashioned approach to literature"; *TLS* 15 Oct. 1971, 1277: "a timely and
useful book," "original and penetrating."

347a.   Eastman, Richard. 1970. *Style: Writing as the Discovery of Outlook*.
New York: Oxford UP. 280 pp. (2nd ed. 1978).
A descriptive and prescriptive manual on how to write. [See Smith, no. 433].
Ling 169, 63–65: "greatly needed."

348.   Fowler, Alastair, ed. 1970. *Silent Poetry: Essays in Numerological Analysis*. London: Routledge. 260 pp.
"Numerological criticism analyzes literary structures . . . ordered by numerical symmetries or expressing number symbolisms." 10 essays, the first 2 on
traditions of arithmological thought (Pythagorean and Platonic, Augustinian and exegetical), the subsequent essays on individual works, arranged
chronologically.
TLS 23 July 1970, 809; *MLR* 67, 161–63.

349.   Greimas, A. J. 1970. *Du sens: Essais sémiotiques* [On Meaning: Semiotic Essays]. Paris: Seuil. 314 pp.
Collection of 15 articles, most of them previously pub. Includes a system of
narrative agents by analogy with syntax in terms of binary oppositions, etc.
BL (1971), 824.

350.   Guiraud, Pierre. 1970. *Essais de stylistique* [Stylistic Essays]. Paris:
Klincksieck. 283 pp.
Theoretical and practical studies dating from 1952 to 1967 based on struc-
tural and functional linguistics.
Ling 101, 112–15: "useful as an introduction to the framework of structuralist
stylistics," although it does not overcome the "shortcomings" of that approach.

351.   Heller, L. G., and James Macris. 1970. *Toward a Structural Theory of
Literary Analysis: Prolegomena to Evaluative-Descriptivism*. Worcester:
Inst. for Systems Analysis. 65 pp.
A theory for description and evaluation based on the linguistic concepts of
function-manifesting units and complementary distribution. The focus is on
schematizations of plot that can be accounted for by these concepts.
Style 12, 315–17: the "formal descriptivism" is "one of severely limited utility" and the "non-subjective evaluative system" is "suspect both in principle
and practice."

351a. Maren-Grisebach, Manon. 1970. *Methoden der Literaturwissenschaft* [Methods of Literary Criticism]. Bern: Francke. 106 pp.
Explains 6 critical approaches in roughly chronological order: positivist, historical, phenomenological, existential, morphological, and sociological or Marxist.

352. Segre, Cesare. 1970. *Crítica bajo control*. Barcelona: Planeta. 316 pp.
The first 10 chs. are a version of *I segni e la crítica*, with 3 new essays on medieval works.
MLR 67, 863–64: "a mixed bag," "useful" exposition of some contemporary critical theory and "particularly interesting" on García Márquez and Pizzuto.

353. Stempel, W.-D. 1970. *Beiträge zur Textlinguistik* [Contribution to Text Linguistics]. Munich: Fink. 302 pp.
MLR 69, 137: the ch. on "genres littéraires" is "brilliant"; *Ling* 121, 123–29 (in Ger.).

354. Turbayne, Colin. 1970. *The Myth of Metaphor*. Rev. ed. New York: Columbia UP. 241 pp.
Minor corrections but includes 2 new forewords and an app. that interpret the book. Name and term index.

355. Wallace, Karl. 1970. *Understanding Discourse: The Speech Act and Rhetorical Action*. Baton Rouge: Louisiana State UP. 150 pp.
An analysis of the speech act as the "unit of meaningful utterance" and the microcosm of the macrocosm of the rhetorical act, rhetoric being the theory of such actions. Name and term index.
QJS 57, 251: "one of the most important statements on rhetorical scholarship in the half century."

356. Williams, C. B. 1970. *Style and Vocabulary: Numerical Studies*. New York: Hafner. 161 pp.
Ch. 1, historical background; chs. 2–3, basic terminology and concepts; ch. 4, word- and sentence-length distributions; chs. 5–6, vocabulary; ch. 7, prosody; ch. 8, discussion of various studies. Bib. 5 pp.; name and term index.
Style 10, 296–99: "a fine introductory study."

357. Dijk, Teun van. 1971. *Taal. Tekst. Teken. Bijdragen tot de literatuurtheorie* [Language. Text. Sign. Contributions to the Theory of Literature]. Amsterdam: Polak. 251 pp.
Collection of papers (in Dutch) about such topics as literary semantics, text grammar, etc.

358. Dixon, Peter. 1971. *Rhetoric*. Critical Idiom Series. London: Methuen. 88 pp.

A study of the historical fluctuations of the meaning and scope of rhetoric, with indication of "some of the ways in which rhetoric has impinged upon literature." Bib. 8 pp.; name and title index.

359.   Fowler, Roger. 1971. *The Languages of Literature: Some Linguistic Contributions to Criticism*. London: Routledge. 256 pp.
A collection of previously pub. essays that "imply the beginnings of a consistent philosophy of language and literature. . . . [T]hey argue and demonstrate the appropriateness of linguistic concepts to a literary education." Bib. 2 pp.; name index.
Ling 141, 79–83: "a document in the personal history of Fowler's progress as a critic and theorist," his search for the cooperation of linguistics and criticism is "finally contradictory"; *MLR* 67, 866: "many positive qualities"; *RES* ns 24, 316; *Choice* 9, 502; *LJ* 97, 875.

360.   Galperin, I. R. 1971. *Stylistics*. Moscow: Higher School. 343 pp.
An introd. discusses the nature of style and other problems. Parts 2–5 discuss vocabulary and phonetic, lexical, and syntactic expressive devices. Part 6 treats functional styles (belles lettres; publicistic, newspaper, scientific prose; and official documents). Bib. 6 pp.; name and term indexes. [See Crystal and Davy, no. 846.]
Style 7, 181–83: a hostile rev.; see Galperin's reply (Winter 1974); *Samlaren* 94, 269–70; *SAS* 35, 198–202.

361.   Guillén, Claudio. 1971. *Literature as System: Essays toward the Theory of Literary History*. Princeton: Princeton UP. 528 pp.
11 previously pub. essays on comparative literature, rewritten in various degrees. Section 1 on literary influence, section 2 on genre, section 5 on theory. An attempt to "show some of the ways in which literature . . . functions historically as a system — i.e., as an order (of interacting parts)." Name and term index.
YR 61, 254: "His book is a great step forward toward the clarification of the problems of literary history, and one of the most distinguished contributions to literary theory in our time"; *Diacritics* 3.1, 9–18; *MLR* 68, 138–40: "dazzling," "destined to be a classic."

362.   Henry, Albert. 1971. *Métonymie et métaphore*. Paris: Klincksieck. 160 pp.
First the figure is explained and then literary examples are examined. Term and name indexes.
Ling 141, 92–97: "confusing complication"; *BL* (1976), 2977.

363.   Jacobs, Roderick, and Peter Rosenbaum. 1971. *Transformations, Style, and Meaning*. Waltham: Xerox. 140 pp.

A generative-transformational model applied to the analysis of the linguistic features that characterize an individual author in order to relate stylistics to meaning. Bib. follows each ch.

Style 7, 177–80: although it "tries to cover too much territory" the book is recommended "to anyone interested in the linguistic bases of literary style"; *KN* 21, 116–20; *CJL* 16, 118–20; *ETC* 30, 326.

364.   Jakobson, Roman. 1971–. *Selected Writings*. The Hague: Mouton. 7 vols. 1: *Phonological Studies*, 1971, 775 pp. Name, language, and term indexes. 2: *Word and Language*, 1971, 752 pp. Name and term indexes. (*AA* 75, 1077–78: "the articles illustrate very well the wide range of Jakobson's interests in linguistics.") 3: *Poetry of Grammar and Grammar of Poetry*, 1981, 814 pp. See no. 587b. 4: *Slavic Epic Studies*, 1966, 752 pp. 5: *On Verse, Its Masters and Explorers*, 1979, 624 pp. 6: *Early Slavic Paths and Crossroads*. Forthcoming. 7: *Studies in Comparative Mythology. Miscellanea. Bibliography*. Forthcoming.

365.   Jakobson, Roman. 1971. *Studies in Verbal Art: Texts in Czech & Slovak*. Michigan Slavic Contributions 4. Ann Arbor: Michigan Slavic Pubs. 412 pp.
A collection of his essays written from 1928 to 1965.

366.   Jameson, Fredric. 1971. *Marxism and Form: Twentieth-Century Dialectical Theories of Literature*. Princeton: Princeton UP. 432 pp.
Analyzes 6 Continental writers (Sartre, Adorno, Marcuse, Benjamin, Bloch, and Lukács) in the process of constructing a dialectical model for literary criticism.

YR 62, 119–26: "This book is misnamed. It has little to say about form"; "the main flaw of the book [is] . . . the uncritical acceptance of the presuppositions of dialectical materialism," but it is "a challenge also to the American intellectual to come to terms with Marxism"; *MLR* 69, 599–601: "the most important work of critical theory to appear in English since Northrop Frye's *Anatomy of Criticism*."

367.   Kinneavy, James L. 1971. *A Theory of Discourse*. Englewood Cliffs: Prentice. 478 pp.
Makes a distinction between *aim* and *mode* of discourse. The 4 primary kinds of discourse are based on aim: reference, persuasive, literary, expressive. The 4 modes (description, narration, classification, evaluation) are secondary to aim in that any or all of them may serve any of the aims. Chs. 1–2 explain the need for a comprehensive theory and justify the communication triangle as an ordering principle. Each of the last 4 chs. sets forth the norms of 1 of the 4 kinds of discourse. Bibs. with each ch.; name and term index. [*A Theory* has been adapted for use in writing classrooms in *Aims and Audiences in Writing* and *Writing—Basic Modes of Organization*.]

Style 12, 52–54: "massive scholarship," "a source of crucial distinctions," "a landmark work"; *QJS* 60, 120; *P&R* 5, 188.

368.   Marin, Louis. 1971. *Etudes sémiologiques* [Semiological Studies]. Paris: Klincksieck.
Previously pub. articles that attempt to establish a field of inquiry encompassing visual art and literature.
Diacritics 7.2, 22–34.

368a.   Miller, David. 1971. *The Net of Hephaestus: A Study of Modern Criticism and Metaphysical Metaphor.* The Hague: Mouton. 173 pp.
A study of metaphor as a fundamental critical problem for the New Critics. The first 3 chs. survey 3 generations of New Critics; ch. 4, "Grammar of Metaphor"; ch. 5, the "location" of verbal art.
Ling 137, 99–107: his "assessment of the difficulties besetting New Critical theory is accurate; however the purgative which he envisions is probably insufficient."

369.   Riffaterre, Michael. 1971. *Essais de stylistique structurale* [Essays on Structural Stylistics]. Paris: Flammarion. 364 pp.
A collection of previously pub. articles and a few new ones. Part 1, principles and methods; part 2, application to specific works (Hugo) and problems; part 3, French structuralism and Baudelaire's "Les chats."
Style 8, 87–91: "the gimmick of the 'Superreader' " is "highly questionable" and a major fault "is the lack of a concluding chapter," but the collection is "an honest attempt to objectify the methods of stylistics," and it constantly provokes the reader "to define his own position"; *TLS* 25 Feb. 1972, 228; *Diacritics* 11.3, 13–26; 11.4, 17–35.

370.   Shibles, Warren. 1971. *An Analysis of Metaphor in the Light of W. M. Urban's Theories.* The Hague: Mouton. 171 pp.
An exposition of Urban's ideas in *Language and Reality* (1939) and a refutation of the literal, or substitution, theory. Bib. 6 pp.; name and term index.
Style 9, 128–30: "important and detailed criticism of the substitution theory"; *Ling* 169, 90–92: "verifies convincingly that Urban's theory . . . is more acceptable than the 'literalist theory,' " "a precious instrument . . . for all those" concerned with metaphor.

371.   Thompson, Ewa. 1971. *Russian Formalism and Anglo-American New Criticism: A Comparative Study.* The Hague: Mouton. 160 pp.
Beneath the surface similarities of these 2 schools (the dependence of thought on language and the practice of close reading of literary texts) exists a "basic polarity." Ch. 1, historical survey; ch. 2, philosophical backgrounds; ch. 3, application of principles to practical criticism. Bib. 4 pp.; name and term index.

372. Žolkovskij, Alexandr, and Juryj Ščeglov. 1971–78. *K opisaniyu smysla svyaznogo teksta* [Toward Description of the Meaning of Liaison Text]. Moscow: Inst. russkogo jazyka AN. 8 vols.
The first 2 parts have been pub. in Eng.: "Towards 'Theme-(Expression Devices)-Text' Model of Literary Structure," in Shukman, no. 218a; "The Poetic Structure of a Maxim by La Rochefoucauld: An Essay in Theme-Text Poetics," *PTL* 3 (1978), 549–92. These works explore the processes by which themes are given expressive linguistic form.

373. Barteau, Françoise. 1972. *Les romans de Tristan et Iseut: Introduction à une lecture plurielle* [The Romances of Tristan and Iseult: Introduction to a Plural Reading]. Paris: Larousse. 319 pp.
An introd. to contemporary critical methods (socioeconomic, semiotic, Freudian, phenomenological, and existential) as applied to the verse romances of Tristan.
MLR 70, 877–79: "a virtuoso performance" but lacks "care with minutiae."

374. Barthes, Roland. 1972. *Critical Essays.* Trans. Richard Howard. Evanston: Northwestern UP. 279 pp. (*Essais critiques.* Paris: Seuil, 1964.)
33 essays written between 1953 and 1963, marking Barthes's "conversion to structuralism understood in its strictest sense, whereby literature and social life are regarded as 'no more than languages,' to be studied not in their content but in their structure, as pure relational systems" (trans.'s note).
PR 40, 294; *NYTBR* 30 July 1972, 5; *CC* 89, 488.

375. Boon, James. 1972. *From Symbolism to Structuralism: Lévi-Strauss in a Literary Tradition.* Oxford: Blackwell; New York: Harper. 250 pp.
An effort to establish the similarity between the symbolist poets (Mallarmé, Baudelaire, et al.) and Lévi-Strauss as to the innate structures of human thought revealed in myths. Includes "Structural Analysis: A View from Baudelaire's 'Les chats'" (38–61). Bib. 14 pp.; name and term index.
MLR 71, 186: discusses "fundamental" issues and provides "a mass of apposite and thought-provoking observations," but fails to develop all these issues, and the arguments are disconnected "like a series of digressions."

376. Dijk, Teun van. 1972. *Beiträge zur generativen Poetik* [Toward a Generative Poetic]. Munich: Bayerischer Schulbuch. 224 pp. (Ital. trans.: *Per una poetica generativa.* Bologna: Il Mulino, 1976.)
Collection of papers about text grammar, literary semantics, etc.

377. Hawkes, Terence. 1972. *Metaphor.* London: Methuen. 102 pp.
A history of metaphor and the argument that "language is reality" by working metaphorically. Ch. 2, "The Classical View"; ch. 3, "Sixteenth, Seventeenth, and Eighteenth Centuries"; ch. 4, "The Romantic View"; ch. 5, "Some

Twentieth-Century Views." Bib. 7 pp.; name and term index.
Style 10, 311–12: "a beautiful book"; *Hermathena* 114, 100; *Choice* 10, 770;
ANQ 11, 74.

378.   Herczeg, Giulio. 1972. *Saggi linguistici e stilistici* [Linguistic and Stylistic
        Essays]. Florence: Olschki. 624 pp.
        A collection of 27 previously pub. articles.
        MLR 70, 640–41: another of the author's "important contributions to our
        knowledge of Italian syntax" and style (*Lo stile indiretto libero in italiano*
        and *Lo stile nominale in italiano*, and numerous articles).

379.   Ihwe, Jens. 1972. *Linguistik in der Literaturwissenschaft: Zur Entwick-
        lung einer modernen Theorie der Literaturwissenschaft* [Linguistics in
        Literary Criticism: The Development of a Modern Theory of Literary
        Criticism]. Munich: Bayerischer Schulbuch. 450 pp.
        Style 11, 76–79: Investigates "the extent to which linguistic ideas and models
        can be made use of in the development of an adequate theoretical frame for
        the description of literature. . . . Although his method of presentation is
        irritating and occasionally borders on obfuscation, Ihwe's ambitious book
        should serve as a stimulus to further study"; *JLS* 3, 121–28; *BL* (1977), 3325.

380.   *Issledovanija po poètike i stilistike* [Analysis in Poetics and Stylistics].
        1972. Leningrad: Gosizdat. 277 pp.

381.   Jameson, Fredric. 1972. *The Prison-House of Language: A Critical Ac-
        count of Structuralism and Russian Formalism*. Princeton: Princeton UP.
        230 pp.
        An evaluation of Fr. structuralism, further limited to theoretical work based
        on the metaphor or model of a linguistic system (thus excluding, e.g., Lucien
        Goldmann and Jean Piaget), with certain exceptions — e.g., the linguistics-
        based Russian structuralism of J. Lotman and others and certain North Amer.
        linguistic structuralists are omitted. Ch. 1, "The Linguistic Model"; ch. 2,
        "The Formalist Projection"; ch. 3, "The Structuralist Projection." Bib. 7 pp.;
        name and term index.
        Style 8, 81–84: "intelligent and well-documented," but the self-imposed
        limitations, especially the absence of practical criticism, and the hostility to
        structuralism itself are dissatisfying; *YR* 62, 290: "it is quite possible that . . .
        Jameson's problem is finally insoluble: to go beyond formalism may be against
        the nature of understanding"; *HR* 26, 413; *TLS* 8 June 1973, 636; *Diacritics*
        3.2, 15–21.

382.   Kawin, Bruce. 1972. *Telling It Again and Again: Repetition in Litera-
        ture and Film*. Ithaca: Cornell UP. 197 pp.

Demonstrates the importance of recurrence (in contrast to repetitiousness) in literature, especially in the manipulation of time. Bib. 4 pp.; name and term index.

ConL 15, 123; *JAAC* 31, 277.

383.   Levin, V. D., ed. 1972. *Stilističeskie issledovanija* [Stylistic Investigations] Moscow: Nauka. 317 pp.

Differentiates between the concept of functional language variation and functional style.

Ling 169, 70–75 (in Ger.): in question still is the stylistic norm, especially the conscious or unconscious mixing of different stylistic elements.

384.   Pautasso, Sergio. 1972. *Le frontiere della critica* [The Frontiers of Criticism]. Milan: Rizzoli. 238 pp.

A survey of modern Ital. criticism.

MLR 69, 365–66: "over-zealous ecumenicism."

385.   Prieto, Antonio. 1972. *Ensayo semiológico de sistemas literarios* [Semiological Essay on Literary Systems]. Barcelona: Planeta. 288 pp.

See the same author's *Morfologia de la novela*, no. 686.

386.   Rasmussen, Jens. 1972. *Stil i sproget* [Style and Language]. Copenhagen: Schlønbergske. 112 pp.

387.   Ruwet, Nicholas. 1972. *Langage, musique, poésie*. Paris: Seuil. 247 pp.

BL (1973), 3081; *FM* 41, 304–06; *LeS* 9, 171–74.

388.   Thavenius, Jan. 1972. *Stil och vocabulär: En undersökning av formord i lyrik och prosa* [Style and Vocabulary: An Examination of Structure Words in Poetry and Prose]. Lund: Gleerup. 236 pp.

Style 9, 117–20: "required reading" regarding analysis of "structure words as potential style markers"; "the apparatus is careful and sophisticated."

389.   Bryant, Donald. 1973. *Rhetorical Dimensions in Criticism*. Baton Rouge: Louisiana State UP. 145 pp.

6 lectures: a commentary on K. Burke, I. A. Richards, and McLuhan; the distinction between rhetorical and literary criticism; rhetorical criticism of 18th-cent. discourse, etc.

MLR 69, 831–32: "uneven but welcome," at its best a "sensitive display of critical intelligence."

390.   Chapman, Raymond. 1973. *Linguistics and Literature*. Totowa: Littlefield. 119 pp.

"I shall work mainly on the assumptions which are common throughout the world of linguistics"—diachronic, synchronic, langue, parole, register (stylistics part of sociolinguistics), and deviation, i.e., choice (individuation through unique patterning, or foregrounding). The first 4 chs. explain these and other concepts and the next 5 treat specific aspects of a text through the concepts—syntax, semantics, figurative language, prosody, and discourse. Bib. following each ch.; name and term index.

Style 8, 425–29: "a valuable . . . introduction" to stylistics; *Lore&L* 2.1, 54; *DQR* 4, 187–89; *Lang&S* 7, 72–73.

391.   Coquet, Jean-Claude. 1973. *Sémiotique littéraire: Contribution à l'analyse sémantique du discours* [Literary Semiotics: A Contribution to the Semantic Analysis of Discourse]. Tours: Mame. 268 pp.
The first half of the book consists of 7 previously pub. essays; the second half is a new analysis of Claudel's play *La ville*.
Diacritics 5.3, 32–38: a favorable rev.; *BL* (1976), 2986.

392.   Derrida, Jacques. 1973. *Speech and Phenomena, and Other Essays on Husserl's Theory of Signs*. Trans. David Allison. Evanston: Northwestern UP. 166 pp.
Contains a trans. of Derrida's famous essay on "la différance." Name and term index.
Centrum 6, 50–60: Derrida's concept of the sign is "beset by serious logical difficulties" and is "indeed partial and misleading."

393.   Doubrovskij, Sergej. 1973. *The New Criticism in France*. Trans. Derek Coltman. Chicago: U of Chicago P. 328 pp. (*Pourquoi la nouvelle critique: Critique et objectivité*. Paris: Mercure, 1967.)
An account of Fr. traditional and new criticism in the 1960s, from the Picard-Barthes controversy to the fundamental issue of the nature of literature. Name and term index.
JAAC 33, 104–07: "contentious," "vigorous" style verging on "legalistic, in zealous congestions of heavyweight phrasing, quasi-syllogistic demolitions and strangulations"; many of his ideas long ago advocated by the American New Critics; *VQR* 50, 81; *PS* 48, 178; *LJ* 98, 3636; *Choice* 11, 442.

394.   Enkvist, Nils E. 1973. *Linguistic Stylistics*. The Hague: Mouton. 179 pp.
"My aim was to attempt a concise, introductory, and general inventory of current problems in linguistic stylistics." Enkvist's own view of style is as "a differential between a text and a contextually related norm," since "response itself is based on . . . comparison of the text with an imagined or explicit norm" in the mind of the reader. "Those linguistic features whose densities in the text are significantly different from those in the norm are called *style markers*." "Style is a notational term, an abbreviation for a concept that can

be defined in terms of other, more basic, concepts. Style is not a linguistic prime. This means that each stylolinguist owes to his readers an explicit report of precisely what he means by *style*, and by what methods he has arrived at his results and conclusions." Bib. 27 pp.; name index.

Style 9, 103–07: "admirable clarity and precision . . . an invaluable book . . . a *guide* to its subject"; *Ling* 169, 65–67: "everything" in this book "facilitates apprehending" the subject; *Lingua* 38, 76–79; *SAP* 8, 193–96.

395. Halliday, M. A. K. 1973. *Explorations in the Functions of Language.* London: Arnold. 135 pp. Rpt. Amsterdam: North-Holland, 1977.
"A functional approach to language means . . . seeing whether language itself has been shaped by use . . . how the form of language has been determined by the functions it has evolved to serve." The first 4 papers lead to the last, "Linguistic Function & Literary Style," in which Halliday applies his ideas to the study of W. Golding's *The Inheritors.* "The key to the study of style lies in semantics."
CP 23, 200: "clear introduction to Halliday's views on language function," Halliday a pioneer in emphasizing function as well as structure in language analysis; *CJL* 21, 196–99; *DQR* 4, 81–85; *LSoc* 4, 247–53; *Choice* 18, 627.

396. Hamburger, Käte. 1973. *The Logic of Literature.* Trans. Marilynn Rose. Bloomington: Indiana UP. 369 pp. (*Die Logik der Dichtung,* 1957; 2nd rev. ed., Stuttgart: Klett, 1968. 284 pp.)
MLR 53, 449–50, and 57, 1–11 (1st ed.); 65, 684–85 (2nd rev. ed.): focuses on the completely rewritten section on lyrical poetry in a generally favorable rev.; Bronzwaer, *Tense in the Novel*; *RM* 28, 123; *Choice* 10, 1376; *LJ* 98, 70.

397. Ingarden, Roman. 1973. *The Cognition of the Literary Work of Art.* Trans. Ruth Crowley and Kenneth Olson. Evanston: Northwestern UP. 436 pp. (Orig. Polish title: *O poznawaniu dzieła literackiego,* 1973. Pub. in a rev. and enl. form in Ger. as *Vom Erkennen des literarischen Kunstwerks,* 1968. This Eng. trans. is based on the Ger. version.)
"*The Literary Work of Art* and *The Cognition of the Literary Work of Art* are companion pieces in establishing certain fundamental principles for dealing with literature as an object of knowledge" (introd.).
JAAC 33, 220: "an important book" about "how to read," excellent trans.; *RM* 28, 554; *LJ* 99, 1390; *Choice* 11, 960.

398. Ingarden, Roman. 1973. *The Literary Work of Art: An Investigation on the Borderlines of Ontology, Logic, and the Theory of Literature.* Trans. George Grabowicz. Evanston: Northwestern UP. 415 pp. (*Das literarische Kunstwerk,* 1931; *O dziele literackim,* 1960.)
An investigation of "the basic structure and the mode of existence of the literary work." Part 1 delimits the topic; part 2 discusses the structure (e.g., stratifica-

tion); part 3, miscellaneous subjects (e.g., drama and film). 2 substantial introds. interpret the book. Bib. of Ingarden's works, 1915–71; name and term index 10 pp.

Strzetelski, *Some Problems of Short Fiction*: Ingarden's work is "the most rounded off, precise, subtle and elegant theory yet known. . . . His analysis of the literary work of art has put the whole field of literary studies into philosophical order" (7); Martínez-Bonati, *Fictive Discourse and the Structures of Literature*: Ingarden "does not see" that individual reading experiences change the structure of the work (99); *JAAC* 33, 217–20; *RM* 28, 555–56.

399.   Jacobs, Roderick. 1973. *Studies in Language: Introductory Readings in Transformational Linguistics*. Lexington: Xerox. 166 pp.

1 ch. on stylistics.

400.   Jakobson, Roman. 1973. *Questions de poétique* [Problems of Poetics]. Paris: Seuil. 507 pp.

A collection of linguistic analyses of literature dating from 1919 to 1972, divided into 2 groups. The first section contains essays written between 1919 and 1937 on the theory of literature and art and on certain authors (Puskin, Pasternak, et al.). The second section is organized around the theme of the poetry of grammar: 4 theoretical studies followed by analyses of 10 poems. Glossary of proper names. No bib. or index.

TLS 25 May 1973, 591: "remarkable consistency," "monumental . . . achievement."

401.   Koch, Walter. 1973. *Das Textem: Gesammelte Aufsätze zur Sememaтik des Texts*. Hildesheim: Olms. 229 pp.

BL (1973), 939.

402.   Kopperschmidt, Josef. 1973. *Allgemeine Rhetorik* [General Rhetoric]. Stuttgart: Kohlhammer. 216 pp.

Style 10, 212–13: "a theoretical treatment of rhetoric and persuasion . . . the *constitutive* rules of rational, persuasive discourse," "significant and scholarly."

403.   Le Guern, Michel. 1973. *Sémantique de la métaphore et de la métonymie* [The Semantics of Metaphor and Metonymy]. Paris: Larousse. 117 pp.

An explanation and defense of Jakobson's distinction of metaphor and metonymy.

Style 8, 92–94: "does not seriously challenge the work of the Liège Group," the "second part of the book . . . might best be overlooked"; *BL* (1976), 3005.

404.   Martín, José L. 1973. *Crítica estilística*. Introd. Helmut Hatzfeld. Madrid: Gredos. 410 pp.
BL (1975), 2974; (1976), 3013.

405.   Moore, Arthur. 1973. *Contestable Concepts of Literary Criticism*. Baton Rouge: Louisiana State UP. 241 pp.
A search for a verifiable criticism. The contestable concepts are sincerity, the identity of poet and poetic speaker; rhetoric, universal intelligibility; the popular ballad; form; and seer writing. In the final ch. he explains his view of literature as an indeterminate verbal object. Name and term index.
Centrum 1, 166–69: fails to work out his notion of literature sufficiently; *JAAC* 33, 108: "clear and suggestive," "informed by wide range of reference."

406.   Oomen, Ursula. 1973. *Linguistische Grundlagen poetischer Texte* [Basic Linguistic Concepts of Literary Texts]. Tübingen: Niemeyer. 132 pp.
Designed for the undergraduate classroom; discusses metaphor, repetition, the use of linguistic concepts in teaching, etc.
AUMLA 47, 119–20: "more explanation of linguistic concepts" needed; *BL* (1977), 3341.

407.   Sanders, Willy. 1973. *Linguistische Stiltheorie: Probleme, Prinzipien, und Moderne Perspektiven des Sprachstils* [Linguistic Theory of Style: Problems, Principles, and Modern Perspectives of Style]. Kleine Vandenhoeck-Reihe 1386. Göttingen: Vandenhoeck. 149 pp.
Style 9, 213–15: an outline of "the basic issues involved in working out any linguistic theory of style"; complements Enkvist's *Linguistic Stylistics*; but 149 pp. "is hardly sufficient for Sanders to cover his subject adequately," *BL* (1977), 3387.

408.   Schmidt, Siegfried. 1973. *Texttheorie: Probleme einer Linguistik der sprachlichen Kommunikation*. Munich: Fink. 184 pp.
Presents a "pragmalinguistic" model of text analysis in which a text is a communicative action game composed of linguistic communicative acts. [See Richard Watts, no. 1427.]
Paideia 29, 111.

409.   Turner, G. W. 1973. *Stylistics*. Harmondsworth: Penguin. 256 pp.
The grammarian isolates forms and constructions, establishes norms, and provides a coherent theory of norm and variation. Style is "what grammar leaves out," i.e., individual performance, "the purpose and circumstances and detailed particularity of speech." Literary language is "language in context, words in relation to other words. Each detail of a literary work takes its quality from the whole work. . . . [S]tylistics is that part of linguistics which concentrates upon variation in the use of language and upon comparing vari-

ations, relating them to contexts and observing patterns." Ch. 1, "Language, Style and Situation"; chs. 2–4 descriptive: sounds, syntax, vocabulary; chs. 5–8 explanatory: context, register, functions of language, use of stylistics. Bib. 2 pp.; name and term indexes.

Style 10, 79–81: "a popular introduction to stylistics," "lucidly" presented, though in the nature of introductions sometimes inadequately developed and supported; *Ling* 169, 92–94: "agrees in every respect with the purpose of a survey on stylistics," although there are "problems," including his "prevailing idea" of style; *BSLP* 69, 71–73; *Lore&L* 2.2, 34–35; *DQR* 4, 187–89; *AS* 48, 274–76; *JC* 26, 223; *MLJ* 59, 69; *JQ* 54, 838.

410.   Ullmann, Stephen. 1973. *Meaning and Style: Collected Papers*. New York: Barnes. 175 pp.

Studies of semantics and stylistics and "their interrelations. It begins with a survey of current trends in semantics. . . . Next, three crucial problems of stylistics are explored," then "two aspects of Proust's attitude to language." The survey of semantics is newly published from 1971–72 lectures.

JLS 4, 124–25: "within its own imposed limits, a solid contribution to stylistics"; *Ling* 168, 109–12: "thought-provoking," "interesting," "useful"; *MLR* 71, 653–54; *BL* (1976), 3049.

411.   Uspenskij, Boris. 1973. *A Poetics of Composition: The Structure of the Artistic Text and Typology of a Compositional Form*. Trans. Valentina Zavarin and Susan Wittig. Berkeley: U of California P. 181 pp. (Orig. pub. in Russ., 1970.)

A typological study of point of view, its functions on various "planes" of a text and in various types of literary and artistic compositions. Point of view is expressed on 4 planes (chs. 1–4): ideological, phraseological, spatiotemporal, and psychological. The phraseological plane involves diction and the characters' idiolects. Ch. 5 deals with interrelations of different levels. Chs. 6–7 add further complexities (e.g., the object of description). Name and term index.

Style 10, 274–77: "a "useful" synthesis and "clearly" illustrated" but "far from exhaustive," and he "represents the audience as generally passive"; *BA* 49, 804; *JLS* 5, 31–37, and 6, 91–93; *CL* 27, 357–60; *MLR* 67, 713–16.

412.   Vološinov, V. N. 1973. *Marxism and the Philosophy of Language*. Trans. Ladislav Matejka and I. R. Titunik. New York: Seminar. 205 pp. (Orig. pub. 1929; 2nd ed., 1930; rpt. 1972.)

A philosopher of language examines the history and presuppositions of linguistics as a science, and especially of linguistic schools, in order to propose a synthesis and a program for the future. 2 interpretive apps. by the translators. Name and term index.

Style 8, 535–43: "one of the best general introductions to linguistic study as a whole"; *RSQ* 4, 14–17: "perhaps the major contribution of the pre-Marxist (pre-Stalinist) period of Soviet linguistics"; *SILTA* 6, 401–03 (rev. of Russ. ed.); *LeL* 3, 174–79.

413.   Zajicek, Jacques. 1973. *Etudes stylistiques comparatives: Neerlandais-français* [Comparative Stylistic Studies: Netherland-French]. The Hague: Mouton. 319 pp.
EG 29, 501–03.

414.   Asmuth, Bernhard, and Luise Berg-Ehlers. 1974. *Stilistik*. Opladen: Westdeutscher. 178 pp. (2nd ed. 1978.)
BL (1975), 2921.

415.   Booth, Wayne. 1974. *A Rhetoric of Irony*. Chicago: U of Chicago P. 294 pp.
An effort to "offer reflections on how one properly argues" about the issues of irony—how one determines the cues of irony and how ironic meanings are transferred from author to reader. The book begins with irony in discursive prose and moves through drama and poetry to fiction, most of the discussion dealing with "stable irony." Bib. 6 pp.; name and term index.
    Style 9, 216–18: "a first rate critical intelligence," "a voice of sanity," "subtle and profound"; *P&R* 8, 123–29; *SCN* 33, 26–27; *CCC* 26, 89–91; *CE* 37, 99–101; *AQ* 31, 367–69; *JGE* 26, 333–41; *JAAC* 33, 361–63; *NCF* 30, 511–13; *SR* 83, xxxiv, xxxvi, xxxviii; *Diacritics* 6.2, 15–21 (rev. article); *ELN* 13, 232–38; *YCGL* 25, 86–90; *MFS* 22, 315–21; *SHR* 10, 378–79; *EIC* 26, 83–90.

416.   Brainerd, Barron. 1974. *Weighing Evidence in Language and Literature: A Statistical Approach*. Toronto: U of Toronto P. 276 pp.
An introd. to statistics for students of language and style. The first 6 chs. present the theories and techniques. The last ch. studies article and pronoun use, distribution of syllables per word, and lexico-statistics. Bib. 4 pp.; name and term index.
    Style 11, 407–09: "The linguist, humanist, or statistician looking for a book to use in classes on style or language will find this a useful text"; *RRL* 22, 114–15; *CHum* 11, 323–24; *FMLS* 12, 371.

417.   Brandi, Cesare. 1974. *Teoria generale della critica* [A General Theory of Criticism]. Torino: Einaudi. 392 pp.
In 2 parts: analysis of semiosis and art and examination of art as manifested by different modes of perception.
    Diacritics 5.3, 16–23.

418.   Broekman, Jan. 1974. *Structuralism: Moscow-Prague-Paris*. Trans. Jan Beekman and Brunhilde Helm. Dordrecht: Reidel. 117 pp. (*Strukturalismus: Moskau, Prag, Paris*. Munich: Aller, 1971. 174 pp.)

Ch. 1 explains the "structuralist endeavour"; the next 3 chs. trace the development of structuralist thought from Moscow through Prague to Paris; and the final ch. explains "What Is Structuralistic Philosophizing." Bib. 5 pp.; name and term indexes.

419.   Bruno, Agnes. 1974. *Toward a Quantitative Methodology for Stylistic Analyses*. Berkeley: U of California P. 65 pp.
An exploratory study of the value of selected statistics for the study of high- and low-formulaic stanzas in the *Nibelungenlied*, illustrating techniques "that have wider application in stylostatistical analyses." Bib. 5 pp.
Style 10, 300–02: "has explored some potentially useful directions for a definitive study" with "care and thoroughness"; *QJS* 62, 329.

420.   Ellis, John. 1974. *The Theory of Literary Criticism: A Logical Analysis*. Berkeley: U of California P. 274 pp.
"Theoretical analysis is, of its very nature, a logical inquiry. . . . for whatever the field of inquiry, its theoretical problems can be resolved only by carefully controlled conceptual analysis." Ch. 2, "The Definition of Literature"; ch. 3, "The Aims of the Study of Literature"; etc. Bib. 8 pp.; name index.
YR 64, 606–12: "a coherent and recommendable theory."

421.   Enkvist, Nils E. 1974. *Stilforskning och stilteori* [History and Theory of Style]. Lund: Gleerup. 211 pp.
Style 9, 103–07: not a translation of *Linguistic Stylistics* but "a Swedish equivalent" containing in addition a condensed history of stylistics and written with "admirable clarity."

422.   Heath, Stephen. 1974. *Le vertige du déplacement: Lecture de Barthes* [The Dizziness of Displacement: A Reading of Barthes]. Paris: Fayard. 214 pp.
TLS 30 Aug 1974, 934: "intelligent," "remarkable achievement" for those interested in Barthes's work.

423.   Hymes, Dell. 1974. *Foundations in Sociolinguistics: An Ethnographic Approach*. Philadelphia: U of Pennsylvania P. 245.
Part 2, "The Status of Linguistics as a Science," contains a rev. of K. Burke's *Language as Symbolic Action* that discovers "underlying parallels . . . between Burke's work and recent trends in linguistics." Part 3 is about "Linguistics as Sociolinguistics." Bib. 21 pp.; name and term indexes.

424.   Lanham, Richard. 1974. *Style: An Anti-Textbook*. New Haven: Yale UP. 142 pp.
This book "argues that the premises from which the study of composition now departs — clarity, plainness, sincerity — are incomplete and seriously mis-

leading. It suggests alternative premises and an alternative pedagogy." This is "a counterstatement to the textbooks now in use." Bib. "Note" 7 pp.

SR 82, lxxiv: "flawed but vital work," "grand but questionable purposes"; *Centrum* 2, 87–89; *NYTBR* 25 Aug 1974, 28; *HM* 248, 94.

425.   Leech, Geoffrey. 1974. *Semantics*. Harmondsworth: Penguin. 286 pp.
A rev. of previous scholarship and a presentation of a theory that distinguishes among conceptual, associative, and thematic meaning, with the main emphasis on conceptual. The book divides into 2 parts, with ch. 5 acting as a bridge: chs. 1–4 offer a general introd.; chs. 6–14 present the semantic theory. Bib. 18 pp.; name and term index.

Style 10, 306–10: "intelligent as well as original"; "Readers primarily interested in style will find much to think about . . . especially his discussion of lexical innovation, subordinating parts of messages, and thematic meaning"; *Semiotica* 26, 151–80 (rev. article); *Ling* 201, 90–92; 202, 69–73; *Anglia* 95, 177–79.

426.   Müller, Günther. 1974. *Morphologische Poetik: Gesammelte Aufsätze* [Morphological Poetics: Collected Essays]. Tübingen: Niemeyer. 590 pp.
18 essays spanning 30 years (the latest 1954), divided into 3 groups: introd., theoretical essays, and interpretations.

427.   Patillon, Michel. 1974. *Précis d'analyse littéraire: 1. Structures et techniques de la fiction* [Manual of Literary Analysis: 1. Structures and Techniques of the Illusion]. Paris: Nathan. 144 pp.
A manual for the students of the "premier cycle" based on recent research (Jakobson, Genette, Benveniste, Todorov, et al.), into literary "fiction." The book is divided into 4 parts—"Who Speaks?" "Who Sees?" "Illusions," and "Constructions"—and each part follows the same procedure: examination of texts, theory, application. Bib. 2 pp.

428.   Pfeiffer, Karl. 1974. *Sprachtheorie, Wissenschaftstheorie und das Problem der Textinterpretation: Untersuchungen am Beispiel des "New Criticism" und Paul Valérys* [Language Theory, Critical Theory and the Problem of Text Interpretation: Investigation and Illustration of the "New Criticism" and Paul Valéry]. Amsterdam: Rodopi. 429 pp.
An analysis of 2 opposing views of language, that of New Criticism and that of Valéry—the objective and the situational views—with discussion of many twentieth-century interpretive theorists (Ingarden, Husserl, et al.).

MLR 72, 378–79: "absorbing"; *BL* (1975), 2984; (1979), 2746.

429.   Quirk, Randolph. 1974. *The Linguist and the English Language*. New York: St. Martin's. 181 pp.
12 essays on a wide range of literary and language subjects, including "Charles

Dickens, Linguist," "a conflation, revision and expansion" of earlier essays
pub. in 1959 and 1961. Name and term index.
Style 11, 80–81: "excellent and suggestive Dickens paper," "rare combination of solidity and vision" in the vol.; *Ling* 213, 95–96; *JL* 14, 124; *RES* 26,
365–66; *ES* 57, 270–71; *YES* 6, 202–04.

430.   Riesel, Elise. 1974. *Theorie und Praxis der linguostilistischen Textin-
        terpretation.* Moscow: Hochschule. 182 pp.
BL (1975), 2988.

431.   Scholes, Robert. 1974. *Structuralism in Literature: An Introduction.* New
        Haven: Yale UP. 223 pp.
An introd. to European critical thinking particularly on narrative, but no discussion of Derrida, Lacan, or Foucault or of film. Structuralism is treated as
a "distinct discipline" separate from semiotics. Structuralism "seeks to establish a model of the system of literature itself. . . . At the heart of the idea
of structuralism is the idea of system." Chs. 1 and 2 on Saussure and Jakobson and others; ch. 3 on the taxonomies of Jolles and Souriau; ch. 4 on many
approaches to fiction; ch. 5 on Todorov, Barthes, Genette; last ch. tries to
pull all together. Annotated bib. 17 pp.; name and term index.
Style 10, 268–70: "manic eclecticism"; "in the end we are left with . . .
a pile of elements that have still to be ordered"; *Diacritics* 5.2, 19–23; *Centrum* 2, 73–83 (compares the book to Culler's *Structuralist Poetics*); *JEGP*
73, 459; *MLQ* 36, 193. [*Humanities Index* identifies many revs.]

432.   Silk, M. S. 1974. *Interaction in Poetic Imagery with Special Reference
        to Early Greek Poetry.* Cambridge: Cambridge UP. 263 pp.
A mainly taxonomic study of metaphor that seeks "to relate and differentiate between particular instances in terms of various . . . provisional categories," using examples chiefly from the original Gk. Bib. 5 pp.; 3 indexes: Gk.
words, passages, and names and terms.
Style 10, 203–08: "all but inaccessible to any reader with little Latin and
less Greek" and "ignores most recent work in linguistics," but offers "some
useful extension of Richards' tenor-and-vehicle approach," and "his concept
of 'interaction' is a useful addition to the stylistic lexicon"; *REG* 89, 117–18;
Phoenix 31, 364–66; *CPh* 72, 146–59 (rev. article).

433.   Smith, Charles K. 1974. *Styles and Structures: Alternative Approaches
        to College Writing.* New York: Norton. 436 pp.
Based on the idea of "alternative" patterns of writing as modes for different
ways of thinking and perceiving, the book presents diverse methods of com-
posing within each mode, concluding with a "rhetoric of reperception."
Style 17, 63–64: a significant context for teaching writing, but the author
applies concepts of style and styles carelessly.

434. Spillner, Bernd. 1974. *Linguistik und Literaturwissenschaft: Stilforschung, Rhetorik, Textlinguistik* [Linguistics and Literary Criticism: Stylistics, Rhetoric, and Text Linguistics]. Stuttgart: Kohlhammer. 147 pp.

An analysis of the theoretical and methodological problems involved in various approaches to style (rhetoric and text linguistics subsidiary topics). Bib. (616 items).

Style 11, 73–75: "a good introduction to the problems involved in working out a descriptive model for stylistic analysis"; *BL* (1977), 3412; (1979), 2761.

435. Stacy, R. H. 1974. *Russian Literary Criticism: A Short History*. Syracuse: Syracuse UP. 267 pp.

Ch. 8 on the formalists, ch. 9 on Marxist and Soviet criticism. Brief "Suggested Reading" follows each ch. Name and term index.

Choice 12, 690: "fills a major gap."

436. Wetherill, P. M. 1974. *The Literary Text: An Examination of Critical Methods*. Berkeley: U of California P. 331 pp.

An introductory survey of "the main lines of thinking which relatively advanced criticism has adopted" (in France, Britain, and the U.S.), though he has not attempted "a systematic formulation of the links between linguistics and literary criticism." The book is arranged inductively and "in order of increasing importance" and "increasing complexity": part 1, "Sounds" (and rhythm), "Grammar," "Meaning I: Words," "Meaning II" (semantics), "Style," "Counting"; part 2, "Construction," "Sequence," "Conclusions." Bib. 43 pp. (786 refs.); name and term index.

Style 10, 214–16: "best . . . linguistically based introduction . . . for the graduate level," "contributes significantly to the very recent effort . . . to synthesize various national theories and approaches"; *JAAC* 34, 501: "the book is to be praised for its judicious assessment of the works of recent . . . critics," "Special praise is due his chapter on style"; *BA* 49, 866; *MFS* 22, 315–21.

437. Yllera, A. 1974. *Estilística, poética y semiótica literaria* [Stylistics, Literary Poetics, and Semiotics]. Madrid: Alianza. 186 pp.
BL (1976), 3058.

438. Abraham, Werner. 1975. *A Linguistic Approach to Metaphor*. Lisse: Peter de Ridder. 54 pp.

A logical, syntactic, and semantic approach: "The concept of metaphorical meaning . . . is developed by integrating both the meaning postulate approach (Carnap) and the componential approach (which plays a decisive role in the semantic theory introduced by Katz and Fodor)."

Style 10, 203–08: "while nothing . . . is startlingly new (save, perhaps, the argument based on retrieval systems), he does pull together some important ideas" for "an advanced seminar on style"; *SLang* 1, 455–59; *Lingua* 38, 359–62; *MLR* 74, 388.

439.   Bloom, Harold. 1975. *A Map of Misreading*. New York: Oxford UP. 206 pp.
"This book offers instruction in the practical criticism of poetry, in how to read a poem, on the basis of the theory of poetry set forth" in *The Anxiety of Influence*.
     Diacritics 7.3, 44–52; *Centrum* 6, 32–49 (2 general rev. articles).

440.   Culler, Jonathan. 1975. *Structuralist Poetics: Structuralism, Linguistics and the Study of Literature*. Ithaca: Cornell UP. 301 pp.
Criticism should pursue not more interpretations of individual works but the deconstruction of conventions of meaning, the analysis of modes of signification in order to understand them, ourselves, and our culture. We need not only a grammar of texts but a grammar of reading, a theory of literary "competence." 11 chs. are divided into 3 parts: "Structuralism and Linguistic Models" (langue, parole, Jakobson, etc.), "Poetics" (competence, genre models, lyric novel), and "Perspectives." Bib. 20 pp.; name and topic index. [James Russell Lowell Prize for an Outstanding Book by an MLA Member, 1975.]
     Style 10, 264–67: "a superb prolegomena" with "rare clarity of discourse" and "breadth of literary understanding"; Lentricchia, *After the New Criticism*: Culler so compromises structuralism in traditional ways as to have created something else (104ff.); *Diacritics* 6.1, 23–26: a "cogent redefinition of the basic orientation" of the "project of a renewed attention to texts"; *Lingua* 46, 383–87; *ES* 58, 174–82; *PTL* 1, 197–202; *RES* 27, 513–15; *MLR* 71, 877–79; *Lang&S* 9, 213–16; *KLit* 5, 51–52; *AUMLA* 46, 364–65.

441.   D'Angelo, Frank. 1975. *A Conceptual Theory of Rhetoric*. Cambridge: Winthrop. 183 pp.
A presentation of linguistic and rhetorical principles, including chs. on syntagmatic and paradigmatic structure and style and structure. Bib. 15 pp.; name and term index.
     Lang&S 13, 191: several topics need further clarification, but the book is "a stimulating blend of deduction, eclectic thinking, and practical applications"; *RSQ* 6, 29–33.

442.   Deimer, Günther. 1975. *Argumentative Dialoge: Ein Versuch zu ihrer sprachwissenschaftlichen Beschreibung* [Argumentative Dialogues: An Experiment in Linguistic Description]. Tübingen: Niemeyer. 162 pp.

443.   Eagleton, Terry. 1975. *Marxism and Literary Criticism*. London: Methuen. 88 pp.

A study of the "four central topics of Marxist criticism": literature and history, form and content, the writer and commitment, and the author as producer.

MLR 79, 151–53: a "cerebral, untested theory. . . . in virtual isolation from the objects of its application."

444.   Fleischer, Wolfgang, and Georg Michel. 1975. *Stilistik der deutschen Gegenwartssprache* [Stylistics of Contemporary German]. Leipzig: Bibliographisches Inst. 394 pp.
BL (1977), 8492.

445.   Deleted.

446.   Gadamer, Hans-Georg. 1975. *Truth and Method.* New York: Seabury. 576 pp. (Orig. *Wahrheit und Methode.* Tübingen: Mohr, 1960.)
Hermeneutics (the understanding and interpretation of texts) leads to knowledge and truth different from that derived from scientific investigation, which seeks to amass ratified knowledge. In contrast, hermeneutics is the investigation of art and historical traditions, not a methodology but an attempt to understand what the human sciences are within the totality of our experience of the world. Name and term indexes.
Diacritics 6.4, 2–9.

447.   Garrido Gallardo, Manuel. 1975. *Introducción a la teoría de la literatura* [Introduction to the Theory of Literature]. Madrid: Soc. General Española de Librería. 168 pp.
BL (1977), 3310.

448.   Guiraud, Pierre. 1975. *Semiology.* Trans. George Gross. London: Routledge. 106 pp. (*La Sémiologie.* "Que sais-je?" Paris: PUF, 1971.)
A study of 3 aspects of semiology: nonlinguistic signals, forms of social communication (rites, etc.), and the arts and literature. Ch. 4 deals with "Aesthetic Codes." Bib. 1 p. (In the foreword Frank Kermode argues that "linguistics will provide a model both for the more general science" of the life of signs in society and "for procedures appropriate to its other departments.")
SocR 23, 930.

449.   Hartman, Geoffrey. 1975. *The Fate of Reading and Other Essays.* Chicago: U of Chicago P. 352 pp.
The first group of essays deals with "psychoaesthetics," the second with literary history, the third with changes in the canon and in conventions or habits of reading, and the fourth with "position papers." Name and term indexes.

JAAC 35, 252: "interesting collection of essays which bears the characteristic impress of insightfulness of the author" yet does not extend the concerns of his previous work, *Beyond Formalism*; *YR* 65, 88; *GaR* 30, 736; *PQ* 55, 260; *SR* 85, 153; *PR* 44, 131; *HR* 28, 601; *WHR* 29, 382.

450.   Hiatt, Mary P. 1975. *Artful Balance, the Parallel Structure of Style*. New
        York: Teacher's CP. 192 pp.
A study of parallel structures in selections from the Brown U Corpus for the purpose of searching for a formal model. 13 chs.; bib. 2 pp.; 5 apps.
    Style 11, 410–11: "commendation is due . . . for giving us a detailed picture of parallel structures"; *CE* 44, 858: "Hiatt's book should have changed the theory and practice of the [teaching] profession regarding coordination and parallelism."

451.   Howell, Wilbur S. 1975. *Poetics, Rhetoric, and Logic: Studies in the
        Basic Disciplines of Criticism*. Ithaca: Cornell UP. 267 pp.
A collection of 8 essays pub. over the last 30 years (1946–74), with a new 27-pp. introd. Name and term index. [Awarded the $1,000 Book Prize by the Speech Communication Assn., 1976.]
    Style 10, 209–11: "Brought together . . . these essays may begin to make the impact that they should have made"; *QJS* 61, 454–59: an attack on the book; *RSQ* 6, 55–57: a reply, describing Howell as "a great thinker on rhetoric"; *QJS* 62, 62–77: Burke vs. Howell; *ELN* 15, 227–29; *MLR* 73, 369.

452.   Kloepfer, Rolf. 1975. *Poetik und Linguistik: Semiotische Instrumente*
        [Poetics and Linguistics: Instruments of Semiotics]. Munich: Fink. 194
        pp.
BL (1977), 3337; (1978), 2535.

453.   Köller, Wilhelm. 1975. *Semiotik und Metapher: Untersuchungen zur
        grammatischen Struktur und kommunikativen Funktion von Metaphern*
        [Semiotics and Metaphor: Studies in Grammatical Structure and Communicative Function of Metaphors]. Stuttgart: Metzler. 388 pp.

454.   Orsini, Gian. 1975. *Organic Unity in Ancient and Later Poetics: The
        Philosophical Foundations of Literary Criticism*. Carbondale: Southern
        Illinois UP. 120 pp.
Focuses on the origins of the concept in Plato and Aristotle. Considers "organic unity" the central issue in literary criticism. Bib. 3 pp.; name index.
    JAAC 35, 248: "laudable" project but "disappointing" product, no more than "preliminary help"; *Choice* 13, 217: "lucid" and a "valuable philosophical introduction" but "no substitute (and does not pretend to be)" for Grube's *The Greek and Roman Critics* or McKeon's *Critics and Criticism*; *LJ* 101, 530.

455.   Pasternack, Gerhard. 1975. *Theoriebildung in der Literaturwissenschaft: Einführung in Grundfragen des Interpretationspluralismus* [The Formation of Theories in Literary Criticism: An Introduction to Basic Issues of Pluralism in Interpretation]. Munich: Fink. 303 pp.

456.   Plett, Heinrich. 1975. *Textwissenschaft und Textanalyse: Semiotik, Linguistik, Rhetorik* [Text Criticism and Analysis: Semiotic, Linguistic, Rhetoric]. Heidelberg: Quelle. 354 pp.
   On the interdisciplinary study of literature based on linguistic theory. *DaF* 13, 304.

457.   Riesel, Elise, and E. Schendels. 1975. *Deutsche Stilistik* [German Stylistics]. Moscow: Hochschule. 315 pp.

458.   Said, Edward. 1975. *Beginnings: Intention and Method*. New York: Basic. 432 pp.
   A defense of "beginnings" in human imagination and will in contrast to absolute "origins." Ch. 3, "The Novel as Beginning Intention."
   Style 11, 82–83: "not at all clear . . . just what Said aims to show or prove, though individual passages are lucid and sometimes brilliant"; *MLR* 73, 582–85: "a manuscript in search of an editor" but "always able to surprise with a striking comment"; *ECS* 1, 282–83; *Novel* 10, 185–88; *BA* 50, 727–28; *GaR* 30, 736–44.

459.   Segre, Cesare. 1975. *Semiotics and Literary Criticism*. The Hague: Mouton. 195 pp. (*I segni e la critica: Fra strutturalismo e semiologia*. Torino: Einaudi, 1969).
   An appraisal of new approaches to literature that developed in the 1960s, especially in France, Italy, and the Soviet Union, in the process rejecting Fr. structuralism (the "nouvelle critique") as antihumanistic in its denial of author and meaning. Segre opposes to this structuralism a semiotic stylistics divided into 2 parts—a stylistics of invention and a stylistics of communication. The book develops from a discussion of structuralism to a synthesis to 5 studies of contemporary authors (none Eng.-speaking—Antonio Machado, et al.).
   Style 10, 281–90: more "discriminating" than J. Culler on the "nouvelle critique"; the 5 essays on authors are a "weakness" because written before Segre's critical synthesis; *PTL* 2, 403–09.

460.   Widdowson, H. G. 1975. *Stylistics and the Teaching of Literature*. London: Longman. 128 pp.
   Defines stylistics as "the study of literary discourse from a linguistics orientation," "a way of mediating between two *subjects*: English language and literature." The linguist studies literature as "*text*," the literary critic "treats literary

works as *messages*," and the stylistic critic "treats literature as *discourse*." Bib.
2 pp.; name and term index.
  Choice 13, 656: "useful" to "sophisticated scholar-teachers and scholar-
teachers-in-the-making"; *PTL* 1, 598–99.

461.   Adam, Jean-Michel, and Jean Goldenstein. 1976. *Linguistique et dis-
        cours littéraire* [Literary Linguistics and Discourse]. Paris: Larousse. 351
        pp.
Explains various (especially Fr.) theories.

462.   Bayley, John. 1976. *The Uses of Division: Unity and Disharmony in Liter-
        ature*. New York: Viking. 248 pp.
A study of "the involuntary divisions, amounting to a total disunity, which
seems to characterize" the art of the writers discussed in the book.
  SR 85, xvi: "erudite, deft, and civilized," "perceptive and often fascinating," yet "the usefulness of his criticism lies in doubt"; *Spec* 236, 24; *TLS*
23 July 1976, 914; *NYRB* 24, 33.

463.   Brütting, Richard. 1976. *"Écriture" und "Texte": Die französische Liter-
        aturtheorie "nach dem Strukturalismus"* ["Écriture" and "Texte": French
        Literary Theory "after Structuralism"]. Bonn: Bouvier. 217 pp.

464.   Bureau, Conrad. 1976. *Linguistique fonctionnelle et stylistique objec-
        tive* [Functional Linguistics and Objective Stylistics]. Paris: PUF. 264 pp.
Style is the operation of strategically chosen superposed codes. Bureau focuses here on the strategic uses of syntactic structures.
  MLR 74, 389: "a practical exercise in stylistic analyses" that seeks to describe a style objectively without considering effects; the reviewer expresses
skepticism regarding this intention; *Pensée* 193, 145–46; *FM* 46, 179–81; *BL*
(1977), 3270; Hervey, *Semiotic Perspective* 219–27.

465.   Eagleton, Terry. 1976. *Criticism and Ideology: A Study in Marxist Literary
        Theory*. New York: Schocken. 191 pp.
An attempt "to construct a materialist aesthetics" in 5 chs.: "Mutations of
Critical Ideology" (on the history of criticism), "Categories for a Materialist
Criticism" (the major constituents of a Marxist theory of literature), "Towards
a Science of the Text" (the relations of the text to ideology and history), etc.
Name index.
  Choice 14, 673: "the 34-year old author's fifth and most remarkable vol-
ume," "indispensable"; *Enc* 49, 90; *TLS* 20 May 1977, 606; *LJ* 102, 495.

466.   Eco, Umberto. 1976. *A Theory of Semiotics*. Bloomington: Indiana UP.
        354 pp.

An account and a critique of sign theory, i.e., the idea that the world is a material reality shaped into systems by cultural conventions that generate communication. Ch. 1 surveys the field of semiotics; ch. 2 offers a model of communication; ch. 3 elaborates and clarifies terms and concepts; ch. 4 presents a typology of modes of sign production. Bib. 26 pp.; name and term indexes. [Cf. Phelan, no. 735.]

N&Q 26, 163–65: "remarkable achievement"; *FI* 11, 409–16 (rev. article); *PTL* 2, 367–83 (rev. article), 385–96 (rev. article); *Diacritics* 7.3, 54–63; 10.1, 50–59; *LeS* 11, 643–46; *SR* 87, 628–38; Fokkema and Kunne-Ibsch consider the book important.

467.   Gutwinski, Waldemar. 1976. *Cohesion in Literary Texts: A Study of Some Grammatical and Lexical Features of English Discourse.* The Hague: Mouton. 183 pp.
Chs. 1–3 provide theory; chs. 4 and 5 compare the density and variety of ties in short passages from Henry James and Hemingway. Bib. 8 pp.; name and term index.

Ling, spec. issue (1978), 339–46: "not really a contribution on cohesion or on James and Hemingway or on the English language, but a demonstration of how different features of cohesion . . . may interact in a text, another example, that is, of what linguistics *can* do for the study of literature"; *Lore&L* 2, 129.

468.   Halliday, M. A. K. 1976. *Halliday: System & Function in Language.* Ed. G. R. Kress. London: Oxford UP. 250 pp.
"[A] selection from about 90 books, articles, reviews, lectures and working papers, many unpublished. It contains none of Halliday's papers on language teaching, stylistics, sociolinguistics, applied linguistics." Bib. 2 pp.; a list of Halliday's pub. books and articles; name and term index.

JLS 8, 36–41: "the papers and their introduction fail the reader primarily in two ways," but they "move towards" the solution of the problems posed, and Halliday has elsewhere attempted their solution "with greater illumination."

469.   Halliday, M. A. K., and Ruqaiya Hasan. 1976. *Cohesion in English.* London: Longman. 374 pp.
"Cohesive relations are relations between two or more elements in a text that are independent of structure; for example, between a personal pronoun and an antecedent proper name, such as John . . . he." The book explains 5 types of "ties": reference, substitution, ellipsis, conjunction, and lexis. Bib. 10 pp.; term index.

Style 14, 47–50: "important new tools," "seminal," "a solid base for the development of more finely tuned systems for particular stylistic analysis"; *JAZA* 16, 77–80; *SS* 40, 59–69; *Lang* 154, 676–78; *AUMLA* 49, 155–57; *Lingua* 45,

333–54 (rev. article); *ES* 58, 470–73; *BSL* 72, 256–59; *ZPSK* 32, 75–78; *N&Q*
25, 352–53; *EA* 32, 214; *RLV* 43, 103.

470.   Hardt, Manfred. 1976. *Poetik und Semiotik: Das Zeichensystem der
        Dichtung* [Poetics and Semiotics: The System of Signs in Literature].
        Tübingen: Niemeyer. 173 pp.
An introd. to a semiotics especially of the nonverbal features of literary works.
MLR 74, 129: "encouraging demonstrations . . . of the role semiotics might
play" within poetics.

471.   Hill, Archibald A. 1976. *Constituent and Pattern in Poetry*. Austin: U
        of Texas P. 157 pp.
A collection of revisions of 12 previously pub. articles (1951–74). All deal with
interpretation of short poems on the assumption that poems are verbal designs and from a conceptual model of the study of literary discourses as analo-
gous to linguistic study, specifically the taxonomic model of neo-Bloomfieldian
linguistics. [Analogy is also fundamental to Hill's approach to meaning.] The
essays are divided into 3 parts of 4 chs. each: part 1, definition of literature
and patterns; part 2, types of meaning and imagery; part 3, principles for
interpreting meaning. Name and term index.
Style 11, 415–19: "a clear, compact, and unified statement of Hill's major
ideas about the relation of linguistics to analysis and interpretation"; *SoQ*
15, 199–208; *Lang* 53, 728–29; *Choice* 13, 1288; *LJ* 101, 2065.

472.   Holenstein, Elmar. 1976. *Roman Jakobson's Approach to Language:
        Phenomenological Structuralism*. Trans. Catherine Schelbert and Tar-
        cisius Schelbert. Bloomington: Indiana UP. 215 pp. (*Jakobson ou le
        structuralisme phénoménologique*. Paris: Seghers, 1974.)
Chronological background, "Philosophical and Methodological Principles,"
and "Comprehensive Theory of Language" are the 3 main divisions of the
book. Bib. 15 pp.; name and term indexes.
Choice 14, 1042: "coherent comprehensive statement," lucid, "essential"
for "advanced programs in linguistics"; *LJ* 102, 494.

473.   Koch, Walter. 1976. *Textsemiotik und strukturelle Rezeptionstheorie*
        [Text Semiotics and Structural Receptions Theory]. Hildesheim: Olms.
        745 pp.
Attempts at description of different sign systems in literature using a socio-
semiotic approach. Koch's introd. gives the Ger. point of view on the subject,
c. 1975; other essays deal with poetry, drama, film, mass communication, advertising, and speech-act theory.
JLS 7, 123–25: "contributes in no small measure" to "theoretical discussion," but "a number of points of criticism . . . need to be made."

474.   Krieger, Murray. 1976. *Theory of Criticism: A Tradition and Its System*.
         Baltimore: Johns Hopkins UP. 250 pp.
         Part 1, "The Problem: The Limits and Capacities of Critical Theory"; part
         2, "The Humanistic Theoretical Tradition"; part 3, "A Systematic Extension."
         "[T]his volume uses its introductory section, in which I set up a general schema
         to account for a variety of theoretical undertakings, and its second section,
         in which I analyze exemplary theories drawn from the history of criticism,
         to move toward my own contribution" in part 3. His own theory is "fundamen-
         tally humanistic, in that at its center is man as the creator of forms." Name
         index.
         JAAC 35, 480: generally disappointing, yet 1 ch. "deserves to become a
         standard anthology piece"; *MFS* 23, 307; *Critm* 19, 275; *VQR* 54, 13; *SR* 85,
         115; *NR* 175, 27 and 30.

475.   Küper, Christoph. 1976. *Linguistische Poetik* [Linguistic Poetics]. Stutt-
         gart: Kohlhammer. 148 pp.

476.   Lotman, Juryj. 1976. *Analysis of the Poetic Text*. Ed. and trans. D. Bar-
         ton Johnson. Ann Arbor: Ardis. 309 pp. (*Analiz poèticeskogo teksta*.
         Leningrad: "Prosveščenie," 1972).
         Puts the theories outlined in his *Structure* to practical test. The "poetic text"
         is defined by its extraordinarily high semantic significance resulting from con-
         vergence of multiple systems. The book also offers an advocacy of the scien-
         tific study of literature. Part 1 sets forth general principles for a scientific literary
         semiotics and examines such issues as parallelism and recurrence. Part 2 pro-
         vides analysis of the dominant features of several Russ. poems. Chronological
         bib. of Lotman's works. Trans.'s introd., "The Structural Poetics of Yury Lot-
         man," where Lotman is described as "the preeminent figure in Soviet literary
         structuralism."
         Style 12, 71–72: "an important, even seminal book, providing a large num-
         ber of exciting integrative concepts," "the best introduction to Lotman's work";
         CL 30, 268; *FR* 50, 937; *TLS* 31 Dec. 1976, 1630; *WLT* 51, 118.

477.   Marino, Adrian. 1976. *Kritik der literarischen Begriffe* [Critique of Liter-
         ary Terms]. Trans. from Romanian by Bernd Kolf. Cluj-Napoca: Dacia.
         479 pp. (*Critica ideilor literare*. Cluj: Dacia, 1974).
         An attempt to present "a theoretical and methodological framework" able
         to deal with a "hundred problems," which he treats within "a specifically
         developed hermeneutic framework."
         JLS 8, 130–31: "an important and impressively well researched contribu-
         tion to the current debate on the terminology of literary criticism."

478.   Mooij, J. J. A. 1976. *A Study of Metaphor: On the Nature of Metaphor-
         ical Expressions*. Amsterdam: North-Holland. 196 pp.

Prevailing theories are divided into 2 major types based on the role played by reference—dualistic and monistic. Mooij's own approach is dualistic, distinguishing 3 varieties, which reflect the degree of strength of reference. Emphasis on literature. Bib. 6 pp.; name index.

Style 13, 385–87: "an excellent study"; *GRM* 29, 353–54; *BJA* 18, 286–87; *FdL* 18, 270–83 (rev. article).

479.   Mukařovský, Jan. 1976. *On Poetic Language.* Trans. John Burbank and Peter Steiner. Lisse: de Ridder. 88 pp. (Orig. pub. 1940.)

Also in *Structure, Sign, and Function.* On the functional nature of poetic language, sound, word, and semantic aspects. Glossary of Czech literary figures. Essay by Peter Steiner and Wendy Steiner on "The Relational Axes of Poetic Language." Name index.

BL (1976), 3025; (1979), 2739.

480.   Ricoeur, Paul. 1976. *Interpretation Theory: Discourse and the Surplus of Meaning.* Ft. Worth: Texas Christian UP. 107 pp.

Ch. 1, "Language as Discourse"; ch. 2, "Speaking and Writing"; ch. 3, "Metaphor and Symbol"; ch. 4, "Explanation and Understanding"; Conclusion (sociocultural and atemporal approaches to a literary text). Name and term index.

Style 14, 41–44: "abundance and richness of thought," "penetrating and forceful."

481.   Waugh, Linda. 1976. *Roman Jakobson's Science of Language.* Lisse: Peter de Ridder. 115 pp.

In 2 parts, Jakobson's general ideas and "specifics of structure." His work on language is "interwoven and interrelated by common threads, by certain overriding principles." Bib. 7 pp.; name and term index.

Choice 14, 1354: "compact and well-organized although the . . . examples are sometimes inadequate and the writing at times graceless"; the book contrasts to Holenstein's *Roman Jakobson's Approach to Language.*

482.   Weimann, Robert. 1976. *Structure and Society in Literary History: Studies in the History and Theory of Historical Criticism.* Charlottesville: UP of Virginia. 273 pp.

An attempt through a comprehensive historical methodology to present a systematic conception of literature as embedded in history: literary structures (verbal and ideational organization) are born of specific historical conditions. Ch. 1, theoretical issues; chs. 2–4, examinations of various concepts and methods of literary history; chs. 5–6, application: Shakespearean imagery and narrative perspective. Name index.

Style 11, 306–08: "Weimann writes remarkably clearly about difficult matters" and "he commands an astonishing erudition" and "an energetic spirit of critical inquiry," but so much space is devoted to discussion of earlier methods of literary history that "little space remains" for the author's own views; *CRCL* 5, 393–99; *CLIO* 6, 89–94; *CLS* 15, 351–52.

483.   Weinrich, Harald. 1976. *Sprache in Texten* [Language in Texts]. Stuttgart: Klett. 356 pp.
Style 15, 86–89: "The present volume is an assembly of Weinrich's papers composed in the years between 1958 and 1976, nearly all of them revised and unified under the notion of 'language *in texts*.' He discusses a breathtaking range of linguistic issues," "the reader is rewarded with new perspectives . . . and with an elegance of style and a humaneness of outlook"; *RPh* 32, 97–100; *RLR* 42, 208–09; *GL* 18, 47–53; *Kratylos* 21, 45–47; *ZFSL* 88, 178–83.

484.   Young, Thomas. 1976. *The New Criticism and After.* Charlottesville: UP of Virginia. 90 pp.
6 essays, assessments of J. C. Ransom and considerations of new directions in literary study.

485.   Anderegg, Johannes. 1977. *Literaturwissenschaftliche Stiltheorie* [Theory of Literary Style]. Göttingen: Vandenhoeck. 114 pp.
Style 15, 32–34: "about stylistics and the concept of style in general," presents an open view of style by rejecting specific concepts of style, though late in the book he defines style himself in a restrictive way. Bib. 4 pp.

486.   Barthes, Roland. 1977. *Image-Music-Text.* Trans. Stephen Heath. New York: Hill. 220 pp.
13 essays covering the period 1961–73, including "Rhetoric of the Image," "Introduction to the Structural Analysis of Narratives," and "From Work to Text." Name and term index.
JAAC 37, 235: "interesting supplement to other writings of this period," "excellent descriptions"; *MFS* 24, 612; *TLS* 9 Dec. 1977, 1443; *TES* 13 Jan. 1978, 18; *NS* 94, 514; *LJ* 103, 973.

486a.   Champagne, Roland. 1977. *Beyond the Structuralist Myth of Écriture.* Berlin: de Gruyter. 142 pp.
4 essays on 3 Fr. critics—Sollers, Kristeva, and Barthes (2 essays)—focusing especially on the controversy between structuralism and semiology. Bib. and index.
MLJ 63, 386: "fascinating reading for all who are interested in the advent of structuralism"; *WLT* 52, 701.

487.   Corno, Dario. 1977. *Il senso letterario: Note e lessico de semiotica della letteratura* [The Literary Sense: Notes and Dictionary of the Semiotic of Literature]. Torino: Giappichelli. 384 pp.

488.   Coulthard, Malcolm. 1977. *An Introduction to Discourse Analysis*. London: Longman. 195 pp.
"Discourse" is defined as "the total verbal process in its context situation."
A survey and integration of diverse theories and studies essential for the analysis of discourse—grammar, speech act, conversation, intonation, etc. Ch. 9 deals directly with literature. Bib. 7 pp.; name and term index.
Style 15, 83–86: even though "he cannot present a unified comprehensive method to replace the old ones" (e.g., the notion of "linguistics beyond the sentence"), the book deserves "an unqualified recommendation" because it is "an absolute prerequisite for a new orientation"; *Ling* 17, 352–53: a "very readable paraphrase of some of the important works in this area" but needs "a clearer definition of its scope and a closer scrutiny of methodological issues"; *QJS* 66, 450–60; *CJVS* 23, 45–47.

489.   Culler, Jonathan. 1977. *Ferdinand de Saussure*. Penguin Modern Masters. New York: Penguin. 140 pp.
An explanation and analysis of the works of "the father of modern linguistics." Chs. on "The Man and the *Course*," "Saussure's Theory of Language," "The Place of Saussure's Theories," and "Semiology: The Saussurian Legend." Annotated bib. 3 pp.; name and term index.
Style 13, 295–99: "Though Culler's book is flawed [the exaggeration of Saussure's revolutionary significance, the prominence given to the arbitrariness of language at the expense of motivation], it ought to lead . . . to deeper study"; *YR* 67, 106: "clear exposition," "excellent initiation"; *AA* 82, 821; *B* 74, 459; *LJ* 102, 1850; *JLS* 6, 112.

490.   Delas, Daniel. 1977. *Poétique/Pratique* [Poetics/Practice]. Paris: CEDIC. 173 pp.
A manual to introduce poetic analysis to Fr. lycée students, divided into 4 parts—13 concepts, 3 illustrative analyses of texts, a bibliographic survey of contemporary criticism (rhetoric, stylistics, structuralism, poststructuralism) and key passages from various contemporary critics. [See Patillon, nos. 427 and 507.]
Style 15, 498–99: "exemplary concision and clarity," "a fine textbook"; *FM* 47, 77–81.

491.   Dijk, Teun van. 1977. *Het Literatuuronderwijs op School: Een kritische analyse* [Teaching Literature at School: A Critical Analysis]. Amsterdam: van Gennep. 351 pp.
A discussion of literary instruction in Dutch secondary schools. Includes analyses of textbooks used on literary history and theory, the *l'art pour l'art* point of view now prevailing, etc.

492. Fokkema, D. W., and Elrud Kunne-Ibsch. 1977. *Theories of Literature in the Twentieth Century: Structuralism, Marxism, Aesthetics of Reception, Semiotics.* New York: St. Martin's. 219 pp.
The "search for a theory of literature" is a "condition of the scientific study of literary texts." This book intends to enable students of literature to "judge the foundations of their discipline" by presenting the "outlines of current theories of literature." Bib. 19 pp.; name index.
JLS 9, 46–48: "useful and informative"; *JAAC* 37, 236: "informative and balanced"; *Choice* 15, 1308; *LJ* 103, 1637; *CLS* 16, 183.

493. Foucault, Michel. 1977. *Language, Counter-Memory, Practice: Selected Essays and Interviews.* Trans. Donald Bouchard and Sherry Simon. Ithaca: Cornell UP. 240 pp.
Deals with language and literature—e.g., "Language to Infinity," "What Is an Author?"
BL (1977), 1235.

494. Gülich, Elisabeth. 1977. *Linguistische Textmodelle* [Linguistic Text Models]. Munich: Fink. 353 pp.
Expansion of the author's paper presented in 1972 under the title "Linguistische Textmodelle, Stand und Moglichkeiten."

495. Hawkes, Terence. 1977. *Structuralism and Semiotics.* New Accents Series. Berkeley: U of California P. 192 pp.
The "boundaries [of semiotics] (if it has any) are coterminous with those of structuralism," both included within the province of communication and, along with linguistics, leading to a poetics of writing and reading conceived as a system of conventions. Ch. 1, introd.: Vico, Piaget, structuralism; ch. 2, "Linguistics and Anthropology": Saussure, Amer. structural linguistics, Lévi-Strauss; ch. 3, "The Structures of Literature": Russ. formalism, European structural linguistics, Jakobson, Greimas, Todorov, Barthes; ch. 4, "A Science of Signs": structuralism and semiotics, Peirce, Saussure, Barthes; ch. 5, "New 'New Criticism' for Old 'New Criticism.'" Annotated bib. 25 pp.; name and term index.
JLS 7, 125: "informative," "successful"; *TLS* 14 Apr. 1978, 418: prefers a "more assertive, speculative and broad-based approach"; *N&Q* 26, 382–84; *AWR* 62, 126–29.

496. Hirsch, E. D., Jr. 1977. *The Philosophy of Composition.* Chicago: U of Chicago P. 200 pp.
Advocates the principle of "relative readability": "One prose style is better than another when it communicates the same meaning as the other does but requires less effort from the reader." Name and term index.

Style 14, 165–70: "Hirsch's central argument is invalid" but students of style "will find much of interest," especially in ch. 5, "The Psychological Bases of Reading"; *MLN* 95, 1181–202.

497.   Kerbrat-Orrecchioni, Catherine. 1977. *La connotation* [On Connotation]. Lyon: PU de Lyon. 254 pp.
A study of connotation by concepts derived from Saussure — signifier and signified, denotation-connotation, etc.
Style 15, 489–90: not a "definitive study on connotation," because crucial "references and suggestions are not followed up or developed systematically and extensively," but has "great value . . . in bringing together the many theories which touch on connotation"; *ZRP* 94, 1978; *BSLP* 74.2, 77–81; *FM* 47, 178–81.

498.   Lemaire, Anika. 1977. *Jacques Lacan*. Trans. David Macey. Boston: Routledge. 266 pp. (*Jacques Lacan*. Brussels: Charles Denart, 1970.)
The ideas of Lacan and his school and the relation between structuralism and psychoanalysis. Bib. 6 pp.; name and term index.
Choice 15, 468: "undecodable English"; *Enc* 50, 57; *TLS* 11 Aug. 1978, 909; *LJ* 103, 671.

499.   Levin, Samuel R. 1977. *The Semantics of Metaphor*. Baltimore: Johns Hopkins UP. 158 pp.
An analysis of the generation and interpretation of linguistically deviant expressions. Ch. 1, "Pragmatic Deviance"; Ch. 3, "Modes of Construal"; etc. Bib. 4 pp,; name and term index.
Style 14, 171–76: "a disappointment"; *Lingua* 48, 264–71; *JLS* 10, 54–56; *LSoc* 8, 281–84; *MLN* 92, 1190–94; *Semiotica* 25, 379–87 (rev. article).

500.   Lodge, David. 1977. *The Modes of Modern Writing: Metaphor, Metonymy, and the Typology of Modern Literature*. Ithaca: Cornell UP. 279 pp.
In part 1, fundamental questions such as What is literature? and What is realism? are applied to a wide range of literary texts. In part 2, a comprehensive typology of literary discourse is proposed based on the poles of metaphor and metonymy, again illustrated by texts. Part 3 examines various schools of modern writing and the works of selected major writers — Joyce, Stein, Hemingway, Lawrence, Woolf, Larkin. Name and term index.
YR 67, 254–59: "a very good" book, "bold and ambitious but always lucid and explicit"; *CL* 20, 369–76; *TLS* 13 Jan. 1978, 28.

501.   Lotman, Juryj. 1977. *The Structure of the Artistic Text*. Trans. Gail Lenhoff and Ronald Vroon. Ann Arbor: Dept. of Slavic Languages and Literatures, U of Michigan. 300 pp. (*Struktura xudožestvennogo teksta*. Moscow: "Iskusstvo," 1970.)

A theoretical approach to the representational arts seen as secondary modeling systems; treats the concept of the text, the system it manifests, its paradigmatic and syntagmatic axes, etc., in a search for a total aesthetic.

Scholes, *Semiotics and Interpretation*: "a major statement by the leading critic in the Soviet group of semioticians known as the Tartu school" (154); *MLR* 67, 713–16: "the product of a vigorous and original mind."

502.   Moreau, Jean. 1977. *La contraction et la synthèse de textes* [The Reduction and Synthesis of Texts]. Paris: Nathan. 159 pp.
A traditional school manual for the analysis of texts.

503.   Mistrík, Josef. 1977. *Kapitolky za štylistiky* [Stylistic Capitalization]. Bratislava: Obzor. 244 pp.

504.   Mukařovský, Jan. 1977. *Structure, Sign, and Function*. Trans. John Burbank and Peter Steiner. New Haven: Yale UP. 269 pp.
The second of 2 vols. of Mukařovský's selected essays (see *The Word and Verbal Art*); this one deals with general aesthetics and nonliterary arts. Bib. of Mukařovský's writings; name and term index.

Choice 15, 561: "an atmosphere so thick with inflationary abstraction that vision is useless"; *LJ* 102, 2424.

505.   Mukařovský, Jan. 1977. *The Word and Verbal Art*. Trans. John Burbank and Peter Steiner. New Haven: Yale UP. 238 pp.
[Mukařovský was the leading literary scholar of the Cercle linguistique de Prague (Prague School, 1926–). This collection of essays and a second, *Structure, Sign, and Function*, attempt to give an overall view of his systematic structural theory of literature.] This vol. of selected essays dating from 1933 to 1946 is devoted to poetics in 9 chs.: "On Poetic Language"; "Two Studies of Poetic Designation" ("The Aesthetic Function of Language" and "The Semantics of the Poetic Image"); "Two Studies of Dialogue," etc. Foreword by René Wellek. Name and term index.

Style 15, 64–68: a "remarkable" anthology that makes Mukařovský substantially available in Eng. for the first time, but the "editors' preference for general and theoretical, rather than specific and analytic, work" has misrepresented both what is best and what is typical in the works of Mukařovský (and the Prague School), for he was foremost an empirical scholar and critic; *DQR* 9, 153–56; *SEER* 22, 232–33; *CL* 31, 170–74; *SR* 87, 628–38; *SEEJ* 22, 282–83; *YR* 67, 111–13.

506.   Nöth, Winfried. 1977. *Dynamik semiotischer Systeme: Vom altenglischen Zauberspruch zum illustrierten Werbetext*. [The Dynamics of Semiotic Systems: From the Old English Spell to the Illustrated Advertisement]. Stuttgart: Metzler. 204 pp.

Diverse topics, literary (narrative) and nonliterary (advertising), united by a semiotic theory of "openness" and "dynamics." An extension of his earlier *Strukturen des Happening* (1972) and *Semiotik: Einführung mit Beispielen für Reklameanalysen* (1975).

JLS 9, 116–18: "a highly stimulating book . . . by virtue of its integrating power concerning heterogeneous phenomena in linguistics and literature both synchronically and diachronically."

507.   Patillon, Michel. 1977. *Précis d'analyse littéraire: 2. Décrire la poésie* [Manual of Literary Analysis: 2. To Describe Poetry]. Paris: Nathan. 142 pp.

A continuation of the author's school manual on the nature of literature, this volume explaining the poetic sign, phonics, grammar, and lexis. Jakobson plays a particularly important role. Bib. 1 p. (Barthes, Greimas, Hjelmslev, Lotman, et al.).

507a.   Pearce, Roger. 1977. *Literary Texts*. Birmingham: U of Birmingham. 99 pp.

A "slightly shortened version of the first part" of the author's thesis, *The Analysis and Interpretation of Literary Texts, with Particular Reference to James Joyce's* A Portait of the Artist as a Young Man. "My basic position in this study is to argue for the usefulness and necessity of a linguistic description of literary texts." Bib. 9 pp.

508.   Pratt, Mary L. 1977. *Toward a Speech Act Theory of Literary Discourse*. Bloomington: Indiana UP. 236 pp.

An attempt to apply the theory of speech acts (Austin, Searle, Ohmann, et al.) to the analysis of prose fiction. Ch. 1, "The 'Poetic Language' Fallacy," refutes the idea that "poetic" language differs in kind from natural language. Ch. 2, "Natural Narrative," compares the narratives of Labov's Martha's Vineyard and Harlem informants and "literary" narratives from Defoe to Borges. Chs. 3 and 4 focus speech act theories on examples of prose fiction; etc. Bib. 8 pp.; name and term index.

Style 12, 404–07: clear and accurate synthesis of sources and "a most interesting theory," but fails "to say just what does distinguish a literary text from a non-literary one"; *JLS* 8, 45–47: "If stylistics is to go beyond the methodology of practical criticism, and remove the opposition of literary and 'ordinary' language by becoming linguistic stylistics, with styles rather than literary style as its object, then it is in the direction *toward* which this book points that we have to turn"; *Lang* 55, 475–77; *JAAC* 36, 225–28; *PTL* 3, 387–90; *P&L* 2, 269–71; *MLN* (rev. article) 92, 1081–98.

509.   Reichert, John. 1977. *Making Sense of Literature*. Chicago: U of Chicago P. 222 pp.

An exploration of basic critical issues — the relations among author and text and reader, the functions of literature, its relations to life, etc. Name and term index.

Style 14, 54–55: "builds up a strong case for literature's" links with a multiplicity of linguistic and nonlinguistic experiences; *CLIO* 9, 311–14: "enthusiastic," the book is "modest, pragmatic, forthright, disposed against fancy, continental fashions and toward old rhetoric"; *P&L* 2, 258–65: "admirably clear-headed approach," but the critical issues "are far from being as simple as that"; *WHR* 32, 361–63: "stronger in philosophy than in linguistics and language," but "often acute and stimulating" on "human cognition and its classificatory powers"; "a stimulating book" although "it raises more problems than it can handle"; *AQ* 35, 393–94; *MFS* 25, 371–76.

510.   Ricoeur, Paul. 1977. *The Rule of Metaphor: Multidisciplinary Studies of the Creation of Meaning in Language.* Trans. Robert Czerny. Toronto: U of Toronto P. 384 pp. (*La métaphore vive.* Paris: Seuil, 1975.)
Discusses metaphor from 8 different points of view from classical rhetoric to semiotics to hermeneutics — from word to sentence to discourse. Bib. 11 pp.; name and term index.

Diacritics 10.4, 15–28: "magisterial," "a minor classic"; *Ling* 18, 159–63: "as fearless as he is knowledgeable," "subtly reasoned and unusually complete in coverage," "rough going for all but the specialist," "curious omission: almost no mention" of "psychological or even psycholinguistic studies" and "no mention" of "Gestalt theories."

511.   Rigolot, François. 1977. *Poétique et onomastique: L'exemple de la Renaissance* [Poetics and Onomastics: The Example of the Renaissance]. Geneva: Droz. 269 pp.
An apparently complete system for the description of names in literature.
MLJ 62, 314: "a solid and exciting investigation, with important implications for poetics in general and for the study of individual authors and periods"; *FR* 53, 121.

512.   Sammons, Jeffrey. 1977. *Literary Sociology and Practical Criticism: An Inquiry.* Bloomington: Indiana UP. 235 pp.
An examination of the development within Ger. literary criticism (*Literaturwissenschaft*) of "literary sociology" (*Literatursoziologie*), the relations of literature and society, of imagination and reality, "literature in its real, local context of human relations and social construction of consciousness." "My thesis . . . is that by regarding the genesis, substance, form, and affectiveness of literature from as realistic and non-mythical, non-fictional a vantage point as we can find, we protect the realm of art and the imagination." Bib. 25 pp. [usefully divided into 14 categories]; name index.
MLR 74, 651: a "judicious, scrupulously middle-of-the-road affair . . .

likely to dissatisfy everybody," "honest, and painfully authentic in its liberal principles" but "lame"; *SR* 86, 588; *MFS* 24, 650; *WLT* 52, 700; *Choice* 14, 1421; *LJ* 103, 2336.

513.   Sandell, Rolf. 1977. *Linguistic Style and Persuasion*. London: Academic. 329 pp.
"This is a psychological study, not a linguistic, nor a literary one. The problem to which this book is devoted is this: can linguistic style influence the persuasive effect of a message?" The style variables involved in 3 experimental field studies range from adjectives to sentence length. The conclusion is that style "has effects on all persuasive criteria tested." Bib. 12 pp.; name and term indexes.
    JLS 7, 56–57: "does not engage at all with current issues in the linguistic study of literature"; *CP* 23, 655; *JQ* 55, 171.

514.   Sanders, Willy. 1977. *Linguistische Stilistik* [Linguistic Stylistics]. Göttingen: Vandenhoeck. 201 pp.
The first third of the book elaborates his theory of style as choice, the remainder investigates stylistic devices, types, and levels in actual texts. Bib. 13 pp.
    Style 15, 31–32: "Sanders' theoretical framework [style as choice] is not finally one that can survive any fundamental analysis," but the book has "practical value"; *BL* (1977), 3388; (1979), 2758.

515.   Shukman, Ann. 1977. *Literature and Semiotics: A Study of the Writings of Ju. M. Lotman*. Amsterdam: North-Holland. 239 pp.
A study of Lotman (chs. 2–6) in the context of the Moscow-Tartu semiotics group (chs. 1 and 7), showing the development of Lotman and the semiotics group and their key ideas in the sixties (secondary modeling systems, etc.) as expressed in pub. and unpub. books, papers, and notes from symposia and summer schools. Ch. 2 treats "Lectures on Structural Poetics," Lotman's first "structuralist" work; ch. 3, 2 articles written in 1963 and 1965 on "Meaning in Literature"; ch. 4, several articles on typology; ch. 5, cultural history and structural analysis of literary texts; ch. 6, "The Structure of the Artistic Text"; ch. 7, practical studies. Bib. 26 pp.; name and term index.
    Style 15, 55–61: "a rich source of information which is generally unobtainable," "Shukman really has no predecessors," but the book has several flaws, including "poorly digested" summaries of texts.

516.   Stacy, R. H. 1977. *Defamiliarization in Language and Literature*. Syracuse: Syracuse UP. 193 pp.
An explanation of what Šklovskij meant by *ostranenie*, illustrated by numerous examples from world literature. Name and term index.

Style 14, 394–95: difficult reading because passages from works in original languages, but this reflects Stacy's "breadth of knowledge."

517.   Szabó, Zoltán. 1977. *A mai stilisztika nyelvelméleti alapjai*. Kolozsvar-Napoca: Dacia. 215 pp.
Fundamentals of linguistic stylistics.
     BL (1979), 2765.

518.   Titzmann, Michael. 1977. *Strukturale Textanalyse: Theorie und Praxis der Interpretation* [Structural Analysis of Texts: Theory and Practice of Interpretation]. Munich: Fink. 470 pp.
     Bib. 13 pp.

519.   Viebrock, Helmut. 1977. *Theorie und Praxis der Stilanalyse: Die Leistung der Sprache für den Stil, dargestellt an Texten der englischen Literatur der Gegenwart* [Theory and Practice of Stylistic Analysis: The Contribution of Language to Style, Illustrated in Texts of Contemporary English Literature]. Heidelberg: Winter. 167 pp.
An attempt to bridge the gap between linguistics and traditional linguistic studies by providing a model based upon the notions of deviation, coherence, foregrounding, competence, and intention. Most of the book involves the application of this combined method to 12 texts, 3 each from poetry, drama, prose fiction, and nonfiction.
     BL (1977), 3430.

520.   Williams, Raymond. 1977. *Marxism and Literature*. Oxford: Oxford UP. 218 pp.
Part 3, "Literary Theory," discusses culture and the multiple processes and kinds of writing, including analysis of "Signs and Notations," "Conventions," "Genres," "Forms," and the "Medium" of language itself. Bib. 4 pp.; name index.
     MLR 75, 826–30: "Williams has done more to shape the critical consciousness of his generation than any writer since Leavis. He has done it in a way that forces his readers to recognize the political dimension of literary discourse"; "There can be no doubt about the importance of this attempt to mediate between" the "particularity of English literary criticism" and the "generalizations of Marxism. But certain difficulties arise . . . ."

521.   Ziolkowski, Theodore. 1977. *Disenchanted Images: A Literary Iconology*. Princeton: Princeton UP. 273 pp.
A study of the image as theme, motif, and symbol expressed through, respectively, character, plot, and recurring image. Name and term index.
     YR 67, 109–11: "enormous variety of concrete illustration," "intelligent control and theoretical awareness"; *HR* 30, 476; *MLJ* 62, 209, *MLR* 73, 579; *JEGP* 77, 313; *SR* 86, 309.

522. Berg, Wolfgang. 1978. *Uneigentliches Sprechen: Zur Pragmatik und Semantik von Metapher, Metonymie, Ironie, Litotes und rhetorische Frage* [Figurative Language: Pragmatics and Semantics of Metaphor, Metonymy, Irony, Litotes, and the Rhetorical Question]. Tübingen: Narr. 167 pp.
Uses modern linguistics to describe types of figurative speech, arguing that figurative sentences are best interpreted inferentially in the contexts of linguistic competence, social expections, and factual knowledge.
Ling 19, 1026–28: "as a whole a well-founded and useful publication" and "interesting," although "important questions are left unanswered."

523. Bisztray, George. 1978. *Marxist Models of Literary Realism.* New York: Columbia UP. 247 pp.
A study of only 2 models—Lukács's critical realism and Gorkij's socialist realism. Bib. 11 pp.; name index.
Style 16, 96–98: tends to see literary realism as the monopoly of party intelligentsia.

524. Coletti, Vittorio. 1978. *Il linguaggio letterario* [The Literary Language]. Bologna: Zanichelli. 169 pp.

525. Corti, Maria. 1978. *An Introduction to Literary Semiotics.* Trans. Margherita Bogat and Allen Mandelbaum. Bloomington: Indiana UP. 176 pp. (*Principi della communicazione letteraria.* Milan: Bompiani, 1976.)
A comprehensive approach to literature—how a culture or a class imposes values and genres, the importance of the historical contexts and personal values of senders and receivers of messages in literature (reading not only a psychological process), etc. Bib. 10 pp.; name index. [Excellent introd. to the totality of a "text."]
Style 15, 89–90: "This approach to the sociology of reading is significant in semiotic research and merits serious investigation," and it is "an informative commentary on the state of the art of Italian semiotics and how it differs [from] or compares to other models in Europe and the United States"; "the central text for a seminar on literary semiotics"; *CRCL* 6, 422–25; *MLR* 75, 349–50; *RES* ns 31, 193–95; *MLN* 94, 866–69.

526. Denham, Robert. 1978. *Northrop Frye and Critical Method.* University Park: Pennsylvania State UP. 262 pp.
An assessment of "each *area* of his work" ("fifteen books, more than 330 essays, reviews, and contributions to books" by the time of this book). Name and term index.
YR 69, 575: "thorough and lucid."

527. Derrida, Jacques. 1978. *Writing and Difference.* Trans. Alan Bass.

Chicago: U of Chicago P. 342 pp. (*L'écriture et la différence*. Paris: Seuil, 1967.)

A collection of the author's essays written between 1959 and 1967. Contains critiques of structuralism, Artaud, Freud and writing, and Husserl, among other essays.

VQR 56, 119: "landmark of contemporary French thought"; *NS* 98, 240; *RM* 33, 172; *Enc* 55, 53.

528. Dijk, Teun van. 1978. *Taal en Handelen: Een interdisciplinaire inleiding in de pragmatiek* [Language and Action: An Interdisciplinary Introduction to Pragmatics]. Muiderberg: Coutinho. 174 pp.

Introd. to speech-act theory and pragmatics from a discourse point of view, including a discussion of the cognitive processes underlying speech-act comprehension and a sociocultural analysis of speech acts and pragmatic conditions.

529. Dijk, Teun van. 1978. *Tekstwetenschap: Een interdisciplinaire inleiding* [Discourse Studies: An Interdisciplinary Introduction]. Utrecht: Spectrum. 323 pp. (Ger. trans., *Textwissenschaft: Eine interdisziplinäre Einführung*. Tübingen: Niemeyer, 1980; Span. trans., Barcelona, 1983.)

Introd. to text grammar, rhetorical and stylistic dimensions of discourse, cognitive discourse processing, and conversational interaction.

530. Epstein, E. L. 1978. *Language and Style*. London: Methuen. 92 pp.

"Style" is the *how* of human behavior and therefore language use. Literary style has 2 aspects—"public and private strategies of perception." Bib. 3 pp.; name and term index.

JLS 9, 48–49: "disappointing" because so "limited in scope"; *PoT* 2, 207–12; *Lang* 56, 477–78; *RES* ns 31, 193–95; *EA* 33, 202.

531. Gaskell, Philip. 1978. *From Writer to Reader: Studies in Editorial Method*. Oxford: Clarendon. 268 pp.

12 studies of problems and issues raised by revision, the author's intention and accuracy of texts "following an extract from a text through its surviving stages." Name and term index.

Style 14, 186–91: poses "intriguing puzzles" that lead to an approach to style as process.

532. Halliday, M. A. K. 1978. *Language as Social Semiotic: The Social Interpretation of Language and Meaning*. London: Arnold; Baltimore: University Park. 256 pp.

Essays "written between 1972 and 1976" with the common theme of language as a "social fact," the "product of the social process," "one of the semiotic systems that constitute a culture, in which the culture itself is interpreted in semiotic terms" (an "information system").

AUMLA 52, 379–81: "a major theory" possessing "power and scope"; *Enc* 50, 48; *JLS* 9, 38–40.

533.   Heintz, Gunter. 1978. *Sprachliche Struktur und dichterische Einbildungskraft: Beitrag zur linguistischen Poetik* [Linguistic Structure and Poetic Imagination: A Contribution to Linguistic Poetics]. Munich: Hueber. 434 pp.

534.   Hoy, David. 1978. *The Critical Circle: Literature, History and Philosophical Hermeneutics*. Berkeley: U of California P. 182 pp.
A survey of hermeneutic critics and concepts, defining hermeneutics broadly as "any theory of criticism emphasizing meaning and its reception rather than psychological intention and genesis." Name and term index.
Style 15, 508–10: "crippled" by "vagueness and arguable assertations," by the attempt to discuss too many critics in such brief space, and by a bias in favor of the hermeneutics of Hans-Georg Gadamer, "but stylisticians should make an effort to read this book because the issues Hoy touches on are central to stylistic analysis"; *MLR* 75, 149–50: "a stimulating, wide-ranging, and acute defence of Gadamer" but weak in its treatment of E. D. Hirsch and the notion of truth.

534a.   Manca, Marie A. 1978. *Harmony and the Poet: The Creative Ordering of Reality*. Berlin: de Gruyter. 197 pp.
Explores the role and form the idea of harmony assumes in the work and thought of 6 poets: Dante, Shakespeare, Whitman, Rimbaud, Char, and Hart Crane.

535.   Medvedev, P. N., and M. M. Baxtin. 1978. *The Formal Method in Literary Scholarship: A Critical Introduction to Sociological Poetics*. Trans. Albert Wehrle. Baltimore: Johns Hopkins UP. 191 pp.
This Marxist account and critique of Russ. formalism was first pub. in 1928. It criticizes the antihistoricism, artistic autonomism, individualism, and psychologism of formalism, which the authors would replace with "sociological poetics." Part 1, "The Objects and Tasks of Marxist Literary Scholarship"; part 2, "A Contribution to the History of the Formal Method"; part 3, "The Formal Method in Poetics"; part 4, "The Formal Method in Literary History." Name and term index.
Style 15, 71–72: a negative rev.: "they are unable to muster a philosophical argument in support of their cause," "very little is said . . . to rebut formalist principles," "its utopian quality and its prescriptive tone," "a remarkable lack of intellectual openmindedness and a schoolmasterish sterility"; Erlich, *Russian Formalism*: "the most extended and scholarly critique of OPOJAZ ever undertaken by a Marxist (92)"; *MLR* 76, 143–44: "forcefully argued"; *SR* 87, 628–38; *SEEJ* 23, 411–12; *SlavR* 38, 154–55.

536. Miko, František. 1978. *Style, Literature, Communication*. Bratislava: Slovenské pedagogické. 183 pp.
BL (1978), 2546.

537. Mistrík, Josef. 1978. *Rétorika* [Rhetoric]. Bratislava: Slovenské pedagogické. 205 pp.
BL (1978), 2552; (1979), 2736.

538. Norris, Christopher. 1978. *William Empson and the Philosophy of Literary Criticism*. London: Athlone. 222 pp.
A scrutiny of Empson's work in its relation to the main movements of 20th-cent. criticism. Name index.
AUMLA 51, 109–10: "many new insights" but "much less rewarding" than reading Empson's works; *MLR* 75, 182–85: "the first serious, sustained, fully informed, and deeply searching examination of Empson's critical work"; *JLS* 9, 49–51.

539. Rogers, Robert. 1978. *Metaphor: A Psychoanalytic View*. Berkeley: U of California P. 159 pp.
A survey of psychoanalytic thinking on metaphor and a theory of metaphor that encompasses poetry, the reader, and language in general. Name and term index.
Style 15, 80–83: "exemplifies the best that the old psychoanalytic framework can offer us while also hinting at . . . the more satisfying information-processing paradigm."

540. Sandig, Barbara. 1978. *Stilistik: Sprachpragmatische Grundlegung der Stilbeschreibung* [Stylistics: Pragmatic Foundations of the Description of Style]. Berlin: de Gruyter. 201 pp.
An action-theory approach to nonliterary style.
Ling 17, 1076–79: "careful steps," "well-defined concepts," "convincing."

541. Schaff, Adam. 1978. *Structuralism and Marxism*. Oxford: Pergamon. 203 pp. (*Strukturalismus und Marxismus*. Vienna: Europa, 1974).
3 essays, the first explaining the concept of structuralism, the second analyzing Marxist structuralism in France, and the third on Chomsky's generative grammar. "The link between these three essays is my zeroing in on the philosophical aspects of structuralism." Name and term indexes.
Choice 16, 239: "extremely well-written."

542. Seidler, Herbert. 1978. *Grundfragen einer Wissenschaft von der Sprachkunst* [A Science of Literature: Basic Issues]. Munich: Fink. 340 pp.
AUMLA 54, 293–94: "concerns the struggle for a theoretical foundation of a systematic and scholarly analysis of literature as an art-form."

543.   Smith, Barbara H. 1978. *On the Margins of Discourse: The Relation of Literature to Language.* Chicago: U of Chicago P. 225 pp.
The first 2 parts of the book offer an investigation of literature as a "fictive utterance," "verbal structures that have been designed or discovered" to "invite" activities of "cognitive play," the "playing with . . . the conventions of linguistic transactions." The third part presents an attack on the essays in *Style and Structure in Literature: Essays in the New Stylistics*, ed. R. Fowler, all of which base their analyses on a linguistic model. Name and term index.
    Style 15, 451–53: "a cultured, intellectual, urbane book," "notable for the cogency and wit" of its examples, but "the basic methodological distinction between natural and fictive utterance fails . . . to offer objective textual criteria for distinguishing the literary and the non-literary"; *JLS* 10, 63–64: "the book I would recommend to all concerned with the relation of language to literature and with the study of their mutual reinforcement as disciplines"; *MLR* 77, 136–37; *JAF* 94, 90–92; *MP* 78, 340–43; *CL* 32, 295–97; *JEGP* 79, 231–35; *YR* 69, 560–76; *Lang&S* 13, 156–73.

544.   Strelka, Joseph. 1978. *Methodologie der Literaturwissenschaft.* [Methodology of Literary Criticism]. Tübingen: Niemeyer. 423 pp.
Part 1, "Studies of Principles"; part 2, "Studies of Methods."
    AUMLA 54, 234–36: "recommendable."

545.   White, Hayden. 1978. *Tropics of Discourse: Essays in Cultural Criticism.* Baltimore: Johns Hopkins UP. 287 pp.
Previously pub. articles. Tropes are inescapable, "for tropics is the process by which all discourse *constitutes* the object which it pretends only to describe realistically and to analyze objectively." Name and term index. [This book develops concepts introduced in White's *Metahistory*, 1973.]
    JLT 3, 31–38: the general theory propounded in this book has "unusual promise, because of its inherent power of analysis, and because it is simple enough to be readily teachable and usable in any university course."

546.   Zimmer, Rudolf. 1978. *Stilanalyse* [Style Analysis]. Tübingen: Niemeyer. 105 pp.
Ch. 1 discusses stylistic approaches by Spitzer, Bally, Riffaterre, and Riesel and quantitative and generative transformational; chs. 2 and 3 deal with special problems, such as phonostylistics and word order.
    BL (1979), 2775.

547.   Bennett, Tony. 1979. *Formalism and Marxism.* London: Methuen. 200 pp.
A comparison of Russ. formalism with Althusserian Marxism (Althusser, Macherey, Eagleton), divided into 2 parts—analysis of formalism and discussion of "recent developments within Marxism" that give hope for a fruitful

dialogue between formalists and Marxists. Bib. 7 pp.; name and term index.
Style 16, 98–100: valuable chiefly for its call "for literary scholarship committed to the social significance of literature and criticism"; *JLS* 9, 121–22: an unfavorable rev.; *MLR* 76, 143–46.

548.   Booth, Wayne. 1979. *Critical Understanding: The Powers and Limits of Pluralism*. Chicago: U of Chicago P. 408 pp.
A book about criticism of criticism of literature. Rejects 5 attitudes (monism, skepticism, etc.) for methodological pluralism — the acceptance of more than 1 critical method, judging each by its method or critical paradigm. Separate chs. on Crane, Burke, and Abrams. Term index 21 pp.; name index.
Style 17, 41–44: fair, openminded, and generous, but "a largely pointless book"; *ConL* 23, 105–13; *JEGP* 79, 429–31; *CritQ* 22, 89–90: *RES* ns 32, 365–67; *ELN* 17, 233–34; *MFS* 26, 372–76; *WHR* 34, 167–70.

549.   Boström Kruckenberg, Anita. 1979. *Roman Jakobsons poetik: Studier i dess teori och praktik* [Roman Jakobson's Poetics: A Study of Theory and Practice]. Uppsala: U Uppsala. 210 pp.

550.   Cassirer, Peter. 1979. *Stil, stilistik, stilanalys* [Style, Stylistics, and Analysis of Style]. Stockholm: Almqvist. 273 pp.

551.   Chambers, Ross. 1979. *Meaning and Meaningfulness: Studies in the Analysis and Interpretation of Texts*. Lexington: French Forum. 197 pp.
Previously pub. essays on such topics as interpretation, description, and meaning. Bib. 3 pp.; name and term index.
AUMLA 55, 104: "I cannot recommend this volume too highly," "a model of clarity, inspired good sense, and scholarliness unencumbered by pedantry"; *MLR* 76, 904–06.

551a.   Cohen, Keith. 1979. *Film and Fiction: The Dynamics of Exchange*. New Haven: Yale UP. 216 pp.
On the influence of film on fictional form and the features common to these narrative arts (discontinuity, mobility of point of view, achronology, cutting, etc.). Part 2 focuses on 5 novels pub. between 1900 and 1925: Stein's *Three Lives*, Romains's *Mort de quelqu'un*, Proust's *A la recherche*, Joyce's *Ulysses*, and Woolf's *To the Lighthouse*.
MLR 78, 391–92: "he has not demonstrated . . . the influential role of cinema," but this does not "undermine the value of the parallels he does demonstrate."

551b.   Dugast, Daniel. 1979. *Vocabulaire et stylistique: I. Théâtre et dialogue*. Geneva: Slatkine. 292 pp.
A statistical approach to language in literature.

Ling 20, 569–70: "beginner and specialist alike will be rewarded with the important statistical material, the wealth of research potentials, and the scientific inventiveness they will find in Dugast's 'experimental stylistics.'"

552.   Eco, Umberto. 1979. *The Role of the Reader: Explorations in the Semiotics of Texts*. Bloomington: Indiana UP. 273 pp.
The focus is on the "semiotics of texts," a theoretical exploration of "closed" and "open" texts (simple and complex, Superman tales vs. *Ulysses*), the structures common to each, and the operations a "model reader" must perform in reading them. 6 of the 9 essays "were written between 1959 and 1971." Bib. 7 pp.
Style 15, 479–82: the book is not about the reader; the distinction between closed and open texts "raises more questions than it answers"; and the book is written in opaque style; *YR* 69, 564: "focuses coherently" on "the reader's active 'production'" of a text; *RM* 35, 126; *AA* 82, 867; *CLIO* 10, 93; *FQ* 34, 59; *MLR* 76, 142; *JAAC* 38, 336; *WLT* 54, 339.

553.   Fónagy, Iván. 1979. *Les métaphores en phonétique* [Metaphors in Phonetics]. Ottawa: Didier. 218 pp. (*Die Metaphern in der Phonetik*. The Hague: Mouton, 1963. 132 pp.)
One of several conclusions of this inductive study of phonetic metaphors (e.g., moisted consonants) is that the preconscious mental data processing that results in metaphors precedes and prepares for conscious conceptual analysis in science as well as in poetry.
ZRP 97, 630.

554.   Freedle, Roy. 1979. *New Directions in Discourse Processing*. Norwood: Ablex. 336 pp.
12 essays focus especially on "schema theory (largely from a psycholinguistic perspective)" and "cultural schemata." Chs. 2 and 4 on narrative. Name and term indexes.
Lang 56, 450; *JL* 17, 40.

555.   Graff, Gerald. 1979. *Literature against Itself: Literary Ideas in Modern Society*. Chicago: U of Chicago P. 260 pp.
An attack on modern critics (New Critics, structuralists, deconstructionists, etc.) who undermine the idea of mimesis. Name index, with a few terms.
Style 16, 65–67; *Diacritics* 10.3, 2–14; 10.4, 75–85; *MLR* 78, 385; *PLL* 18, 428.

556.   Guerin, Wilfred, et al. 1979. *A Handbook of Critical Approaches to Literature*. 2nd ed., rev. New York: Harper. 350 pp.
An explanation of 5 "major" approaches (traditional, formalistic, psychological, mythological, and exponential) and 12 others (sociological, linguistic,

appreciative, Aristotelian, generic, genetic, feminist, history of ideas, phenomenological, rhetorical, structuralist, and stylistic), applied to "Young Goodman Brown," *Huckleberry Finn*, *Hamlet*, and "To His Coy Mistress." Bib. 6 pp.; name and term index.

CEAF 10, 16–17: "Even with its limitations" (e.g., failure to examine its own critical assumptions), "this text should be required reading for all undergraduate literary students."

557. Hayden, John. 1979. *Polestar of the Ancients: The Aristotelian Tradition in Classical and English Literary Criticism*. Newark: U of Delaware P. 237 pp.

The mimesis-instruction-pleasure tradition—Aristotle, Sidney, Dryden, Johnson, Arnold—offers a critique of period divisions applied to literary criticism and a challenge to the relativism of much recent criticism.

MLR 77, 690–91: "useful observations . . . written in a direct, common sense way," but "the studies of particular critics often seem rather rushed."

558. Kress, Gunther, and Robert Hodge. 1979. *Language as Ideology*. London: Routledge. 163 pp.

An attempt to construct a linguistics that directly confronts human belief, power, and action. Who does what to whom with words, and how, and why? The "real task, namely to relate forms of thought to the existence of the producers of those thoughts, as individuals living in a material world under specific conditions in specific societies at given times." Bib. 7 pp.; name and term index.

Style 16, 90–94: "Their analysis, furry around the edges, less than rigorous in many places, is genuinely interesting enough to be turned upon them"; *MLR* 76, 139–42: "will challenge those who know something about linguistics but will confuse the common reader"; *CL* 35, 362–73: rev. article comparing to *Language and Control* by Fowler, Hodge, Kress, and Trew and to *Literature, Language and Society in England, 1580–1680* by Aers, Hodge, and Kress; *JLS* 12, 92–95.

559. Pieper, Ursula. 1979. *Über die Aussagekraft statistischer Methoden für die linguistische Stilanalyse* [On the Value of Statistical Methods for Linguistic Style Analysis]. Tübingen: Narr. 157 pp.

560. Ruthven, K. K. 1979. *Critical Assumptions*. Cambridge: Cambridge UP. 263 pp.

12 chs. for particular theories or sets of assumptions: "Books as Heterocosms," "Organic and Inorganic Forms," "Criteria of Complexity and Simplicity," "Inspiration," "Making," etc. Focus on "four recurrent problems . . . genesis, form, meaning, and value." An argument for a literary history and criticism grounded in theory. Name index, term index (5 pp.)

MLR 76, 139–40: with "remarkable powers of organization" the author "resurrects the amiable genre of the complexion or cento—a quilt of quotations stitched together by the author's own commentary"; *AUMLA* 54, 232.

560a.   Searle, John. 1979. *Expression and Meaning: Studies in the Theory of Speech Acts*. Cambridge: Cambridge UP. 187 pp.
A collection of papers applying the theory developed in *Speech Acts* (1969). *Centrum* ns 1, 149–57: "a 'must'," "well-written, clear, interesting," "significant."

561.   Belsey, Catherine. 1980. *Critical Practice*. London: Methuen. 168 pp. (Port. trans., *A prática crítica*, 1982.)
Advocates the ideas of Lacan, Althusser, and Derrida and their attacks on the commonsense assumptions of intentionalism, New Criticism, humanism, empiricism, and idealism, and the literary reflection of those assumptions— expressive realism. Bib. 12 pp.; name and term index.
JLS 11, 39–42: an original and significant book; *PN Review* 30, 80: "lively, lucid and committed"; *CritQ* 23, 72–77; *BJA* 21, 186–89.

562.   Blanchard, Marc Éli. 1980. *Description: Sign, Self, Desire; Critical Theory in the Wake of Semiotics*. The Hague: Mouton. 299 pp.
The first section ("Sign") investigates the relation of linguistic to narrative structures; section 2 ("Self") examines the problem of the subject by making the experiences of the subject a condition of the interpretation of the text; the last section ("Desire") deals with the other language-governing narrative, the language of desire. Bib. 8 pp.
CL 35, 87–89: "delivers little," the arguments "left so unfinished."

563.   Dijk, Teun van. 1980. *Macrostructures: An Interdisciplinary Study of Global Structures in Discourse, Interaction, and Cognition*. Hillsdale: Erlbaum. 317 pp.
Summarizes and expands his past work on macrostructures, especially in a cognitive model.

564.   Fehrman, Carl. 1980. *Poetic Creation: Inspiration or Craft*. Trans. Karin Petherick. Minneapolis: U of Minnesota P. 229 pp. (*Diktaren och de skapande ögonblicken*. Stockholm: Norstedt, 1974.)
The genesis of a work results from an extremely complex and contradictory dialectical process of craftsmanship and inspiration, "of rules and chance, of technique and impulse." Examples are drawn mainly from Scandinavian literature (Ibsen, Lagerlof) but also from world literature (Valéry). Name and term index.
Style 15, 474–76: "a relentless exploration of method and theory relevant to the genesis of a work of art," "sound scholarship."

565.   Grassi, Ernesto. 1980. *Rhetoric as Philosophy: The Humanist Tradition*. University Park: Pennsylvania State UP. 122 pp.
An effort to reestablish the Lat. tradition, from Cicero to Vico, as the foundation for rhetoric, in "rejection of formal semiotics, strict linguistics, and rhetoric understood only as an art of persuasion." No bib. or index.
RM 35, 131–32: "exciting fresh departures"; *Ren&R* 6, 211.

566.   Hartman, Geoffrey. 1980. *Criticism in the Wilderness: The Study of Literature Today*. New Haven: Yale UP. 323 pp.
A study of such topics as the proper form and language for the critical essay, the situation of professional literary study today, hermeneutics, practical criticism. Bib. 13 pp.; name and term index.
YR 71, 129–33: "range, incisiveness, and revelatory intelligence"; *CL* 34, 177–81: this "speculative essay on the nature of understanding" is "exemplary."

567.   Hockey, Susan. 1980. *A Guide to Computer Applications in the Humanities*. Baltimore: Johns Hopkins UP. 248 pp.
Chs. include material on concordances, vocabulary, collocation, dialect, morphology, syntax, style, authorship, and sound patterns. Bib. 2 pp.; glossary of terms; useful addresses; name and term index.
ELN 18, 153–56: "although far from perfect . . . a generally sound introduction"; *WHR* 34, 375–78.

568.   Juhl, P. D. 1980. *Interpretation: An Essay in the Philosophy of Literary Criticism*. Princeton: Princeton UP. 332 pp.
A conservative defense of intention and unitary interpretation.
MLR 77, 130–32: "a philosophy of interpretation as doctrinaire in principle as it must seem unworkable in practice"; *JLS* 11, 38–39.

569.   Kennedy, George A. 1980. *Classical Rhetoric and Its Christian and Secular Tradition from Ancient to Modern Times*. Chapel Hill: U of North Carolina P. 291 pp.
A history of the classical tradition from the earliest times through the synthesis of classical and Christian elements in the 4th cent., to its decline at the end of the 18th. Bib. 10 pp.; name and term index.
CW 73, 372–73: "an essential tool"; *CL* 33, 282; *QJS* 67, 206; *RenQ* 34, 79.

570.   Kristeva, Julia. 1980. *Desire in Language: A Semiotic Approach to Literature and Art*. Ed. L. S. Roudiez. Trans. T. Gora et al. New York: Columbia UP. 305 pp.
10 previously pub. essays (1969–77). Ch. 1, "The Ethics of Linguistics"; ch. 2, "The Bounded Text"; ch. 3, "Word, Dialogue, and Novel," etc. The ed. provides definitions of key terms in his introd. Name and term index.
MFS 28, 723: "impressive"; *Critm* 23, 261–63; *Comw* 109, 120; *BRMMLA* 35, 314; *Enc* 57, 56; *JAAC* 40, 93.

571.   Kurzweill, Edith. 1980. *The Age of Structuralism: Lévi-Strauss to Fou-
        cault.* New York: Columbia UP. 256 pp.
On Fr. structuralists mainly; chs. on Lévi-Strauss, Althusser, Barthes, Lefebvre,
Foucault, Ricoeur, Lacan, and Touraine, other structuralists, poststructuralists,
and antistructuralists. Name and term index.
        AHR 86, 571–72; *AA* 83, 964–65; *Choice* 18, 521; *RSR*, 177; *AJS* 87, 989;
SRNB 8, 26; *WLT* 55, 538.

572.   Lentricchia, Frank. 1980. *After the New Criticism.* Chicago: U of Chicago
        P. 384 pp.
A history of contemporary U.S. theory but concentrating on Krieger, Hirsch,
de Man, and Bloom, "the major theorists in American criticism since about
1957" (the year of Frye's *Anatomy*). His main objection to this criticism is
its isolation, its tendency to operate oppositionally, especially to separate literature from history and humanity. Name index.
        Style 17, 37–41: for his grasp of the lineage of critical theories and his de-
termination to discover connections among the disparate theories and to af-
firm the relations between literature and actual human experience, the book
should be priority reading; *MLR* 78, 386: "learned, allusive, carefully written" with "an extraordinary knack of exposing the contradictions and uncer-
tainties of those whom he seems to advocate," but "he misses some vital
figures" and his "own theory remains unclear"; *Diacritics* 11.3, 57–73; *ConL*
23, 105–13; *MFS* 27, 759–62; *SAQ* 81, 114–16; *EIC* 32, 89–93.

573.   Norrman, Ralf, and Jon Haarberg. 1980. *Nature and Language: A Semi-
        otic Study of Cucurbits in Literature.* London: Routledge. 232 pp.
This study of squashes in literature "is paradigmatic, panchronic and, to some
extent, interdisciplinary" (see definitions, pp. 2–8). Bib. 11 pp.; name and
term index.
        MLR 78, 395–97: a "firm riposte to the structuralist idea that signs are al-
ways 'arbitrary'" and "a persuasive argument for the existence" of "natural
symbols."

573a.   Oakman, Robert. 1980. *Computer Methods for Literary Research.*
        Columbia: U of South Carolina. 236 pp. (Rev. ed. 1984.)
An introductory guide and history to the subject, explaining computers, input and output, the making of bibiographies, style analysis, etc. Bib. 33 pp.
Name and term index.
        MP 79, 233–39: a better book than Susan Hockey's: though both are "ex-
cellent guides," Oakman's is "more thorough, more scholarly, more extensive"; *MLJ* 65, 111; *TheatJ* 33, 265; *TLS* 9 May 1980, 533.

574.   Silverman, David, and Brian Torode. 1980. *The Material Word: Some
        Theories of Language and Its Limits.* London: Routledge. 354 pp.

An analysis of recent criticism of language divided into 2 types: "interpretation" and "interruption." Interpretation approaches a text with a version of reality presupposed; interruption approaches a text in a spirit of interrogation toward the view of reality proposed in the text. The authors claim to be in the "interruption" camp. Bibs. follow each ch.; name and term indexes.
NS 100, 21; *Choice* 17, 667–68; *SocR* ns 28, 914–16; *Soc* 15, 287–93.

575.   Slaughter, Cliff. 1980. *Marxism, Ideology, and Literature.* Atlantic Highlands: Humanities. 228 pp.
Chs. on Marx, Trotsky, Lukács, Goldmann, Benjamin. Name and term index.
Choice 18, 264: "excellent analysis"; *SocR* 29, 373; *TES* 21 Nov. 1980, 23.

576.   Tiefenbrun, Susan. 1980. *Signs of the Hidden: Semiotic Studies.* Amsterdam: Rodopi. 237 pp.
Studies of subliminal or nonexplicit levels of meaning with examples from 17th-cent. Fr. texts; most of the essays previously pub.
MLR 76, 965–66: main idea formulated with "vigour" and "fruitfulness."

577.   Traugott, Elizabeth, and Mary L. Pratt. 1980. *Linguistics for Students of Literature.* New York: Harcourt. 444 pp.
An introd. to many of the important subfields in contemporary linguistics (transformational grammar, case grammar, generative semantics, sociolinguistics) and an effort to demonstrate their usefulness to literary critics by special attention to phonology and phonetics, morphology, lexis, syntax, semantics, speech acts, etc. "Suggested Further Readings" follow each ch.; bib. 12 pp.; glossary; name and term indexes.
Style 15, 490–92: "consistently well-written, lucid and entertaining," although "not without weaknesses" (their discussion of articulatory phonetics "neglects the organs of articulation," their stress on Eng.-language linguistics minimizes the role of Saussure, Hjelmslev, Benveniste, Jakobson and other influential linguists, etc.); *Lang* 57, 782–83: complains about various omissions (little reference to phonological patterns, neglect of rhetorical devices) but considers the book "exceedingly well-written," a "skillful and very useful introduction to linguistics as applied to literature."

578.   Valesio, Paolo. 1980. *Novantiqua: Rhetorics as a Contemporary Theory.* Bloomington: Indiana UP. 321 pp.
An interdisciplinary overview of the philosophy of rhetoric, employing modern linguistics to provide a grammar and lexicon within a structural framework. "Rhetorics" in the title means the empirically grounded study of rhetoric, defined as "the functional organization of discourse." Bib. 27 pp.
QJS 68, 91: "an important book"; *Choice* 18, 942: "a remarkable book."

578a.   Weathers, Winston. 1980. *An Alternate Style: Options in Composition.* Rochelle Park: Hayden. 131 pp.

Encourages beginning writers to attempt what he calls the "Grammar B" style
of writing, with characteristics of variegation, synchronicity, discontinuity, and
ambiguity.
EJ 71, 87: "Exciting. Provocative. Stimulating."

579.   Zima, Peter. 1980. *Textsoziologie: Eine kritische Einführung* [Text So-
       ciology: A Critical Investigation]. Stuttgart: Metzler. 192 pp.
JLS 11, 42–43: "a concise but comprehensive critical introduction" to the Fr.
school within the context of both Amer. and European thought.

580.   Altieri, Charles. 1981. *Act and Quality: A Theory of Literary Meaning
       and Humanistic Understanding.* Amherst: U of Massachusetts P. 343 pp.
Defends the value of literature as a special kind of cognitive activity on the
basis of meaning as use and provides a survey of recent theoretical debates.
Bib. 8 pp.; name index.
JEGP 82, 124–27: "scope and depth," "he bears listening to"; *CL* 35,
376–80: "a dreadful muddle from beginning to end"; *CC* 98, 1214; *LJ* 106,
1421.

581.   Culler, Jonathan. 1981. *The Pursuit of Signs: Semiotics, Literature,
       Deconstruction.* Ithaca: Cornell UP. 242 pp.
A denunciation of further interpretation of literary works. "Criticism is the
pursuit of signs" ("signifying structures"), which are "never simply given as
such but must be pursued, and different modes of criticism can be distinguished by the accounts they give of this pursuit. . . . This book investigates
. . . a semiotics of literature." Part 1 examines 2 overviews of recent criticism and semiotics; part 2, the problems of literary semiotics in more detail;
part 3, deconstruction. Name and term index.
JLT 3, 26–30: "its main interest is as a kind of guide-book to what has been
going on in the last five years"; *JLS* 12, 73–91: useful in many ways but "fundamentally flawed" in its "particular stance in relation to literature"; *JAAC*
40, 329; *MFS* 27, 759; *TLS* 1 Jan. 1982, 3.

582.   Dijk, Teun van. 1981. *Studies in the Pragmatics of Discourse.* The Hague:
       Mouton. 331 pp.
Collection of papers written between 1972 and 1979 on topic and comment,
macro-speech acts, speech acts in cognition, literary pragmatics, pragmatic
connectives, the role of pragmatics in text grammar and linguistic theory, and
the theory of action as the basis for a pragmatic theory. Bib. 7 pp.; index.
LaS 13, 369.

583.   Dubois, Jacques, et al. 1981. *A General Rhetoric.* By Group M. Trans.
       Paul Burrell and Edgar Slotkin. Baltimore: Johns Hopkins UP. 254 pp.
       (*Rhétorique générale.* Paris: Larousse, 1970.)

A trans. of the second Fr. ed. of *Rhétorique générale* (1976), to which has been added a later article, "Seven Years of Reflection." The book is mostly a study of tropes and schemes, "what classical rhetoric called *elocutio*. It attempts to set forth the basic principles by which all figures of language and thought are derived and can be described." The main principle is that of the transformation of (deviation from) the nonliterary use of language, and is thus a study of *metabole* ("any kind of change of whatever aspect of language"), especially of metaplasms, metataxes, metasememes, and metalogisms. "The principle figures appear in an orthogonal schema, deriving from some fundamental operations." Part 2, chs. 7 and 8, add figures of narrative voice and narration. Index to authors. [A better title would be "a treatise on figures" or "a schema of figures."]

   MLN 96, 1179–84: "brief, clear, and symmetrical," "outstanding" translation; *Critm* 24, 273–77: several serious shortcomings—e.g., "much of the analysis" must "be taken on trust," "a stilted and unreliable translation"; *Ling* 121, 105–13 (orig. ed., in Ger.); *FM* 46, 157–60; *ArsS* 2, 103–11; *FL* 8, 436–46.

584.   Falk, Eugene. 1981. *The Poetics of Roman Ingarden*. Chapel Hill: U of North Carolina P. 213 pp.
   "An exposition of Ingarden's works on literature." Name and term index.
   CL 34, 275: "this is one of the most significant books ever written to clarify and settle the most fundamental problems of literary theory, literary criticism, and literary aesthetics"; *JAAC* 40, 345; *WLT* 56, 188.

585.   Fowler, Roger. 1981. *Literature as Social Discourse: The Practice of Linguistic Criticism*. Bloomington: Indiana UP. 215 pp.
   A collection of Fowler's essays "written ca. 1973–1978" on "language, literary styles, and their social contexts and functions. . . . I argue that first and foremost, literature is a kind of *discourse* . . . within social structure like other forms of discourse." Bib. 11 pp.; name index.
   RMR 97–98: "repeatedly and vehemently beats a number of long-dead horses" and suffers from "an egregious lack of cohesiveness," but much in the book is "profitable."

585a.   Hamon, Philippe. 1981. *Introduction à l'analyse du descriptif*. Paris: Hachette. 268 pp.
   A reevaluation of the importance of description to poetry and narrative divided into 5 chs. on competence, construction, typology, configuration, and the topos of description.
   RR 57, 101–04: "an important contribution" to "a genre neglected or mistreated" by "contemporary narratology."

586.   Harris, Roy. 1981. *The Language Myth*. New York: St. Martin's. 212 pp.
   An attack on Saussure and other "fixed code" linguists and an advocacy of

a linguistics from a user's perspective, an "integrational linguistics" in which communication is effected by "total behavior" and language is "a continually creative process." Bib. 4 pp.; name and term index.
Choice 19, 910: "lively, lucid, and literate"; *LRB* 4, 9; *Lis* 106, 311.

587.   Hartman, Geoffrey. 1981. *Saving the Text: Literature/Derrida/Philosophy*. Baltimore: Johns Hopkins UP. 184 pp.
Mainly a study of the ideas and the style of Derrida's *Glas* (which juxtaposes in alternating columns a commentary on Hegel with one on Genet). Bib. 7 pp.; name and term indexes.
      GQ 55, 387: "Hartman is ever appropriate to his task" in spite of Derrida's misunderstanding of Hegel and the "disordered aphoristic farrago" of the style of *Glas*; *YR* 71, 133–38; *Lang&S* 16, 238.

587a.   Hoek, Leo. 1981. *La marque de titre* [The Significance of the Title]. Amsterdam: Mouton. 368 pp.
Presentation of a semiological framework for the description of the structures and functions of book titles, particularly of novels.

587b.   Jakobson, Roman. 1981. *Poetry of Grammar and Grammar of Poetry*. Ed. Stephen Rudy. Vol. 2 of *Selected Writings*. The Hague: Mouton. 814 pp.
"Of the five volumes of Roman Jakobson's *Selected Writings* now in print, the present volume has the most direct bearing on his manifold contribution to literary studies . . . reveals the full scope of his inquiry into the theory and practice of 'poetics,' conceived in Jakobson's terms as that discipline which studies 'the *differentia specifica* of verbal art in relation to other arts and in relation to other kinds of verbal behavior,' in other words, a discipline closely related to the science of language and general semiotics" (from Rudy's pref.). Part 1 contains his chief theoretical papers on the relation of linguistics to poetics.
      CLit 9, 236.

588.   Jameson, Fredric. 1981. *The Political Unconsciousness: Narrative as a Socially Symbolic Act*. Ithaca: Cornell UP. 305 pp.
A study of the historical "dynamics of the act of interpretation," which foregrounds "the interpretive categories or codes through which we read and receive the text in question": "we apprehend" texts "through sedimented layers of previous interpretations." "I will here argue the priority of a Marxian interpretation in terms of semantic richness." Name and term index. [A significant effort to reorganize literary studies.]
      Diacritics 12 (spec. iss. on Jameson, mainly on this book), 23–72; *JLT* 3, 12–17: "My whole objection to the historical matrix for literature . . . is that it is too complex for any community to gather around it"; *MLN* 98, 780–87:

enthusiasm for a work of "high quality"; *MFS* 28, 723: "dazzling," "the sixty pages on *Lord Jim* contain some of the most brilliant arguments ever devoted to Conrad," but perhaps the book expresses too "relentless" a "push for completeness."

589.   Koch, Walter. 1981. *Poetizität* [Poeticalness]. Hildesheim: Olms. 254 pp.
A semiotic-genetic model of the basic qualities of a poetic based on 3 modalities: the concrete-aesthetic, the concrete-metalingual, and the concrete-metaphysical.

590.   Lodge, David. 1981. *Working with Structuralism: Essays and Reviews on Nineteenth- and Twentieth-Century Literature.* Boston: Routledge. 207 pp.
A collection of pub. articles written during the 1970s. Lodge assumes that the European tradition of literary theory and practice loosely called "structuralism" has been established and that critics of all persuasions should employ its insights and methods. Name index only.
    NCF 37, 250: "his own use of the method seems partial and arbitrary. . . . The result leads to some idiosyncratic and partial readings"; *AUMLA* 57, 72–74: "considerably slighter than" *The Modes of Modern Writing* (1977), "not a sustained argument but an uneven collection of sixteen occasional pieces," and "most of the pieces contain nothing particularly structuralist"; *MLR* 77, 907: the essays are "sensible, perceptive, and readable" though "hardly any trace of the methods of structuralism," "has little that is new to tell."

591.   Martínez-Bonati, Félix. 1981. *Fictive Discourse and the Structures of Literature: A Phenomenological Approach.* Trans. Philip Silver. Ithaca: Cornell UP. 176 pp. (Rev. ed., with additions, of *La estructura de la obra literaria.* Santiago: U of Chile, 1960.)
On "the nature of literary discourse and the fundamental architecture of the literary work." Ch. 1, "the logical properties of fictional sentences"; ch. 2, "the functions of discourse and the semiotic analysis of communication; ch. 3, "the ontological status of literary discourse"; and *passim* "the analysis of the art of reading and of literary competence." Name and term indexes.
    Choice 18, 1410: "dated and rigid conceptual repertoire"; *VQR* 57, 129; *LJ* 106, 1308.

592.   Pike, Kenneth L. 1981. *Tagmemics, Discourse, and Verbal Art.* Ann Arbor: Michigan Studies in the Humanities. 47 pp.
Pike applies his tagmemical theories to different aspects of verbal art. Ch. 1, "Linguistic Complexity in a Two-Page Instruction Sheet"; ch. 2, "Levels of Observer Relationship in Verbal Art"; ch. 3, "Grammar versus Reference

in the Analysis of Discourse." Introd. Richard W. Bailey, "Tagmemics and the Universe of Discourse." Bib. 3 pp.

592a.   Raval, Suresh. 1981. *Metacriticism*. Athens: U of Georgia P. 289 pp.
Argues the interdependence of the many schools of criticism with rhetoric and history, using Kant's theory of beauty as norm for the tracing of subjective (Holland, Fish, Bleich) and absolute (Frye, Hirsch) tendencies. Name and term index.
MFS 28, 725: successfully maps out the diffuse territory of modern criticism; only Lentricchia's *After the New Criticism* is its equal and then with qualifications.

593.   Skura, Meredith. 1981. *The Literary Use of the Psychoanalytic Process*. New Haven: Yale UP. 280 pp.
5 models used by the Freudian analyst are a bridge to the interaction among all levels of the text to discover how meaning emerges: case history, fantasy, dream, analyst-patient exchange, and "entire psychoanalytic process . . . the most promising for literary criticism." Name and term index.
YR 71, 288–93: "a definitive account of the new relations between two complex and changing disciplines"; *Choice* 18, 1540: "a landmark," "indispensable."

594.   Stafford, William. 1981. *Books Speaking to Books: A Contextual Approach to American Fiction*. Chapel Hill: U of North Carolina P. 165 pp.
A method of examining a work with other works that share its thematic elements; e.g., the images of whiteness in *Moby-Dick*, *The Wings of the Dove*, and *Absalom, Absalom!* Name index.
MFS 28, 301: "the method . . . appears to be a happenstance, and not a very sophisticated one"; *AL* 54, 141.

595.   Strickland, Geoffrey. 1981. *Structuralism or Criticism? Thoughts on How We Read*. New York: Cambridge UP. 209 pp.
An attack on the principal structuralist theories of the past 2 decades, especially on the theory that we can construe a closed system of literary signs. The second part defends certain presuppositions about the act of reading and authorial intention. In the final section the author compares the writings of Roland Barthes unfavorably to the criticism of F. R. Leavis. Bib. 6 pp.; name and term index.
AUMLA 57, 70–72: "an attempt by a traditionalist" to prove that the "structuralist 'revolution'" will never surpass "the manifesto stage"; the "uneven" book "does not fulfill the high expectations aroused." *MLR* 77, 907–10: the book "poses a false dilemma," its "radical skepticism" is "untenable," and it is not possible, "as Mr. Strickland seems to advocate," to "return to an antitheoretical, almost instinctive, pre-conceptual practical criticism."

596.   Taylor, Talbot J. 1981. *Linguistic Theory and Structural Stylistics.* Oxford: Pergamon. 111 pp.
Stylistics profoundly reflects its acceptance of the fundamental assumption of linguistics that the function of language is to enable the communication of meaning between speakers. "The aim of this book is to examine some of the theoretical dilemmas to which such a view of style, language, and communication leads." Ch. 1, "The Concept of Style"; ch. 2, "Bally and the Saussurian Origins of Structural Stylistics"; ch. 3, "Jakobson and the Poetic Function of Language"; ch. 4, "Riffaterre and Affective Stylistics"; ch. 5, "Generative Stylistics and the Stylistics of Processing Strategies"; ch. 6, "Stylistics Theories and Communications." Brief bib. (1 1/2 pp.), author and subject indexes. [A highly skeptical critique of stylistics, "the extreme vulnerability of every new proposal," the mentalist "hocus-pocus" employed to explain how communication works.]
PoT 3, 200; *Choice* 19, 620: "clearly written," "recommended for . . . upper-division undergraduates and graduate students"; *Lingua* 60, 96–97.

597.   Todorov, Tzvetan. 1981. *Introduction to Poetics.* Trans. Richard Howard. Minneapolis: U of Minnesota P. 83 pp. (Orig. pub. in *Qu'est-ce que le structuralisme: Poétique*, 1968; rev. ed., *Poétique*, 1973; both Paris: Seuil).
After a definition of "poetics," Todorov establishes the elements essential to the analysis of a literary text: semantics; registers; verbal aspects of mode, time, perspective, voice; syntax (sentence and narrative). In the final ch. he enlarges his discussion to "perspectives" of literary history and aesthetics in general. Name and term index.
MLR 78, 636: a "lucid" "primer on formalist and structuralist poetics" but contains some contradictions and ambivalences; *JAAC* 41, 112; *BW* 12, 12.

598.   Todorov, Tzvetan. 1981. *Mixail Baxtin le principe dialogique suivi de écrits du cercle de Baxtin* [Mixail Baxtin, the Dialogical Principle, Followed by the Writings of Baxtin's Circle]. Paris: Seuil. 318 pp.
An introd. to Baxtin.
MLR 77, 398–402: a "clear and thorough guide" but advances "inordinate claims" for the thought of Baxtin.

599.   Aarsleff, Hans. 1982. *From Locke to Saussure: Essays on the Study of Language and Intellectual History.* Minneapolis: U of Minnesota P. 422 pp.
14 essays moving from "the rise of science in the seventeenth century to the publication of Saussure's" *Cours.* Includes "Wordsworth, Language, and Romanticism." Name and term index 21 pp.
LRB 4, 11; *NYRB*, 29, 36; *Obs* 23 May 1982, 31; *TLS* 9 July 1982, 734.

600.   Barthes, Roland. 1982. *A Barthes Reader.* Ed. Susan Sontag. New York:
        Hill. 495 pp.
        Previously pub. material (1942–79) except for 2 newly translated essays. Son-
        tag's introd. places him in the Fr. tradition — from Montaigne through Gide —
        of exploration of the self.
        AR 41, 120: "essential" for anyone "with an interest in comtemporary cul-
        tural and literary criticism"; *HR* 36, 411; *TLS* 10 Dec. 1980, 1372; *Nat* 235, 525.

601.   Bruss, Elizabeth. 1982. *Beautiful Theories: The Spectacle of Discourse
        in Contemporary Criticism.* Baltimore: Johns Hopkins UP. 519 pp.
        An attempt to explain how, "in little more than a decade, the practices and
        the very subject matter of Anglo-American literary studies have shifted so pro-
        foundly" and criticism has become "theory as literature" (part 1). Separate
        chs. on Gass, Sontag, Bloom, and Barthes. Name and term index.
        Choice 20, 699: "clear, levelheaded, and in several places ground-breaking,"
        "indispensable" for graduate libraries; *LJ* 107, 995.

602.   Chapman, Raymond. 1982. *The Language of English Literature.* Lon-
        don: Arnold. 148 pp.
        Literature is not a special code but "the planned and skillful use of what all
        speakers of English can share," nor does the "examination of language de-
        pend upon any school or theory." Evaluates a feature easily identifiable out-
        side literature yet different from the expectations of normal language. 11 chs.:
        "Strange and Familiar Language," "The Use of English," "Literature and
        Style," "Literature and Everyday Language," "The Special Language of Liter-
        ature," etc. Bib. 2 1/2 pp.; author and general indexes.
        BBN Dec. 1982, 760; *TES* 14 Jan. 1983, 24.

603.   Culler, Jonathan. 1982. *On Deconstruction: Theory and Criticism in
        the 1970s.* Ithaca: Cornell UP. 302 pp.
        A sequel to *Structuralist Poetics,* i.e., a discussion of the criticism of the 1970s,
        especially an analysis of the problems raised by the recent critical emphasis
        on the reading experience and an exposition of the ideas and methods of
        deconstruction as related to other strands of contemporary criticism. Ch. 1,
        "Readers and Reading," deals with structuralism and reader response criti-
        cism, "Reading as a Woman," and "Stories of Reading" (Holland, Fish, Bleich,
        Hirsch, Booth, Riffaterre, Iser); ch. 2, "Deconstruction," is mainly about Der-
        rida; ch. 3, "Deconstructive Criticism," "analyses a range of studies from the
        growing store of deconstructive criticism" — Michaels, B. Johnson, de Man,
        Brenkman, et al. Bib. 21 pp.; name and term index.
        CE 46, 818: "in many respects, the best, most authoritative account of its
        subject"; *HR* 36, 542: "authority" on "decon." but "likes all resisting read-
        ings equally well," "inside the formidably thorough, patient, well-read per-

son of Jonathan Culler beats an unproblematical heart of common sense";
LJ 108, 744: "in general admirably crisp and concise," "eminently readable";
AR 41, 373; *NS* 105, 24; *NR* 188, 28; *LRB* 5, 17.

604.   Deely, John. 1982. *Introducing Semiotic: Its History and Doctrine.*
         Bloomington: Indiana UP. 246 pp.
Part 1 gives the history, especially the importance of Poinsot; part 2 deals with
the 20th cent. 2 apps.; bib. 30 pp.; term and name indexes. [The historical-
theoretical body of the book is only about 120 pp.]
    Choice 20, 701: contrasts the book to Eco's *A Theory of Semiotics* and Se-
beok's *The Sign and Its Masters,* "a welcome perspective on the evolution of
semiotic thought."

605.   Derrida, Jacques. 1982. *Margins of Philosophy.* Trans. Alan Bass.
         Chicago: U of Chicago P. 448 pp. (*Marges de la philosophie.* Paris:
         Minuit, 1972.)
Essays on linguistics (Saussure, Benveniste, Austin), metaphor, and the languages of philosophy.
    LJ 107, 2259: "true illumination for those prepared to follow his arduous
path"; *SHR* 18, 289.

606.   Fiske, John. 1982. *Introduction to Communication Studies.* London:
         Methuen. 174 pp.
The book identifies 2 main schools. "One is that which sees communication
as the encoding, transmission and decoding of messages" (the process school).
"The other sees communication as the generation of meanings, and is concerned with the interaction of communicator, text and audience" (the semiotic school). The author favors the semiotic approach in combination with
the process approach. Chs. 1–5 give the main models, theories, and concepts;
chs. 6–7, methods and applications of analysis; ch. 8, ideology and meaning.
Bib. 10 pp.; name and term index.
    Western Teacher 11, 7: "cohesive and illuminating," "clear argument, in-
teresting illustration and logical presentation"; *BBN* Sept. 1982: "lucid and
balanced summaries": "This will undoubtedly and deservedly become a widely
used text" [but elsewhere critical].

607.   Genette, Gérard. 1982. *Figures of Literary Discourse.* Trans. Alan
         Sheridan. New York: Columbia UP. 303 pp.
Trans. of 11 essays from *Figures I* (1966), *II* (1969), and *III* (1972) divided into
7 theoretical essays and the remainder readings of specific literary texts. Name
and term index.
    JAAC 41, 454: "strong readings of major works and insightful analyses of
concepts . . . written in a prose clearer than that of his contemporaries";
Critm 25, 67; *ECr* 23, 109; *LRB* 4, 8.

607a.   Genette, Gérard. 1982. *Palimpsestes: La littérature au second degré*
        [Palimpsests: Literature with a Second Level of Meaning]. Paris: Seuil.
        472 pp.
An examination of a wide range of critical concepts—intertext, architext,
paratext, avant-text, hypertext, metatext—and texts, with focus on "parody"
(reading 1 text by its relation with another text).
    MLN 98, 761–64: "c'est le meilleur Genette (mais sans doute aussi le plus
prévisible) qui cherche à reprendre du terrain"; *WLT* 57, 243: the strength
of this taxonomy of the dependencies of texts "is found in the explanations
linking various primary texts" to their models.

608.   Green, Geoffrey. 1982. *Literary Criticism and the Structures of History:
        Erich Auerbach and Leo Spitzer.* Lincoln: U of Nebraska P. 186 pp.
"He shows us" how their contributions to literary study are linked "to their
personal histories and the longer history of their times" (from the foreword
by Robert Scholes). Name and term index.
    SAQ 83, 467.

609.   Gumperz, John. 1982. *Discourse Strategies.* Cambridge: Cambridge UP.
        225 pp.
An exploration of how linguistic knowledge and social factors interact in oral
exchanges. Ch. 9 deals with "Ethnic Style in Political Rhetoric." Bib. 8 pp.;
name and term indexes. [Marginally relevant to literary criticism.]
    Choice 20, 825: "excellent"; *BBN* May 1983, 305; *TLS* 14 June 1983, 37.

610.   Hervey, Sándor. 1982. *Semiotic Perspectives.* London: Allen. 273 pp.
Explanations of the kinds of semiotics. After a ch. on Saussure and Peirce,
individual chs. treat "Semiotics as a Behavioural Theory: Charles Morris,"
"Semiotics as a Theory of 'l'Acte Sémique': Luis Prieto," "Semiotics as a The-
ory of 'Speech Acts': Austin and Searle," "Semiology as an Ideology of Socio-
Cultural Signification: Roland Barthes," "Semiology as a Theory of Semio-
logical Systems and of Indices: Functionalism," "An Integrated Theory of
Semiotics: Axiomatic Functionalism," "Semiotics as a Stylistic Theory: Bureau and Riffaterre," "Semiotics of the Cinema: Christian Metz," and "Zoo-
Semiotics." Bib. 4 pp.; name and term index.
    QJS 70, 90; *Choice* 20, 976.

611.   Hohendahl, Peter. 1982. *The Institution of Criticism.* [Articles trans.
        from Ger.] Ithaca: Cornell UP. 287 pp.
7 essays pub. 1971–79 giving a social history of Ger. criticism and discussion
of modern criticism as an institution. Name and term index.
    MFS 28, 727: "goes a long way toward providing" a "thorough examina-
tion" of "the ways in which the literary system was embedded in the larger
social system"; *GQ* 55, 572 (in Ger.).

612.   Kenny, Anthony. 1982. *The Computation of Style: An Introduction to Statistics for Students of Literature and Humanities.* New York: Pergamon. 176 pp.

A minicourse in statistical methods for literary analysis. Pt. 1 discusses descriptive statistics and computing. Pt. 2 deals with inferential statistics and cross-sectional sampling.

MLJ 67, 176: "clearly and consistently presented," "an excellent springboard for the neophyte"; *BBN* Dec. 1982, 761; *TLS* 26 Nov. 1982, 1290. [See Brainerd, no. 416, and Oakman, no. 573a.]

613.   Lavers, Annette. 1982. *Roland Barthes: Structuralism and After.* Cambridge: Harvard UP. 300 pp.

A chronological examination of Barthes's books and essays reveals the continuity of his aims and the shifts of his views. Apps. on structuralism, semiology, synchrony and diachrony, language and meaning. Bib. 25 pp.; name index. [Lavers, a translator of Barthes, communicated the ideas of her book to him during its composition.]

RR 74, 502–04 (in Fr.): the best-documented book, at least on the first half of Barthes's work; *Choice* 20, 576: "excellent" in the first four-fifths of the book on Barthes as a synthesizer "of linguistic, structuralist, semiotic, and Marxist thought."

614.   Lunn, Eugene. 1982. *Marxism and Modernism: An Historical Study of Lukács, Brecht, Benjamin, and Adorno.* Berkeley: U of California P. 332 pp.

A study of a group of Ger. Marxist writers of the 1930s and 1940s who express a flexible response to modernism. Bib. 33 pp.; name and term index.

LJ 107, 2340: "impressive scholarship"; *Choice* 20, 978.

615.   Norris, Christopher. 1982. *Deconstruction: Theory and Practice.* London: Methuen. 157 pp.

Deconstruction is an aggressively skeptical attack on the assumption that literary texts possess meaning and that literary criticism is the way to that meaning. The challenge is made partly by denying any distinction between literature and literary criticism and partly by arguing "the powerlessness of ready-made concepts to explain or delimit the activity of writing." The book is mainly about Derrida, the influence on him and his influence on U.S. critics. Chs. on structuralism and New Criticism, Derrida, Nietzsche, Marx and Nietzsche, U.S. deconstructionists, and Wittgenstein. Bib. 14 pp.; proper name and topical indexes.

CE 46, 815: "over-values the deconstructionists," but "on the whole, an excellent guide"; *CL* 35, 283: "reliable," even "excellent," though "reservations about both its style and content"; *MLR* 78, 137; *RSR* 9, 6; *LRB* 4, 9.

615a.   Posner, Roland. 1982. *Rational Discourse and Poetic Communication: Methods of Linguistic, Literary and Philosophical Analysis*. Berlin: de Gruyter. 258 pp.
Ch. 1, semiotic framework for texts as instruments of purposive behavior; ch. 2, meaning and signs, semantics and pragmatics; ch. 3, iconicity, grammar, style; ch. 4, pragmatic differences between sentences which have the same meaning applied to dialogue; ch. 5, creativity in poetry. Chs. 6, 7, and 8 apply the approach in ch. 5 to Baudelaire's "Les chats," Goethe's *An den Mond*, and Sterne's *Tristram Shandy*; ch. 9, socially positive roles of rational discourse and poetry.

616.   Quirk, Randolph. 1982. *Style and Communication in the English Language*. London: Arnold. 136 pp.
Previously pub. but rev. essays, only 1 of which deals with belles lettres. Quirk's theme is that "Style and communication are inseparable." Name and term index.
    Lang&S 16, 504: "an extraordinary range of scholarly reference, a constantly alert intelligence," but limited by the "model of language" the author uses; *LRB* 5, 17; *TES* 11 Feb. 1983, 28; *Choice* 21, 90.

616a.   Schmidt, Siegfried. 1982. *Foundation for the Empirical Study of Literature: The Components of a Basic Theory*. Trans. and rev. Robert de Beaugrande. Hamburg: Buske. 207 pp. (Based on *Grundriss der empirischen Literaturwissenschaft*. Wiesbaden: Braunschweig, 1980.)
An interdisciplinary study of text based on the action theory of literary and aesthetic communication, involving literary production, mediation, perception, postprocessing, cognition, norm, and emotion. The author announces a next vol. to exemplify the theory regarding literary history, pedagogy, and criticism.
    Ling 20, 764–68: "impressive results," "contains components of a new theory of literature," "certain inadequacies" but "a remarkable achievement."

617.   Scholes, Robert. 1982. *Semiotics and Interpretation*. New Haven: Yale UP. 161 pp.
Explains the concepts and terminology of semiotics in the context of contemporary literary theory and applies them to fiction, poetry, drama, and film. Out of these arguments the author has developed a theory of literature. 1 ch. presents "Semiotic Approaches to Joyce's 'Eveline,' " another discusses the role of literature and language in shaping consciousness of the female body. "Glossary of Semiotic Terminology." Annotated bib. 5 pp.; name and term index.
    JLT 3, 22–26: "a stimulating and useful book" because it focuses "on the public matter of working with literature in the classroom"; *Critm* 24, 382:

"little that is new about either theory or literature"; *AL* 54, 476; *AR* 40, 368; *TLS* 15 Oct. 1982, 1140; *Choice* 20, 79.

617a.   Seung, T. K. 1982. *Semiotics and Thematics in Hermeneutics*. New York: Columbia UP. 242 pp.

"My objective is to reinstate contextual understanding as the foundation of all our interpretive activities, as installed long ago in the German hermeneutic tradition. . . . I will show how the recent developments in linguistics and semiotics can be used for articulation of various contexts. I will further show the indispensability of contextual articulation for the thematic explication of textual meaning." Name and term index.

Choice 20, 1131: "concerned with important critical issues . . . for research libraries"

618.   Seung, T. K. 1982. *Structuralism and Hermeneutics*. New York: Columbia UP. 310 pp.

An explication of the "transition from structuralism to post-structuralism." Concentrates on philosophy (Heidegger, Husserl, Derrida) but literary criticism also discussed (Fish, Barthes).

JAAC 41, 348–50: "convincing" and "at a number of points . . . original," but his "polemical intentions" "skew" his line of argument; *Choice* 19, 1554: "lapses," but a "well-written book"; *TLS* 9 July 1982, 734.

619.   Todorov, Tzvetan. 1982. *Symbolism and Interpretation*. Trans. Catherine Porter. Ithaca: Cornell UP. 175 pp. (*Symbolisme et interpretation*. Paris: Seuil, 1978.)

Rhetoric and hermeneutics, the production and interpretation of discourse, united. 2 parts: "Symbolics of Language" (general theory) and "Strategies of Interpretation" (patristic vs. philological exegesis). Bib. 2 pp.; name index.

MLN 98, 765–71: a generally negative rev., partly because the book needs the substantiation found in Todorov's *Theories of the Symbol*; *PoT* 2, 231–36.

620.   Todorov, Tzvetan. 1982. *Theories of the Symbol*. Trans. Catherine Porter. Ithaca: Cornell UP. 302 pp. (*Théories du symbole*. Paris: Seuil, 1977, shortened and updated.)

A history of semiotics, the tradition of sign theory, from classical rhetoric to the present; a discussion of the ways words become symbols; and theories of the symbol in Freud, Saussure, and Jakobson. Bib. "Notes" 4 pp.; name index.

CL 35, 286–89: some parts "interesting and valuable," other parts "odd or misconceived"; "I am very disappointed in this book"; *Choice* 20, 421: "very good translation," "the most important study of symbolism to appear in English since Angus Fletcher's *Allegory*"; *PoT* 2, 231–36; *BL* (1977), 3423; (1978), 2573; (1979), 2767.

621.   Wellek, René. 1982. *The Attack on Literature and Other Essays*. Chapel
        Hill: U of North Carolina P. 199 pp.
        Chs. on "Science, Pseudoscience, and Intuition in Recent Criticism," "The
        New Criticism: Pro and Contra," and "Russian Formalism," etc. Name and
        term indexes.

621a.   Adams, Hazard. 1983. *Philosophy of the Literary Symbolic*. Tallahas-
        see: UP of Florida. 466 pp.
        A survey of significant contributions to the idea of the symbolic by Vico, Kant,
        Blake, Cassirer, Campbell, Wheelright, et al. Bib.; index.
        PoT 5, 212; *TLS* 6 Apr. 1984, 370.

621b.   Atkins, G. Douglas. 1983. *Reading Deconstruction/Deconstructive Read-
        ing*. Lexington: UP of Kentucky. 158 pp.
        The first half of the book examines and defends deconstructive critics, the
        second half applies deconstructive concepts to 18th-cent. literary works. Name
        and term index.
        CE 46, 814: "cogent survey" but "tendency to lapse into caricature."

621c.   Bartel, Roland. 1983. *Metaphors and Symbols: Forays into Language*.
        Urbana: NCTE. 83 pp.
        An informal discussion for secondary and undergraduate courses. Chs. on
        "Popular Metaphor" (riddles, slang, etc.), "Humor in Metaphor," etc.

622.   Deleted.

623.   Culler, Jonathan. 1983. *Roland Barthes*. New York: Oxford UP. 130 pp.
        Introductory guide to Barthes as (the ch. titles) man of parts, literary historian,
        mythologist, critic, polemicist, semiologist, structuralist, hedonist, writer, and
        man of letters. Bib. 3 pp.; name and term index.
        LJ 108, 1363: "knowledgeable, jargon-free, balanced, and well-written";
        Choice 21, 430; *WLT* 58, 70.

623a.   Cummings, Michael, and Robert Simmons. *The Language of Literature:
        A Stylistic Introduction to the Study of Literature*. Foreword M. A. K.
        Halliday. Oxford: Pergamon, 1983. 235 pp.
        The authors employ the approach of the "systemic" school of modern lin-
        guistics, because of "the advantages of a grammar which is less complex than
        some of the alternatives, and an approach to lexis which we have found in-
        triguing to students and useful in the analysis of texts. In addition systemic
        linguistics has always been very text-oriented and empirical in its approach,
        and this pays off in stylistic applications." The book "progresses through the
        systemicists' 'levels of language'" — from phonology and graphology to gram-
        mar and lexis to literary context: each of the eleven units builds on "the knowl-

edge gained so far." The book is designed as a text book "for use at the third- and fourth-year college and graduate levels." Bib.; index.

Style 18, 221: "some things to admire" but the authors "let their grammatical model *limit* . . . what they say about style."

624. Eagleton, Terry. 1983. *Literary Theory: An Introduction*. Oxford: Blackwell; Ithaca: Cornell UP. 244 pp.

After tracing the rise of Eng. as an academic discipline, the author sets forth the main features of the major schools in modern literary theory—phenomenology, hermeneutics, reception theory, structuralism, semiotics, post-structuralism, and psychoanalysis. Bib. 8 pp.; name and term index.

Nat 238, 59: "clear and cogent" but as "a Marxist, he has axes to grind" and with space for only "roughly ten pages of text for each theory" the book is superficial; *In These Times* 8.13, 18: "remarkable and important"; *PoT* 5, 149, and 5, 429; *CE* 47, 407–19.

625. Felman, Shoshana. 1983. *The Literary Speech Act: Don Juan with J. L. Austin, or Seduction in Two Languages*. Ithaca: Cornell UP. 176 pp. (*Le Scandale du corps parlant: Don Juan avec Austin ou la séduction en deux langues*. Paris: Seuil, 1980.)

Imagines an encounter between Molière's *Don Juan* and J. L. Austin, showing that Molière studies the performance of seduction and that speech-act theory reflects eros as well. Most of the book is an explanation and virtual panegyric of Austin's ideas.

MLR 76, 963–64 (rev. of the Fr.): deserves a "careful perusal"; one may question its "overall coherence," but argument developed "logically and with enough examples"; *Diacritics* 11.3, 27–28.

626. Fónagy, Iván. 1983. *La vive voix: Essais de psycho-phonétique* [The Living Voice: Essays on Psychophonetics]. Paris: Payot. 346 pp.

Introd. Roman Jakobson. The distinctive features of "live speech," in contrast to "dead letters," are investigated by means of physiological, acoustic, and semantic analysis in the conceptual framework of psychoanalysis. 87 figs., 32 tables.

626a. Foulkes, A. P. 1983. *Literature and Propaganda*. London: Methuen. 124 pp.

Ch. 2 defines propaganda; ch. 3 examines literature and "the schemes of interpretation which have collected" around it, etc., for an exploration of the relations between literature and propaganda. Bib. 5 pp.; name and term index.

Choice 21, 699; *TES* 14 Oct. 1983, 30; *VLS* Apr. 1984, 17.

626b. Fry, Paul. 1983. *The Reach of Criticism: Method and Perception in Literary Theory*. New Haven: Yale UP. 239 pp.

Treats some landmark texts in the history of criticism to argue against preoccupation with method. A discussion of "how method goes wrong" in Aristotle's *Poetics* leads to Longinus's *On the Sublime* "as a model of non-Aristotelian thinking" that leads to non-Longinian extremes—Dryden's "Preface to *Fables*" and Shelley's *Defence of Poetry*—and finally to "a personal view of method" mediated by the work of Walter Benjamin. Name and term index. *VQR* 60, 9; *LRB* 6, 16; *TLS* 18 May 1984, 580.

627.   Hutchinson, Peter. 1983. *Games Authors Play*. London: Methuen. 131 pp.
Application of the concept of "game" to literature—sound play, puzzles, irony, pun, paradox, ambiguity, allusion, etc. Part 1 is "an introduction to literary games in general." Part 2 presents various literary games in alphabetical order.
    Choice 21, 1602: too brief for "readers with a strong literature background"; *Enc* 63, 50; *TLS* 25 May 1984, 580.

628.   Jakobson, Roman, and Krystyna Pomorska. 1983. *Dialogues*. Cambridge, MA: MIT P; Cambridge, Eng.: Cambridge UP. 183 pp. (*Dialogues*. Paris: Flammarion, 1980.)
A collaboration between Jakobson and Pomorska to "explore" Jakobson's "career." The 15 chs. include such topics as poetics, folklore, phonology, time, space, parallelism, metaphor and metonymy, and semiotics. Afterword by Pomorska. Bib. 1 p.
    Choice 20, 1590: "a valuable bird's-eye view" but "fully accessible only to readers already familiar with much of Jakobson's work"; an easier introd. is Jakobson and Waugh, *The Sound Shape of Language*.

629.   King, James R. 1983. *The Literary Moment As a Lens on Reality*. Columbia: U of Missouri P. 213 pp.
A study of significant moments in the works of 9 writers arranged in chronological order—Donne, Bacon, Sterne, Wordsworth, Melville, Paul Goodman, Borges, and Durrell. The book is not a history of the moment in literature, however, but is an exploration of kinds of significant moments. Name index, with a few terms.

629a.   Koch, Walter. 1983. *Poetry and Science, Semiogenetical Twins: Towards an Integrated Correspondence Theory of Poetic Structures*. Tübingen: Narr. 608 pp.
This "semiogenetic" approach to "poeticity" combines the ideas of Roman Jakobson and other semioticians with points of view shared by literary theory, anthropology, biology, and systems theory. Among the arguments in the book: poetic theory must include 3 modes of "poeticity" (aesthetic, stylistic, and metaphysical); each mode evinces three different phases of structure (prosphory, diaphory, symphony). Analyses of concrete texts are included.

630. Lehmann, Winfred. 1983. *Language: An Introduction*. New York: Random. 241 pp.

"*Language: An Introduction* is a successor to the two earlier editions of *Descriptive Linguistics*. . . . [T]he interests of linguists have been extended, especially to the consideration of texts as well as sentences, to typological structures, and to applications." Ch. 12, "Language in Its Diversity": sections on the uses of language by politicians, poets, scientists, priests. Bib. 4 pp.; name and term index.

631. Leitch, Vincent. 1983. *Deconstructive Criticism: An Advanced Introduction*. New York: Columbia UP. 304 pp.

The book deals with the questions What is a text? and What is interpretation? by attempting to "portray" deconstruction. Deconstruction as a mode of textual theory and analysis "subverts almost everything in the tradition, putting in question received ideas of the sign and language, the text, the context, the author, the reader," etc. Part 1 "focuses on modern theories of language"; part 2 "investigates theories of literature and tradition"; and part 3 "surveys various influential contemporary practices of critical reading and writing"—Derrida, Barthes, Deleuze, Hartman.

CE 46, 816: "a more substantial and meticulous account of deconstruction than either Norris or Atkins offers"; *LJ* 7, 2258: "the extensive coverage . . . turns out to be wordiness and archness more than real insight and penetrating critical evaluation."

631a. Lentricchia, Frank. 1983. *Criticism and Social Change*. Chicago: U of Chicago P. 173 pp.

A "meditation" on the importance of Kenneth Burke and the destructiveness of Paul de Man. No bib. or index.

CE 47, 407–19: compares the book to Cain (no. 634b3) and Eagleton (no. 624), books that envision English studies as cultural analysis.

632. McGann, Jerome. 1983. *A Critique of Modern Textual Criticism*. Chicago: U of Chicago P. 146 pp.

A book on editing texts but related to criticism by McGann's attack on severing literary texts from their nonliterary contexts: authors are not autonomous, intention is an evolutionary matter, and a literary work is a "series of specific 'texts,' a series of specific acts of production." Name index.

TLS 21 Sept. 1984, 1058; *RSR* 10, 170.

632a. Man, Paul de. 1983. *Blindness and Insight: Essays on the Rhetoric of Contemporary Criticism*. 2nd ed., rev. Minneapolis: U of Minnesota P. 308 pp.

The first edition of this diverse collection of essays is here augmented by several essays, all printed "exactly as they were first published." Name and term index 18 pp.

Introd. Wlad Godzich: "his pre-eminence in the field of literary theory is generally acknowledged"; *CLit* 9, 245: "the most important essay" is "The Rhetoric of Blindness: Jacques Derrida's Reading of Rousseau," where he "proposes his own version of deconstruction"; "it is here that American deconstruction is born"; *NR* 188, 28.

632a1.   Nuttall, A. D. 1983. *A New Mimesis: Shakespeare and the Representation of Reality*. London: Methuen. 209 pp.
This attempt "to show that literature can engage with reality" is also an argument "against formalism, that is, against the resolution of matter into form, reality into fiction, substance into convention." Name and term index.

632b.   Robson, W. W. 1983. *The Definition of Literature and Other Essays*. Cambridge: Cambridge UP. 267 pp.
Attacks purely descriptive criticism, for an honorific criticism "which commits its users to decisions about values and quality."
Choice 21, 88: "lucid, judicious, and urbane."

633.   Shukman, Ann. 1983. *The New Soviet Semiotics*. London: Methuen. 180 pp.
Special emphasis on literature, especially the work of Uspensky and Lotman.

634.   Silverman, Kaja. 1983. *The Subject of Semiotics*. New York: Oxford UP. 309 pp.
Examines Freud, Lacan, Saussure, Peirce, Barthes, Derrida, Benveniste, et al., with many references to literary and cinematic works. Bib. 5 pp.; name and term index.
Choice 21, 269: "a pioneering synthesis"; *LJ* 108, 1138; *FQ* 38, 53; *TLS*, 16 Mar. 1984, 278.

634a.   Thurley, Geoffrey. 1983. *Counter-Modernism in Current Critical Theory*. New York: St. Martin's. 261 pp.
12 chs. on hard- and soft-core modernism, art languages, stylistics and structural poetics, etc. Name and term index.
WLT 58, 482; *LRB* 6, 16; *BBN* June 1984, 365; *Obs* 5 Feb. 1984, 53.

634b.   Ziolkowski, Theodore. 1983. *Varieties of Literary Thematics*. Princeton: Princeton UP. 267 pp.
A group of essays, all but 2 of which have appeared previously, that "use the same basic procedures to explore" thematic material and that illustrate how "themes, motifs, and images constitute an important link between the literary work and the social, cultural, and historical contexts." App. on "A Practical Guide to Literary Thematics." Name and term index.
Choice 21, 826: "entertaining and informative" but short on explaining the "why?" of his examples; *TLS* 20 Apr. 1984, 434.

634b1. Abercrombie, John. 1984. *Computer Programs for Literary Analysis.* Philadelphia: U of Pennsylvania P. 206 pp.

634b2. Chapman, Raymond. 1984. *The Treatment of Sounds in Language and Literature.* Oxford: Blackwell. 272 pp.
Treats the ways in which imaginative writers use the written code of language to convey auditory experience—dialogue, dialect, stress, intonation, qualities of individual voices, etc. Chs. on natural and mechanical sounds, music and the nonverbal signals of conversation; writers who have been particularly aware of the problems in visual expression of sound; and texts in which the tension between sight and sound has been deliberately exploited for literary effect.

634b3. Cain, William. 1984. *The Crisis in Criticism: Theory, Literature, and Reform in English Studies.* Baltimore: Johns Hopkins UP. 307 pp.
CE 47, 407–19: "the most comprehensive book I have seen on its topic."

634c. Eco, Umberto. 1984. *Semiotics and the Philosophy of Language.* Bloomington: Indiana UP. 242 pp.
Conceives of human beings as "signifying animals" whose "ability to produce and to interpret signs, as well as their ability to draw inferences, is rooted in the same cognitive structures." 7 chs.: "Signs," "Dictionary vs. Encyclopedia," "Metaphor," "Symbol," "Code," "Isotopy," "Mirrors." Some parts of the book previously pub. in England. Bib. 8 pp.; name and term indexes.
Choice 21, 1479: "lively yet erudite," "superbly clear and patient"; *NYTBR* 13 May 1984, 17.

634c1. Jakobson, Roman. 1984. *Verbal Art, Verbal Sign, Verbal Time.* Ed. Krystyna Pomorska and Stephen Rudy. Minneapolis: U of Minnesota P. 232 pp.
11 essays selected by Jakobson shortly before his death in 1982 to serve as an introd. to some of his linguistic theories and especially to his work in poetics.

634d. Ray, William. 1984. *Literary Meaning: From Phenomenology to Deconstruction.* Oxford: Blackwell. 228 pp.
Traces the search of literary critics for an adequate sense of the "meaning" of a novel or poem, from its phenomenological beginning to today's deconstruction. Name and term index 7 pp.
LRB 6, 14.

635. Sčeglov, Yuryj, and Alexandr Zolkovskij. 1984. *Poetics of Expressiveness: A Theory and Application.* Amsterdam: Benjamins. C. 330 pp.
The volume presents—for the first time in book form in Eng.—the work of 2 major representatives of the Moscow-Tartu school. The introd. outlines their

project for a "poetics of expressiveness" against the background of the structural-semiotic movement of the 1960s and 1970s. Pt. 1 is a systematic exposition of the theory, concentrating on the concepts of theme, expressive device, poetic world, etc. Pts. 2 and 3 apply these concepts to a structuralist portrayal of Tolstoy's tales for children (shown to be a "*War and Peace* in miniature") and of the medieval Lat. author Archpoet of Cologne (with special emphasis on his "Mock Penitent"). Bib. of the poetics of expressiveness; glossary of its metalanguage.

635a.   Steiner, Peter. 1984. *Russian Formalism: A Metapoetics*. Ithaca: Cornell UP. 276 pp.

636.   Žolkovskij, Alexandr. 1984. *Themes and Texts: Toward a Poetics of Expressiveness*. Ithaca: Cornell UP. 256 pp.
A collection of the author's writings that appeared between 1960 and 1980, supplemented by an introd. written for inclusion here. An attempt to define the devices by which themes are given expressive force. Glossary; bib. 12 pp.; name and term index.

636a.   Bojtár, Endre. 1985. *Slavic Structuralism in Literary Science*. [Trans. from Hungarian.] Amsterdam: Benjamins. 150 pp.

637.   Dijk, Teun van, ed. 1985. *Handbook of Discourse Analysis*. 4 vols. London: Academic. Vol. 1, 320 pp.; 2, 288 pp.; 3, 264 pp.; 4, 240 pp.

3.0 Culture, History, and Style: The Period, the Nation, the Genre (638–1012b)

3.1 Theory (638–758)

638.   Lehnert, Herbert. 1966. *Struktur und Sprachmagie: Zur Methodik der Lyrik-Interpretation* [Structure and Language-Magic: On the Methods of Interpretation of the Lyric]. Stuttgart: Kohlhammer. 159 pp.
An analysis of poetic form and the creative process.
MLR 64, 451–52: "sensitive interpretations."

639.   Ritchie, J. M., ed. 1966. *A Symposium*. Vol. 1 of *Periods in German Literature*. London: Wolff. 320 pp.
General discussions of the extent to which various periods are intellectual or stylistic unities and of the adequacy of the terms used to describe those unities.
MLR 65, 945: "partly successful."

640.   Kuehl, John, ed. 1967. *Creative Writing and Rewriting: Contemporary American Novelists at Work*. New York: Appleton. 308 pp. Also pub.

under title *Write and Rewrite: A Study of the Creative Process* (New York: Meredith, 1967).
Compares portions of original drafts and final published works of 10 writers: Welty, Boyle, Jones, Malamud, Morris, Fitzgerald, Roth, Warren, Hawkes, and Styron.
Style 2, 86–87: "rewarding"; *Sat Rev* 50, 28; *LJ* 92, 2411.

641.   Kempf, Roger. 1968. *Sur le corps romanesque* [On the Imaginative Body]. Paris: Seuil. 189 pp.
An examination of how authors render the physical presence of their characters through gestures, facial expressions, clothes, movement, etc.
MLR 65, 417–18: a favorable rev.

642.   Smith, Barbara H. 1968. *Poetic Closure: A Study of How Poems End.* Chicago: U of Chicago P. 289 pp.
Closure, "the sense of finality, stability, and integrity," depends "primarily upon the reader's experience of the structure of the entire poem." Chs. 2 and 3 deal with closure and formal and thematic "structures"; ch. 4 on "terminal features"; final ch. on failures of closure, on "anti-closure" and other topics. Bib. 6 pp.; name and term index. [See Torgovnick, no. 738.]
RES ns 20, 383–85: "thoroughly clear and logical," but "there is a gap, a thinness in the argument"; *AS* 38, 324; *NYTBR* 3 Aug. 1969, 4; *Choice* 5, 1576.

643.   Sonnino, Lee. 1968. *A Handbook to Sixteenth-Century Rhetoric.* London: Routledge. 278 pp.
The terms are divided into 4 categories: the figures of rhetoric (Lat. names), the figures (Gk. names), style, and genre. Bib. 10 pp.; indexes of tropes and schemes, Gk. terms, Lat. terms, and Ital. terms.
Choice 6, 1374: "has succeeded admirably in her intent"; *QJS* 55, 327.

644.   Barrette, Paul, and Monique Fol. 1969. *Un certain style ou un style certain? Introduction à l'étude du style français* [A Kind of Style or a Certain Style? Introduction to the Study of French Style]. New York: Oxford UP. 351 pp.
A general textbook for courses in Fr.
Style 6, 315–16: the book does not fulfill the promise of the title.

645.   Heilman, Robert. 1969. *Tragedy and Melodrama: Versions of Experience.* Seattle: U of Washington P. 326 pp.
A look at what certain works of different ages have in common, on the assumption that "generic formulations of human truth endure behind the multiplicity of phenomenal variations." Name and term index.

MLR 66, 165–67: the "usefulness of the categories" is "open to question," but the author continually displays "critical insight."

646.   Hodgart, Matthew. 1969. *Satire.* London: Weidenfeld. 255 pp.
A study not only of formal satire but of satire wherever it occurs.
MLR 65, 588–89: a "powerful plea" for studying formal satire.

647.   Leech, Geoffrey. 1969. *A Linguistic Guide to English Poetry.* London: Longman. 237 pp.
Linguistics is seen as fundamental to an explanation of the constituents of poetry—meter, figurative language, etc. Bib. 4 pp.; name and term index.
    RES ns 22, 114: best on meter, but on syntax and semantics "rarely goes beyond what one might expect to find in a traditional school grammar book"; *N&Q* 16, 434; *Choice* 6, 1396; *Lingua* 25, 165: insufficient and too simple exposition of linguistic concepts and application of those concepts to literature; *Poetics* 9, 116: "an elementary textbook in stylistics intended for use by beginning undergraduates."

648.   Nurse, Peter, ed. 1969. *The Art of Criticism: Essays in French Literary Analysis.* Edinburgh: Edinburgh UP. 317 pp.
Analyses of passages from 5 cents. of Fr. literature by critics of diverse orientation.
    MLR 65, 619–20: "practical value," "interesting reading."

649.   Ritchie, J. M., ed. 1969. *Texts and Contexts.* Vol. 2 of *Periods in German Literature.* London: Wolff. 265 pp.
Offers interpretations of representative works.
    MLR 66, 941–42: certain periods receive too partial a treatment, but "the book is by no means a complete failure," since it "contains a number of admirable chapters."

650.   Weissenberger, Klaus. 1969. *Formen der Elegie von Goethe bis Celan* [Forms of the Elegy from Goethe to Celan]. Bern: Francke. 163 pp.
An attempt to identify an ideal type, a timeless inner structure.
    MLR 66, 456: "perceptive analysis of contemporary German poetry."

651.   Brower, Reuben, ed. 1970. *Forms of Lyric.* New York: Columbia UP. 187 pp.
7 diverse essays.
    Style 6, 192–93: the contributors' interest in the process of lyric poems gives some unity to the collection, but otherwise "the essays are each quite distinct."

652.   Kristeva, Julia. 1970. *La texte du roman: Approche sémiologique d'une structure discursive transformationnele* [The Text of the Novel: A Semi-

ological Approach to a Transformational Discursive Structure]. The Hague: Mouton. 209 pp.

Bib. 11 pp.; name and term index.

MLR 68, 900–02: "a collection of suggestions to be developed" rather than "a coherent theoretical enterprise"; *TLS* 3 Sept. 1971, 1055; *RR* 63, 76–78; *RLR* 80, 195–98; *LeS* 6, 509–12.

653. Young, Richard, Alton Becker, and Kenneth Pike. 1970. *Rhetoric: Discovery and Change.* New York: Harcourt. 383 pp.

A textbook based on the idea of rhetoric as concerned primarily with a creative process, from the writer's first choices to the final editing of the final draft. Chs. 2–7, therefore, focus on prewriting or invention, chs. 8–12 on the relation of writer and reader, chs. 13–15 on language and editing, ch. 16 on style. Name and term index.

Centrum 1, 61–76: "a liberating text" based upon "modern linguistic principles," yet "it is embarassingly short on data" (the rev. offers a close comparison with Brooks and Warren's *Modern Rhetoric*).

654. Alonso, Dámaso. 1971. *Pluralità e correlazione in poesia* [Plurality and Correlation in Poetry]. Bari: Adriatica. 390 pp.

A study of the theory and application of correlation in poetry.

MLR 69, 655–57: an "extremely interesting and stimulating" book by "one of the masters of modern literary and stylistic studies."

655. Greimas, A. J., et al. 1971. *Essais de sémiotique poétique* [Essays on Poetic Semiotics]. Paris: Larousse. 240 pp.

Studies of a wide range of Fr. writers—Bataille, Baudelaire, Hugo, et al.—through a great variety of critical theory, method, and language.

Diacritics 4.3, 20–27.

656. Howell, Wilbur S. 1971. *Eighteenth-Century British Logic and Rhetoric.* Princeton: Princeton UP. 742 pp.

A chronological account of the various rhetorical movements during the time when rhetoric was reshaped by the rise of the elocution movement, the affiliation of logic with science, and the development of a "new rhetoric" by Smith, Campbell, and Blair. [See the same author's earlier *Logic and Rhetoric in England, 1500–1700*.] Name and term index 24 pp. [Awarded the $1,000 Book Prize by the Speech Communication Assn., 1972.]

Style 7, 207–10: "comprehensive" and "judicious," "the last word" on the subject; *PhS* 21, 275–77; *WMQ* 3rd ser. 29, 637–43; *QJS* 58, 346–49; *ECS* 7, 353–62; *MP* 72, 205–08.

657. Levitt, Paul. 1971. *A Structural Approach to the Analysis of Drama.* The Hague: Mouton. 119 pp.

A study of "the place, relation, and function of scenes in episodes and in the whole play." Ch. 5, "Rhythm"; ch. 6, "The Whole Analysis: *Riders to the Sea.*" Name index.

658.   Mossop, D. J. 1971. *Pure Poetry: Studies in French Poetic Theory and Practice, 1746 to 1945.* Oxford: Clarendon; London: Oxford UP. 264 pp.
An attempt "to determine the meanings attached to the term" *poésie pure* "by the writers most closely associated with its use": Bremond, Baudelaire, Mallarmé, and Valéry. Bib. 5 pp.; name index.
    MLR 71, 178–79: "at all times lucid, fair, rigorous . . . subtle, shrewd, sensitive."

659.   Neuhaus, Volker. 1971. *Typen multiperspektivischen Erzählens* [Types of Multiperspective Narratives]. Cologne: Böhlau. 179 pp.
Covers a wide diversity of narratives.
    MLR 69, 467–68: "performs a valuable service."

660.   States, Bert. 1971. *Irony and Drama: A Poetics.* Ithaca: Cornell UP. 243 pp.
An analysis of the dialectic of ironic tension in drama, the "unlimited capacity" to "oppose" ideas, based on the criticism of Kenneth Burke. Name and term index.
    MLR 68, 142–44: "despite the shakiness of his theoretical underpinnings" he "produces stimulating insights."

661.   Champigny, Robert. 1972. *Ontology of the Narrative: An Analysis.* The Hague: Mouton. 114 pp. (*Ontologie du narratif.* Paris: St.-Germain-des-Prés, 1972. 127 pp.)
A study of the essentials of narrative fiction and the ways in which they relate to and are distinguished from other literary modes.
    MLJ 58, 142 (on Fr. ed.): "cuts through many confusions"; *Ling* 169, 59–63 (on Eng. ed.).

662.   Genette, Gérard. 1972. *Figures III* [Forms III]. Paris: Seuil. 286 pp.
Most of the book deals with narrative — *ordre, durée, fréquence, mode, voix* — and this part was trans. as *Narrative Discourse.* Bib. 3 pp,; term index.
    Style 8, 139–42.

663.   Hernadi, Paul. 1972. *Beyond Genre: New Directions in Literary Classification.* Ithaca: Cornell UP. 244 pp.
Chs. 1–3 summarize "sixty or so modern theories"; ch. 4 discusses Lukács and Frye; ch. 5 classifies "sixteen or so modes."
    MLR 69, 134–37: "the title's promise is not honoured" and ch. 5 offers a "very simplistic taxonomy," but the book is "extremely learned."

663a.   Howe, James. 1972. *The Making of Style*. Philadelphia: Chilton. 216 pp. An introductory text for composition that focuses on kinds of discourses: argumentation, news story, description, narrative satire, riddles, letters, etc. No bib. or index.

664.   Scaglione, Aldo. 1972. *The Classical Theory of Composition from Its Origins to the Present: A Historical Survey*. Chapel Hill: U of North Carolina P. 447 pp.
A descriptive, chronological survey of what has been said of significance about "the structure of sentences and the ordering of their elements, both on the linguistic and artistic levels," in Gk. and Lat. and, since 1600, in Eng., Fr., and Ital. Bib. 29 pp.; name index 14 pp. [An updated Ger. version appeared in 1981 as vol. 1 of a 2-vol. work, the second vol. of which covers the Germanic area.]
Style 11, 309–10: the author "has read" all the primary texts and "an enormous amount of secondary commentary" and "replicated it with a condensed clarity," the "notes and bibliography constitute in themselves a valuable reference work," and there is an "excellent index"; *Ling* 200, 65–68: "overall solidity"; *ZRP* 93, 110–12; *RPh* 24, 522–38; *LeS* 9, 1–30; *SAQ* 40, 106–09.

665.   Zumthor, Paul. 1972. *Essai de poétique médiévale* [An Essay on Medieval Poetics]. Paris: Seuil. 518 pp.
Diacritics 4.2, 2–11: "extraordinary" achievement.

666.   Bremond, Claude. 1973. *Logique du récit* [The Logic of Narrative]. Paris: Seuil. 349 pp.
Plot analysis of diverse genres, "The Principal Narrative Roles," and critiques of Bédier, Greimas, Todorov, et al.
Diacritics 7.1, 2–17: "(a) Brémond's *Logique du Récit* appears to offer valid criteria for the study of narrative at the level of the *narrated* and in the form of a general theory of roles and role-playing. (b) However, neither this theory nor any other theory of narrative should be considered apart from the stylistic processes, which it implies, and on which it eventually becomes dependent for its elaboration and its application."

667.   Chabrol, Claude, ed. 1973. *Sémiotique narrative et textuelle* [Narrative and Textual Semiotics]. Paris: Larousse. 223 pp.
Diacritics 4.3, 2–8: "a collection of papers exemplifying the richness and variety of narratological activity," including the ed.'s "masterful" rev. of the field of narrative and verbal semiotics since 1966.

668.   Delas, Daniel, and Jacques Filliolet. 1973. *Linguistique et poétique* [Linguistics and Poetics]. Paris: Larousse. 206 pp.
An attempt to define the nature and functioning of poetry in scientific terms.

Style 8, 106–08: the authors "excel at the analytic method and carefully
define many pertinent and potentially problematical terms," but "this book
will be difficult reading for the uninitiated" and it is "unnecessarily wordy,"
"over-organized and compartmentalized"; *BL* (1976), 2961.

669.   Hendricks, William O. 1973. *Essays on Semiolinguistics and Verbal Art.*
        The Hague: Mouton. 210 pp. (Span. tr.: *Semiologia del discurso liter-
        ario.* Madrid: Cátedra, 1976.)
An inquiry into the "upward extension" of linguistics in 7 essays previously
pub. between 1966 and 1971. "Semiolinguistics" is the author's label for a
subfield within semiotics that deals with verbal signs beyond the sentence,
the linguistic study of structures in literature, or texts (here specifically narrative texts). In general the book explores the relation between linguistics and
literary theory. Bib. 9 pp.; name and term indexes.
Style 9, 210–12: "well documented and a sound and exciting discussion of
a very important growing point of our knowledge"; *CJL* 22, 219–21; *LSoc* 5,
110–15; *SAS* 37, 247–48; *AA* 80, 154–55.

670.   Prawer, S. S. 1973. *Comparative Literary Studies: An Introduction.* New
        York: Barnes. 180 pp.
Chs. on definition; national character and literature; reception and communication; influence, analogy and tradition; translation and adaptation; themes
and prefigurations; genres, movements, periods; structure and ideas; "plac-
ing"; theory and criticism. Bib. 4 pp.; name index.
MLR 70, 841: "conscientious," "impressive range of reference," " 'a useful
conspectus in briefest compass,' " but insufficiently empirical; *TLS* 1 May 1974,
105; *LJ* 99, 1304; *Choice* 11, 430.

671.   Prince, Gerald. 1973. *A Grammar of Stories: An Introduction.* The
        Hague: Mouton. 106 pp.
An attempt "to show that a finite number of explicit rules could account for
the structure of all the sets and only the sets which are generally and intui-
tively recognized as stories. . . . Furthermore, I have followed very closely
the early versions of the theory of generative grammar developed by Chomsky."
Bib. 3 pp.; name and term index.

672.   Stern, J. P. 1973. *On Realism.* London: Routledge. 199 pp.
Attempts to define literary realism by philosophical perspectives, contrasts
with alternatives (symbolism, naturalism, socialist realism, etc.), and examples drawn from European literature. Name index.
MLR 69, 137–41: "lucid."

673.   Todorov, Tzvetan. 1973. *The Fantastic: A Structural Approach to a Liter-
        ary Genre.* Trans. Richard Howard. Cleveland: Case Western Reserve UP.

179 pp. (Paperback ed. Cornell UP, 1975; orig. *Introduction à la littér-ature fantastique*, Paris: Seuil, 1970.)
An examination of both generic theory and a particular genre, an essay in fictional poetics in search of the linguistic bases for the structural features in fantastic texts. The author strives for a methodological rigor and system that approaches the scientific. Name index.
Style 8, 98–100: the "snubbing" of data is "damaging" because the book addresses a European literary history "that is only imaginary, a critic's unicorn."

674.   Bruns, Gerald L. 1974. *Modern Poetry and the Idea of Language*. New Haven: Yale UP. 300 pp.
A historical and critical analysis of the "Hermetic" (words refer to other words) and "Orphic" (words signify and give meaning to experience and world) ideas of language. Name and term index.
Style 10, 189–93: "generally . . . saying things that clarify"; *MLR* 70, 386: "a timely book," "a most useful set of concepts" written in "the most ad-mirable lucidity of style"; *DQR* 6, 78–81; *ES* 57, 89–91.

675.   Levin, Samuel R. 1974. *Estructuras lingüísticas en la poesia*. Madrid: Cátedra. 106 pp. (*Linguistic Structures in Poetry*. The Hague: Mouton, 1962.)
BL (1976), 3007.

676.   Mehlman, Jeffrey. 1974. *A Structural Study of Autobiography: Proust, Leiras, Sartre, Lévi-Strauss*. Ithaca: Cornell UP. 246 pp.
A Fr. structuralist and psychoanalytic analysis of recurrent narrative patterns, stylistic details, puns, etc., in the discovery of deviation and absence.
MLR 72, 456–57: "an important contribution to structuralist literature"; *MLJ* 59, 459–60: "brilliantly traverses" the four authors; *CL* 28, 93.

677.   Murphy, James J. 1974. *Rhetoric in the Middle Ages: A History of Rhe-torical Theory from Saint Augustine to the Renaissance*. Berkeley: U of California P. 395 pp. (Ital. trans. Naples: Liqueri, 1983.)
A "medieval history . . . of the preceptive rhetorical tradition," i.e., works that advise how discourse should be composed, showing the stages by which teaching of rhetorical theory evolved. Part 1 (3 chs.) surveys the ancient (mainly Roman) influence; part 2, the main part of the book, traces the preceptive tradition over a one-thousand-year period. Name and term index 21 pp.
Style 9, 234–37: "clear," "valuable, up-to-date"; *RSQ* 5, 6–11: "the history of the medieval arts of discourse has not yet been adequately written, except for Professor Murphy's good work with the *ars dictaminis* and the *ars praedicandi*" (see Murphy's reply); *QJS* 61, 336–40: "Whatever the faults of *Rhetoric in the Middle Ages*, it surely marks a giant step forward"; *P&R* 9, 181–85; *RPh* 30, 663–65.

678.   Weisstein, Ulrich. 1974. *Comparative Literature and Literary Theory: Survey and Introduction.* Trans. William Riggan. Bloomington: Indiana UP. 340 pp. (*Einführung in die vergleichende Literaturwissenschaft.* Stuttgart: Kohlhammer, 1968.)
Chs. on definition; influence and imitation; reception and survival; epoch, period, generation, and movement; genre; thematology; literature and the other arts. Long app. on the history of the discipline. App. 2 on "Bibliographical Problems." Bib. 34 pp,; name index.
    Centrum 2, 90–93: "not a step forward."

679.   Bloch, Maurice, ed. 1975. *Political Language and Oratory in Traditional Society.* London: Academic. 240 pp.
Ethnography of language ("Maori Oratory and Politics," etc.) but potentially applicable to literature, and ch. 10, "Ambiguity in Political Discourse," offers "a sociolinguistic investigation into a corpus of French political tracts of May '68." Bib. 5 pp.; name and term index.
    Choice 13, 107: "intriguing start," "for professionals and specialized graduate students"; *TLS* 26 Mar. 1976, 357; *CS* 6, 330.

680.   Fries, Udo. 1975. *Studien zur Textlinguistik: Frage und Antwortsätze. Eine Analyse an neuenglischen Dramatexten* [Studies in Text Linguistics: Questions and Responses. An Analysis of New English Dramatic Texts]. Vienna: Braumüller. 256 pp.
Examination of the structure and content of questions and answers.

681.   Gülich, Elisabeth, and Wolfgang Raible, eds. 1975. *Textsorten: Differenzierungskriterien aus linguistischer Sicht* [Types of Texts: Linguistic Criteria for Differentiation]. Wiesbaden: Athenäum. 241 pp.

682.   Gunter, Richard. 1975. *Reading Poems.* Columbia: Hornbeam. 87 pp.
With special attention to grammar the author confronts the problem of teaching linguistics and stylistics simultaneously. Chs. on "The Question of Meaning," "The Inner System of English," "The Politics, Action and Geography of the Poem," and "Reading the Poem."
    HQ 3, 83–88; *CCC* 29, 92–95.

683.   Gurewitch, Morton. 1975. *Comedy, the Irrational Vision.* Ithaca: Cornell UP. 245 pp.
Aims "to focus on comedy's interest in illogic and irreverence, in disorder and disinhibition"; consequently, farce is the primary subject (chs. 4–5), with satire, humor, and irony secondary. Name and term index.
    Style 10, 109–13: "highly original" on farce but leaves out the linguistic aspect: "Still another study remains to be written on the language and style of irrational comedy."

684.   Martínez García, José. 1975. *Propiedades del lenguaje poético* [Attrib-
       utes of Poetic Language]. Oviedo: U de Oviedo. 602 pp.
Starting from a general definition of poetry and through the analysis of over
400 short and simple illustrative extracts, an attempt is made to deduce a
series of progressively more complex and specific concepts. The book is arranged into 10 chapters plus a summary of conclusions. The aim of the book
is to prove that the only system that underlies the poetic text is the linguistic
system (from the author's summary in Eng. by letter).
      BL (1977), 3350.

685.   "Narratology." 1975. *Poétique* 6.24. 111 pp.
       7 essays.

686.   Prieto, Antonio. 1975. *Morfología de la novela* [Morphology of the
       Novel]. Barcelona: Planeta. 427 pp.
A study of the novel as an aesthetic sign composed of linguistic sign, symbol,
and symptom in a two-way communication.
      MLR 71, 611: a generally negative rev.

687.   Wicker, Brian. 1975. *The Story-Shaped World: Fiction and Metaphysics.
       Some Variation on a Theme*. Notre Dame: U of Notre Dame P. 230 pp.
An account of how the world is shaped by metaphor and narrative. The first
part of the book is organized by an elaborate binary system (especially meta-
phor/analogy); the second part assesses the adequacy of modern stories to shape
the world (Lawrence, Joyce, Waugh, Beckett, Robbe-Grillet, and Mailer). Bib.
7 pp.; name index.
      Style 11, 94–95: "interesting but sometimes very confusing," the "theoret-
ical underpinnings . . . too weak"; *AUMLA* 46, 305–07: "a challenging and
ambitious book."

688.   Zumthor, Paul. 1975. *Langue, texte, énigme* [Language, Text, and Rid-
       dle]. Paris: Seuil. 266 pp.
Diverse essays extending in approach the author's earlier *Essai de poétique
médiévale*, no. 665.
      MLR 72, 434–35: "The views adumbrated" here "are too complex to be
easily summarized and too important to be ignored."

689.   Frye, Northrop. 1976. *The Secular Scripture: A Study of the Structure
       of Romance*. Cambridge: Harvard UP. 199 pp.
"There are four primary narrative movements in literature. These are, first,
the descent from a higher world; second, the descent to a lower world; third,
the ascent from a lower world; and, fourth, the ascent to a higher world."
Chs. (originally lectures) on the world of man, the context of romance, heroes
and heroines, themes of descent, themes of ascent, and the recovery of myth.
Name index.

Style 11, 212–13: "clarity and comprehensibility," but such a theoretical and wide-ranging subject necessarily results in "oversimplification" and insufficient evidence; *PQ* 56, 531; *PLL* 14, 359; *TLS* 5 Nov. 1976, 1399.

690.   Hendricks, William O. 1976. *Grammars of Style and Styles of Grammar.* Amsterdam: North-Holland. 253 pp.
A collection of independent essays on prose style, dividing the subject into 2 parts—group style and individual style—and defining style as a differential manner of linguistic expression, in an effort to limit and thereby define "style." "Grammatical" includes semantics and text grammar (intersentence). Bib. 11 pp.; name and term indexes.
    Style 11, 119–204; "a disappointing [methodological] contraction in the scope of stylistics" (see Hendricks's extended reply following); *Ling* spec. issue 1978, 316–21: "an original contribution" that "makes up largely for the lack of coherence and systematic treatment"; *Lingua* 48, 276–79.

691.   Shapiro, Michael. 1976. *Asymmetry: An Inquiry into the Linguistic Structure of Poetry.* Amsterdam: North-Holland. 231 pp.
Chs. on language as semiotic; symmetry, asymmetry, and parallelism; a semiotic theory of poetic language; and rhyme. "The chief aim of this book is to offer a theory of poetic language which facilitates a synthetic understanding of the linguistic structure of poetry. This is achieved by the introduction of a concept—*markedness*. . . . It is via markedness that the several levels of linguistic structure in poetic texts are interrelated." Bib. 20 pp.; name index.
    BL (1977), 3259.

692.   Bal, Mieke. 1977. *Narratologie: Essais sur la signification narrative dans quatre romans modernes* [Narratology: Essays on Narrative Signification in Four Modern Novels]. Paris: Klincksieck. 199 pp.
Narratology is the science that formulates the theory of the relations between narrative text, narration, and story. Summary in Eng. Bib. 11 pp.; index.

693.   Dubois, Jacques, et al. 1977. *Rhétorique de la poésie: Lecture linéaire, lecture tabulaire* [Rhetoric of Poetry: Linear Reading and Tabular Reading]. Paris: PUF. 299 pp.
    BL (1978), 2517.

694.   Fowler, Roger. 1977. *Linguistics and the Novel.* London: Methuen. 145 pp.
"I have attempted to draw together several threads in a preliminary sketch" of "a new approach in the criticism of fiction"—Chomsky's transformational grammar, Halliday's functional approach, etc. "The main preoccupation of the present book is the significance . . . of sentence-structures, and of 'trans-

formations,' both in the individual sentence and cumulatively in a complete work." Bib. 7 pp.; name and term index.

Style 12, 389–91: "many virtues — concision and lucidity," "model" use of linguistic concepts, but "two serious failings"; *JLS* 7, 126–27: "cannot be recommended without reservation"; *Novel* 12, 274–76; *JES* 9, 216–17; *TLS* 14 Apr. 1978, 418; *RRL* 24, 551–52; *ArsS* 2, 237–41; *DuJ* 40, 281–83; *BJA* 18, 380–81; *MFS* 25, 371.

695.   "Genres." 1977. *Poétique* 8.32. 127 pp.
7 essays.

696.   Hamon, Philippe. 1977. *Semiologia lessico leggibilità del testo narrativo* [Semiotics, Lexicon, and Readability of the Narrative Text]. Parma/Lucca: Pratiche. 219 pp.
A trans. from Fr. of 4 articles pub. 1972–73.
JLS 8, 129–30: "fruitful and suggestive."

697.   Hartveit, Lars. 1977. *The Art of Persuasion: A Study of Six Novels*. Bergen: Universitetsforlaget. 152 pp.
The subject of this study is "the strategies with which the novelist shapes and guides the reader's response to his work," particularly pattern and emphasis. Each ch. "focuses on a particular aspect of the art of persuasion" in 1 novel, e.g., the door imagery in *Silas Marner*. Bib. 3 pp.; name index.
MFS 24, 306: "quaint" "innocence" and "naiveté" in critical theory but "more or less persuasive as interpretative readings" of the novels; *Choice* 15, 398.

698.   Karrer, Wolfgang. 1977. *Parodie, Travestie, Pastiche* [Parody, Travesty, and Pastiche]. Munich: Fink. 275 pp.
Bib. 24 pp.

699.   Mistrík, Josef. 1977. *Štylistika slovenského jazyka* [Stylistics of the Slovakian Tongue]. Bratislava: SPN. 451 pp.

700.   Nowakowska, Nina. 1977. *Language of Poetry and Generative Grammar: Toward Generative Poetics?* Poznań: U im. Adama Mickiewicza w Poznaniu. 137 pp.
Tests a "theory of language known as generative grammar upon the poetic use of language," using sample analysis of T. S. Eliot's poems. Bib. 7 pp.

701.   Pfister, Manfred. 1977. *Das Drama: Theorie und Analyse* [The Drama: Theory and Analysis]. Munich: Fink. 454 pp.
An attempt to present a systematic description, analysis, and terminology for

drama, which includes performance, machinery (set, props), and audience in addition to the text.
MLR 75, 832–33: "For those who are prepared to face and overcome the terminology barrier the book will . . . prove most rewarding."

702.   Rohrich, Lutz. 1977. *Der Witz: Figuren, Formen, Funktionen* [The Joke: Figures, Forms, Functions]. Stuttgart: Metzler. 343 pp.
BL (1979), 2755.

703.   Todorov, Tzvetan. 1977. *The Poetics of Prose*. Trans. Richard Howard. Ithaca: Cornell UP. 272 pp. (*La poétique de la prose*. Paris: Seuil, 1971.) Collection of 16 essays written between 1964 and 1969 on verisimilitude, grammar of narrative, formalism, etc. Name and term index.
Scholes, *Semiotics and Interpretation*: "formidable," "lucid, logical," "together with Genette's *Narrative Discourse* and Barthes's *S/Z*, this is one of the major texts in the semiotic study of fiction" (155); *MLR* 68, 900–02: "exemplary clarity," "a good introduction" to "the contemporary French attempt to develop a literary semiology or poetics."

704.   Varga, A. Kibédi. 1977 *Les constantes du poème: Analyse du langage poétique* [The Constants of a Poem: Analysis of Poetic Language]. Paris: Picard. 309 pp.

705.   Chatman, Seymour. 1978. *Story and Discourse: Narrative Structure in Fiction and Film*. Ithaca: Cornell UP. 277 pp.
A comprehensive approach to a general theory of narrative, the ways plot, character, and settings are transmitted, through a synthesis of recent Continental critical concepts and methods. Name and term indexes.
PoT 1, 171–86: "reviews much important theoretical material from French sources, organizes it in a coherent way, introduces a number of original ways of approaching narrative," and offers "specific examples from a wide range of narrative," "a basic guide to the study of narrative"; *MLR* 75, 823–25: "a loosely-classified collection of interesting observations," but "theory the book is not"; *Critm* 22, 81; *FQ* 33, 23; *JAAC* 38, 207; *QRFS* 5, 527.

706.   Cohn, Dorrit. 1978. *Transparent Minds: Narrative Modes for Presenting Consciousness in Fiction*. Princeton: Princeton UP. 331 pp.
A classification and analysis of methods of presenting thought in fiction: "psychological-narration" (traditional authorial narration), "quoted monologue" (narrator's discourse about a character's consciousness), "narrated monologue" (free indirect style), etc. A wide range of fiction in Eng., Fr., Ger., and Russ. are used as examples. Bib. (eds. of literary texts only, no critical works); name index.

Style 14, 392–94: "an exciting, groundbreaking study," "sensitive, coherent readings," "ability to combine identification of literary types with close
stylistic readings"; *MLR* 76, 645–46: "a definitive treatise on a special sector
of narrative technique."

707.   Forrest-Thomson, Veronica. 1978. *Poetic Artifice: A Theory of Twentieth-
         Century Poetry*. Manchester: U of Manchester P; New York: St. Mar-
         tin's. 168 pp.
A polemical assertion of the autonomy of poetry—"all the rhythmic, phonetic, verbal, and logical devices which make poetry different from prose."
    Choice 16, 664: "fascinating" but "irritating," "idiosyncratic" yet "neces-
sary . . . for getting at recent poetry"; *Enc* 53, 77; *NS* 97, 958.

708.   Kennedy, William. 1978. *Rhetorical Norms in Renaissance Literature*.
         New Haven: Yale UP. 229 pp.
An account of the norms governing the strategies for characterizing speakers
and establishing their relation to an audience and of how these norms "generate larger structures of mode, style, and genre." Name and term index.
    Diacritics 10.1, 77–87: "important in taking account of methodological prob-
lems"; *Critm* 221, 164–65; *RSQ* 10, 33–35.

709.   Kestner, Joseph. 1978. *The Spatiality of the Novel*. Detroit: Wayne State
         UP. 203 pp.
An attempt to create a "spatial poetics of the novel." The author assumes
temporality and shows how spatiality supplements it, positing 3 kinds of
spatiality: "geometric" (point, line, plane), "virtual" (pictorial, sculptural,
architectural), and "genidentic" (text and reader relationship). Bib. 6 pp.
Name and term index.
    MLR 78, 389–95: "does its work of consolidation effectively," "some sus-
tained and sophisticated readings of major works"; *Style* 15, 42–49: recommends Louis Mink's "History and Fiction as Modes of Comprehension" as
a corrective.

710.   Laferrière, Daniel (now Rancour-Laferrière). 1978. *Sign and Subject:
         Semiotic and Psychoanalytic Investigations into Poetry*. Lisse: de Rid-
         der. 103 pp.
"This book reaches toward a synthesis of the linguistic semiotics initiated by
Roman Jakobson with the psychoanalytic psychology invented by Sigmund
Freud." Bib. 8 pp.; name and term indexes.
    Choice 16, 384: "small but important," too complex for undergraduates.

711.   Marin, Louis. 1978. *Le récit est un piège* [Narrative Is a Trap]. Paris:
         Minuit. 145 pp.
On the power of narrativity and narrative strategies in La Fontaine et al.

712.   Murphy, James J., ed. 1978. *Medieval Eloquence: Studies in the Theory and Practice of Medieval Rhetoric.* Berkeley: U of California P. 354 pp.
6 essays on the theory of rhetoric, 8 on practice. Name and term index 20 pp. [See the author's *Renaissance Eloquence*, no. 748.]
QJS 65, 445: "well written," "major contribution"; *Choice* 16, 73.

713.   Sternberg, Meir. 1978. *Expositional Modes and Temporal Ordering in Fiction.* Baltimore: Johns Hopkins UP. 338 pp.
An exploration (1) of the ways of introducing expositional materials during the sequential unfolding of a novel and (2) of beginnings. Name and term index.
Style 15, 42–49: "contrary to Sternberg's bizarre objection, literary theory and interpretation must always come ultimately to the second reading . . . critical reading is . . . re-reading."

714.   Todorov, Tzvetan. 1978. *Les genres du discours* [The Genres of Discourse]. Paris: Seuil. 309 pp.
16 essays written 1971–77, generally addressed to the question of the idea of literature.

715.   Valdés, Mario, and Owen Miller, eds. 1978. *Interpretation of Narrative.* Toronto: U of Toronto P. 202 pp.
14 essays edited from a 1976 colloquium, 4 dealing with the methodology of formalist text-oriented criticism (McDonald, Miller, Riffaterre, Fitch) and 4 using the hermeneutic method and reception theory; 3 papers appear under "Metacriticism." Bib. 7 pp,; name index.
MLR 78, 389–95: some of the contributors assume "unattractive postures of neo-scholastic obfuscation and monopolization," but Riffaterre's essay is a notable exception.

716.   Bloom, Edward, and Lillian Bloom. 1979. *Satire's Persuasive Voice.* Ithaca: Cornell UP. 305 pp.
A study of the features and strategies of satire as structures of humanistic persuasion. Ch. 1, didactic intention; ch. 2, particular satires (especially Dryden's "Absalom and Achitophel"); ch. 3, indignation and ridicule, wit and irony; chs. 4–6, religious, political, and "manners" satire. Name index, with a few terms.
Style 15, 477–78: "perceptive, illuminating, and convincing" but weakened by "conceptual narrowness"; *MLR* 77, 149–50.

717.   Genette, Gérard. *Introduction à l'architexte* [Introduction to the Essential Text]. Paris: Seuil. 89 pp.
The importance of knowing the generic tradition of a text for understanding and interpretation.

718.   Holloway, John. 1979. *Narrative and Structure: Exploratory Essays*. Cambridge: Cambridge UP. 156 pp.

6 chs. explore various aspects of narrative, several of which employ mathematical models of analysis. 2 apps., 1 on poetic structures, the other on oratory. No bib. or index.

AUMLA 55, 102–03: "a considerable contribution to speech act theory," "offers exciting new hypotheses"; *MLR* 78, 389–95: "original, spare, strange"; *CL*, 33, 375–76; *N&Q* 28, 476–77; *RES* ns 32, 498–99.

719.   Mistrík, Josef. 1979. *Dramatický text* [The Dramatic Text]. Bratislava: SPN. 221 pp.

Includes linguistic, paralinguistic, and metalinguistic problems (*BL* [1979], 131).

BL (1980), 129.

720.   Rose, Margaret A. 1979. *Parody/Meta-Fiction: An Analysis of Parody as a Critical Mirror to the Writing and Reception of Fiction*. London: Croom Helm. 197 pp.

Part 1, a discussion of the ways in which parody has been defined and of the relation of parody to other forms (e.g., satire, irony, burlesque). Part 2, a theory of parody as metafiction. Bib. 5 pp.; name and term index.

MFS 27, 383: "erudite" but "needs a leaven of levity" and wit; *PoT* 3, 231–33; *Enc* 55, 44; *Choice* 16, 1576.

721.   Segre, Cesare. 1979. *Structures and Time: Narration, Poetry, Models*. Trans. John Meddemmen. Chicago: U of Chicago P. 271 pp. (*Le strutture e il tempo*. Torino: Einaudi, 1974. 279 pp.)

8 rpt. essays from the early 1970s plus 1 new theoretical essay, treating such subjects as the relations among point of view, narrative levels, and theme in *Don Quixote* and a plot analysis of the *Decameron* based on Brémond's schema.

Style 17, 52–56: The essays are only loosely connected by the concept of time, and only a few can be said to be "structuralist" in method but are "conventional"; *MLR* 76, 429–30: "a new and important theoretical chapter, 'Analysis of the Tale, Narrative Logic, and Time,'" but the 8 interpretations "fail to live up to" its "methodological promise"; *MLR* 71, 609–10 (on the Ital.).

721a.   Weisz, Jutta. 1979. *Das Epigramm in der deutschen Literatur des 17. Jahrhunderts*. Stuttgart: Metzler. 307 pp.

Provides a taxonomy of 4 primary types and 9 subcategories based on the analysis of over 100 Ger. and Lat. epigram collections.

GQ 55, 233: "will undoubtedly remain the most comprehensive treatment on the subject for many years to come."

722.   Bonnet, Henri. 1980. *Roman et poésie: Essai sur l'esthétique des genres*
        [Novel and Poetry: Essay on the Aesthetics of Genres]. Paris: Nizet. 294
        pp.
Part 1 on novel and poetry; part 2 on art, style, genre.

723.   Dijk, Teun van, ed. 1980. "Story Comprehension." *Poetics* 9.1–3. 334 pp.
        16 essays and a bib. on "story processing."

724.   Elam, Keir. 1980. *The Semiotics of Theatre and Drama*. London:
        Methuen. 248 pp.
Opening 2 chs. on semiotics, poetics, signs, Prague structuralism; ch. 3 on
theatrical communication (codes, systems, performance); ch. 4 on dramatic
logic; ch. 5 on dramatic discourse. Bib. 28 pp.; name and term index.
    JAAC 40, 439: "generally lucid," "frankly introductory book helps enor-
mously" with extensive bib. and suggestions for further reading; *TLS* 23 Oct.
1981, 1244; *BBN* Feb. 1981, 112; *JC* 32, 214.

725.   Genette, Gérard. 1980. *Narrative Discourse: An Essay in Method*. Trans.
        Jane Lewin. Ithaca: Cornell UP. 285 pp.
This is "Discours du récit" from *Figures III*. Builds a systematic theory of narrative identifying the basic constituents and techniques of narrative, through
an analysis particularly of *Remembrance of Things Past*. Chs. on order, duration, frequency, mood, and voice. Foreword by Jonathan Culler. Bib. 5 pp.;
name and term index.
    Culler: "the most thorough attempt we have" to fill the need "for a sys-
tematic theory of narrative"; Scholes, *Semiotics and Interpretation*: "one of
the two or three most important works of semiotic analysis of fiction currently
available in English" (153–54).

726.   George, Kathleen. 1980. *Rhythm in Drama*. Pittsburgh: U of Pittsburgh
        P. 194 pp.
Ch. 1 is "a sampling" of critics "who have tried to describe rhythm"; suc-
ceeding chs. "contain observations on the ways of rhythm" — repetition, alternation, scenes, etc. Name index.
    TJ 33, 550: "excellent," "well researched," "insightful observations"; *Choice*
18, 965.

727.   Guetti, James. 1980. *Word-Music: The Aesthetic Aspect of Narrative
        Fiction*. New Brunswick: Rutgers UP. 226 pp.
An effort to establish an "aural fiction" in contrast to "visual," realistic
(representational) fiction, through examples from Burgess, Conrad, Crane,
Faulkner, Nabokov, Pynchon, and other novelists.

Style 17, 61: never establishes with sufficient concreteness what prose rhythm is; omits Gertrude Stein.

727a.   Hutcheon, Linda. 1980. *Narcissistic Narrative: The Metafictional Paradox.* Waterloo: Wilfrid Laurier UP. 168 pp.
A typology and analysis of examples of metafiction—self-reflective fiction about fiction. Separate chs. on Fowles's *The French Lieutenant's Woman*, Volponi's *La macchina mondiale*, etc. Name and term index.
MFS 27, 765: "reads like a dissertation" but provokes "new insights and appreciation"; *Choice* 19, 69.

728.   Jefferson, Ann. 1980. *The "Nouveau Roman" and the Poetics of Fiction.* Cambridge: Cambridge UP. 218 pp.
"The *nouveau roman* invites us to elaborate a new poetics of fiction . . . so that we see all the pre-existing fiction in a new light. . . . The first two chapters will demonstrate how the novels explore and redefine" character and plot. Ch. 3, "Narrative Strategies and the Discovery of Language," investigates "the ways in which the apparently realistic use of certain narrative techniques encourages reflexivity." The final ch., "The Novel and the Poetics of Quotation," "will attempt to determine the generic features of fiction." Bib. 6 pp.; name index.
CL 34, 93–96: "disappoints in three major respects"; *MLR* 77, 218–19; *PoT* 3, 211–27.

729.   Baxtin, Mixail. M. 1981. *The Dialogic Imagination: Four Essays.* Ed. Michael Holquist. Trans. Caryl Emerson and Michael Holquist. Austin: U of Texas P. 444 pp.
Essays on the novel by a critic (1895–1975) whom the editor describes "as one of the leading thinkers of the twentieth century." Glossary of terms.
CL 34, 174–76: "Baxtin is a critic of major importance"; *MLR* 77, 398–401.

729a.   Dillon, George. 1981. *Constructing Texts: Elements of a Theory of Composition and Style.* Bloomington: Indiana UP. 199 pp.
Ch. 2 specifies "the conventions governing the expository essay"; the remaining chs. "discuss the way the conventions of the essay function as patterns of order and expectation in constructing texts." The author cites from essays by "acclaimed masters of the essay": Samuel Johnson et al. Name and term index.
Choice 19, 618: "Cogently argued, intensely practical, and intelligently humanistic," on the "need for a theory of discourse that views it as human action and interaction"; *LJ* 106, 1633.

730.   Gould, Eric. 1981. *Mythical Intentions in Modern Literature.* Princeton: Princeton UP. 279 pp.

Employs contemporary theories of language, anthropology, interpretation, and psychoanalysis to define myth as part of the symbolic order of language and to suggest a synthesis of structuralism and interpretation theory. Primary attention to Joyce, Eliot, and Lawrence. Bib. 3 pp.; name and term index. *WLT* 56, 577: "informative," "erudite"; *Choice* 19, 1062.

731.   Lanser, Susan S. 1981. *The Narrative Act: Point of View in Prose Fiction*. Princeton: Princeton UP. 308 pp.
Point of view is expressed on 3 levels: status, the narrator's relation to the speech act; contact, the relation between narrator and audience; and stance, the narrator's relation to the textual world. Bib. 6 pp.; name and topic index.
    MLR 78, 642: "general insights . . . not new" (a rather negative rev.); *MFS* 28, 720: "this book will help students—immensely," "very fine readings"; *Critm* 25, 69; *WLT* 56, 760; *Choice* 19, 1395.

732.   Leech, Geoffrey, and Michael Short. 1981. *Style in Fiction: A Linguistic Introduction to English Fictional Prose*. London: Longman. 402 pp.
Shows how linguistic analysis and literary appreciation can be related through the linguistic study of literary style. Concentrates on Eng. fiction from the 18th to the 20th cents. for practical examples and analysis, which means "that we leave in the background the larger issues of authorial, genre and period style." Part 1 explains style and stylistics, and part 2 applies those concepts and methods. Exercises and passages for further study are provided. Bib. 11 pp.; name and term index.
    MFS 28, 653: "not a linguistic introduction to the study of style in English fiction" but "an introduction to linguistic terminology" that may or may not be "of some use to stylistics"; *BBN* Feb. 1981, 115.

733.   Miller, D. A. 1981. *Narrative and Its Discontents: Problems of Closure in the Traditional Novel*. Princeton: Princeton UP. 300 pp.
A study of the "narratable": "the instances of disequilibrium, suspense, and general insufficiency from which a given narrative appears to arise." Part 1, the longest section, deals with Jane Austen, part 2 with *Middlemarch*, part 3 with Stendhal. Bib. 11 pp.; name and term index.
    MFS 28, 345: obscure and jargon-ridden but "worth the struggle"; *CL* 35, 82–85: questions many of the book's conceptions; *MP* 80, 287; *VS* 26, 354; *JEGP* 81, 543; *WLT* 56, 410; *Critm* 24, 78.

734.   Mitchell, W. J. T., ed. 1981. *On Narrative*. Chicago: U of Chicago P. 270 pp.
A collection of 1979 symposium papers accompanied by responses, the whole unified by the issues of the relation between temporal and narrative sequence and between literature and the human sciences and of narrative as a mode of knowledge.

JAAC 41, 456–61: the collection is "riven in two" by a split between questions external and questions internal to narrative, but the essays "represent the best work being done in this country"; *AA* 85, 195: "richly argumentative; *Style* 17, 297.

735.   Phelan, James. 1981. *Worlds from Words: A Theory of Language in Fiction.* Chicago: U of Chicago P. 259 pp.
Establishes his theory in part 1 by an application of other critics' (Fish, Lodge, Miller) theories to novels (*The Ambassadors, Sister Carrie, Persuasion*) and then in part 2 tests his theory by the same tactic (Olson and *Lolita*, Eco and *Willie Masters' Lonesome Wife*). "It is an essay on style and an inquiry into hermeneutics, an analysis of five novels and an experiment in theory construction." Bib. 6 pp.; name and term index.
WLT 56, 410: "despite shortcomings . . . might prove useful to some readers."

736.   Scaglione, Aldo. 1981. *Die Theorie der Textkomposition in den Klassischen und den Westeuropäischen Sprachen* and *Die Theorie der Wortstellung im Deutschen.* Vols. 1 and 2 of *Komponierte Prosa von der Antike bis zur Gegenwart.* [The Theory of Composition in Classical and Western European Languages and The Theory of German Word Order. Vols. 1 and 2 of The Composition of Prose from Antiquity to the Present Time]. Stuttgart: Klett.
Vol. 1 is an updated version of *The Classical Theory of Composition*; vol. 2 is the sequel (*The Theory of German Word Order from the Renaissance to the Present.* Minneapolis: U of Minnesota P, 1981).
Rhetorik (1983), 165–67.

737.   Smitten, Jeffrey, and Ann Daghistany. 1981. *Spatial Form "in" Narrative.* Ithaca: Cornell UP. 275 pp.
10 essays on "the techniques by which novelists subvert the chronological sequence inherent in narrative. . . . through such devices as image patterns, leitmotifs, analogy, and contrast." Includes Joseph Frank's "Spatial Form: Thirty Years After." Bib. 20 pp.; name and term index.
MFS 28, 349: the essays demonstrate the "usefulness and resiliency of the concept"; *MP* 80, 340; *JEGP* 81, 543; *VQR* 58, 7; *SAQ* 81, 475; *CLit* 10, 212; *SR* 90, 575.

738.   Torgovnick, Marianna. 1981. *Closure in the Novel.* Princeton: Princeton UP. 238 pp.
Closure is the "process by which a novel reaches . . . what the author . . . believes is an adequate, appropriate conclusion" in regard to the beginning and middle. The author discusses 11 19th- and 20th-cent. novels from George Eliot to Virginia Woolf, employing 4 sets of terms to describe various rela-

tionships and perspectives regarding the closure of a novel. Bib. 7 pp.; name
and term index. [Cf. Miller, no. 733.]

MFS 28, 345: "conventional and traditional," author deserves praise for her
"dedication" and "enthusiasm"; *JEGP* 81, 543; *MP* 80, 287; *Critm* 24, 78;
WLT 56, 410.

739.   Ward, J. P. 1981. *Poetry and the Sociological Idea*. Atlantic Highlands:
         Humanities; Brighton: Harvester. 242 pp.
Posits a fundamental opposition between every kind of poetry and the sociological outlook to which the poet was aligned (phenomenological, interac-
tionist, Marxist, etc.). Modern poetry can be read in the light of the deflection
of language from its uses in sociological discourse. Name and term index.
[Cf. Forrest-Thomson, no. 707.]

WLT 56, 579: argues his general viewpoint "with vigor" but is "less convincing in his discussion of particular poets"; *SRNB* 9, 115; *TLS* 27 Nov. 1981,
1402; *Choice* 19, 619.

740.   Allen, Judson. 1982. *The Ethical Poetic of the Later Middle Ages: A
         Decorum of Convenient Distinction*. Toronto: U of Toronto P. 327 pp.
An attempt to define the medieval theory of literature by an analysis of "what
medieval commentators wrote about their classic literature, and about the
making of their own." Name and term index.

MP 81, 61: "a remarkable collection of primary source material," "consistently rewards its user."

741.   Altman, Janet. 1982. *Epistolarity: Approaches to a Form*. Columbus:
         Ohio State UP. 235 pp.
Evaluates the development and significance of the epistolary novel, using Fr.
and Eng. examples and drawing on a wide range of recent narrative criticism.

Choice 20, 258: "strongly recommended"; *TLS* 7 Jan. 1983, 20.

742.   Banfield, Ann. 1982. *Unspeakable Sentences: Narration and Represen-
         tation in the Language of Fiction*. Boston: Routledge. 340 pp.
Sets forth a theory of the language of narrative fiction based on Chomskyan
linguistic practice. The first 5 chs. develop a grammar of narrative style by
various sentence types (represented speech and thought, direct speech, narration per se). Ch. 6 discusses of the historical development of narrative style.
The conclusion finds narrative fiction in the cognitive processes externalized
by "narration" and "representation." Bib. 11 pp.; name and term index.

PoT 4, 17–45: this "ambitious bid to undermine current narrative theory
and resettle it" on the new foundation of "generative grammar of narrative
sentences" is "wrong in principle" and "orientation" but "far from valueless,
although its value is largely negative"; *TLS* 19 Nov. 1982, 1280: "important
new book," "sharp tools of analysis"; *Style* 18, 229; *LRB* 4, 8.

743. Bruns, Gerald L. 1982. *Inventions: Writing, Textuality, and Understanding in Literary History*. New Haven: Yale UP. 201 pp.
"The history of interpretation is the history of writing, textuality, and understanding, which I take to be practices that make their appearance within traditions." Part 1, "The Ancients"; part 2, "The Moderns" (Descartes compared to Paul de Man et al.); part 3, "Romantic Hermeneutics" (chs. on Jane Austen and G. M. Hopkins); part 4, "Modern Textuality" (chs. on W. C. Williams's *Kora in Hell*, Joyce's *Ulysses*). Name and subject indexes.
   CL 35, 280–83: "extensive and accurate learning" expressed tersely and unpretentiously, but the historical part and the critical essays do not mesh well; *Choice* 20, 576: "an important step in redefining the literary enterprise in more human terms and should be read by anyone seriously interested in current issues in literary theory."

744. Di Pietro, Robert. 1982. *Linguistics and the Professions: Proceedings of the Second Annual Delaware Symposium on Language Studies*. Norwood: Ablex. 272 pp.
20 essays divided into 4 parts: "Language and the Medical Profession," "Language and the Law," "Language in Commercial and Official Uses," and "Language in Employment and Public Services." Name and term indexes.

745. Donker, Marjorie, and George Muldrow. 1982. *Dictionary of Literary-Rhetorical Conventions of the English Renaissance*. Westport: Greenwood. 268 pp.
"A collection of essays describing the literary norms and rhetorical controls that inform English poetry of the later sixteenth and earlier seventeenth centuries." Bib. references follow many entries. Name and term index.
   LRN 8, 73–74: "substantial" research, "accurate and thorough," "lucid and concrete."

746. Fónagy, Iván. 1982. *La repetizione creativa: Ridondanze espressive nell'opera poetica* [Creative Repetition: Expressive Redundance in Poetic Work]. Bari: Dedalo. 127 pp.

746a. Johnson, W. R. 1982. *The Idea of Lyric: Lyric Modes in Ancient and Modern Poetry*. Berkeley: U of California P. 214 pp.
Within the basic idea of the genre, which is "immutable and universal," various modes and emphases function. Not a historical survey but samples lyrics of classical antiquity and of the past 150 years to exemplify the form.
   CL 35, 374–76: a "rich" and "fine treatment of difficult and elusive subject."

747. McFadden, George. 1982. *Discovering the Comic*. Princeton: Princeton UP. 268 pp.

A definition and history of the comic and an analysis of comic texts in a framework of modern critical thought.
Critm 24, 387–88: "attempts too many things"; *AL* 54, 316; *Choice* 19, 1234.

748.   Murphy, James J., ed. 1982 (rev. 1984). *Renaissance Eloquence: Studies in the Theory and Practice of Renaissance Rhetoric.* Berkeley: U of California P. 474 pp.
23 essays define Renaissance rhetoric and explore its contributions to diverse fields in various countries over 3 centuries. Part 1, "The Scope of Renaissance Rhetoric"; part 2, "Rhetorical Trends in Renaissance Europe"; part 3, "Ethics, Politics, and Theology"; part 4, "Rhetoric and Other Literary Arts."
QJS 69, 441: "tremendously useful act of cultural recovery"; *SCN* 40, 87.

749.   Petro, Peter. 1982. *Modern Satire: Four Studies.* Berlin: Mouton. 162 pp.
With the intention of correcting the frequently negative view of 20th-cent. satire, the author discusses four satirical novels: Hašek's *The Good Soldier Švejk*, Bulgakov's *The Master and Margarita*, Orwell's *Nineteen Eighty-Four*, and Vonnegut's *Breakfast of Champions*. Selected bib.

750.   Prince, Gerald. 1982. *Narratology: The Form and Functioning of Narrative.* Berlin: Mouton. 184 pp.
Chs. on narrating (narrator, narratee, narration) narrated, narrative grammar, reading narrative, and narrativity. "I attempt to answer three questions": "what are the features of narrative which allow us to characterize its possible manifestations in pertinent terms (Chapters one and two)? what would a formal model accounting for these features and manifestations look like (Chapter three)? what are the factors which affect our understanding of a narrative and our evaluation of its narrativity (Chapters four and five)?" "I try to discuss, however briefly, most of what I think must be known." Bib. 5 pp.; name and term indexes.
Style 17, 290: "clear and concise organization of a difficult, large, and rapidly evolving field of study"; *Choice* 20, 1590.

751.   Wright, Austin. 1982. *The Formal Principle in the Novel.* Ithaca: Cornell UP. 317 pp.
A defense and demonstration of neo-Aristotelian critical theory. First 8 chs. (171 pp.) redefine concepts of formal unity by a sifting of recent critical disputes; the next 4 chs. analyze the plots of *The Portrait of a Lady*, *The Sound and the Fury*, *Invisible Man*, and *Pale Fire*. Name and term index. [Cf. Booth's *The Rhetoric of Fiction* and Friedman's *Form and Meaning in Fiction*.]
Choice 20, 433: "well-written . . . its value . . . high"; *LJ* 107, 1464: "knowledgeable exposition which, however, opens no really new perspectives."

752.   Easthope, Antony. 1983. *Poetry as Discourse.* London: Methuen. 182 pp.
Part 1 presents a theory of discourse as language, ideology, and subjectivity.

Part 2 applies this theory to poetry (pentameter and language, ideology, and subjectivity) from the Renaissance to modernism. *"Poetry As Discourse* has applied to poetry a theoretical approach very close to that put forward by Catherine Belsey" in *Critical Practice*. Bib. 12 pp.; name and term index.
   Choice 21, 268: "excellent," "rigorous lucidity"; *TES* 14 Oct. 1983, 30, and 28 Oct. 1983, 22; *VLS* Apr. 1984, 17.

753.   Fowler, Alastair. 1983. *Kinds of Literature: An Introduction to the Theory of Genres and Modes*. Cambridge: Harvard UP. 357 pp.
An effort to "recover a sense of the variety of literary forms," mainly in Eng. literature, by asking how genres function and relate to mode—i.e., not by building systems but by discussing problems. Bib. 7 pp.; name and term index 22 pp.
   Choice 20, 1129: "A long, thorough, methodical, useful and slightly disappointing survey"; *THES* 4 Mar. 1983, 14.

753a.   Higgins, Dick. 1983. *Horizons: The Poetics and Theory of the Intermedia*. Carbondale: Southern Illinois UP. 152 pp.
A study of new arts—visual poetry, sound poetry, etc.; the final section, entitled "Literary Poetics," deals with current experimental literature. Glossary.

754.   Rimmon-Kenan, Shlomith. 1983. *Narrative Fiction: Contemporary Poetics*. London: Methuen. 173 pp.
A definition of narrative fiction and a classification of its basic aspects—"the events, their verbal representation, and the act of telling or writing," or story, text, and narration—in a synthesis of contemporary approaches (New Criticism, Russ. formalism, Fr. structuralism, phenomenology, etc.). Bib. 15 pp. (many annotated); name and term index 10 pp.
   Choice 21, 566: "very good in what it does and vulnerable . . . for what it ignores or under-emphasizes," "well-organized and cogently argued"; *TES* 14 Oct. 1983, 30; *MFS* 30, 413; *VLS* Apr. 1984, 133.

755.   Rogers, William. 1983. *The Three Genres and the Interpretation of Lyric*. Princeton: Princeton UP. 277 pp.
Genre theory based on ideas from Heidegger's hermeneutics. Ch. 1 constructs an "interpretive model" for the definition of lyric. Ch. 2 deals with 2 problematical cases—poems of anomalous voice and impersonal poems. Ch. 3 addresses the problem of interpretation. Ch. 4 "applies the model to particular poems from various literary periods."
   LJ 108, 586: "usefully complements Alastair Fowler" (1983).

756.   Schmid, Herta, and Aloysius van Kesteren, eds. 1983. *Semiotics, Theatre and Drama*. Amsterdam: Benjamins. 500 pp.

757.   Siebenschuh, William. 1983. *Fictional Techniques and Factual Works.*
        Athens: U of Georgia P. 183 pp.
An effort to define a factual prose that employs fictional techniques but does
not therefore become "fiction." For illustration he discusses Boswell's *Life of
Johnson*, Newman's *Apologia*, and Gosse's *Father and Son*. In the conclusion
he sets forth a program for "a true rhetoric of fictional effects in factual contexts . . . still waiting to be written."
        Choice 20, 1591: "modest but important."

758.   Wald, Alan. 1983. *The Revolutionary Imagination: The Poetry and Pol-
        itics of John Wheelwright and Sherry Mangan.* Chapel Hill: U of North
        Carolina P. 288 pp.
On a political aesthetic in poetry as exemplified by these 2 poets. Name and
term index.
        Choice 21, 283: "impressive and impeccable scholarship."

758a.   Bürger, Peter. 1984. *Theory of the Avant-Garde.* Trans. Michael Shaw.
        Minneapolis: U of Minnesota P. 135pp. (*Theorie der Avantgarde*. Frank-
        furt: Suhrkamp, 1974.)
Offers "a categorical framework" within which individual analyses can be undertaken. Chs. on "critical literary science" (hermeneutics, ideology, functions),
the avant-garde and that science (aesthetic categories, Benjamin's theory of
art), the autonomy of art, the avant-gardist work of art, and avant-garde and
engagement. Lengthy foreword by Jochen Schulte-Sasse on "Theory of Modernism versus Theory of the Avant-Garde." Bib. 3 pp.; name and term index.
        AAm 72, 19.

758b.   Pepicello, W. J., and Thomas A. Green. 1984. *The Language of Rid-
        dles: New Perspectives.* Columbus: Ohio State UP. 180 pp.

758c.   Thiher, Allen. 1984. *Words in Reflection: Modern Language Theory and
        Postmodern Fiction.* Chicago: U of Chicago P. 256 pp.

3.2 Practice (759–1012)

3.2.1 Diction, Imagery, Tropes (759–87)

759.   Colie, Rosalie. 1966. *Paradoxia Epidemica: The Renaissance Tradition
        of Paradox.* Princeton: Princeton UP. 553 pp.
Examines "the ways in which some writers made conscious use of the paradoxical tradition." Organized topically: scientific paradoxes, paradoxes of self-
reference, etc. Bib. 21 pp.; name and term index.
        NYRB 8, 26; *Choice* 4, 528.

760.   Frohock, W. M., ed. 1969. *Image and Theme: Studies in Modern French Fiction. Bernanos, Malraux, Sarraute, Gide, Martin du Gard.* Cambridge: Harvard UP. 156 pp.
Articles on "Image-conveying Abstractions" and "Dream Imagery" in the various authors.
MLR 66, 196–98: some of the classifications result in excessive simplification, but several articles are very worthwhile.

761.   Glicksberg, Charles. 1969. *The Ironic Vision in Modern Literature.* The Hague: Nijhoff. 261 pp.
An effort to describe the literary expression of the modern temper in chs. on "irony in modern poetry, fiction, and drama" "irony and the diabolical," and "the nihilism of the absurd and the absurdity of art."
Style 13, 381–82: "cogent reading," especially in combination with Booth's *A Rhetoric of Irony* (no. 415), Muecke's *The Compass of Irony* (no. 336), and Thurley's *The Ironic Harvest.*

762.   Burgess, Glyn. 1970. *Contribution à l'étude du vocabulaire pré-courtois* [Contribution to the Study of Pre-Courtois Vocabulary]. Geneva: Droz. 187 pp.
A study of the evolution of 10 terms from their origins to the 3 great romances of antiquity—*Thèbes, Eneas,* and *Troie.*
MLR 66, 892–93: "thorough as well as perceptive," though "no spectacular discoveries have emerged" and "his sociological interpretations" will "not convince every reader."

763.   Knobloch, Eberhard. 1971. *Die Wortwahl in der archaisierenden chronikalischen Erzählung: Meinhold, Raabe, Storm, Wille, Kolbenheyer* [Word Choice in Archaizing Narratives in the Form of Chronicles: Meinhold, Raabe, Storm, Wille, Kolbenheyer]. Goppingen: Kummerle. 228 pp.
The use of archaisms in 5 works of 19th- and 20th-cent. fiction.
MLR 69, 228: description only, no assessment.

764.   Miner, Earl, ed. 1971. *Seventeenth-Century Imagery: Essays on the Uses of Figurative Language from Donne to Farquhar.* Berkeley: U of California P. 202 pp.
11 papers on diverse topics—Donne's introversion, Milton's Church government, etc. Name and term index.
Style 7, 202–06: "no attempt to discuss or define seventeenth-century imagery"; some of the essays "have nothing at all to do with imagery."

765.   Freytag, Wiebke. 1972. *Das Oxymoron bei Wolfram, Gottfried und andern Dichtern des Mittelalters.* [The Oxymoron in the Works of Wolfram, Gottfried, and Other Medieval Poets]. Munich: Fink. 290 pp.

A study of the use of the oxymoron figure in the Middle Ages, particularly by Wolfram and Gottfried.
MLR 68, 935–37: "admirable clarity."

766.   Lavis, Georges. 1972. *L'expression de l'affectivité dans la poésie lyrique française du moyen âge (XIIe–XIIIe siècles)* [The Expression of Feeling in French Lyrical Poetry of the Middle Ages (12th–13th Centuries)]. Paris: Belles Lettres. 625 pp.
A semantic study of the expression of joy and suffering in the entire corpus of the Old French courtly love song.
MLR 71, 401: "this book indicates most encouragingly how modern linguistic techniques can serve the ends of literary research."

767.   Miles, Josephine. 1974. *Poetry and Change: Donne, Milton, Wordsworth, and the Equilibrium of the Present.* Berkeley: U of California P. 243 pp.
A wide-ranging collection of the author's previously pub. writings dating from 1955, mainly on diction. The first section classifies poets and prose writers according to their dependence on adjectives and verbs and also traces the use of connectives since the 16th cent. The second section presents data on Browne, Milton, and Addison to argue that style shifted from dependence on adjectives to dependence on verbs. Bib. 24 pp. [James Russell Lowell Prize for an Outstanding Book by an MLA Member, 1974.]
Style 11, 327–29: defective and misleading data; *Enc* 34, 58: "she takes English poetry seriously and helps one understand it better"; *SR* 84, 684–95; *AL* 47, 492–93; *RenQ* 28, 416–17; *TLS* 25 Apr. 1975, 442; *Choice* 11, 1779; *LJ* 99, 1820; *PQ* 54, 879.

768.   Wyatt, Kathryn. 1974. *Unanimistic Imagery in 20th Century French Literature.* University: Romance Monographs. 210 pp.
Follows Leo Spitzer's analysis of the imagery of Jules Romains, classifying the images according to the concepts involved. Bib. 8 pp.
MLR 72, 214–15: "a brave attempt at assessing Romains's influence in the field of language and style."

769.   Dumonceaux, Pierre. 1975. *Langue et sensibilité en France au XVIIe siècle: L'évolution du vocabulaire affectif* [Language and Sensibility in Seventeenth-Century France: The Evolution of the Vocabulary of Feeling]. Geneva: Droz. 509 pp.
Traces the evolution of the meaning of groups of words with evidence from the main literary works plus extraliterary texts.
MLR 72, 684–85: "invaluable as a storehouse" of information.

770.   Hallyn, Fernand. 1975. *Formes métaphoriques dans la poésie lyrique de l'âge baroque en France* [Metaphorical Forms in the Lyric Poetry of the Baroque Age in France]. Geneva: Droz. 261 pp.

A study of poetry written between about 1580 and 1660.
MLR 72, 948–49: "furthers our understanding of baroque poetry" and "a valuable contribution to the theory of metaphor."

771.   Knapp, Fritz. 1975. *Similitudo: Stil- und Erzählfunktion von Vergleich und Exempel in der lateinischen, französischen und deutschen Grossepik des Hochmittelalters* [Similitude: Stylistic and Narrative Function of Parable and Exemplum in the Latin, French, and German Epic of the High Middle Ages]. Vienna: Braumüller. 444 pp.
Comparison and example in the medieval Lat., Fr., and Ger. epic.
BL (1976), 2992; (1978), 2536.

772.   Sherbo, Arthur. 1975. *English Poetic Diction from Chaucer to Wordsworth*. East Lansing: Michigan State UP. 214 pp.
A chronological history and listing of poetic diction, each ch. a compendium of devices to be found in Chaucer, Spenser, Shakespeare, Milton, Dryden, Pope, Thompson, and Wordsworth. The author argues that the strongest sources of poetic diction were Spenser and the translations by Dryden and Pope. Name index.
Style 11, 319–20: each ch. is "more of an appendix than part of a discursive text" and "many more questions are raised than Professor Sherbo undertakes to answer," but the "painstaking tracing" of terms is a "pleasure."

773.   Ziegler, Vickie. 1975. *The Leitword in "Minnesang": Stylistic Analysis and Textual Criticism*. University Park: Pennsylvania State UP. 200 pp.
A study of the use of groups of synonyms in the medieval Ger. lyric, particularly in the work of Reinmar der Alte. Bib. 3 pp.
LJ 100, 1327: "shows convincingly" that *"Leitwörter* can be a powerful tool of textual criticism," "authoritative"; *GQ* 50, 44.

774.   Perry, Menakhem. 1976. *Ha-miBne ha-semanti šel šire Bialik: Trumalate'orya šel pitu'amašma'uyot berezeP ha-ṭeqst ha-siPruti* [Semantic Dynamics in Poetry: The Theory of Semantic Change in the Text Continuum of a Poem, Especially in the Hebrew Poetry of Kh. N. Bialik]. Tel Aviv: Porter Inst. for Poetics & Semiotics. 244 pp.

775.   Hemeldonck, Walter van. 1977. *Antieke en Bijbelse metaforiek in de moderne Nederlandse letteren (1880–ca. 1914): Een bijdrage tot de Europese stijlgeschiedenis* [Classical and Biblical Metaphors in Modern Netherlands Letters (1880–c. 1914): A Contribution to the History of European Style]. Gent: Secretariaat van de Koninklijke Acad. voor Nederlandse Taal en Letterkunde. 319 pp.
An investigation of the influence of Greco-Roman and biblical imagery on modern Dutch and Flemish writers.

MLR 75, 954–55: many new aspects, "recommended" to modern language, folklore, and anthropology libraries.

776.   Matthews, J. H. 1977. *The Imagery of Surrealism*. Syracuse: Syracuse UP. 320 pp.
A "simultaneous examination of pictorial and verbal expressions" because understanding of one depends on understanding of the other. Bib. 9 pp.; name index.
FR 53, 135: "brilliant insights and suggestive arguments," "useful introductory book"; *AR* 37, 119; *TLS* 13 Jan. 1978, 33; *SR* 86, 317.

777.   Kelly, Douglas. 1978. *Medieval Imagination: Rhetoric and the Poetry of Courtly Love*. Madison: U of Wisconsin P. 330 pp.
A survey of several centuries of Fr. and Eng. literature to show how the process of imagination or image making was expressed in allegory to create the literature of *fin' amors*. Bib. 17 pp.; name and term index.
Style 15, 39–40: "workers with style will benefit from Kelly's discussion of a pre-Coleridgean history of imagination"; *MLR* 76, 149.

778.   Mead, Gerald. 1978. *The Surrealist Image: A Stylistic Study*. Bern: Lang. 161 pp.
A search for the underlying principles of the surrealist image in its phonetic, syntactic, and semantic aspects. Bib. 11 pp.; name and term index.
MLR 76, 206: "too theoretical" and does not "study the poem, or even the image in the context of the poem."

779.   Brown, Marshall. 1979. *The Shape of German Romanticism*. Ithaca: Cornell UP. 241 pp.
Describes a group of geometrical terms present in all the writings of the period: the circle, ellipse, center, etc. These references and images reflect an organic worldview. Bib. 11 pp.; name and term index.
Style 15, 35–37: "formidably learned" but insufficiently attentive to evidence and "contextual meanings" and "finally uncritical."

780.   Green, D. H. 1979. *Irony in the Medieval Romance*. Cambridge: Cambridge UP. 431 pp.
Draws examples mainly from Ger. writers in an attempt to provide a conservative methodology and classification for the study of medieval irony. All examples in their original language. Bib. 25 pp.; name and term index.
Style 17, 72–75: reveals a thorough awareness of mainstream scholarship up to about 1970; *AUMLA* 54, 238; *MLR* 75, 929–33.

781.   Quilligan, Maureen. 1979. *The Language of Allegory: Defining the Genre*. Ithaca: Cornell UP. 305 pp.

The author ranges from *De planctu naturae* to *Gravity's Rainbow* to explore the operations — especially the analogical operations — of language. Bib. 9 pp.; name and term index.

Style 17, 68–72: a scholarly achievement; more taxonomical than Barney (no. 949).

782. Schilling, Michael. 1979. *Imagines Mundi: Metaphorische Darstellungen der Welt in der Emblematik* [Imagines Mundi: Metaphorical Representations of the World in Emblematical Works]. Bern: Lang. 290 pp.

Emblematical images or metaphors of the world by Ger. baroque writers.
MLR 77, 758–59: "rather heavy-going survey."

783. Wheeler, Michael. 1979. *The Art of Allusion in Victorian Fiction*. New York: Barnes. 182 pp.

Chs. on the "aesthetics of allusion," the Victorian novel-reading public and typical uses of allusion, 8 novels within the period 1840–90 (*Jane Eyre, Mary Barton, Hard Times, Middlemarch, The Egoist, Robert Elsmere, The Return of the Native,* and *Tess of the d'Urbervilles*), and developments in the 20th cent. Allusion is shown to be a conventional literary device with specific functions (illuminate character, etc.) and types (reference to literary character, etc.). Name and term index.

Style 15, 463–64: except for the neglect of allusion as an aspect of style (devoting most attention to the meaning of the reference), the book "provides an excellent model"; *MLR* 76, 450–51.

784. Sloane, Mary C. 1981. *The Visual in Metaphysical Poetry*. Atlantic Highlands: Humanities. 110 pp.

The interaction of emblem, meditation, and the epistemological upheaval of the period had a profound effect on visualization in metaphysical poetry. Name index.

Choice 19, 1245: lukewarm rev., previous works "will supply all the needed information found here."

785. Wilde, Alan. 1981. *Horizons of Assent: Modernism, Post-Modernism, and the Ironic Imagination*. Baltimore: Johns Hopkins UP. 209 pp.

Irony in the 20th cent. as a response to an absurd and fragmented world. 3 forms of irony accompanied the development of 20th-cent. literature: mediate irony, disjunctive irony, and suspensive irony. E. M. Forster, Ivy Compton-Burnett, and Donald Barthelme particularly illustrate the progression through these ironical forms. Name and term index.

GQ 55, 570: lacks a "solid footing in literary theory" but has "lucid style and humanist wit"; *ConL* 23, 244–53; *PoT* 3, 211–27; *Boundary* 10, 263–70; *TLS* 6 Nov. 1981, 1310.

786.   Quinn, William, and Audley Hall. 1982. *Jongleur: A Modified Theory of Oral Improvisation and Its Effects on the Performance and Transmission of Middle English Romance.* Washington: UP of America. 423 pp.
A statistical analysis of the rhyme recurrences in *King Horn* that shows that the performers of such Middle Eng. romances used a stock of readily recallable words (rather than phrases) to improvise their recitals.
    Spec 58, 801: "a new way to gauge the differences among extant romances . . . that should help us interpret each romance."

787.   Shell, Marc. 1982. *Money, Language, and Thought: Literary and Philosophical Economies from the Medieval to the Modern Era.* Berkeley: U of California P. 219 pp. & 24 pp. illus.
The participation of economic form in literature and philosophy is defined by "the tropic interaction between economic and linguistic symbolization and production." The thinkers studied in this book (Goethe, Hegel, et al.) have tried "to account self-critically for the money of the mind informing their own thought." Name and term index. [See author's *The Economy of Literature.* Baltimore: Johns Hopkins UP, 1978.]
    Style 13, 303–04; *Diacritics* 10.1, 37–48.

787a.   Rice, Donald, and Peter Schofer. 1983. *Rhetorical Poetics: Theory and Practice of Figural and Symbolic Reading in Modern French Literature.* Madison: U of Wisconsin P. 243 pp.
Concentrates on "the point of view of the reader. Reading is thus treated here as a fundamentally rhetorical activity: the reader constructs a text by establishing *figural* and *symbolic traces,* based on *metaphorical, metonymical, synecdochal,* and *ironic relationships.*" The author "redefines key rhetorical and poetical terms" and argues that rhetoric is "the primary force of the text." The introd. treats "Jakobson's New Rhetoric"; part 1, "Rhetorical Theories"; part 2, "Rhetorical Readings" (Balzac, Baudelaire, Mallarmé, Simon). Bib. 5 pp.; name and term index.

787b.   Saldívar, Ramón. 1984. *Figural Language in the Novel: The Flowers of Speech from Cervantes to Joyce.* Princeton: Princeton UP. 267 pp.
An examination of "the processes by which narrative establishes the grammar and syntax proper to the expression of its particular meaning." Name and term index.

3.2.2 Syntax, Schemes (788–95)

788.   Aspland, C. W. 1970. *A Syntactical Study of Epic Formulas and Formulaic Expressions Containing the -ant Forms in Twelfth-Century French Verse.* St. Lucia: U of Queensland P. 175 pp.
A study of the interrelation between the pattern of the formulaic expression and its syntax.
    MLR 66, 891–92: "a most valuable and scholarly contribution."

789.　Bronzwaer, W. J. M. 1970. *Tense in the Novel: An Investigation of Some Potentialities of Linguistic Criticism.* Groningen: Wolters-Noordhoff. 160 pp.

An effort to demonstrate that the insights of linguistics can be valuable in literary criticism, testing the claim on Murdoch's *The Italian Girl*, Frayn's *A Very Private Life*, and Halliday's explication of "Leda and the Swan," by focusing on 1 feature of language: tense.

JLS 1, 119–23: "a more earnest, more cosmopolitan, version of David Lodge's *Language of Fiction*," treats linguistics judiciously, and "challenges two major arguments on tense and the language of fiction": Hamburger's *The Logic of Poetry* and Weinrich's *Tempus*; *MLR* 67, 394–95.

790.　Tufte, Virginia. 1971. *Grammar as Style.* New York: Holt. 280 pp.

A composition manual that approaches composition through grammatical analyses of style: "a study of grammatical patterns and the way they work in the hands of contemporary professional writers . . . addressed to anyone interested in stylistic theory and practice. . . . Each chapter except the first ["The Relation of Grammar to Style"] concentrates on a major syntactic structure or concept and considers its stylistic role in sentences from twentieth-century fiction and nonfiction. In all, the book includes fifteen major grammatical topics and more than a thousand samples of modern prose." Bib. 21 pp.; term index. [Another forceful defense of the study of grammar may be found in the works of Roman Jakobson — e.g., "A Postscript to the Discussion on Grammar of Poetry." *Diacritics* 10.1, 22–35.]

791.　Casparis, C. Paul. 1975. *Tense without Time: The Present Tense in Narration.* Bern: Francke. 212 pp.

A study of the historical (or narrative) present (tense outside time) in prose fiction in Eng. from Dickens to the present. Bib. 12 pp.; name index.

Style 11, 210–11: "the first extended account of the Historical Present as a narrative resource of modern authors writing in English," has a "strong" theoretical framework, "an essential work, despite a rather scattered expository style"; *MLR* 73, 151–52: an "interesting and competent dissertation" especially "because it reflects that welcome trend towards linking language with literature and to applying advanced linguistics to recent and contemporary creations."

792.　Cluett, Robert. 1976. *Prose Style and Critical Reading.* New York: Teachers CP. 316 pp.

"[I]ntelligently handled [quantitative] data derived from objectively chosen samples can illuminate much in literature. . . . can also confirm or refute intuitions that cannot be tested in any other way." Chs. 1–3, introductory and theoretical; ch. 4, the sentence; ch. 5, stylistic types (14 authors); ch. 6, Sidney and the Elizabethan novelists; ch. 7, Hemingway; ch. 8, Carlyle (compared to 13 other writers); ch. 9, historical, using 50 samples from the late 16th cent. to the 20th cent. Bib. 3 pp., name and term index.

Style 11, 330–35: "minor statistical shortcomings" but "impeccable documentation," "an important book, the first to systematically apply quantitative methods on a large scale to literary criticism"; *Choice* 14, 673.

793.   Kohonen, Viljo. 1978. *On the Development of English Word Order in Religious Prose around 1000 and 1200 A.D.* Publications of the Research Inst. of the Åbo Akad. Foundation 38. Åbo, Finland. 242 pp.

793a.   Kanyó, Zoltán. 1981. *Sprichworter: Analyse einer einfachen Form* [Proverbs: Analysis of a Simple Form]. Amsterdam: Mouton. 310 pp. A semiotic and linguistic analysis of the grammar of the Ger. proverb as a poetic form.

794.   Kugel, James L. 1981. *The Idea of Biblical Poetry: Parallelism and Its History*. New Haven: Yale UP. 339 pp.

"The present study consists of two fairly distinct undertakings. . . . The first, represented by chapters 1 and 2, is an attempt to arrive at some comprehensive notion of biblical parallelism. . . . The second, longer part is a history of ideas about parallelism — and biblical poetry generally — from antiquity to the present." Name and term index.

CL 34, 361: "immensely learned and closely argued"; *TLS* 25 Dec. 1981, 1506; *TT* 39, 331.

795.   Scaglione, Aldo. 1981. *The Theory of German Word Order from the Renaissance to the Present*. Minneapolis: U of Minnesota P. 241 pp. (*Die Theorie der Wortstellung im Deutschen*. Stuttgart: Klett, 1981).

This is a sequel to *The Classical Theory of Composition* (no. 664) and covers the Germanic area (not covered in that work). A study of the way theorists and stylists through the cents. have interpreted the uniquely systematic character of Ger. word order and sentence structure. Bib. 13 pp.; term and name indexes.

MLJ 66, 341–42: "three concise chapters" addressed to the general linguist, "a valuable reference"; *Lang* 59, 231: "comprehensive and competent"; *BL* (1977), 3390.

795a.   Austin, Timothy. 1984. *Language Crafted: A Linguistic Theory of Poetic Syntax*. Bloomington: Indiana UP. 171 pp.

Sets forth the standards that a general theory of stylistics must meet and outlines a linguistic theory of syntax in poetry based on these standards. His "interpretive stylistics" combines technical analysis by transformational generative grammar and perceptual analysis of patterns. Bib.; term and name indexes.

LJ 109, 1849.

3.2.3 Prosody, Sound Patterns in Prose (796–832)

796.   Parent, Monique, ed. 1967. *Le vers français au vingtième siècle* [French
Verse in the Twentieth Century]. Paris: Klincksieck. 324 pp.
A collection of papers on prosody.
MLR 65, 430–34.

797.   Piper, William B. 1969. *The Heroic Couplet.* Cleveland: Case Western
Reserve UP. 454 pp.
10 chs. of "A Brief History" and 48 chs. of "Essays and Illustrations" trace the
practice and achievement in the Eng. heroic couplet from Chaucer to Keats.
Name, poem, and term indexes.
Style 7, 191–92: "thoroughgoing and often eloquent."

798.   Faure, Georges. 1970. *Les éléments du rythme poétique en anglais
moderne.* [The Elements of Poetic Rhythm in Modern English]. The
Hague: Mouton. 336 pp.
An attempt to refute the concept of the "foot" on the basis of a distinct sepa-
ration of ordinary speech from poetic composition.
MLR 66, 885–87: "illuminating and scholarly," "a considerable contribution."

799.   Guiraud, Pierre. 1970. *La versification.* Paris: PUF. 128 pp.
On meter, rhyme, stanzas, function, the "grammar" of Fr. verse, stylistics, evolution. Bib. 1 p.

800.   Klausenburger, Jurgen. 1970. *French Prosodics and Phonotactics: An
Historical Typology.* Tübingen: Niemeyer. 92 pp.
"The purpose of this study is (1) to trace the evolution of the prosodic structure of French, from LSL over OF to the modern period, in terms of a
nexus/cursus typology; and (2) to describe the phonotactic structures of OF
and MF, and to outline their diachronic relationship." Bib. 4 pp.

801.   Malof, Joseph. 1970. *A Manual of English Meters.* Bloomington: Indiana UP. 236 pp. Rpt. Greenwood, 1978.
Introd. on basic terms, chs. on "Foot Verse (Syllable-Stress Verse)," "Simple-
Stress Verse," "Stress-Verse: The Native Meters," "Syllabic Verse," "Free Verse,"
and "Using the Scansion" (application to lines from *King Lear*). 6 apps., 4
of them glossaries, 1 a bib., 1 a key to quotations.
Style 7, 189–90: "a good book about prosody"; *Choice* 8, 48: outstanding
"clarity," "supersedes all the partial treatments available (Hillyer, Shapiro,
Deutsch, Hamilton, et al.)," "indispensable."

802.   Palmer, F. R., ed. 1970. *Prosodic Analysis.* London: Oxford UP. 256 pp.
16 previously pub. articles (1948–61) mainly about prosody in diverse foreign

languages, but Firth's "Sounds and Prosodies" (1948) and Robins's "Aspects of Prosodic Analysis" (1957, on Firthian analysis) have general relevance. *Ling* 169, 81–82: "substantial and interesting."

803.   Halle, Morris, and Samuel J. Keyser. 1971. *English Stress: Its Form, Its Growth, and Its Role in Verse.* New York: Harper. 206 pp.
A theory of meter arranged in 3 sections: the generative theory of Eng. stress set forth in Chomsky and Halle, *The Sound of English Stress* (1968); the historical evolution of stress rules; and the theory of meter—of iambic pentameter and "stress maxima." Bib. 4 pp.; word and term indexes.
Style 9, 231–33: "evident incompleteness" of the generative theory, the iambic pentameter theory has been "strenuously debated"; *Lang* 53, 655–66, and 49, 606–11 (rev. articles); *DQR* 2, 137–40; *LingR* 13, 12–13; *HAB* 24, 133; *Ling* 121, 5–19; *LingB* 19, 1–19 (rev. article).

804.   Léon, Pierre. 1971. *Essais de phonostylistique* [Essays on Phonological Stylistics]. Montreal: Didier. 185 pp.

805.   Newton, Robert. 1971. *Form in the "Menschheitsdämmerung": A Study of Prosodic Elements and Style in German Expressionist Poetry.* The Hague: Mouton. 270 pp.
An attempt to establish the persistent presence of traditional poetic forms and patterns (stanza, line, meter, rhyme) in poetry generally characterized as formless. Bib. 5 pp.
Style 11, 99–100: an "able" study that proves its thesis with an "almost elaborately cautious" methodology; *MLR* 68, 702; *GQ* 48, 389.

806.   Pendlebury, B. J. 1971. *The Art of the Rhyme.* New York: Scribner's. 112 pp.
An attempt to show rhyme's function "as a metrical resource" and its importance to the achievements of many poets. Rhyme "has an important function to fulfill in tightening stress-patterns, giving definition to stanza-forms, and so intensifying the emotional quality of a poem"—pointing and binding. Name and term index.

807.   Mölk, Ulrich, and Friedrich Wolfzettel. 1972. *Répertoire métrique de la poésie lyrique française des origines à 1350* [Metrical Catalog of French Lyrical Poetry from Its Origins to 1350]. Munich: Fink. 682 pp.
A catalog of the metrical structures of trouvère lyric poetry.
MLR 70, 873: "long-awaited," "meticulous care," "admirable."

808.   Wimsatt, W. K., ed. 1972. *Versification: Major Language Types. Sixteen Essays.* New York: New York UP for MLA. 252 pp.
On meter. A general ch., "Elements of Versification," is followed by 11 chs. on the meters of various languages, 3 chs. on Eng., and a final ch. entitled "Verse and Music." No bib. or index.

Style 9, 227–29: "very stimulating," "invaluable" for providing information about many verse systems and for presenting essential questions and problems.

809.   Wlassics, Tibor. 1972. *Interpretazioni di prosodia dantesca* [Interpretations of Dante's Prosody]. Rome: Signorelli. 161 pp.
Mainly on Dante's use of rhyme, but also assonance, consonance, onomatopoeia, enjambment, etc.
MLR 69, 427–29: "a valuable work" for students of the *Commedia*.

810.   Allen, W. S. 1973. *Accent and Rhythm: Prosodic Features of Latin and Greek: A Study in Theory and Reconstruction.* Cambridge: Cambridge UP. 394 pp.
An examination of the suprasegmental features of Lat. and Gk.
Style 9, 225–26: "a careful, exhaustive study of the intimate relations between language and verse"; *ArL* 8, 87–92; *Em* 45, 197–201; *Gnomon* 48, 1–8; *Gymnasium* 83, 116–18; *LangS* 9, 70–74; *JRS* 65, 240–41; *Phonetica* 30, 239–41; *Lang* 51, 472–75.

811.   Attridge, Derek. 1974. *Well-Weighed Syllables: Elizabethan Verse in Classical Metres.* New York: Cambridge UP. 258 pp.
Explains Elizabethan pronunciation and scansion of Lat. in the first part of the book, in the second part surveys Elizabethan experimental programs in classical meters, and in the third treats the theory and practice of quantitative poets (Spenser, Sidney, Campion especially).
RenQ 30, 109–10: "both a masterful treatise on the state of prosody in the Renaissance and an illuminating study in cultural history"; *MLR* 74, 407–11; *PTL* 1, 214; *CCr* 29, 255; *EA* 30, 92.

812.   Gauthier, Michel. 1974. *Système euphonique et rhythmique du vers français* [Euphonic and Rythmic System of French Verse]. Paris: Klincksieck. 164 pp.

813.   Beaver, J. C., and J. F. Ihwe, eds. "Generative Metrics." 1974 and 1975. *Poetics* 12 (152 pp.) and 16 (63 pp.).

814.   Bailey, James. 1975. *Toward a Statistical Analysis of English Verse.* Lisse: de Ridder. 83 pp.
An "application of the Russian linguistic-statistical method" to selected iambic tetrameter poems by 10 Eng. poets.
Style 11, 336–37: "difficult to give much credence to Bailey's findings."

815.   Hollander, John. 1975. *Vision and Resonance: Two Senses of Poetic Form.* New York: Oxford UP. 314 pp.

A prosodic study. The 12 chs. (most of them previously pub.) "move along
an axis from the aural to the visual." Name and term index.
MLR 72, 649–51: "rich in perceptive detail."

816.   Kuryłowicz, Jerzy. 1975. *Metrik und Sprachgeschichte* [Metrics and the
        History of Language]. Wroclaw: Wydaw. Polskiej Akad. Nauk. 254 pp.

817.   Touber, A. H. 1975. *Deutsche Strophenformen des Mittelalters* [German
        Stanza Structures of the Middle Ages]. Stuttgart: Metzler. 164 pp.
A computer-based study of the metrical schemes of medieval Ger. lyric poetry,
excluding the *Leich*.
MLR 72, 738: "invaluable tool."

818.   Harding, D. W. 1976. *Words into Rhythm: English Speech Rhythm in
        Verse and Prose*. Cambridge: Cambridge UP. 166 pp.
A rev. version of lectures given 1970–71. Opposes reducing Eng. verse to metrical variations on metrical schemes in favor of "speech rhythms." Two chs. deal
with prose rhythm, mainly via Saintsbury's and Croll's approaches. Bib. 3 pp.;
name and term index.
Style 12, 392–93: "a thorough and scholarly investigation," but "the need
still remains for a more precise analysis"; *MLR* 76, 920–22: the book "has many
virtues," "lean and lucid."

819.   Adams, Percy. 1977. *Graces of Harmony: Alliteration, Assonance, and Con-
        sonance in Eighteenth-Century Poetry*. Athens: U of Georgia P. 253 pp.
A study of "consonant and vowel echoes that occur not in rhymes but in stressed
syllables anywhere in the lines" because "more subtle than rhymes" and comprehensive and dominant in the tradition of Eng. poetry. Ch. 1, "The Tradition That Dryden Was Given"; separate chs. on Dryden, Pope, and Thompson;
ch. 5 surveys the use of acoustic devices by other 18th-cent. poets and dramatists;
final ch. surveys 19th- and 20th-cent. poets. Name and term index.
Style 12, 68–70: "the most important book yet to appear on Restoration and
eighteenth-century poetic technique" because "painstakingly" related "to the
entire history of English poetry"; *ArQ* 34, 181–83.

820.   Tsur, Reuven. 1977. *A Perception-Oriented Theory of Metre*. Tel Aviv:
        Tel Aviv U. 244 pp.
Uses Halle and Keyser as his foundation but modifies their theory in various
ways — the existence of the foot, concern for units larger and smaller than the
line, etc. Bib. 3 pp.
Style 14, 397–99: "evidence and organization prevent Tsur's theory from being fully convincing," but "potentially useful."

821. Roubaud, Jacques. 1978. *La vieillesse d'Alexandre: Essai sur quelques états récents du vers français* [The Old Age of Alexander: Essay on Some Recent Conditions of French Verse]. Paris: Maspero. 214 pp.
A study of the alexandrine.
MLR 75, 673–75: "[I]t is impossible to imagine anyone who is alive to the situation of poetry in the Western world reading these two hundred pages without passionate involvement in the argument they propose."

822. Volkoff, Vladimir. 1978. *Vers une métrique française* [Toward a French Metrics]. Columbia: French Literature Pubs. 200 pp.
Fr. verse rests on a relatively stable system based on the anapest and iamb. Introd. on terminology, the alexandrine, etc.: ch. 2, rhythm and meter; ch. 3, phonetics; ch. 4, the alexandrine, etc. Bib. 3 pp.
MLR 76, 689: "worth reading" but could have been a "substantial article" and doubtful whether the "French themselves will ever accept such a metrical view."

823. Avalle, D'Arco. 1979. *Le origini della versificazione moderna* [The Origins of Modern Versification]. Torino: Giappichelli. 94 pp.

824. Golomb, Harai. 1979. *Enjambment in Poetry: Language and Verse in Interaction.* Tel Aviv: Porter Inst. for Poetics & Semiotics. 310 pp.
A study of the run-on line "as a central phenomenon in the relationships between intonation, syntactic segmentation and lineation (i.e., line-division) in poetry." Bib. (systematically compiled to 1973) in Eng. and Russ. 40 pp.; name and term index.

825. Jakobson, Roman, and Linda Waugh. 1979. *The Sound Shape of Language.* Bloomington: Indiana UP. 308 pp.
Only a few short sections deal directly with literature, such as "Sound Symbolism," "Inferences from a Cummings Poem." Bib. 50 pp.; term index.
JLS 11, 63–66: "acute insights" but "grave defects," "the book falls flat"; *Ling* 19, 531–40: "seems rambling only at first sight" for "turns around one idea, that of the basic constituents of speech. . . . a hymn to distinctive features . . . in phonology, grammar, semantics and poetry," "difficult book to read and to review" but "the message is constantly reinforced and the story itself remains always interesting and new"; *Diacritics* 11.1, 29–43.

826. Hartman, Charles. 1980. *Free Verse: An Essay on Prosody.* Princeton: Princeton UP. 199 pp.
Analyzes the rhythmic correlatives of meter, of free verse prosody, and especially line length and syntax. Bib. 7 pp.; name and term index.
Style 17, 75–77: employs an idiosyncratic definition of counterpoint as the

relation between the elements of prosody; *Critm* 23, 367; *SR* 89, 117; *TLS* 29 May 1981, 597; *WLT* 55, 680.

826a.   Léon, Pierre, and Mario Rossi, eds. 1980. *Problèmes de prosodie, I: Approches théoriques* [Problems of Prosody, I: Theoretical Approaches]. Ottawa: Didier. 109 pp.
Essays on theories of intonation. [See Léon and Rossi, no. 829.]
   FR 55, 588–89: "much remains to be done."

826b.   O'Connor. M. 1980. *Hebrew Verse Structure*. Winona Lake: Eisenbrauns. 630 pp.
The first 9 chs. study the individual units of the verse, especially the syntax; ch. 10 applies that analysis to determine the subdivisions of a poem.
   JLS 12, 91–96: "a significant book."

826c.   Wesling, Donald. 1980. *The Chances of Rhyme: Device and Modernity*. Berkeley: U of California Press. 170 pp.
Examines the formal, historical, and social influence of rhyme on poetry. Bib. 5 pp.; name index.
   CL 33, 298: "densely written, very ambitious" with "finely considered technical criticism," but "a longer or more limited book might have proved more adequate"; *JEGP* 80, 431; *SR* 89, xvii.

827.   Grotjahn, Rüdiger, ed. 1981. *Hexameter Studies*. Bochum: Brockmeyer. 262 pp.
Includes "Annotated Bibliography on the Statistical Study of Hexameter Verse" (37 pp.).

828.   Hollander, John. 1981. *Rhyme's Reason: A Guide to English Verse*. New Haven: Yale UP. 64 pp.
Brief survey of line, sound, and stanzaic patterns and larger arrangements of these. Bib. 2 pp.

829.   Léon, Pierre, and Mario Rossi, eds. 1981. *Problèmes de prosodie, II: Expérimentations, modèles et fonctions* [Problems of Prosody, II: Experimentations, Models, and Functions]. Ottawa: Didier. 195 pp.
[See Léon and Rossi, no. 826a.]

830.   Newton, Robert P. 1981. *Vowel Undersong: Studies of Vocalic Timbre and Chroneme Patterning in German Lyric Poetry*. The Hague: Mouton. 456 pp.
"The present studies aspire to extend the methodology of probing effective features" via pattern analysis of vowel and stress "frequency hierarchies."

831. Wagenknecht, Christian. 1981. *Deutsche Metrik: Eine historische Einführung* [German Metrics: A Historical Introduction]. Munich: Beck. 139 pp.
Mainly about metrics from the 16th cent. to the present.
MLR 78, 479: "supersedes" Kayser's *Kleine deutsche Versschule.*

832. Attridge, Derek. 1982. *The Rhythms of English Poetry*. London: Longman. 395 pp.
A nonchronological study of the rhythm and meter of the main tradition of regular accentual-syllabic verse that extended over 600 years in Middle and modern Eng. (Scant attention is given to alliteration or rhyme or to metrical interaction with syntax.) Part 1, "Approaches": ch. 1, "Traditional Approaches"; ch. 2, "Linguistic Approaches." Part 2, "Rhythm": ch. 3, "Rhythms of English Speech"; ch. 4, "Four-Beat Rhythm"; ch. 5, "Five-Beat Rhythms." Part 3, "Metre": ch. 6, "Metrical Rules"; ch. 7, "Rules of English Metre"; ch. 8, "Metrical Rules and Structures of Language." Part 4, "Practice": ch. 9, "Functions of Poetic Rhythm"; ch. 10, "Rhythm at Work: Some Examples." App., "Rules and Scansion." Bib. 13 pp.; proper name and terminological index. [Scholarly, erudite, closely reasoned; for advanced students.]
Lang&S 16, 244: "the most rigorous, sustained, and wide-ranging linguistic theory of English metre so far produced on this side of the Atlantic"; *BBN* Feb. 1983, 115: "fine critical sense of continuities and contrasts."

3.2.4 Studies on Several Linguistic Levels (833–1012)

833. Weinberg, Bernard. 1966. *The Limits of Symbolism: Studies of Five Modern French Poets*. Chicago: U of Chicago P. 430 pp.
Close analysis of 13 poems based on the belief that every feature of every poem resulted from conscious choice and that therefore the critic should try to determine the reason for the presence and placement of each word. The bulk of the book concerns whether the poems are symbolist or impressionist.
MLR 64, 181–84: the rev. challenges both postulate and analysis.

834. Frohock, W. M. 1967. *Style and Temper: Studies in French Fiction, 1925–1960*. Cambridge: Harvard UP. 153 pp.
Separate efforts "to help define a number of major talents"—mainly Malraux, Sartre, Camus, Montherlant, Saint-Exupéry, Bernanos, Céline, Giono. Bib. 5 pp.; name and term index.
Style 1, 179–80: unenthusiastic.

835. Meier, Erika. 1967. *Realism and Reality: The Function of the Stage Directions in the New Drama from Thomas William Robertson to George Bernard Shaw*. Bern: Francke. 334 pp.
The development of stage directions and dialogue to Shaw's "perfectly balanced whole."
MLR 65, 404: a "solid achievement but only occasional relevance to its title."

836.   Peterson, Douglas. 1967. *The English Lyric from Wyatt to Donne: A History of the Plain and Eloquent Styles.* Princeton: Princeton UP. 391 pp.
Focuses on the influence on the poetry of the theory and practice of rhetoric.
MLR 64, 860–61: "scholarly."

837.   Wrenn, C. L. 1967. *Word and Symbol: Studies in English Language.* London: Longman. 197 pp.
10 previously pub. essays, 4 of which deal with the continuity of Eng. poetry and the language of Spenser, Milton, and Eliot.
MLR 65, 860–61: praises the literary essays [yet they are brief and unsystematic].

838.   Adolph, Robert. 1968. *The Rise of Modern Prose Style.* Cambridge: MIT P. 372 pp.
In opposition to Croll and R. F. Jones, Adolph argues that prose shifted from Elizabethan expressiveness to Restoration "plain" style because of the new utilitarian ethic. Bib. 3 pp.; name and term index.

839.   Habicht, Werner. 1968. *Studien zur Dramenform vor Shakespeare: Moralität, Interlude, romaneskes Drama* [Studies in Dramatic Form before Shakespeare: Morality Play, Interlude, Romance Drama]. Heidelberg: Winter. 259 pp.
An account of the interweaving of genres, forms, and techniques in drama before Shakespeare—the morality play, the interlude, tragicomedy, sermon, novella, romance, prose fiction, etc. Bib., index, 3-pp. summary in Eng.
MLR 67, 165–66: reassesses the plays "in a new light."

840.   Levine, George, and William Madden, eds. 1968. *The Art of Victorian Prose.* New York: Oxford UP. 378 pp.
A study of Victorian nonfiction prose by 15 contributors, divided into 3 parts: "aspects of the history of nineteenth-century prose," "particular authors," and "theoretical problems." Name and term index.
Style 4, 177–86: mainly traditional literary studies, but as a "forceful assertion of the art of Victorian non-fiction . . . the book is an important collection."

841.   Lewicka, Halina. 1968. *La langue et le style du théâtre comique français des XVe et VXIe siècles: Les composés* [Language and Style of the French Comic Theater of the Fifteenth and Sixteenth Centuries: The Compounds]. Warsaw: Panstwowe Wydawnictwo Naukowe; Paris: Klincksieck. 225 pp.
A classification and analysis of the compounds.
MLR 65, 623–24: "an essential work of reference for all researchers in the field."

842. Meyer, Herman. 1968. *The Poetics of Quotation in the European Novel.* Trans. T. Ziolkowski and Y. Ziolkowski. Princeton: Princeton UP. 278 pp. (*Das Zitat in der Erzählkunst.* Stuttgart: Metzler, 1967.)

A study of "what the literary quotation signifies and achieves as a structural element in the novel from Rabelais to the present," treating "quotation" broadly to include literary reference, allusion, pastiche, parody, and plagiarism. Name index.

Style 7, 184–88: "amazing and amusing" erudition; *MLR* 60, 143–44; 65, 207–09.

843. Raban, Jonathan. 1968. *The Technique of Modern Fiction: Essays in Practical Criticism.* London: Arnold. 203 pp.

Analyses of the techniques of fiction divided into 3 areas: "Narrative," "Character," and "Style and Language." Each section is divided into 5 chapters or topics, each providing a general introd., a quotation from a modern novel, and an analysis of the quotation. Bib. 8 pp.; name index.

MLR 65, 617–18: "most of what he says is acceptable enough" but there are "two serious shortcomings": a failure "to show how his fifteen technical subsections may cohere in a formal unity" and to relate the extracts to the whole novels.

844. Steinmetz, Horst. 1968. *Die Trilogie: Entstehung und Struktur einer Grossform des deutschen Dramas nach 1800* [The Trilogy: Origin and Structures of a Dramatic Genre in Germany after 1800]. Heidelberg: Winter. 192 pp.

An investigation into the formal implications of the genre "trilogy," whether it possesses an inner form.

MLR 66, 230: "thoughtful contribution."

845. Webber, Joan. 1968. *The Eloquent "I": Style and Self in Seventeenth-Century Prose.* Madison: U of Wisconsin Press. 298 pp.

Comparison of the styles and themes of autobiographical passages by 8 17th-cent. authors (4 Anglican—Donne, Burton, Browne, Traherne; 4 Puritan—Bunyan, Lilburne, Milton, and Baxter) reveals the Puritans expressed themselves most readily in action and the Anglicans in meditation. Bib. 8 pp.; name index.

Style 3, 200–04: praises Webber's analysis of specific passages but questions her general thesis and methodology; *MLR* 65, 142–44.

846. Crystal, David, and Derek Davy. 1969. *Investigating English Style.* Bloomington: Indiana UP. 264 pp.

Treating style within the framework of general language variation, the authors scrutinize the linguistic differences to be observed primarily within the repertoire of Eng. used in everyday life. Part 1 gives the various theoretical con-

cepts needed to classify the varieties of language into types and outlines a
set of techniques for describing any piece of language; part 2 illustrates the
approach by describing in detail extracts of 5 kinds of Eng.: conversation, commentary, religion, newspaper reporting, legal documents. Name and term index. [Cf. Galperin's *Stylistics*, no. 360. A reviewer calls this book "general
stylistics" to contrast the study of belles lettres.]

Style 5, 300–08: clarifies the study of style; *Ling* 122, 68–78: "despite its
undoubted merits, seems in the final analysis to be somewhat premature and
in many respects peculiarly sterile"; *LL* 23, 155–58; *Anglia* 90, 500–05, *BSLP*
66, 172–73; *Vir* (1971), 421–23; *SN* 43, 600–02; *Ind Ling* 31, 126–28; *Lingua*
27, 288–93; *ZPSK* 24, 437–38; *Lang&S* 4, 153–54; *PP* 14, 54–56; *ES* 53,
181–83.

847.   Dorfman, Eugene. 1969. *The Narreme in the Medieval Romance Epic:
         An Introduction to Narrative Structures.* Toronto: U of Toronto P. 259 pp.
"This book has 2 principal aims: first, to present an experimental theory on
the functional analysis of literary structures into constituent units, *narremes*,
parallel with the phonemes and morphemes of linguistic analysis; second,
to exemplify the theory in practice, mainly by the detailed analysis of two
major Romance epics, the *Roland* and the *Cid*, supported by a less detailed
examination of 12 additional Romance narratives." Bib. 17 pp.; name and
term index.
     Pierre Guiraud's foreword: "no man is better qualified or prepared than
Eugene Dorfman"; Scholes, *Structuralism in Literature*: "a rather feeble attempt to apply structuralism" (207); *MLR* 67, 413–14.

848.   Garrett, Peter. 1969. *Scene and Symbol from George Eliot to James Joyce:
         Studies in Changing Fictional Mode.* New Haven: Yale UP. 284 pp.
A study of the use of scenic presentation (vs. narrative summary) and symbolism (rather than realism) as they developed from Eliot through James, Conrad, and Lawrence to Joyce. It is a development from mimesis to poiesis, the
novel becoming constitutive of meaning rather than imitating life. Bib. 8 pp.;
name index.
     Style 6, 77–78: "an argument based on the fallacy of relevance. . . . some
acceptable and conventional remarks."

849.   Georgi, Annette. 1969. *Das lateinische und deutsche Preisgedicht des
         Mittelalters in der Nachfolge des "genus demonstrativum"* [The Latin
         and German Panegyric of the Middle Ages in Succession of the "Genus
         Demonstrativum"]. Berlin: Schmidt. 205 pp.
A study of the medieval panegyric.
     MLR 67, 686–87: "very useful."

850.   Houston, John. 1969. *The Demonic Imagination: Style and Theme in
         French Romantic Poetry.* Baton Rouge: Louisiana State UP. 177 pp.

A study of the "presiding themes and symbols" of the "first decades of the nineteenth century," particularly the attribution of evil to God or nature, with humankind as victim, against "the background of the evolution of prosody and poetic language." Name and term index.

MLR 65, 910–11: some "regrettable" lacunae, but "refreshing and helpful pioneer," "remarkable sensitivity toward poetic language."

851. Inglis, Fred. 1969. *The Elizabethan Poets: The Making of English Poetry from Wyatt to Ben Jonson.* London: Evans. 168 pp.
Traces the development of the "plain style" in Elizabethan poetry, which comes to perfection in the poetry of Jonson.

MLR 65, 372–73: popularized history which "will create as many problems as it will solve."

852. Lawler, James R. 1969. *The Language of French Symbolism.* Princeton: Princeton UP. 270 pp.
"I have tried to combine linguistic and formal study with reference to other parts of each author's work." Usually focuses on a single poem by each of 6 poets: Mallarmé, Verlaine, Rimbaud, Claudel, Apollinaire, and Baudelaire. Name index.

Style 7, 214–16: "scholarly, judicious and reponsible"; *MLR* 66, 413–15.

853. Milic, Louis. 1969. *Stylists on Style: A Handbook with Selections for Analysis.* New York: Scribner's. 527 pp.
An introd. gives Milic's view of style: an entity separable from content to be analyzed as deviations from norms. Traditional rhetorical analysis (anaphora, parallelism, etc.) are combined with 2 analytical innovations—"propositional reduction" and the "logical diagram." 100 British and American prose writers are selected in reverse chronological order. Over a third of the book contains annotations on the selections. Bib. 3 pp.; name and term index.

Style 6, 71–73: "handsome format" and "unusually effective" in explicating the terms of rhetorical art, but "does not demonstrate the value" of his "propositional reduction" and logical diagrams methods.

854. Murrin, Michael. 1969. *The Veil of Allegory: Some Notes toward a Theory of Allegorical Rhetoric in the English Renaissance.* Chicago: U of Chicago P. 224 pp.
Traces 1 strand in the history of allegory, the revival in Florence of the late classical mode that veils truth from the multitude, its development in Elizabethan critics and poets, its demise in the 17th cent. and its partial revival in the Romantics. Name and term index.

Style 7, 193–97: "compact, useful, and occasionally annoying".

855. Smith, William R. 1969. *The Rhetoric of American Politics: A Study of Documents.* Westport: Greenwood. 464 pp.

Analyzes 5 speeches, 3 manifestos, 3 laws, and 2 court decisions spanning 2 1/2 cents. Ch. 1 explains his Aristotelian conception of rhetoric as the use of all available means of persuasion in a given situation, and his 4-part method of analysis: purpose, materials, form, and effect. Bib. 17 pp.; name and term index.

Style 8, 566–69: "worthy" method but "his indifference to recent criticism . . . causes wonder."

855a.   Bateson, Mary. 1970. *Structural Continuity in Poetry. A Linguistic Study in Five Pre-Islamic Odes*. Paris: Mouton. 176 pp.

An effort to develop precise methods out of descriptive linguistics for describing the structure of the pre-Islamic ode. 7 chs. on background of the form, the 5 poems, phonological deviation, morphological repetition, order, and span of pattern.

Ling No. 141, 83–86: "numerous virtues," "highly important contribution to the Arabic linguistics."

856.   Bersani, Leo. 1970. *Balzac to Beckett: Center and Circumference in French Fiction*. New York: Oxford UP. 340 pp.

Discusses each author's attitude toward language and reality underlying the narrative strategies he employs to communicate his meaning. The novels of these writers (and the novel in general) are composed of 2 movements — a central thematic core and the narrative devices that diversify and enrich it. Name index.

MLR 67, 423–24: "impressive."

857.   Block, Haskell. 1970. *Naturalistic Triptych: The Fictive and the Real in Zola, Mann, and Dreiser*. New York: Random. 114 pp.

A comparison of Zola's *L'assommoir*, Mann's *Buddenbrooks*, and Dreiser's *An American Tragedy*, particularly of the substantial documentation and research preceding composition, for accurate depiction of reality.

MLR 67, 160–61: "valuable."

858.   Brandt, William. 1970. *The Rhetoric of Argumentation*. New York: Bobbs. 288 pp.

A 2-part system for analyzing the structures of this kind of discourse. "Structural Rhetoric" offers a 2-part framework for analyzing parts of an argument and their relation to one another: argument using (1) deduction and induction and (2) the classical 6 parts (Brandt adds a seventh). The second section of the book, "Textual Rhetoric," subsumes all rhetorical figures under 4 intentions of an author. The third section discusses flaws in arguments, and the last section deals with reportorial writing. Name and term index. [See Lanham, no. 51.]

Style 8, 560–63: "well-done" but "no real analysis of semantic or linguistic bases from which the figures derive their effect."

859.   Braudy, Leo. 1970. *Narrative Form in History and Fiction*. Princeton: Princeton UP. 318 pp.
Studies of late 18th-cent. historical and fictional narratives, particularly those of Hume, Gibbon, and Fielding. Bib. 12 pp.; name and term index.
Style 13, 42–44: "subtly argued and carefully crafted" but leaves many important questions unanswered.

859a.   Deloffre, F. 1970. *Stylistique et poétique françaises*. Paris: Soc. d'édition d'enseignement supérieur. 214 pp.
A college text with a general introd. to stylistics applied to Fr. literature – 2 poems from the 16th cent., a fable by La Fontaine, the ending of a poem by Chénier, etc.
Ling 141, 105–06: "excellent manuel," "clair et attrayant."

860.   Hahnloser-Ingold, Margrit. 1970. *Das englische Theater und Bert Brecht: Die Dramen von W. H. Auden, John Osborne, John Arden in ihrer Beziehung zum epischen Theater von Bert Brecht und den gemeinsamen elisabethanischen Quellen* [The English Theater and Bert Brecht: The Plays of W. H. Auden, John Osborne, John Arden in Relation to the Epic Theater of Bert Brecht and to Their Common Elizabethan Sources]. Bern: Francke. 281 pp.
The influence of Brecht's technical devices (self-introductions, presenters, etc.) on 3 British dramatists.
MLR 67, 409–10: an unfavorable rev.

861.   Patterson, Annabel. 1970. *Hermogenes and the Renaissance: Seven Ideas of Style*. Princeton: Princeton UP. 240 pp.
Traces the influence of the second cent. AD Greek rhetorician's *Concerning Ideas* (that part of his *Art of Rhetoric* devoted to 7 categories of style) on rhetoricians and poets in the Renaissance. Bib. 10 pp.; name and term index.
Style 7, 198–201: inadequate evidence or analytic precision but offers "a more flexible, perceptive rhetorical description of styles" than do similar studies; *MLR* 67, 868–69.

862.   Rosenthal, Erwin. 1970. *Das fragmentarische Universum* [The Fragmentary Universe]. Munich: Nymphenburger. 183 pp.
A study of how changes in perception are reflected in the language and structure of the modern novel.
MLR 67, 955–56: chs. not "consistent in quality," covers "too many authors," weak analysis.

863.   Stone, Robert K. 1970. *Middle English Prose Style: Margery Kempe and Julian of Norwich*. The Hague: Mouton. 220 pp.

A study of *The Book of Margery Kempe* and *The Relevations of Divine Love* by Dame Julian in search of an understanding of medieval prose style. Chs. 1 and 2 examine the writers' personalities and the general characteristics of their writing. Chs. 3–5 deal with diction, alliteration, and sentence structure. Apps. on assonance and consonance and on alliteration. Bib. 4 pp.; name and term index.

Style 9, 131–33: "too many lists," an "over-reliance on secondary material," and a failure to compare with other works of medieval prose; *Choice* 8, 678: "modest, painstaking, clearly written."

864.   Strzetelski, Jerzy. 1970. *The English Sonnet: Syntax and Style.* Crakow: Jagellonian U. 146 pp.
"This study, an investigation in descriptive stylistics, a branch of applied linguistics, presents an examination of the contribution of the syntax to the style of the English sonnet." 278 sonnets are examined "to find out what describable formal syntactic features of the sonnets differentiate the style of the English sonneteers from one another." Bib. 5 pp.

865.   Vickers, Brian. 1970. *Classical Rhetoric in English Poetry.* London: Macmillan; New York: St. Martin's. 180 pp.
The use of classical figures of speech, particularly in Renaissance poetry. Ch. 1 traces the idea of rhetoric from ancient Greece into the 18th cent. Ch. 2 discusses the aspects of rhetoric (invention, arrangement, etc.). Chs. 3–5 deal with *elocutio*, the figures, with ch. 5 discussing specific figures in 4 Renaissance poets. Bib. 5 pp.; name and term index.

Style 9, 238–41: regrets the "unnecessarily narrow" limit to British poetry and neglect of 19th and 20th cents., but finds the book "lucid, well-written"; *QJS* 58, 35: "deserves oblivion"; *MLR* 66, 380–82.

866.   Wells, Stanley. 1970. *Literature and Drama, with Special Reference to Shakespeare and His Contemporaries.* London: Routledge. 117 pp.
On the strengths and limitations of reading and performing plays, the importance of additions and extensions in performance (movement, music, silence, gesture, voice, etc.), and the inexhaustibility of interpretation in performance. Bib. 3 pp. [Studies of the diversity of performance of plays contribute to our understanding of reader-author interaction; see section 6.0.]

MLR 67, 400–01: "a work of refreshing good sense."

867.   Witke, Charles. 1970. *Latin Satire: The Structure of Persuasion.* Leiden: Brill. 280 pp.
"Studies of satirists working in Latin" from "the Augustan Age through the high Middle Ages."

RSQ 3, 7–8.

868. Angress, R. K. 1971. *The Early German Epigram: A Study in Baroque Poetry*. Lexington: UP of Kentucky. 134 pp.
A study of 17th-cent. Ger. epigrammatic writing.
MLR 69, 224–25: "well-written and soundly documented."

869. Ball, Patricia. 1971. *The Science of Aspects: The Changing Role of Fact in the Work of Coleridge, Ruskin, and Hopkins*. London: Athlone. 163 pp.
How the 3 react to their "shared capacity for observation differently, interpret it differently, and evaluate it differently." Bib. 2 pp.; name index.
MLR 67, 404–05: "modest and soberly written."

870. Bennett, James R., ed. 1971. *Prose Style: A Historical Approach through Studies*. San Francisco: Chandler/Intext. 286 pp.
Chronologically arranged essays from Ælfric to Joyce. Each section is followed by "Suggestions for Research" and "Selections for Analysis." Includes "A Contextual Method for the Description of Prose Style" and a "Glossary of Historical and Critical Terms." Bib. 30 pp.; name index.

871. Bowers, John W., and Donovan Ochs. 1971. *The Rhetoric of Agitation and Control*. Reading: Addison. 152 pp.
Definitions in introd. 3 examples of the rhetoric of agitation and its control in actual situations follow, including a description of the ideology and language of the agitators and their opponents in each instance.
Style 8, 564–65: "a scholarly debriefing of what happened" in 3 cases, its style "that of the textbook."

872. Brettschneider, Werner. 1971. *Die moderne deutsche Parabel: Entwicklung und Bedeutung* [The Modern German Parable: Development and Significance]. Berlin: Schmidt. 80 pp.
A history and definition of the parabolic mode.
MLR 69, 472–73: "concentrated and lucidly written."

873. Burrow, J. A. 1971. *Ricardian Poetry: Chaucer, Gower, Langland, and the "Gawain" Poet*. London: Routledge. 165 pp.
A case for sufficient common characteristics in the poetry of these 4 writers to justify designating a Ricardian period of Eng. literature — ironic sophistication, use of significant detail in descriptions, use of the simile, etc. Name and term index.
MLR 67, 612–13: "excellent critical account."

874. Forster, Leonard. 1971. *The Poet's Tongues: Multilingualism in Literature*. London: Cambridge UP. 101 pp.

A brief chronological but unsystematic survey of the use of languages other than the mother tongue in poetry. Name index.
MLR 68, 132–34: "mastery of the subject."

875.   Gradon, Pamela. 1971. *Form and Style in Early English Literature*. London: Methuen. 398 pp.
A chronological study of aspects of language and narration — image, emblem, plot, semantic range — from Old Eng. to the late 15th cent. Bib. 9 pp.; glossary of terms.
Style 11, 311–13: "the most substantial and provocative study" of medieval form and style "to have appeared in a good many years."

876.   Hassan, Ihab. 1971. *The Dismemberment of Orpheus: Toward a Postmodern Literature*. New York: Oxford UP. 297 pp. (2nd ed., introd. and postlude expanded, 1982.)
Orphic dismemberment and regeneration is the author's metaphor for a radical crisis in art and language. Focuses especially on Hemingway, Kafka, Genet, and Beckett. Name index.
VQR 47, clxviii: "a remarkably compassionate diagnosis," "convincing and helpful"; *HR* 24, 519; *Sat Rev* 54, 23; *CC* 88, 570.

877.   Jung, Marc-René. 1971. *Etudes sur le poème allégorique en France au moyen âge* [Studies of the Allegorical Poem in France during the Middle Ages]. Bern: Francke. 334 pp.
Studies of the ways in which allegory is used in the Middle Ages from Prudentius to Guillaume de Lorris.
MLR 69, 166–68: "scholarly, informative, and stimulating."

878.   Kroeber, Karl. 1971. *Styles in Fictional Structure: The Art of Jane Austen, Charlotte Brontë, George Eliot*. Princeton: Princeton UP. 293 pp.
A study of the art of fiction with the hope of "building up an objective, cumulatively rewarding discipline of studies of fictional styles" for a future "aesthetic history of fiction." Ch. 2, "Words in Fiction," evaluates computer studies. Other chs.: "Forms of Characterization," "Point of View," "Style and Change: Jane Austen," "Image and Metaphor," "Novel and Romance," "Resolution Scenes," "The Total Design of Novels," "A Contrast of Passages from *Emma, Villette,* and *Middlemarch*," "Narrative and Dialogue: Large and Small Structures," "Evaluations." Bib. 10 pp.; app. of tabulations, 78 pp.; name and term index.
Style 7, 238–40: "timely . . . the product of enormous labor," but the pursuit of a scientific criticism "transforms a literary study into a technological treatise"; *YR* 61, 132: hostile rev.: "the commentary in general errs," etc.; *PP* 19, 154–56; *JEGP* 70, 680–82; *RES* 23, 514–15; *CHum* 8, 115–18; *SNNTS* 5, 406–08; *ES* 54, 597–600; *ELN* 10, 233–36.

879.　Kugel, James. 1971. *The Techniques of Strangeness in Symbolist Poetry.* New Haven: Yale UP. 123 pp.

A brief history and analysis of the sources of mystery in symbolist poems (incomplete information, frustrated allusion, etc.). Bib. 6 pp.; name and term index.

VQR 47, clxix: "succeeds admirably," "unobtrusively scholarly"; *LJ* 96, 1713.

880.　Partridge, A. C. 1971. *The Language of Renaissance Poetry: Spenser, Shakespeare, Donne, Milton.* London: Deutsch. 348 pp.

A study of word choice, metrics, grammar, semantics, and rhetorical figures during the period 1575–1675 as expressed by 4 poets. Bib. 12 pp.; name and term index.

TLS 11 Feb. 1972, 162: "comprehensive," "detailed," most important on "rhetorical training of Renaissance poets."

881.　Riha, Karl. 1971. *Cross-Reading and Cross-Talking: Zitat-Collagen als poetische und satirische Technik* [Cross-Reading and Cross-Talking: Quotation Collage as Poetic and Satiric Technique]. Stuttgart: Metzler. 104 pp.

A study of the collage in Dadaist, Expressionist, and postwar experimental poets.

MLR 69, 228–29: not a "serious attempt."

882.　Spencer, Sharon. 1971. *Space, Time, and Structure in the Modern Novel.* New York: New York UP. 251 pp.

Space has replaced time as the major structuring device, space conceived as "virtually inexhaustible" in its relationships and impossible to describe "from a single point of reference." Meaning in the modern "architectonic" novel is found "in the relationships among the juxtaposed portions of the work": Cortázar, Robbe-Grillet, Musil, Saporta, et al. Bib. 9 pp.; name and term index.

Style 9, 443–45: "not only pioneering, but prophetic"; *CL* 14, 398–405.

883.　Stanzel, Franz. 1971. *Narrative Situations in the Novel:* Tom Jones, Moby-Dick, The Ambassadors, Ulysses. Trans. James Pusack. Bloomington: Indiana UP. 186 pp. (*Die typischen Erzählsituationen im Roman.* Vienna: Braumüller, 1963.)

A study of the "mediacy of presentation" or "narrative situation" (point of view) and the structures that derive from it in 4 novels. The last ch. presents a typology of the novel based on the preceding argument. Name index (of authors studied).

MLR 68, 159–61: mainly favorable rev.

884.　Steinberg, Günter. 1971. *Erlebte Rede: Ihre Eigenart und ihre Formen in neuerer deutscher, französischer und englischer Erzählliteratur* [Interior Monologue: Its Peculiarity and Its Forms in Modern German, French, and English Prose]. 2 vols. Göppingen: Kümmerle.

885.   Boa, Elizabeth, and J. H. Reid. 1972. *Critical Strategies: German Fiction in the Twentieth Century*. London: Arnold. 206 pp.
An introd. to both the general themes and the techniques (chs. on point of view, patterns, imagery, etc.) in an attempt to relate technique, fictional subject matter, and the world around us. Bib. 4 pp.; name index.
MLR 70, 226–28: the authors have attempted too much.

886.   Campbell, Karlyn. 1972. *Critiques of Contemporary Rhetoric*. Belmont: Wadsworth. 217 pp.
3 chs. discuss the principles and methods of rhetorical criticism, for an understanding of persuasive discourse. Reprints 4 speeches and 6 essays and provides analysis of each. Name and term index.
Style 8, 566–69: better suited to the analysis of radical rhetoric than W. R. Smith's classical system.

887.   Fish, Stanley. 1972. *Self-Consuming Artifacts: The Experience of Seventeenth-Century Literature*. Berkeley: U of California P. 432 pp.
An attempt to demonstrate a method of literary analysis, to define a literary genre and establish its canon, and to interpret several Renaissance texts. The self-consuming artifacts of the title (mainly works by Bacon, Herbert, Bunyan, Burton, Milton, and Browne) involve the reader in discursive activities that they then subvert. Name index.
Belsey, *Critical Practice*: fails "to recognize that a plurality of readers must necessarily produce a plurality of readings. Fish's reader is disarmingly singular. . . . There is no recognition that experience is in any sense ideologically or discursively constructed. . . . [W]hat he practices is on the whole a sophisticated form of New Criticism" (33–34); *Diacritics* 4.2, 24–27; 5.1, 26–31.

888.   Garke, Esther. 1972. *The Use of Songs in Elizabethan Prose Fiction*. Bern: Francke. 132 pp.
The function of songs in the prose of the best writers.
MLR 70, 141: "careful and systematic classification of the techniques."

889.   Houston, John. 1972. *Fictional Technique in France, 1802–1927: An Introduction*. Baton Rouge: Louisiana State UP. 159 pp.
Traces from Chateaubriand to Proust, with chs. on "Stendhal and Pseudorealism," "Balzac and *La comédie humaine*," "Minor Genres: Romance and Confession Novel," "Flaubert, His Disciples, and Impersonal Narration," "Beyond Impersonal Narration," and "Proust and First-Person Narration." Name and term index.
MLR 69, 879–80: "very scrappy," "so many points raised are not developed."

890.　Chabrol, Claude, and Louis Marin, eds. 1973. *Sémiotique narrative: Récits bibliques* [Narrative Semiotics: Biblical Narratives]. Paris: Larousse. 130 pp.

891.　Doležel, Lubomír. 1973. *Narrative Modes in Czech Literature*. Toronto: U of Toronto P. 152 pp.
A theory and taxonomy of narrative modes, followed by 4 studies of specific literary works. The classification depends on 2 optional narrator functions — interpretation and action. This "taxonomy of functions is complemented by a 'verbal model,' based on the systems of pronouns, verb tenses, references to time and place (deixis), address to the reader (allocution), and 'subjective semantics.'" Bib. 4 pp.; name and term index.
　Style 11, 96–98: "interesting and useful," the "avenues which this book defines . . . deserve full exploration"; *CRCL* 1, 194–98; *SlavR* 34, 445–46; *PTL* 1, 569–78; *CL* 29, 265–67; *AUMLA* 41, 140.

892.　Lorian, Alexandre. 1973. *Tendances stylistique dans la prose narrative française au XVIe siècle* [Stylistic Tendencies in French Narrative Prose of the Sixteenth Century]. Paris: Klincksieck. 343 pp.
Mainly in 2 parts: exaggeration and "overlapping." Name and term indexes.

893.　Mohrmann, G. P., et al., eds. 1973. *Explorations in Rhetorical Criticism*. University Park: Pennsylvania State UP. 245 pp.
12 essays on a wide variety of subjects — "Kennedy vs. Big Steel," Cicero's orations, Black Power rhetoric, "Rhetorical Criticism in Twentieth-Century America," etc.

894.　Page, Norman. 1973. *Speech in the English Novel*. London: Longman. 172 pp.
Citing examples from 30 novelists spread over 2 cents. and stylistically diverse, Page shows how authors use speech to individualize character and establish local and class identity. Chs. 1–4 "general and theoretical"; chs. 5–6 "on selected novels and novelists"; ch. 6 on Dickens, "the supremely original and versatile exponent of dialogue writing." Bib. follows each ch.; name and term index. [An important contribution to the effort to create an aesthetic history of fiction; see Kroeber, no. 878.]
　Style 8, 265–66: this extension of the author's *The Language of Jane Austen* contains among other commendable parts a "persuasive" ch. on Dickens.

895.　Spencer, Jeffry. 1973. *Heroic Nature: Ideal Landscape in English Poetry from Marvell to Thomson*. Evanston: Northwestern UP. 319 pp.
The study of the visual and pictorial in literature, specifically of pictorialism in the verbal landscapes of Marvell, Milton, Dryden, Pope, and Thompson. Name and term index.
　MLR 69, 844–46: "a good deal" is "derivative," but "it is useful."

896.   Stapleton, Laurence. 1973. *The Elected Circle: Studies in the Art of Prose.*
        Princeton: Princeton UP. 297 pp.
A study of the ways nonfiction prose writers develop their themes by metaphor, rhythm, and tone ("the interaction of the prose writer's sense of human life and his means of identifying it in language"). Donne, Browne,
Felltham, Hazlitt, De Quincey, Emerson, Thoreau, and T. S. Eliot receive separate chs. Name and term index (mainly the former).
    RES 26, 363: "pleasantly written but superficial"; *AL* 46, 393; *VQR* 50, cxxii.

897.   Turco, Lewis. 1973. *Poetry: An Introduction through Writing.* Reston:
        Reston. 406 pp.
A college-level introd. to the reading of poetry in contrast to prose. Bib. 1
p.; name and term index 36 pp., double columns.
    Style 10, 86–92: "seems hasty in production . . . and in organization"
but "teases the student into new ways of perceiving poetry."

898.   White, James. 1973. *The Legal Imagination: Studies in the Nature of
        Legal Thought and Expression.* Boston: Little. 986 pp.
Especially see ch. 6, "The Imagination of the Lawyer," commentaries on sample
arguments.
    RSQ 4, 6–8: "a milestone."

899.   Caws, Mary Ann, ed. 1974. *About French Poetry from Dada to "Tel
        Quel": Text and Theory.* Detroit: Wayne State UP. 298 pp.
A highly diverse collection of essays "arranged by approach rather than by
chronology" (the first essay is about juxtaposition) "so that the general and
the comparative precede the analytic and the linguistic." Name and term index. [Continuation of her earlier books—*The Poetry of Dada and Surrealism*
(1969) and *The Inner Theatre of Recent French Poetry* (1972; reviewed in *Diacritics* 4.1, 25)).]
    Choice 12, 398: "important," "articles uniformly excellent"; *LJ* 100, 128.

900.   Fell, John L. 1974. *Film and the Narrative Tradition.* Norman: U of Okla-
        homa P. 284 pp.
An explanation of the genesis of film narrative out of 19th-cent. prose narrative sources that stressed the sense of physical space, temporal duration, and
objects as determinants of human action. Bib. 13 pp.; name and term index.
    Style 9, 533–36: "It is the best and most fully researched, eminently intel-
ligent discussion of the origins of narrative film out of late-Victorian dime
novels, comic strips, optics, and advertising art."

901.   Gay, Peter. 1974. *Style in History.* New York: Basic. 242 pp.
A study of the importance of individual (habitual) expression in historical
writings, focusing mainly on Gibbon, Ranke, Macaulay, and Burckhardt. Bib.
20 pp.; name index, a few terms.

Style 8, 549–54: "excellent" but "an insufficient demonstration of style *at work* in historical writing."

902.   Gilman, Sander. 1974. *The Parodic Sermon in European Perspective: Aspects of Liturgical Parody from the Middle Ages to the Twentieth Century.* Wiesbaden: Steiner. 244 pp.
A chronological survey especially of parodies in major literary works; concentrates on technique.
   MLR 72, 230–31: "weaknesses in the general approach" and "difficult to read."

903.   Grawe, Christian. 1974. *Sprache im Prosawerk: Beispiele von Goethe, Fontane, Thomas Mann, Bergengruen, Kleist und Johnson* [Language in Prose: Examples from Goethe, Fontane, Thomas Mann, Bergengruen, Kleist, and Johnson]. Bonn: Bouvier. 111 pp.
The verbal patterns developed through characters' conversations.
   MLR 71, 472: 2 of the essays "admirably coherent and compact."

903a.   Kristeva, Julia. 1974. *La révolution du langage poétique: L'avant-garde à la fin du XIXe siècle, Lautréamont et Mallarmé* [The Revolution of Poetic Language: The Avant-Garde to the End of the Nineteenth Century: Lautréamont and Mallarmé]. Paris: Seuil. 645 pp.
Semiotic approach.

904.   Nims, John F. 1974. *Western Wind: An Introduction to Poetry.* New York: Random. 466 pp.
A college-level introd. to the reading of poetry, especially focusing on the metrical expressiveness of variation from a norm. 6 main sections: the images of sense perception (chs. on metaphor, symbol, synesthesia, paradox, understatement; images and emotions; sounds; rhythms; structures. Postscript on concrete poetry. Name and term indexes.
   Style 10, 86–92: "apart from metrics . . . a powerful mixture of sense and wisdom."

905.   "Politics and Style I." 1974. *Style* 8.3. 149 pp.
3 essays, 11 reviews, bib.

906.   Richter, David. 1974. *Fable's End: Completeness and Closure in Rhetorical Fiction.* Chicago: U of Chicago P. 214 pp.
In contrast to Kermode's reader-focused *The Sense of an Ending* and like Smith's *Poetic Closure*, this book focuses on "how the literary work provides the 'consoling' form" Kermode discusses, the rhetorical strategies in the creation of form. The form discussed here is "rhetorical fiction," or fable (apologue)—*Rasselas, Candide, Lord of the Flies, The Stranger, V., Catch-22.*

Checklist of "Formally Interesting Rhetorical Fiction"; bib. 6 pp.; name and term index.

VQR 51, ci: "useful insights," "wide-ranging," "fascinating thesis"; *Genre* 8, 379; *TLS* (N 7 '75), 1329; *Choice* 12, 526; *LJ* 100, 131.

907. Sebeok, Thomas. 1974. *Structure and Texture: Selected Essays in Cheremis Verbal Art*. The Hague: Mouton. 158 pp.

The first half of these 12 previously pub. essays (1950s mainly) analyze the interplay between structure and texture in the charms, prayers, etc., of the Cheremis culture. The second half of the anthology discusses the statistical and comparative analysis of texts. Name index.

Style 12, 61–62: "a valuable model of structural analysis within the positivistic tradition."

908. Sloan, Thomas O., and Raymond Waddington, eds. 1974. *The Rhetoric of Renaissance Poetry from Wyatt to Milton*. Berkeley: U of California P. 247 pp.

10 original essays ranging from the general to explications of single poems. Name and term index.

Style 11, 84–86: "excellent"; *Ren&R* 12, 126–27; *Critm* 18, 77–82; *P&R* 9, 127; *RES* ns 28, 72–74; *QJS* 62, 87–89; *SCN* 34, 91; *SR* 84, 684–95; *VQR* 51, civ; *Choice* 12, 396; *LJ* 99, 1714; *SCN* 34, 91.

909. Williams, Ioan. 1974. *The Realist Novel in England: A Study in Development*. Pittsburgh: U of Pittsburgh P. 221 pp.

A survey of the 19th-cent. realist novel, from Austen to James. Name index.

AR 33, 116: "like good history . . . attempts to recover the viewpoints of another time," "sanity," "fresh and persuasive"; *DR* 54, 379; *RES* 27, 493; *NCF* 30, 522; *MFS* 21, 591.

910. Bartel, Roland, et al. 1975. *Biblical Images in Literature*. Nashville: Abingdon. 383 pp.

Essays arranged in 3 parts by genre: the Bible in fiction, poetry, and drama. Index to biblical texts alluded to or discussed.

Choice 13, 650: "indispensable" for class use, but "limited" as a reference tool.

911. Carlson, Richard S. 1975. *The Benign Humorists*. Hamden: Archon. 154 pp.

Mainly on Carroll, de la Mare, Grahame, Milne, Potter, Wodehouse. Ch. 6, "The Language of Benign Humor."

Style 10, 109–13: a "whimsical," pixyish study.

912. Ciardi, John, and Miller Williams. 1975. *How Does a Poem Mean?* 2nd ed. Boston: Houghton. 408 pp.

Sections of commentary on language, tone, imagery, meter, and syntax of poems. A college text. Term and name index.

913.   Hardy, Barbara. 1975. *Tellers and Listeners: The Narrative Imagination.* London: Athlone–U of London. 279 pp.
Proclaiming that literature and narratives in literature are not autonomous but closely related to storytelling in daily life, Hardy goes on with 5 chs. on "Forms and Themes" and 4 on "Authors." E.g., the ch. on "Narrative Imagination" presents ways in which stories are used to "persuade, encourage," etc.
    MLR 73, 145–51: negative rev.: "heavy going—often puzzling," "lack of defined thesis," etc.

914.   "Innovative Fiction." 1975. *Style* 9.3. 168 pp.
7 essays, a bib., and 2 revs.

915.   Kennedy, Andrew. 1975. *Six Dramatists in Search of a Language: Studies in Dramatic Language.* London: Cambridge UP. 271 pp.
Uses the methods of "three areas of inquiry: aesthetics, dramatic criticism, and stylistics," with an emphasis on dramatic approaches, for an examination of 6 dramatists. Bib. 16 pp.; name and term index.
    Style 10, 217–18: too "narrow" in scope but valuably interweaves analysis of "different styles and techniques"; *AUMLA* 45, 116–18.

916.   Martindale, Colin. 1975. *Romantic Progression: The Psychology of Literary History.* New York: Wiley. 225 pp.
A quantitative study of verbal "regression" in Eng. poetry from Pope to Keats and in Fr. poetry from Chénier to Char, a "progression" from rational, discursive writing to the parataxis and metaphysical distance of modern poetry and the writing of schizophrenics. Bib. 13 pp.; name and term indexes.
    Style 11, 325–26: insufficient evidence, conclusions "hardly justified," "this is not good literary history"; *AL* 8, 249; *JAAC* 34, 501.

917.   Paterson, Linda. 1975. *Troubadours and Eloquence.* Oxford: Clarendon. 244 pp.
"Just as each troubadour has his own ideal of eloquence, so his methods vary within the general style of *clus, leu* or *braus*. . . . The concept of a poetry of clichés, uniform by accident or design . . . is foreign to the aims and methods of any of these poets." Bib. 6 pp.; name and term index.
    MLR 72, 675–76: "an outstanding contribution to our understanding of troubadour styles."

918.   Rhode, Robert D. 1975. *Setting in the American Short Story of Local Color: 1865–1900.* The Hague: Mouton. 189 pp.
Introd. on approach and definitions; ch. 2, "Setting as Background and Or-

nament"; ch. 3, "Setting in Close Relation to Character"; ch. 4, "Setting Personified." Bib. 11 pp.; name and term index. [Extremely inadequate attention to setting; a good book on setting is greatly needed.]
   AL 48, 423: "helpful," offers a "fresh method"; *Choice* 13, 371.

919.   Rodríguez-Pasqués, Petrona de. 1975. *El discurso indirecto libre en la novela argentina* [Free Indirect Discourse in the Argentinian Novel]. Rio Grande do Sul, Braz.: Pontficia U Católica. 232 pp.
Style 12, 408–09: "the first systematic and quantitative attempt to trace the appearance and use of free indirect discourse (*discurso indirecto libre*), in the Argentine novel."

920.   Røstvig, Maren-Sofie, ed. 1975. *Fair Forms: Essays in English Literature from Spenser to Jane Austen.* Cambridge: Brewer; Totowa: Rowman. 248 pp.
6 essays on the careful designs found in Spenser's *Fowre Hymnes* (complex patterns of cross-reference and parallelism), Milton's "On the Morning of Christ's Nativity" (conceptual structure and stanzaic design), Dryden's *An Essay of Dramatick Poesie* (network of allusions), *Tom Jones* and *Rasselas* (elaborately patterned cross-references in *Rasselas*), and *Pride and Prejudice* (structured on a process of clarification). Name and term index.
   MLR 72, 393–94: a valuable "challenge delivered collectively by this group of scholars from Oslo University."

921.   Veeder, William. 1975. *Henry James—The Lessons of the Master: Popular Fiction and Personal Style in the Nineteenth Century.* Chicago: U of Chicago P. 287 pp.
Argues that James's mature style grew out of the popular fiction of midcentury. Mainly an analysis of 2 novels—*Portrait* and *Washington Square.* Ch. 1, "Tradition and Style"; ch. 3, "Style, Character, and Social Commentary"; ch. 4, "Style, Character, and the Process of Portraiture." Name and term index.
   Style 11, 103–04: "demonstrates convincingly" by "painstaking tabulation and comparative analysis of a full range of stylistic effects"; *QQ* 83, 683; *MFS* 22, 610. [Honorable mention for best book of explication pub. 1975–76 in Eng. or Amer. Literature, Explicator Literary Foundation.]

922.   Brodhead, Richard. 1976. *Hawthorne, Melville, and the Novel.* Chicago: U of Chicago P. 216 pp.
"Their affair with the novel is my subject." The novels of these 2 authors are made of "distinctly different representational modes," which partly derived from the authors' modification of "the constitutive conventions" of the novel. Name and term index.
   YR 66, 277–82: despite "grave faults," the book has "many fine things to say about these authors and the novel"; *Centrum* 4, 50–56.

923. Bruss, Elizabeth. 1976. *Autobiographical Acts: The Changing Situation of a Literary Genre*. Baltimore: Johns Hopkins UP. 184 pp.
"Two separate interests converged to produce this study: first, a concern to explain the mode of existence of a literary genre, how it changes while remaining the same; second, a desire to make more flexible and relevant use of linguistics in literary criticism." Chs. on Bunyan, Boswell, De Quincey, and Nabokov. Name and term index.
VQR 53, 88: "substantial contribution," "penetrating analysis"; *Critm* 19, 367; *CL* 30, 181; *SR* 85, xlvi.

924. Gumpel, Liselotte. 1976. *"Concrete" Poetry from East and West Germany: The Language of Exemplarism and Experimentalism*. New Haven: Yale UP. 268 pp.
Explains the differences in meaning of concrete poetry in West and East Germany, radical experimentalism in the West, more "lyrical" in the East (continuity with traditional verse). Bib. 14 pp.; name and term index.
Style 12, 308–09: "throughout the terminology is extremely heavy-handed," "much is explained that is obvious and much left unexamined that is not"; *MLR* 73, 954.

925. Lanham, Richard. 1976. *The Motives of Eloquence: Literary Rhetoric in the Renaissance*. New Haven: Yale UP. 234 pp.
A study of the "ludic" (verbal performance, playfulness, extravagance) in mainly Renaissance writings, especially Shakespeare's, based on the assumption that humans and language are social, complex, diverse and therefore always rhetorical, satirical, pleasurable, etc. Bib. 2 pp.; name and term index.
Style 13, 230–32: "witty and bracing" and "always gives you something to think about," but the "theoretical uncertainty of the book" mars the performance; *MLR* 74, 139–41: "lapses of taste and violations of decorum," "frequent . . . refusals to get to the point."

926. Lottinville, Savoie. 1976. *The Rhetoric of History*. Norman: U of Oklahoma P. 258 pp.
A manual for the writing of effective historical prose, each ch. dealing with a different step in the process—conceptualization, narrative, continuity, etc. Bib. 13 pp.; name and term index.
Style 13, 37–38: "highly instructive."

927. Maisani-Léonard, Martine. 1976. *André Gide ou l'ironie de l'écriture* [André Gide or the Irony of Writing]. Montreal: PU de Montréal. 271 pp.
Style 12, 397–98: a study of "récit," fictional works that combine the use of a fictive "I" with that of the aorist, concluding that all literary texts are simultaneously "récit" and "discours." The Gidean "récit" is employed to illustrate the argument. "Important as the first study of Gide from a linguistic point of view."

928.   Neumann, Gerhard. 1976. *Ideenparadiese: Untersuchungen zur Aphoristik bei Lichtenberg, Novalis, Friedrich Schlegel und Goethe* [Paradise of Ideas: Investigations on the Aphorism in Lichtenberg, Novalis, Friedrich Schlegel, and Goethe]. Munich: Fink. 863 pp.
MLR 75, 450–52: "In spite of some reservations, this book is to be highly recommended to any scholar who is interested in aphorisms, in the Age of Goethe, and in the philosophical problems of knowledge."

929.   "Politics and Style II." 1976. *Style* 10.4. 116 pp.
5 essays, 4 revs.

930.   Spiegel, Alan. 1976. *Fiction and the Camera Eye: Visual Consciousness in Film and the Modern Novel.* Charlottesville: UP of Virginia. 203 pp.
The novel became more visual and concrete particularly in the latter half of the 19th cent., 1 development in the 20th cent. the "cinematographic" novel. Name and term index.
Style 11, 323–24: scanty evidence and imprecise methodology; *FQ* 30.4, 44: "serious, responsible, and interesting" and "full of excellent insights and engaging passages" but "not overwhelmingly original," "contains several factual errors," and is "schematically too neat"; *Choice* 14, 58; *LJ* 101, 2393.

931.   Strzetelski, Jerzy. 1976. *Some Problems of Short Fiction: The Dramatic Short Story.* Cracow: U Jagiellońskiego. 116 pp.
A study of 4 short stories (Boccaccio's "The Falcon," Maupassant's "The Necklace," Mansfield's "Bliss," and Kipling's "The Man Who Would Be King") based on Roman Ingarden's *O budowie obrazu* (*The Pictorial Work of Art*). Bib. 1 p.

931a.   Black, Michael. 1977. *Poetic Drama as Mirror of the Will.* London: Vision. 203 pp.
The author's main idea is that the convention of verse developed by Shakespeare and Racine is a better vehicle than prose for the revelation of character.
MLR 78, 409–10: "raises several interesting questions without substantially contributing to their resolution," " 'high' journalism."

932.   Blake, Norman. 1977. *The English Language in Medieval Literature.* London: Dent; Totowa: Rowman. 190 pp.
"An attempt to show how a knowledge of the English language of the medieval period helps us to understand the nature and type of literature written then." Chs. on words, wordplay, parody, themes, syntax, and levels of discourse. Bib. 2 pp.; name index.
Spec 53, 788: "well intended" but the "attempt" will not "succeed"; *RES* 29, 330; *TLS* 20 Jan. 1978, 68; TES 10 Feb. 1978, 24.

933.   Cohen, Murray. 1977. *Sensible Words: Linguistic Practice in England, 1640–1785*. Baltimore: Johns Hopkins UP. 188 pp.
A wide-ranging study of the linguistic systems of the 17th and 18th cents., covering such topics as pronunciation, the shift in emphasis from words to sentences, spelling, and phonetics. Cohen argues against the labels and influences and continuities of traditional histories, emphasizing the complexity and individuality of writers and works. Extensive notes (41 pp.); name and term index.
Style 12, 297–98: "formidable" research, "often" analyzes "acutely and sensitively," but in several ways the book is superficial.

934.   Felperin, Howard. 1977. *Shakespearean Representation: Mimesis and Modernity in Elizabethan Tragedy*. Princeton: Princeton UP. 199 pp.
A study of literary conventions in a variety of classic works from Homer to Shakespeare (3 of the 5 chs.) and an analysis of how these authors transformed and received sign systems for universal meaning and continuing "modernity." Name and term index.
JEGP 77, 588–90: "often I remain unconvinced," but "the comments on individual plays . . . are astute"; *YR* 68, 453–60; *VQR* 55, 24; *SR* 88, 447; *Choice* 15, 544.

935.   Deleted.

936.   Hiatt, Mary. 1977. *The Way Women Write*. New York: Teachers CP. 152 pp.
A statistical examination of 50 books by male and 50 by female authors reveals that men and women write differently, but "popular stereotypes of the feminine style" are false. Bib. 3 pp.
Style 15, 456–57: "has successfully dispelled some of the myths about the 'feminine' style of writing"; *CLIO* 8, 318; *Verbatim* 4, 2.

937.   Higdon, David. 1977. *Time and English Fiction*. London: Macmillan. 168 pp.
A study of how the "time scheme of a novel" affects "structure, theme, and the reader's experience of the work." 4 basic modes of narrative presentation are established: "process time," "barrier time," "polytemporal time," and "retrospective time." Bib. 15 pp.; name index.
MLR 75, 839–40: More about narrative techniques and a system of fictional types than about time: "a critical study of the element of time in English fiction still needs to be written."

938.   Pascal, Roy. 1977. *The Dual Voice: Free Indirect Speech and Its Functioning in the Nineteenth-Century European Novel*. Manchester: Manchester UP; Totowa: Rowman. 150 pp.

Part 1, "Theory", an examination of the device; part 2, "Texts," practical criticism of 19th-cent. works—Goethe, Austen, Büchner, Dickens, Thackeray, Eliot, Trollope, Flaubert, Zola, Dostoevskij.

MLR 74, 146–49: "probing and suggestive," "performs a very great service."

939.   Weimann, Robert, ed. 1977. *Realismus in der Renaissance: Aneignung der Welt in der erzählenden Prosa* [Realism in the Renaissance: Appropriation of the World in Narrative Prose]. Berlin: Aufbau. 808 pp.

Attempts to identify the chief features of realistic Renaissance prose (*Gargantua and Pantagruel*, *Don Quixote*, etc.).

MLR 75, 834–35: "a substantial" work, "though the verbosity and Marxist jargon of several sections impede easy reading."

940.   Canary, Robert, and Henry Kozicki, eds. 1978. *The Writing of History: Literary Form and Historical Understanding.* Madison: U of Wisconsin P. 165 pp.

5 essays treating "the relationship between the content of historical writing and the literary form in which it is presented," by 2 historians, 2 literary critics, and 1 philosopher. Bib. 7 pp.; name and term index.

Style 13, 39–41: "should be read."

941.   Coletti, Vittorio. 1978. *Momenti del linguaggio poetico novecentesco* [Moments of Poetic Language in the Twentieth Century]. Genoa: Melangolo. 127 pp.

ASNP 9, 2027.

942.   Kästner, Hannes. 1978. *Mittelalterliche Lehrgespräche: Textlinguistische Analysen, Studien zur poetischen Funktion und pädagogischen Intention* [Medieval Didactic Discourse: Text-Linguistic Analyses, Studies of Poetic Function and Pedagogical Intention]. Berlin: Schmidt. 319 pp.

A study of the semantics of the didactic conversation in Ger. literature between 1170 and 1270.

MLR 76, 731–32: generally "useful" though sometimes confusing, and excessive theory and method at expense of illustration.

943.   Kennedy, X. J. 1978. *An Introduction to Poetry.* 4th ed. Boston: Little. 455 pp.

Sections on "voice" (tone), words, imagery, figures, song, sound, rhythm, closed and open forms, etc. First-line and name indexes.

944.   Ragussis, Michael. 1978. *The Subterfuge of Art: Language and the Romantic Tradition.* Baltimore: Johns Hopkins UP. 243 pp.

Writers from Wordsworth to D. H. Lawrence who use language "to awaken" people from illusion by employing subterfuge, dissembling, evasion, and an "incomplete style" (gaps, fragmentation, lacunae, ellipses) in response to experience difficult to decipher.

JEGP 79, 134: "brilliant," "splendid"; *RES* 31, 93; *SR* 88, 298; *Critm* 21, 271; *Choice* 15, 1520; *LJ* 103, 2241; *Style* 18, 106.

945.   Russell, John. 1978. *Style in Modern British Fiction. Studies in Joyce, Lawrence, Forster, Lewis, and Green*. Baltimore: Johns Hopkins UP. 196 pp.

A study of 9 "not highly experimental" novels, supported by quantitative and comparative data. "To give an account of their styles and . . . to have some sort of norm . . . a norm of realistic fiction." Name index.

Style 15, 50–52: "a treasure of subtle critical observations"; *RES* ns 31, 365–66; *MLR* 76, 941–42; *CL* 20, 369–76; *MFS* 25, 306–09; *SNNTS* 10, 462–64.

946.   Weissman, Frida. 1978. *Du monologue intérieur à la sous-conversation* [From Interior Monologue to Non-Verbalized Conversation]. Paris: Nizet. 139 pp.

Previously pub. essays on the theory, history, and practice of inner monologue and stream of consciousness.

MLR 76, 428–29: "at best, a reasonably lucid and well-documented restatement."

947.   Welsh, Andrew. 1978. *Roots of Lyric: Primitive Poetry and Modern Poetics*. Princeton: Princeton UP. 276 pp.

A "search . . . for basic structures of poetic language, whether they are found in a Bantu riddle or a poem by Donne, in a Cherokee charm or a song by Shakespeare." Welsh's "modern poetics" are those of Pound (*melopoeia*, etc.) and others, plus Frye's taxonomy (*melos*, etc.). Name and term index. [James Russell Lowell Prize for an Outstanding Book by an MLA member, 1978.]

JEGP 78, 278–80: extremely hostile attack on its elitist formalism devoid of "social responsibility"; *JAF* 94, 88–90; *CL* 32, 199–202; *RES* ns 31, 366–67.

948.   Wittig, Susan. 1978. *Stylistic and Narrative Structures in the Middle English Romances*. Austin: U of Texas P. 223 pp.

A study of 25 Middle Eng. metrical romances (*Sir Gawain and the Green Knight* omitted), classifying the formulaic shorter verbal patterns, analyzing stanzas and other groups of lines (prayers, synopses, etc.) and larger structural units (scenes and episodes). Ch. 1, "Problems of Stylistic Analysis in Middle English Romance"; ch. 2, "Larger Structural Units: The Motifeme"; ch. 3, "Larger Structural Units: The Type-Scene and Type-Episode." Bib. 7 pp.; name and term index.

AUMLA 54, 242: "a much needed 'linguistic-based explanation' for the stylistic and structural redundance . . . that informs every level of the Middle English non-cyclic verse romances"; *Style* 13, 228–29.

949.   Barney, Stephen. 1979. *Allegories of History, Allegories of Love.* Hamden: Shoe String. 323 pp.
Focuses especially on allegory and myth as mirrors, revealers of correspondences. A work of practical criticism of the "best works of allegory" — *Psychomathia, The Faerie Queene, Piers Plowman, The Confidence Man, The Romance of the Rose,* "Rappacinni's Daughter," and *The Castle.* Name and term index.
   Style 17, 68–72: a scholarly study of the metaphorical basis of allegory; *MLR* 77, 139.

950.   Burton, Frank, and Pat Carlen. 1979. *Official Discourse: On Discourse Analysis, Government Publications, Ideology and the State.* London: Routledge. 148 pp.
5 reports of official committees of inquiry into cases of apparent breakdown in law and order are analyzed through an eclectic synthesis of ideas and methods from linguistics, Marxism, and psychoanalysis. "Our concern has been to deconstruct official texts and to expose for analysis the structures of knowledge and modes of knowing realised in state publications" and generally to investigate "the connection between knowledge and power relations." Bib. 5 pp.; name and term index.
   Style 16, 67–70: a "laudable" project but "would be much more persuasive if they utilized detailed linguistic analysis," and their writing suffers from "considerable and at times infuriating . . . obscurity."

951.   Calder, Daniel, ed. 1979. *Old English Poetry: Essays on Style.* Berkeley: U of California P. 174 pp.
6 essays, 5 based on papers delivered at a symposium in 1977 on diverse problems.
   Spec 56, 366: "useful and instructive"; *LJ* 107, 510.

952.   Caserio, Robert L. 1979. *Plot, Story, and the Novel: From Dickens and Poe to the Modern Period.* Princeton: Princeton UP. 304 pp.
Advocates the direct bearing of literatue on life by the capacity of story and plot to discriminate our moral values, particularly through structures "at whose center is the experience of reversal." Name and term index.
   YR 69, 466–69: "a critical speculation of the highest order"; *CL* 34, 286: lacks "charm of style" and is entangled in "a series of dubious claims" but has some "virtues."

953.   Cave, Terence. 1979. *The Cornucopian Text: Problems of Writing in the French Renaissance.* Oxford: Clarendon. 386 pp.
A study of "fundamental questions concerning the nature and status of writing" in the work of Erasmus, Rabelais, Ronsard, and Montaigne. "While language in general is a major theme of this book, language is always considered in its organized form as 'discourse.'" Part 1 explores the theory of discourse, part 2 the writers with special attention to "a group of figurative themes"

that connect them — the figures of abundance, cornucopia. Bib. 13 pp.; name index.

MLR 75, 654: "a major step" in communication between "intellectual historians and textual critics"; *TLS* 14 Dec. 1979, 140; *MP* 78, 419; *RenQ* 33, 458; *CL* 33, 95.

954.   Ermert, Karl. 1979. *Briefsorten: Untersuchungen zu Theorie and Empirie der Textklassifikation* [Types of Letters: Studies in the Theory and Empiricism of Text Classification]. Tübingen: Niemeyer. 226 pp.
A study of text linguistics and theory of text classification via the nonliterary letter.
AUMLA 54, 302: "a full and readable account."

955.   Fussell, Paul. 1979. *Poetic Meter & Poetic Form*. Rev. ed. New York: Random. 188 pp.
A traditional introd. "to help aspiring readers deepen their sensitivity to the rhythmical and formal properties of poetry." This rev. ed. adds examples and a new ch. on free verse. Part 1 deals with meter, part 2 with stanzas. Bib. 2 pp.; name and term index. [Helpful for beginners on functional uses of meter and stanzas.]

955a.   Gilbert, A. J. 1979. *Literary Language from Chaucer to Johnson*. New York: Barnes. 224 pp.
A study of the literary registers of the period (low, middle, high) as contexts for discerning the styles of the writers, since style is "a relationship between form and meaning." Name and term index.
Choice 18, 245: "maddening qualities" but "always interesting on syntax"; *NS* 99, 481; *TLS* 14 Mar. 1980, 300.

956.   Heitmann, Klaus. 1979. *Der französische Realismus von Stendhal bis Flaubert* [French Realism from Stendhal to Flaubert]. Wiesbaden: Athenäon. 137 pp.
Balzac is a third writer studied, with brief attention to Sue.
MLR 76, 470–71: favorable review.

957.   "History as Art." 1979. *Style* 13.1. 44 pp.
Bib., 3 revs. In the same number: "Language of War Literature" (1 essay and bib.).

958.   Irwin, Michael. 1979. *Picturing: Description and Illusion in the Nineteenth-Century Novel*. London: Allen. 161 pp.
An analysis of descriptions, especially of persons and places (faces, clothes, houses, towns, etc.), mainly in Dickens, Eliot, and Hardy. Focus on facts and details of description, but some recognition of the functional relations between setting and character, action, and theme. Name index.

Style 15, 467–68: "this book, despite ignoring the language and theory of most style studies, can prove worthwhile as a stimulus for further analysis."

959.   Johnson, Barbara. 1979. *Défigurations du langage poétique: La seconde révolution baudelairienne* [Deformations of Poetic Language: The Second Baudelairian Revolution]. Paris: Flammarion. 213 pp.
On Baudelaire's and Mallarmé's prose poems.
TLS 4 July 1980, 761: "brilliant," "varied and powerful readings," "one of the most exciting books on nineteenth-century French literature to have appeared in recent years."

960.   Kennedy, Alan. 1979. *Meaning and Signs in Fiction*. New York: St. Martin's. 148 pp.
A "try at a history of the way meaning is structured in the novel," allowing the novelists "to speak for themselves." [I.e., the author denies any knowledge of contemporary structuralism.] Name index.
Choice 16, 820: "Kennedy's style is often difficult and his thesis possibly reducible to the traditional notion . . . that a writer must find a set of symbols that adequately express the inner life of the characters"; *MLR* 76, 643–45.

961.   Korg, Jacob. 1979. *Language in Modern Literature: Innovation and Experiment*. New York: Barnes; Brighton: Harvester. 244 pp.
"This book takes the view that linguistic experiment is an essential element of literary modernism" (c. 1910–30). Ch. 4, "Form and Language" (fragmentation, etc.); ch. 5, "Abstraction and Language"; ch. 6, "Imagery and Other Resources" (parody, etc.); ch. 7, "The Language of *Finnegans Wake*." Name and term index.
JEGP 80, 457: "competent, informative and well written" "for undergraduates," but as literary history it is "superficial and derivative" and its theoretical and methodological framework "weak"; *CR* 236, 218–19: "a valuable handbook"; *Enc* 55, 48: "useful"; *MLR* 78, 386; *MFS* 27, 388.

962.   Lewalski, Barbara. 1979. *Protestant Poetics and the Seventeenth-Century Religious Lyric*. Princeton: Princeton UP. 536 pp.
"The spectacular flowering of English religious poetry in the seventeenth century occurred in response to a new and powerful stimulus to the imagination of the pervasive Protestant emphasis upon the Bible as a book, as God's Word . . . and in the linguistic features of a variety of texts." Name index. [James Russell Lowell Prize for an Outstanding Book by an MLA member, 1979.]

963.   MacAndrew, Elizabeth. 1979. *The Gothic Tradition in Fiction*. New York: Columbia UP. 289 pp.
A study of how the Gothic authors used their devices to make manifest "the effects and sometimes the cause of evil in the mind." Concentrates on such

works as *The Castle of Otranto, Frankenstein, Dr. Jekyll and Mr. Hyde, Wuthering Heights*, and *The Turn of the Screw*. Bib. 8 pp.; term and name index.
VQR 56, lxxxix: "informative" but "not good enough"; *AL* 52, 517; *TLS* 14 Mar. 1980, 290.

964.   Seidel, Michael. 1979. *Satiric Inheritance, Rabelais to Sterne*. Princeton: Princeton UP. 283 pp.
Separate chs. on Butler's *Hudibras*, Marvell's *Last Instructions* and Dryden's *Absalom and Achitophel*, Swift's *A Tale of a Tub, Gulliver's Travels*, Pope's *The Rape of the Lock* and *The Dunciad*, and Sterne's *Tristram Shandy*. A book "about the satiric violation of narrative lines." Bib. 7 pp.; name and term index.
VQR 56, 765; *YR* 69, vi; *Choice* 17, 64.

965.   Steinberg, Erwin, ed. 1979. *The Stream-of-Consciousness Technique in the Modern Novel*. Port Washington: Kennikat. 198 pp.
27 previously pub. essays and excerpts, each abstracted by the ed.
MFS 25, 751: "a representative collection," "critically satisfying and informative," but "hampered" by lack of writing after 1970; *Choice* 16, 822.

966.   Stewart, Susan. 1979. *Nonsense: Aspects of Intertextuality in Folklore and Literature*. Baltimore: Johns Hopkins UP. 228 pp.
On techniques of nonsense, "the relationships between . . . the universe of common sense and the universe of nonsense" fictions, using a "concept of intertextuality to describe these relationships." Bib. 10 pp.; name and term index.
JAAC 39, 101: "intelligent, well-written, and absorbing," "interest to a variety of specialists" as well as to laymen; *JC* 30, 236; *AL* 52, 517; *Choice* 18, 84; *LJ* 105, 406.

967.   Aronson, Alex. 1980. *Music and the Novel: A Study in Twentieth-Century Fiction*. Totowa: Rowman. 267 pp.
Deals with "the function of the musical experience . . . fiction written in the first half of the twentieth century." 10 chs.: ch. 1, "experiment with musical analogies" leading up to the 20th-cent. novel; ch. 2, musical texture in works of James Joyce; etc. Bib. 10 pp.; name and term index.
MLR 78, 391: raises many issues "without discrimination"; *WLT* 55, "very perceptive"; *MFS* 26, 728; *Spec* 245, 18; *Choice* 18, 387.

968.   Bayley, Peter. 1980. *French Pulpit Oratory, 1598–1650: A Study in Themes and Styles, with a Descriptive Catalogue of Printed Texts*. Cambridge: Cambridge UP. 323 pp.
An analysis of 313 sermons—their diversity within certain common themes revealed by recurrent imagery.
MLR 76, 697–98: "scrupulous attention to detail and diversity."

969.   Bishop, Michael, ed. 1980. *The Language of Poetry: Crisis and Solu-
        tion: Studies in Modern Poetry of French Expression, 1945 to the Pres-
        ent.* Amsterdam: Rodopi. 268 pp.
An introd. by the ed. on the relation between poetic word and the world
in modern francophone poetry, with 12 essays on 8 European Fr. poets and
4 non-European poets.
   MLR 77, 736–77: some admirable essays but "the four studies of post-
colonial poets" are a "digression."

970.   Boase, Paul, ed. 1980. *The Rhetoric of Protest and Reform, 1878–1898.*
        Athens: Ohio UP. 354 pp.
The author proposes "to describe, analyze and evaluate the issues and the
colorful, articulate men and women who used the public platform." The 13
essays are arranged into 5 groups: industrial protest, agrarian revolt, women's
rights, religion vs. science, and the intellectuals. Name index.
   Style 16, 74–76: "This volume gives the reader an excellent flavor of the
rhetorical style of the period."

971.   Burton, Deirdre. 1980. *Dialogue and Discourse: A Sociolinguistic Ap-
        proach to Modern Drama Dialogue and Naturally Occurring Conver-
        sation.* London: Routledge. 210 pp.
" 'Dialogue' contains studies of specific modern drama texts, and is basically
an exercise in a new area of literary-linguistic stylistics. Chapters 1, 2, and
3 demonstrate how recent advances in the sociolinguistic description of spoken discourse . . . can be drawn on to account for reader and audience intuitions about the dialogue in those texts. . . . 'Discourse' is an attempt to
expand one powerful linguistic theory of naturally occurring talk," to show
that analysis of dialogue style must draw on a theoretical framework for the
analysis of naturally occurring conversation. Ch. 8, suggestions for further research. Bib. 12 pp.; name and title index; subject index.
   AUMLA 58, 222–24: a "powerful" model of spoken discourse, "perceptive, convincing and even exciting," "more successful than were Sinclair and
Coulthard (1975) or Goffman in his *Frame Analysis* (1974)"; *JLS* 12, 100–01.

972.   Fumaroli, Marc. 1980. *L'âge de l'éloquence: Rhétorique et "res literaria"
        de la Renaissance au seuil de l'époque classique* [The Age of Eloquence:
        Rhetoric and the "Literary Thing" from the Renaissance to the Begin-
        ning of the Classical Age]. Geneva: Droz. 882 pp.
A history of Fr. rhetoric and prose in the 16th cent. and the first half of the
17th.
   MLR 77, 203–05: "splendid."

973.   Holden, Jonathan. 1980. *The Rhetoric of the Contemporary Lyric.*
        Bloomington: Indiana UP. 136 pp.

7 essays on recent poets' strategies of persuasion and on the major trends in American poetry in the 1970s, contending that syntax plus "tone" play a more important role in today's lyric than do rhythm, sound, or image. Uses revisions of texts to reveal their elements.

JEGP 81, 466: "value" in "Holden's various ruminations on the technical problems facing poets," although his method of rewriting poems or prose passages tends to trivialize his subject; *TLS* 5 June 1981, 644; *Choice* 18, 659.

973a.   Houston, John P. 1980. *French Symbolism and the Modernist Movement: A Study of Poetic Structures.* Baton Rouge: Louisiana State UP. 298 pp.

"This book is intended to elucidate the structural and stylistic difference that distinguish what is usually called modern poetry [Mallarmé, Rilke, Pound et al.] from that which preceded it." Name and term index.

MLR 78, 415–16: "ambitious and successful," "fluent and precise."

974.   Lang, Berel, ed. 1980. *Philosophical Style.* Chicago: Nelson. 545 pp. Literary analyses of philosophical texts in the contexts of the history of philosophy and the various schools of philosophical discourse. 25 commentators from Plato and Aristotle to Stephen Pepper and D. T. Suzuki are divided into 3 sections: "Philosophers on the Writing of Philosophy," "Philosophical Style: The Search for Categories," "Style and the Reading of Philosophy." Bib. 2 pp.; name index.

Choice 18, 806: "provides little in the way of real help."

975.   Mellard, James. 1980. *The Exploded Form: The Modernist Novel in America.* Urbana: U of Illinois P. 208 pp.

Calls attention to the "dialectical pattern of destruction and reconstruction . . . in the history of the traditional/modernist novel" as "identified in paradigmatic attitudes . . . *naive*, *critical*, and *sophisticated*," modes illustrated by *The Sound and the Fury*, *Catch-22*, and *Trout Fishing in America*. Name and term index.

MFS 27, 712: "comprehensive"; *AL* 53, 742; *JEGP* 81, 148; *Enc* 57, 68; *TLS* 1 May 1981, 421; *Choice* 18, 952; *LJ* 105, 2413.

976.   Nash, Walter. 1980. *Designs in Prose: A Study of Compositional Problems and Methods.* London: Longman. 228 pp.

A manual of composition concerned with "the relationship between cohesion (particularly syntactic and lexical cohesion) and the creation of effective rhetorical designs in expository or simple descriptive prose." Bib. 5 pp.; term index.

TLS 23 Jan. 1981, 86: "should be a prescribed text in . . . writing programmes"; *BBN* Jan. 1981, 86.

977.   "Philosophy as Style and Literature as Philosophy." 1980. *The Monist*
        63.4. 141 pp.
9 articles, about half on the language of philosophical writings.

977a.   Reiss, Timothy. 1980. *Tragedy and Truth: Studies in the Development
        of a Renaissance and Neoclassical Discourse*. New Haven: Yale UP. 334
        pp.
In the 16th and 17th cents., tragedy played an important part in establishing
the belief that language described an independently existing reality. Reiss sup-
ports this argument with analyses of plays by Buchanan, Jodelle, Garnier,
Shakespeare, Marlowe, and Racine. Name and term index.
    MLR 78, 408–09: does not make "a persuasive case for his major proposi-
tion that tragedy before Racine was not based on a referential view of
language."

978.   Rhodes, Neil. 1980. *Elizabethan Grotesque*. London: Routledge. 207 pp.
A study of the bizarre juxtapositions and unexpected incongruities that produce laughter and revulsion, with special attention to Nashe. Bib. 12 pp.;
index.
    Enc 57, 60: "excellent in its kind"; *RenQ* 35, 327; *BBN* May 1981, 306.

979.   Scott, Clive. 1980. *French Verse-Art: A Study*. Cambridge: Cambridge
        UP. 252 pp.
Begins with a ch. on Eng. metrics contrasted to Fr. and follows with chs. on
such topics as rhyme and the caesura. Not merely a description of genres and
elements, but includes interpretations to show the relation between metrics
and meaning.
    MLR 76, 953–55: "useful introductory chapter," "sensible middle-of-the-
road approach," but examples limited mainly to late 19th cent.

980.   Blake, N. F. 1981. *Non-Standard Language in English Literature*. Lon-
        don: Deutsch. 217 pp.
A tradition of nonstandard spelling, vocabulary, and syntax has developed
in literary writing since the time of Chaucer: "writers borrow from other writers
and so non-standard representations become traditional." Separate chs. on
Chaucer and his predecessors; from Chaucer to Shakespeare: nondramatic and
dramatic traditions; Shakespeare; the 17th cent.; the 18th cent.; the Romantics; the Victorians; early modern; and modern. Bib. 5 pp.; indexes of authors
and works referred to and of words and phrases.
    Choice 20, 579: "well written" and "well done."

980a.   Brooke-Rose, Christine. 1981. *A Rhetoric of the Unreal: Studies in Nar-
        rative and Structure, Especially of the Fantastic*. Cambridge: Cambridge
        UP. 416 pp.

Ch. 1 deals with the reality crisis of the 20th cent. Ch. 2 discusses a wide range of critics, from the Russ. formalists to Wayne Booth and the Chicago School to Derrida and Lacan. Other chs. deal with science fiction, *Rip Van Winkle*, *The Turn of the Screw*, etc., applying her model of analysis.

PoT 3, 211–27; 233–38 (2 revs.): "a curious disparity . . . is perceptible throughout the book: slight uneasiness on the level of theoretical issues combined with subtle and illuminating exploration of the individual texts."

981.   Caws, Mary Ann. 1981. *A Metapoetics of the Passage: Architectures in Surrealism and After.* Hanover: UP of New England. 202 pp.
A study of surrealistic writers particularly as a "work refers to the structure of the connecting passage . . . between elements as it relates to the material of the text or to that stretching between two texts": attention to the connections of the individual text to a larger whole and to surface tension and texture. Name and term index.
WLT 57, 354: "freshness and intelligence" [her 1981 *The Eye in the Text*, on painting, literature, and film, was extolled as "an extraordinarily profound book" in *WLT* 56, 580].

981a.   Christensen, Inger. 1981. *The Meaning of Metafiction: A Critical Study of Selected Novels by Sterne, Nabokov, Barth and Beckett.* Oslo: Universitetsforlaget. Distr. by Columbia UP. 155 pp.
A comparison of the 4 authors' conceptions of the narrator, narrative, and narratee.
MFS 28, 732: "easily described and readily dismissed."

982.   Gage, John T. 1981. *In the Arresting Eye: The Rhetoric of Imagism.* Baton Rouge: Louisiana State UP. 188 pp.
A study of attitudes toward rhetoric, the rhetoric, and the practice of the imagists. Bib. 7 pp.; name and term index.
Choice 19, 626: "a useful new tool . . . about Imagism."

983.   Gent, Lucy. 1981. *Picture and Poetry, 1560–1620: Relations between Literature and the Visual Arts in the English Renaissance.* Leamington Spa, Eng.: Hall. 100 pp.
The way the Eng. poets "looked at pictures influenced, in some respects, the way they wrote their poetry" — especially in their "impressive verbal display." Name index.
TLS 19 June 1981, 696; *BC* 31, 230.

984.   Gura, Philip. 1981. *The Wisdom of Words: Language, Theology, and Literature in the New England Renaissance.* New York: Columbia UP. 203 pp.

A study of the linguistic matrix "from which our classic American writers emerged" (Emerson, Thoreau, Hawthorne, and Melville, mainly), especially the development in perception of religious language and symbolism. Bib. 4 pp.; name and term index.

CC 98, 1106; *AA* 84, 751; *AL* 54, 296; *Choice* 19, 51; *NEQ* 55, 132; *RSR* 8, 275; *RR* 42, 150.

985.   Houston, John. 1981. *The Traditions of French Prose Style: A Rhetori-*
         cal Study. Baton Rouge: Louisiana State UP. 278 pp.
Concentrates on "the developing picture of French style" and rhetoric in order to permit one "to situate" an author's prose "historically." "Significant texts," not statistics "about a writer's whole work," are studied, and "more than simply the occurrence of figures like anaphora or metonymy; levels of style and the relation of genre to style are central." Name and term index.

SR 90, xxiv–xxvi: "stimulating guidebook," "closely-worked arguments."

985a.   Krysinskij, Vladimir. 1981. *Carrefours de signe* [Intersections of Signs].
         Amsterdam: Mouton. 452 pp.
Semiotic-narrative and hermeneutic analysis of the evolution in form and content of the modern novel in a comparative and international perspective.

986.   Levine, George. 1981. *The Realistic Imagination: English Fiction from*
         Frankenstein to Lady Chatterley. Chicago: U of Chicago P. 357 pp.
An attempt to show how the 19th- and early 20th-cent. novel was a process to escape convention and to create new language for expressing reality. A "challenge to the antireferential bias of our criticism and to the method of radical deconstruction that has become commonplace." Name and term index.

Choice 19, 240: "An important new study . . . certain to influence all subsequent consideration of realism."

987.   Lucente, Gregory. 1981. *The Narrative of Realism and Myth: Verga,*
         Lawrence, Faulkner, Pavese. Baltimore: Johns Hopkins UP. 189 pp.
A study of the combination of components of realistic and mythic discourse in modern narrative.

MFS 28, 352: "firmly rooted in textual specificities" compared to Eric Gould's *Mythic Intentions in Modern Literature* (1981); *Choice* 19, 1234.

987a.   Perloff, Marjorie. 1981. *The Poetics of Indeterminacy: Rimbaud to Cage*.
         Princeton: Princeton UP. 346 pp.
An exploration of an important aspect of modernism and postmodernism through the study primarily of U.S. poetry and secondarily of Fr. literature and modern art. Roman Jakobson's dichotomy between metaphor and metonymy figures importantly, for Perloff finds indeterminate poetry mainly metonymic. Name index.

CL 34, 181–83: "remarkable for the breadth and depth of its insight," each ch. "a significant contribution"; *Critm* 24, 64: takes issue with the book on many levels, a negative rev.

987b.   Riggan, William. 1981. *Picaros, Madmen, Naifs, and Clowns: The Unreliable First-Person Narrator*. Norman: U of Oklahoma P. 206 pp.
A discussion of 4 types of unreliable "fictional autobiographer who recounts his own life . . . in his own voice and in a conscious act of writing," in the writings of Defoe, Sterne, Fowles, Nabokov, et al. Bib. 16 pp.; name index.
MFS 28, 721: "good essays."

988.   Rubin, David. 1981. *The Knot of Artifice: A Poetic of the French Lyric in the Early Seventeenth Century*. Columbus: Ohio State UP. 109 pp.
Identifies the techniques that distinguish between poets of the mid-16th cent. and the poets of the early 17th cent.
MLR 77, 952–53: the book makes many "interesting points" but is open "to serious objections."

989.   White, Allon. 1981. *The Uses of Obscurity: The Fiction of Early Modernism*. London: Routledge. 190 pp.
"The present book examines the moment when obscurity began to appear as an important, positive aspect of nineteenth-century English fiction" (Meredith, James, and Conrad). Specifically a study of shifts "backwards and forwards" in "referential fixity and clarity" by "dissolving both" into "the dense 'textualité' of metaphor, obscure syntax, broken narrative and anomic subjectivism." Bib. 6 pp.; name and term index.
MFS 28, 365: "very convincing and perceptive"; *BBN* Dec. 1981, 755; *LRB* 4, 13; *TES* 4 Sept. 1981, 22; *TLS* 13 Nov. 1981, 1337; *Choice* 19, 922.

990.   Winn, James. 1981. *Unsuspected Eloquence: A History of the Relations between Poetry and Music*. New Haven: Yale UP. 381 pp.
"My book is in part a history of some basic components of poetic and musical creation—formal construction, emotional expression, and initiation in all its guises—and in part a history of the metaphors by which people have tried to explain the mystery of making." Bib. 18 pp.; name and term index.
Critm 24, 379–82: "well-schooled and articulate," a "master work"; *MLR* 78, 397–400: "well informed and well written" but "not a work of original scholarship."

991.   Berke, Bradley. 1982. *Tragic Thought and the Grammar of Tragic Myth*. Bloomington: Indiana UP. 119 pp.
"Whereas the rules of a performance model specify actions, the rules of a grammar specify possibilities for action. Thus, a grammar of tragic myth is a description of the possibilities for expressing and understanding tragic myth

and not an account of the actual psychological activity of doing so." The author sets up a transformational generative grammar of 13 rules. Bib. 4 1/2 pp.; no index.

Lang 59, 943–44: "a fascinating theoretical combination of linguistic and literary scholarship," "further testing" needed.

992.   Bishop, Lloyd. 1982. *In Search of Style: Essays in French Literary Stylistics.* Charlottesville: UP of Virginia. 187 pp.
9 studies of "various aspects of French literary style and stylistic theory" — comic catharsis, romantic irony, euphony, etc. Bib. 3 pp.; name index.

993.   Craige, Betty. 1982. *Literary Relativity: An Essay on Twentieth-Century Narrative.* Lewisburg: Bucknell UP. 136 pp.
An investigation of the origins and diversity of "the avant-garde narrative of our age — in its extremes of subjectivism, objectivism, and absurdism" — focused mainly on the issue of how form reflects meaning. Bib. 4 pp.; name index.

MFS 29, 360: "clarity and precision in defining the notion of relativity in literature"; *WLT* 57, 357; *Choice* 20, 700.

994.   Greene, Thomas. 1982. *The Light in Troy: Imitation and Discovery in Renaissance Poetry.* New Haven: Yale UP. 354 pp.
"This is a book about the literary uses of *imitatio* during the Renaissance era in Italy, France, and England." Name and term index 14 pp. [James Russell Lowell Prize for an Outstanding Book by an MLA member, 1982.]

Choice 20, 824: "learned, graceful, and penetrating"; *SR* 92, 290: "a major work."

995.   McKay, Janet. 1982. *Narration and Discourse in American Realistic Fiction.* Philadelphia: U of Pennsylvania P. 212 pp.
The Bostonians, The Rise of Silas Lapham, and *The Adventures of Huckleberry Finn* reveal their authors' attention to narrative technique, especially the narrator's voice and directly and indirectly reported discourse. Ch. 1 presents selected current research in narratology and discourse analysis as the basis for the analysis of the novels. Bib. 8 pp.; name and term index.

MFS 29, 328: important for offering "confirmations rather than innovations," valuable for "insights into the complex acts of reading a novel"; *CLit* 10, 221; *Choice* 20, 1140.

996.   Miller, J. Hillis. 1982. *Fiction and Repetition: Seven English Novels.* Cambridge: Harvard UP. 250 pp.
A study of "the complex tissue of repetitions" in novels as sources of meaning, particularly the "grounded" and "ungrounded" kinds of repetition. Name index.

JAAC 41, 452–54: "exemplifies clarity, generosity . . . unpretentious erudition, attention to detail, and caution," but "his larger conclusions seem to me unpersuasive"; *PoT* 4, 783–94: "I recommend" the book; *MFS* 29, 261; *CLit* 10, 72 and 75; *AR* 40, 361; *RSR* 9, 1; *TLS* 10 Sept. 1982, 975; *BBN* Aug. 1982, 503.

997.   "Newspaper Writing as Art." 1982. *Style* 16.4. 87 pp.
6 essays, 2 revs., bib.

998.   Obler, Loraine, and Lise Menn, eds. 1982. *Exceptional Language and Linguistics*. New York: Academic. 372 pp.
Research on exceptional language behavior illuminates linguistic theory. The exceptional situations covered include legal-bureaucratic, translation, poetry, and proverb.
Choice 20, 701: "exceptional," "exceedingly well written and edited."

999.   Orr, Leonard. 1982. *De-Structing the Novel: Essays in Applied Postmodern Hermeneutics*. Troy: Whitston. 261 pp.
"These essays tend towards the hermeneutics of the Heidegger-Gadamer-Ricoeur line rather than the Schleiermachian and intentionalist 'hermeneutics' recently popularized by E. D. Hirsch in his *Validity in Interpretation*." Bib. 37 pp. ("intended to complement but not duplicate" the bib. in Harari's *Textual Strategies*); no index.
MFS 28, 728.

1000.   O'Toole, L. M. 1982. *Structure, Style, and Interpretation in the Russian Short Story*. New Haven: Yale UP. 272 pp.
The main categories of narrative structures are redefined in the light of the theoretical work of the Russ. formalists, the Prague School, recent structuralists, and "occasional semiotic insights" as an integrated set of analytical procedures, and applied to examples of 19th-cent. Russ. short stories. Chs. on "Narrative Structure," "Point of View," "Fable," "Plot," "Character," "Setting." Bib. 3 pp.; name and term index.
WLT 57, 311: "meticulous and systematic" yet "none . . . revolutionary"; *TES* 18 June 1982, 29; *Choice* 20, 437.

1001.   Pearce, Richard. 1982. *The Novel in Motion: An Approach to Modern Fiction*. Columbus: Ohio State UP. 155 pp.
The fracturing and displacement of narrative time in Joyce, Beckett, Pynchon, and other novelists. "The novel *in* motion . . . engages us directly in the dislocations of the narrative medium." Name index.
Choice 21, 416: "cogent" and "compelling"; *AL* 56, 452; *MFS* 30, 409; *AR* 42, 383.

1001a. "Poetics of the Avant-Garde." 1982. *PoT* 3.3. 239 pp.
6 essays on current trends, 6 essays on concrete poetry, a rev. article, and 3 revs.

1002. "Politics and Style III." 1982. *Style* 16.1. 160 pp.
4 articles, 14 revs., bib.

1003. Reiss, Timothy. 1982. *The Discourse of Modernism.* Ithaca: Cornell UP.
410 pp.
Examines aspects of the development and growth to dominance "of modern
Western discourse — or . . . the 'analytico-referential,'" employing principally
"science fictions and utopias drawn from the critical historical moment of
the European Renaissance and Neoclassicism." Bib. 15 pp.; name and term
index.
SR 91, lviii: "supplement" to Foucault's *Archaeology of Knowledge,*
"rigorously grounded"; *MLN* 98, 799: "not as convincing as it might be,"
but "sound and significant points"; *RenQ* 36, 278; *Choice* 20, 78.

1004. Smith, Stan. 1982. *Inviolable Voice: History and Twentieth-Century Poetry.* Dublin: Gill & Macmillan; Atlantic Highlands: Humanities. 243
pp.
A study of Hardy, T. S. Eliot, Edward Thomas, Ezra Pound, and others to
demonstrate the ways in which poetry has its origins in a particular history.
Bib. 4 pp.; name index.
BBN Dec. 1982, 762; *Choice* 20, 432.

1005. Steiner, Wendy. 1982. *The Colors of Rhetoric: Problems in the Relation between Modern Literature and Painting.* Chicago: U of Chicago
P. 263 pp.
A study of the "semiotic concreteness" of modern painting and literature —
"no longer stressing their mirroring function but their paradoxical status as
signs of reality and as things in their own right." Ch. 1, "the history of the
painting-literature analogy"; ch. 2, "post-Renaissance notions of artistic reference, particularly the contrast between scientific prose and nonsense"; ch.
3, "the homology between cubist painting, modern writing, and recent concepts of history and periodization." Bib. 8 pp.; name and term index.
MFS 29, 377–79: "a wealth of material" presented with "acumen" but "disappointing" in "practical criticism"; *Critm* 25, 282.

1006. Barnett, Richard. 1983. *Dynamics of Detour: Codes of Indirection in
Montaigne, Pascal, Racine, and Guilleragues.* Tübingen: Narr. C. 170 pp.
A study of antiphrastic expression in France's eminent neoclassical writers.
A rereading of Fr. classical textuality that reveals the hidden codes of linguis-
tic indirection.

1007.   Church, Margaret. 1983. *Structure and Theme:* Don Quixote *to James Joyce.* Columbus: Ohio State UP. 207 pp.
The structural elements that underlie 13 novels: *Madame Bovary, The Magic Mountain, Mrs. Dalloway,* etc.
MFS 30, 415: "traditional, straightforward, honest, and humanely liberal."

1007a.   Fletcher, Pauline. 1983. *Gardens and Grim Ravines: The Language of Landscape in Victorian Poetry.* Princeton: Princeton UP. 277 pp.
On the significance of landscape in the poetry of 7 poets: Tennyson, Arnold, Browning, D. G. Rossetti, Morris, Swinburne, and Hardy. Bib. 16 pp.; name index.
Choice 21, 422: "fresh approach and sound analysis."

1008.   Géfin, Laszlo. 1983. *Ideogram: History of a Poetic Method.* Austin: U of Texas P. 181 pp.
The first history of Ezra Pound's ideogrammic method and its use by 2 generations of Amer. poets; i.e., a history of a modernist mode of composition. Bib. 4 pp.; name and term index 6 pp.
JEGP 83, 104: "excellent."

1009.   Kennedy, Andrew. 1983. *Dramatic Dialogue: The Duologue of Personal Encounter.* Cambridge: Cambridge UP. 283 pp.
Chs. on "The Duologue of Recognition in Greek Tragedy," "Duologues of Transformation in Shakespeare," "The Combat of Wit" (in Shakespeare, Jonson, and Restoration comedy), "The Confessional Duologue from Ibsen to Albee," "Duologues of Isolation," and "The Impersonal/Personal Duologue from Brecht to Shepard." Name and term index.
Choice 21, 268: "highly recommended"; *CD* 18, 280; *BBN* Aug. 1983, 508.

1009a.   Lang, Berel. 1983. *Philosophy and the Art of Writing: Studies in Philosophical and Literary Style.* Lewisburg: Bucknell UP. 246 pp.
"I attempt to demonstrate . . . three related theses": first, "that philosophical discourse is a form of making as well as of knowing"; second, "that the process of making . . . is itself a version of praxis or doing" (connected to historical contexts); and third, that "the role of a persona . . . within the individual work is a condition of intelligibility" (through style). Bib. 6 pp.; name and term index.
Choice 21, 268: "a pleasure to read" but some lack of "proportion."

1010.   Lanham, Richard. 1983. *Analyzing Prose.* New York: Scribner's. 255 pp.
A traditional taxonomy using rhetorical terminology to describe a variety of styles. Chs. on "Noun and Verb Styles," "Parataxis and Hypotaxis," "The Periodic Style and the Running Style," etc. Glossary of rhetorical terms. No bib. or index.

1010a.   Meisel, Martin. 1983. *Realizations: Narrative, Pictorial, and Theatrical Arts of the Nineteenth Century*. Princeton: Princeton UP. 416 pp.
On the collaboration between storytelling and picture making in painting, drama, and fiction of 19th-cent. Britain (with some attention to France and Germany). 200 illustrations; bib. 15 pp.; name and term index 17 pp.
Choice 22, 73: "authoritative . . . erudite, highly academic"; *LJ* 109, 900; *TLS* 10 Aug. 1984, 883.

1010b.   "Narratology." 1983. *Style* 17.2. 207 pp.
8 articles and 3 revs.

1010c.   Rivers, Elias. 1983. *Quixotic Scriptures: Essays on the Textuality of Hispanic Literature*. Bloomington: Indiana UP. 164 pp.
Focuses on "linguistic pragmatics." The author claims to be "indebted to recent developments in Anglo-American sociolinguistics, speech-act theory, and reader-response criticism, as well as to the European traditions of philology and the suggestions of French structuralism," in this survey of Hispanic literature. Bib. "note" 3 pp.
Hisp 67, 665: "eminently readable," "extremely useful," "quite fulfills its promise."

1011.   Stowe, William. 1983. *Balzac, James, and the Realistic Novel*. Princeton: Princeton UP. 203 pp.
How the 2 authors solved the problems of fictional representation. A comparison of interpretation in *Le père Goriot* and *The American*, of representation in *Illusions perdues* and *The Princess Casamassima*, and of drama in *La cousine Bette* and *The Wings of the Dove*.
AL 55, 655: "excellent," "useful," "valuable"; *MFS* 30, 295; *Choice* 21, 283.

1012.   Waugh, Patricia. 1983. *Metafiction*. London: Methuen. 200 pp.
A study of contemporary self-conscious fiction—Barth, Coover, Lessing, Fowles, et al.

1012a.   Mueller, Janel. 1984. *The Native Tongue and the Word: Developments in English Prose Style, 1380–1580*. Chicago: U of Chicago P. 429 pp.
Introd. contains "A Stylistics of the Sentence." Chs. follow chron. order. Name and term index.

1012a1.   Norris, Christopher. 1984. *The Deconstructive Turn: Essays in the Rhetoric of Philosophy*. London: Methuen. 201 pp.
A study of philosophical texts as rhetorical constructions, particularly focusing on the disjunctive relation between logic and language. Name and term indexes.
Choice 22, 116: "succeeds in making the claims and ideas of deconstruc-

tion more available to a wider audience" but "only minimally successful" in showing "the superiority of Derrida's reading"; *LRB* 6, 12; *TLS* 17 Aug. 1984, 923.

1012b.   Spires, Robert. 1984. *Beyond the Metafictional Mode: Directions in the Modern Spanish Novel.* Lexington: UP of Kentucky. 176 pp.
The evolution of metafiction (textual strategies involved in turning fiction back into itself) from Cervantes to the 1970s, with critical focus on the 20th-cent. — Unamuno, Jarnés, Ballester, Cunquiero, Goytisolo, Gaite.

4.0 Habitual Usage: The Author (1013–276d)

See the Bennett bibliography on author styles, no. 104.

4.1 Theory (1013–16)

1013.   Roland, Alan, ed. 1978. *Psychoanalysis, Creativity, and Literature: A French-American Inquiry.* New York: Columbia UP. 368 pp.
17 essays with diverse approaches, divided into 4 sections: "A Sociology of Psychoanalysis," "Psychoanalysis," "Creativity," "Psychoanalysis and Literature." Name and term indexes.
   Critm 21, 157: "the volume as a whole seems a Tower of Babel," though the work of "deeper translation" is begun here.

1014.   de Man, Paul. 1979. *Allegories of Reading: Figural Language in Rousseau, Nietzsche, Rilke, and Proust.* New Haven: Yale UP. 305 pp.
Part 1, "Rhetoric," explains how to read part 2, "Rousseau," a method that stresses skepticism about language (because necessarily metaphorical) and about traditional assumptions and interpretations. The book focuses on how texts communicate secretly, between the lines, allegorically. This secret plot of texts has three parts: putting into question, undecidability, and the undoing of reference. Name index.
   Style 15, 75–77: "De Man's great gift is to read diverse traditions," e.g., "the criticism of Rousseau — as so many compounds of mistake"; *Diacritics* 11.4, 36–57; *YR* 69, 573–74.

1015.   Donoghue, Denis. 1981. *Ferocious Alphabets.* Boston: Little. 211 pp.
A defense of the importance of authors against recent antihumanist critical depreciation or dismissal in which authority is ascribed to the language of the author's work alone. The first part of the book treats the New Critics — Ransom, Blackmur, Richards, Empson, Eliot, and, in addition, Kenner and Gass. The second part examines "epireaders," humanists who believe that each work of literature reflects a speaker — Burke, Ricoeur, Bloom, Poirier. The

third part considers the enemies of the imagination, mainly deconstructionists, who separate writing from the writer's individual voice—Derrida especially, early Barthes, de Man.

JLT 3, 18–23: the theme of the relation between the writer and the audience is "of major importance, and I am very impressed by what Donoghue has to say about it"; *HR* 34, 631; *Enc* 58, 61.

1016.   Carroll, David. 1982. *The Subject in Question: The Languages of Theory and the Strategies of Fiction*. Chicago: U of Chicago P. 231 pp.
An assertion of the "inevitability of theory" and an examination of the relation between critical theory and literary fiction, arguing that each shares dimensions of the other. Each ch. "consists of a critical analysis of a different theoretical position which holds an important place in contemporary critical theory (structuralism, linguistics, Marxism, contemporary historiography, formalism, etc.) and a reading of one or more of the novels of the contemporary French novelist, Claude Simon." Name and term index.
Style 18, 218: "may well be the very best book of/on deconstructive criticism available to us at this particular moment"; *Choice* 20, 976.

4.2 Practice (1017–276d)

4.2.1 Diction, Imagery, Tropes (1017–64b)

1017.   Jones, Grahame. 1966. *L'ironie dans les romans de Stendhal*. Lausanne: Grand Chêne. 205 pp.
The constantly changing contexts and techniques of irony. [The study goes far beyond figurative language.]
MLR 65, 170–72: "remarkably original study."

1018.   Weinstock, Horst. 1966. *Die Funktion elisabethanischer Sprichwörter und Pseudosprichwörter bei Shakespeare* [The Function of Elizabethan Proverbs and Pseudoproverbs in the Works of Shakespeare]. Heidelberg: Winter. 227 pp.
Shakespeare's artistic uses of proverbs and quasi-proverbs.
MLR 64, 397: "invaluable aid."

1019.   Loeb, Ernst. 1967. *Die Symbolik des Wasserzyklus bei Goethe* [The Symbolism of the Water Cycle in the Work of Goethe]. Paderborn: Schöningh. 204 pp.
Traces Goethe's water symbolism through his writings.
MLR 65, 217–18: does not cover "any new ground" but "provides an excellent panorama."

1020.   Murray, Roger. 1967. *Wordsworth's Style: Figures and Themes in the Lyrical Ballads of 1800*. Lincoln: U of Nebraska P. 166 pp.

Wordsworth controls "figurative departures from literal discourse" especially by "quiet metaphors," equivocation, repetition, predication, synecdoche, and personification. Bib. 11 pp.; name and term index.

Style 1, 165–68: "significant," "a model."

1021.   Stahl, August. 1967. *"Vokabeln der Not" und "Früchte der Tröstung": Studien zur Bildlichkeit im Werke Rainer Maria Rilkes* ["Vocabulary of Poverty/Misery" and "The Fruit of Consolation": Studies of Imagery in the Work of Rainer Maria Rilke]. Heidelberg: Winter. 164 pp.

The title indicates the 2 main groups of images that are analyzed.

MLR 65, 710: "refreshing and worthwhile."

1022.   Haidu, Peter. 1968. *Aesthetic Distance in Chrétien de Troyes: Irony and Comedy in* Cligés *and* Perceval. Geneva: Droz. 272 pp.

Ironic unification in the 2 romances, irony linking all elements of the narratives through parallelism, comparison, etc. Bib. 7 pp.

MLR 67, 626–31: "criticism of very great value."

1023.   Neumann, Peter. 1968. *Zur Lyrik Paul Celans* [Paul Celan's Lyrics]. Göttingen: Vandenhoeck. 100 pp.

A study of the metaphors, compounds, symbols, and politics in 5 collections of lyric poetry.

MLR 65, 713–16: a rave rev.

1024.   Ansari, K. H. 1969. *John Webster: Image Patterns and Canon.* New Delhi: Jalaluddin Rumi. 296 pp.

Imagery analysis is employed to explain character, plot, and theme.

MLR 68, 384–85: "a deep understanding."

1025.   Howard-Hill, Trevor. 1969–78. *Oxford Shakespeare Concordances.* 30 vols. Oxford: Clarendon.

Based on the Folio old-spelling texts and the first authoritative eds. See Howard-Hill's account of the preparation of the concordances in *SB* 22 (1969), 143–64.

RenQ 24, 90–92: "not for the general public but for a small group of highly trained technician-scholars"; *TLS* 14 Aug. 1969, 903; *RenQ* 25, 366.

1026.   Nesselroth, Peter. 1969. *Lautréamont's Imagery: A Stylistic Approach.* Geneva: Droz. 123 pp.

Concentrates especially on his figures of speech.

MLR 65, 912–13: "scholarly" and admirably integrates "various approaches," but an application of academic criteria to such poetry has "certain dangers."

1027.   Zuberbühler, Rolf. 1969. *Holderlins Erneuerung der Sprache aus ihren etymologischen Ursprüngen* [Holderlin's Renewal of Language through His Etymological Sources]. Berlin: Schmidt. 119 pp.

A study of the special origin of Holderlin's poetic power—his use of words in their original etymological sense. 3 phases of Holderlin's "etymological renewal" of language are identified.

MLR 66, 463–64: "fully documented and supported," "rich in fine observations."

1028.   Brook, G. L. 1970. *The Language of Dickens*. London: Deutsch. 269 pp.
Dickens quarried for linguistic and philological material. Ch. 1, the language of description and narration; chs. 2–6, the language of his characters, from dialect (chs. 2–4) to idiolect (ch. 5) to language used for a specific occasion (ch. 6); and a final ch. on proper names. Bib. 2 pp.; name and term index.
Style 10, 100–01: a "wealth of information" but "methodological disorder" within chapters.

1029.   Dowden, Wilfred. 1970. *Joseph Conrad: The Imaged Style*. Nashville: Vanderbilt UP. 200 pp.
An analysis of pervasive and "controlling" or "conditioning" images in individual works—nature imagery in *Almayer's Folly*, avian imagery in *The Nigger of the Narcissus*, etc., and especially light-dark imagery in many novels. Name index.
Style 7, 245–48: overinterprets at times but has addressed "significant aspects of Conrad's narrative art."

1030.   Schier, Rudolf. 1970. *Die Sprache Georg Trakls* [The Language of Georg Trakl]. Heidelberg: Winter. 107 pp.
On Trakl's diction, imagery, and metaphor.
MLR 67, 951–52: "somewhat uneven"; ch. 3 is "a good one" and the last is "competent."

1031.   Schleiner, Winfried. 1970. *The Imagery of John Donne's Sermons*. Providence: Brown UP. 254 pp.
The concept of "field of imagery" provides the critical center for analysis of Donne's 7 conventional "fields." Ch. 2, "Imagery and Decorum"; ch. 3, "Fields of Imagery"; ch. 4, "Imagery and Exegesis of Scripture." Bib. 7 pp.; name index.
Style 6, 203–06: subjects of imagery and sermons excessively detached from their rhetorical context; *JEGP* 70, 541; *RES* ns 22, 342; *SAQ* 70, 120.

1032.   Göbel, Helmut. 1971. *Bild und Sprache bei Lessing* [Lessing's Imagery and Language]. Munich: Fink. 233 pp.
A classification and analysis of Lessing's imagery.
MLR 68, 456: "original and valuable contribution to the study of Lessing's style."

1033. Rivero, Eliana. 1971. *El gran amor de Pablo Neruda* [The Great Love of Pablo Neruda]. Madrid: Plaza Mayor. 182 pp.
A study of Neruda's symbols.
MLR 67, 932–33: "a useful and welcome book."

1034. Schick, Edgar. 1971. *Metaphorical Organicism in Herder's Early Works: A Study of the Relation of Herder's Literary Idiom to His World-View.* The Hague: Mouton. 135 pp.
Mainly about organic metaphors and their origin in Herder's antirationalism.
MLR 68, 456–57: negative rev.; *Choice* 9, 373: "attention to detail and a thoroughness of presentation."

1035. Kofman, Sarah. 1972. *Nietzsche et la métaphore* [Nietzsche and Metaphor]. Paris: Payot. 210 pp.

1036. Graham, Ilse. 1973. *Goethe and Lessing: The Wellsprings of Creation.* London: Elek. 356 pp.
A study mainly of the recurrent images in 4 novels by each author.
MLR 71, 728–29: "a book that no one interested in either of these writers or in poetic creation can neglect."

1037. Schäfer, Jürgen. 1973. *Shakespeares Stil: Germanisches und romanisches Vokabular* [Shakespeare's Style: Germanic and Romance Vocabulary]. Frankfurt am Main: Athenäum. 240 pp.
Partly a statistical study of the distribution of Germanic and Latinate elements but mainly an analysis of words in context.
Style 10, 97–99; *MLR* 72, 890–91: both revs. generally favorable.

1038. Barnard, Robert. 1974. *Imagery and Theme in the Novels of Dickens.* Bergen: Universitetsforläget; New York: Humanities. 164 pp.
A study of imagery patterns in 9 novels that show Dickens to be "a highly aware and sophisticated artist trying to find a satisfactory form for his all-embracing vision of life in society." Bib. 4 pp.
NCF 29, 489; *Choice* 11, 1774: "aimed at the beginning student," "incomplete," "a poor investment."

1039. Celler, Morton. 1974. *Giraudoux et la métaphore: Une étude des images dans ses romans* [Giraudoux and Metaphor: A Study of the Images in His Novels]. The Hague: Mouton. 150 pp.
MLR 71, 687: confirms "what was already known," fails to take account of recent work on metaphor.

1040. Doody, Margaret. 1974. *A Natural Passion: A Study of the Novels of Samuel Richardson.* Oxford: Clarendon. 410 pp.

Mainly interpretations and appreciations but discussion of techniques enters in, especially of imagery, which receives 2 separate chs.: "he is a master of the cumulative and intricate effect made possible by imagery."
MLR 72, 151–54: "an outstanding study."

1041.   Hellge, Rosemarie. 1974. *Motive und Motivstrukturen bei Ludwig Tieck* [Motif and Motif Structure in Ludwig Tieck]. Göppingen: Kümmerle. 285 pp.
The structural significance of major motifs mainly in the *Märchen* and early novels.
MLR 71, 470–71: some interpretations "unconvincing" because "they fail to take in the full literary and biographical context of the works concerned."

1041a.   Juhasz, Suzanne. 1974. *Metaphor and the Poetry of Williams, Pound, and Stevens*. Lewisburg: Bucknell UP. 292 pp.
"The essays in this book closely examine each poet's characteristic use of metaphor and the function it fulfills in his work, especially in long poems." Bib. 5 pp.; name index.
MP, 73, 431: a negative rev.

1042.   Koubourlis, Demetrius. 1974. *A Concordance to the Poems of Osip Mandelstam*. Ithaca: Cornell UP. 704 pp.
Groups words of the same "family" together; separates homographs and homonyms.
Choice 12, 662: "necessary addition" for scholars.

1043.   Solomon, Philip. 1975. *Life after Birth: Imagery in Samuel Beckett's Trilogy*. University, MS: Romance Monographs. 155 pp.
A study of 5 categories of image in which "the three dimensions of the trilogy—existential, epistemological, aesthetic—are crystallized." Bib. 3 pp.
MLR 72, 705–06: "provides some sharp new insights into detailed patterns of meaning," but "only the final section of the book conveys an adequate sense of the imagery as an expression of the artist's sensibility."

1044.   Frappier-Mazur, Lucienne. 1976. *L'expression métaphorique dans* La comédie humaine: *Domaine social et physiologique* [Metaphorical Expression in *The Human Comedy*: The Social and Physiological Domain]. Paris: Klincksieck. 357 pp.
The importance and consistency of the alimentary and economic imagery are demonstrated.
MLR 73, 191–92: "very substantial," "a valuable aid."

1045.   Bryans, John. 1977. *Calderón de la Barca: Imagery, Rhetoric and Drama*. London: Támesis. 207 pp.

Ch. 2, "Verbal Structure"; ch. 4, "Conceit"; chs. 6–7, imagery, etc.
MLR 74, 478: "ambitious and masterly."

1045a.   McClelland, Denise. 1977. *Le vocabulaire des* Lais *de Marie de France*. Ottawa: U d'Ottawa. 203 pp.
A computerized frequency study organized by topics: man, society, universe.
Spec 55, 147: complains about the difficulty of the organization and the insufficiency of context.

1046.   Rodríguez, Israel. 1977. *La metáfora en la estructura poética de Jorge Guillén y Federico García Lorca* [Metaphors in the Poetic Structures of Jorge Guillén and Federico García Lorca]. Madrid: Hispanova. 163 pp.
Ch. 1, theory; ch. 2, Guillén; ch. 3, Lorca; ch. 4, comparative.
Hisp 62, 180: "a worthy contribution to the study of style."

1047.   Berry, Ralph. 1978. *The Shakespearean Metaphor: Studies in Language and Form*. London: Macmillan; Totowa: Rowman. 128 pp.
"Some ways in which Shakespeare exploits the possibilities of metaphor" in 8 plays. Name index.
MLR 75, 620–21: a favorable rev.

1048.   Clark, Carol. 1978. *The Web of Metaphor: Studies in the Imagery of Montaigne's* Essais. Lexington: French Forum. 191 pp.
Chs. on earlier studies, Montaigne's images in relation to traditional contexts, the development of his innovative vocabulary, and close analysis of 3 passages. Images are shown to be central to the *Essais*. Bib. 6 pp.
MLR 76, 465–66: a favorable rev.

1049.   Gallasch, Linda. 1978. *The Use of Compounds and Archaic Diction in the Works of William Morris*. Bern: Lang. 179 pp.
"The systematic study of the diction, that is the individual words and locutions as bearers of meaning, in the works, particularly the late prose romances, of William Morris is the object of study in this dissertation." Ch. 5, "Archaic and Obsolete Words in Morris' Works"; ch. 6, "Compounds in Morris' Works." Bib. 7 pp.; word index.

1050.   Pasley, Malcolm, ed. 1978. *Nietzsche: Imagery and Thought: A Collection of Essays*. London: Methuen. 262 pp.
Nietzsche's animal and height imagery, his idea of metaphor, his masks, etc.
MLR 75, 709–11: "a number of most stimulating essays"; *GQ* 53, 234–36: "most of the essays are simply studies of image-clusters . . . and as such are of limited value to readers looking for a fresh perspective," except for "two notable exceptions."

1051.   Roster, Peter, Jr. 1978. *La ironía como método de análisis literario: La poesía de Salvador Novo* [Irony as a Method of Literary Analysis: The Poetry of Salvador Novo]. Madrid: Gredos. 226 pp.
A quarter of the book discusses irony, the remainder Novo's techniques.
Hisp 63, 442–43: "focus gives the book greater significance."

1052.   Burnley, J. D. 1979. *Chaucer's Language and the Philosopher's Tradition.* Totowa: Brewer/Rowman. 196 pp.
A study of Chaucer's vocabulary ("saint," "gentleman") by an investigation of the philosophical tradition underlying his language. Word index; name and term index.
Style 15, 499–501: "clarity and precision"; *MLR* 77, 404–05.

1053.   Mantiega, Robert. 1979. *The Poetry of Rafael Alberti: A Visual Approach.* London: Támesis. 130 pp.
An analysis mainly of the role of color and color symbolism and of the moods created.
MLR 75, 918–19: "thorough and valuable."

1054.   Prodaniuk, Ihor. 1979. *The Imagery in Heinrich Böll's Novels.* Bonn: Bouvier. 146 pp.
An analysis of the "literary imagery" in his "major works." "Images are collected from each book and subsequently classified according to the traditional and yet current terminology of *metaphor, simile, personification, symbol,* and *allusion.* Then, these basic materials are categorized according to the motifs that they convey." Bib. 2 pp.
AUMLA 54, 286–88: "reliable" textual analysis but poor literary scholarship, "largely uncritical and at times painfully obvious."

1055.   Cowart, David. 1980. *Thomas Pynchon: The Art of Allusion.* Carbondale: Southern Illinois UP. 154 pp.
Traces references not only to science but also to literature, film, music, and painting. Concludes that Pynchon's allusions "lend unity not only to the individual stories and novels, but to the author's work as a whole." Bib. 2 pp.; name and term index.
Style 17, 84–86: needs a more "workable" theory of allusions; *MFS* 26, 675; *RMR* 35, 155.

1056.   Earle, T. F. 1980. *Theme and Image in the Poetry of Sá de Miranda.* Oxford: Oxford UP. 153 pp.
Part 2 offers a study of the imagery of the 16th-cent. Portugese poet Francisco de Sá de Miranda, particularly the images of violence. Bib. 7 pp.; name and term index.
Choice 18, 666: "too brief" for the subject; *RenQ* 34, 608; *BBN* Nov. 1980, 695.

1057.   Personneaux, Lucie. 1980. *Vincente Aleixandre ou une poésie du sus-
        pens: Recherches sur le réel et l'imaginaire* [Vicente Aleixandre's Sus-
        pended Poetry: Inquiries into the Real and the Imaginary]. Montpellier:
        U Paul Valéry. 389 pp.
A study of metaphorical procedures, the vocabulary of sense perceptions, and
surrealist poetry.
        MLR 77, 978–79: "elements of real substance" but far too long.

1058.   Sandford, John. 1980. *Landscape and Landscape Imagery in R. M. Rilke.*
        London: U of London Inst. of Germanic Studies. 159 pp.
The second half of the book discusses landscape features (land, water, etc.) either as real experience or as motif or symbol.
        MLR 77, 997–98: simplifies Rilke's ideas and poetry but does marshall the
materials needed to explore how locality "feeds . . . symbolic range."

1059.   Stark, John. 1980. *Pynchon's Fictions: Thomas Pynchon and the Litera-
        ture of Information.* Athens: Ohio UP. 183 pp.
Offers information about the range, manner, and implications of Pynchon's
allusions in chs. on literature, film, history, psychology, religion, and science
and technology.
        Style 17, 84: his method sometimes excessively isolates items from relations
with other elements.

1060.   Went-Daoust, Yvette. 1980. *Le symbolisme des objets et l'espace myt-
        hique dans le théâtre de Jean Genet* [The Symbolism of Props and Set-
        tings in the Plays of Jean Genet]. Oegstgeest: Drukkerij de Kempenaer.
        233 pp.
An investigation of the symbolic meaning of objects and settings to show how
conflict of symbols structure the plays.
        MLR 76, 976–77: "convincing," "worthwhile."

1060a. Crouzet, Michel. 1981. *Stendhal et le langage.* Paris: Gallimard. 424 pp.
Beyle's struggle with language — misquoting, misspelling, repetition, banality,
personal attraction to silence, etc.
        MLN 98, 795–99: "meticulous," "flawless" knowledge of Stendhal's works,
"it will doubtless" become essential to Stendhal scholars.

1061.   Sharma, T. R. S. 1981. *Robert Frost's Poetic Style.* Atlantic Highlands:
        Humanities. 150 pp.
A study of Frost's figures of thought, such as metonymy, synecdoche, and metaphor, following certain theories of Roman Jakobson. "The metonymic method,
then, is basic to Frost's style." The author defines style as "choices of words
and rhythm a poet makes in his poems." Chs. on metonymy, synecdoche, metaphor. Bib. 4 pp. (all critical references predate 1970); name and term index.

Style 18, 114: insufficient evidence for claims, not "always analytically careful" (e.g., on "colloquial"), lacks a "comprehensive theory," but welcome as
literary history; *Choice* 20, 88: "does not supersede" Gerber's *Robert Frost* (1967)
or Potter's *Robert Frost Handbook* (1980); *AL* 54, 474.

1062.   Bernheimer, Charles. 1982. *Flaubert and Kafka: Studies in Psychopoetic
         Structure.* New Haven: Yale UP. 280 pp.
A study of early and late works by each author (*La tentation de saint Antoine*
and "The Judgment," *Bouvard et Pécuchet* and *The Castle*) to show the conflict between Eros and Thanatos, metonymy and metaphor, in each author.
Name and term index.
    CLit 10, 209: "stimulating and challenging" but "effectiveness greatly reduced
by the preponderance of linguistic and structuralistic jargon"; *Choice* 20, 575:
"whether he augments and sharpens one's understanding of Flaubert's and
Kafka's work remains a question."

1063.   Harris, Susan. 1982. *Mark Twain's Escape from Time: A Study of Pat-
         terns and Images.* Columbia: U of Missouri P. 169 pp.
Especially about Twain's "preferred imagery" of alienation, despair, and escape
from time — his images of space, water, childhood, and women (the "imagery
of contentment"). Bib. 5 pp.; name and term index.
    Choice 20, 1137: "not powerful criticism" but often "insightful" and "offers
generally balanced judgements"; *WCRB* 9, 37.

1064.   Vivante, Paolo. 1982. *The Epithets in Homer: A Study in Poetic Values.*
         New Haven: Yale UP. 222 pp.
Argues that the noun-epithet phrases in the *Iliad* and the *Odyssey* are more
than formulaic devices serving to complete a metric line; rather, they further
action and theme. Name and term index.

1064a.   Mann, Karen. 1983. *The Language That Makes George Eliot's Fiction.*
         Baltimore: Johns Hopkins UP. 226 pp.
Begins with figures of speech — particularly metaphors — within each ch. and
the human relationships they illuminate and progresses to "the longest units
of fictional discourse," relating current ideas about language to Eliot's effort
to represent the world. Bib. 9 pp.; name and term index.

1064b.   Springer, Marlene. 1983. *Hardy's Use of Allusion.* Lawrence: UP of
         Kansas. 207 pp.
Hardy "out-alluded virtually every allusionist — not only in substance, but in
skill as well," even in an age of abundant allusions. The book progresses chronologically from the early novels to the "masterful selection that is to mark his
late masterpieces." Bib. 6 pp.; name index.
    Choice 21, 824: "vigorous and direct," "a significant addition to studies on
Hardy"; *MFS* 30, 358; *BBN* Dec. 1984, 714.

4.2.2 Syntax, Schemes (1065–71)

1065.   Behre, Frank. 1967. *Studies in Agatha Christie's Writings: The Behavior of "A Good (Great) Deal, a Lot, Lots, Much, Plenty, Many, a Good (Great) Many."* Gothenburg: Acta Universitatis. 203 pp.
A study of the use of 9 intensifiers and quantifiers in Christie's novels published from 1920 to 1965.
MLR 65, 592: "lucid demonstration of precise linguistic analysis"; *ES* 49, 86.

1066.   Margetts, John. 1969. *Die Satzstruktur bei Meister Eckhart* [Sentence Structure in the Works of Meister Eckhart]. Stuttgart: Kohlhammer. 216 pp.
A study mainly of Eckhart's sentence structure.
MLR 67, 687–88: "admirable," of interest beyond Eckhart.

1067.   Schwarze, Christoph. 1970. *Untersuchungen zum syntaktischen Stil der italienischen Dichtungssprache bei Dante* [Investigations of the Syntactical Style of the Italian Poetic Language in the Work of Dante]. Bad Homburg: Gehlen. 400 pp.

1068.   Fairley, Irene. 1975. *E. E. Cummings and Ungrammar: A Study of Syntactic Deviance in His Poems.* Searingtown: Watermill. 191 pp.
Cummings's syntactic deviances have definite pattern and often have thematic or dramatic function. Chs. on syntactic innovations, adjective-adverb displacement, subject-verb-object displacement, syntactic deviance and structural patterns, and other topics. Bib. 6 pp.; name and term index.
Style 11, 224–28: "successful in showing the defining characteristics of Cummings' style," "admirably aware of the underlying problems in the study of poetic deviance"; *PTL* 3, 180–83: "an important contribution"; *MSpr* 69, 368–70: regrets the lack of "thorough comparisons" with other writers, but "a stringent and lucid description of Cummings's deviant language" which raises "some basic questions fundamental to all analyses of communication."

1069.   Stavely, Keith. 1975. *The Politics of Milton's Prose Style.* New Haven: Yale UP. 136 pp.
An analysis mainly of the sentences of 11 of Milton's pamphlets, employing Morris Croll's methodology (Ciceronian, etc.). The author concludes that "an exalted 'poetic' texture limits the political effectiveness of Milton's prose." Ch. 1, "Syntax and Persuasion," compares passages in Milton, Browne, Hooker, Lilburne, and Walwyn. The next 4 chs. trace the development of Milton's style, noting a sharp change in 1649. Bib. 2 pp.; name and term index.
JEGP 75, 430–33: "sensitivity to the prose textures" but a "difficult book to read at times"; *Style* 10, 504–07; *MP* 74, 204; *VQR* 51, cliv; *Choice* 12, 847; *LJ* 100, 856.

1070.   Ando, Sadao. 1976. *A Descriptive Syntax of Christopher Marlowe's Language*. Tokyo: U of Tokyo P. 721 pp. Dist. U.S.: ISBS, Inc., Forest Grove, OR.

A transformational generative grammatical concordance (mainly of verbal constructions) for all of Marlowe's works. Bib. 10 pp.; term index 16 pp.

ES 58, 77–79: "conscientious precision," "will take an honourable place beside Visser's *More*, Franz's *Shakespeare*, and Söderlind's *Dryden*."

1071.   Flowers, Mary. 1979. *Sentence Structure and Characterization in the Tragedies of Jean Racine: A Computer-Assisted Study*. Teaneck: Fairleigh Dickinson UP; London: Associated UP. 223 pp.

Explores the literary implications of the sentence as "one of Racine's main instruments for characterization." Racine's use of language is not homogeneous; rather, characters reveal themselves and their situations by the way they use sentences. 3 apps. on the computer program; bib. 4 pp.; name and term index.

FR 53, 604–05: "persuasive if sometimes punctilious use of her material," "unwieldy methodological apparatus."

4.2.3 Prosody, Sound Patterns in Prose (1072–75c)

1072.   Robinson, Ian. 1971. *Chaucer's Prosody: A Study of the Middle English Verse Tradition*. Cambridge: Cambridge UP. 251 pp.

A study of what we need to know about Middle Eng. to read Chaucer, whether there is any point in distinguishing rhythm and meter, and whether there is a gap between Chaucer and his disciples. His central thesis is that Chaucer did not write regular iambic pentameter. Bib. 3 pp.; name and term index. [See Conner, no. 1074.]

JEGP 72, 238–41: "lively if overlong," "contentious," "valuable . . . for its fresh views . . . and for the author's many sensitive and convincing readings"; *Choice* 8, 1021.

1073.   Wagenknecht, Christian. 1971. *Weckherlin und Opitz: Zur Metrik der deutschen Renaissancepoesie* [Weckherlin and Opitz: On the Meter of German Renaissance Poetry]. Munich: Beck. 126 pp.

A prosodic analysis of the poetry of Weckherlin and Opitz.

MLR 69, 225: "one puts down this conscientiously presented book, almost convinced."

1073a.   Baligand, Renée. 1972. *Les poèmes de Raymond Queneau: Etude phonostylistique*. Studia Phonetica 6. Paris: Didier. 124 pp.

Ling 141, 102–05 (in Ger.): Baligand does not show anything new.

1074.   Conner, Jack. 1974. *English Prosody from Chaucer to Wyatt*. The Hague: Mouton. 104 pp.

An investigation of the evidence for determining the iambic base of Chaucer's meter, an attempt to demonstrate that Chaucer "regularly released his final consonants," and an attack on Ian Robinson (no. 1072). Bib. 2 pp.; name and term index.

MLR 72, 147–48: the argument that the final released consonants functioned as metrical syllables "offers something for everyone" to "disagree with"; "the author presents Chaucer's verse" as a "linguistic fossil."

1075.   Beaver, Joseph. 1976. *The Prosody of John Donne*. Chicago: Dept. of Linguistics, Northeastern Illinois U. 142 pp.
A study of the metricality of Donne's iambic lines by an application of Halle-Keyser metrics to the entire corpus of Donne's poetry. Beaver concludes that only approximately one-half of one percent of the lines are unmetrical. Bib. 2 pp.
Style 12, 55–57: "does not warrant a revaluation of Donne's reputation as a metricist" but "does raise a number of useful questions for a 'grammar of prosody.'"

1075a.   Le Mée, Katharine. 1978. *A Metrical Study of Five Lais of Marie de France*. The Hague: Mouton; Berlin: de Gruyter. 202 pp.
Includes study of rhyme, syllable count, word length, grammatical forms, narrative devices, and special methods for analysis of medieval texts. 13 charts; 78 figs.; 16 tables.
Spec 55, 141: the ch. on stress patterns is "questionable," the argument of another ch. is "forced," a lukewarm rev.; *FR* 53, 735.

1075b.   Beltrami, Pietro. 1981. *Metrica, poetica, metrica dantesca*. Pisa: Pacini. 163 pp.
5 essays based on structural and descriptive linguistics, pulled together by an introductory essay.
MLN 98, 140: "basically incomplete," "a modest contribution."

1075c.   Cercignani, Fausto. 1981. *Shakespeare's Works and Elizabethan Pronunciation*. Oxford: Clarendon. 432 pp.
An attempt to refute Kökeritz's 1953 argument that Shakespeare's pronunciation was so far advanced as to be almost identical with that of present educated Southern Eng.
Lang 59, 915–17: "missed an opportunity," corroborates "what was already rather well-known"; *JEGP* 82, 227.

4.2.4 Studies on Several Linguistic Levels (1076–276d)

1076.   Frohock, W. M. 1963. *Rimbaud's Poetic Practice: Image and Theme in the Major Poems*. Cambridge: Harvard UP. 250 pp.
Chs. 1–3 an introd. to the pre-*voyant* poetry; chs. 4–6 an analysis of the *Lettre du Voyant* and the poems "Le bateau ivre" and "Le coeur volé"; ch. 7 on the late verse, etc. Bib. 4 pp.; name index.

Style 4, 59–67: "as an introductory study for the general reader it is largely successful," with some "excellent analysis."

1077.   Sternfeld, F. W. 1963. *Music in Shakespearean Tragedy*. London: Routledge. 334 pp.
A study of the contribution of music to the dramatic effects of the plays, showing Shakespeare an innovator in employing song to enhance tragic speech and action. Bib. 26 pp.; index of lyrics; name and term indexes.
MLR 64, 133–35: "fascinating, and knowledgeable."

1078.   Axton, William. 1966. *Circle of Fire: Dickens' Vision and Style and the Popular Victorian Theater*. Lexington: UP of Kentucky. 294 pp.
Dickens composed his plots and scenes in the modes of the popular theater—the apostrophe, invocation, direct address, soliloquy, aside, the grotesque and burlesque, incompatible juxtapositions, incongruous scenes, etc. Name and term index.
Style 4, 81–84; *JAAC* 26, 408; *JEGP* 67, 169; *RES* 19, 348; *WHR* 22, 173.

1079.   Brill, Siegfried. 1967. *Die Komödie der Sprach: Untersuchungen zum Werke Johann Nestroys* [The Comedy of Language: Investigations of the Work of Johann Nestroy]. Nürnberg: Carl. 232 pp.
Analyzes 10 techniques of linguistic comedy.
MLR 64, 947–48: the "classification is not always enlightening," but he "succeeds in bringing out" Nestroy's "central concern" and "complexity."

1080.   Cook, Richard. 1967. *Jonathan Swift as a Tory Pamphleteer*. Seattle: U of Washington P. 157 pp.
A study of writings that "are among the most accomplished examples of political writing in the English language," directed "toward discussion and analysis of specific rhetorical techniques and approaches in the tracts themselves." Name index.
Style 8, 570–74: pedagogical value, no "new interpretations or new information," but arranges Swift's political writings into "coherent patterns"; *AHR* 73, 1523; *NS* 75, 618; *PQ* 47, 429.

1081.   Dembo, L. S., ed. 1967. *Nabokov: The Man and His Work*. Madison: U of Wisconsin P. 282 pp.
A wide-ranging collection. The essays that analyze Nabokov's writings (including his trans. of Pushkin) stress his artificiality—the verbal games, puns, cross-references, parodies, allusions, etc. Bib. of criticism of Nabokov up to 1967.
Style 5, 88–91.

1082.   Erken, Gunther. 1967. *Hofmannsthals dramatischer Stil: Untersuchungen zur Symbolik und Dramaturgie* [Hofmannsthal's Dramatic Style: Investigations of Symbolism and Dramaturgy]. Tübingen: Niemeyer. 271 pp.
An analysis of the principles of Hofmannsthal's dramatic style.
MLR 65, 467: "important" for Hofmannsthal research.

1083. Higman, Francis. 1967. *The Style of John Calvin in His French Polemical Treatises.* London: Oxford UP. 191 pp.

An opening ch. on his principles and organizational strategies, followed by chs. on vocabulary, syntax, and imagery, all of which show Calvin's basic polarizing method.

MLR 64, 667–68: "able and interesting," "lucid expositions and analyses"; *TLS* 15 Feb. 1968, 163.

1084. Rudenstine, Neil. 1967. *Sidney's Poetic Development.* Cambridge: Harvard UP. 313 pp.

By attention to Sidney's use of "plain style," Ciceronianism, and other kinds of choices of syntax, diction, and ornamentation, the author traces the "unbroken continuity" of Sidney's styles. Name and term index.

Style 5, 196–202: favorable; *MLR* 64, 631–32.

1085. Stedmond, John. 1967. *The Comic Art of Laurence Sterne: Convention and Innovation in* Tristram Shandy *and* A Sentimental Journey. Toronto: U of Toronto P; London: Oxford UP. 178 pp.

Discusses the influence of Rabelais, Burton, et al. (esoteric learning, digressions, rhetorical and stylistic devices, etc.), and the new uses Sterne made of those writers and traditions.

MLR 64, 648–49: "a solid book, well written, sound in its scholarship, and stimulating in its criticism"; *JEGP* 67, 311.

1086. Alazraki, Jaime. 1968. *La prosa narrativa de Jorge Luis Borges* [The Narrative Prose of Jorge Luis Borges]. Madrid: Gredos. 240 pp.

A study of themes and style—adjectivization, figures of speech (antinomy, oxymoron, paradox, etc.), distance, etc.

MLR 65, 661: with some exceptions "a sound contribution."

1087. Baxtin, Mixail. 1968. *Rabelais and His World.* Trans. Helene Iswolsky. Cambridge: MIT P. 484 pp. (*Tvorčestvo Fransua Rable.* Moscow: Xudožestvennija literatura, 1965; written in 1940.)

"The method which Baxtin introduces for an analysis of literary phenomena is largely based on the structure of the dialogue and the function of a word in a discourse. . . . His study is concerned with semiotic operation" and compares different sign systems, "such as verbal, pictorial, and gestural" (foreword by K. Pomorska). Name and term index.

Style 4, 73–76: "closer to myth criticism than stylistics, but is postulated on close reading," yet "frequently tends to sweeping and unproved generalities"; *NYRB* 13, 16; *NYTBR* 19 Jan. 1969, 36; *RM* 23, 737.

1088. Blatt, Thora. 1968. *The Plays of John Bale: A Study of Ideas, Technique, and Style.* Copenhagen: Gads. 267 pp.

The language, structure, and dramatic technique of the plays.
MLR 65, 371–72: "valuable."

1089.   Brophy, James. 1968. *Edith Sitwell: The Symbolist Order.* Carbondale:
         Southern Illinois UP. 170 pp.
Argues a theory of internal order in Sitwell's poetry based on word texture
and sounds in opposition (what Sitwell called "shadow"), which in recurrence
become symbols. Bib. 3 pp.; name index.
MLR 65, 409: "merits praise," but the task still remains of showing how
the concept of "shadow" provides order; *ConL* 10, 147; *LJ* 93, 2007.

1090.   Cooper, Sherod. 1968. *The Sonnets of Astrophel and Stella.* The Hague:
         Mouton. 183 pp.
An analysis of versification, rhyme schemes, vocabulary, rhetoric, and imagery
using quantitative methods.
MLR 66, 857: several reservations.

1091.   Haggis, Donald. 1968. *C.-F. Ramuz, ouvrier du langage* [C.-F. Ramuz,
         Craftsman of Language]. Paris: Minard. 156 pp.
A study of 3 of Ramuz's works that span his career, comparing the texts from
manuscript to print.
MLR 66, 193–94: an admiring rev.

1092.   Just, Gottfried. 1968. *Ironie und Sentimentalität in den erzählenden
         Dichtungen Arthur Schnitzlers* [Irony and Sentimentality in the Nar-
         rative Fiction of Arthur Schnitzler]. Berlin: Schmidt. 149 pp.
MLR 65, 223–24: too narrow a range of evidence but "clear, intelligent," "precise, acute."

1093.   Lindberg-Seyersted, Brita. 1968. *The Voice of the Poet: Aspects of Style
         in the Poetry of Emily Dickinson.* Cambridge: Harvard UP. 290 pp.
Chs. 2–4 on diction, prosody, and syntax show how primary is the technique
of contrast in Dickinson's poetry. Bib. 8 pp.; name and term index.
Style 5, 319–22: "the first full-length attempt to put the theories and
methods of modern linguistics and stylistics to work in analyzing the poems";
ES 52, 562–63; *ZAA* 20, 88–90; *JbAm* 14, 298–301; *JEGP* 68, 320–23; *AL*
41, 437–38; *NEQ* 42, 281–84.

1094.   Mitchell, Jerome. 1968. *Thomas Hoccleve: A Study in Early Fifteenth-
         Century English Poetic.* Urbana: U of Illinois P. 151 pp.
Mainly a study of themes, genres, handling of sources, language, and meter.
Annotated bib. 21 pp.; name index.
MLR 66, 851–52: "a very carefully produced book" that sheds "much light"
on an "unduly neglected range of poetry."

1095. Newell, Kenneth. 1968. *Structure in Four Novels by H. G. Wells.* The Hague: Mouton. 120 pp.
Mainly a macrostructural study of how the narratives are blocked out in sequence, but metaphorical organization also receives attention — indigestion in *Mr. Polly* and the 2 unifying metaphors of *Tono-Bungay*. No bib. or index.
MLR 67, 407–08: "as an unpretentious short study of a section of Wells's work this is a useful and sensible book."

1096. Vickers, Brian. 1968. *The Artistry of Shakespeare's Prose.* London: Methuen. 452 pp.
Documents the development of Shakespeare's treatment of conventional devices (e.g., witty repartee of Beatrice and Benedick to satire of Timon and Apemantus) and examines the distinction between prose and poetry. Name and term index.
Style 4, 159–62: "disappointing as stylistics"; *JEGP* 68, 178–80: inexpert, "tedious"; *MLR* 64, 393–94: "the most searching, detailed, and comprehensive account of Shakespeare's prose that we have"; *EA* 23, 440–41; *QQ* 76, 150–51; *RES* 20, 215–18; *ELN* 6, 203–05; *N&Q* ns 4, 157–58.

1097. Vickers, Brian. 1968. *Francis Bacon and Renaissance Prose.* Cambridge: Cambridge UP. 316 pp.
Contrary to Morris Croll's argument, Bacon was influenced stylistically not by Seneca or Tacitus but by the law, traditional rhetorical theory (*partitio* particularly), the pre-Socratics (especially Hippocrates), and the Renaissance habit of heaping up commonplaces. Bib. 6 pp.; name index, with a few terms.
Style 3, 200–01: "towers over everything else written on Bacon as a literary man"; *JEGP* 68, 178–80: "garrulity," "hasty"; *MLR* 65, 375–77: "a genuine reassessment."

1098. Wetzel, Heinz. 1968. *Klang und Bild in den Dichtungen Georg Trakls* [Sound and Image in the Poetry of Georg Trakl]. Göttingen: Vandenhoeck. 195 pp.
A study of the rhythmic and tonal effects and the imagery in Trakl's poetry.
MLR 65, 711–22: "useful," "demonstrates the importance of the musical elements"; *Ling* 121, 114–20: "demands wider recognition than it has received."

1099. Booth, Stephen. 1969. *An Essay on Shakespeare's Sonnets.* New Haven: Yale UP. 218 pp.
A Shakespeare sonnet "is organized in a multitude of different coexistent and conflicting patterns" (ch. 1); these patterns are the source of the unique reading experience of the poems.
JEGP 70, 296–97: "lucid and empirical," but his attack on interpretation is "perverse" and "large parts" of the book are "unreadable"; *NYRB* 15, 33; *MP* 68, 383; *Choice* 6, 1390.

1100.   Chambers, Ross. 1969. *Gérard de Nerval et la poétique du voyage* [Gérard de Nerval and the Poetics of Travel]. Paris: Corti. 409 pp.
Applies structuralist and stylistic techniques to identify and explain the patterns in Nerval's travel narratives and pen sketches: the idea of freedom in the images of rapidity and immobility, rhythms of time and space, etc.
MLR 65, 637–38: "an interesting theory."

1101.   Ellrich, Robert. 1969. *Rousseau and His Reader: The Rhetorical Situation of the Major Works.* Chapel Hill: U of North Carolina P. 108 pp.
Rousseau's concern for his different kinds of readers (both real and imaginary). "My initial principle is simple and familiar: All use of speech implies convention and therefore at least duality of minds. The problem of communication through language may in this light be seen as the search for the means supplied by the conventions (or code) to transmit a message from one mind to another." [Were the book written in the 1980s it would probably have "semiotics" in its title.]
MLR 67, 637–38: "perceptive and lively."

1102.   Garland, H. B. 1969. *Schiller, the Dramatic Writer: A Study of Style in the Plays.* Oxford: Clarendon. 301 pp.
Schiller's mastery of language — his use of speech to characterize, the functional effectiveness of vocabulary and imagery, etc. Bib. 2 pp.
MLR 66, 215–17: "deserves a warm welcome."

1103.   Hamilton, K. G. 1969. *John Dryden and the Poetry of Statement.* East Lansing: Michigan State UP. 193 pp. (Brisbane: U of Queensland P, 1967.)
Dryden is the master stylist of "the poetry of statement" during a time of great stylistic transition. Chs. on imitation, meaning, sound imagery, and amplification. Bib. 12 pp.; name index.
Style 7, 223–26: imprecise theory and terms but his readings of passages "well worth" attention.

1104.   Jacobs, Jürgen. 1969. *Wielands Romane* [Weiland's Novels]. Bern: Francke. 122 pp.
A study of style and narrative techniques — conversational dialogue with the reader, etc.
MLR 66, 456–57: "breaks little new ground" but "presents" in "sensible terms the characteristic features of Wieland's styles."

1105.   Jones, John A. 1969. *Pope's Couplet Art.* Athens: Ohio UP. 217 pp.
A study of balanced antithesis and parallelism, rhyme, closure, and sentence form in 8 major poems. Jones finds a different "style" in each poem, "tailored to the thematic content." Name and term index.

Style 6, 198–202: "remarkably sensitive and skillful"; *JEGP* 69, 177–79: sometimes vague, "too often his assertions raise more questions . . . than they answer"; "offers no significant new insight into the total import of poems" but "often illuminates the intricacies of structure, tone, and meaning"; *PQ* 49, 370–71; *UTQ* 40, 183–84; *ECS* 3, 419–21; *ES* 53, 258–63; *QQ* 77, 140–41.

1106. Kiechler, John. 1969. *The Butterfly's Freckled Wings: A Study of Style in the Novels of Ronald Firbank*. Bern: Francke. 121 pp.
7 chs.: "Local Colour," "Reported Speech," "Dialogue," "Imagery," etc.
MLR 65, 614–15: the ch. on reported speech is "adroit."

1107. Klopfenstein, Eduard. 1969. *Erzähler und Leser bei Wilhelm Raabe* [Narrator and Reader in the Works of Wilhelm Raabe]. Bern: Haupt. 166 pp.
A study of the author-reader relationship by discussion of the dialogue between author, narrator, characters, and reader.
MLR 66, 469–70: "necessarily somewhat sketchy" but "nevertheless stimulating."

1108. Mills, John A. 1969. *Language and Laughter: Comic Diction in the Plays of Bernard Shaw*. Tucson: U of Arizona P. 176 pp.
After 2 introductory chs., ch. 3 examines "Shaw's use of various dialects, especially cockney vocabulary and syntax"; ch. 4 treats "the ways which Shaw makes comic capital of various literary styles and of professional jargon"; ch. 5 deals with "the comic effectiveness of repetition of words and of punning"; the conclusion gives an account of Shaw's "neutral voice," the general style of most of his characters.
Style 5, 309–14: "well worth the reading (and is handsomely written)"; *MP* 68, 215; *Choice* 7, 1066.

1109. Ross, David, Jr. 1969. *Style and Tradition in Catullus*. Cambridge: Harvard UP. 188 pp.
A study of the vocabulary and meter of Catullus's poetry. Bib. 5 pp.; index of passages; name and term index.
Style 5, 315–18: "a serious, excellent study."

1110. Salzmann, Wolfgang. 1969. *Molière und die lateinische Komödie* [Molière and Latin Comedy]. Heidelberg: Winter. 272 pp.
The uses Molière made of Latin comedy (especially of Plautus): riposte, handling of dialogue, ambivalence of speech, etc.
MLR 66, 689: a lukewarm rev.

1111. Stallworthy, Jon. 1969. *Vision and Revision in Yeats's "Last Poems."* Oxford: Clarendon. 181 pp.

The author's second book on Yeats's poems from draft to print. Bib. 2 pp.; name index.

MLR 65, 893–94: "no very great contribution" as a study of the manuscripts but praises the "civilized manner" of his reading of Yeats.

1112.   Wortley, W. V. 1969. *Tallemant des Réaux: The Man through His Style.* The Hague: Mouton. 95 pp.

Discusses the variety of Tallemant's devices — using physical traits to imply moral ones, narrative pace, *badinage*, etc. — in his *Historiettes.*

MLR 67, 414–15.

1113.   Chevalier, Jean-Claude. 1970. *"Alcools": Analyse des formes poétiques.* Paris: Minard. 208 pp.

A linguistic analysis of the process of poetic composition, how words generate one another on every level.

MLR 68, 184–85: a "serious step forward" in understanding the poetic process.

1114.   Colie, Rosalie. 1970. *"My Ecchoing Song": Andrew Marvell's Poetry of Criticism.* Princeton: Princeton UP. 315 pp.

The elements of Marvell's poetry constitute the first 2 parts of the study: "Studies in Theme and Genre" and "Stylistic and Rhetorical Devices." Part 3 offers "a composite reading" of "Upon Appleton House." Name and term index.

MLR 68, 156–57: "persistent tact, intelligence, and good sense"; *Critm* 13, 210; *JEGP* 70, 665; *RES* 22, 496.

1115.   Gordon, Alex. 1970. *Ronsard et la rhétorique* [Ronsard and Rhetoric]. Geneva: Droz. 244 pp.

A study of the importance of rhetoric to Ronsard and in the 16th cent. generally.

MLR 67, 885–86: "his conclusions carry conviction."

1116.   Griffiths, Richard. 1970. *The Dramatic Technique of Antoine de Montchréstien: Rhetoric and Style in French Renaissance Tragedy.* Oxford: Clarendon. 236 pp.

Treats scenes, stichomythia, imagery, etc.

MLR 66, 686–87: "masterly"; *FS* 25, 192; *TLS* 23 Oct. 1970, 1219; *Choice* 8, 234.

1116a.   Gullón, Ricardo. 1970. *Técnicas de Galdós.* Madrid: Taurus. 222 pp.

Discusses various narrative devices used in 4 novels.

1117.   Kloepfer, Rolf, and Ursula Oomen. 1970. *Sprachliche Konstituenten moderner Dichtung: Entwurf einer deskriptiven Poetik: Rimbaud* [Linguistic Constitutents of Modern Literature: A Plan for a Descriptive Poetics: Rimbaud]. Bad Homburg: Athenäum. 231 pp.

1118.   Kobs, Jörgen. 1970. *Kafka: Untersuchungen zu Bewusstsein und Sprache seiner Gestalten* [Kafka: Investigations into the Consciousness and Language of His Characters]. Bad Homburg: Athenäum. 559 pp.
An attempt to relate characters' consciousness and perception to particular stylistic traits.
MLR 68, 706: too long but the analysis is "most illuminating."

1119.   Parent, Monique. 1970. *Cohérence et résonance dans le style de "Charmes" de Paul Valéry* [Coherence and Resonance in the Style of "Charmes" by Paul Valéry]. Paris: Klincksieck. 222 pp.
An analysis of the vocabulary (key words), syntax, imagery, and variants of a collection of separate poems linked in theme and vocabulary.
MLR 68, 424–25: "something of a *pot-pourri*," but "author has knack of saying all that usefully can be said in the space of a few pages."

1120.   Patterson, Gertrude. 1970. *T. S. Eliot: Poems in the Making*. Manchester: Manchester UP; New York: Barnes. 198 pp.
A study of the influences on Eliot's "methods of composition" and resultant modes and structures—imagism, symbolism, etc. Bib. 5 pp.; name and term index.
MLR 67, 177–79: "an accomplished and discerning book."

1121.   Phillipps, K. C. 1970. *Jane Austen's English*. London: Deutsch. 229 pp.
Chs. on vocabulary, sentence structure, and modes of address. Bib. 3 pp.; name and term indexes.
MLR 69, 382–83: Page (*The Language of Jane Austen* [no. 1146]) and Phillipps "go over the same ground, but *Jane Austen's English* is to be preferred as the more erudite, the more sensitive to literary nuance, and accordingly as the more illuminating"; *TLS* 30 July 1971, 920; *ES* 53, 365.

1122.   Rogers, T. J. 1970. *Techniques of Solipsism: A Study of Theodor Storm's Narrative Fiction*. Cambridge: Modern Humanities Research Assn. 219 pp.
A study of the technical expressions of Storm's anxiety of being trapped in a solipsistic world: lack of omniscient narrator, inconclusive endings, indirection via sense impressions, shifting narrational perspective, in short, pervasive ambiguity.
MLR 66, 467–69: "has much to offer the general student of nineteenth-century literature as well as the Storm specialist."

1123.   Samaras, Zoe. 1970. *The Comic Element of Montaigne's Style*. Paris:
         Nizet. 252 pp.
A study of the ways Montaigne's words and sentences differ from normal usage and sentence construction — i.e., the rich display of tropes and schemes
for "comic" effects.
MLR 68, 405–07: a negative rev.; *FR* 45, 526; *RR* 64, 306.

1124.   Sherrington, R. J. 1970. *Three Novels by Flaubert: A Study of Tech-
         niques*. Oxford: Clarendon. 363 pp.
An analysis of point-of-view techniques in *Madame Bovary*, *Salammbô*, and
L'education sentimentale. One conclusion is that *Salammbô* improves on
Bovary.
MLR 68, 422–23: "subtle, argumentative and interesting."

1125.   Sutherland, R. D. 1970. *Language and Lewis Carroll*. The Hague: Mou-
         ton. 245 pp.
A study of Carroll's linguistic principles underlying and revealed by his liter-
ary works. Bib. 2 pp.; name and term index.
Semiotica 5, 89–92; *TLS* 4 Dec. 1970, 1415.

1126.   Affron, Charles. 1971. *A Stage for Poets: Studies in the Theatre of Hugo
         and Musset*. Princeton: Princeton UP. 254 pp.
A study of the relation between poetry and drama by analysis of specific fea-
tures of a few plays (figurative language, rhythm, etc.).
MLR 69, 880–81: "stimulating."

1127.   Boyde, Patrick. 1971. *Dante's Style in His Lyric Poetry*. London: Cam-
         bridge UP. 359 pp.
Traditional rhetorical categories and terms from medieval rhetoric, combined
with statistical counts and percentages, are applied to the description of 13
groups of lyrics (the *Vita nuova* mainly).
MLR 69, 657–69: "an original and valuable contribution."

1128.   Cash, Arthur, and John Stedmond, eds. 1971. *The Winged Skull: Papers
         from the Laurence Sterne Bicentenary Conference*. London: Methuen.
         315 pp.
Section 5, "Style and Composition," contains 4 essays.
MLR 67, 403–04.

1129.   Coleman, Dorothy. 1971. *Rabelais: A Critical Study in Prose Fiction*.
         London: Cambridge UP. 241 pp.
A study of the modalities of Rabelais's narrative — burlesque, word games,
irony, Ciceronian and other styles, poetic prose, etc.
MLR 69, 866–68: the investigation is "triumphantly shown" by an "acute
mind"; *TLS* 5 Nov. 1971, 1389.

1130. Gilman, Sander. 1971. *Form und Funktion: Eine strukturelle Unter-suchung der Romane Klabunds* [Form and Function: A Structural Analysis of Klabund's Novels]. Frankfurt: Athenäum. 188 pp.
An examination of interspersed lyrics, symbols, leitmotifs, anecdote, narrator, etc.
MLR 69, 469–70: Klabund's characteristics as a novelist "are realized."

1131. Jones, Emrys. 1971. *Scenic Form in Shakespeare.* Oxford: Clarendon. 269 pp.
Shakespeare's "mastery of scenic construction," the scene being the "primary dramatic unit" of his plays. *Othello, King Lear, Macbeth,* and *Antony and Cleopatra* receive separate chs. Name index.
MLR 67, 871–73: "lucid, scholarly, exceptionally sensitive to both literary and theatrical considerations, this is an original and important book."

1132. McMaster, Juliet. 1971. *Thackeray: The Major Novels.* Manchester: Manchester UP. 230 pp.
Thackeray is a conscious artist particularly in his use of irony. Ch. 1, "Narrative Technique" in *Vanity Fair*; ch. 2, "Tone and Theme" in *Pendennis*, etc. Name and term index.
MLR 68, 396–97: generally favorable rev.; *TLS* 14 July 1972, 794.

1133. Risset, Jacqueline. 1971. *L'anagramme du désir: Essai sur la "Délie" de Maurice Scève* [Anagram of Desire: An Essay on the "Delie" of Maurice Scève]. Rome: Bulzoni. 112 pp.
Diacritics 4.3, 9–14: "her promise is unfortunately not fulfilled in her book."

1134. Rizzuto, Anthony. 1971. *Style and Theme in Reverdy's* Les Ardoises du toit. University: U of Alabama P. 204 pp.
A study of an early collection of Reverdy's poems, with chs. on metaphor, rhyme, meter, "visual verse," and a holistic analysis of 1 poem. Bib. 12 pp.; index to poems.
Style 7, 227–30: "reservations" but praises "the analysis of the verse"; *MLR* 69, 422–23.

1135. Ueding, Gert. 1971. *Schillers Rhetorik: Idealistische Wirkungsästhetik und rhetorische Tradition* [Schiller's Rhetoric: Idealistic Effect Aesthetic and Rhetorical Tradition]. Tübingen: Niemeyer. 204 pp.
A study of the tension between Schiller's idealism and his commitment to the rhetorical tradition of the enlightenment.
MLR 68, 944–45: "Despite so many good things, the book is not easy to read."

1136. Ullman, Pierre. 1971. *Mariano De Larra and Spanish Political Rhetoric.* Madison: U of Wisconsin P. 428 pp.

A combination of "Parliamentary history and stylistic analysis" (mainly pointing out classical tropes). Bib. 9 pp.; name and term index.
Style 10, 508–11; *MLR* 67, 200–01: negative rev. of the "stylistics" material.

1137.   Vogel, Joseph. 1971. *Dante Gabriel Rossetti's Versecraft.* Gainesville: U of Florida P. 111 pp.
A statistical and analytical description of the meter (ch. 1), stanzas (ch. 2), and rhyme (ch. 3) of Rossetti's poetry, with a concluding ch. on "The Blessed Damozel" showing how Rossetti employed poetic devices functionally together. The author believes Rossetti is a "remarkably fine craftsman." No index.
Style 9, 143–44: an admirable, traditional author study but sometimes uncritical with evidence.

1138.   Allen, Rupert. 1972. *The Symbolic World of Federico García Lorca.* Albuquerque: U of New Mexico P. 205 pp.
A Jungian analysis of the "collective unconscious" as manifested in Lorca's works. Bib. 2 pp.; name and term index. [By the same author: *Psyche and Symbol in the Theater of Federico García Lorca: "Perlimplin," "Yerma," "Blood Wedding."* Austin: U of Texas P, 1974.]
MLR 69, 209–10: "the literary critic is left gasping with bewilderment"; *Choice* 10, 462: "penetrating and even brilliant insights bound to cause controversy"; *Hisp* 57, 183.

1139.   Berry, Ralph. 1972. *The Art of John Webster.* Oxford: Clarendon. 174 pp.
The 3 plays known to be Webster's own are interpreted through stylistic analysis, particularly in the context of the baroque since his plays are "attempts to achieve in literature the effects of the baroque." Name and term index.
MLR 70, 148–51: the analysis of techniques "frequently illuminates" the plays "in new and unexpected ways," and "the reader comes away from this part of the book with a strong sense of their stylistic unity."

1140.   Bien, Peter. 1972. *Kazantzakis and the Linguistic Revolution in Greek Literature.* Princeton: Princeton UP. 291 pp.
The first half of the book concerns the revolution, the second half treats Kazantzakis's role, in whose demotic novels—*Zorba, Christ Recrucified*, and *The Last Temptation*—style reflected "the concrete reality of everyday existence."
Style 10, 508–11: "a pleasure to read"; *MLR* 69, 239–40.

1141.   Chatman, Seymour. 1972. *The Later Style of Henry James.* New York: Barnes. 135 pp.
19 sections explain the linguistic bases of James's "abstractness"—deixis, nominalization of psychological verbs, cleft sentences, ellipsis, etc.

Style 7, 241–44: "assiduously detailed evidence . . . is most persuasive," but book gives us "little sense of the larger effects of Jamesian" paragraphs and chapters; *Novel* 7, 187–89: "a considerable achievement"; *NCF* 28, 492–94: Chatman's method faulty: he "discovers what he already knows," and he "fosters the view that the style is vague and attenuated," which is "not the case"; *AL* 44, 494–96; *MFS* 19, 267–70.

1142.   Conroy, Peter, Jr. 1972. *Crébillon fils: Techniques of the Novel.* Banbury: Voltaire Foundation. 238 pp.
A study of the point of view, methods of characterization, use of plot, and general representational format in 3 epistolary novels (1732–42).
   MLR 70, 901: analyses of the 3 novels are "acute," but fuller contexts are needed.

1143.   Deleuze, Gilles. 1972. *Proust and Signs.* Trans. Richard Howard. New York: Braziller. 167 pp. (*Proust et les signes.* Paris: PUF, 1964.)
"The word sign, *signe*, is one of the most frequent in the work. . . . The Search is presented as the exploration of different worlds of signs which are organized in circles and intersect at certain points." Ch. 6 presents an analysis of "serial repetition." Ch. 8, an addition to the original ed., deals with Proust's conception of his work as "an apparatus . . . *producing signs of different orders*, which will have an effect on the reader."
   Choice 9, 1137: "brief but significant and original"; *Crit* 27, 1060; *FS* 26, 472; *TLS* 13 Apr. 1973, 423; *LJ* 97, 876.

1144.   Eliason, Norman. 1972. *The Language of Chaucer's Poetry: An Appraisal of the Verse, Style, and Structure.* Copenhagen: Rosenkilde. 250 pp.
Ch. 1, "Sound"; ch. 2, "Style"; ch. 3, "Structure." "I am concerned with the particular way Chaucer used his language." Term index.
   MLR 68, 889: "particularly readable and interesting whether one agrees or disagrees"; *MP* 72, 60; *RES* 25, 74.

1145.   James, E. Anthony. 1972. *Daniel Defoe's Many Voices: A Rhetorical Study of Prose Style and Literary Method.* Atlantic Highlands: Humanities; Amsterdam: Rodopi. 269 pp.
"Defoe was pre-eminently" a "conscious" literary artist in his "many voices," down to the smallest stylistic details. Chs. 1–4 on Defoe's literary values and techniques; Chs. 5–7 on *Crusoe, Moll,* and *Roxanne.* Name and term index.
   Style 11, 101–02: "a careful and sensible reader of Defoe," analyzes Defoe's voices "effectively," but does not avoid the pitfalls of "circularity," the "leaps from detail to thesis"; *MLR* 69, 151–52.

1146.   Page, Norman. 1972. *The Language of Jane Austen.* New York: Barnes. 208 pp.

"[T]he triumph of the novels is to a large extent a triumph of style." Chs. on Austen's ability to make common subjects significant through style; vocabulary; syntax; dialogue; epistolary techniques; her predecessors and successors. "My aim has been not . . . to use the novels as a quarry for linguistic or philological material [e.g., Brooks on Dickens] . . . as to endeavour to reach a deeper understanding of their meaning and artistry." Bib. 7 pp.; name and term index.

MLR 69, 382–83: Page and Phillipps (no. 1121) "go over the same ground" but Phillipps's book "is to be preferred"; *Style* 8, 265–66; *PP* 17, 41–42; *ES* 54, 595–96.

1147.   Rigolot, François. 1972. *Les langages de Rabelais*. Geneva: Droz; Paris: Minard. 186 pp.
Not a study, e.g., of the military or legal or medical terms, but a series of explications of selected passages in which the linguistic interest is pronounced, in order to establish certain basic traits and principles underlying those elements.
MLR 70, 176: "brave approach to a truly gargantuan task," but reader is "too frequently dazzled and further mystified by the author's own linguistic *tour de force*"; *TLS* 7 July 1972, 784.

1148.   Rubin, David L. 1972. *Higher, Hidden Order: Design and Meaning in the Odes of Malherbe*. Chapel Hill: U of North Carolina P. 124 pp.
An analysis of stylistic patterns (allusive motifs, systems of images, etc.) in 6 odes to demonstrate the "higher order" of Malherbe's odes. Bib. 1 p.
MLR 69, 869: a "superficial analysis" of style; *ECr* 17, 271.

1149.   Vannier, Bernard. 1972. *L'inscription du corps: Pour une sémiotique du portrait balzacien* [The Description of the Body: Toward a Semiotics of Balzac's Portraits]. Paris: Klincksieck. 197 pp.
On Balzac's description of human characters, especially the visual aspects. Bib. 7 pp.
Diacritics 4.1, 2–6.

1150.   Burgess, Anthony. 1973. *Joysprick: An Introduction to the Language of James Joyce*. London: Deutsch. 187 pp.
Mainly a miscellaneous description of stylistic devices in *Ulysses* and *Finnegans Wake* (pastiche, interior monologue, etc.) by a novelist who is not a professional linguist. Bib. 2 pp.; name and term index.
Style 9, 252–54: "overstresses the formal elements," "many valuable insights"; *TLS* 15 June 1973, 669; *JJQ* 11, 175; *Spec* 230, 815.

1151.   Debicki, Andrew. 1973. *La poesía de Jorge Guillén*. Madrid: Gredos. 361 pp.

A formal study (imagery, tone, point of view, etc.).
MLR 70, 921–23: "originality" and "subtlety" but "the central thesis is missing" because he adopts an "autotelic line of criticism."

1152. Drew-Bear, Annette. 1973. *Rhetoric in Ben Jonson's Middle Plays: A Study of Ethos, Character Portrayal, and Persuasion.* Salzburg: Inst. für Englische Sprache und Literatur, U Salzburg. 311 pp.
The rhetoric of evil in the plays and the connection between culture and the abuse of language.
MLR 70, 145; *Choice* 10, 1716: "repetitive, obvious, and tiring."

1153. George, Emery. 1973. *Hölderlin's "Ars poetica": A Part-Rigorous Analysis of Information Structure in the Late Hymns.* The Hague: Mouton. 684 pp.
Analysis based on information theory.
MLR 70, 945–46: "impressive."

1154. Godshalk, William. 1973. *Patterning in Shakespearean Drama.* The Hague: Mouton. 199 pp.
An eclectic study of the patterns (image, scene, theme, action, etc.) in 10 plays (e.g., circularity in *Macbeth*).
MLR 70, 391–92: the results are "modest," the readings tending to "lack force and persistence, in spite of the occasional fresh insight"; *Choice* 12, 220.

1155. Hawkes, Terence. 1973. *Shakespeare's Talking Animals: Language and Drama in Society.* Totowa: Rowman; London: Arnold. 247 pp.
The plays express Shakespeare's awareness of the conflicting definitions of language and embody a conception of language in speech as superior to literacy in writing. Name and term index.
YR 64, 432: argument "doubtful," "strained interpretations"; *MLR* 70, 392–94; *Enc* 43, 64; *LJ* 99, 1954; *Choice* 11, 1631.

1156. Heinze, Norbert. 1973. *Zur Gliederungstechnik Hartmanns von Aue: Stilistische Untersuchungen als Beitrag zu einer strukturkritischen Methode* [Hartmann von Aue's Structuring Technique: Stylistic Analysis as a Contribution to a Method of Structural Criticism]. Göppingen: Kümmerle. 281 pp.
On the verbal pointers used to indicate turning points in Hartmann's works.
MLR 70, 455: has strengths but his method is in question.

1157. Hunter, Edwin R. 1973. *William Faulkner: Narrative Practice and Prose Style.* Washington: Windhover. 267 pp.
Part 2, "Prose Style," discusses "clusters," "the retained discard," "negative constructions," rhythm, imagery, and sentences. Name and term index.

Style 10, 127–28: "The whole study lacks focus, point, and cogency"; "poorly conceived, poorly informed, and poorly executed"; *JML* 4, 313; *MFS* 20, 281.

1158.   Johnson, Lee. 1973. *Wordsworth and the Sonnet.* Copenhagen: Rosenkilde. 186 pp.
An analysis of the formal characteristics of the sonnets, which reveal Wordsworth's craftsmanship in his use of the Petrarchan form, syntax, rhyme, etc. Name and term index.
Style 9, 134–38: lacks adequate contexts of Wordsworth's life and times, but "a good deal of useful information is offered" with "thoroughness and patience" and with "few distortions"; *MLR* 70, 396.

1159.   Knight, Stephen. 1973. *Rymyng Craftily: Meaning in Chaucer's Poetry.* London: Angus. 247 pp.
"There is great craft in the way he handles 'metres,' 'rymyng' and other aspects of the poet's art. The purpose of this study is to show how Chaucer often writes with great attention to the detailed working of the poetry in a passage." App. on "The Figures of Style." Name and term index.
Choice 11, 1777: careful, lucid, "more useful than the standard works of Manly or Baldwin"; *AUMLA* 44, 268.

1160.   Lokrantz, Jessie T. 1973. *The Underside of the Weave: Some Stylistic Devices Used By Vladimir Nabokov.* Uppsala: Acta U Upsaliensis. 133 pp.
A discussion mainly of diction — "intrusive voice [of the "author," the "narrauthor," and other narrators], puns, proper names, and patterns of sounds." Bib. 4 pp.
Style 9, 258–59: "short, simple, and clear," "useful," but "does not sufficiently relate these devices to the rest of the particular novel"; *SN* 46, 279.

1161.   Perloff, Marjorie. 1973. *The Poetic Art of Robert Lowell.* Ithaca: Cornell UP. 209 pp.
A study of the "purely literary aspects of the poetry" — imagery, genre, convention, syntax, and tone. The aim is to discriminate between the "permanently valuable" and the "second rate." Name index.
JEGP 73, 270–72: "the book is good — a well-written, first-rate, balanced, and objective study"; *MP* 72, 333; *Enc* 43, 58; *AL* 46, 414; *Comw* 100, 286.

1162.   Peters, Margot. 1973. *Charlotte Brontë: Style in the Novel.* Madison: U of Wisconsin P. 175 pp.
The first 2 chs. stress the role of gramatical and syntactial inversion; chs. 3 and 4 discuss antithesis on multiple levels; and the final ch. demonstrates the importance of legal terminology in *Jane Eyre.* Bib. 6 pp.; name and term index.

Style 9, 139–42: "originality and significance," "shows convincingly how well traditional and linguistic methods combine to illuminate the relationship of form and content, prose style, and the mind of Charlotte Brontë"; *ES* 56, 167–70; *N&Q* 22, 473–74; *MLR* 69, 627; *VS* 17, 343–44; *SNNTS* 6, 371–72; *MLQ* 34, 339–42; *NCF* 28, 360–62; *Centrum* 2, 95–97.

1163. Reed, Joseph, Jr. 1973. *Faulkner's Narrative.* New Haven: Yale UP. 303 pp.
A traditional analysis beginning with a ch. on Faulkner's ideas about story telling, followed by a ch. on short stories, and then chs. on the novels. Name and term index 14 pp.
Style 12, 77–81: several crucial weaknesses, but "may be the definitive treatment."

1164. Ringbom, Håkan. 1973. *George Orwell as Essayist: A Stylistic Study.* Åbo: Acta Acad. Åboensis, ser. A., vol. 44, no. 2. 78 pp.
An analysis that uses Enkvist's approach of a "contextually related norm" and focuses on the series, punctuation and sentence length, and "plus words." Bib. 2 pp. [Admirable critical restraint: "the apparent exactness of the figures and tables in this study is, in many respects, a spurious exactness . . . because the norm chosen, Section G of Kučera-Francis, is far from ideal," etc.]
Style 9, 146–51: "lucid presentation," "excellent beginning"; *MSpr* 67, 380–84; *N&Q* 21, 397.

1165. Silver, Isidore. 1973. *The Intellectual Evolution of Ronsard, 2: Ronsard's General Theory of Poetry.* St. Louis: Washington UP. 478 pp.
A study not only of Ronsard's theoretical statements but also of his poems on poetry and the revisions of his poetry that demonstrate his convictions. Bib. 11 pp.; name and term index.
MLR 71, 916–17: "the considerable positive qualities of this informative study far outweigh the minor methodological weaknesses."

1166. Stamm, Ralf. 1973. *Ludwig Tiecks späte Novellen: Grundlage und Technik des Wunderbaren* [Ludwig Tieck's Late Novellas: Basis and Technique of the Fantastic]. Stuttgart: Kohlhammer. 156 pp.
A study of 8 novellas, tracing the use of variations on the theme of the wondrous (fantastic, etc.).
MLR 71, 471–72: "well-documented and ably-written."

1167. Thole, Bernward. 1973. *Die "Gesänge" in den Stücken Bertolt Brechts: Zur Geschichte und Ästhetik des Liedes im Drama* [The "Songs" in the Plays of Bertolt Brecht: On the History and Aesthetics of the Song in Drama]. Göppingen: Kümmerle. 262 pp.
A study of a major aspect of the epic theater.
MLR 71, 231–32: "a significant contribution to Brecht criticism."

1168.   Burger, Hermann. 1974. *Paul Celan: Auf der Suche nach der verlore-
nen Sprache* [Paul Celan: On the Search for the Lost Language]. Zurich:
Artemis. 149 pp.
A study of Celan's poetic language and his attitudes to language via analysis
of paradox, syntax, imagery, etc., in a limited number of works.
MLR 72, 249–50: "well-balanced and informative," "very persuasive."

1169.   Culler, Jonathan. 1974. *Flaubert: The Uses of Uncertainty*. Ithaca: Cornell UP; London: Elek. 264 pp.
Ch. 1 on the juvenilia; ch. 2 on the 4 uses of uncertainty in Flaubert's mature
work (the way "the mature novels resist recuperation"); ch. 3 on ways Flaubert
manipulates his reader with instances of stupidity and irony. Bib. 2 pp.; name
and term index.
MLR 72, 197–98: "brings to the discussion of literature a new level of
sophistication, but it is not certain that he gives a new coherence to Flaubert";
MLJ 59, 403; *SR* 83, 316; *YR* 64, 266.

1170.   Dentan, Michel. 1974. *C. F. Ramuz: L'espace de la création*. Neuchâtel:
Baconnière. 145 pp.
An analysis of recurrent images, vocabulary, and syntax as they reveal the per-
sonality of Ramuz.
MLR 72, 208: the author goes too far in submerging the characters in Ramuz.

1171.   Elliott, Ralph. 1974. *Chaucer's English*. London: Deutsch. 447 pp.
Ch. 1 on "the more important facts of Chaucer's pronunciation and grammar and a few hints about his prosody." The remaining chs. deal with collo-
quialisms and slang, technical language, literary terms, proper names, oaths,
etc. Ch. 3 "looks at the language of the four prose works," and the final ch.
"probes the question of characterization through language in Chaucer's poetry." Bib. 5 pp.; word index; name and term index.
Style 10, 95–96: "competence and thoroughness" as a Chaucer scholar but
uses "loose" and "casual" procedures; *ES* 57, 258–60.

1172.   Gray, Floyd. 1974. *Rabelais et l'écriture* [Rabelais and Writing]. Paris:
Nizet. 215 pp.
A study of diverse aspects of Rabelais's use of language — e.g., bookish and
everyday languages. Bib. 6 pp.
MLR 72, 176–77: several reservations, but "unusually thought-provoking."

1173.   Huonder, Eugen. 1974. *The Functional Significance of Setting in the
Novels of Francis Scott Fitzgerald*. Bern: Lang; Frankfurt: Lang. 128 pp.
Discusses places of the actions in 4 novels. Bib. 11 pp. [Extremely weak on
the nature of setting, typical of works on setting.]

1174. Levine, Robert. 1974. *A Comparison of Sidney's "Old" and "New Arcadia."* Salzburg: Inst. für Eng. Sprache und Literatur. 122 pp.
Uses the revision to argue that the "New" is an ironic comedy.
MLR 72, 148–49: mixed praise and criticism.

1175. McGowan, Margaret. 1974. *Montaigne's Deceits: The Art of Persuasion in the* Essais. London: London UP. 207 pp.
An attempt to show Montaigne's techniques for engaging and controlling reader response: incomplete or inappropriate titles, suspending arguments with anecdotes, elliptical expressions, reversal of assumptions, dialogue, tone alteration, paradox, etc.
MLR 71, 665–66: "Subtlety of approach does not preclude forceful argument and the book often penetrates to the very core of the *Essais*"; *MLJ* 59, 401; *QJS* 61, 348.

1176. Meir, Colin. 1974. *The Ballads and Songs of W. B. Yeats: The Anglo-Irish Heritage in Subject and Style.* London: Macmillan. 141 pp.
A study of the ways in which Yeats employed linguistic usages current in Ireland among Eng.-speaking people who nevertheless expressed the influence of their Gaelic background.
MLR 71, 152–54: "a welcome contribution to the study of Yeats's earlier verse."

1177. Rexheuser, Adelheid. 1974. *Sinnsuche und Zeichensetzung in der Lyrik des frühen Celan: Linguistische und literaturwissenschaftliche Untersuchungen zu dem Gedichtband* Mohn und Gedächtnis [Search for Sense and Punctuation (Positioning of Signs) in the Early Poetry of Celan: Linguistic and Literary Studies of the Volume *Poppies and Memory*]. Bonn: Bouvier. 201 pp.
A study of metaphors using Brooke-Rose's classification in *Grammar of Metaphor* and a transformational framework.
MLR 72, 251–52: the "very concentration on method" produces "far closer readings" than those of predecessors.

1178. Richard, Jean-Pierre. 1974. *Proust et le monde sensible.* Paris: Seuil. 238 pp.
On descriptions, food, structure, sense impressions, and other aspects of *A la recherche*.
MLR 71, 183–84: "rich study."

1179. Riddel, Joseph. 1974. *The Inverted Bell: Modernism and the Counter Poetics of William Carlos Williams.* Baton Rouge: Louisiana State UP. 308 pp.

An antiformalist, deconstructive reading of Williams's canon. "This is a study in 'poetics,' as distinguished from a study of poetry; a study of neither intentions nor forms, but of the problematic of language and of 'intention.' " Name and term index.

Diacritics 5.2, 24–31: "of great importance for literary criticism now. Perhaps it is even a main task for American criticism in the immediate future"; *MLR* 71, 156–58: "provocative but ultimately exasperating study."

1180.   Romanowski, Sylvie, 1974. *L'illusion chez Descartes: La structure du discours cartésien.* Paris: Klincksieck. 204 pp.
A structuralist and broadly stylistic study of the organization of Descartes's 3 main themes, the chief of which is the theme of illusion.
MLR 71, 669–70: "the author's central contention is somewhat elusive."

1181.   Scheick, William. 1974. *The Will and the Word: The Poetry of Edward Taylor.* Athens: U of Georgia P. 181 pp.
Chs. 1–3 on ideas, ch. 4 on "verbal piety," ch. 5 on the poet's "artistry" — use of metaphor, etc. Final ch. on his mysticism. Bib. 9 pp. Name index. Ch. 4 originally appeared in *Lang&S.*
AL 46, 397: "deucedly difficult to penetrate and appreciate" yet shows "Taylor exceedingly well"; *NEQ* 48, 434; *Choice* 11, 1140; *LJ* 99, 1713.

1182.   Willow, Mary. 1974. *An Analysis of the English Poems of St. Thomas More.* Nieuwkoop: De Graaf. 285 pp.
Examines the prosody, rhetoric, and innovations (from medieval to Renaissance) in More's verse.
AUMLA 46, 298–99: "significant in its own conclusions" but "unnecessarily long and repetitive" and "takes no account of Morean scholarship since the mid nineteen-fifties."

1183.   Bassoff, Bruce. 1975. *Toward Loving: The Poetics of the Novel and the Practice of Henry Green.* Columbia: U of South Carolina P. 179 pp.
A study of the "intrasystemic aspects of the novel, with the fact that novels signify as well as refer" and "a discussion of some of the salient problems one faces in criticism of the novel" through the novels of Green, leading to an analysis particularly of *Loving.* Bib. 7 pp.; name and term index.
Scholes, *Semiotics and Interpretation*: "Insufficiently recognized" as "a pioneering" attempt "to apply semiotic concepts to the analysis of an English novel" (153); *ConL* 18, 110.

1184.   Clark, John W. 1975. *The Language and Style of Anthony Trollope.* London: Deutsch. 238 pp.
Mainly a traditional linguistic study of data in the history of language; the first 6 chs. on how the novels reflect the grammar, slang, dialects, etc., of the times. No index.

Style 12, 386–87: "a storehouse of information" on "how Trollope's novels exemplify the language system," of more interest to philologists than to readers of literature.

1185.   Copeland, Carolyn F. 1975. *Language and Time and Gertrude Stein.* Iowa City: U of Iowa P. 182 pp.
A description of certain representative works that show Stein to be a serious experimentalist with narrators, whose roles developed through distinct formal phases (1903–12, 1913–32, 1932–44). Bib. 4 pp.
Style 11, 217: "not bound by a coherent argument," too impressionistic, and "most of the eight posthumous volumes of Stein" are "missing from the bibliography" and "undiscussed in the text," but valuable for displaying Stein's "devices" of "linguistic expressiveness."

1186.   Ghertman, Sharon. 1975. *Petrarch and Garcilaso: A Linguistic Approach to Style.* London: Támesis. 144 pp.
A structural linguistics syntactical analysis of Garcilaso's first 4 *canciones* and his first eclogue.
MLR 72, 472–73: a disapproving rev.; *RenQ* 30, 92; *MLN* 92, 363.

1187.   Kanes, Martin. 1975. *Balzac's Comedy of Words.* Princeton: Princeton UP. 299 pp.
Part 1, Balzac's ideas about language; part 2, the role of language in the *Comédie humaine*; part 3 an analysis of *Illusions perdues*. Bib. 17 pp.; name and term index.
MLR 72, 698–99: an unfavorable rev.; *Choice* 13, 526: "of interest to Balzac scholars"; *FR* 50, 927; *NCFS* 5, 344; *MFS* 22, 685; *VQR* 53, 160.

1188.   Kimmich, Flora. 1975. *Sonnets of Catharina von Greiffenberg: Methods of Composition.* Chapel Hill: U of North Carolina P. 129 pp.
An evaluative classification of the sonnets into 3 groups according to the quality of integration. Bib. 3 pp.
MLR 72, 741–43: an unfavorable rev.; *GQ* 50, 540: generally unfavorable; *JEGP* 76, 74; *MLN* 92, 627.

1189.   Kuhfuss, Walter. 1975. *Mässigung und Politik: Studien zur politischen Sprache und Theorie Montesquieus* [Moderation and Politics: Studies in Montesquieu's Political Language and Theory]. Munich: Fink. 242 pp.

1190.   Schmaltz, Wiebke. 1975. *Reinmar der Alte: Beiträge zur poetischen Technik* [Reinmar the Older: Contributions to Poetic Technique]. Göppingen: Kümmerle. 258 pp.

A study of recurring linguistic features in the poetry of Reinmar.
MLR 72, 738–39: "very useful contribution to Reinmar studies."

1191.   Stephens, James. 1975. *Francis Bacon and the Style of Science.* Chicago:
         U of Chicago P. 188 pp.
A study of Bacon's tradition and innovation within philosophical unity and
growth. Ch. 1, Bacon's relation to a rhetorical tradition that united rhetoric,
philosophy, and style; chs. 2–3, the development of Bacon's rhetorical theory
for a philosophical style; ch. 4, his use of myth, parable, fable. Name and
term index.
   Style 11: 314–16: "the originality of Stephens lies in his recognizing Bacon's figurative language as a style appropriate to science"; *RSQ* 11, 103–06:
"a well-ordered study . . . based on a host of research"; *JEGP* 76, 129–31
"offers valuable new insights" but "at times . . . frustrating" (first half too
abstract, etc.); *RenQ* 29, 456–58; *MP* 76, 401–03.

1192.   Valentini, Alvaro. 1975. *Lettura di Montale: "Le Occasioni"* [Reading
         Montale: "The Circumstances"]. Rome: Bulzoni. 248 pp.
Explications of the poems of one of Montale's collections, using paraphrase
and semantic analysis mainly.
   MLR 72, 218–19: "over-explanation."

1193.   Bailey, Kenneth. 1976. *Poet and Peasant: A Literary Cultural Approach
         to the Parables in Luke.* Grand Rapids: Eerdmans. 238 pp.
A study of 4 parables by a methodology that combines a delineation of Oriental culture and literary structure. Bib. 12 pp.; name and biblical reference
indexes. [Sequel: *Through Peasant Eyes: More Lucan Parables, Their Culture
and Style.* Grand Rapids: Eerdmans, 1980].
   Style 15, 497–98: "the discussion drags when the author pursues his structural analysis and sparkles with literary insight when it explicates the text within
a framework of Oriental culture."

1193a.   Boos, Florence. 1976. *The Poetry of Dante Gabriel Rossetti: A Critical
         Reading and Source Study.* The Hague: Mouton. 311 pp.
Ch. 1, "Style in 'The House of Life'" (formal development of the sonnets,
characteristic devices, etc.); ch. 2, "Evolution of a Narrative Ballad Style"; etc.
Apps.; bib. 20 pp.; name and term index.
   VS 22, 230: mixed blame and praise, "more often than not, her procedure
leads to illuminating observations."

1194.   Doran, Madeleine. 1976. *Shakespeare's Dramatic Language.* Madison:
         U of Wisconsin P. 253 pp.
8 lectures and articles, 5 of them previously pub. (1 written 13 years earlier,

the app. 34 years earlier), united for a book on distinctive single features of language in individual plays. 2 of the 6 chs. deal with syntax, 2 with rhetorical devices, 1 with diction, and 1 with the effect of linguistic variety.
Style 14, 401–03: "many sensitive" insights, but "without a rigorous enough method of quantitative analysis"; *MLR* 76, 663–64: a "fine collection."

1195.   Franklin, Ursula. 1976. *An Anatomy of Poesis: The Prose Poems of Stéphane Mallarmé*. Chapel Hill: Dept. of Romance Langs., U of North Carolina. 267 pp.
"A detailed analysis of each prose poem" not as a representative of the genre or as a product of the symbolist movement but as whole units in a whole. Bib. 3 pp.
FR 51, 440: "an insightful analysis of a neglected aspect of Mallarmé's creativity."

1196.   Grow, L. M. 1976. *The Prose Style of Samuel Taylor Coleridge*. Salzburg: Inst. für Eng. Sprache und Literatur, U Salzburg. 161 pp.
Describes the development of Coleridge's style and distinguishes between his journalistic and philosophical styles. Separate ch. on *Biographia Literaria*. Bib. 13 pp.
MLR 79, 168–69.

1197.   Kravis, Judy. 1976. *The Prose of Mallarmé: The Evolution of a Literary Language*. London: Cambridge UP. 239 pp.
Examines a selection to show that the prose has poetic effects and "rhythms more subtle than those of poetry."
MLR 74, 703–04: "the general rejection of analytic technique in favour of private response is unnecessary"; *MLN* 92, 869–73: "sometimes unjustifiable intuitive statements" but "lucid" and "lays the foundation for more specific work."

1198.   Nevius, Blake. 1976. *Cooper's Landscapes: An Essay on the Picturesque Vision*. Los Angeles: U of California P. 127 pp.
Cooper employed description and landscape more for picturesque than for sublime effects. Nevius attempts "to identify the distinguishing qualities of Cooper's visual imagination" and "to explain their origins." Name index.
MLR 73, 620: "excellent short study"; *NCF* 31, 230.

1199.   Newman, A. S. 1976. *Une poésie des discours: Essai sur les romans de Nathalie Sarraute* [A Poetry of Discourses: Essay on the Novels of Nathalie Sarraute]. Geneva: Droz. 200 pp.
A formalist, linguistic guide to reading Sarraute.
MLR 75, 415–16: "illuminating."

1200.   Pavel, Thomas. 1976. *La syntaxe narrative des tragédies de Corneille: Recherches et propositions* [The Narrative Syntax of Corneille's Tragedies: Inquiries and Proposals]. Paris: Klincksieck. 159 pp.
Style 12, 402–03: "recommended as an introduction to narratological problems and technique . . . goes into the specific nature of transformations in narrative and . . . deep and surface structures."

1201.   Relyea, Suzanne. 1976. *Signs, Systems, and Meanings: A Contemporary Semiotic Reading of Four Molière Plays.* Middletown: Wesleyan UP. 148 pp.
An attempt "to identify semiotic systems and ways of functioning within and without them in seventeenth-century comedy"; not a "complete analysis of the plays involved" but the identification of "the elements of a specific semiology of meaning inseparable" from certain dramatic characters and a dilemma within Molière. Bib. 3 pp.
    FR 51, 432, and 52, 160: "rewarding," "giant step forward . . . bringing together semiotics and classical theatre"; *Choice* 13, 1606; *LJ* 101, 1860.

1202.   Yeazell, Ruth. 1976. *Language and Knowledge in the Late Novels of Henry James.* Chicago: U of Chicago P. 143 pp.
James's "late style" exhibits the efforts of characters to escape from or transform the facts of the world. Name index. [Cf. Chatman's much more systematic study of this style, no. 1141.]
    Centrum 4, 50–56: "beautifully written."

1203.   Anderson, Charles. 1977. *Person, Place, and Thing in Henry James's Novels.* Durham: Duke UP. 308 pp.
James's characters "arrive at relations only indirectly through the places and things that symbolize what they are and hence reveal their true meanings to each other." A study of 6 of the main novels, omitting *The Golden Bowl.* Name and term index.
    Style 15, 468–71: "a really fine and rewarding book, well-organized, and beautifully written"; *MLR* 75, 639–42.

1204.   Carlson, Patricia A. 1977. *Hawthorne's Functional Settings: A Study of Artistic Method.* Atlantic Highlands: Humanities; Amsterdam: Rodopi. 208 pp.
On the importance of setting and scene to meaning in Hawthorne's writings.
    Style 12, 306–07: "lack of rigorous methodology and . . . indifference to any of the techniques of analysis and classification of fictional processes developed in recent years"; *Choice* 14, 857: a mixed rev., e.g., "usually well written" but "develops what careful readers . . . already know."

1205.   Creighton, Joanne. 1977. *William Faulkner's Craft of Revision.* Detroit: Wayne State UP. 182 pp.

An interpretive study of "the changes that Faulkner made in the process of revision and composition," "the governing purposes which inspired the changes," and "the success or failure of Faulkner's craftmanship," using the Snopes trilogy, *The Unvanquished*, and *Go Down, Moses* for evidence. "My primary objective is to gain insight into the structural designs of these works." Bib. 5 pp.; name index.

Style 14, 186–91: Creighton's approach "seems true to Faulkner's own approach to his art."

1206.   Grabes, Herbert. 1977. *Fictitious Biographies: Vladimir Nabokov's English Novels*. The Hague: Mouton. 140 pp.
A study of allusions, word games, and particularly the relation between fact and fiction.
MFS 25, 515: "there are worse approaches to these novels."

1207.   Graham, Ilse. 1977. *Goethe: Portrait of the Artist*. Berlin: de Gruyter. 381 pp.
An attempt to define the unique quality of Goethe's structuring principle.
MLR 74, 748; *CG* 133, 364; *GQ* 51, 367; *JEGP* 77, 124.

1207a.   Knapp, Peggy A. 1977. *The Style of John Wyclif's English Sermons*. The Hague: Mouton; Berlin: de Gruyter. 116 pp.
A study of the diction, allusions, irony, syntax, allegorical method, metaphor, and rhetoric of the sermons in the context of late 14th-cent. prose.
Spec 54, 161: although some chapters are helpful, ch. 6 on grammar is a "disaster," but the "chief shortcoming" is the "failure to take account of the textual problem"; *RSR* 6, 138.

1208.   Lorenzo-Rivero, Luis. 1977. *Larra: Lengua y estilo* [Larra: Language and Style]. Madrid: Playor. 204 pp.
Chs. on historical and cultural background, vocabulary, figurative language, humor, etc.

1209.   Norrman, Ralf. 1977. *Techniques of Ambiguity in the Fiction of Henry James, with Special Reference to "In the Cage" and "The Turn of the Screw."* Åbo: Åbo Akad. 197 pp.
James employed 2 types of ambiguity—complex and vague. Complex ambiguity operates particularly through "the incomplete reversal," vague through "blanks" or gaps. A key technique is the linguistic or nonlinguistic movement from symbol through repetition or explanation to unambiguous neocode. Another is the extensive use of misunderstandings in conversations. These techniques require the reader to participate actively in the creation of meaning. Bib. 7 pp; critic index.

MLR 76, 938–39: a favorable rev.; *Style* 14, 67–70: cataloguing tedious because of the "and then" format and "the obviousness of many of the devices."

1210.   Regosin, Richard. 1977. *The Matter of My Book: Montaigne's Essais as the Book of the Self.* Berkeley: U of California P. 249 pp.
See especially part 2, which has 3 chs. on Montaigne's attitudes on style.
MLR 75, 656–57: "has the great merit of containing a detailed working out of the implications of self-portraiture."

1211.   Artiss, David. 1978. *Theodor Storm: Studies in Ambivalence, Symbol, and Myth in His Narrative Fiction.* Amsterdam: Benjamins. 215 pp.
Storm's technique of ambivalence produces an ironical style, and much of his fiction was written in a "system of signs and symbols, that . . . enables us to chart his landscapes in almost cartographic terms."
GQ 53, 233: does not define ambivalence and gives only 2 examples to prove his thesis about irony; *MLR* 75, 455–56.

1212.   Fort, Bernadette. 1978. *Le langage de l'ambiguité dans l'oeuvre de Crébillon fils.* [Language of Ambiguity in the Work of Crebillon the Younger]. Paris: Klincksieck. 204 pp.
Examination of words and syntax of the author's writings—clausal embedding, dialogue, ambiguity.
MLR 75, 890: "penetrating analysis of this author's way with words," "brilliant."

1212a. Gasché, Rodolphe. 1978. *System und Metaphorik in der Philosophie von Georges Bataille.* Bern: Lang. 391 pp.
Focuses on myth, image, word, etc., to examine the interrelations of philosophy and literature in selected works by Bataille.
MLN 98, 822: "brings Bataille's works into a clearly essential position with respect to the questioning of boundaries in philosophy and literature."

1213.   Gray, Floyd. 1978. *La poétique de Du Bellay* [The Poetics of Du Bellay]. Paris: Nizet. 166 pp.
A study of the poetic techniques of Du Bellay's sonnets only—naming, rhythm, rhyme, etc.
MLR 75, 883: "the book is worth more than one reading."

1214.   Jeanneret, Michel. 1978. *La lettre perdue: Écriture et folie dans l'oeuvre de Nerval* [The Lost Letter: Writing and Obsession in the Work of Nerval]. Paris: Flammarion. 234 pp.
A study of the recurrent obsessions in some of Nerval's major works and the methods by which he turns them into art.
MLR 76, 472–73: a "work which all university libraries should possess."

1215. Kinney, Arthur. 1978. *Faulkner's Narrative Poetics: Style as Vision*. Amherst: U of Massachusetts P. 286 pp.
Faulkner's organization of narrative consciousness, its roots, techniques, and accomplishments. Part 1 reviews "our current state of knowledge" about the narration of consciousness; part 2 "examines those techniques most recurrent in his body of fiction." Name and term index.
   Style 14, 293–94: has "carefully read Faulkner's work" and "background of sources"; *AL* 51, 287–89; *LJ* 103, 1411.

1216. Lazaridès, Alexandre. 1978. *Valéry: Pour une poétique du dialogue* [Valéry: For a Poetics of Dialogue]. Montreal: P de l'U. 258 pp.
An examination of dialogues by Valéry toward a definition and classification.
   MLR 75, 205: "commendable clarity" except in the final ch. of "systematic ideological critique."

1217. Partridge, A. C. 1978. *John Donne: Language and Style*. London: Deutsch. 259 pp.
An analysis of each of Donne's literary forms. "My objectives have been to adapt linguistic expositions to the merits of style." Bib. 6 pp.; name and term index.
   Choice 16, 1445: a negative rev.; *NS* 97, 368.

1218. Phillipps, K. C. 1978. *The Language of Thackeray*. London: Deutsch. 205 pp. Dist. U.S. and Canada by Westview.
9 chs. provide information about the historical usage of words and grammar and Thackeray's brilliant deployment of that language: "Style," "Regency English in the Victorian Period," "Slang," "Register," "Grammar, Word-Formation, Lexis," "Regional Dialects," "The Language of *Henry Esmond*," "Proper Names," "Modes of Address." Bib. 3 pp.; word index. [The fourth book of a series on the language of 19th-cent. novelists; others on Austen, Trollope, and Dickens.]
   Style 14, 287–88: lacks "unity and system," "too readily generalizes on incomplete evidence," "glances at too many topics," and neglects Thackeray's narrators, but a rich source of historical linguistic information; *Dickensian* 75, 113; *RES* 30, 488, *NCF* 33, 517.

1219. Pinsker, Sanford. 1978. *The Languages of Joseph Conrad*. Amsterdam: Rodopi. 87 pp.
The languages of "the East," "Narration," "the Sea," and "Politics," with a final note on *Victory*. "I have tried to focus on those areas of Conrad's fiction where his doubts about the efficacy of verbal construct were most pronounced. . . . The result is a series of 'languages' which combine subject matter and posture into those identifying characteristics we know as Conrad's *style*."

MFS 25, 298: "well worth reading," "written with good humor and healthy critical cynicism"; *Choice* 15, 1520.

1220.   Porter, Charles. 1978. *Chateaubriand: Composition, Imagination, and Poetry*. Saratoga: Anma Libri. 145 pp.
A study especially of discontinuity in Chateaubriand's writings—i.e., the use of abrupt juxtapositions, ellipsis, etc.
   MLR 76, 970: "excellent contribution" but best on the paragraph, "on less sure ground" in his chs. on larger structural features.

1221.   Regn, Gerhard. 1978. *Konflikt der Interpretationen: Sinnrätsel und Suggestion in der Lyrik Mallarmés* [Conflicting Interpretations: Semantic Riddles and Suggestion in the Poetry of Mallarmé]. Munich: Fink. 268 pp.
Bib. 19 pp.
   RF 93, 273.

1222.   Schackel, Peter. 1978. *The Poetry of Jonathan Swift: Allusion and the Development of a Poetic Style*. Madison: U of Wisconsin P. 218 pp.
A study of Swift's borrowings and allusive range and artistry as a way of describing Swift's development as a poet. Name and term index.
   Style 15, 40–42: the examination of sources is "admirably fulfilled," but the study of allusions is marred by the lack of definition and classification. [See Perri et al., no. 120.]

1223.   Scheick, William. 1978. *The Slender Human Words: Emerson's Artistry in Prose*. Knoxville: U of Tennessee P. 162 pp.
Treats Emerson's essays as "prose poems or prose paintings" organized by central images (called "hieroglyphs"). Part 1 presents Emerson's epistemology and aesthetic; part 2 examines the hieroglyph in 17 essays, concentrating on 3 major hieroglyphs—One Man, Traveling Geographer, and Human Logos. Name and term index. [Named outstanding academic book, *Choice*, May 1979].
   Style 14, 64–66: "a valuable first" examination of Emerson as an artist in prose, though he forces some interpretations and his method "does not account very well for movement within the essays."

1224.   Steele, Peter. 1978. *Jonathan Swift: Preacher and Jester*. Oxford: Clarendon; London: Oxford UP. 252 pp.
On the craft of Swift the satirist in historical context. Bib. 14 pp.; name and term index.
   MLR 75, 163–64: "outstanding" in "critical insight and statement."

1225.   Steiner, Wendy. 1978. *Exact Resemblance to Exact Resemblance: The Literary Portraiture of Gertrude Stein*. New Haven: Yale UP. 225 pp.

A study of the theory of Stein's portraiture (chs. 1–2) divided into 3 chronological phases (ch. 3)—the typologized portraits (1908–11), the visually oriented portraits (1913–25), and the portraits of self-contained movement (last 20 years of her life). Bib. 4 pp.; name and term index.

Style 13, 226–27: "thoughtful and carefully argued."

1226.   Wright, Elizabeth. 1978. *E. T. A. Hoffmann and the Rhetoric of Terror: Aspects of Language Used for the Evocation of Fear*. London: Inst. of Germanic Studies. 307 pp.

An investigation of the uncanny and of the devices used to make the flesh creep, and an attempt to show Hoffmann's control over his materials.

MLR 76, 509–10: "firm grip" on "diverse material" and demonstrates "Hoffmann's control."

1227.   Alkon, Paul. 1979. *Defoe and Fictional Time*. Athens: U of Georgia P. 276 pp.

Analysis of such techniques as reading time and read-about time, memory, narrative sequence, tempo, emblematic time. Name and term index.

MLR 76, 164–65: "shrewd observations."

1228.   Borroff, Marie. 1979. *Language and the Poet: Verbal Artistry in Frost, Stevens, and Moore*. Chicago: U of Chicago P. 198 pp.

A study of authors' voices apprehended in historical and cultural contexts. The first ch., "Words, Language, and Form," explains the theoretical approach exemplified in the essays on individual authors, which focus on diction and syntax. Apps. giving Romance-Latinate, finite verb, and word frequency counts. Bib. 4 pp.; name and term index.

Style 14, 294–95: "a very clear theory of style emerges in conjunction with illustrations of its particular fruits," "brilliantly demonstrates" the many levels of formality in texts; *AL* 52, 495–97; *Choice* 16, 1014; *WLT* 54, 289.

1229.   Cameron, Sharon. 1979. *Lyric Time: Dickinson and the Limits of Genre*. Baltimore: Johns Hopkins UP. 280 pp.

A discussion of about 70 Dickinson poems as illustrative of the lyric, with main focus on time "in a particular body of poetry as it teaches us to be aware of the temporal characteristics of a genre." Name and term index.

Style 17, 65–68: a "bifurcated study of individual and genre" but "densely argued" with "bracing, challenging, searching readings of a range of poems."

1230.   Chothia, Jean. 1979. *Forging a Language: A Study of the Plays of Eugene O'Neill*. Cambridge: Cambridge UP. 242 pp.

The first part of the book sets "O'Neill's search for form and his twenty years of experimentation" within the contexts of the Amer. theater and his private literary interests. "Then, after an examination of the more specifically linguistic contexts of contemporary interest in the American vernacular," the "real critical discourse" begins "with an examination of the language of selected plays from the early and middle years. . . . This examination serves as a prelude to the chapter-length studies of *The Iceman Cometh* and *Long Day's Journey into Night.*" Bib. 11 pp.; name and term index.

CD 14, 374–77: "clarity of observation" often "remarkable"; *RES* 33, 232.

1231.   Eversmann, Susanne. 1979. *Poetik und Erzählstruktur in den Romanen Italo Calvinos* [Poetic Elements and Narrative Structure in the Novels of Italo Calvino]. Munich: Fink. 198 pp.

A wide-ranging study of Calvino's techniques: the dualism of authorial narrative and fictional narrator, allegory, irony, allusion, parody, symbolism, etc.

MLR 76, 979–80: "the most thorough analysis so far of everything Calvino has written," "erudite."

1232.   Franklin, Ursula. 1979. *The Rhetoric of Valéry's Prose "Aubades."* London: U of Toronto P. 151 pp.

Examination of 13 prose poems or poetic prose fragments published by Valéry himself.

MLR 76, 710: "does not entirely fulfill the expectations aroused by its title" but "most rewarding" on "the texture of the Valéryan moment."

1232a.   Groupe d'Entrevernes. 1979. *Analyse sémiotique des textes: Introduction-théorie-pratique.* Lyon: PU de Lyon. 208 pp.

Covers surface structure (narrative sequencing), the discursive component (figures, themes), and deep structures (semantics, isotopic series, semiotic square) and applies the concepts to the story of the Tower of Babel. Term index.

PoT 2, 204–06: "the best introduction to Greimas aside from the works of Greimas himself" but suffers from "information overload" and "epistemological narrowness."

1233.   Jameson, Fredric. 1979. *Fables of Aggression: Wyndham Lewis, the Modernist as Fascist.* Berkeley: U of California P. 190 pp.

The first 4 chs. deal with style, the next 5 with politics. Ch. 1 offers close analysis of selected passages; ch. 2, narrative structure; ch. 3, use of clichés; ch. 4, generalizations about stylistic practices. Name and term index.

Style 16, 87–90: "a highly intelligent and sophisticated piece of criticism, obscured from time to time with billowing clouds of formalist-structuralist rhetoric"; *MLR* 77, 944–45: "stimulating and rewarding."

1234.   Kofman, Sarah. 1979. *Nerval: Le charme de la répétition* [Nerval: The Fascination of Repetition]. Lausanne: L'age d'homme. 124 pp.

1235.   MacCabe, Colin. 1979. *James Joyce and the Revolution of the Word.* London: Macmillan. 186 pp.

A novel-by-novel study of Joyce's politics and the political "use of language," employing ideas and tools provided by a wide range of contemporary linguistic and psychoanalytic critics (Lacan, Derrida, et al.). Bib. 10 pp.; name and term index.

Style 16, 70–72: "a "good example" of how "literary criticism may be served by language analysis" and how both may be employed in "an assessment of Joyce's politics."

1236. Nuiten, Henk. 1979. *Les variantes des* Fleurs du mal *et des "Epaves" de Charles Baudelaire* [Variants of *Fleurs du Mal* and "Epaves" by Charles Baudelaire]. Amsterdam: Holland UP. 432 pp.
An analysis of corrections made for clarity and variants that change the expressive meaning.
MLR 76, 706–07: the "crucial topic" is "excellently treated."

1237. Porter, Joseph. 1979. *The Drama of Speech Acts: Shakespeare's Lancastrian Tetralogy.* Berkeley: U of California P. 208 pp.
A study of "language and speech" in the 4 plays. Bib. 11 pp. (includes a section on "Speech Action"); name and term index.
MLR 78, 137: shows "that modern linguistic approaches can be a literary critical tool of some subtlety"; *CLit* 7, 166; *SR* 88, 447; *Choice* 16, 1174.

1237a. Pozuelo Yvancos, José María. 1979. *El lenguaje poético de la lírica amorosa de Quevedo.* Murcia: Secretariado de Pub. de la U de Murcia. 362 pp.
A study of Quevedo's linguistic innovations in the post-Petrarchan mode of his love poetry, especially in ch. 3 on specific devices—epithets, hyperbaton, etc.
MLR 78, 210–11: a "pioneering work, but marred" in various ways.

1238. Schlack, Beverly. 1979. *Continuing Presences: Virginia Woolf's Use of Literary Allusion.* University Park: Pennsylvania State UP. 195 pp.
Woolf's use of the literary allusion is significantly appropriate to her "indirect, inferential, and ambiguous" style. Bib. 3 pp.; name index.
CLit 8, 103: "a useful reference tool"; *HR* 32, 540; *SNNTS* Summer 1980, 179.

1239. Sykes, Stuart. 1979. *Les romans de Claude Simon.* Paris: Minuit. 195 pp.
A chronological survey particularly of the spatial form of the novels.
MLR 77, 219–20: a "worthy complement" to Loubere's earlier book.

1240. Walker, Keith. 1979. *La cohésion poétique de l'oeuvre césairienne* [Poetic Cohesion in the Work of Césaire]. Tübingen: Narr; Paris: Place. 140 pp.
ECr 21, 108: "convincing," "welcome addition to Césaire scholarship."

1241.   Baxter, John. 1980. *Shakespeare's Poetic Styles: Verse into Drama*. London: Routledge. 255 pp.
Focuses on *Richard II* and the 2 main styles available to Shakespeare — "plain" and "eloquent". Name and term index.
MLR 78, 137–39: "keen sense of the strong subtleties of Shakespeare's dramatic verse," yet follows an obfuscating critical method.

1242.   Edwards, Philip, et al., eds. 1980. *Shakespeare's Styles: Essays in Honour of Kenneth Muir*. Cambridge: Cambridge UP. 247 pp.
16 essays, mainly on the early and the late plays, with particular analysis of the matter of language, sincerity, and context. Name index.
AUMLA 58, 198–200: "an important collection" even though the "mature comedies and major tragedies" are neglected, "the final three essays do not concern themselves with style," and the definition of style is treated loosely; *MLR* 78, 136–37: "several contributors" need the "sharper instruments and more precise vocabulary" that "modern linguistic approaches" provide.

1242a.   Gerstenberg, Renate. 1980. *Zur Erzähl-Technik von Günter Grass*. Heidelberg: Winter. 194 pp.
This chronological study of Grass's narrative techniques examines syntax, perspectives, and time as bases for explication of texts.
GQ 57 335–36: "deals successfully with a very difficult subject" but "reads rather tediously."

1243.   Janus, Dieter. 1980. *"Pervenci": Untersuchungen zur Sprache der frühen Lyrik von Petar Preradović* ["Pervenci": A Study of the Language in the Early Poetry of Peter Preradović]. Frankfurt am Main: Lang. 244 pp.
A study of the first collection of poems by Preradović.
Slavia 50, 229.

1244.   Kritzman, Lawrence. 1980. *Destruction/Découverte: Le fonctionnement de la rhétorique dans les* Essais *de Montaigne* [Destruction/Discovery: The Function of Rhetoric in the *Essays* of Montaigne]. Lexington: French Forum. 184 pp.
Through fragments, antitheses, etc., Montaigne undermined the linear movement traditionally expected in essays.
MLR 78, 178–79: "a very rewarding experience."

1245.   Simons, Madeleine. 1980. *Sémiotisme de Stendhal* [The "Semiotism" of Stendhal]. Geneva: Droz. 335 pp.
On Stendhal's understanding of language as signs.
MLR 76, 970–71: "probably . . . the most successful attempt till now to bring to the study of Stendhal the linguistic and historical insights of the new semiology."

1246. Sprinker, Michael. 1980. *"A Counterpoint of Dissonance": The Aesthetics and Poetry of Gerard Manley Hopkins.* Baltimore: Johns Hopkins UP. 149 pp.
Chs. on Hopkins's aesthetics, theory of language, problematic of writing, "The Wreck of the Deutschland," and late poems. Introd. on "The Windhover" as a specimen of the author's "strategy of reading" Hopkins. A poststructuralist approach inspired by Derrida and especially Harold Bloom. Name index.
JEGP 81, 139: "will spark debate"; *VS* 25, 102; *CLit* 9, 73.

1246a. Tucker, Herbert, Jr. 1980. *Browning's Beginnings: The Art of Disclosure.* Minneapolis: U of Minnesota P. 257 pp.
A study of Browning's addiction to anticipation: "He kept beginning . . . in the course of any one of his distinctly nervous poems." And this formal method derives from his moral doctrine of incompleteness. "From the formal effects of its largest structures to the minutiae of its verbal style, Browning's is . . . an art that resists its own finalities" by prolonging action and deferring climax. Focuses on early poems and plays, with some attention to the dramatic poems of the middle years. Bib. 3 pp.; name and term index.
JEGP 81, 444: "the most challenging and perceptive book-length analysis of Browning's poetry to appear in recent years"; *HR* 34, 416; *SAQ* 81, 239; *Choice* 18, 1267.

1247. Tulloch, Graham. 1980. *The Language of Walter Scott: A Study of His Scottish and Period Language.* London: Deutsch. 351 pp.
A study especially of the vocabulary and grammar of the period language in Scott's historical novels that occur outside Scotland and of "Scots" in the Scottish novels. Bib. 5 pp.; term and word indexes.
Style 15, 461–62: "very thorough," "underlines how clever and inventive . . . was Scott."

1248. Béchade, Hervé. 1981. *Les romans comiques de Charles Sorel: Fiction narrative, langue, et langages* [The Comic Novels of Charles Sorel: Narrative Fiction, Speech, and Languages]. Geneva: Droz. 333 pp.
A study of the evolution of Sorel's narrative techniques and an analysis of his use of language to portray the various social classes in early 17th-cent. France.
MLR 78, 183–84: the second part of the study is "original," "the first complete and well-researched treatment of this aspect of Sorel's writings."

1248a. Birgander, Pia. 1981. *Boris Vian romancier: Etude des techniques narratives.* Lund: Etudes romanes de Lund. 230 pp.
A computational study of the vocabulary and syntax of Vian's works.
MFS 28, 712: "an unpalatable, dry, difficult-to-follow, and generally unsatisfying text."

1249.   Burnett, Archie. 1981. *Milton's Style: The Shorter Poems,* Paradise
Regained, *and* Samson Agonistes. London: Longman. 187 pp.
Each poem is discussed "on its own terms," i.e., with no "single principle
of analysis," except for attention to "adjective usage." No introd. or conclusion. App. on problems of definition and quantification as evidence; strongly
attacks previous studies by Miles and Emma on Milton's use of adjectives. Name
and term index.
   RenQ 36, 482–84: too limited to grammatical style and overstates the "fruitfulness of quantitative analysis," but "much" readers can learn about Milton; *Style* 18, 111; *BBN* June 1982, 380; *TES* 15 Apr. 1983, 32.

1249a.   Cottrell, Robert. 1981. *Sexuality-Textuality: A Study of the Fabric of Montaigne's* Essais. Columbus: Ohio State UP. 182 pp.
An evolutionary approach to the essays, stressing the chronological layers of
the text's composition from masculine to feminine valorization.
   MLN 98, 815: "intelligent, scholarly, valiant attempt to operate in a new
and still somewhat undigested critical mode"; *CL* 35, 70–75: a negative rev.

1249b.   Doyle, Mary. 1981. *The Sympathetic Response: George Eliot's Fictional
Rhetoric.* Rutherford: Fairleigh Dickinson UP. 183 pp.
Eliot selects and "manages" her fictional materials to "produce the desired
effects of understanding and sympathy" in her readers. Doyle examines the
rhetoric in 5 novels "with a focus on her increasing achievement of right distance according to the requirements of the formal whole." Bib. 5 pp.; name
and term index.
   NCF 38, 112: "a thin, intelligent, and old-fashioned Aristotelian reading."

1250.   Egan, James. 1981. *The Inward Teacher: Milton's Rhetoric of Christian
Liberty.* University Park: Pennsylvania State UP. 99 pp.
Correlates Milton's choice of logic, genre, and language with his particular
audience and traces the development of his prose styles within "the oration,
the disputation, the history, and the sermon."
   Style 15, 476–77: Egan's "new correlation" of the development of Milton's
styles with his personal development "recommends" the book.

1250a.   Gilman, Stephen. 1981. *Galdós and the Art of the European Novel:
1867–1887.* Princeton: Princeton UP. 413 pp.
A study of Galdós's novels written during the 20 year span of the title, focusing particularly on *Fortunata y Jacinta.*
   CL 35, 186–91: "one of the major contributions to our knowledge of Galdós
the novelist"; *MLN* 98, 311: a "dense and highly original study" from which
we emerge "with an immensely richer insight into the art of narration"; *MP*
81, 94.

1251.   Hermann, John, and John Burke, Jr., eds. 1981. *Signs and Symbols in Chaucer's Poetry*. University: U of Alabama P. 257 pp.
9 essays on the meaning of simple signs from everyday life in Chaucer's poetry, on particular signs with larger meanings, Chaucer's musical references, etc. Name and term index.
   MP 81, 407: all the essays "deal with matters of importance"; *RES* 35, 357.

1252.   Horton, Susan. 1981. *The Reader in the Dickens World: Style and Response*. Pittsburgh: U of Pittsburgh P. 136 pp.
An attempt to identify the structural and stylistic causes of the complex feelings of surprise, puzzlement, delight, etc., prompted in readers of Dickens's novels. The vision of the world as moral and rational presented by the narrator is contradicted by the images of suffering humanity. Name index.
   SR 90, 83–89; *Choice* 18, 1416: "mainly a series of uneven and ununified essays that say mostly obvious . . . things"; *VS* 26, 93.

1253.   Kars, Hendrik. 1981. *Le portrait chez Marivaux: Étude d'un type de segment textuel: Aspects métadiscursifs, définitionnels, formels* [The Portrait in Marivaux: Study of a Type of Textual Segment: Aspects Metadiscursive, Definitional, Formal]. Amsterdam: Rodopi. 252 pp.
Ch. 2 offers a definition of "portrait"; ch. 3 examines the techniques of the portrait (placement in context, internal syntax, etc.). Name and term index.
   MLR 77, 725–26: "rich fund of documentation" but sometimes "remorselessly laborious" and "no really firm conclusions are arrived at."

1254.   Kirschke, James. 1981. *Henry James and Impressionism*. Troy: Whitston. 333 pp.
Traces "possible Impressionist influences" on James. Ch. 1, impressionist techniques in visual and plastic arts; ch. 2, possible Continental literary sources; ch. 3, British and U.S. influences; ch. 4, the relations between James's theory of fiction and impressionism. Bib. 20 pp.; name index.
   MFS 28, 290: "well worth reading" but needs to place James in "a larger context"; *MP* 81, 207; *Choice* 19, 626.

1255.   Kucich, John. 1981. *Excess and Restraint in the Novels of Charles Dickens*. Athens: U of Georgia P. 290 pp.
A study of the tension between the excesses of Dickens's language, sentimentality, and melodrama and the rigid social restraints to thought and action that he acknowledged. The author bases his analysis on a model of the psyche derived from Roland Barthes, Norman O. Brown, Morse Peckham, and especially Georges Bataille. He concentrates on *The Old Curiosity Shop*, *Bleak House*, *A Tale of Two Cities*, and *Great Expectations*. Ch. 6, "Mechanical Style," on the tension between satire and parody. Name and term index.
   VQR 58, 117; *VS* 26, 459; *Choice* 19, 1401: "stimulating."

1256.   Lambert, Mark. 1981. *Dickens and the Suspended Quotation*. New Haven: Yale UP. 208 pp.
The direct quotation split by an authorial utterance was a favorite device of Victorian novelists and particularly of Dickens. The author connects this minor device to such larger subjects as the personality of Dickens and the difference between the early novels and the late. Name and term index.
 MLR 78, 164–66: "his ingenuity does not seem to work"; *Choice* 19, 80: "not very persuasive in substantiating his major premise"; *CL* 35, 85.

1257.   Minogue, Valerie. 1981. *Nathalie Sarraute and the War of the Words*. Edinburgh: Edinburgh UP. 225 pp.
Sarraute's war against stereotypes in language, focusing mainly on her first 5 novels.
 MLR 77, 466–67: "an excellent introduction"; *MFS* 27, 651; *WLT* 56, 485.

1258.   Porter, David. 1981. *Dickinson: The Modern Idiom*. Cambridge: Harvard UP. 316 pp.
A study of the composition and revision of the poems to get at her unique "otherness"—"the intense concentration, the surprise of her violations of selectional rules, the short aggressive lines that catch motion, the intimacy of the voice, the polysyllabic tours de force, the linguistic control over destructive emotions, the metonymic deftness. . . ." Name index.
 Critm 24, 87: "that rare thing, an excitingly written, carefully thought-out critical judgement"; *AL* 54, 298; *TLS* 26 Mar. 1982, 357.

1258a.   Veldman, Hendrik. 1981. *Tentation de l'inaccessible: Structures narratives chez Simenon*. Amsterdam: Rodopi. 272 pp.
A Proppian, "functions" analysis of the plots of 35 novels and an analysis of the narrative stances of the novels based on Genette and Mieke Bal.
 MLR 78, 197–98: "shows that simplified structuralist tools are useful expository devices, but it does not quite bring Simenon . . . back to literary life."

1259.   Abel, Elizabeth, ed. 1982. *Writing and Sexual Difference*. Chicago: U of Chicago P. 324 pp.
Essays originally pub. in *CritI* on how gender informs and complicates both the writing and the reading of texts, how attitudes toward sexual difference generate and structure literary texts, and how critical methods can effectively disclose traces of gender in literature.
 WCRB 9, 59; *Nat* 237, 183; *MLR* 79, 879.

1260.   Casagrande, Peter. 1982. *Unity in Hardy's Novels: "Repetitive Symmetries."* Lawrence: Regents P of Kansas. 249 pp.

An attempt to establish "two basic patterns" in the fiction: return and restoration. Bib. 4 pp.; name and term index.

BBN July 1982, 442; *SR* 90, 313; *Choice* 20, 82.

1261.   Corns, Thomas. 1982. *The Development of Milton's Prose Style.* Oxford: Clarendon. 118 pp.
Computerized attempt to define what is "really unique" to Milton and "how his style changes," by comparing his writing "against contemporary stylistic norms for the same genre": "I compare each group of Miltonic tracts with pamphlets by other writers contributing to the same controversies." Bib. 4 pp.; name index.

RenQ 36, 479–82: data excessively isolated from subject and meaning.

1261a.   Crow, Christine. 1982. *Paul Valéry and the Poetry of Voice.* Cambridge: Cambridge UP. 302 pp.
Close examinations of each of the poems in his main collection, *Charmes,* including a 36-pp. analysis of "Le cimetière marin."

MLR 78, 720: "in conception . . . an exciting book" but "falls short of its aspirations"; *Choice* 20, 273: "important"; *WLT* 57, 245.

1262.   Fabricant, Carole. 1982. *Swift's Landscape.* Baltimore: Johns Hopkins UP. 307 pp.
A study of "the actual features of his physical surroundings and the idiosyncratic, highly distinctive way in which he perceived them," a "pervasively *political* landscape." Name and term index.

Choice 20, 1136: "continually interesting, fresh, and absolutely essential to the serious student"; *LJ* 108, 131.

1262a.   Fitch, Brian. 1982. *The Narcissistic Text: A Reading of Camus' Fiction.* Toronto: U of Toronto P. 128 pp.
A study of the self-reflexive, intertextual, intratextual "act of quoting" in *L'étranger, La peste,* and *La chute.*

MFS 28, 713: corroborates the "already shown thematic quoting"; *MLR* 78, 723; *RSR* 9, 166.

1263.   Harper, Howard. 1982. *Between Language and Silence: The Novels of Virginia Woolf.* Baton Rouge: Louisiana State UP. 346 pp.
A phenomenological approach to the "narrative consciousness" in its search for escape from conformity and its recognition of the importance of silence. The novels are concerned primarily with "perception and expression" in a style that sometimes approaches "expressionism." Bib. 3 pp.

MFS 29, 287: "first-rate readings" particularly of the openings of the novels; *VQR* 59, 88; *LJ* 107, 1326.

1264.   Helsinger, Elizabeth. 1982. *Ruskin and the Art of the Beholder.* Cambridge: Harvard UP. 424 pp.
Part 1, "Looking at Landscapes"; part 2, "Looking at Art." Examines the reforms in perception Ruskin's first work effected and the part Ruskin played in the development of a new aesthetic tradition.
Choice 20, 414: "greatly enriches one's understanding of how Ruskin's aesthetic perceptions and prose style evolved"; *LJ* 107, 1745; *TLS* 22 Oct. 1982, 1153.

1265.   Houston, John P. 1982. *The Shape and Style of Proust's Novel.* Detroit: Wayne State UP. 141 pp.
"Style is an absolute manner of seeing things for Proust, a question of vision, and so constitutes the ultimate reality of literature. My argument therefore builds up to a long examination of Proust's verbal art" (40 pp.). Part 1 on intellectual structure, part 2 on techniques (e.g., point of view), part 3 on verbal texture. Name and term index.
Choice 20, 273: "careful" and "intelligent," though sometimes "pedantic"; *FR* 57, 562: "clearly and gracefully written" mainly "to the undergraduate or lay reader"; *MLR* 79, 201.

1266.   Lonoff, Sue. 1982. *Wilkie Collins and His Victorian Readers: A Study in the Rhetoric of Authorship.* New York: AMS. 298 pp.
"Like his fellow novelists, he was conscious of a bond between himself and his readers, and that consciousness affected every aspect of his novels, from format to content to significance." Bib. 17 pp.; name and term index. [This book could be classified under 6.0; it suggests a rich field of author-audience research.]
NCF 37, 610: "thoroughly researched and written with vigor and clarity"; *VS* 27, 247; *Choice* 20, 986.

1267.   Matthews, John. 1982. *The Play of Faulkner's Language.* Ithaca: Cornell UP. 278 pp.
An attempt to redefine Faulkner's artistic significance through an approach based on Derrida's critique of the metaphysics of presence. "I hope to show that Faulkner's major fiction elevates fabrication over representation . . . and celebrates the playfulness of writing in space (or play) between the written and the written about." Name index.
Critm 25, 80–82: "closely reasoned, exciting, and often illuminating," but "several minor and two major flaws" weaken the book; *MFS* 28, 676: "uses Derrida's concepts with tact and discernment" for "close and careful readings of Faulkner's texts"; *TLS* 14 Jan. 1983, 43.

1268.   Packman, David. 1982. *Vladimir Nabokov: The Structure of Literary Desire.* Columbia: U of Missouri P. 122 pp.

Nabokov's 3 major novels in Eng. (*Lolita, Pale Fire,* and *Ada*) "are reflexive considerations of the literary game." A study of "the play-element" in the novels. Bib. 4 pp.; name index.

Choice 20, 1130: "gracefully written" but not as profound as Maurice Couturier's similar 1979 Fr. study, *Nabokov;* "a useful primer on deconstruction" but "little substance as a critical study of Nabokov"; *MFS* 29, 736.

1269. Trousdale, Marion. 1982. *Shakespeare and the Rhetoricians.* Chapel Hill: U of North Carolina P. 206 pp.

Because Shakespeare and his contemporaries distinguished words from things, their fictions were consciously structured verbal artifices "creating an almost bewildering sense of possible significances." Name index.

CL 35, 180–82: superior to Brian Vickers's *Classical Rhetoric in English Poetry* and *The Artistry of Shakespeare,* and in spite of several problems the book's thesis is "persuasive"; *Choice* 19, 1562: "a difficult book—full of technical language and old-spelling quotations . . . but it is well worth the effort"; *TLS* 8 Oct. 1982, 1110.

1269a. Wetherill, P. M., ed. 1982. *Flaubert: La dimension du texte.* Manchester: Manchester UP. 272 pp.

9 papers from a 1980 conference on such topics as theme, description, realism, and coherence.

MLR 78, 190–91: "an absorbing array of contributions."

1270. Blake, N. F. 1983. *Shakespeare's Language: An Introduction.* New York: St. Martin's. 154 pp.

A guide to the language of Shakespeare and his contemporaries—varieties, vocabulary, grammar, and syntax. Bib. 3 pp.; table of passages quoted (all from Shakespeare).

Choice 21, 418: "a sensible introduction" but also "valuable to advanced students"; *TES* 30 Dec. 1983, 22.

1271. Deleted.

1271a. Finneran, Richard. 1983. *Editing Yeats's Poems.* New York: St. Martin's. 144 pp.

On the problems of establishing a definitive ed. of the poems. Name index.

1271b. Fleishman, Avrom. 1983. *Figures of Autobiography: The Language of Self-Writing in Victorian and Modern England.* Berkeley: U of California P. 486 pp.

The introd. discusses such issues as truth, meaning, myth, and convention. Part 1 deals with "traditional figures": Augustinian, spiritual, and Romantic. Parts 2–5 discuss individual writers: Carlyle, Mill, Newman, Ruskin,

Dickens, C. Brontë, G. Eliot, Butler, Yeats, Sassoon, O'Casey, Muir, Lawrence, Joyce, Richardson, Woolf. Name and term index.
CC 100, 378: a "basic volume"; *Choice* 20, 1596; *LJ* 108, 500.

1272.   Gordon, Lois. 1983. *Robert Coover: The Universal Fiction-Making Process.* Carbondale: Southern Illinois UP. 192 pp.
An introd. to Coover's variety of forms and styles, especially his transposition of traditional literary forms and genres and forms from other art forms, such as film montage or operatic interlude. Coover's method is to counterpoint (his musical term is "descants") with numerous mythic, legendary, or symbolic levels "which serve to explode any final meaning or resting point." Bib. 3 pp.; name index.
AL 55, 492: "first complete study" of Coover, "detailed analyses"; *Choice* 21, 276.

1272a. Hily-Mane, Genevieve. 1983. *Le style de Ernest Hemingway: La plume et le masque.* Paris: PUF. 356 pp.

1273.   McCarthy, Mary S. 1983. *Balzac and His Reader: A Study of the Creation of Meaning in* La comédie humaine. Columbia: U of Missouri P. 155 pp.
Balzac's strategies for shaping his readers' responses: metaphor, description, structure (a short story), and the "reappearing character." Bib. 4 pp.; name and term index.
AR 41, 372: a favorable rev.

1274.   Moorjani, Angela. 1983. *Abysmal Games in the Novels of Samuel Beckett.* Chapel Hill: U of North Carolina P. 166 pp.
Uses deconstructive theories and recent studies on narratology to examine the novels' broken symmetries, repetitions, gaps, and discontinuities. "This essay . . . analyzes how Beckett's novels undermine textual linearity, on the one hand, and the myths of self-transparency, on the other, by turning words into toys, writing into abysmal play." Bib. 15 pp.

1275.   Quilligan, Maureen. 1983. *Milton's Spenser: The Politics of Reading.* Ithaca: Cornell UP. 256 pp.
An examination of *The Faerie Queene* and *Paradise Lost* in an attempt to define the means by which they move their readers to make ethical and political choices — how they make rhetorical appeals to their readers, how they address readers specifically in terms of their gender, etc.

1275a. Ruppersburg, Hugh. 1983. *Voice and Eye in Faulkner's Fiction.* Athens: U of Georgia P. 189 pp.
Narrative viewpoint and structure in 4 novels: *Light in August, Pylon, Absa-*

lom, Absalom!, and *Requiem for a Nun.* Faulkner employs point of view "in a way more complex . . . than any other successful novelist of the English language." Bib. 5 pp.; name and term index 8 pp.
SR 92, 474: "a first-rate study," "thoroughly accurate"; *MFS* 30, 319.

1275b.   Wallace, Robert. 1983. *Jane Austen and Mozart: Classical Equilibrium in Fiction and Music.* Athens: U of Georgia P. 320 pp.
Compares 3 Austen novels with 3 Mozart piano concertos.
GaR 38, 621: "ingenuity," but "only dimly does it illuminate the texts of Jane Austen."

1276.   Wooten, Cecil. 1983. *Cicero's "Philippics" and Their Demosthenic Model: The Rhetoric of Crisis.* Chapel Hill: U of North Carolina P. 199 pp.
An analysis of Cicero's use of Demosthenes in creating the style and narrative techniques of his most mature speeches. In the process he defines a type of oratory that he terms "the rhetoric of crisis." Name index.
QJS 70, 483: "a model for critical studies proposing to show the influence of someone on someone else."

1276a.   Elliott, Ralph. 1984. *Thomas Hardy's English.* Oxford: Blackwell; London: Deutsch. 384 pp.
Primarily on Hardy's vocabulary but also examines his syntax and pronunciation. Bib. and "Index of Words."
Choice 22, 554: "succeeds admirably" in showing how "effectively Hardy drew upon the rich resources of the English language"; *BBN* Oct. 1984, 627; *TLS* 3 Aug. 1984, 860.

1276b.   Hartwig, Joan. 1984. *Shakespeare's Analogical Scene: Parody as Structural Syntax.* Lincoln: U of Nebraska P. 243 pp.
A study of how the interludes with minor characters comment on their neighboring long scenes particularly through parody. Chs. on *Macbeth, Romeo & Juliet, Richard II, Twelfth Night,* and *Hamlet.* Name and term index 10 pp.

1276c.   Keach, William. 1984. *Shelley's Style.* London: Methuen. 269 pp.
Examines Shelley's ideas of language and the relation to his practice of writing. Ch. 1 on *A Defence of Poetry*, chs. 2–4 on imagery, 5 on speed, 6 on rhyme, 7 "Shelley's Last Lyrics." Works discussed and name and term indexes.

1276d.   Olken, I. T. 1984. *With Pleated Eye and Garnet Wing: Symmetries of Italo Calvino.* Ann Arbor: U of Michigan P. 157 pp.
Chs. on structural, thematic, natural symmetry, concentrating on the trilogy *I nostri antenati* (1960). No bib. or index.
WHR 38, 301: "a necessary" but "naive guide," tending to be "somewhat conservative, linear, mechanical."

5.0 Individual Choice: The Text (1277–434)

5.1 Theory (1277–89)

1277.   Meschonnic, Henri. 1970–75. *Pour la poétique* [For Poetics]. Paris: Gallimard. Vol. 1: *Essai* [An Essay]. 1970. 178 pp. Vol. 2: *Epistemologie de l'écriture, poétique de la traduction* [Epistemology of Writing, Poetics of Translation]. 1973. 458 pp. Vol. 3: *Une parole écriture* [The Written Word]. 1973. 342 pp. Vol. 4: *Le signe et le poème* [The Sign and the Poem]. 1975. 547 pp.
   Style 8, 101–05 (of first 3 vols.): For Meschonnic, "style is the whole system of the work, inseparable from its signification"; thus "monism is the dynamic core" of his thought; "Meschonnic plays an important part in the renewal of . . . literary study in France"; *Ling* 121, 120–21 (in Fr., on vol. 1).

1278.   Dijk, Teun van. 1972. *Some Aspects of Text Grammars: A Study in Theoretical Linguistics and Poetics*. The Hague: Mouton. 375 pp.
   "The aim of this book is to present a provisional framework for the theoretical description of discourse. The formal device needed for such a description will be called a 'Text Grammar' as distinguished from the current type of generative-transformational 'Sentence Grammars.' . . . Especially the role of linguistics in literary scholarship (poetics) is crucially linked with an explicit insight into the structure of texts." The second half of the book discusses generative poetics and a theory of metaphor. Bib. 9 pp.; name and term indexes. [Van Dijk's *Text and Context*, no. 1284, corrects and extends this book.]
   Diacritics 7.4, 34–46: "For those involved in the critical fields that opened or reopened recently (reader criticism, hermeneutics, phenomenology of reading), van Dijk's book is both a solid foundation and gold mine of suggestions. The shafts may be hard to open — but they reach a motherlode, out of which scores of books are yet to come"; *FdL* 14, 207–15, *Centrum* 1, 155–64; *Ling* 141, 72–75.

1279.   Petöfi, János, and Hannes Rieser, eds. 1973. *Studies in Text Grammar*. Dordrecht: Reidel. 348 pp.
   7 essays "of recent linguistic research which aim at the description of discourses and at the development of a formal theory." Bib. (following most of the essays).
   Ling 188, 81–88: "will provide a number of theoretical principles for the study of concrete problems"; *Spektator* 4, 377–82; *LeS* 11, 636–38; *JOP* 1, 177–92.

1280.   Cluysenaar, Anne. 1975. *Aspects of Literary Stylistics*. 1976. New York: St. Martin's. 160 pp.
   Pub. in London as *Introduction to Literary Stylistics: A Discussion of Domi-*

nant Structures in Verse and Prose. Critics using linguistics to analyze literary texts ought to study "texts as wholes" (i.e., the dominant structures and unity). The author uses the scale and category grammar of British linguistics, involving analysis of the frequency and distribution of stylistic features within the various linguistic levels and within the total structure as those features function as communication and aesthetically. Term and name indexes.

Style 11, 420–22: The book "does not provide a literary critical framework in which to place the stylistic analysis," but "the strengths . . . are considerable," "some excellent analyses of literary texts"; *PTL* 1, 597–98; *Lore&L* 2.5, 53; *LJ* 101, 1531; *Choice* 13, 1286.

1281.   Grimes, Joseph. 1975. *The Thread of Discourse.* The Hague: Mouton. 408 pp.
The result of workshops in 7 countries to explain how "we can use linguistic tools to understand the way complete discourses go together." Bib. 15 pp.; name and term index.
JL 13, 320–21: "valuable and stimulating survey"; *Lang* 53, 956–59.

1282.   Mistrík, Josef. 1975. *Štruktúra textu* [The Structure of the Text]. Bratislava: Ceskoslovenský rozhlas. 91 pp.

1283.   Petöfi, János. 1975. *Vers une théorie partielle du texte* [Toward a Partial Theory of the Text]. Hamburg: Buske. 148 pp.
Bib. 15 pp.
CLing 22, 117–19.

1284.   Dijk, Teun van. 1977. *Text and Context: Explorations in the Semantics and Pragmatics of Discourse.* London: Longman. 261 pp. (Span. trans., Madrid: Catedra, 1980; Ital. trans., Bologna: Il Mulino, 1981).
An examination of the methods of linguistic analysis that transcend the sentence level. "I am acutely aware of the weaknesses" of *Some Aspects of Text Grammars* (1972). "The present study therefore aims at providing some corrections by a more explicit and more systematic approach." Each of the 2 parts begins with a ch. giving theoretical background. Part 1 on semantics—formal or logical semantics, connection and connectives, coherence, macro-structures; part 2 on pragmatics—theory of action, speech acts, macro-speech acts. Bib. 7 pp.; term index.
Ling 19, 190–95: "an important stage in the development of text linguistics," "students of style will profit much," "many merits"; *LB* 68, 242–47; *Zagadnienia Informacji Naukowej* 1979.1, 152–61; *NJL* 2, 61–62; *ES* 60, 824–27; *BSLP* 74, 81–83; *LeS* 13, 586–88.

1285.   Riffaterre, Michael. 1978. *Semiotics of Poetry.* Bloomington: Indiana UP. 213 pp.

An exploration of the ways indirection and ungrammaticalness direct meaning and mediate reality. A "semiotic" approach because "the unit of meaning peculiar to poetry is the finite, closed entity of the text." Ch. 1, "The Poem's Significance" (the formal and semantic unity in contrast to mimetic information); ch. 2, "Sign Production"; ch. 3, "Text Production" (a poem develops by "hypogrammatic" derivation—a succession of variations generated by its initial [usually unexpressed] *datum* or "matrix"). Bib. 4 pp.; name and term index.

Style 15, 72–74: "This is a very important book—necessary reading for anyone concerned with the devices of poetic language"; *Centrum* ns 1, 36–47 (article illustrated by a poem by Emily Dickinson); *Diacritics* 11.3, 13–26; *SR* 87, 628–38; *CL* 33, 74–76; *Lang* 56, 456–58; *RR* 71, 197–201; *MLJ* 63, 229–30; *MLN* 94, 1199–202.

1286.   Petőfi, János, ed. 1979. *Text vs. Sentence: Basic Questions of Text Linguistics.* Hamburg: Buske. 2 vols., 341 and 247 pp.
46 papers that respond to the ed.'s 5 questions dealing with the basic issues in the field of text linguistics: What constitutes a text? What are the tasks of text linguistics?, etc. Mainly in Eng. 1 essay is about "Stylistics within the Interdisciplinary Framework of Text Linguistics" (in vol. 2). Bib. (references follow each essay).

1287.   Beaugrande, Robert de. 1980. *Text, Discourse, and Process: Toward a Multidisciplinary Science of Texts.* Norwood: Ablex. 351 pp.
1 of a series of vols. from diverse disciplines "which share a common interest in discourse . . . prose comprehension and recall, dialogue analysis, text grammar construction," etc. Beaugrande defines texts as "meaningful configurations of language intended to communicate" and argues that "text linguistics would constitute the *verbal domain of semiotics*, dealing with the entire range from one-word texts (e.g., 'Fire!') to texts as vast as *The Divine Comedy.*" 9 chs.: "Basic Issues" (systems, models, levels, text, sentence, etc.), "Sequential Connectivity," "Conceptual Connectivity," etc. Bib. 28 pp.; name and term indexes.
JLS 10, 120–27: "one of the finest, most innovative contributions to the field of text linguistics within the last decade."

1288.   Beaugrande, Robert de, and Wolfgang Dressler. 1981. *Introduction to Text Linguistics.* London: Longman. 270 pp.
An attempt "to introduce the general public to a newly emerging science of text and discourse. . . . We have undertaken to synthesize traditional beyond-the-sentence linguistics with a wide range of interdisciplinary research on the production, reception, and utilization of texts in human interaction." Bib. 28 pp.; name and term indexes. [Relates to criticism in 6.1.]
RRL 27, 596; *BCILA* 35, 72.

1289. McKeon, Zahava. 1982. *Novels and Arguments: Inventing Rhetorical Criticism*. Chicago: U of Chicago P. 260 pp.
A rhetoric of the novel, showing the ways in which the objects of critical analysis are constituted as discourse, using concepts from ancient rhetoric, particularly those of Aristotle and Cicero. Part 1 sets forth her definition of rhetoric; part 2 applies the theory to 20th-cent. fiction, especially the works of Günter Grass and Flannery O'Connor. Name and term indexes.
MFS 29, 360: "convincingly and comprehensively argues for a rhetorical approach to the study of the novel," "brilliantly demonstrates" her thesis.

5.2 Practice (1290–434)

5.2.1 Diction, Imagery, Tropes (1290–312)

1290. Monsonego, S. 1966. *Etude stylo-statistique du vocabulaire des vers et de la prose dans la chantefable* Aucassin et Nicolette [Stylo-Statistic Study of the Vocabulary of the Verse and Prose in the *Chantefable Aucassin et Nicolette*]. Paris: Klincksieck. 154 pp.

1291. Gittleman, Anne. 1967. *Le style épique dans* Garin le Loherain [Epic Style in *Garin le Loherain*]. Geneva: Droz; Paris: Minard. 333 pp.
A study of formulaic techniques.
MLR 64, 895–96: "an excellent foundation for any further study of medieval literary technique."

1292. Kühne, Jorg. 1968. *Das Gleichnis: Studien zur inneren Form von Robert Musils Roman* Der Mann ohne Eigenschaften [The Metaphor: Studies of the Inner Form of Robert Musil's Novel *Der Mann ohne Eigenschaften*]. Tübingen: Niemeyer. 201 pp.
A study of metaphor as the key to the novel.
MLR 67, 228: "a difficult but fascinating book not just on Musil but on certain aspects of metaphor."

1293. Sices, David. 1968. *Music and the Musician in* Jean-Christophe: *The Harmony of Contrasts*. New Haven: Yale UP. 189 pp.
An inquiry into the extent to which the novel is musical, including a discussion of imagery patterns.
MLR 64, 680–82: "well worth doing," "a pleasure to read."

1294. Herzog, Valentin. 1970. *Ironische Erzählformen bei Conrad Ferdinand Meyer, dargestellt am "Jürg Jenatsch"* [Ironical Narrative Structures in the Works of Conrad Ferdinand Meyer, Exemplified by the Story "Jurg Jenatsch"]. Bern: Francke. 156 pp.
A detailed analysis of the irony in this novel—characters, actions, symbols, quotations, speeches, etc.
MLR 68, 234–35.

1295.   Hornsby, Roger. 1970. *Patterns of Action in the* Aeneid*: An Interpretation of Vergil's Epic Similes.* Iowa City: U of Iowa P. 156 pp.
Topically organized—the world of nature, gods and men, the city, etc. Bib.
2 pp.; name and term index.
CW 64, 204: "a book of potential, marred by preconceptions."

1296.   Bender, John. 1973. *Spenser and Literary Pictorialism.* Princeton: Princeton UP. 218 pp.
On the iconographic dimension of *The Faerie Queene*, the importance of the image as a visual experience, and the distinction between description and pictorialism. 3 main techniques of the pictorial are defined: focusing, framing, and scanning. Compares "Spenser's use of visual material with that of other writers: Chaucer, Shakespeare, Milton, Keats, Flaubert," and especially Ariosto and Tasso. Bib. 10 pp.; name and term index.
MLR 69, 618–19: "the system is employed with intelligent flexibility."

1297.   Freilich, Joan. 1973. *Paul Claudel's* Le Soulier de satin*: A Stylistic, Structuralist and Psychoanalytic Interpretation.* Toronto: U of Toronto P. 227 pp.
Mainly about the use of imagery in the narrative, structural, emotional, and thematic levels of the play, but syntax and meter are also discussed.
MLR 71, 686: "painstaking and thorough" but cliché- and jargon-laden.

1298.   La Quérière, Yves de. 1973. *Céline et les mots: Etude stylistique des effets de mots dans le* Voyage au bout de la nuit [Céline and Words: Stylistic Study of the Effects of Words in the *Journey to the End of the Night*]. Lexington: UP of Kentucky. 170 pp.
An examination of the lexical techniques of this experimental novel: neologisms, archaisms, startling associations, paradox, wordplay, cliché, etc. Bib. 3 pp.; term index.
MLR 71, 688–89: "a readable and non-technical introduction."

1299.   McConnell, Joan. 1973. *A Vocabulary Analysis of Gadda's "Pasticciaccio."* University: Romance Monographs. 194 pp.
A discussion of archaic, literary, and foreign words; dialectal forms; and neologisms.
MLR 69, 892–93: does not recommend; *MLJ* 58, 137.

1300.   Stephens, A. R. 1974. *Rilkes* Malte Laurids Brigge*: Strukturanalyse des erzählerischen Bewusstseins* [Rilke's *Malte Laurids Brigge*: An Analysis of the Structure of the Narrative Conscience]. Bern: Lang. 269 pp.
The metaphoric system of Rilke's important prose work.
AUMLA 46, 346–50: "has the qualities necessary to become a standard work."

1301.   Crosland, Andrew. 1975. *A Concordance to F. Scott Fitzgerald's* The Great Gatsby. Detroit: Gale. 425 pp.
Uses the 1925 unpub. first printing of the novel for the Key Word in Context (KWIC) program written in assembler language. Lists each word type with frequency of occurrence followed by a line of context for each occurrence. 3 apps.: vocabulary in alphabetical order with frequency of each, vocabulary in order of decreasing frequency, and a chart for converting page references to the 1974 Scribner Library ed.
Style 10, 303–05: "shows considerable care in its preparation and represents more than a competent job."

1302.   Kutzner, Patricia. 1975. *The Use of Imagery in Wolfram's* Parzival: *A Distributional Study.* Bern: Lang. 235 pp.
MLR 73, 458–59: questions "the numerical reliability" of the data; *Monatshefte* 70, 425.

1303.   Charpentier, Colette. 1976. *Le thème de la claustration dans* The Unicorn *d'Iris Murdoch: Etude lexicale et sémantique* [The Theme of Claustration in *The Unicorn* by Iris Murdoch: Lexical and Semantic Study]. Paris: Didier. 223 pp.
A statistical study of recurring words and phrases to show that the ambiguity of the central image of the unicorn is implicit throughout the novel.
MLR 77, 712–13: the argument is demonstrated, but the apparatus is "cumbersome."

1304.   Pasco, Allan. 1976. *The Color-Keys to* A la recherche du temps perdu. Geneva: Droz. 231 pp.
Proust's structural use of colors, each ch. devoted to an individual color.
MLR 73, 434: in spite of the "elaborate support" his "conclusion is only tentative"; *FR* 51, 307; *MLJ* 62, 199.

1305.   Kakar, H. S. 1977. *The Persistent Self: An Approach to* Middlemarch. Delhi: Doabar. 144 pp.
The interactions of metaphor in the novel.
MLR 75, 862–63: "serious, sensitive," "reinvigorates."

1306.   O'Connor, Daniel, and Jacques Jimenez. 1977. *The Images of Jesus: Exploring the Metaphors in Matthew's Gospel.* Minneapolis: Winston. 187 pp.
A study of the "synectic" (problem-solving) process by which Jesus metaphorically explored his relationship with God (the central father-son metaphor), as interpreted by Matthew.
Style 15, 503–06: "contains fresh insights and intriguing possibilities," but "basic errors are made."

1307.   Bolchazy, Ladislaus, ed. 1978. *A Concordance to the* Utopia *of St. Thomas More and a Frequency Word List.* Hildesheim: Olms. 388 pp.
Uses the Key Word in Context (KWIC) format accompanied by a simple word-frequency list that gives the number of times the word occurs and the percentage of the total word count this recurrence represents. Based on an authoritative critical ed. of *Utopia* (Yale UP, 1965). [The reader is reminded that only a few of the now hundreds of concordances in existence are cited in this bib. See the bib. by Crosland, no. 153.]
   Style 15, 49–50: generally favorable.

1308.   Crosman, Inge. 1978. *Metaphoric Narration: The Structure and Function of Metaphors in* A la recherche du temps perdu. Chapel Hill: North Carolina Studies in the Romance Langs. and Lits. 230 pp.
An analysis of the metaphors of time in the novel, beginning with the simplest and progressing to sustained, multiple, accumulating, and other complex forms. Bib. 12 pp.
   Style 14, 290–91: a useful classification of metaphors but almost nothing on the function of them in the design of the novel; *MLR* 75, 895: "a useful handbook of textual analysis" even though the author believes "images are separable from the text."

1309.   Bacigalupo, Massimo. 1980. *The Formèd Trace: The Later Poetry of Ezra Pound.* New York: Columbia UP. 512 pp.
Concentrates on the form of the lyrical mythic passages to demonstrate the formal unity (especially associative motifs) in the late *Cantos* (1945–60). Name index.
   Style 14, 291–93: "His chosen subject, the associations in the lyric passages, is important and fully treated"; *MLR* 78, 173–74: "careful, subtle, and weighty," but not always.

1310.   Murtaugh, Kristen. 1980. *Ariosto and the Classical Simile.* Cambridge: Harvard UP. 195 pp.
Part 1, terms, approaches, predecessors; part 2, the *Furioso.* Bib. 13 pp.
   KRQ 29, 435.

1310a.   McKinley, Mary. 1981. *Words in a Corner: Studies in Montaigne's Latin Quotations.* Lexington: French Forum. 134 pp.
A study of the contexts and resonances of the over 1,300 quotations in the *Essais.*
   MLR 78, 179–81: "deserves to be read by both scholars and undergraduates for its suggestive power, its liveliness of approach, and its ability to afford pleasure"; *FR* 56, 628: "an eye-opener"; *RenQ* 36, 123.

1311.   Mancing, Howard. 1982. *The Chivalric World of* Don Quixote*: Style, Structure, and Narrative Technique.* Columbia: U of Missouri P. 240 pp.

An analysis of the novel as a repository of chivalric style—i.e., of archaic language and chivalric rhetoric so prominent throughout the novel. Bib. 9 pp.; name and term index.

MLN 98, 297: "an unfortunately off-putting book" but in general "stimulating"; *CL* 35, 79: "impressive"; *Choice* 20, 92.

1312.   Brown, Frank. 1983. *Transfiguration: Poetic Metaphor and the Languages of Religious Belief.* Chapel Hill: U of North Carolina P. 250 pp.
A study of the metaphoric structure of T. S. Eliot's *Four Quartets* that shows the interdependence of poetic and conceptual modes of discourse.
TT 41, 373; *TS* 45, 391.

1312a.   Tucker, Lindsey. 1984. *Stephen and Bloom at Life's Feast: Alimentary Symbolism and the Creative Process in James Joyce's* Ulysses. Columbus: Ohio State UP. 177 pp.
Joyce's use of the ingestion-elimination process for metaphoric, mythic, and ritualistic purposes.
Choice 22, 562: "well worth the attention of serious students."

5.2.2 Syntax, Schemes (1313–21)

1313.   Kałuza, Irena. 1970. *The Functioning of Sentence Structure in the Stream-of-Consciousness Technique of William Faulkner's* The Sound and the Fury: *A Study in Linguistic Stylistics.* Norwood: Norwood Eds. 108 pp. (Orig. pub. in Crakow in 1967.)
After an introd. on aim and method, chs. on "Basic Structures: Unmodified Clauses and Appended Groups," "The Idiolect of Intuition," "The Idiolect of Subjectivity," "The Idiolect of Rationalism." Summary in Polish. Bib. 3 pp.
MFS 26, 654.

1314.   Treip, Mindele. 1970. *Milton's Punctuation and Changing English Usage, 1582–1676.* London: Methuen. 189 pp.
A study of the punctuation in the 3 major texts of *Paradise Lost* (manuscript, 1667 variants, and 1674). Also, punctuation provides "a valuable tool for the analysis of style in earlier prose and verse and a gauge to some of the puzzling phenomena of stylistic change." Bib. 5 pp.; name index.
Style 11, 321–22: "reward in its pages"; *MLR* 66, 863–64: "careful and detailed."

1315.   Louria, Yvette. 1971. *La convergence stylistique chez Proust* [Stylistic Convergence in Proust]. Paris: Nizet. 214 pp. (Orig. pub. 1957.)
A grammatical analysis of phrases or words linked together by grammatical function—called "convergence."
MLR 71, 181: "the most conscientious exploration in Proust criticism of the stylistic feature" called "convergence."

1316.   Spillner, Bernd. 1971. *Symmetrisches und asymmetrisches Prinzip in der Syntax Marcel Prousts* [The Principle of Symmetry and Asymmetry in the Syntax of Marcel Proust]. Meisenheim am Glan: Hain. 223 pp.
Style 13, 233: "a carefully planned attempt at an in-depth analysis of the basic classical symmetry underlying the sentence structure in *A la recherche*, a structure modified to a great extent by asymmetrical syntax."

1317.   Burton, Dolores. 1974. *Shakespeare's Grammatical Style: A Computer-Assisted Analysis of* Richard II *and* Antony and Cleopatra. Austin: U of Texas P. 364 pp.
Ch. 1, "Style as a Function": definitions of style in process of formulating a definition; ch. 2, "Locating Style in Literature": various problems — sentence mood, etc.; ch. 3, "Reflections on Stylistic Analysis": style as proportions, grammatical oppositions, etc.; ch. 4, "Grammar as Meaning": nominal group words beginning with determiners; ch. 5, "Charting the Dimensions of Style": deletions. The final ch., "From Stylistics to Poetics," interprets the 2 plays. 2 apps. Bib. 12 pp.; name and term index 12 pp.
Style 12, 383–85: sometimes uses terminology "not adequately defined," uses an inferior text, and does not discuss her computer methodology, but "a major study. . . . exciting, useful, and provocative of further thought"; *KN* 26, 401–07; *RES* 27, 61–64.

1318.   Brooke-Rose, Christine. 1976. *A Structural Analysis of Pound's Usura Canto: Jakobson's Method Extended and Applied to Free Verse*. The Hague: Mouton. 76 pp.
A detailed examination particularly of the grammatical patterns in the short canto 45 to explain how they generate meaning. Bib. 4 pp.
Style 11, 221–23: the subtitle "is a little misleading" since "not applying Jakobson's remarks on metrics to a study of free verse" (prosody discussed "only in passing"), but otherwise a "thorough job," "careful and intelligent," though the author's "ingenious" linkages of patterns and meaning are not always convincing.

1319.   Loukopoulos, Wassili. 1978. *Heinrich von Kleist, "Der Zweikampf ": Eine Strukturanalyse der Syntax unter dem Aspekt des Subjektgebrauchs* [Heinrich von Kleist, "The Duel": An Analysis of Syntax in View of the Use of the Grammatical Subject]. Stuttgart: Hochschulverlag. 182 pp.

1320.   Gotoff, Harold. 1979. *Cicero's Elegant Style: An Analysis of the "Pro Archia."* Urbana: U of Illinois P. 255 pp.
Seeks to analyze the sentence structure of one speech "and in so doing to develop a vocabulary for making precise and specific observations on Cicero's prose style." Apps. on the author's syntactical notation and on prose rhythm. Glossary of critical terms 21 pp.

Choice 17, 66: "highly useful" for "appreciating one of the great figures of Western humanism"; *CW* 73, 429.

1321. Gottfried, Roy. 1980. *The Art of Joyce's Syntax in* Ulysses. Athens: U of Georgia P. 185 pp.
Not a quantitative study but an examination of Joyce's expressive use of syntax, the violations of normal syntax that richly individualize ideas, events, and characters. Bib. 4 pp.; name and term index.
Style 17, 89–91: "a fine exercise in practical criticism," the "heart of the book, pages 48 to 66[,] . . . is as intelligent as anything yet written about the novel's linguistic peculiarities"; *MLR* 77, 190.

5.2.3 Prosody, Sound Patterns in Prose (1321a–25a)

1321a. Stevick, Robert. 1968. *Suprasegmentals, Meter, and the Manuscript of* Beowulf. The Hague: Mouton. 88 pp.
Uses the spacing in the manuscript to "establish some further information about scribal practices, about the meter of *Beowulf,* and about some suprasegmental features of Old English."
Ling 62, 110–17: the "evidence is slippery," "one wishes Stevick had used his evidence to arrive at a hypothesis, rather than vice-versa," but the author proves the facsimile is essential to the study of the prosody of *Beowulf.*

1322. Fónagy, Iván. 1974. *Dallamfejtés: Füst Milán "Öregség"* [Interpretation of Prosody: Milan Füst's "Old Age"]. Budapest: Akad. Kiado. 220 pp.
With a record of the poet's voice reading his poem. A short Eng. version, "The Voice of the Poet: Acoustic and Functional Analysis of Poems Recited by the Poet," is in *Toward a Theory of Context,* ed. Adam Makkai (The Hague: Mouton, 1975), 81–124. An Eng. version, *The Voice of the Poet* (Budapest: Akad. Kiado), is in preparation. 116 figs., 38 tables, subject index.

1323. Chesters, Graham. 1975. *Some Functions of Sound-Repetition in* Les fleurs du mal. Hull: U of Hull. 91 pp.
Sonic recurrences support rhythms and meanings.
MLR 72, 961: "excellent."

1324. Reinhard, Mariann. 1976. *On the Semantic Relevance of the Alliterative Collocations in* Beowulf. Bern: Francke. 277 pp.
Chs. on complementary, contrastive, and specific collocations, the relation between the collocations and syntax, and the relevance of 2 patterns within a larger context. Bib. 4 pp.; index of lines.
Spec 53, 839: "works out Quirk's theory in detail," "well written," but unconvincing.

1325. Tatilon, Claude. 1976. *Sonorités et texte poétique: Examen des structures phonématiques impressives et expressives, suivi d'une application aux* Fables *de La Fontaine* [Sonorities and Poetic Text: A Study of "Impressive" and Expressive Phonemic Structures, Followed by an Application to the *Fables* of La Fontaine]. Montreal: Didier. 144 pp.

1325a.   Luecke, Jane-Marie. 1978. *Measuring Old English Rhythm: An Application of the Principles of Gregorian Chant Rhythm to the Meter of* Beowulf. Madison: U of Wisconsin P. 158 pp.
Spec 55, 147: "confused and her model unconvincing" but does undermine some "inherited presuppositions" and "employs a commendable flexibility in scansion."

5.2.4 Studies on Several Linguistic Levels (1326–434)

1326.   Benstock, Bernard. 1965. *Joyce-Again's Wake: An Analysis of* Finnegans Wake. Seattle: U of Washington P. 312 pp.
An attempt to bridge the gap between the professional reader and the intelligent and industrious general reader. Sections on prose rhythms, puns, etc. Bib. 4 pp.; name and term index.
Style 2, 83–85: wavers between introductory and scholarly but "strengths . . . more striking than its weaknesses."

1327.   Alpers, Paul. 1967. *The Poetry of* The Faerie Queene. Princeton: Princeton UP. 415 pp.
An analysis of the language of the epic, showing how Spenser alternates language of facts and language of awareness of them, and how he controls syntax line by line. Name and term index.
Style 4, 163–68: positive; *MLR* 65, 869–70: "in every sense substantial."

1328.   Kallich, Martin. 1967. *Heav'n's First Law: Rhetoric and Order in Pope's "Essay on Man."* DeKalb: Northern Illinois UP. 152 pp.
4 essays on imagery, antitheses, and recurrences in the poem.
Style 6, 82–84: "little that is new, much that is obvious"; *PQ* 47, 406; *GaR* 23, 107; *MP* 66, 369.

1329.   Lillyman, William. 1967. *Otto Ludwig's* Zwischen Himmel und Erde: *A Study of its Artistic Structure.* The Hague: Mouton. 190 pp.
Undertakes "to show the function and significance" of the novel's "motifs, leitmotifs, symbols, images, and method of narration."
CL 21, 374–75: the "most substantial" criticism of the book; *MLR* 64, 951.

1330.   Todorov, Tzvetan. 1967. *Littérature et signification* [Literature and Signification]. Paris: Larousse. 118 pp.
Revision of doctoral thesis *Analyse semiologique des* Liaisons dangereuses: *Contribution a l'étude du sens.* Includes a discussion of the epistolary form, an analysis of *Les liaisons dangereuses*, and a classification of rhetorical devices.
Style 8, 143.

1331. Cooper, John R. 1968. *The Art of* The Compleat Angler. Durham: Duke UP. 184 pp.
7 chs.: an introd.; 3 chs. on the relation between the *Angler* and the georgic, pastoral, and dialogue traditions; other chs. on prose style, sources, and revisions. Bib. 6 pp.; name index.
Style 4, 69–72: "questions unsatisfactorily answered and problems unsatisfactorily solved"; *ELN* 6, 291.

1332. Irving, Edward, Jr. 1968. *A Reading of* Beowulf. New Haven: Yale UP. 256 pp.
A study of the way the poem says what it says, much of the meaning traceable to the "inherited rhetoric of Germanic poetic style." The world of the poem is one of radical contrasts, and the chief quality of Old Eng. poetic style is its ability to emphasize these contrasts. Bib. 5 pp.
Style 5, 206–09: praise.

1333. Proffer, Carl. 1968. *Keys to* Lolita. Bloomington: Indiana UP. 160 pp.
Analysis of the rich verbal texture of the novel: allusions, the web of clues in the quest for Quilty, prose rhythm, imagery, pun, naming, phonics.
MLR 65, 618–19: "useful."

1334. Schmidt, Jochen. 1968. *Hölderlins Elegie* Brod und Wein*: Die Entwicklung des hymnischen Stils in der elegischen Dichtung.* [Hölderlin's Elegy *Bread and Wine*: The Development of Hymnal Style in Elegiac Poetry]. Berlin: de Gruyter. 229 pp.
Focuses on rhetorical figures.
MLR 64, 943–44: his "task is executed with commendable efficiency."

1335. Thornton, Weldon. 1968. *Allusions in* Ulysses*: An Annotated List.* Chapel Hill: U of North Carolina P. 554 pp.
A page-by-page list from the Random House (Modern Library) 1961 and 1934 eds. that intends to be complete in "the areas of literature, philosophy, theology, history, the fine arts, and popular and folk music." Bib. 15 pp.; index 31 pp.
MLR 71, 155–56: "a great deal sounder and more valuable than some more recent compilations of notes purporting to assist the reader of *Ulysses*."

1336. Versini, Laurent. 1968. *Essai sur les sources et la technique des* Liaisons dangereuses*: Laclos et la tradition.* Paris: Klincksieck. 793 pp.
Discusses Laclos's skill with the epistolary form, etc.
MLR 64, 672–75: partly very skilled, partly unconvincing.

1337. Blanch, Robert, ed. 1969. *Style and Symbolism in* Piers Plowman*: A Modern Critical Anthology.* Knoxville: U of Tennessee P. 275 pp.
The 13 previously pub. essays elucidate the "literary value" of the poem. Name and term index.

Choice 7, 384: "the whole business [of reprinting articles culled from journals] is to be deplored"; *LJ* 95, 498.

1338.   Chaillet, Jean. 1969. *Etudes de grammaire et de style*. Paris: Bordas. 2 vols., 416 and 400 pp.
Vol. 1, 28 explications of poems and passages from the 16th, 17th, and 18th cents. Vol. 2, 27 explications from the 19th and 20th cents., with detailed grammatical and stylistic indexes.
    BSLP 68, 196–99.

1339.   Charney, Maurice. 1969. *Style in* Hamlet. Princeton: Princeton UP. 333 pp.
Sections on imagery, on staging and structure, and on the language of characterization. [No definition or theory of style.] Name and term index.
    Style 6, 85–89: "raising more questions than it answers," tends to be a "listing of certain details"; *Lang&S* 4, 77.

1340.   Deleted.

1341.   Todorov, Tzvetan. 1969. *Grammaire du* Décaméron [A Grammar of the *Decameron*]. The Hague: Mouton. 100 pp.
Establishes a method based on analogy with universal grammar, then treats the elements of "narrative grammar" as illustrated in the *Decameron*.
    TLS 18 Sept. 1970, 1045: "single, profitably restricted purpose: to test the possibilities of isolating . . . the rules" of "a 'narratology.'"

1342.   Cambon, Glauco. 1970. *Dante's Craft: Studies in Language and Style*. Minneapolis: U of Minnesota P; London: Oxford UP. 215 pp.
Diverse essays, some close textual analysis of the *Commedia*.
    MLR 66, 200–01: a "sound" approach though "vitiated by certain weaknesses in the treatment."

1343.   Goldsmith, Margaret. 1970. *The Mode and Meaning of* Beowulf. London: Athlone. 282 pp.
A study of the symbolism and allegory of the epic in the context of Christian doctrine, *Beowulf* being the first great medieval allegory of human life and death based on the beliefs of the Western Church. Bib. 5 pp.; name and term index.
    Style 7, 71–73: the historical method neglects language.

1344.   Gopnik, Irwin. 1970. *A Theory of Style and Richardson's* Clarissa. The Hague: Mouton. 140 pp.
Chs. 1–2 present the concepts of "automatization" and "manipulation" derived from the Prague Linguistic Circle. Ch. 3 offers "An Analysis of the Verbal Structure in *Clarissa*" based on the foregoing. Bib. 4 pp.; name index.
    Style 6, 74–76: "does not lead anywhere"; *MP*, 69, 352–55; *PQ* 50, 475.

1345. Huppé, B. F. 1970. *The Web of Words.* Albany: State U of New York P. 197 pp.

A study of how the stylistic features of 4 Old Eng. Christian poems (*Vainglory, The Wonder of Creation, The Dream of the Rood, Judith*) serve each poem's didactic unity. Name and term index.

Style 7, 64–69: "a sound procedure."

1346. Jakobson, Roman, and Lawrence G. Jones. 1970. *Shakespeare's Verbal Art in "Th' Expense of Spirit."* The Hague: Mouton. 33 pp.

A grammatical analysis of sonnet 129. Rpt. in vol. 3 of Jakobson's *Selected Writings,* no. 587b.

JL 12, 21–73: "I regard both Jakobson's methods and his conclusions as invalid"; *NYRB* 15, 33 and 16, 32; *Comt* 50, 70.

1347. Kehl, D. G., ed. 1970. *Literary Style of the Old Bible and the New.* Indianapolis: Bobbs. 64 pp.

A collection of essays by diverse traditional critics and translators. Bib. 1 p.

Style 6, 185–91.

1348. Leaska, Mitchell. 1970. *Virginia Woolf's* Lighthouse: *A Study in Critical Method.* New York: Columbia UP. 221 pp.

An evaluation of this multiple-point-of-view novel through a critical method that combines point-of-view analysis (chs. 3–5) and stylistics (ch. 6). Ch. 6 studies the sentence and word lengths, etc., to confirm each character's individuality. 2 apps., 1 on clauses, the other statistical tables on aspects of syntax and diction. Bib. 9 pp.; name index.

Style 6, 212–15: "moderately useful"; *PS* 45, 370.

1349. Lott, Robert. 1970. *Language and Psychology in* Pepita Jiménez. Urbana: U of Illinois P. 284 pp.

A study of the vocabulary, imagery, and structure of Valera's novel to reveal the purposefulness of technique in an aesthetic whole. Bib. 6 pp.; term and name indexes.

MLR 67, 678–79: a generally favorable rev.; *Hisp* 55, 180; *MLN* 87, 375.

1350. Morhange-Bégué, Claude. 1970. *"La chanson du mal aimé": Analyse structurale et stylistique.* Paris: Minard. 306 pp.

A line-by-line analysis of Apollinaire's poetic forms that reveals 3 structures.

MLR 68, 185–86: "not only a challenging" study but "a serious step forward" into the "poetic process."

1351. Rossum-Guyon, Françoise van. 1970. *Critique du roman: Essai sur* La modification *de Michel Butor* [A Critique of the Novel: An Essay on *La modification* by Michel Butor]. Paris: Gallimard. 311 pp.

TLS 3 Sept. 1971, 1055: "exhaustive analysis of the structure."

1352.   Delbouille, Paul. 1971. *Genèse, structure et destin d'*Adolphe [Genesis, Structure, and Destiny of *Adolphe*]. Paris: Belles lettres. 643 pp.
MLR 69, 415–16: a traditional "comprehensive and judicial compendium."

1353.   Field, P. J. C. 1971. *Romance and Chronicle: A Study of Malory's Prose Style*. Bloomington: Indiana UP. 202 pp.
An examination of the narrative devices of *Morte Darthur* in the context of 15th-cent. Eng. prose. Defines style as the way the language of the book contributes to meaning. Name and term index 2 pp.
Style 7, 236–37: "admirable".

1354.   Howarth, W. D., and C. L. Walton. 1971. *Explications: The Technique of French Literary Appreciation*. London: Oxford UP. 270 pp.
The introd. gives an account of the development of *explication de texte*, followed by 25 explications. Based "squarely on stylistic analysis — the study of the way in which linguistic phenomena combine to produce literary effect," *explication de texte* reconciles the study of literature and language.
MLR 69, 164–66: "stimulating" but discrepancies between "their precepts and their practice" and an "uneven collection" of explications.

1355.   Junker, Hedwig. 1971. *Drama und "Pseudodrama": Studien zur theatertheoretischen Reflexion in Eugène Ionescos* Victimes du devoir [Drama and "Pseudodrama": Studies of Reflection on Theater Theory in Eugene Ionesco's *Victimes du devoir*]. Frankfurt am Main: Athenäum. 145 pp.
An analysis especially of the "Pseudodrama."
MLR 69, 426–27: "a wholly original appreciation of the immense subtlety" of the play.

1356.   Marin, Louis. 1971. *Sémiotique de la Passion: Topiques et figures* [Semiotics of the Passion: Themes and Images]. Bibliothèque de sciences religieuses. Paris: Aubier-Montaigne. 255 pp.
Semiotic treatment of the Gospels.
Diacritics 7.2, 35–43: an admiring rev. of Marin's "virtuoso performance."

1357.   Sinfield, Alan. 1971. *The Language of Tennyson's* In Memoriam. Oxford: Blackwell. 223 pp.
Chs. on diction, syntax, imagery, sound, and rhythm test the author's belief that *In Memoriam* is "rather a good poem." Name and term index.
Style, 15, 455: a refreshing alternative to the chronological, ad hoc approach to Tennyson's verse; *Ling* 147, 112–15: "interesting" and "convincing."

1358.   Wilder, Amos. 1971. *Early Christian Rhetoric: The Language of the Gospel*. Cambridge: Harvard UP. 135 pp. (Orig. pub. Harvard UP, 1964.)

A study of the literary forms and style of the New Testament writings, called "early Christian rhetoric" because of the oral speech that lies behind the writings: "It is not only a question of how the first Christians wrote but how they spoke and talked." Ch. 1, "The New Utterance," on the new speech modes of Jesus; ch. 2, "Modes and Genres"; ch. 3, "The Dialogue"; ch. 4, "The Story"; ch. 5, "The Parable"; ch. 6, "The Poem"; ch. 7, "Image, Symbol, Myth." Name and reference indexes.

1359.   Barrett, Gerald R., and Thomas L. Erskine. 1972. *From Fiction to Film: Conrad Aiken's "Silent Snow, Secret Snow."* Belmont, CA: Dickenson. 193 pp.
A study of the short story and its transformation into film form, including 12 articles on the story and a shot-by-shot analysis of the film compared to the story. [This new approach may be found in other volumes in this series, including Bierce's "An Occurrence at Owl Creek Bridge" and Lawrence's "The Rocking-Horse Winner."]
Style 9, 563.

1360.   Highet, Gilbert. 1972. *The Speeches in Vergil's* Aeneid. Princeton: Princeton UP. 380 pp.
A substantial rev. of previous criticism is followed by a detailed analysis of all the speeches. Name and term index.
Style 8, 260–62: "full of both shrewd observation and real literary criticism" but provides too little context from whole poem.

1361.   Le Hir, Yves. 1972. *Styles.* Paris: Klincksieck. 225 pp.
24 brief analyses of short poems or passages from plays or fiction.
BL (1972), 216.

1362.   Requadt, Paul. 1972. *Goethes* Faust I: *Leitmotivik und Architektur* [Goethe's *Faust I*: Leitmotifs and Architecture]. Munich: Fink. 394 pp.
A structure of expansion and contraction through motifs, symbols, images shapes the experience of human erring at the heart of the work.
MLR 72, 244–45: "clear-headed," "objective."

1363.   Bleikasten, André. 1973. *Faulkner's* As I Lay Dying. Trans. Roger Little. Bloomington: Indiana UP. 180 pp. (Orig. Fr. Paris: Colin, 1970.)
Ch. 3, "Language and Style," treats diction, syntax, and figures; ch. 4, "Technique," discusses structures (arrangement of events, time and tense, points of view, interior monologue); ch. 6 treats setting. Bib. 9 pp.; name index.
Style 10, 102–06: "uneven and too often inaccurate"; *MFS* 20, 281: "genuinely rewarding"; *JML* 4, 313.

1364.   Crespo, Ángel. 1973. *Aspectos estructurales de "El moro expósito" del Duque de Rivas* [Structural Aspects of Rivas's "El moro expósito"]. Uppsala: Acta U Upsaliensis. 257 pp.
A study of the play's themes, symbols, plot, narrative modes, versification, setting, etc.
MLR 70, 671–74: praises the strictly formal analysis but condemns the failure to place Rivas's techniques in their ideological contexts.

1365.   Kavanagh, Thomas. 1973. *The Vacant Mirror: A Study of Mimesis through Diderot's* Jacques le fataliste. Banbury: Voltaire Foundation. 184 pp.
A structuralist study (i.e., the relations between narrator and subject, narrative components, verb tenses, etc.) of a novel that questions its own fictional status.
MLR 71, 172: a "useful" book, but it confuses "meaning and reference."

1366.   Nøjgaard, Morten. 1973. *Elévation et expansion: Les deux dimensions de Baudelaire* [Elevation and Expansion: The Two Dimensions of Baudelaire]. Odense: Odense UP. 175 pp.
A study of the imagery (*signes poétiques*) and structure of *Les fleurs du mal.*
MLR 71, 676–77: a luke-warm rev.; *FR* 48, 435.

1367.   Raitz, Walter. 1973. *Zur Soziogenese des bürgerlichen Romans: Eine literatursoziologische Analyse des* Fortunatus [The Social Genesis of Bourgeois Novels: A Socioliterary Analysis of *Fortunatus*]. Düsseldorf: Bertelsmann. 177 pp.
An analysis of the content and structure of the novel as an objectivization of historical conditions.
MLR 71, 217–18: a generally unfavorable rev.; *ZDPh* 95, 460.

1368.   Balbert, Peter. 1974. *D. H. Lawrence and the Psychology of Rhythm: The Meaning of "Form" in* The Rainbow. The Hague: Mouton. 130 pp.
An attempt to show the connections between the ideas and the art of the novel, the thematic and linguistic "rhythms."
MLR 71, 907–10: "the fullest study so far" of the novel, a consistent achievement "of showing in detail" how the novel fuses "psychology and rhythm."

1369.   Barthes, Roland. 1974. *S/Z*. Trans. Richard Miller. New York: Hill. 271 pp. (Paris: Seuil, 1970.)
A minute dissection of a short novel by Balzac, *Sarrasine*, which is divided into 561 numbered fragments, or "lexias," varying in length from 1 word to several lines. Analyzed according to 5 "codes" (hermeneutic, semantic, proairetic, cultural, and symbolic). In addition there are 93 sections of commentary of a page or 2 identified by Roman numerals.

Richard Howard, "A Note on *S/Z*": "These divagations . . . constitute the most sustained yet pulverized meditation on *reading* I know in all of Western critical literature" (x); Scholes, *Semiotics and Interpretation*: "the fullest, richest, and most successful application of semiotic methods to the analysis of a single fictional text," but the translation contains "a number of errors" (153); *YR* 64, 609: "an important essay in deconstruction," "a seminal work"; *MLR* 66, 191–92.

1370. Bovon, François, ed. 1974. *Structural Analysis and Biblical Exegesis*. Pittsburgh: Pickwick. 164 pp. (*Analyse structurale et exégèse biblique*. Neuchâtel: Delachaux, 1971.)
Essays by structuralists (Barthes et al.) and traditional exegetes. Bib. 54 pp.

1371. Cooper, Judith. 1974. Ubu Roi: *An Analytical Study*. New Orleans: Tulane UP. 120 pp.
Analysis of plot and episodes, comedy, and language.
MLR 72, 203–04: "well-trodden ground" but "useful to have the material assembled in one book."

1372. "Holistic Criticism." 1974. *Style* 8.2. 147 pp.
5 essays suggest various methods for apprehending the design of a text.

1373. Iser, Wolfgang. 1974. *The Implied Reader: Patterns of Communication in Prose Fiction from Bunyan to Beckett*. Baltimore: Johns Hopkins UP. 303 pp.
Mainly a chronologically arranged series of analyses of 10 literary texts from *Pilgrim's Progress* to Beckett's *Trilogy*, which combines consideration of the intentions of both author (a text is a web of strategems to affect readers) and reader (who participates in generating the text's meaning). [Thus the author presents a traditional rhetorical addresser-message-addressee framework. The book would be assigned to 6.0 more for what the author claims than for what he performs.] Name and term indexes.
Style 10, 344–47: "an original contribution to the phenomenology of reading," but "frustrating" because of the "persistent confusion between a rhetorical approach . . . and a phenomenological one" in spite of Iser's stated rejection of rhetoric; *YR* 64, 610: "disappointing"; *Diacritics* 5.3, 13–15; 7.4, 20–33.

1374. Núñez de Villavicencio, Laura. 1974. *La creatividad en el estilo de Leopoldo Alas, Clarin* [Creativity in the Style of Leopoldo Alas's *Clarin*]. Oviedo: Inst. de Estudios Asturianos. 285 pp.
A study based on a taxonomy of grammatical categories but including metaphor.
MLR 71, 940–41: "only scratches the surface, but it does so suggestively."

1375.   Provost, William. 1974. *The Structure of Chaucer's* Troilus and Criseyde. Copenhagen: Rosenkilde. 117 pp.
A description of the arrangement of books and groups of stanzas within books, time units, and narrative units and of patterns connecting each structural level. The last ch. describes several minor structural devices.
MLR 71, 372–73: "admirably clear" description, but "we must seek to criticize and to evaluate" also.

1376.   Richard, Jean-Pierre. 1974. *Proust et le monde sensible* [Proust and the Sensory World]. Paris: Seuil. 238 pp.
A study of description, sensory images, connections, unity, and other aspects of *A la recherche*.
MLR 71, 184: "this rich study will no doubt now count as one of the group of key critical commentaries" on the novel.

1377.   Wing, Nathaniel. 1974. *Present Appearances: Aspects of Poetic Structure in Rimbaud's* Illuminations. University, AL: Romance Monographs. 172 pp.
A study of 25 of the *Illuminations* to show how they function as self-sufficient verbal artifacts. Bib. 6 pp.
Style 10, 223–25: demonstrates "often extremely well."

1378.   Almansi, Guido. 1975. *The Writer as Liar: Narrative Technique in the* Decameron. London: Routledge. 166 pp.
A formalist-Fr. structuralist "anti-realist and anti-psychological reading of the Hundred Tales" in 5 chs. Ch. 1, "Narrative Screens," the tales self-contained and disconnected from the real world; ch. 2, "Literature and Falsehood," 2 stories offer key to whole as counterfeit; etc.
Style 11, 214–16: "readable and sometimes witty chapters," a "sharp and persuasive little book," but treats the referential-self-reflexive, realism-formalism conflicts narrowly.

1379.   Lambert, Mark. 1975. *Malory: Style and Vision in* Le Morte Darthur. New Haven: Yale UP. 255 pp.
A study of selected tales. Ch. 1, "Aspects of Period Style" (dialogue, narration); ch. 2, "Malorian Style" (particularity, narrative, landscape, setting, etc.); ch. 3, "The Last Tales." Name and term index.
Style 10, 219–22: "a stimulating demonstration that Malory's prose style . . . is a reverberation of the major theme"; *AUMLA* 47, 73; *MLR* 73, 874.

1380.   Lejeune, Philippe. 1975. *Lire Leiris: Autobiographie et langage* [To Read Leiris: Autobiography and Language]. Paris: Klincksieck. 192 pp.
A close linguistic analysis of Leiris's *L'âge d'homme*.
MLR 72, 963–64: "stimulating."

1381.   Percas de Ponseti, Helena. 1975. *Cervantes y su concepto del arte: Es-
        tudio crítico de algunos aspectos y episodios del* Quijote [Cervantes and
        His Conception of Art: A Critical Study of Some Aspects and Episodes
        of *Quijote*]. Madrid: Gredos. 2 vols. 690 pp.
An explanation of Cervantes's unique verisimilitude and his narrative inno-
vations. Analysis of the Cave of Montesinos episode consumes 177 pp. Bib.
18 pp.; name and general indexes.
   Hisp 59, 545: "one of the most original and intelligent contributions of
Cervantine criticism in recent years"; *TLS* (3 Sept. 1976), 1066; *MLR* 73, 213–15.

1382.   Wlassics, Tibor. 1975. *Dante narratore: Saggi sullo stile della* Comme-
        dia [Dante Story-Teller: Essays on the Style of the *Comedy*]. Florence:
        Olschki. 234 pp.
10 diverse studies.
   MLR 72, 964–66: critical of method but praises "a number of interesting
insights."

1383.   Brody, Robert. 1976. *Julio Cortázar:* Rayuela. London: Támesis. 86 pp.
Mainly a stylistic study, with chs. on "the quest," "structures," "language and
authenticity," and "style and spontaneity."
   MLR 72, 727–78: "good, clear, introduction" but almost turns the novel
into "a set-book."

1384.   Carrard, Philippe. 1976. *Malraux ou le récit hybride: Essai sur les tech-
        niques narratives dans* L'espoir [Malraux, or the Hybrid Narrative: An
        Essay on the Narrative Techniques in *L'espoir*]. Paris: Minard. 293 pp.
Mainly about point of view.
   MLR 73, 652–53: "precise and concentrated."

1385.   *"Finnegans Wake."* 1976. *Poétique* 7.26. 120 pp.

1386.   French, Marilyn. 1976. *The Book as World: James Joyce's* Ulysses. Cam-
        bridge: Harvard UP. 295 pp.
" . . . a close, chapter-by-chapter reading of the text, with emphasis on discovering the point of view underlying each episode, and on considering the
effect of the style in each episode." Name and item index.
   MLR 74, 188–89: "sharp critical insight, intelligent observation, and com-
mendably high standards of scholarship"; *MP* 76, 435–38; *Cithara* 17, 75–78.

1387.   Greimas, A. J. 1976. *Maupassant: La sémiotique du texte: Exercices pra-
        tiques* [Maupassant: The Semiotics of the Text: Practical Exercises]. Paris:
        Seuil. 276 pp.
Applies his semantic theory mainly to the analysis of 1 short story, "Deux
amis."

FR 50, 501: "an informative journey of a semiotic exercise" but perhaps "too tight and too complex"; *Diacritics* 7.1, 18–40; *RR* 67, 320.

1388.   Hirschberg, Dagmar. 1976. *Untersuchungen zur Erzählstruktur von Wolframs* Parzival: *Die Funktion von erzählter Szene und Station für den doppelten Kursus* [Studies in the Narrative Structure of Wolfram's *Parzival*: The Function of Narrated Scene and Station for the Twofold Quest]. Göppingen: Kümmerle. 379 pp.
An analysis of structure and function of the scene as the basic narrative unit.
   MLR 73, 937–39: successfully advances our knowledge of the work but sometimes does not take the argument "far enough."

1389.   Nohrnberg, James. 1976. *The Analogy of* The Faerie Queene. Princeton: Princeton UP. 870 pp.
An exploration of the unifying function of analogy in the poem — e.g., the "analogy of inner and outer government" that shapes books 2 and 5 and "sexual and social love" that informs books 3 and 4. Analytical table of contents; name and term index 60 pp.; index to Scriptures.
   Style 12, 299–301: "often diffuse" but "enormously learned" in showing the "multiform patterns of analogy."

1390.   Tiefenbrun, Susan. 1976. *A Structural Analysis of* La Princesse de Clèves. The Hague: Mouton. 185 pp.
An attempt to apprehend the patterns of the novel partly by testing readers' reactions and partly by employing mathematical procedures to corroborate the analyst's conclusions. "The first half of this study is a paradigmatic analysis based on progressive, sentence by sentence, microstylistics" to explain how the novel "is structured according to a limited number of binary oppositions. . . . The second half of the study constitutes a syntagmatic sequential analysis in which long-range patterns are traced on levels beyond the sentence." Bib. 6 pp.; name and term index.
   Style 12, 75–76: "theoretical and methodological weaknesses" but "some very interesting statements about the style and structure"; *MLR* 73, 184–86.

1391.   DeJean, Joan. 1977. *Scarron's* Roman comique: *A Comedy of the Novel, a Novel of Comedy*. Bern: Lang. 109 pp.
A study of *Roman comique* and the burlesque, employing the apparatus and concepts and techniques of linguistic and formalist criticism.
   MLR 75, 661–62: "a sensitive and subtle account" of the novel.

1392.   Dijk, Teun van, and János Petöfi, eds. 1977. *Grammars and Descriptions: Studies in Text Theory and Text Analysis*. Berlin: de Gruyter. 402 pp.

13 essays written "in the years 1972 to 1974 . . . to present a wide choice of different" concepts and methods "of linguistic text descriptions" of the same text—James Thurber's "The Lover and His Lass." Eng., Fr., and Ger. Bib. references follow each essay. [See Carroll, no. 1016, and Davis, no. 1405.]

JLS 8, 58–59: "an important step towards" the goal of "dialogue between the different directions of text linguistics."

1393.   Fitch, Brian. 1977. *Dimensions, structures et textualité dans la trilogie romanesque de Beckett* [Scope, Structures, and Textuality in Beckett's Novel Trilogy]. Paris: Minard. 207 pp.

MLR 74, 712: much prefers Dina Sherzer's *Structure de la trilogie de Beckett* (1976).

1394.   Gontarski, S. E. 1977. *Beckett's "Happy Days": A Manuscript Study.* Columbus: Ohio State U Libraries. 86 pp.

An examination of the 9 stages of the composition of the play. Bib. 4 pp.; name index.

   MLR 75, 876: the book "I will remember most clearly and return to most frequently is perhaps the least ambitious" (of the several books appraised in the rev.).

1395.   Greiner, Thorsten. 1977. *Die poetische Gleichung: Funktionale Analyse moderner Lyrik am Beispiel von Saint-John Perses "Neiges"* [The Poetic Equation: A Functional Analysis of Modern Poetry Using the Example of Saint-John Perse's "Neiges"]. Munich: Fink. 333 pp.

MLR 74, 950: "His object is to present all facets of the poem, its semantic, syntactic, phonological, and metric-rhythmic 'levels,' as 'functions' of one another, creating a web of 'equivalences and oppositions' which alone reveals the meaning"; "succeeds in revealing the poem in a new light."

1396.   Groden, Michael. 1977. Ulysses *in Progress.* Princeton: Princeton UP. 235 pp.

A study of the 3-stage process by which *Ulysses* was written and the importance of the pivotal "Cyclops" episode, where Joyce turned from writing a book about Stephen and Bloom to a book of parodies, schematic correspondences, and encyclopedism. Bib. 7 pp.; name and term index.

   Style 14, 71–73: "for the Joyce specialist," one of the 2 most "informative books published on Joyce in the last five years"; *MP* 77, 59–61; *JJQ* 18, 93–97; *MLR* 75, 179.

1397.   Jakobson, Roman, and Stephen Rudy. 1977. *Yeats' "Sorrow of Love" through the Years.* Lisse: de Ridder. 55 pp.

Compares 18 features of the 1892 version and the 1925 final version. Bib. 1 p. Rpt. in vol. 3 of Jakobson's *Selected Writings*, no. 587b.

MLN 92, 1106–16: biased and limited but "suggests fruitful ways of understanding Yeats" and "poetry itself."

1398.   Mercken-Spaas, Godelieve. 1977. *Alienation in Constant's* Adolphe: *An Exercise in Structural Thematics*. Bern: Lang. 173 pp.
A structuralist study of *Adolphe* as a system of aspects of alienation, with a section on modes of expression.
MLR 76, 195–96: "Acute and detailed as far as it goes."

1399.   Norris, Margot. 1977. *The Decentered Universe of* Finnegans Wake: *A Structuralist Analysis*. Baltimore: Johns Hopkins UP. 151 pp.
The book is a dream, its time synchronic, its universe decentered (no fixed point to define it), its structure determined by play; and it is expressed in a new language to escape encrusted concepts and to reproduce a dream world. Bib. 2 pp.
Style 12, 399–401: several parts of the book need longer treatment, but "it casts light on a good many passages" and it "makes a very good case for the necessity of Joyce's unconventional language"; *MLR* 75, 381.

1400.   Peale, C. George. 1977. *La anatomía de* El diablo cojuelo: *Deslindes del género anatomístico* [Anatomy of *The Lame Devil*: A Method of Generic Analysis]. Chapel Hill: U of North Carolina P. 139 pp.
An analysis of the book as a Menippean satire. Includes analysis of the juxtaposition of divergent styles, Vélez's use of literary techniques borrowed from other writers, and oral influences.
MLR 75, 220–21: "sensible," "has a great deal to teach us," but not well written.

1401.   Polzin, Robert. 1977. *Biblical Structuralism: Method and Subjectivity in the Study of Ancient Texts*. Philadelphia: Fortress. 216 pp.
The book is divided into 3 parts: an introduction to a structuralist approach to literature in informal language, an application of that approach to the Book of Job, and an examination of the extent to which basically structuralist methods have informed biblical studies in the past. Bib. 11 pp.; name index.
Style 15, 68–71: "significant ground-breaking exercise in structural thinking about Biblical literature," a "clear and helpful" summary of structuralist theory (with 1 exception), and an *"invaluable"* assessment of the assumptions beneath modern biblical scholarship; but his "purely formalistic" analysis in part 2 does "not relate to the subjective questions which . . . seem to be fundamental to Biblical literature" and to Job in particular.

1402.   Swearingen, James E. 1977. *Reflexivity in* Tristram Shandy: *An Essay in Phenomenological Criticism*. New Haven: Yale UP. 271 pp.

The novel is "an incipient phenomenology the ultimate aim of which is an ontological analysis of the meaning of Tristram's being." Ch. 4 examines questions of language. Bib. 8 pp.; name and term index.

GaR 32, 675: "excellent"; *VQR* 54, 56: very negative rev.; *MP* 77, 339; *PQ* 57, 515.

1403.   Watts, Cedric. 1977. *Conrad's* Heart of Darkness: *A Critical and Contextual Discussion*. Milan: Mursia. 171 pp.

Includes analysis of Conrad's verbal adroitness, narrative techniques, multiple perspectives, etc.

MLR 75, 866: "a very helpful introduction."

1404.   Wolff, Reinhold. 1977. *Strukturalismus und Assoziations-psychologie: Empirisch-pragmatische Literaturwissenschaft im Experiment: Baudelaires "Les chats"* [Structuralism and Associative Psychology: An Experiment in Empirical-Pragmatic Literary Criticism: Baudelaire's "Les chats"]. Tübingen: Niemeyer. 124 pp.

BL (1979), 2772.

1405.   Davis, Walter. 1978. *The Act of Interpretation: A Critique of Literary Reason*. Chicago: U of Chicago P. 194 pp.

An examination of various methodologies of literary interpretation and the presentation of a unified program of criticism, a "radical pluralism" of "multiple working hypotheses." Richard McKeon's "modes of thought" ("problematic," "operational," and "dialectical") provide the philosophical bases for 3 interpretations (hypotheses) of Faulkner's *The Bear* (R. S. Crane, Kenneth Burke, and "Hegel-Davis"), each to be tested by evidence. Name and term index. [See Carroll, no. 1016, and Dijk and Petöfi, no. 1392.]

Style 15, 98–101: "brilliant and subtle," but the sections on McKeon's philosophy are "too brief" and the appendix is "ill-judged"; *CLIO* 9, 311–14: "an eloquent appeal for recognizing human purpose . . . in literary works"; *MLR* 74, 897: "well-informed" but "highly abstract, often convoluted and repetitious" and "embraces the most forced and confused theory" of the 3.

1406.   Freedman, William. 1978. *Laurence Sterne and the Origins of the Musical Novel*. Athens: U of Georgia P. 213 pp.

A study of the role of music in *Tristram Shandy*: "the styles, forms, techniques, and rhythms of the music he played and heard so often worked their way . . . into his novel." Name index.

ECS 13, 112: rides his musical metaphor excessively, but the book is "well written and almost always interesting"; *MP* 78, 185; *SR* 87, cviii–cx.

1407.   Gardner, Helen. 1978. *The Composition of* Four Quartets. New York: Oxford UP. 239 pp.

Part 1 deals with the documents, growth, and sources. Part 2 presents Eliot's final text, each passage followed by a record of revisions and pertinent correspondence with Eliot himself in reply to Gardner's comments and questions.
Style 14, 186–91: "Gardner's choice to focus on the final text is appropriate" for Eliot.

1408.   Maddox, Donald. 1978. *Structure and Sacring: The Systematic Kingdom in Chrétien's* Erec et Enide. Lexington: French Forum. 221 pp.
An interpretation based on methods of modern semiotics and narratology—bipartite and tripartite structures, etc.
MLR 75, 186–87: lacks the historical material to support the structuralist analysis; *FR* 53, 442: "successful," "convincing"; *Spec* 54, 831.

1409.   Maddox, James, Jr. 1978. *Joyce's* Ulysses *and the Assault upon Character*. New Brunswick: Rutgers UP. 244 pp.
An analysis of Joyce's use of epiphany, allusion, "parallax" (perspectives), and other methods to convey character indirectly. Name index.
MFS 25, 287–90: "The most impressive aspect . . . the ways in which Joyce utilizes style to support, test, and otherwise set off his characters"; *MLR* 75, 178–80.

1410.   Diaz Migoyo, Gonzalo. 1978. *Estructura de la novela: Anatomia de* El Buscón [Structure of the Novel: Anatomy of *El Buscón*]. Madrid: Fundamentos. 177 pp.
Ch. 1, plot of cause-effect; chs. 2–3, author vs. narrator (Pablos's style); ch. 4, verisimilitude.
HR 49, 357: "methodologically consistent," "even elegant at times in its argumentation."

1411.   Freeman, Michelle. 1979. *The Poetics of "Translatio Studii" and "Conjointure": Chrétien de Troyes's* Cligés. Lexington: French Forum. 199 pp.
Examines such techniques as placement of metaphors, symbol, inversion, ironic juxtaposition.
MLR 76, 181–82: a "welcome" study, but the coverage is too selective and ignores "almost completely the style and scholastic vocabulary of the poem."

1412.   Kermode, Frank. 1979. *The Genesis of Secrecy: On the Interpretation of Narrative*. Cambridge: Harvard UP. 169 pp.
Explains the differences between hermeneutic and semiotic interpretation through an examination of the Gospel of Mark. Name and term index.
Centrum 6, 133–40: "settles nothing about St. Mark, but it will make any reader think anew about the interpretive act"; *NR* 180, 27; *NS* 98, 107; *Choice* 16, 1010.

1413.   Smith, Frederik. 1979. *Language and Reality in Swift's* A Tale of a Tub. Athens: Ohio State UP. 172 pp.
A nonquantitative study of many of the uses of language in Swift's book, with chs. entitled "Words and Things," "Wordplay," "Lexical Fields," "Syntax and Rhythm," etc. Smith defines style as habitual choice, following the Sapir-Whorf hypothesis and Richard Ohmann's "epistemic" approach from *Shaw: The Style and the Man.*
Style, 17, 79–84: Smith's eschewal of quantification weakens some of his generalizations.

1414.   Johnson, Barbara. 1980. *The Critical Difference: Essays in the Contemporary Rhetoric of Reading.* Baltimore: Johns Hopkins UP. 156 pp.
A collection of 7 essays (4 of them reprints) on specific texts, loosely connected by the deconstruction of the oppositions (a critical or literary text's own disagreements with itself) studied in each ch. "In each essay, the text or its pattern of previous readings is seen to be setting up a network of differences" or oppositions — "masculine/feminine . . . syntax/semantics," etc. Name index.
MLR 78, 381–83: "remarkably adept at drawing out these twists of implication"; *CL* 34, 369: "excellent readings of texts" but too little on the implications of deconstructive theory.

1415.   Nöth, Winfried. 1980. *Literatursemiotische Analysen: Zu Lewis Carrolls Alice-Büchern* [Literary Semiotics Analyses: The *Alice* Books]. Tübingen: Narr. 106 pp.
Uses various semiotic models to explain how patterns of communication are structured and function in *Wonderland* and *Looking-Glass,* dealing mainly with nonsense and anomaly. Bib. 4 pp.
JLS 11, 37–38: a successful application of different semiotic models and systems.

1416.   Oppenheim, Lois. 1980. *Intentionality and Intersubjectivity: A Phenomenological Study of Butor's* La modification. Lexington: French Forum. 187 pp.
An investigation of the way meaning is constituted in the novel via the modification experience in the temporal structure.
MLR 77, 734–35: though aims limited, a "convincing defence" of her method in ch. 1; rev. compares book to Mary Lydon's *Perpetuum Mobile* on Butor ("wide-ranging and perceptive") *FR* 55, 911.

1417.   Pickering, Wilbur. 1980. *A Framework for Discourse Analysis.* Arlington: U of Texas P. 189 pp.
Part 1, "Framework," presents 5 "macrosystems": ch. 2, "Hierarchy"; ch. 3, "Cohesion"; ch. 4, "Prominence"; ch. 5, "Style"; ch. 6, "Strategy." Ch. 7

adds "Medium, Language and Culture." Part 2, "Application": analysis of Paul's letter to the Colossians by the macrosystems (text in Gk.). He follows a decoding approach, questioning the validity of an encoding perspective, and argues that a sentence grammar cannot operate outside a discourse grammar. Bib. 13 pp.

1418.   Spitzer, Leo, and Jules Brody. 1980. *Approches textuelles des* Mémoires *de Saint-Simon* [Textual Approaches to Saint-Simon's *Mémoires*]. Tübingen: Narr; Paris: Place. 107 pp.
Spitzer's essay was written in 1931; Brody has 2 essays; and there is a bib. of criticism of Saint-Simon, 1959–78.
    FR 56, 480.

1419.   Thoiron, Philippe. 1980. *Dynamisme du texte et stylostatistique: Élaboration des index et de la concordance pour* Alice's Adventures in Wonderland: *Problèmes, méthodes, analyse statistique de quelques données* [Dynamism of the Text and Stylostatistics: Preparation of the Index and Concordance for *Alice's Adventures in Wonderland*: Problems, Methods, Statistical Analysis of Some Data]. Geneva: Slatkine. 691 pp.
A first vol. to be followed by *Index et concordance pour* Alice's Adventures in Wonderland. Bib. 43 pp.; name and term index 7 pp.; tables, charts 75 pp.; table of contents 15 pp.
    Ling 20, 571–72: His "dynamic norm" is "original," "a very readable handbook on many difficult points of methodology," "a fine example of intelligent interdisciplinary research" and "a new interpretation of *Alice*."

1420.   Villaverde, Yolanda. 1980. *Vicente Aleixandre, poeta surrealista* [Vicente Aleixandre, Surrealist Poet]. Santiago de Compostela: U de Santiago de Compostela. 183 pp.
Mainly a stylistic analysis of *Espadas como labios*.
    MLR 76, 982: "a disappointing book"; *Hisp* 238, 466.

1420a. Alter, Robert. 1981. *The Art of Biblical Narrative.* New York: Basic. 195 pp.
A close study of how the Hebrew biblical narratives employ stylistic choices to illuminate the complex individuality of the characters.
    JAAC 41, 340–43: contrasts this "very fine book" to Frye's (1982) very different book; *GaR* 36, 900–04: "his method is radically and brilliantly inductive," also contrasted to Frye's book.

1420b. Azar, Inés. 1981. *Discurso retórico y mundo pastoral en la "Egloga segunda" de Garcilaso.* Amsterdam: Benjamins. 172 pp.
An analysis of the rhetorical strategies in Garcilaso's Second Eclogue, employing especially Benveniste's *Problèmes de linguistique générale*.

MLN 98, 289: "adds several new dimensions to Garcilaso studies"; *MLR* 78, 733: "diligent and sensitive," "admirable clarity and thoroughness."

1421.   Chao, Denise. 1981. *Le style du* Journal d'un curé de campagne *de Georges Bernanos* [The Style of *Diary of a Country Priest* by Georges Bernanos]. Washington: UP of America. 120 pp.
A study of the semantic and syntactic characteristics of the novel. Bib. 3 pp.; index.

1422.   Dowling, William C. 1981. *Language and Logos in Boswell's* Life of Johnson. Princeton: Princeton UP. 185 pp.
The *Life* is a paradigm of antithetical structure in narrative, of a plurality of worlds in antithetical relation to one another, of discontinuous orders of discourse. The author proposes a "grammar of discontinuity" for interpreting similar texts. Name index.
Biography 5, 267; *JEGP* 82, 131; *MP* 80, 191; *LJ* 106, 1079.

1423.   Lawrence, Karen. 1981. *The Odyssey of Style in* Ulysses. Princeton: Princeton UP. 229 pp.
The changes in style away from the personal voice and novelistic conventions of the first half of the novel to the various stylistic masks of the second half are rhetorical experiments intended by Joyce to disrupt the reader's expectations. This unique movement of styles changes the idea of style as the "signature" of the writer in the first half of the novel to one of a "citational process" as "language is flooded" by the history of language, which "leads us to doubt the authority" of any one of the novel's styles. Author and term index.
MFS 28, 629: "delightful reading," "orderly," "no serious fault to be found"; *Style* 18, 227; *Choice* 19, 1069; *BRD* 78.10, 57; *TLS* 20 Aug. 1982, 909.

1424.   Lévy, Sidney. 1981. *The Play of the Text: Max Jacob's "Le cornet à Dés."* Madison: U of Wisconsin P. 159 pp.
An analysis of the antireferential techniques of Jacob's text: riddles, parodies, etc.
MLN 98, 831–34: helps us understand 20th-cent. poetry, "clearly organized" with "several enlightening and astute analyses of single poems"; *MLR* 78, 194: "ingenuity"; *VQR* 58, 80; *WLT* 56, 305.

1424a. Miller, Robin. 1981. *Dostoevsky and* The Idiot: *Author, Narrator, and Reader*. Cambridge: Harvard UP. 296 pp.
An analysis of the ambiguous narrator-chronicler—his wily strategies, his development in the notebooks for the novel, his different voices, his development within the novel. Name and term index.
MLR 78, 250–52: "solid, honest, and thorough."

1425.   Ogburn, Floyd, Jr. 1981. *Style as Structure and Meaning: William Brad-*
        ford's Of Plymouth Plantation. Washington: UP of America. 163 pp.
        Bradford's history is "tightly unified and structured in a unique manner."
        Ogburn employs the tools of foregrounding and collocation "to present a new
        approach to the history." Bib. 8 pp.; name and term index.

1426.   Terras, Victor. 1981. *A Karamazov Companion: Commentary on the*
        Genesis, Language, and Style of Dostoevsky's Novel. Madison: U of Wis-
        consin P. 482 pp.
        An admiring appraisal of many aspects of the language and narrative devices
        of this "polyphonic" novel. Bib. 10 pp.; name and term index.
        Style 17, 91.

1427.   Watts, Richard. 1981. *The Pragmalinguistic Analysis of Narrative Texts:*
        Narrative Co-operation in Charles Dickens's Hard Times. Philadelphia:
        Benjamins. 239 pp.
        "I shall develop a model of the written narrative text as a vehicle of commu-
        nication, by drawing on recent developments in theories of language use"
        (sociolinguistics, pragmalinguistics, philosophy of language, etc.), especially
        Siegfried Schmidt's pragmalinguistic model of text analysis. "I shall then ap-
        ply that model to an interpretation of sections of Charles Dickens's novel *Hard*
        Times." Bib. 7 pp.; name and term indexes.
        PoT 5, 221: "a performance-based narratology" versus competence-based.

1427a. Wilson, R. B. J. 1981. *Henry James's Ultimate Narrative:* The Golden
        Bowl. St. Lucia: U of Queensland P. 329 pp.
        The chs. discuss different aspects of the novel: ch. 2 on how 5 critics have
        dealt with 1 sentence in the last ch.; ch. 3, a summary of the final stages
        of the novel and centers of consciousness; ch. 4 on character; ch. 5 on the
        final scene. Bib. 16 pp.; name and term index.
        MFS 28, 662: "powerful and endlessly interesting — if the reader will reread
        [the novel] as he goes."

1427b. Amossy, Ruth. 1982. *Parcours symboliques chez Julien Gracq: "Le Rivage*
        des Syrtes" [Symbolic Routes in the Work of Julien Gracq: "The Borders
        of the Syrtes"]. Paris: Soc. d'Edition d'Enseignement Supérieur. 310 pp.
        An explication of the syntax, language, and symbolism of Gracq's surrealistic
        story.
        MFS 28, 713: a "scholarly study of synthesis" expressed in "unassuming
        style."

1428.   Cowan, Bainard. 1982. *Exiled Waters:* Moby-Dick *and the Crisis of Al-*
        legory. Baton Rouge: Louisiana State UP. 194 pp.

Moby-Dick progresses through 5 different kinds of allegory — ironic, diagram-matic, carnivalistic, anagogic, and prophetic — each constituted by a signifi-cant event in Ishmael's life and by the change in his attitude toward life. Bib. 8 pp.; name and term index.

    WHR 37, 174–77: an enthusiastic rev.: "rich allusiveness," "wide range of reference"; *SR* 91, 86; *Choice* 20, 426.

1429.   Frye, Northrop. 1982. *The Great Code: The Bible and Literature.* New York: Harcourt. 261 pp.

"A study of the Bible from the point of view of a literary critic. . . . my own personal encounter." Part 1, "The Order of Words" (language, myth, metaphor, typology); part 2, "The Order of Types" (typology, metaphor/im-agery, myth/narrative, language/rhetoric). Name and term index.

    GaR 36, 900–04: in contrast to Alter (no. 1420a), Frye is "theoretical and deductive" in his "emphasis on the general comedic pattern of the Christian Bible"; *JAAC* 41, 340–43: also contrasts Frye and Alter; Frye has not written a book about the Bible as much as "a great book about language, myth and metaphor"; *VQR* 59, 86; *Comw* 109, 475.

1430.   Lindheim, Nancy. 1982. *The Structures of Sidney's* Arcadia. Toronto: U of Toronto P. 224 pp.

3 kinds of structure (rhetorical, tonal, and narrative) "operate simultaneously . . . within themselves as well as being structurally functional in the work as a whole." Rhetorical: local organization of language and ideas; tonal: ar-rangement of sequences of events; narrative: episodes and plot. Name and topic index.

    JEGP 82, 544: "considerable merits" but sometimes prefers neatness over insight; *RenQ* 36, 650.

1430a.   Rodway, Allan. 1982. *The Craft of Criticism.* Cambridge: Cambridge UP. 192 pp.

"The bulk of the book consists of practical critiques of poems of various kinds . . . illustrating *a variety of critical methods.*" Rodway limits the meaning of "criticism" by distinguishing it from scholarship (information about a text) and metacriticism (what a text is a sign of); criticism is the study of the lin-guistic integrity and unity of a text. Glossary 22 pp.

    BBN Apr. 1983, 255; *TES* 24 Dec. 1982, 24.

1431.   Hollis, C. Carroll. 1983. *Language and Style in* Leaves of Grass. Baton Rouge: Louisiana State UP. 277 pp.

A wide-ranging feature study employing computational, linguistic, and semiotic-structuralist principles and methods. Explains linguistically the changes between the first ed. and the later rev. eds. of the poem. Bib. 13 pp.; name and term index.

Choice 21, 571: "for a book applying" recent linguistic methods it is "remarkably well written and convincingly argued," "an important study"; *Style* 18, 113.

1432.   Svoboda, Frederic. 1983. *Hemingway and* The Sun Also Rises: *The Crafting of a Style*. Lawrence: UP of Kansas. 148 pp.
A study of the notebook draft, typescript second draft, typist's copy, galley proofs, and Hemingway's notes to himself to reveal how he worked out the plot, characters, and style of the novel. Focuses particularly on 4 extensively revised scenes. 45 pp. of illus.
Choice 21, 427: "a fascinating piece of scholarly detective work."

1433.   Tengström, Emin. 1983. *A Latin Funeral Oration from Early 18th Century Sweden: An Interpretive Study*. Göteborg: Acta U Gothoburgensis. 217 pp.
A holistic analysis of 1 oration: genre, language, structure, social context, ideology, whole message. Bib. 6 pp.; name and term indexes.

1434.   Williams, Gordon. 1983. *Technique and Ideas in the* Aeneid. New Haven: Yale UP. 312 pp.
In the first part the author studies large-scale figural structures; the second part examines various features that are adapted to convey a point of view and to express emotionally charged ideas. Companion to his *Figures of Thought in Roman Poetry* (1980). Index of passages discussed; name and term index.
Choice 20, 1132: "difficult" but "exciting," a "must for all college libraries"; *AJP* 105, 228: a "searching addition to his notable critiques of Latin literature."

6.0 Individual Response: The Reader (1435–84)

6.1 Theory (1435–71a)

1435.   Holland, Norman. 1968. *The Dynamics of Literary Response*. New York: Oxford UP. 378 pp. Rpt. Norton, 1975.
Develops a transformational model of literary experience in the first 6 chs. and applies the model to various literary forms in the last 6. Holland postulates that every text contains 2 complementary levels of meaning—the central meaning of the themes supplied by text and reader, and the central fantasy in the text and the reader's mind. Glossary; name and term index. [Could be classified under 4.0.]
JEGP 68, 560: "a continuing confusion between the work and the response to it" but illuminates "certain aspects of the critical acts"; *NYRB* 12, 33; *KR* 31, 573.

1436. Purves, Alan, and Victoria Rippere. 1968. *Elements of Writing about a Literary Work: A Study of Response to Literature*. Urbana: NCTE. 90 pp.

An analysis of the constituents of writing about literature, by dividing the written response into statements and assigning each statement to 1 of 4 major categories: engagement-involvement, perception, interpretation, and evaluation.

1437. Rosenblatt, Louise. 1968. *Literature as Exploration*. 2nd rev. ed. New York: Noble. 304 pp. (3rd ed. New York: Noble, 1976; rpt. New York: MLA, 1983; orig. pub. 1938).

On the importance of the reader's contribution to a literary work. Little change in "general pattern" but "considerable revision in presentation and illustrative materials. As a coda, I have included a recent article." Bib. 5 pp.; name and term index.

EJ 57, 1359–60: "rich and skillfully written"; Tompkins, *Reader-Response Criticism* xxvi; Suleiman and Crosman, *The Reader in the Text* 45.

1438. Slatoff, Walter. 1970. *With Respect to Readers: Dimensions of Literary Response*. Ithaca: Cornell UP. 212 pp.

Explores "some of the questions which arise when we do seriously acknowledge that books require readers." Name and term index.

Belsey, *Critical Practice*: "Slatoff's admiration for 'open' texts . . . slides . . . back into a conventional respect for texts as authorial soliloquies" (31); *BJA* 11, 200; *Choice*, 8, 544; *LJ* 95, 2920.

1439. Eaton, Trevor. 1972. *Theoretical Semics*. The Hague: Mouton. 176 pp.

In the first part of the book Eaton attacks the impressionism of traditional criticism and argues for the systematic linguistic study of literature. In the second part he provides a theory of discourse as a basis for rigorous stylistics, dividing literary discourse into *literary semantics* (what was in the mind of the author, which is largely unretrievable) and *semics* (what is in the mind of a reader). Semics is the real foundation for stylistics since a reader's response is alone accessible to investigation. [See his distinction between theoretical and empirical semics, no. 245.] Glossary of terms for literary semantics. Bib. 5 pp.; name and term indexes.

Style 9; 108–11: fails to show that his model "has greater explanatory power than previous models," but "otherwise interesting and unusually well-written," and the theory of "semantic space is an important attempt to interconnect the fields of psychology, linguistics, and literary criticism"; *ES* 56, 174–76: "serves the vital function of alerting literary critics" to the need for a new, viable theory; *MLR* 70, 579–81; *RES* ns 26, 361–63; *JLS* 9, 94–103.

1440. Purves, Alan, ed. 1972. *How Porcupines Make Love: Notes on a Response-Centered Curriculum*. Lexington: Xerox. 218 pp.

10 essays on classroom practice.
EJ 63.3, 111: "delightful, informative . . . provocative," might be used "in conjunction" with Rosenblatt (no. 1437).

1441.   Purves, Alan, and Richard Beach. 1972. *Literature and the Reader: Research in Response to Literature, Reading Interests, and the Teaching of Literature.* Urbana: NCTE. 208 pp.
Chs. on studies of response to literature, reading interests, and teaching literature, each followed by a substantial bib. App. of "Summaries of Significant Studies."
Choice 10, 827: cool rev.; *EJ* 63.3, 113: they "attempt too many studies and so really do justice to only a few."

1442.   Graevenitz, Gerhart von. 1973. *Die Setzung des Subjekts: Untersuchungen zur Romantheorie* [The Positioning of the Subjects: Analysis in the Theory of the Novel]. Tübingen: Niemeyer. 163 pp.
Examines the perceptual process between the reader and the linguistic text.
MLR 71, 729–30: "particularly successful when calling into question hallowed methodological assumptions, and for this reason his study will contribute to a newly differentiated awareness of the hermeneutic relationship of reader to novel fiction."

1443.   Swanger, David. 1974. *The Poem as Process.* New York: Harcourt. 256 pp.
The way language is used in poetry requires the reader to be a "co-poet, creating the poem anew." "*The Poem as Process* stresses the activity and process common to the reader and the poet." Name index.
Choice 12, 66: "well informed and current for undergraduates," "for class use mainly."

1444.   Barthes, Roland. 1975. *The Pleasure of the Text.* Trans. Richard Miller. New York: Hill, 1975; London: Cape, 1976. 67 pp. (*Le plaisir du texte.* Paris: Seuil, 1973.)
The pleasures offered by the reading of "writerly" texts (signifiers have free play, author and reader cooperate) are of 2 kinds: *plaisir* (pleasure) and *jouissance* (bliss, ecstasy). The book is composed of fragments in alphabetical order.
NYTBR 14 Sept. 1975, 38: a "self-indulgent meditation on the solitary vice of reading," "an assertive book, Nietzschean in its manner, aiming at effect rather than persuasion"; *MLR* 69, 362–65: an "avante-garde manifesto," "purely and tautologously subjective" in attack against structuralism; *KR* 43, 409; *YR* 65, 261; *NYRB* 23, 31.

1445.   Bleich, David. 1975. *Readings and Feelings: An Introduction to Subjective Criticism.* Urbana: NCTE. 114 pp.

A course of study divided into 4 phases: "Thoughts and Feelings," "Feelings about Literature," "Deciding on Literary Importance," "Interpretation as a Communal Act."

QJS 62, 318: "a significant book" but Bleich is subverting "the humanities as an inherited tradition"; *JAAC* 34, 217.

1446. Foulkes, A. P. 1975. *The Search for Literary Meaning: A Semiotic Approach to the Problem of Interpretation in Education.* Frankfurt: Lang. 159 pp.
A study of literary responses to lexical connotation, particularly those that derive from the shared values of a community.
JLS 5, 102–03: mainly positive rev.

1447. " 'The' Reader, and Real Readers." 1975. *CE* 36.7. 8 pp.
Articles by Bleich, Erlich, Friedman, Holland, Schwartz, and Tsur.

1448. Warning, Rainer, ed. 1975. *Rezeptionsästhetik: Theorie und Praxis* [The Aesthetics of Reception: Theory and Practice]. Munich: Fink. 504 pp. Bib. and indexes.

1449. Link, Hannelore. 1976. *Rezeptionsforschung: Eine Einführung in Methoden und Probleme* [The Study of Reception: An Introduction to Methods and Problems]. Stuttgart: Kohlhammer. 184 pp.
Ch. 1, the categories of author and reader; ch. 2, *Rezeptionsgeschichte* and *Rezeptionsästhetik*; ch. 3, various theoretical methods (Ingarden et al.); ch. 4, ways of reading a specific poem.
MLR 74, 130: "though extremely demanding in parts," the book "is clear and precise . . . . without oversimplifying the issues involved."

1450. Charles, Michel. 1977. *Rhétorique de la lecture* [A Rhetoric of Reading]. Paris: Seuil. 298 pp.
Roles of the reader in various Fr. works.

1451. Magliola, Robert. 1977. *Phenomenology and Literature: An Introduction.* West Lafayette: Purdue UP. 208 pp.
Part 1, the Geneva School (Marcel Raymond et al.) and their accomplices (Emil Staiger et al.) and Heidegger. Part 2, Hirsch, Husserl, Ingarden, and Dufrenne. Name and term index.
Style 12, 313: "a work of formidable erudition" with "careful exposition" except for his treatment of Heidegger; *PLL* 14, 368; *P&L* 3, 122; *Diacritics* 9.2, 30–41.

1452. Bleich, David. 1978. *Subjective Criticism.* Baltimore: Johns Hopkins UP. 309 pp.

Argues that knowledge is developed through the "resymbolization" of experience, a series of acts of explanation to oneself. A work "becomes a reflection of a particular reader." The book makes an argument for the superiority of the subjective paradigm over the objective. Ch. 1, "The Subjective Paradigm"; ch. 2, "The Motivational Character of Language and Symbol Formation"; chs. 6–10, on actual classroom experiences. Name and term index.

MLR 75, 156–57: "deserves the widest and most serious discussion"; *Centrum* ns 1, 74–78: "reads like a bad social science textbook"; *Style* 13, 300–02.

1453.   Iser, Wolfgang. 1978. *The Act of Reading: A Theory of Aesthetic Response*. Baltimore: Johns Hopkins UP. 239 pp. (*Der Akt des Lesens.* Munich: Fink, 1976.)

A description of his process of reading (reconstructing) the structural object of the literary text: the cultural conventions (social and literary) reproduced and transformed into a literary text by such strategies as foregrounding and indeterminacy (gaps) engage the reader in acts of completing or reconstituting the text. Ch. 2, a "functionalist" model of a literary text; ch. 3, "processing" the literary text; ch. 4, interaction of text and reader. Name and term indexes.

Style 14, 179–82: disagrees with Iser in "seven points" — rejecting Iser's premise of the aesthetic object, condemning his dogmatic generalizations based only on his own responses, criticizing his lack of metatheory of literary discourse, etc., but concedes the book displays "breadth of learning" and "intellectual elegance"; *NCF* 34, 337–43: "subtlety and complexity," "an important contribution . . . though one wishes Iser had been more up to date in his arguments with other reader-oriented critics," "assimilable . . . to traditional criticism," closer to E. D. Hirsch than to Stanley Fish; Belsey, *Critical Practice* 36; *Diacritics* 10.2, 47–85 (2 revs. and an interview), and 11.1, 2–13; *Centrum* ns 1, 65–73; *YR* 69, 560–61.

1454.   Miko, František, and Anton Popovič. 1978. *Tvorba a recepcia: Estetická komunikácia a metakomunikácia* [Form and Reception: Aesthetic Communication and Metacommuncation]. Bratislava: Tatran. 385 pp.

BL (1978), 2550; (1979), 2735.

1455.   Rosenblatt, Louise. 1978. *The Reader, the Text, the Poem: The Transactional Theory of the Literary Work*. Carbondale: Southern Illinois UP. 196 pp.

"A physical text" becomes a poem "by virtue of its relationship with the reader who can thus interpret it and reach through it to the world of the author." Rosenblatt distinguishes between "efferent" and "aesthetic" reading — a disengaged concentration on content and an engaged attention to "the actual experience" of reading. Name and term index. [Assumes reality of text and author; compare Eco and Iser; contrast the "empirical semics" of Eaton (and Segers and Kintgen).]

Style 14, 183–85: nothing new, but a clear synthesis of transactional theory; more appropriate for teachers "than for specialists in the field of literary criticism and scholarship"; *CE* 41, 223–27: "a triumph of original thinking on a central subject beautifully and powerfully expressed"; *EJ* 69, 82; *JAAC* 38, 91–93; *JAE* 14, 107–10; *MLR* 76, 923; *MP* 78, 343; *SR* 87, 640; *YR* 69, 560–76.

1456.   Segers, Rien. 1978. *The Evaluation of Literary Texts: An Experimental Investigation into the Rationalization of Value Judgments with Reference to Semiotics and Esthetics of Reception.* Lisse: de Ridder. 234 pp.
Part 1, chs. 1–2 explain "the background" of the approach; ch. 3 discusses auxiliary disciplines; ch. 4, the structure of literary evaluation. Part 2, the experimental research: ch. 5 provides a methodology for the analysis of value judgments; ch. 6, the results and problems of the experiments. Bib. 27 pp. Name index.
JLS 8, 109–17 (rev. article): "a very important contribution to the problem of value in literature" but "provides no way of compensation for the distortion of the concept of value which such useful studies necessarily entail."

1457.   "Théorie de la réception en Allemagne." 1979. *Poétique* 10.39. 125 pp.

1458.   Chafe, Wallace, ed. 1980. *The Pear Stories: Cognitive, Cultural, and Linguistic Aspects of Narrative Production.* Norwood: Ablex. 327 pp.
Research into how people process experience into oral narratives. Name and term indexes.
AA 84, 184: "offers great insight into the nature of discourse processes"; *Choice* 18, 289.

1459.   Fish, Stanley. 1980. *Is There a Text in This Class? The Authority of Interpretive Communities.* Cambridge: Harvard UP. 394 pp.
Part 1, "Literature in the Reader," presents 12 previously pub. essays. Part 2, "Interpretive Authority in the Classroom and in Literary Criticism," gives the author's present conclusions. The whole offers a history of the development of the author's views. Name index.
NR 184, 36–38: "Fish's last chapter all but concedes the triviality of his previous argument"; *SR* 90, 119–23: "While Fish claims to be analyzing reader response, he is actually analyzing the text, and he is treating the text in the way that he learned from the New Critics"; *CC* 99, 801; *MP* 80, 113; *Critm* 23, 177; *Enc* 57, 54; *LJ* 106, 559; *NYRB* 28, 64; *TLS* 8 May 1981, 507; *Diacritics* 12.4, 40–57.

1460.   Suleiman, Susan, and Inge Crosman, eds. 1980. *The Reader in the Text: Essays on Audience and Interpretation.* Princeton: Princeton UP. 441 pp.
17 essays present varieties of "audience-oriented criticism." Bib. 24 pp. (annotated); name and term indexes.

MLR 76, 906–09: contains several excellent essays; *CL* 35, 169–72: Suleiman's 6-category typological introd. "presents one of the best overviews of reader-oriented criticism currently available"; "good essays," but questions inclusion of deconstruction as a variety of such criticism.

1461.   Tompkins, Jane, ed. 1980. *Reader-Response Criticism: From Formalism to Post-Structuralism*. Baltimore: Johns Hopkins UP. 275 pp.
12 essays plus the editor's introd. on "authors' attitudes toward their readers, the kinds of readers various texts seem to imply, the role actual readers play in the determination of literary meaning, the relation of reading conventions to textual interpretation. . . . [T]he essays represent a variety of theoretical orientations: New Criticism, structuralism," etc. Bib. 30 pp.
IFR 8, 162; *WLT* 55, 540; *MFS* 27, 753: "superb introd."

1462.   Graesser, Arthur. 1981. *Prose Comprehension beyond the Word*. New York: Springer. 310 pp.
A report about psychological research in discourse processing and a schema-based framework for exploring prose comprehension. Bib. 25 pp.; name and term indexes.
AJPs 95, 336.

1463.   Ruthrof, Horst. 1981. *The Reader's Construction of Narrative*. London: Routledge. 231 pp.
An attempt to relate new narrative concepts with the phenomenology of reading. Since story is dependent on the reader's realization of the presentational process, story cannot be equated with action sequence but is the reader's construction of the interrelationship of the presented world and the process. Name and term indexes. [Terminologically specialized.]
MFS 28, 358: an "instructive enterprise" though "too taxonomic"; *Choice* 19, 232: "succeeds in integrating the strands of his argument to a very considerable degree," his own contribution to the critical debate "considerable"; *JAE* 16, 113; *MLJ* 66, 76.

1464.   Jauss, Hans. 1982. *Aesthetic Experience and Literary Hermeneutics*. Trans. Michael Shaw. Minneapolis: U of Minnesota P. 357 pp. (*Aesthetische Erfährung und literarische Hermeneutik, I: Versuche im Feld der ästhetischen Erfährung*. Munich: Fink, 1977. 382 pp.)
A theory of the reader within the framework of literary history and aesthetic response. Bib. 5 pp.; name and term index.
JAAC 37, 363–65: Jauss a "courageous pioneer," the book a "substantial contribution"; *CLS* 16, 358–60: a "true *summa*" by a "brilliant theoretician."

1465.   Jauss, Hans. 1982. *Toward an Aesthetic of Reception*. Trans. Timothy Bahti. Introd. Paul de Man. Minneapolis: U of Minnesota P. 231 pp.

5 articles pub. 1969–80 on assumptions prevailing at time text created, the structure and language of the text, the reader's response, and the historical development of the text's reception. Name and term index.

JAAC 41, 354–56: "significant as an emblem" of "criticism's attempt to break away from an obeisance to the text and move toward an engagement with historicity"; *Choice* 20, 700: "indispensable."

1466.   Mailloux, Steven. 1982. *Interpretive Conventions: The Reader in the Study of American Fiction.* Ithaca: Cornell UP. 228 pp.

An introd. to reader-response criticism. In chs. 1–2 the author presents a critique of Fish, Culler, Iser, Holland, and Bleich. In chs. 3–7 he offers a "social reading model" based on "communities and conventions rather than psychological categories." Bib. 3 pp.; name and term index.

Choice 20, 428: "significant achievement"; *JEGP* 83, 256: "the net effect" of the book "is to leave things much as they were"; *JAS* 17, 471; *RMR* 37, 275; *WHR* 37, 172.

1467.   Sharratt, Bernard. 1982. *Reading Relations, Structures of Literary Production: A Dialectical Text/Book.* Atlantic Highlands: Humanities. 341 pp.

A study of the complex set of relations between the reader and the book being read, seeking to establish the concept of a fundamental dialectic that takes place between the reader and the text. Special attention is given to the relation between the novel, especially the novel of crime and detection, and the ideological apparatus of the law in society at different historical periods. [An unusual book difficult to describe or categorize, sometimes close to creative writing.]

Choice 20, 260: "highly original," "playful," "intelligent and complex"; *TLS* 23 Apr. 1982, 458; *Enc* 58, 66.

1468.   Cooper, Charles, ed. 1983. *Researching Response to Literature and the Teaching of Literature.* Norwood: Ablex. 400 pp.

Papers presented at a conference (Bleich, Holland, Purves, Rosenblatt, Kintgen, et al.).

1469.   Dijk, Teun van, and Walter Kintsch. 1983. *Strategies of Discourse Comprehension.* New York: Academic. 418 pp.

1470.   Mitchell, W. J. T. ed. 1983. *The Politics of Interpretation.* Rev. ed., with new introd. Chicago: U of Chicago P. 386 pp.

A collection of essays (most of them previously pub.) that explores the proposition that criticism and interpretation are inseparable from politics — that the arts of understanding and explanation derive from and depend on the structures of power and social value that organize human life in each particular culture, time, or nation. [See 3.0 for similar works.] Name and term index.

MFS 30, 399: "a volume whose considerable parts are greater than its sum."

1471.   Riffaterre, Michael. 1983. *Text Production.* Trans. Terese Lyons. New York: Columbia UP. 341 pp. (*La production du texte.* Paris: Seuil, 1979. 285 pp.)
A work about textual analysis. By the definition of style as the text itself, textual analysis should explain the uniqueness of a literary work. The author develops a typology of intertextuality, a theory of reading, and an approach to literariness as a dialectic between text and reader. Name and term index. [See 2.0 and 5.0.]
   Style 17, 279: some of the "best . . . close textual analysis" of the "last decade" (rev. of Fr. ed.); *PoT* 5, 218: a "continuation" of the "essential tenets" of *Semiotics of Poetry* "in particular clarity"; *TLS* 16 Mar. 1984, 278.

1471a.   Holub, Robert. 1984. *Reception Theory: A Critical Introduction.* London: Methuen. 189 pp.
A study of Ger. reader-response theory, *Rezeptions-theorie,* and its roots in Russ. formalism, Czech structuralism, phenomenology, hermeneutics, literary sociology, and West Ger. society. Annotated bib. 12 pp.; name and term index.
   Choice 21, 1602: "exceptional achievement."

6.2 Practice (1472–84)

1472.   Frey, Eberhard. 1970. *Franz Kafkas Erzählstil: Eine Demonstration neuer stilanalytischer Methoden an Kafkas Erzählung "Ein Hungerkünstler"* [Franz Kafka's Narrative Style: A Demonstration of New Methods of Stylistic Analysis Using Kafka's Story "The Hunger Artist"]. Bern: Lang. 372 pp.
A study of students' reactions to the story. Bib. 8 pp.
   AUMLA 47, 103–05: "a significant study," "the first half . . . a genuine contribution to stylistics."

1473.   Holland, Norman. 1973. *Poems in Persons: An Introduction to the Psychoanalysis of Literature.* New York: Norton. 182 pp. Rpt. Norton, 1975.
A study of how writers create texts and readers re-create them out of their desires and defenses, their "identity themes." The first ch. offers an examination of H.D.'s syntax and imagery through the filter of her autobiographical *Tribute to Freud.* [Thus this portion of the book is part of 4.0.] The second ch. examines the response of 2 students to a poem by H.D., while the third gives Holland's reading of the poem. The book concludes with "A Polemical Epilogue and Brief Guide to Further Reading."

Style 10, 348–49: "a clear and forthright introduction"; *MFS* 20, 292–96: "an admirable introduction" that "serves a number of useful purposes"; *HSL* 6, 72–79: the idea of the identity theme is "a very real advance for psychological criticism," but Holland continues to be too reductionist; *C&L* 25.1, 57–62; *CE* 36, 815–17; *GaR* 28, 170–73; *JAAC* 33, 226–28.

1474. Ledebur, Ruth von. 1974. *Deutsche Shakespeare-Rezeption seit 1945* [German Shakespeare Reception since 1945]. Frankfurt: Akademische. 391 pp.
The history of postwar Germanies is reflected in Ger. Shakespeare criticism. *MLR* 72, 892–94: "impressively rich in materials."

1475. Süssenberger, Claus. 1974. *Rousseau im Urteil der deutschen Publizistik bis zum Ende der Französischen Revolution: Ein Beitrag zur Rezeptionsgeschichte* [The Treatment of Rousseau in German Journalism until the End of the French Revolution: A Contribution to Reception History]. Bern: Lang. 352 pp.
Ger. reactions to Rousseau from the 1750s until the end of the 18th cent., based on the work of Hans R. Jauss.
MLR 71, 466–67: "this new methodology frequently becomes opaque" in the author's hands.

1475a. Frey, Eberhard. 1975. *Stil und Leser: Theoretische und praktische Ansätze zur wissenschaftlichen Stilanalyse* [Style and the Reader: Theoretical and Practical Approaches to a Scientific Analysis of Style]. Bern: Lang. 149 pp.
Studies of responses of average readers to various texts in search for a valid, empirical stylistics.
MLJ 61, 207: "innovative" but "questionable" in attempting to apply this kind of statistical data to the description and evaluation of literary style.

1476. Holland, Norman. 1975. *5 Readers Reading*. New Haven: Yale UP. 418 pp.
An analysis of the responses of 5 readers to Faulkner's "A Rose for Emily." Name and term index 8 pp.
Diacritics 5.3, 24–31: "for all my admiration" for the book "I hesitate before its conclusions"; *Choice* 12, 1303: "a massive challenge to the orthodox assumptions that dominate education"; *QJS* 62, 213; *LJ* 100, 764; *TLS* 18 July 1975, 801.

1477. "Response to Literature." 1976. *RTE* 10.3. 97 pp.
5 essays. The first, by Lee Odell and Charles Cooper, sets forth a technique for analyzing the processes by which a written response is formulated.

1478.   Deleted.

1479.   Dillon, George L. 1978. *Language Processing and the Reading of Literature: Toward a Model of Comprehension.* Bloomington: Indiana UP. 208 pp.
Focusing mainly on syntactical problems, Dillon explores 2 levels of reading—perception (propositional structure of sentences) and comprehension (contextual frame of sentences)—especially in the work of Spenser, Milton, James, Faulkner, and Stevens. (The third level of reading—interpretation of intention—"exceeds the bounds of this study.") Chs. on "Phrases and Their Functions," "Clause Boundaries," "Reference, Coreference, and Attachment," "Consciousness of Sentence Structure" (by literary authors), "Integration into Context," "Some Values of Complex Processing." Bib. 6 pp.
Style 15, 77–79: a strong introd. and first 4 chs. on perception and comprehension based on "solid" linguistics and psychological research, but the sections on interpretation "go little beyond intuition"; also, there is little in the book "specific to reading," and the analytical model "ties the author to analysis of the individual sentence" (in contrast to Halliday and Hasan's more inclusive *Cohesion in English*); *MLR* 75, 351–52: "a well-informed application of the results . . . from research into language *performance*"; *RES* ns 31, 322–24; *Ling* 17, 930–33.

1480.   Horton, Susan. 1979. *Interpreting Interpreting: Interpreting Dickens's Dombey.* Baltimore: Johns Hopkins UP. 136 pp.
"Interpretive strategies bring into being the interpretations they describe"; the structure we attribute to a text is "determined by the structure of an interpreter's inquiry." But there are practical limits to the number of interpretations. *Dombey and Son* is shown to have permitted many interpretive paradigms, Horton's own model being a historical and biographical investigation of Dickens's intentions. Name index. [See 5.2.4, where this book could be classified.]
Style 17, 44–46: "an important and highly intelligent book"; *Critm* 22, 274; *Choice* 17, 220.

1481.   Berry, Ralph. 1981. *Changing Styles in Shakespeare.* London: Allen. 123 pp.
Perceptions of Shakespeare on the contemporary British stage. [I use this 1 critical work to represent the field, largely unexplored, of changing interpretations of plays on the stage.]
TLS 1 Jan. 1982, 18.

1482.   Cardinal, Roger. 1981. *Figures of Reality.* London: Croom Helm; Totowa: Barnes. 245 pp.

Partly about strategies of suggesting unreality and reality in poems, partly about the author's and other readers' responses to these strategies. Ger. Romantic and Fr. surrealist poetry predominate. Bib. 9 pp.; name and term index.

MLR 77, 913–15: negative rev.; *WLT* 56, 577: the "finest" book by "one of the best minds in the field"; *BBN* Apr. 1981, 242; *SR* 89, lxxvi; *Choice* 18, 1091.

1483. Rancour-Laferrière, Daniel. 1982. *Out from under Gogol's Overcoat: A Psychoanalytic Study*. Ann Arbor: Ardis. 251 pp.
The author claims to be making a "depth psychoanalysis of the ways sensitive readers respond" to "The Overcoat" by consulting "numerous native speakers of Russian" and "the enormous critical and scholarly literature" on "The Overcoat." Bib. 12 pp.; no index.
Choice 20, 709: "little short of brilliant"; *MLR* 79, 509.

1484. Kintgen, Eugene. 1983. *The Perception of Poetry*. Bloomington: Indiana UP. 269 pp.
A study of the reading process, "the actual experience of reading." Ch. 1, critique of diverse approaches to readers reading; ch. 2, the elementary operations of the processes of reading; ch. 3, the processes exemplified from 1 reader's protocol on Shakespeare's sonnet 94; ch. 4, 4 readers' protocols on the same sonnet; ch. 5, 1 reader reading 3 poems; ch. 6, appraisal of protocol analysis and speculation on "what all readers have in common." 81 pp. of protocols; no bib. or index. [The empirical study of a text at its most extreme limit. See Eaton on empirical semics, no. 245.]

Appendix 1. Chronology

1878   Ferdinand de Saussure, *Mémoire sur le système primitif des voyelles dans les langues Indo-Européennes*. The origin of what later came to be called structural grammar or linguistics because of the argument that a language is a self-contained system consisting of structures entering into relationships in which each part is dependent on every other part.

1893   Charles S. Peirce, "What Is a Sign?" Peirce is "one of the two (with Saussure) founding fathers of modern semiotic studies" (Hawkes, *Structuralism and Semiotics*).
        Buchler in *Philosophical Writings of Peirce*, ch. 7, "Logic as Semiotic: The Theory of Signs," brings together fragments written 1892–1910.

1900–01 Edmund Husserl, *Logische Untersuchungen*. "Seminal for much recent work in the humanities," "very close" in certain aspects to Eco's *Theory of Semiotics* (1977) (Fokkema and Kunne-Ibsch, *Theories of Literature in the Twentieth Century*).

1905   Charles Bally, *Traité de stylistique française* (2 vols.; rpt. 1963).

1906–11 Saussure's lectures on linguistics at the University of Geneva.

1911   Franz Boas, "Introduction" to *Handbook of American Indian Languages*. Like Saussure, Boas concluded each language had to be described in terms of its own structural system.

1915   Saussure's lectures published posthumously as *Cours de linguistique générale*. Its argument that a language should be studied synchronically as a self-regulating system of conventions and relationships was to have momentous influence.

1915   Moscow Linguistic Circle founded.

1916   Petrograd Society for the Study of Poetic Language (OPAJAZ or OPOIAZ) founded. Its *Theory of Poetic Language* appeared the same year.

1917   Viktor Šklovskij, "Art as Technique."
        The revolution proposed by the Russian formalists resided in their giving primacy not to reference but to form by viewing literature as a self-sufficient entity, content as a function of literary form; the parallel with Saussure's conception of language seems apparent.

1919   Boris M. Eixenbaum, "How Gogol's 'Overcoat' Is Made" (trans. 1971).

1921   Edward Sapir, *Language*. Whereas Saussure is the father of European structural linguistics, Sapir and others introduced modern structural linguistics to North America. The essential insight is the same: a language by operating on self-regarding, inherent structuring principles controls perception of reality; a culture is determined by its language; we experience as we do largely because our language predisposes certain perceptions and choice of interpretation.
        Viktor Žirmunskij, "Problems of Poetics." Perhaps introduced the notion of style as the system of devices of an individual work of literature.

1922   Leonard Bloomfield's praise of Sapir's *Language* for attending to synchronic matters prior to diachronic.
        Eixenbaum, *Melodika russkogo liricheskogo stikha*. The role of intonation in verse.

1923   I. A. Richards and C. K. Ogden, *The Meaning of Meaning.*

1924   Bloomfield's review of Saussure's *Cours* in *Modern Language Journal* 8 (1924): Saussure "has given us the theoretic basis for a science of human speech." Richards, *Principles of Literary Criticism.*
Jurij Tynjanov, *The Problem of Verse Language.* Perhaps the first systematic exposition of the idea of structuralism (that all elements in a literary structure are mutually linked by numerous relationships).

1925   Šklovskij, *On the Theory of Prose.* One of the first attempts at a poetics of fiction, that is, an analysis of the conventions of plot. "The Formalists' strategy paralleled that of the New Critics" (Lemon and Reis, *Russian Formalist Criticism*).
Sapir, "Sound Patterns in English."

1926   Prague Linguistic Circle had coalesced into a relatively stable group, with Roman Jakobson as one of its leaders.
Marguerite Lips, *Le style indirect libre.*
Richards, *Science and Poetry.*

1927   Eixenbaum, "The Theory of the Formal Method."
E. M. Forster, *Aspects of the Novel.*

1928   First International Congress of Linguists, The Hague.
Medvedev and Baxtin, *The Formal Method in Literary Scholarship* (trans. 1978).
Jan Mukařovský's analysis of Macha's poem *Máj.* Uses techniques of Russian formalists to analyze the relationships between sound/grammar and meaning/theme.
V. I. Propp, *Morphology of the Folktale.* Another important advance toward a fiction poetics.
Tynjanov and Jakobson, *Problems of the Study of Literature and Language.* Perhaps the first manifesto of structuralism. "Formalism of the nineteen twenties, structuralism of the pre-war years and the semiotics of today share the fundamental presupposition, that literature, like other cultural orders, has its own general principles which can be objectively described, and that these general principles are ultimately socially or historically conditioned. Common to the three movements also is the central place accorded to linguistics in literary theory" (Shukman, *Literature and Semiotics*).

1929   Richards, *Practical Criticism.* Introduces the laboratory method in the investigation of interpretation. The importance of the linguistic structure of literature and of verbal analysis was reinvigorated in the 1920s and 1930s by Richards and his student William Empson and institutionalized as "practical criticism" at Cambridge and as the "New Criticism" in North America.

1930   Empson, *Seven Types of Ambiguity.* A classic of New Criticism now increasingly appreciated by structuralists.
André Jolles, *Einfache Formen.*
Valentin Nikolaevič Vološinov, *Marxism and the Philosophy of Language* (in Russ., trans. 1973). Has been "rightly called a prolegomenon for Soviet semiotics" (Scholes, *Semiotics and Interpretation*).
Prague Linguistic Circle (Prague School, Prague structuralism) flourished during the 1930s as a continuation and reassessment of Russian formalism through the application of both Peirce's semiotic and Saussure's semiology.

1931   Roman Ingarden, *Das literarische Kunstwerk: Eine Untersuchung aus dem Grenzgebiet der Ontologie, Logic und Literaturwissenschaft* (*O dziele literackim*, 1960; *The Literary Work of Art*, 1973).

1932   Mukařovský, "Standard Language and Poetic Language" (the title of Garvin's partial translation of a longer essay). Makes a sharp distinction between different "functional" languages, poetic language a special language within language.

1933   Bloomfield, *Language*. This book, which followed Sapir's and Saussure's insights, is "the most important single publication concerning the scientific study of language during the last thirty-five years" (Fries, *Linguistics and Reading*).

1934   "An ambitious attempt was made" by the Prague Linguistic Circle "to develop a coherent theory of literature and aesthetics which they called *structuralism*, at least as early as 1934. Long before the present fashion for the term, a doctrine was evolved in the Prague Circle and applied concretely which anticipates many of the newest speculations in literary theory and aesthetics or, at least, parallels some of the most active and promising movements in the West: the American New Criticism, the semantics of Charles Morris, the *style as meaning* view of William K. Wimsatt, etc., even though there were no direct contacts among them" (Wellek, *The Literary Theory and Aesthetics of the Prague School*).

1935   *Slovo a slovesnost* (Word and Language Culture) founded by the Prague Circle. The introductory article (Jakobson et al.) proclaimed semiotics to be the crucial intellectual issue of modern times.

1936   Mukařovský, *Aesthetic Function, Norm, and Value as Social Facts* (in Czech). The "best statement" of his general theory of signs, the aesthetic object conceived "as a system of 'autonomous signs' " (Wellek, *Literary Theory*).
           Richards, *The Philosophy of Rhetoric*.

1937   Ingarden, *O poznawaniu dziela literackiego* (*The Cognition of the Literary Work of Art*, 1973). "Just as there is no science or practice of medicine without a model of man, i.e., without anatomy and physiology, there is no systematic knowledge or competent treatment of literature as art without a knowledge of the 'anatomical' structure and of the 'organic' functions of the basic model of the literary work of art as such—of its general idea. Ingarden's work supplies that fundamental knowledge" (Falk, *The Poetics of Roman Ingarden*).
           John Crowe Ransom, "Criticism, Inc." Sometimes cited as the essay that ushered in the era of formal criticism in the U.S.

1938   Cleanth Brooks and Robert Penn Warren, *Understanding Poetry*. Powerfully influential on the way teachers and students in the U.S. perceived literature as formal organizations.
           Charles Morris, *Foundations of the Theory of Signs*.
           Louise Rosenblatt, *Literature as Exploration*. A pioneering work on reader response, the reader counting "for at least as much as the book or poem."

1939   Benjamin Lee Whorf, "The Relation of Habitual Thought and Behavior to Language."

1940   Mukařovský, "On Poetic Language."
           Whorf, "Science and Linguistics."

1941   Kenneth Burke, *The Philosophy of Literary Form: Studies in Symbolic Action*.
           Ransom, *The New Criticism*.

1942   René Wellek and Austin Warren, *Theory of Literature*. This book contains insights from the Prague Linguistic Circle, of which Wellek was a member 1930–35.

1943   Louis Hjelmslev, *Prolegomena to a Theory of Language* (in Danish; trans. Russ., 1960; Eng., 1953 and 1961).

1945   Burke, *A Grammar of Motives*.

1946   Wimsatt and Beardsley, "The Intentional Fallacy."

1947   Brooks, *The Well Wrought Urn*.
           Marcel Cressot, *Le style et ses techniques*.

1948   Leo Spitzer, *Linguistics and Literary History*. Spitzer, Erich Auerbach, Karl Vossler, and Ernst Curtius had exerted a significant influence on European literary studies through their interdisciplinary practice of Romance philology.
1949   Wimsatt and Beardsley, "The Affective Fallacy."
1950   Burke, *A Rhetoric of Motives*
        Etienne Souriau, *Les deux cent mille situations dramatiques.*
1951   Empson, *The Structure of Complex Words.*
        George L. Trager and Henry Lee Smith, Jr., *Outline of English Studies.* In the line of structural linguistics, building on Sapir and Bloomfield.
1952   *Voprosy Jazykoznanija* journal founded (Moscow).
        A. A. Mendilow, *Time and the Novel.*
        Critics and Criticism. A collection of essays by the "Chicago Critics," who are linked by their association with the University of Chicago and their exploration of Aristotelian principles as a basis for criticism ("Neo-Aristotelianism") and their study of the role of theory and method in critical variation ("pluralism").
1953   Roland Barthes, *Le degré zero de l'écriture* (trans. *Writing Degree Zero*, 1967).
        R. S. Crane, *The Languages of Criticism and the Structure of Poetry.* A statement of the pluralism (the importance of theory and method) of the Chicago School.
1954   Robert Humphrey, *Stream of Consciousness in the Modern Novel.*
        Wimsatt, *The Verbal Icon.*
1955   Ongoing debate in *Voprosy Jazykoznanija* during the mid-1950s.
        Maurice Blanchot, *The Space of Literature* (in Fr., trans. 1983).
        Donald Davie, *Articulate Energy: An Inquiry into the Syntax of English Poetry.*
        Victor Erlich, *Russian Formalism.* The earliest and still standard account in English.
        Melvin Friedman, *Stream of Consciousness.*
        A. A. Hill, "An Analysis of *The Windhover*: An Experiment in Structural Method." U.S. structural linguistics applied in the criticism of a poem.
        Claude Lévi-Strauss, *Tristes tropiques.* Follows Sapir and Whorf that language is the chief distinguishing feature whereby all forms of social life can be studied through concepts similar to those employed in linguistics. The beginning of structuralism as a "mass movement" (Jameson, *The Prison-House of Language*).
1956   Jakobson and Halle, *Fundamentals of Language.*
1957   *Voprosy Literaturyj* journal founded (Moscow).
        Barthes, *Mythologies* (trans. 1972). The "classic exposition" of the ways in which ideological myths are naturalized to form common sense in our society (Belsey, *Critical Pactice*).
        Noam Chomsky, *Syntactic Structures.* A profoundly important new paradigm.
        J. R. Firth, *Papers in Linguistics, 1934–1951.*
        Northrop Frye, *Anatomy of Criticism.*
        Käte Hamburger, *Die Logik der Dichtung* (trans. *The Logic of Literature*, 1973).
        Stephen Ullmann, *Style in the French Novel.*
1958   Indiana University Conference on Style organized by Thomas Sebeok. This conference "marked a significant watershed between the casual consideration of literary style from a linguistic point of view and the treatment of linguistic stylistics as a discipline worthy of serious scholarly interest" (Bailey, "Current Trends in the Analysis of Style," *Style* 1.1 [1967]); it included Jakobson's highly influential "Closing Statement: Linguistics and Poetics."
        Christine Brooke-Rose, *A Grammar of Metaphor.*

Lévi-Strauss, *Anthropologie structurale* (trans. *Structural Anthropology*, 1963). "Lévi-Strauss sought to ensure the scientific nature of his observations by his use of the linguistic and particularly the phonological method. The wish to be scientific in his procedure" he shares "with formalists of more than one generation. For linguistics has but one universal object: the articulated language" (Broekman, *Structuralism*).

Jean-Pierre Vinay and Jean Louis Darbelnet, *Stylistique comparée du français et de l'anglais.*

1959 Saussure's *Cours de linguistique générale* translated into Eng. as *Course in General Linguistics.*

1960 *Tel Quel* journal founded, a significant event in the rise of structuralism.
Stephen Ullmann, *The Image in the Modern French Novel.*

1961 Cybernetics endorsed by the Communist Party of the Soviet Union. Conference at Gorkij University on the application of mathematical methods to the study of literary language.
Wayne Booth, *The Rhetoric of Fiction.*
Henry Allan Gleason, Jr., *Introduction to Descriptive Linguistics.*
John Thompson, *The Founding of English Metre.*

1962 Moscow symposium on the structural study of sign systems: the idea of "modeling systems" well represented.
J. L. Austin, *How to Do Things with Words* (lectures delivered in 1955).
Umberto Eco, *L'opera aperta.* Early study of the "open" work.
Jakobson and Lévi-Strauss, " 'Les chats' de Charles Baudelaire."
Thomas Kuhn, *The Structure of Scientific Revolutions.*
Samuel R. Levin, *Linguistic Structures in Poetry.*
Winifred Nowottny, *The Language Poets Use.*
Richard Ohmann, *Shaw: The Style and the Man.*
Bertil Romberg, *Studies in the Narrative Technique of the First Person Novel.*

1963 Barthes, *Sur Racine* (trans. *On Racine*, 1964).
Ivan Fónagy, *Die Metaphern in der Phonetik.* On sound symbolism, etc.

1964 First summer school of the Moscow-Tartu semiotics group held at Kaariku in Estonia.
Travaux Linguistique de Prague revived by the Linguistic Association and the Group for Functional Linguistics.
Semeiotika, journal of Russian structuralist semiotics founded at Tartu University.
Alan Dundes, *The Morphology of North American Indian Folktales.*
Nils Enkvist, John Spencer, and Michael Gregory, *Linguistics and Style.*
Paul Garvin, ed., *A Prague School Reader on Aesthetics, Literary Structure and Style.*
Lucien Goldmann, *Pour une sociologie du roman.* An attempt to unite a Marxist view with a structuralist methodology into a "genetic structuralism."
Ullmann, *Language and Style.*

1965 Seymour Chatman, *A Linguistic Theory of English Meter.*
Chomsky, *Aspects of the Theory of Syntax.* A significant effort to include semantics.
Gleason, *Linguistics and English Grammar.*
William Handy, *A Symposium on Formalist Criticism.*
Lemon and Reis, eds. and trans., *Russian Formalist Criticism.* Translation of essays by Šklovskij, Tomaševskij, and Eixenbaum.
Raymond Picard, *Nouvelle critique ou nouvelle imposture?* An attack on *Sur Racine.*

Tzvetan Todorov, ed., *Théorie de la littérature: Textes des formalistes russes.* Translation of essays by members of the Moscow Linguistic Circle and the Petrograd Society for the Study of Poetic Language.

1966   *Computers and the Humanities* journal founded.

Langages: Sémiotiques textuelles journal founded (Paris).

Lingua e stile journal founded (Bologna).

Second summer school of the Moscow-Tartu semiotics group, Jakobson and Pomorska as guests.

International symposium at Johns Hopkins on "The Languages of Criticism and the Sciences of Man" (pub. 1970 as *The Structuralist Controversy*).

Louis Althusser, *For Marx* (in Fr., trans. 1969).

Emile Benveniste, *Problems in General Linguistics* (in Fr., trans. 1971).

Burke, *Language as Symbolic Action.*

Sergej Doubrovskij, *Pourquoi la nouvelle critique* (trans. *The New Criticism in France,* 1973).

Roger Fowler, *Essays on Style and Language.*

Gérard Genette, *Figures I.*

Algirdas J. Greimas, *Sémantique structurale.*

Jacques Lacan, *Ecrits* (in Fr., trans. 1977).

Pierre Machery, *A Theory of Literary Production* (in Fr., trans. 1978).

Mukařovský, *Studies in Aesthetics.* Reprints his structuralist writings since 1931 with papers written during the war years from manuscript.

Michael Riffaterre, "Describing Poetic Structures: Two Approaches to Baudelaire's 'Les chats' " (reply to Jakobson and Lévi-Strauss, 1962).

Robert Scholes and Robert Kellogg, *The Nature of Narrative.*

Josef Vachek, *The Linguistic School of Prague.*

1967   *Poetica* journal founded.

Style journal founded.

"The annual bibliography of the Modern Language Association (which had made no official mention of 'literary theory' until 1960, and then continued to group it together, indifferently, with 'aesthetics' and 'literary criticism' until 1967) was reorganized to create a separate subdivision devoted exclusively to 'Literary Criticism and Literary Theory'— and the number of entries immediately began to swell from a scant two hundred in 1967 to over six hundred in 1975" (Bruss, *Beautiful Theories*).

Chatman and Levin, eds., *Essays on the Language of Literature.*

E. D. Hirsch, Jr., *Validity in Interpretation.*

Engler's critical edition of Saussure's *Cours,* volume 1.

Frank Kermode, *The Sense of an Ending.*

Josephine Miles, *Style and Proportion: The Language of Prose and Poetry.*

Louis Milic, *A Quantitative Approach to the Style of Jonathan Swift* and *Style and Stylistics: An Analytical Bibliography.*

C. K. Ogden, *Opposition: A Linguistic and Psychological Analysis.*

Todorov, *Littérature et signification.*

1968   *Language and Style* journal founded.

Section on stylistics in *MLA International Bibliography,* volume 3, initiated.

Third summer school of the Moscow-Tartu semiotics group.

Robert Adolph, *The Rise of Modern Prose Style.*

Richard W. Bailey and Lubomír Doležel, eds., *An Annotated Bibliography of Statistical Stylistics.*

Bailey and Dolores M. Burton, *English Stylistics: A Bibliography.*

Eco, *La struttura assente* (with *Le forme del contenuto,* 1971, and other work, reworked into *A Theory of Semiotics,* 1976).
Firth, *Studies in Linguistic Analysis.*
Norman Holland, *The Dynamics of Literary Response.*
1969   Style in Language Conference, Villa Serbelloni, Bellagio.
Semiotica journal founded.
Paul Barrette and Monique Fol, *Un certain style ou un style certain?*
Stephen Booth, *An Essay on Shakespeare's Sonnets.*
David Crystal and Derek Davy, *Investigating English Style.*
Edward Corbett, *Rhetorical Analyses of Literary Works.*
Doležel and Bailey, eds., *Statistics and Style.*
Bernard Dupriez, *L'étude des styles.*
Michel Foucault, *The Archaeology of Knowledge* (in Fr., trans. 1972).
Genette, *Figures II.*
Bennison Gray, *Style: The Problem and Its Solution.*
Graham Hough, *Style and Stylistics.*
Geoffrey N. Leech, *A Linguistic Guide to English Poetry.*
Glen A. Love and Michael Payne, eds., *Contemporary Essays on Style.*
D. C. Muecke, *The Compass of Irony.*
John R. Searle, *Speech Acts.*
Cesare Segre, *I segni e la critica* (trans. *Semiotics and Literary Criticism,* 1975).
Todorov, *Grammaire du* Décaméron.
Karl Uitti, *Linguistics and Literary Theory.*
1970   *Poétique* journal founded (Paris).
Barthes, *S/Z* (trans. into Eng. in 1975). In the 1970s Barthes turned to "decentered," personal, autobiographical writing.
W. J. M. Bronzwaer, *Tense in the Novel.*
Wallace Chafe, *Meaning and the Structure of Language.*
Donald C. Freeman, ed., *Linguistics and Literary Style.*
Greimas, *Du sens.* Stresses the signifying role of binary opposition (derived from Saussure and Jakobson) to create a "grammar" of narrative.
Group M. *Rhétorique générale* (trans. *A General Rhetoric,* 1981). A redefinition of rhetorical figures in modern linguistic terms.
Pierre Guiraud, *Essais de stylistique.*
Guiraud and Kuentz, *La stylistique.*
Jakobson and Jones, *Shakespeare's Verbal Art in "Th'Expence of Spirit."*
Michael Lane, *Structuralism.*
Juryj Lotman, *Struktura khudozhestvennogo teksta* (trans. *The Structure of the Artistic Text,* 1977). The year 1970 was both "the end of a stage" for the Moscow-Tartu semiotics group, with the appearance of "two major works of literary theory," Lotman's *Struktura* and Uspensky's *Poetika kompozitsii,* and "the beginning of a new trend" (Shukman, *Literature and Semiotics*).
Henri Meschonnic, *Pour la poétique* (4 vols., 1970–75).
Todorov, *Introduction à la littérature fantastique* (trans. *The Fantastic,* 1973).
Boris Uspenskij, *A Poetics of Composition* (trans. into Eng., 1973).
C. B. Williams, *Style and Vocabulary.*
1971   *Diacritics* journal founded.
Journal of Literary Semantics founded.
LiLi journal founded.
Poetics journal founded.
Sub-Stance journal founded.

James Bennett, *Prose Style*.
François Bovon, *Analyse structurale et exégèse biblique* (trans. *Structural Analysis and Biblical Exegesis*, 1974).
Jan Broekman, *Strukturalismus: Moskau, Prag, Paris* (Eng. trans. 1974).
Chatman, ed., *Literary Style: A Symposium*. The 1969 Villa Serbellone papers.
Fowler, *The Languages of Literature*.
I. R. Galperin, *Stylistics*.
Greimas, *Essais de sémiotique poétique* and *La sémiologie*.
Claudio Guillén, *Literature as System*.
Morris Halle and Samuel J. Keyser, *English Stress: Its Form, Its Growth, and Its Role in Verse*.
James L. Kinneavy, *A Theory of Discourse*.
Karl Kroeber, *Styles in Fictional Structure*.
Pierre Léon, *Problems of Textual Analysis*.
Paul Levitt, *A Structural Approach to the Analysis of Drama*.
Ladislav Matejka and Krystyna Pomorska, eds., *Readings in Russian Poetics*.
Riffaterre, *Essais de stylistique structurale*.
Joseph Strelka, *Patterns of Literary Style*.
Ewa Thompson, *Russian Formalism and Anglo-American New Criticism*.
Todorov, *Poétique de la prose*. (trans. *The Poetics of Prose*, 1977)
Virginia Tufte, *Grammar as Style*.

1972   Olga Akhmanova, *Linguostylistics*.
Howard S. Babb, ed., *Essays in Stylistic Analysis*.
Teun van Dijk, *Some Aspects of Text Grammars*.
Oswald Ducrot and Todorov, *Dictionnaire encyclopédique des sciences du langage* (trans. *Encyclopedic Dictionary of the Sciences of Language*, 1979).
Trevor Eaton, *Theoretical Semics*.
Norman Eliason, *The Language of Chaucer's Poetry*.
Genette, *Figures III*.
M. A. K. Halliday, *Language as Social Context*.
Jens Ihwe, *Linguistik in der Literaturwissenschaft*.
Fredric Jameson, *The Prison-House of Language: A Critical Account of Structuralism and Russian Formalism*.
Braj B. Kachru and Herbert F. W. Stahlke, eds., *Current Trends in Stylistics*.
Lotman, *Analysis of the Poetic Text* (trans. into Eng., 1976).
Norman Page, *The Language of Jane Austen*.
Warren Shibles, *Essays on Metaphor*.
Jan Thavenius, *Stil Och Vocabulär*.
Wimsatt, *Versification*.

1973   *Association for Literary and Linguistic Computing Bulletin* founded.
Centrum journal founded.
Degrés: Revue de synthèse à orientation sémiologique founded.
Aitken, Bailey, and Hamilton-Smith, eds., *The Computer and Literary Studies*.
Between Language and Literature (Cracow).
Claude Bremond, *Logique du récit*.
Raymond Chapman, *Linguistics and Literature*.
Chatman, ed., *Approaches to Poetics* and *The Later Style of Henry James*.
Jean-Claude Coquet, *Sémiotique littéraire*.
Daniel Delas and Jacques Filliolet, *Linguistique et poétique*.
Doležel, *Narrative Modes in Czech Literature*.
Enkvist, *Linguistic Stylistics*.
Kenneth Goodman, *The Psycholinguistic Nature of the Reading Process*.

M. A. K. Halliday, *Explorations in the Functions of Language.*
William O. Hendricks, *Essays on Semiolinguistics and Verbal Art.*
Holland, *Poems in Persons.*
Jakobson, *Main Trends in the Science of Language.*
Michel Le Guern, *Sémantique de la métaphore et de la métonymie.*
Norman Page, *Speech in the English Novel.*
Margot Peters, *Charlotte Brontë: Style in the Novel.*
Gregory Polletta, *Issues in Contemporary Literary Criticism.*
Gerald Prince, *A Grammar of Stories.*
Willy Sanders, *Linguistische Stiltheorie.*
G. W. Turner, *Stylistics.*
Ullmann, *Meaning and Style.*

1974   *Critical Inquiry* journal founded.
International Society for Semiotic Studies founded in Milan in June.
Booth, *A Rhetoric of Irony.*
Barron Brainerd, *Weighing Evidence in Language and Literature.*
Agnes Bruno, *Toward a Quantitative Methodology for Stylistic Analyses.*
Burton, *Shakespeare's Grammmatical Style.*
John Ellis, *The Theory of Literary Criticism.*
Enkvist, *Stilforskning och Stilteori.*
Wolfgang Iser, *The Implied Reader.*
Geoffrey Leech, *Semantics.*
Miles, *Poetry and Change.*
Scholes, *Structuralism in Literature.*
Thomas Sebeok, *Current Trends in Linguistics.*
Bernd Spillner, *Linguistik und Literaturwissenschaft.*
P. M. Wetherill, *The Literary Text.*

1975   *Linguistic Analysis* journal founded.
C. Paul Casparis, *Tense without Time.*
Anne Cluysenaar, *Aspects of Literary Stylistics.*
Jonathan Culler, *Structuralist Poetics.*
Irene Fairley, *E. E. Cummings and Ungrammar.*
Fowler, *Style and Structure in Literature.*
Joseph Grimes, *The Thread of Discourse.*
Holland, *5 Readers Reading.*
John Hollander, *Vision and Resonance.*
Andrew Kennedy, *Six Dramatists in Search of a Language.*
Don Nilsen and Alleen Nilsen, *Semantic Theory: A Linguistic Perspective.*
János Petöfi, *Vers une théorie partielle du texte.*
Håkan Ringbom, ed., *Style and Text.*
H. G. Widdowson, *Stylistics and the Teaching of Literature.*

1976   *International Review of Slavic Linguistics and Poetics* founded.
PTL: A Journal for Descriptive Poetics and Theory (Tel-Aviv).
Jean-Michel Adam, *Linguistique et discours littéraire.*
Christine Brooke-Rose, *A Structural Analysis of Pound's Usura Canto.*
Conrad Bureau, *Linguistique fonctionnelle et stylistique objective.*
Robert Cluett, *Prose Style and Critical Reading.*
van Dijk, *Pragmatics of Language and Literature.*
Norbert Dittmar, *A Critical Survey of Sociolinguistics.*
Madeleine Doran, *Shakespeare's Dramatic Language.*
Eco, *A Theory of Semiotics.*
Greimas, *Maupassant: La sémiotique du texte.*

Waldemar Gutwinski, *Cohesion in Literary Texts.*
Halliday and Ruqaiya Hasan, *Cohesion in English.*
Stanley Fish, "How to Do Things with Austin and Searle."
William O. Hendricks, *Grammars of Style and Styles of Grammar.*
Archibald A. Hill, *Constituent and Pattern in Poetry.*
Elmar Holenstein, *Roman Jakobson's Approach to Language*
Iser, *Der Akt des Lesens* (trans. *The Act of Reading: A Theory of Aesthetic Re-
sponse,* 1978).
Matejka and Titunik, eds., *Semiotics of Art: Prague School Contributions.*
J. J. A. Mooij, *A Study of Metaphor.*
Paul Ricoeur, *Interpretation Theory.*

1977   *Semiotic Scene* journal founded.
Mieke Bal, *Narratologie.*
Malcolm Coulthard, *An Introduction to Discourse Analysis.*
Culler, *Ferdinand de Saussure.*
Daniel Delas, *Poétique/pratique.*
van Dijk, *Text and Context.*
Fokkema and Kunne-Ibsch, *Theories of Literature in the Twentieth Century.*
Fowler, *Linguistics and the Novel.*
Elisabeth Gülich, *Linguistische Textmodelle.*
Terence Hawkes, *Structuralism and Semiotics.*
Mary Hiatt, *The Way Women Write.*
Catherine Kerbrat-Orrechioni, *La connotation.*
Levin, *The Semantics of Metaphor.*
David Lodge, *The Modes of Modern Writing.*
Daniel Lucid, *Soviet Semiotics: An Anthology.*
Robert Magliola, *Phenomenology and Literature.*
Mihály Péter, *The Structure and Semantics of the Literary Text.*
Mary L. Pratt, *Toward a Speech Act Theory of Literary Discourse.*
Ricoeur, *The Rule of Metaphor*
Sanders, *Linguistische Stilistik.*
Ann Shukman, *Literature and Semiotics: A Study of the Writings of Ju. M.
Lotman.*
R. H. Stacy, *Defamiliarization in Language and Literature.*
Todorov, *Théories du symbole* (trans. 1982).

1978   *Structuralist Review* founded.
Bailey, *The Sign: Semiotics around the World.*
Wolfgang Berg, *Uneigentliches Sprechen* [Figurative Language].
A. Berrendonner, *Stratégies discursives.*
David Bleich, *Subjective Criticism.*
Chatman, *Story and Discourse.*
Dorrit Cohn, *Transparent Minds: Narrative Modes for Presenting Conscious-
ness in Fiction.*
Maria Corti, *An Introduction to Literary Semiotics.*
Walter Davis, *The Act of Interpretation.*
George Dillon, *Language Processing and the Reading of Literature.*
Wolfgang Dressler, *Current Trends in Textlinguistics.*
Trevor Eaton, *Essays in Literary Semantics.*
E. L. Epstein, *Language and Style.*
Veronica Forrest-Thompson, *Poetic Artifice.*
Halliday, *Language as Social Semiotic.*
Joseph Kestner, *The Spatiality of the Novel.*

K. C. Phillipps, *The Language of Thackeray*.
Riffaterre, *Semiotics of Poetry*.
Rosenblatt, *The Reader, the Text, the Poem*.
John Russell, *Style in Modern British Fiction*.
Barbara H. Smith, *On the Margins of Discourse*.
Todorov, *Symbolisme et interprétation* (trans. 1982).
Hayden White, *Tropics of Discourse*.

1979   *Journal of Practical Structuralism* founded.
            Poetics Today founded.
            D. J. Allerton, *Essentials of Grammatical Theory: A Consensus View of Syntax and Morphology*.
            Tony Bennett, *Formalism and Marxism*.
            Burghardt and Hölker, *Text Processing*.
            Chatman et al., *A Semiotic Landscape*.
            Daniel Dugast, *Vocabulaire et stylistique*
            Eco, *The Role of the Reader*.
            Greimas and J. Courtés, *Sémiotique: Dictionnaire raisonné de la théorie du langage* (trans. *Semiotics and Language: An Analytical Dictionary*, 1982).
            John Holloway, *Narrative and Structure*.
            Jakobson and Waugh, *The Sound Shape of Language*.
            Kress and Hodge, *Language as Ideology*.
            Berel Lang, ed., *The Concept of Style*.
            John Odmark, ed., *Language, Literature and Meaning I*.
            Andrew Ortony, ed., *Metaphor and Thought*.
            Petöfi, *Text vs. Sentence*.
            Joseph Porter, *The Drama of Speech Acts*.
            Riffaterre, *Production du texte* (trans. *Text Production*, 1983).

1980   *Association for Literary and Linguistic Computing Journal* founded.
            Issues in Stylistics (Hyderabad).
            Robert de Beaugrande, *Text, Discourse, and Process*.
            Burton, *Dialogue and Discourse*.
            M. L. Ching et al., *Linguistic Perspectives on Literature*.
            David Crystal, *A First Dictionary of Linguistics and Phonetics*.
            Fish, *Is There a Text in This Class?*
            Roy Gottfried, *The Art of Joyce's Syntax in Ulysses*.
            Susan Hockey, *A Guide to Computer Applications in the Humanities*.
            Jakobson and Pomorska, *Dialogues* (trans. 1982).
            Barbara Johnson, *The Critical Difference*.
            Lang, *Philosophical Style*.
            Frank Lentricchia, *After the New Criticism*.
            Robert Oakman, *Computer Methods for Literary Research*.
            Elizabeth C. Traugott and Mary L. Pratt, *Linguistics for Students of Literature*.
            Jane Tompkins, *Reader-Response Criticism*.
            Eugene White, *Rhetoric in Transition*.

1981   Beaugrande and W. Dressler, *Introduction to Text Linguistics*.
            Culler, *The Pursuit of Signs*.
            Fowler, *Literature as Social Discourse*.
            Freeman, ed., *Essays in Modern Stylistics*.
            Philippe Hamon, *Introduction à l'analyse du descriptif*.
            Roy Harris, *The Language Myth*.
            Horton, *The Reader in the Dickens World*.
            Jakobson, *Selected Writings, 3: Poetry of Grammar and Grammar of Poetry*.

Susan Lanser, *The Narrative Act.*
Karen Lawrence, *The Odyssey of Style in* Ulysses.
Geoffrey N. Leech and Michael Short, *Style in Fiction.*
George Levine, *The Realistic Imagination.*
David Lodge, *Working with Structuralism.*
James Phelan, *Worlds for Words: A Theory of Language in Fiction.*
Kenneth Pike, *Tagmemics, Discourse, and Verbal Art.*
Horst Ruthrof, *The Reader's Construction of Narrative.*
Talbot Taylor, *Linguistic Theory and Structural Stylistics.*
Robert Young, *Untying the Text: A Post-Structuralist Reader.*
Peter Zima, *Semiotics and Dialectics.*

1982 Derek Attridge, *The Rhythms of English Poetry.*
Ann Banfield, *Unspeakable Sentences.*
Bradley Berke, *Tragic Thought and the Grammar of Tragic Myth.*
Lloyd Bishop, *In Search of Style.*
Ronald Carter, ed., *Language and Literature: An Introductory Reader in Stylistics.*
Carter and Deirdre Burton, eds., *Literary Text and Language Study.*
Chapman, *The Language of English Literature.*
Crystal, *Linguistic Controversies.*
Culler, *On Deconstruction: Theory and Criticism after Structuralism.*
Hans Jauss, *Toward an Aesthetic of Reception.*
Annette Lavers, *Roland Barthes: Structuralism and After.*
Janet McKay, *Narration and Discourse in American Realistic Fiction.*
James J. Murphy, *The Rhetorical Tradition and Modern Writing.*
Prince, *Narratology.*
Siegfried Schmidt, *Foundations for the Empirical Study of Literature*
Scholes, *Semiotics and Interpretation.*
T. K. Seung, *Semiotics and Thematics in Hermeneutics.*

1983 Norman Blake, *Shakespeare's Language.*
Culler, *Roland Barthes.*
Terry Eagleton, *Literary Theory.*
Alastair Fowler, *Kinds of Literature.*
C. Carroll Hollis, *Language and Style in* Leaves of Grass.
Eugene Kintgen, *The Perception of Poetry.*
Walter Koch, *Poetry and Science, Semiogenetical Twins.*
Shlomith Rimmon-Kenan, *Narrative Fiction.*
Shukman, *The New Soviet Semiotics.*
Kaja Silverman, *The Subject of Semiotics.*
Peter Steiner, *The Prague School.*

1984 Timothy Austin, *Language Crafted.*
William Cain, *The Crisis in Criticism* and *Philosophical Approaches to Literature.*
Eagleton, *The Function of Criticism.*
Chapman, *The Treatment of Sounds in Language and Literature.*
Eco, *Semiotics and the Philosophy of Language.*
Jakobson, *Verbal Art, Verbal Sign, Verbal Time.*
William Ray, *Literary Meaning.*
Ščeglov and Žolkovskij, *Poetics of Expressiveness.*
P. Steiner, *Russian Formalism.*
Allen Thiher, *Words in Reflection.*
Alexandr Žolkovskij, *Themes and Texts.*

1985 van Dijk, *Handbook of Discourse Analysis.*
Elaine Showalter, *The New Feminist Criticism.*

Appendix 2. Approaches:
A Classification of Critics by Theory and Method

The following list of critics provides a succinct guide to this bibliography. Names of additional representatives of each approach can be found under the appropriate category in the bibliography proper or in the subject-terminological index. For definitions and further sources of many of these approaches (and for a few references not in the bibliography because prior to 1968) see James R. Bennett's stylistics checklists and glossaries in *Style*. Not every individual listed under a specific approach necessarily advocates that approach but sometimes merely employs it in at least one piece of criticism, or gives an account of it, or edits a collection of essays about it. Several of the labels designate more than one approach (e.g., paradigmatic, contextual). Probably most of the critics listed are more or less eclectic and could be included under other labels. Some of these critics distinctly altered their theoretical or methodological position at some point in their careers, and many evolved in different ways and degrees. With only a few exceptions, all of those cited wrote in English or have been translated.

aesthetic or text monism (form-content inseparable): Henri Meschonnic. *See also* synonymy
aesthetics of reception: *See* 6.0
affective stylistics: Stanley Fish. *See also* reader response
analogy: Archibald Hill
Aristotelian: John Hayden. *See also* Neo-Aristotelian
artistic text: Juryj Lotman. *See also* literariness *and* reflexivity
author monism: *See* 4.0, style as idiosyncrasy, *and* epistemic
author styles: *See* 4.0, epistemic, *and* propensity
autonomy of poetry: Veronica Forrest-Thomson. *See also* literariness
beginning: Meir Sternberg. *See also* closure
binary analysis: Robert Scholes. *See also* opposition
case grammar: Elizabeth Traugott
choice: G. W. Turner
classical rhetoric: Edward P. J. Corbett, George Kennedy, John Mackin
closure: James R. Bennett, D. A. Miller, Barbara Smith. *See also* beginning
code: Roland Barthes, Jonathan Culler, Robert Scholes. *See also* semiotics
cognition: Roman Ingarden. *See also* reader response, phenomenology, psycholinguistics
cohesion: Waldemar Gutwinski, M. A. K. Halliday. *See also* text linguistics
communication: John Fiske, Randolph Quirk. *See also* rhetoric, pragmatics

comparison (simile, metaphor, figure): Marsh McCall. *See also* 3.2.1, 4.2.1, and 5.2.1
comparative: Nils Enkvist, D. W. Fokkema, Elrud Kunne-Ibsch
competence, literary: Jonathan Culler
computer: Richard Bailey, Susan Hockey, Louis Milic. *See also* statistics, quantitative
concordance: Andrew Crosland, Marvin Spevack
concretization: Roman Ingarden
connotation: Catherine Kerbrat-Orrecchioni
constant form: Robert Cluett. *See also* habitual usage, propensity
content analysis: George Gerbner, Joseph Raben, Sally Sedelow. *See also* statistics
contextual differential: Nils Enkvist
contextualism: Nils Enkvist (comparing textual features to relevant norms), J. R. Firth, Hans-Georg Gadamer, Murray Krieger (verbal structure, the autonomous context), George Levine (referentiality), Håkan Ringbom, G. W. Turner (language and its diverse situations)
convention: Jonathan Culler, Raymond Williams. *See also* semiotics
correlation: Dámaso Alonso. *See also* artistic text
coupling: Samuel R. Levin. *See also* parallelism
cybernetics: Daniel Lucid
Czechoslovakian: Jan Broekman, John Odmark
deconstruction: Harold Bloom, Jacques Derrida, Paul de Man, Geoffrey Hartman, J. Hillis Miller. *See also* poststructuralism
defamiliarization: R. H. Stacy. *See also* foregrounding
description (setting): Charles Anderson, Patricia Carlson
descriptive linguistics, structural linguistics: Leonard Bloomfield
deviation (syntax): Irene Fairley
diachronic: *See* 3.0, 4.0
dialogue: Deirdre Burton
differential, style as: Nils E. Enkvist
discourse, kinds and modes: James Kinneavy. *See also* rhetoric *and* text grammar
discourse analysis, total verbal process of a text: Malcolm Coulthard, Teun van Dijk, Joseph Grimes, Wilbur Pickering. *See also* 5.0
drama: Keir Elam. *See also* 3.0 *and* dialogue
dramatistic: Kenneth Burke
dualism: William Hendricks. *See also* ornate form
epistemic, style expresses author's worldview: Kenneth Burke, Richard Ohmann. *See also* 4.0
exponential (motif): Wilfred Guerin. *See also* symbolic *and* imagery
expressiveness: I. R. Galperin, Juryj Ščeglov
figurative language: *See* 3.2.1, 4.2.1, and 5.2.1 *and* tropes
foregrounding: Raymond Chapman
formalism: William Handy. *See also* New Criticism
formalism (Prague): Ladislav Matejka, Peter Steiner
formalism (Russian): Victor Erlich, Fredric Jameson, Lee Lemon, Daniel Lucid, Ladislav Matejka
French: James R. Bennett, Jan Broekman
frequency: Mary Hiatt. *See also* statistics *and* computer
functional styles: I. R. Galperin. *See also* "general" stylistics
functionalist: I. R. Galperin, Roman Jakobson, Prague School
game: Peter Hutchinson
"general" stylistics (non–belles lettres): David Crystal, Derek Davy
generative metrics: J. C. Beaver, Jens Ihwe
generative poetics: Nina Nowakowska
generative-transformational: Roderick Jacobs, Richard Ohmann, J. P. Thorne (in Lyons)

generic, genre styles: Jonathan Culler, Alastair Fowler, Northrop Frye, Tzvetan Todorov.
    See also 3.0
genetic (genesis, creativity): Carl Fehrman. *See also* revision
Geneva school: Sarah Lawall
gestaltist: Barbara Smith. *See also* closure *and* unity
glossematic: Louis Hjelmslev
grammars of style: William Hendricks
grammar (syntax): W. J. M. Bronzwaer. *See also* 3.2.2, 4.2.2, and 5.2.2
graphicology (graphetics, graphemics, graphology, typography): James R. Bennett
Great Britain: James R. Bennett, Roger Fowler
group styles: William Hendricks. *See also* functional styles *and* genre
habitual usage: Louis Milic. *See also* author styles, propensity, *and* statistics
hermeneutics: Roland Barthes, Hans-Georg Gadamer, David Hoy
historical study of style: Robert Adolph, James R. Bennett, Robert Cluett. *See also* 3.0,
    contextualism, literary history, Marxist, *and* sociology
holistic: *See* 5.0 *and* text grammar
Hungary: John Odmark
ideology: Fredric Jameson, Gunther Kress, Diana Laurenson. *See also* Marxist
imagery: *See* 3.2.1, 4.2.1, and 5.2.1
information theory: Louis Milic
intentionalism: P. D. Juhl, David Newton–De Molina
interpretation: Ross Chambers, E. D. Hirsch
intersentence grammar: William Hendricks. *See also* text grammar
intertextuality: Harold Bloom, Jeanine Plottel. *See also* influence
key word: David Lodge
language-action: Bernard Brock. *See also* text processing
lexical proportion: Josephine Miles
linguostylistics: Olga Akhmanova
literariness: Roman Jakobson, Michael Riffaterre
literary history: Ralph Cohen, Claudio Guillén, Geoffrey Hartman, Terry Eagleton, Robert
    Weismann, Peter Widdowson
literary semantics: Trevor Eaton. *See also* reader response *and* semics
literary semiotics: Maria Corti. *See also* poetics *and* stylistics
literary stylistics (holistic): Anne Cluysenaar. *See also* text grammar
literature, theory of: John Ellis, D. W. Fokkema, Paul Hernadi, Roman Ingarden
macrostructural: Teun van Dijk. *See also* text linguistics *and* discourse analysis
macrostylistics: *See* macrostructural *and* text grammar
Marxist: Terry Eagleton, Fredric Jameson
mathematics: Dolores Burton, John Holloway
meaning: Marcus Hester, Archibald Hill, William Ray, Stephen Ullmann. *See also*
    semantics
metacriticism: Catherine Belsey, Elizabeth Bruss, Geoffrey Hartman, Frank Lentricchia.
    See also 2.0
metaphor: J. J. A. Mooij. *See also* semantics *and* tropes
metaphor/metonymy: A. Henry, Roman Jakobson, Michel Le Guern, David Lodge
metrics: *See* 3.2.3, 4.2.3, *and* 5.2.3
mimesis: A. P. Foulkes. *See also* referentiality
modeling systems: Juryj Lotman
modernism: Eugene Lunn
monism: *See* author monism *and* aesthetic or text monism
morphology: Maren-Grisebach
motif: William Scheick, Massimo Bacigalupo. *See also* exponential *and* thematic criticism

music and literature: Wendy Steiner
narrative grammar: A. J. Greimas, Gerald Prince
narratology (narrativics, fiction poetics): Wayne Booth, Robert Champigny, Lubomír Doležel, Gerald Prince, Franz Stanzel, Boris Uspensky. *See also* 3.0
national styles: *See* 3.0
neo-Aristotelian: Austin Wright
new criticism (French): Laurent LeSage
new criticism (Anglo-American): Ann Jefferson, Ewa Thompson
normalization: W. O. Hendricks
numerology: Christopher Butler
objectivism (literary text explicable intrinsically): I. A. Richards, Michael Riffaterre, W. K. Wimsatt. *See also* formalism *and* reflexivity
opposition: Roman Jakobson. *See also* binary analysis
organic form: Gian Orsini, G. S. Rousseau. *See also* aesthetic monism
ornate form: Richard Lanham. *See also* dualism *and* expressiveness
paradigmatic: Frank D'Angelo, Thomas Kuhn, Richard Lanham
paragraph: James R. Bennett, Virginia Burke
parallelism: Roman Jakobson. *See also* correlation, coupling, *and* symmetry
paramessage: Ronald Carpenter
period styles: *See* 3.0
personality (author styles): *See* 4.0
phenomenological structuralism: Elmar Holenstein, Roman Jakobson
phenomenology: Patrick Brady, Robert Magliola. *See also* reader response
pictorialism (landscape): Jeffry Spencer. *See also* description
pluralism: Roland Barthes, Wayne Booth, Walter Davis, Roger Fowler (sociolinguistics), Norman Friedman
poetic text and language: Jan Mukařovský, I. A. Richards. *See also* literariness, artistic text
poetics: Bert States, Tzvetan Todorov. *See also* formalism *and* literary semiotics
poetry: *See* 3.0
point of view: Boris Uspensky. *See also* narratology
politics and style: James R. Bennett, Dennis Jackson, Fredric Jameson, John Seaman. *See also* ideology, Marxist, *and* sociolinguistics
positivism: Maren-Grisebach
poststructuralism: Harold Bloom, Paul de Man, Jacques Derrida, Josué Harari, J. Hillis Miller, Robert Young. *See also* deconstruction
practical criticism: I. A. Richards. *See also* new criticism
pragmatics: Robert de Beaugrande, Teun van Dijk. *See also* context, discourse analysis, *and* processing
Prague school: Peter Steiner
process: *See* genetic
processing: George Dillon. *See also* text processing *and* reader response
propensity: Robert Cluett, Louis Milic. *See also* personality
propositional reduction, paraphrase: Louis Milic. *See also* synonymy
prose rhythm: *See* 3.2.3, 4.2.3, *and* 5.2.3
prose styles: *See* 3.0
prosody: *See* 3.2.3, 4.2.3, *and* 5.2.3
psychoanalytic: Norman Holland, Jacques Lacan, Martin Lindauer, Meredith Skura
quantitative: Agnes Bruno, Louis Milic. *See also* computer *and* statistics
quantitative semantics: *See* content analysis
reader response: *See* 6.0
realism: George Bisztray. *See also* mimesis *and* referentiality

register: David Crystal, Derek Davy, G. W. Turner
repetition: Norman Holland, Bruce Kawin. *See also* exponential
revision: Philip Gaskell, Ronald Sudol. *See also* genetic
rhetoric: Bernard Brock, Donald Bryant, Edward P. J. Corbett, Jacques Dubois, Richard
  Lanham. *See also* classical rhetoric *and* holistic
Russian: Victor Erlich
scale and category: David Crystal, M. A. K. Halliday
schema theory: Roy Freedle. *See also* discourse analysis *and* pragmatics
scientific study of literature: Seymour Chatman, D. W. Fokkema, Elrud Kunne-Ibsch,
  Juryj Lotman
semantics: Miroslav Červenka, G. N. Leech, Stephen Ullmann
semics: Trevor Eaton. *See also* reader response
semiolinguistics: William O. Hendricks. *See also* text grammar, text linguistics, *and* intersentence grammar
semiotics: Maria Corti, Umberto Eco, Robert Scholes, Cesare Segre, Michael Riffaterre
semiotics (Soviet): Ann Shukman
setting: *See* description
sociolinguistics: Roger Fowler, Dell Hymes
sociology of literature: Jeffrey Sammons, Jane Routh. *See also* sociolinguistics *and* Marxism
sonics: Lewis Turco. *See also* phonology, prosody
spatial form, association: Joseph Kestner, Jeffrey Smitten. *See also* paradigmatic
speech acts: J. L. Austin, Marcia Eaton, Mary Pratt, John Searle
statistics: Richard Bailey, Barron Brainerd, Agnes Bruno, Lubomír Doležel. *See also*
  computer
structuralism: Roland Barthes, Jan Broekman, Jonathan Culler, Josué Harari, Terence
  Hawkes, Thomas Sebeok
structuralism and Marxism: Adam Schaff
structuralism and psychoanalysis: Anika Lemaire
structural metrics: Seymour Chatman, Roger Fowler
structural poetics: Teun van Dijk
style, concept of: Berel Lang, Håkan Ringbom. *See also* 2.0
style as idiosyncrasy (style reveals author's personality): Louis Milic, Richard Ohmann,
  Stephen Ullmann. *See also* 4.0
stylistic ontogeny: William Hendricks
stylistic phylogeny: William Hendricks
stylistics: Seymour Chatman, Michael Ching, Donald Freeman, Roger Fowler, *Issues in
  Stylistics*, Braj Kachru, Barbara Sandig, Karl Uitti. *See also* app. 3, "Introductory
  Reading List on Stylistics"
stylobehavioristics: Nils Enkvist
stylolinguistics: Nils Enkvist
subjective criticism: David Bleich. *See also* reader response
substitution: Bernard Dupriez
Sweden and Finland: James R. Bennett
symmetry: Lubomír Doležel
synonymy: E. D. Hirsch, Jr. *See also* propositional reduction
syntagmatic: Raymond Chapman, Frank D'Angelo
syntax: *See* 3.2.2, 4.2.2, *and* 5.2.2
system structure theory: J. R. Firth, M. A. K. Halliday, G. R. Kress
systemic functional linguistics: M. A. K. Halliday
tagmemics: L. G. Heller, Kenneth Pike
Tartu school of semiotics: Juryj Lotman

text grammar: Teun van Dijk. *See also* 5.0
text linguistics: Robert de Beaugrande, Wolfgang Dressler, I. R. Galperin, János Petöfi. *See also* text grammar *and* discourse analysis
text processing: Wolfgang Burghardt. *See also* processing *and* discourse analysis
text-reading dialectic: Michael Riffaterre
thematic criticism: Eugene Falk, John Smith. *See also* motif *and* textlinguistics
tropes: Hayden White. *See also* rhetoric *and* figures
typology: Robert Cluett
typography: *See* graphicology
vertical context: Claes Schaar. *See also* allusion *and* referentiality
variety, style as: David Crystal, Derek Davy. *See also* discourse
vocabulary: I. R. Galperin, G. W. Turner. *See also* 3.2.1, 4.2.1, *and* 5.2.1

Appendix 3. Introductory Reading List on Stylistics

The following titles have been arranged roughly in order of increasing difficulty within each category, but all could be assigned in an undergraduate criticism course since all are clearly written and most are less than 200 pages.

General

Heather Dubrow, *Genre* (1982)
> Up-to-date, clearly written, 133 small pages. The entire Critical Idiom Series can be recommended for undergraduate classes (books on metaphor, irony, meter, etc.).

Raymond Chapman, *Linguistics and Literature* (1973)
> One reviewer says of this book that it requires only an intelligent reader who understands any elementary school grammar (119 pp.).

Michael Cummings and Robert Simmons, *The Language of Literature* (1983)
> Designed as a textbook for third- and fourth-year college and graduate levels. Each of the 11 sections introduces a new step in the "systemic" approach to a literary text, from phonology to context. Each unit has the same format: analysis of a literary text, exposition of the linguistic principles employed in the analysis, engagement of the student in analysis by the principles, and review (235 pp.).

H. G. Widdowson, *Stylistics and the Teaching of Literature* (1975)
> This book clarifies the activity of stylistics with regard to linguistics and literary criticism and literature — discourse, text, and messages (128 pp.).

Raymond Chapman, *The Language of English Literature* (1982)
> A commonsense, nontechnical approach to ways "the language of daily life . . . is adapted and heightened" in British literature written after 1500 (148 pp.).

Anne Cluysenaar, *Aspects of Literary Stylistics* (1975)
> The focus on the whole text via the Scale and Category grammar gives this book its special perspective as an introduction to practical criticism (158 pp.). Chs. on language and reality, translation, poetry, and narrative (Lawrence's short story "The Blind Man" is printed in full) provide useful scope.

Hilda Schiff, ed., *Contemporary Approaches to English Studies* (1977)
> 6 essays on literature in society, structuralism, Marxism, etc. (105 pp.).

G. W. Turner, *Stylistics* (1973)
> An illuminating distinction between descriptive study (of sounds, etc.) and explanatory study (of context, etc.) makes this a helpful book (256 pp.).

Ronald Carter, ed., *Language and Literature: An Introductory Reader in Stylistics* (1982)
> 12 practical essays that explore ways in which language and literature study and teaching can be integrated. Each chapter has an introduction by the editor and most are followed by exercises (256 pp.).

Norman Holland, *Poems in Persons* (1975)
> Although the psychoanalytic theory of "identity theme" that pervades this book may seem too reductionist to some readers, the book does provide an easy introduction to one way of exploring the dynamic relation of authors, their texts, and their readers (182 pp.).

John Spencer, ed., *Linguistics and Style* (1964)
> An early work on the linguistic study of literature. Nils Enkvist's essay "On Defining Style" and Spencer and Michael Gregory's "An Approach to the Study of Style" offer a fine theoretical introduction (105 pp.). No analysis of literature.

George Dillon, *Language Processing and the Reading of Literature* (1978)
> An introduction to the syntactical problems involved in the initial levels of reading—perception and comprehension—with examples drawn from British and American literature (208 pp.).

P. M. Wetherill, *The Literary Text* (1974)
> An advanced text, but its plain language and numerous examples ensure accessibility to the better students, and its comprehensiveness makes it particularly useful (331 pp.).

Robert Scholes, *Semiotics and Interpretation* (1982)
> The minimal technical terminology (and a glossary for those terms) and maximum examples make this a highly accessible introduction to semiotics (161 pp.).

John Fiske, *Introduction to Communication Studies* (1982)
> Although not about literature, this is an up-to-date general introduction to process and semiotic communication theories (models, codes, signification, ideology, etc.) (174 pp.).

Tzvetan Todorov, *Introduction to Poetics* (1981)
> A program (not an elaborated system) for investigating the general laws and properties of literary discourse, or literariness (83 pp.). Chapter 1 defines poetics. Chapter 2 considers 3 formal aspects of texts essential to signification: semantic (registers, etc.), manner (mode, time, perspective, voice), and syntactic (minimal units and their temporal and spatial ordering). Chapter 3 discusses literary history as a diachronic poetics. There is also an excellent introduction by Peter Brooks.

Ronald Carter and Deirdre Burton, eds., *Literary Text and Language Studies* (1982)
> The interdisciplinary approach to language and literature and the separate essays on poetry, narrative, and drama make this a good introduction for teachers (and future teachers) and for use in the classroom (115 pp.).

Terence Hawkes, *Structuralism and Semiotics* (1977)
> A clear and brief introduction to the development of these essentially similar critical provinces so important to literary study today (192 pp.).

Elizabeth Traugott and Mary Pratt, *Linguistics for Students of Literature* (1980)
> Technical and long (444 pp.); for advanced students.

Narrative

Roger Fowler, *Linguistics and the Novel* (1977)
> A brief (145 pp.) introduction to the linguistic study of narrative.

Shlomith Rimmon-Kenan, *Narrative Fiction: Contemporary Poetics* (1983)

Draws on Anglo-American New Criticism, Russian formalism, French structuralism, the Tel-Aviv School of Poetics, and the phenomenology of reading for analysis of the elements of narrative fiction: events, time, speech, etc. (173 pp.).

Gerald Prince, *Narratology* (1982)
Similar to Rimmon-Kenan, more technical, highly taxonomical, but clear (184 pp.).

Karl Kroeber, *Styles in Fictional Structure* (1971)
In difficulty and length (293 pp.) this book exceeds an introductory text, but if read selectively it offers a clarifying introduction to the comparative study of styles.

Geoffrey Leech and Michael Short, *Style in Fiction* (1981)
Designed to show how linguistic analysis and literary appreciation are interrelated (402 pp.).

Poetry

Paul Fussell, *Poetic Meter and Poetic Form* (1979)
An elementary explanation of the functionality of meter and stanzas "to help aspiring readers deepen their sensitivity to the rhythmical and formal properties of poetry."

Allan Rodway, *The Craft of Criticism* (1982)
Practical critiques of the unity of poems of various kinds employing diverse critical methods (192 pp.).

Geoffrey Leech, *A Linguistic Guide to English Poetry* (1969)
Advanced (237 pp.).

Nonfiction Prose

Richard Lanham, *Analyzing Prose* (1983)
Long (255 pp.) but designed for freshmen in college. Employs traditional rhetorical terminology to provide a taxonomy of basic strategies.

David Crystal and Derek Davy, *Investigating English Style* (1969).
An accessible introduction to "general" stylistics (newspaper reporting, etc.) easily applicable to belles lettres (264 pp.).

Critiques of Traditional English Studies

Terry Eagleton, *The Function of Criticism* (1984).
A history from the *Spectator* to poststructuralism and a plea for a social criticism.

Catherine Belsey, *Critical Practice* (1980)
A polemical explanation of the rejection of the commonsense literature and criticism of "expressive realism" by recent critics, based on the conviction that language is the condition not the reflection of thought and reality (168 pp.). (Placed last not because of its difficulty but because of its uncompromising criticism of almost all theories and methods of literary criticism.)

Index 1. Terms

absolute form *See* organic form
abstraction, 629a, 1141
accentual syllabic meter, 832
accumulation, 858
achrony, 144, 551a, 721
acoustics, 819, 1322
act, 925
actant, 144, 178, 349, 431, 440, 724. *See also* narrative
action assertions, 669
action game, 408
actualization, 144, 397, 727a, 1285
addresser-addressee, 295, 1093, 1275
adjective, 483, 767, 772, 790, 936, 1109, 1249, 1374
adjective-verb ratio, 416
adumbration, 627
adverb, 483, 790, 936, 1109, 1162
adverbial style, 1009a
advertising, 473
aesthesis, 1464. *See also* reader response
aesthetic codes, 448
aesthetic experience, 397, 684, 1464. *See also* poetics *and* reader response
aesthetic function of language, 466, 505
aesthetic irony, 761
aesthetic monism *See* monism *and* organic form
aesthetic reading, 1455. *See also* efferent reading *and* reader response
aesthetics of reception *See* reception aesthetics
affect, 425
affective functions of rhythm, 832
affective stylistics, 197, 222, 592a, 596, 887, 1459. *See also* reader response
agent, 925
agnation, 467
alexandrine, 821, 822
algebra, 1303
aliterature, 876
allegory, 217, 255, 281, 511, 621a, 627, 673, 758a, 777, 781, 854, 875, 877,

allegory (*cont.*)
906, 949, 988, 1165, 1207a, 1251, 1327, 1343, 1389, 1428. *See also* Middle Ages *and* symbolism
alliteration, 194, 327, 819, 828, 863, 1098, 1324, 1333. *See also* phonology *and* sound
alloscenes, 948
allusion, 120, 255, 268, 627, 783, 842, 853, 910, 920, 1055, 1059, 1064b, 1081, 1109, 1184, 1206, 1207a, 1222, 1223, 1238, 1310a, 1333, 1335, 1394, 1409. *See also* reflexivity
alternating rhythm, 832
alternation, 726
ambiguity, 274, 300, 319, 548, 577, 578a, 627, 647, 679, 758b, 899, 987a, 1076, 1122, 1125, 1132, 1209, 1212. *See also* polysemy
ambivalence, 1110
American criticism, 155, 167, 196, 232, 243, 247, 253, 288, 305, 307, 313, 572
American poetry, modern, 93, 1008
American structural linguistics, 495
amplification *See* expansion
anacrusis, 814
anagram, 511, 516, 1133
analogical matrix, 182
analogy, 270, 289, 471, 548, 687, 781, 949, 961, 1175, 1203, 1276b, 1389, 1482. *See also* correlation
anaphora, 466, 467, 690, 1115, 1158. *See also* repetition *and* syntax
anironic, 785
anomaly, 577, 1415
antanaclasis, 1099
anthropology, 495
antiaesthetic, 161
anti-Ciceronianism, 182, 838, 870. *See also* plain style
antihistorical criticism, 572
antilanguage, 585
antimetabole, 194

beginning and ending sentences, 664
belles lettres, 322
beyond the sentence, 669. *See also* discourse
    and macrostructure
biblical styles, 70, 775, 826b, 1232a, 1347,
    1356, 1370, 1420a
bilingualism, 874
bilingual texts, 221
binary, 687
binary opposition, 144, 197, 369, 381, 431,
    440, 515, 618, 1346, 1390, 1414, 1480.
    See also structuralism
biography, 86, 240, 757, 1422. *See also* au-
    tobiography
biplanar model, 596
blanks, 1209
blank verse, 359
branching, 790 *See also* syntax
bricolage, 1016, 1399
brisure, 293
British stylistics, 162, 359, 390, 395
Brown Corpus, 148a, 450
buccal miming, 530. *See also* phonology
Buffalo School, 1473, 1476. *See also* psy-
    choanalytic criticism
bureaucratic language, 998. *See also* legal
    documents, legal language, legal style,
    and register
burlesque, 627, 698, 720, 1129, 1391. *See
    also* comedy *and* satire
cadence, 818, 945. *See also* prose rhythm
caesura, 979, 1158. *See also* prosody
cancellation, 1285
canny and uncanny criticism, 603
canons of interpretation, 319
caricature, 646, 1139. *See also* burlesque
case grammar, 273, 577, 1372
categories, 846
catharsis, 1464. *See also* rhetoric *and* tragedy
catachresis, 1285
causality (deconstruction), 603
Cercle linguistique de Prague *See* Prague
    School
channel, 606. *See also* communication theory
chantefable, 1290
characterization, 440, 705, 728, 894, 1000,
    1146, 1339. *See also* narration
Chicago School, 255, 548. *See also* poetics
choice, 169, 173, 213, 230, 273, 394, 407,
    409, 436, 471, 514, 577, 732, 853, 992,
    1119, 1145, 1250, 1373. *See also*
    deviation

chroneme, 830
chronology, 165
Ciceronian style (Ciceronianism), 301, 1069,
    1084, 1097, 1320. *See also* anti-
    Ciceronianism, balance, *and* nonfic-
    tion prose
cinematic fiction, 590
cinematographic, 930, 1120
circularity, 738
circumlocution, 921, 1225
citationality, 1423
clarity, 424
class (social), 894. *See also* Marxist criticism
classeme, 1285
classical approach, 832. *See also* meter
classical rhetoric, 51, 129, 164, 335, 510,
    569, 620, 712, 865, 955a, 1289. *See
    also* arrangement, invention, *and* style
classical versification, 132, 811
classic vs. romantic (symbols), 620
classicism, 639
clause, 295, 790, 846, 1071, 1313, 1479. *See
    also* grammar
clause number, 1348
clausula, 1285
cleft sentences, 1141
cliché, 369, 786, 921, 917, 1233, 1285, 1291,
    1298, 1423
closed text *See* complexity
closure, 89, 636, 642, 657, 733, 738, 741,
    906, 1105, 1122, 1423, 1246a. *See also*
    gestalt *and* poetics
code, 144, 255, 293, 431, 440, 448, 466,
    470, 495, 568, 579, 581, 585, 606, 634,
    634c, 669, 694, 724, 732, 758b, 935,
    1087, 1285, 1369, 1471. *See also* con-
    vention *and* semiotics
cognition, 144, 183, 371, 397, 528, 554,
    563, 582, 584, 661, 1284, 1458. *See
    also* psycholinguistics *and* reader re-
    sponse
cognitive narrative, 862
cognitive play, 543
coherence, 319, 462, 509, 519, 1269a, 1284,
    1288, 1423. *See also* unity
cohesion, 169, 267, 273, 286, 394, 467, 469,
    496, 577, 694, 732, 790, 976, 1240,
    1281, 1288, 1392, 1417
collage, 627, 881. *See also* montage, ex-
    perimental, *and* innovation
collective discourse, 1379

dramatistic persuasive discourse, 886
dream and literature, 593, 1399. *See also*
    psychoanalytic criticism
dual sign, 1285
duologue, 1009
duplex structure, 351. *See also* plot
duration, 662, 725. *See also* time
dynamics, 713. *See also* narrative
dystopian novel, 905
Eastern European criticism, 21, 156, 162,
    179, 193, 198, 212, 215, 220, 229, 235,
    236. *See also* 2.0, Prague School, Rus-
    sian formalism, *and* Soviet semiotics
Eastern European literature, 111
eclecticism, 279, 548
economics and literature, 787
écriture, 440, 486a. *See also* structuralism
écrivain/écrivant, 495
editing, 632, 1271a
editions, production of, 531
efferent reading, 1455. *See also* reader re-
    sponse
elegy, 650, 753
elevated style, 1145. *See also* decorum, elo-
    quent style, *and* levels
elision, 814, 832
Elizabethan verse, 811
Elizabethan narrative, 888
Elizabethan prose style, 838
ellipsis, 469, 944, 1141, 1175, 1220. *See also*
    punctuation
elocution, 656, 1191
eloquent style, 389, 836, 1241
embedding, 1285
emblem, 782, 784, 875, 895, 962, 1191,
    1296, 1327
emotion, 467
emotive and referential language, 340
emphatic stress (meter), 832
empirical reception theory, 1471a, 1475a
empirical semics, 13, 245, 1456, 1472, 1473,
    1474, 1476, 1481, 1483, 1484
empiricism, 561, 616a
encomium, 1115
ending *See* closure
engagement, 758a. *See also* aesthetic read-
    ing, politics and style, *and* reader re-
    sponse
enjambment, 809, 815, 824, 979, 1158. *See
    also* prosody
enthymeme, 858
enumeration, 992

epic, 339, 708, 753, 771, 788, 847, 861,
    1064, 1067
epic conventions, 1326
epic theater, 860, 1167
epideictic, 569. *See also* oratory
epigram, 721a, 753, 868, 1109
epiphany, 1409
episode, 948, 1371
episteme, 977a
epistemic choice, 182, 1413. *See also* author
    style
epistemology, 183, 1413
epistle, 954, 1417
epistolary, 677, 1142, 1146, 1336
epistolary form, 1330
epistolary novel, 741
epithet, 921, 1064, 1237a
equilibrium *See* balance
equipoise, 921
equivalence, 130, 460, 590, 1285. *See also*
    parallelism
equivocation, 1020
erlebte Rede, 938, 1426. *See also* free in-
    direct speech
essay, 729a, 753, 1048, 1175, 1244
essence, 584
ethos, 164. *See also* classical rhetoric
etymology, 1027
euphemisms, 1184
euphony, 255, 812, 992
European structural linguistics, 495
evaluation, 319, 351, 509, 548, 560, 590,
    1010, 1188, 1436, 1455, 1456. *See also*
    poetics
exaggeration, 892
example, 771, 858
exclamation, 936
exclamatory sentence, 790
exegesis, 1370
exemplum, 771
existential, 373
existentialism, 351a, 572
expansion, 316, 1103, 1285
expectation, 1373
experimental, 753a, 881, 924, 961, 1185,
    1215. *See also* innovation
expletive, 1141
explication de texte, 502, 648, 1147, 1338,
    1354, 1361
exploration, literature as, 1437
exponential, 556. *See also* imagery, repeti-
    tion, *and* symbol

French narrative, 692, 760, 834, 889, 892, 956
French poetry, 658, 788, 850, 877, 899, 969, 1261a
French prose, 985
French prosody, 796, 800, 812, 821
French Renaissance, 953
French rhetoric and prose, 972
French structuralism, 57, 136, 149, 191, 369, 381, 393, 418, 458, 463, 492, 703, 1378
French styles, 664, 992
French stylistics, 12, 201, 992
French symbolism (1870–1920), 852, 1246
frequency, 148a, 662, 725, 732, 1307, 1045a. *See also* statistics
Freudian criticism, 373. *See also* psychoanalytic criticism
Fries-Milic Syntactic Code, 792
function, 409, 431, 440, 468, 495, 504, 585, 888, 942, 971, 1167, 1401, 1405
functional linguistics, 350, 464
functional sentence, 56
functional styles, 224, 322, 360, 630, 955a, 1431. *See also* register
functional stylistics, 744. *See also* "general" stylistics
functionalism, 418, 610. *See also* organic
function/manifesting units, 351
function words, 356
funeral oration, 1433
game, 627
game theory, 1274
gap, 713, 944, 1274, 1285, 1373, 1453. *See also* deconstruction *and* discontinuity
gender and style, 1259
"general" stylistics, 744, 846, 855, 898. *See also* register
generative, 187
generative metrics, 91, 168, 813, 832
generative poetics, 700
generative semantics, 363, 577, 700
generative semantics and style, 260
generative stylistics, 596
generative-transformational grammar, 118, 125, 165, 168, 171, 178, 182, 194, 222, 260, 286, 347, 379, 394, 440, 558, 577, 585, 630, 668, 700, 795a, 1068, 1070, 1141, 1269
generative-transformational model, 363
genetic criticism (process), 159, 1432. *See also* revision

Geneva School, 172, 191, 325, 615, 1451. *See also* phenomenology
genidentic, 709
genre, 25, 118, 161, 169, 173, 202, 208, 265a, 265b, 277, 319, 337, 353, 361, 431, 508, 520, 525, 545, 564, 588, 643, 645, 650, 663, 663a, 666, 670, 673, 676, 678, 689, 695, 698, 701, 702, 708, 713, 714, 717, 722, 728, 734, 744, 753, 755, 780, 781, 839, 844, 849, 854, 861, 866, 867, 868, 901, 907, 922, 923, 926, 934, 940, 948, 949, 954, 963, 977, 978, 991, 1085, 1094, 1126, 1161, 1166, 1225, 1229, 1250, 1355, 1433. *See also* discourse, narrative, poetry, *and* prose
geometric, 709
geometrical imagery, 779
German baroque, 782, 868
German criticism, 457, 611
German literature, 639, 649, 885
German lyric, 817
German metrics, 831
German prose, 736, 795
gestalt, 642, 830, 1453. *See also* closure
Gestalt psychology, 820
gesture, 1155
glossary, 150a
Glossomatics, 118, 379
gnosis *See* hermeneutics
gothic, 963
graffiti, 305
grammar, 113, 148a, 164, 178, 187, 197, 218, 359, 363, 364, 400, 407, 409, 436, 468, 501, 507, 558, 577, 587b, 630, 682, 729a, 758b, 790, 792, 793a, 808, 841, 846, 880, 933, 942, 1061, 1113, 1141, 1144, 1162, 1171, 1184, 1194, 1218, 1236, 1247, 1270, 1276a, 1314, 1315, 1317, 1318, 1319, 1320, 1321, 1337, 1338, 1374, 1397
grammar (cohesion), 467
grammar and meaning, 1318
grammar and poetry, 18, 587b, 628
grammar of narrative, 349, 671, 703. *See also* narratology
grammar of style, 690
grammar of texts, 495, 577
grammatical hierarchy, 592
grammatical model, 394
grammaticality, 394, 407, 1068. *See also* deviation

Middle Ages, 688, 712, 771, 786, 817, 1066, 1207a *See also* allegory *and* medieval

middle style, 358, 656, 861, 1010, 1250. *See also* decorum

mime, 646

mimesis, 199, 213, 227, 247, 298, 368, 454, 474, 555, 557, 591, 617, 632a1, 661, 728, 731, 751, 783, 848, 869, 934, 952, 986, 1005, 1064a, 1285, 1365. *See also* realism *and* referentiality

mimetic discourse, 451

mind style, 732

minus devices, 476

misprision, 293, 439, 615. *See also* influence

modality, 846, 935, 1281, 1463

mode, 431, 597, 753

model, 381, 606, 1285, 1287

modeling systems, 235

model reader, 552

Model T, 168

model theory, 354

modernism, 142a, 255, 500, 614, 758a, 785, 826, 961, 975, 987a, 989, 1001, 1003, 1005, 1179, 1215, 1254

modes of address, 1121, 1218

modes of discourse, 95, 367

modifiers, 530

modifying style, 792

moment, 629

monism, 548, 732, 1277. *See also* dualism

monologue, 706, 1087

monosyllabic-polysyllabic, 1093

monosyllables, 809

montage, 231, 551a, 627, 758a

mood, 662, 725

morality play, 934

morphology, 315, 351a, 426, 567, 577, 855a

morphophonemics, 168

morphosyntax, 178

Moscow Linguistic Circle, 371, 495. *See also* Russian formalism

Moscow-Tartu semiotics group, 515. *See also* Tartu School

motif, 118, 178, 492, 521, 773, 948, 1041, 1058, 1130, 1166, 1223, 1291, 1309, 1329, 1362, 1386. *See also* imagery *and* repetition

motifeme, 948

motion, 1001. *See also* narrative

motivation, 713

motivation (language), 489

movement, 926, 1139

multilingualism, 874

multimedia *See* collage *and* innovation

multiplanar (text), 501

multiple position occupancy, 1075

multivariate techniques, 419

music (fiction), 967, 1150, 1275b, 1293, 1406

music (poetry), 990

music in Shakespeare, 1077

mutation, 381

myth, 223, 281, 526, 556, 621a, 689, 730, 854, 987, 1191, 1272, 1358, 1399, 1429

names, 108. *See also* onomastics

naming, 411, 627, 1125

narrated monologue, 706, 1423

narrated, 750

narratee, 731, 750, 981a

narrative, 48, 54, 64, 74, 107, 135, 175, 177, 180, 185, 193, 201, 203, 213, 221, 223, 235, 245, 247, 255, 276, 288, 298, 300, 302, 305, 306, 308, 431, 433, 436, 440, 448, 482, 486, 500, 551, 552, 554, 562, 574, 581, 583, 587a, 588, 590, 597, 600, 607, 617, 641, 649, 659, 661, 662, 666, 667, 669, 671, 672, 673, 685, 686, 687, 689, 692, 694, 696, 697, 703, 705, 706, 711, 714, 715, 718, 721, 722, 723, 725, 727, 727a, 728, 729, 731, 732, 733, 734, 735, 738, 741, 742, 750, 751, 753, 754, 760, 789, 791, 834, 843, 847, 856, 859, 873, 875, 878, 882, 883, 884, 885, 889, 890, 891, 892, 900, 906, 909, 913, 914, 922, 926, 927, 931, 937, 940, 946, 952, 956, 963, 964, 965, 967, 975, 985a, 986, 987, 993, 995, 996, 1000, 1001, 1010a, 1011, 1012, 1016, 1017, 1022, 1028, 1029, 1036, 1038, 1039, 1040, 1041, 1044, 1049, 1052, 1054, 1055, 1059, 1062, 1063, 1065, 1095, 1104, 1106, 1107, 1116a, 1122, 1124, 1128, 1129, 1130, 1132, 1142, 1145, 1149, 1156, 1163, 1169, 1174, 1183, 1184, 1187, 1193, 1199, 1200, 1206, 1215, 1227, 1231, 1233, 1245, 1250a, 1253, 1255, 1260, 1263, 1265, 1272, 1273, 1274, 1275a, 1276, 1287, 1289, 1292, 1294, 1298, 1303, 1316, 1327, 1329, 1341, 1351, 1352, 1353, 1365, 1367, 1368, 1373, 1378, 1379, 1384, 1385, 1386, 1387, 1390, 1399, 1403, 1406, 1408, 1410, 1412, 1420a, 1426, 1427, 1427a, 1429, 1430, 1442, 1458, 1463, 1471

redundancy, 247, 606, 746, 948, 1029, 1225
reference, 1281
reference discourse, 367
referent, 1285
referential, 1003
referential hierarchy, 592
referentiality, 727a, 757, 977a, 986, 989, 1009a. *See also* allusion, meaning, *and* realism
reflected meaning, 425
reflected speech, 1426
reflexivity, 159, 213, 728, 1081, 1262a, 1268, 1285, 1377, 1378, 1402. *See also* autonomy, autotelic, intratextual, figurative language, *and* unity
register, 169, 173, 187, 390, 409, 585, 597, 602, 630, 843, 846, 885, 1172, 1199, 1218, 1230, 1250
reification, 588
relational (reality), 495
relativism, 551a, 580, 618, 993
religion and literature, 984
religious language, 846, 1312
religious satire, 716
religious writing, 1066
Renaissance, 708, 745, 953, 994
Renaissance, English, 983
Renaissance poetry, 908
Renaissance prose, 939
Renaissance rhetoric, 749
repartée, 1096
repertoire, 1453
repetition, 187, 192, 194, 214, 265b, 382, 406, 476, 501, 515, 641, 647, 669, 726, 727, 746, 855a, 966, 988, 996, 1020, 1041, 1108, 1127, 1143, 1190, 1214, 1234, 1260, 1274, 1285, 1303, 1315, 1323, 1346, 1390, 1399, 1420a, 1425, 1426. *See also* recurrence
reported speech, 179, 412, 927, 1106. *See also* free indirect speech
reposte, 1110
representation, 368, 398, 742. *See also* referentiality *and* visual imagery
representationalism, 727
represented discourse, 891
represented speech, 742
repression, 293
retardation, 713. *See also* narration
retopicalization, 438. *See also* metaphor
revision, 134, 291, 304, 531, 640, 743, 973, 1091, 1097, 1111, 1119, 1165, 1174,

revision (*cont.*)
1205, 1236, 1271a, 1394, 1396, 1397, 1407. *See also* genetic
Rezeptionstheorie, Rezeptionsästhetik See reader response
rhetoric, 84, 118, 121, 126, 129, 150, 150a, 151, 157, 164, 176, 180, 208, 214, 217, 219, 221, 237, 243, 253, 263, 280, 292, 301, 305, 321, 335, 338, 345, 355, 358, 367, 389, 402, 405, 434, 441, 451, 456, 510, 513, 522, 529, 537, 545, 565, 569, 578, 607, 620, 643, 653, 656, 677, 697, 708, 712, 716, 743, 745, 748, 777, 787a, 836, 853, 855, 858, 861, 865, 871, 880, 886, 893, 898, 908, 925, 929, 953, 970, 972, 982, 985, 1010, 1012a, 1031, 1035, 1045, 1080, 1084, 1085, 1090, 1101, 1115, 1127, 1135, 1144, 1145, 1152, 1175, 1191, 1207a, 1217, 1249a, 1250, 1252, 1275, 1276, 1289, 1311, 1314, 1360, 1373, 1423, 1429, 1455
rhetorical devices, 1194
rhetorical figures *See* figurative language
rhetorical, functional and structural, 164
rhyme, 110, 268, 291, 450, 476, 691, 786, 797, 799, 805, 806, 809, 814, 815, 819, 826, 826b, 828, 917, 979, 1075a, 1090, 1093, 1105, 1134, 1137, 1158, 1159, 1213, 1217, 1346. *See also* 3.2.3, 4.2.3, *and* 5.2.3
rhyme statistics, 819
rhythm, 132, 179, 390, 436, 476, 810, 812, 818, 826, 896, 973, 1098, 1126, 1213, 1217, 1249, 1357, 1368, 1413. *See also* 3.2.3, 4.2.3, 5.2.3, *and* meter
rhythm (drama), 657, 726
rhythm (prose), 1157
rhythmemes, 830
riddle, 758b, 1326
ridicule, 716
Rococo, 639
romance, 588, 689, 753, 780, 878, 922, 1022
romantic aesthetics, 620
romantic irony, 336, 992
Romantic period, 223
running sentence, 664
running style, 1010
Russian criticism, twentieth century, 212
Russian formalism, 179, 193, 218a, 264, 283, 352, 371, 379, 381, 394, 418, 431, 435,

sentence opener, 790
sententia (apothegm), 1127
sentimentality, 1092
sequence, 398, 436, 732
sequence, 713. *See also* spatiality
sequences of sentences, 1284
serial, 1143
series, 418, 1164
sermon, 677, 902, 968, 1031, 1066, 1250
setting, 213, 705, 918, 958, 1000, 1060,
    1173, 1198, 1203, 1204, 1227, 1262,
    1363, 1364, 1379. *See also* description
    and referentiality
seventeenth century, 764, 769, 838
shifters, 480
short story, 206, 276, 931, 1000
sign, 118, 198, 241, 255, 284, 291, 293, 298,
    300, 312, 381, 440, 448, 466, 504, 520,
    573, 581, 591, 606, 634, 634a, 724,
    875, 1087, 1125, 1143, 1251, 1285. *See
    also* semiotics
sign, literary work as, 265b
significance, 1285
significant form, 1230
signification, 293, 349, 381, 448, 466, 581,
    583, 606, 617, 1277
significative units, 118
signified, 293, 489, 583
signifier, 293, 489, 583
silence, 634, 634a, 1263, 1378
similarity, 266, 628, 710
simile, 266, 334, 403, 410, 770, 936, 1020,
    1061, 1127, 1295, 1308, 1310
simplicity, 560
simultaneity, 551a, 1406. *See also* modern-
    ism, montage, *and* time
singularity, 846
situational irony, 415
situationality, 1288
sixteenth-century prose narrative, 892
sixteenth-century rhetoric, 643
skepticism, 548, 615
slang, 921, 980, 1171, 1184, 1218, 1230
slogans, 305
slot (formulaic pattern), 948
social context, 183, 1392. *See also* referen-
    tiality
social dialects, 630
social discourse, 585
sociolect, 579
sociolinguistics, 118, 203, 239, 240, 250,
    330, 390, 395, 412, 423, 473, 508, 512,

sociolinguistics *(cont.)*
    525, 528, 532, 535, 547, 558, 577, 579,
    585, 609, 630, 744, 826a, 935, 948,
    971, 1004, 1248, 1284, 1427, 1470,
    1471a
sociological criticism, 611, 1367. *See also*
    Marxist criticism
sociology, 221, 373, 556, 739
sociology of the text, 579
sociosemantics, 532
soliloquy, 705, 1078
song, 1167
sonnet, 114, 143, 618, 864, 955, 1090, 1099,
    1137, 1158, 1188, 1213
sound, 103, 110, 132, 567, 634b2, 638, 973,
    1357, 1397. *See also* phonology
sound and meaning, 797
sound and sense, 1105, 1125
sound formation, 398, 584. *See also* layers,
    layeredness
sound patterns, 1326
sound symbolism (phonesthetics), 577, 819,
    1098. *See also* onomatopoeia
Soviet semiotics, 492, 515, 633. *See also*
    Russian semiotics
space, spatiality, 223, 411, 628, 709, 882,
    900, 1005, 1416. *See also* correlation,
    paradigmatic, *and* structure
Spanish classical prose style, 1349
spatial form, 275, 1239, 1276b, 1398
spatiality, 709
speaker, 427
speech, 220, 411, 732, 894, 1102, 1146, 1155,
    1360
speech acts 73, 102, 144, 145, 187, 195, 197,
    213, 225, 247, 262, 273, 276, 286, 305,
    355, 402, 480, 488, 508, 528, 540,
    560a, 563, 577, 582, 585, 591, 610,
    617a, 625, 724, 731, 732, 971, 1237,
    1284, 1427, 1431, 1453, 1459
speech-act theory, 241, 473
speeches, 929, 1360. *See also* oratory
speech event, 201
speech genres, 577
speech representation, 754. *See also* narrator
speech rhythm, 818, 1093
spelling, 980, 1346
Sprachstil, 407
stable irony, 415
stage directions (drama), 835
stage props (drama), 1060
stance (narrative), 731, 805

stylostatistics, 323
subjective criticism, 1452. *See also* reader
    response
subjectivity, 187
sublime, 1246
subliminal meaning, 576, 587b
subordination, 467, 1071. *See also* syntax
substitution, 469
substitution classes, 592
substitution hypothesis, 438. *See also*
    metaphor
sujet, 713
superreader, 369
supersession, 718
superstructure, 300. *See also* Marxist
    criticism
supposition, 718
suprasegmental, 810. *See also* prosody
surface/deep structure, 118, 596, 935, 1278
surrealism, 231, 776, 778, 981, 1057, 1420,
    1427b, 1471, 1482
suspended quotation, 1256
Sweden, 162
syllable, 796, 1075a
syllabic verse, 801
syllepsis, 1115
symbol, 343, 348, 403, 480, 521, 573, 591,
    606, 617, 621a, 621c, 634c, 760, 787,
    848, 875, 1033, 1053, 1058, 1060,
    1076, 1130, 1138, 1251, 1294, 1329,
    1358, 1362, 1364, 1396, 1427b. *See
    also* allegory *and* imagery
symbolic, 440
symbolic structure, 973a
symbolism, 217, 370, 375, 732, 833, 843,
    848, 850, 852, 879, 885, 984, 1019,
    1023, 1089, 1120, 1203, 1211, 1343,
    1378, 1476
symbolist poetry, 879
symmetry, 343, 348, 359, 587b, 691, 891,
    1097, 1239, 1260, 1265, 1276d, 1316,
    1345, 1375. *See also* balance
synchronicity, 578a
synchrony, 118, 314, 316, 381, 390, 431, 472,
    489, 613, 1016. *See also* diachrony
syncopation, 815
syncretism, 1422
synecdoche, 217, 270, 362, 500, 545, 590,
    1020, 1061, 1086, 1317. *See also*
    metonymy
syneresis, 1075
synesthesia, 403

synonym, 773
synonymy, 220, 363, 596, 700
syntactic level, 732
syntagm, 634
syntagmatic, 118, 390, 431, 441, 489, 501,
    602, 669, 1366, 1387, 1390. *See also*
    paradigmatic
syntax, 118, 165, 167, 182, 192, 194, 203,
    213, 218, 220, 226, 234, 240a, 245,
    273, 274, 277, 286, 315, 347, 359, 360,
    363, 378, 390, 398, 409, 412, 464, 480,
    567, 577, 578, 597, 602, 615a, 664,
    690, 694, 712, 729a, 732, 778, 794,
    795a, 797, 808, 824, 826, 826b, 828,
    840, 843, 863, 864, 912, 916, 932, 942,
    943, 945, 955a, 973, 989, 1010, 1065,
    1066, 1067, 1068, 1069, 1070, 1071,
    1083, 1084, 1091, 1093, 1094, 1096,
    1105, 1108, 1109, 1113, 1119, 1121, 1127,
    1134, 1141, 1146, 1150, 1158, 1161,
    1162, 1164, 1168, 1170, 1186, 1190,
    1194, 1196, 1202, 1207a, 1212, 1217,
    1228, 1229, 1230, 1242a, 1248a, 1253,
    1258, 1261, 1265, 1270, 1280, 1313,
    1316, 1317, 1319, 1320, 1321, 1327,
    1342, 1345, 1347, 1357, 1363, 1374,
    1395, 1413, 1421, 1425, 1427b, 1431,
    1473, 1479. *See also* 3.2.2, 4.2.2, 5.2.2,
    and grammar
syntax and characterization, 1071
system, 385, 412, 492, 501, 724, 1287, 1398,
    1408
system, literature as, 361. *See also* linguis-
    tics, science, semiotics, *and* stylistics
systemic grammar, 295, 394, 623a
tagmemics, 163, 263, 305, 653, 948, 1417.
    See also grammar
tangential, 738
Tartu School, 235. *See also* Soviet semiotics
tautology, 1285
taxonomy, 690. *See also* system
teaching, 310. *See also* approaches *and* liter-
    ary history
teaching literary analysis, 227, 306, 491,
    502, 1446
teaching literary theory, 581
technical language, 1171
tempo, 912, 1227
temporal approach, 832. *See also* meter
temporal sequence vs. narrative sequence,
    734
temporality, 713. *See also* time

Index 2. Authors and Works Studied

Index 3. Critics Discussed

Index 4.   Contributors

Doak, Robert, 72
Doležel, Lubomír, 46, 165, 178, 187, 193, 229, 245, 256, 891
Donato, Eugenio, 172, 258, 302a
Donker, Marjorie, 745
Donoghue, Denis, 199, 1015
Donow, Herbert, 143
Doody, Margaret, 1040
Doran, Madeleine, 1194
Dorfman, Eugene, 847
Dorfmüller-Karpusa, Käthi, 285
Doubrovskij, Sergej, 178, 393
Dowden, Wilfred, 1029
Dowling, William C., 1422
Doyle, Mary, 1249b
Dressler, Wolfgang, 68, 244, 1288
Drew-Bear, Annette, 1152
Dubois, Jacques, 583, 693
Ducrot, Oswald, 118
Dugast, Daniel, 551b
Dumonceaux, Pierre, 769
Dumont, J. P., 655
Dunn, C. W., 808
Dupriez, Bernard, 328
Dworkin, Ronald, 1470
Eagleton, Terry, 240, 443, 465, 624, 1470
Earle, T. F., 1056
Easson, Kay, 305
Easthope, Antony, 752
Eastman, Richard, 347a
Eaton, Marcia, 73
Eaton, Trevor, 227, 245, 1439
Eco, Umberto, 193, 298, 311, 466, 552, 634c
Edel, Leon, 240
Edwards, Philip, 1242
Egan, James, 1250
Egri, Peter, 265a
Eixenbaum, Boris, 156, 193
Elam, Keir, 724
Eliason, Norman, 1144
Elliott, Ralph, 1171, 1276a
Ellis, John, 287, 420
Ellrich, Robert, 1101
Empson, William, 270
Eng, Jan van der, 198
Enkvist, Nils E., 162, 203, 226, 240a, 244, 394, 421
Enzensberger, Hans, 199
Epstein, E. L., 187, 213, 218, 286, 530
Erken, Gunther, 1082
Erlich, Victor, 197, 212
Ermert, Karl, 954

Erskine, Thomas L., 1359
Escarpit, Robert, 133
Esslin, Martin, 287
Eversmann, Susanne, 1231
Fabricant, Carole, 1262
Fairley, Irene, 273, 286, 1068
Falk, Eugene, 180, 584
Faure, Georges, 798
Fehrman, Carl, 564
Fell, John L., 900
Felman, Shoshana, 625
Felperin, Howard, 934
Field, P. J. C., 1353
Filiollet, Jacques, 668
Finneran, Richard, 1271a
Firbas, Jan, 218
Fish, Stanley, 197, 286, 287, 288, 302a, 887, 1459, 1461, 1470
Fiske, John, 606
Fitch, Brian, 1262a, 1393
Fizer, John, 265a
Fleischer, Wolfgang, 444
Fleishman, Avrom, 1271b
Flescher, J., 808
Fletcher, Pauline, 1007a
Flowers, Mary, 1071
Fokkema, D. W., 154, 255, 492
Fol, Monique, 644
Folejevskij, Zbigniev, 246
Fónagy, Iván, 553, 626, 746, 1322
Forrest-Thomson, Veronica, 707
Forster, Leonard, 874
Fort, Bernadette, 1212
Foster, Robert, 113
Foucault, Michel, 160, 258, 293, 493
Foulkes, A. P., 227, 245, 626a, 1446
Foust, Ronald, 737
Fowler, Alastair, 348, 753
Fowler, Roger, 69, 162, 168, 213, 245, 256, 359, 558, 585, 694
Francis, W. Nelson, 148a
Franco, Jean, 227
Frank, Joseph, 737
Frankel, H. H., 808
Franklin, Ursula, 1195, 1232
Frappier-Mazur, Lucienne, 1044
Freedle, Roy, 554
Freedman, Sanford, 149
Freedman, William, 1406
Freeman, Donald C., 92, 168, 187, 213, 286
Freeman, Michelle, 1411
Freilich, Joan, 1297